POLITICAL
CONTINUITY
AND
CHANGE

POLITICAL CONTINUITY AND CHANGE

Revised Edition

Peter H. Merkl

University of California, Santa Barbara

Harper & Row, Publishers
New York, Evanston, San Francisco, London

To Lisa, Jacqueline, and John Peter

CONTENTS

PREFACE

This book is an introduction to the study of politics and aims at ac-
quainting students of this subject with most of its major aspects.
Each topic is dealt with from an analytical point of view and is presented in its proper place in the discipline as a whole. For this purpose, the book is divided into three parts. Part I is devoted to the
broad flow of concepts and developments which make up the Western
political tradition. Included are a brief survey of seminal political
thinkers and ideas of the past 2500 years, an examination of the
nineteenth-century ideologies that set the pattern for the political
values of our time, and an essay on the tradition of constitutionalism,
law, and representative government that has formed Western political institutions.

Part II comprises a number of topical chapters about specific processes, institutions, and institutional problems that have resulted
from the broad tradition of Western political thought. It opens with
chapters on legislative and executive policy-making, different types
of executive-legislative relations, and then deals with political parties
and interest groups, the judiciary, public administration, and with
federal forms of government.

Part III examines the processes of social change and revolution, and the transformation of the political and institutional fabric of the Western tradition. It begins with some remarks on the great revolutions of the Western world and a chapter on political modernization, followed by chapters on totalitarian ideologies and practices of the Communist and Fascist variety. The book ends with an appraisal of the challenge posed by the dynamics of international politics to peace and democracy.

Political Continuity and Change grew from years of teaching the general introduction to political science. Its final form and content owe at least as much to the expressed needs and feelings of the students as to the reflections of the writer and his colleagues and teaching assistants on what an introductory text should contain. Although I am unable to account for the motives of my students, I will attempt to set forth my own and those resulting from long discussions with colleagues and assistants.

The most important reason for writing this book was dissatisfaction with the available texts, none of which quite seemed to fit the needs of instruction for the students at this level. Comparative government texts had too little basic political theory and were not truly comparative. General introductory texts often had too little comparative government, and sometimes no political theory either. Beginning students, moreover, whether political science majors or nonmajors, generally approach the introductory course in political science with expectations of drama and conflict and with minds hungry for philosophical insight, historical perspective, and sociological realism that pose widely varying challenges with each topic. How to combine political philosophy, historical drama, and analytical sociology in a ratio that allows introducing the student to each major subarea of the discipline without going too deeply into it was one major problem of writing the book. How to hold the student's attention, involve him in the issues, and teach him to see politics from many angles and at many levels of generalization was another. Whether the years of experimentation have resulted in an introductory text useful to the teaching purposes of my dear colleagues in the field is for them to decide. Suggestions and criticisms are always welcome.

The briefness of this text also deserves mention, because it is intentional. In the last analysis, every teacher likes to fashion his introductory course to his own liking and according to his own interpretation of what is important and merits greater detail. By limiting the coverage of any particular subject to a general framework and topical reflections, this book invites the use of supplementary paperbacks. Some professors may prefer to shift more stress, for example, to international relations, or to topics of political theory or of partisan politics. Some may wish to add case studies, political novels, or monographs about a particular country or problem. Others may like to change the emphasis from year to year as their own interests or the issues of real political life suggest. A Selected Bibliography, by chapter, containing suggestions of paperbacks for added emphasis or enrichment is included at the back of this book. For the convenience of the instructor, the same bibliography for each chapter is included in the *Instructor's Manual* to accompany the book.

The writer owes a special debt of gratitude to his colleagues, Gordon E. Baker and Stanley V. Anderson, who read parts of the manuscript, and to Rollin Posey, who contributed countless improvements to the entire piece. Alfred E. Prettyman and Jere Grant of Harper & Row added numerous helpful suggestions and supplied the final editorial polish which turns a draft into a book. The greatest contribution by far, however, was made by the legions of question-asking students whose anonymity should not obscure their part in the final product.

PETER H. MERKL

PART I THE WESTERN POLITICAL TRADITION

Of all the traditional fields of study of more than two thousand years of Western civilization, few are more imposing than political science, the study of politics and government. Almost all of the great philosophers of the Western world, Plato, Thomas Aquinas, John Locke, and countless others, recognized its importance by thinking and writing about politics at great length. Some of the most basic issues of the human condition, of living together in communities, are raised by the study of politics. Aristotle called it the "master science" to indicate that it deals with the process by which humans attempt to control their fate on earth. Politics is indeed the foremost arena in which throughout history some men have established their dominion over others. And the means by which intelligent people have striven to achieve and safeguard a maximal amount of personal freedom are also primarily political. Even the recurrent movements of social reform or of radical renewal, however dissatisfied they may be with politics, invariably learn that there can be no lasting change without political thinking and political arrangements.

Whether it is called the master science or the science of engineering human freedom in this world, the study of politics has often supplied the standards of judgment for the merits of whole civilizations and ages of the West as well as of other cultures of the world. Historians have never hesitated to condemn the ancient oriental despotisms for their oppressions or the Greeks for their failure to create a state large and powerful enough to withstand the onslaught of its adversaries. Today, as in just about every decade of the past, there are waves of devastating political criticism both from the left and the right. And, with the benefit of hindsight, someday historians will judge the political failures and triumphs of the liberal civilization in which we live.

By its very nature, such a political judgment will include an assessment of the soundness of our understanding of politics. If politics is the arena of human community-building, of exercising control over people, and of securing human freedom, then optimal political performance requires a thorough understanding of the "master science." The apprentice of the difficult arts of statesmanship and citizenship has to become above all a systematic student of politics past and present. His (or her) political perception needs to be honed by exposure to the most profound thought and the most sophisticated research methods used on political problems. His sense of political values and of direction in a confusing age requires a study of what great thinkers and previous generations have thought and felt. Understanding ourselves as a product of the past need not imply that we accept or conform to its errors and failures. Last but not least important, the student of politics also benefits from a grasp of historical perspective in the evolution of political ideas and institutions.

This book will attempt to capture the essentials of political continuity and change in three major parts. Parts I and II deal with the strands of continuity both in the political ideas and the institutions of the Western tradition, including some problems of adaptation in non-Western countries. Part III is concerned with the impact of political change and revolution on these traditions, especially in developing countries, Western and non-Western, and examines also the challenge of totalitarianism and imperialism in this context.

Part I, entitled "the Western political tradition," begins with an introduction to political science. What is politics? What is scientific about political science? What are some of the contemporary trends of political science research? These and other questions are to focus the mind of the student on the nature of the problem. Then, in Chapter 2, some of the seminal concepts and perennial issues of Western political thought are marshaled to provide the background for the modern interplay between political realities and ideas. The dialogue between Plato and the Athenian democrats about the nature of the best political community and Aristotle's systematic approach to political understanding stand out at the beginning of political thought as well as today. The perennial discussion over the rights of the individual and his obligations toward the community likewise runs like a red thread through the history of thought— from Plato to twentieth-century thought.

In Chapter 3, the harsh realities of the contemporary world become visible in the form of the modern, sovereign nation-state. The contribution of the modern state to the creation of law and order within is contrasted with its propensity toward oppression and the criticisms of the international system of states. A world of sovereign nation-states tends toward international anarchy and war. The contemporary struggle to tame this anarchy by means of international law and organization will very likely play a significant role when historians pass judgment on the political achievements of our age several hundred years from now. Another important factor will be the advancement of the institutions and political realities of democracy from its Western origins throughout the world, the subject of Chapter 4.

Untangling the confusing maze of ideologies—Liberalism, Conservatism, and Democratic Socialism—is the task of Chapter 5. These "isms" originated one by one, as a result of rapid social change and mass mobilization, engaging the loyalty of whole social classes fighting for a place in the sun, or defending their status against challengers. Although these ideologies and their mass support began to crumble in the twentieth century and went into a total eclipse in the 1950s, the contemporary political scene continues to be dominated in the main by Liberal, Conservative, and Democratic Socialist parties and viewpoints derived from these isms, whatever their given name may be today. A student of contemporary politics simply cannot understand what is going on without a firm grasp of the content of the historical three moderate ideologies. The extremist ideologies of Communism and Fascism will be dealt with later in the context of revolutionary change.

Chapter 6, the last chapter of Part I, is devoted to what is doubtless the most enduring political achievement of Western civilization, constitutionalism and representative government. The crowning triumph of the master science, the science of securing personal freedom, the tradition of constitutional government readily shows the accumulation of important contributions from Greek and Roman antiquity, the Middle Ages, and from different national traditions of the modern age. The chapter also discusses the problems of establishing constitutional government in the developing nations.

This, then, is the Western political tradition which enables us contemporaries to stand on the shoulders of our forebears and thus to stand twice as tall. It is a precious heritage which is well worth the effort to explore back to its true sources. Such effort is all the more important, since there are always false prophets and scoundrels who, as with any good thing, try to borrow the mantle of the Western tradition, of constitutional government, or the cultural heritage of the West, for their own nefarious causes. A serious student of politics should feel obliged not to let such semantic skulduggery turn him away from the study of what the Western political tradition really is.

CHAPTER 1   THE STUDY OF POLITICS

In our day and age we have become so accustomed to using the word *science* lightly—to describe the most commonplace activities—that a newcomer to the science of politics could easily mistake it for just another newfangled course of studies with a pompous name. In reality, political science is one of the oldest scientific disciplines of the Western world and one of the central concerns in the life of man and society. Aristotle called it the "master science" in tribute to its crucial role in the ordering of the various relationships within human society. To arrive at a clear conception of what political science involves, we shall first explore three intimately related topics: (1) the nature of politics; (2) what is scientific about political science; and (3) the place of political science among and in relation to the other sciences.

What is politics?

In the broadest sense of the word, politics is a process at work everywhere and continuously, in the smallest groups as well as among great powers on the international level. Every day the news-papers carry considerable news about it, because the public wants to know what is going on in politics. Everyone is vitally affected by questions of whether or not there is going to be a war or who will be elected in the next elections, or what the President will say in a speech. Every day an enormous news-gathering apparatus of thou-sands of news reporters and information services swings into action to satisfy the need of the public for news about politics. The news media cannot report everything that happens, and there is always a great deal more to every political story than does get into print. It is here, where the work of the news reporter leaves off, that the interest of the political scientist begins. He would like to know what really happened, why it happened that way, and what antece-dents led to the present events. The political scientist wants to learn in a general and systematic way what means will best achieve particular political goals. He wants to find out by what standards one can appraise events and actions in the realm of politics. Finally, he ponders the goals, principles, and ideals of politics that give meaning and direction to man's political existence.

The story of the words "politics" and "political" began with the *polis,* the city-state community of ancient Greece. Plato, Aristotle, and many of their Greek contemporaries considered the affairs of the *polis* as worthy of being the subject of a master science because they saw in the participation of the individual in the life of the *polis* a necessary condition of human self-realization. Only "gods or beasts" could live outside the intimately integrated community life of the *polis* without sinking below the level of full human self-realization. The politics of other peoples outside of Greece, more-over, were looked down upon as too barbarian even for consideration.

Because these city-states were small by our standards, and the Greeks did not distinguish sharply between public and private affairs or among different functions of their community life (such as politics, education, and religious worship), practically all behavior of the citizens of the *polis* was regarded as in some sense *political:* it had a bearing on their patterns of living together. Politics to the Greeks was a concept about as all-embracing as the use of the words "society" and "social" today.

Later, the decline of the Greek city-state and the rise of great multinational empires, such as those of Alexander the Great or of Rome, reduced the meaning of the words "politics" and "political" to something nearer in scope to their current meanings. Private concerns were separated from public affairs, and the stigma was removed from withdrawal into private life and from life in the country. A cosmopolitan attitude replaced the narrow nationalism of the Greeks as people began to distinguish between political activities and those of a religious, economic, educational, or military character. Political action became only one of several concerns a man might have, and the political realm, or what is called the *state* today, became one of several communities of which a man might be a member. The erstwhile supremacy and monopoly of politics over the loyalty of a citizen had to be shared in particular with communities of religious belief, which entreated their members to "render unto Caesar [only] the things which are Caesar's, and unto God the things which are God's." In more recent times, the claims of Caesar were similarly precluded from interfering with economic activities, cultural life, and certain basic freedoms of man. Today only the totalitarian movements or regimes tend to reassert a monopoly of political control over all the other activities of man.

Yet the student of politics must not lose sight of the important mutual relationships between politics and economics, politics and religion, and politics and culture. The total activities of men and women in society and the complexities of different aspects of social life are all of one piece. Politics is so deeply embedded in the cultural, economic, and religious life of society that we cannot fully analyze it and understand it without an awareness of the profound influences these other aspects of social life have on it. Between the whole of social life and its component parts, including politics, there has always been interaction as well as tension. Political philosophy from Plato and Aristotle to Karl Marx and classical Liberalism has tended to disagree on which to emphasize more, the unity of the whole (monism) or the autonomy of the parts (pluralism). In contemporary political systems there are extreme differences ranging from the pronounced pluralism of the United States to the monism of the Soviet Union or China. Even in the most pluralistic systems, however, movements of passionate reform and renewal may temporarily bring about a monistic reorientation. In most other systems, also, a delicate balance is maintained between the common interests and those of the constituent parts, and the safeguarding of the common interests is largely through *political* processes and institutions. The pluralistic forces of society, on the other hand, not only resist political direction as much as possible, they exert powerful influences of their own which permeate the whole system. The various cultural influences mold the values and life styles of everyone in the system; economic institutions channel goods and services and thus provide potent incentives and discouragements. On a deeper level yet, family life, peer groups, and other social organisms mold the minds and habits of the young citizens-to-be. All these pluralistic influences generally have a more profound impact on the politics of the community than politics can ever have on them.

We must not, however, be misled by the interdependence of politics and other social activities into a view of politics as merely a reflection of something else. Politics is one of the most important areas for the exercise of human freedom and for man's choice among different ends. It is true that some men deny the ability of man to shape his own fate by the conscious employment of political means. Karl Marx and his followers, for example, saw politics as nothing more than a reflection of prevailing economic conditions, especially of economic technology and the distribution of the ownership of capital. Some adherents of Sigmund Freud and of other psycho-analytical schools have tried to reduce political activities to the operations of subconscious, uncontrollable images and volitions. Some sociologists and cultural anthropologists have regarded the political decisions of man as the automatic outcome of his conditioning by his upbringing, family life, religious observances, ethnic customs, or by his place in the social structure or among the groups of his society—in short, by his cultural and social setting. Some historians would have us believe that we are mere products of the history and traditions of our nation, religion, locality, and family; that our actions have been largely shaped by what happened to our forefathers or what they did. Geographers of the school of geopolitics have explained national character and political decisions exclusively through geographic location, climate, topography, natural resources, and strategic possibilities. Each of these schools of thought contains a grain of truth in that it studies important factors which undoubtedly have an effect on politics. But at the same time each school is tempted to transform its grain of truth into a mountain of fallacy by committing two cardinal mistakes: by attributing all of politics to a single cause to the exclusion of all other possible causes and by denying the existence of free will—the essential freedom of choice, the freedom to change things—which is implicit in politics.

Man has often used his political freedom to change onerous economic conditions, to restrain psychological urges, to alter bad social customs, and to improve the social structure, to overcome geopolitical obstacles, or to break with historical tradition. Examples of the exercise of free will in politics are the prohibition of economic monopolies, laws to restrain individuals from indulging in aggressive urges, social reforms of all kinds to cope with the imperfections of society, the drive of many a modern nation for unity in the face of considerable geographic barriers, and abrupt breaks with historical tradition as momentous as the American, French, Russian, and Chinese Revolutions.

It must be remembered, however, that there are many and real limitations on freedom of political choice. Full political awareness recognizes the limits of our freedom of choice and understands the economic, historical, and cultural conditions that constrain it. But when all is accounted for, there still remain in man's political role spontaneity, creativity, and the power to begin anew. Man is the master of his own fate and responsible for what he does with his freedom. Man can be the prime mover in shaping his secular destiny —and therein lies the dignity of political man.

The essence of politics lies in this fundamental freedom of man in society to *master his own fate* by political means. Hence, politics also rests on the fundamental purposes of man in a social setting. It has to do with the *preservation (or creation) of the community* of human beings in which he wants to live. Politics involves the *basic human values*, religious or ideological, which furnish the goals and principles he sets for himself. It also includes his ideas of the *kind of order* that will prevail among the members of his community, his ideas about the *utilization of the available resources* to supply the physical wants of his community, and his preferences for a particular *form of government* for the articulation and enforcement of his kind of order. The basic order considered desirable in a given community is intimately related to the basic values of the community—values that are rarely consciously thought of until they have been violated or are called into question by a new set of values. As Aristotle put it:

Every state is a community of some kind, and every community is established with a view to some good—for mankind always acts in order to obtain that which they think good. But, if all communities aim at some good, the state or political community, which is the highest of all, and which embraces all the rest, aims at good in a greater degree than any other, and at the highest good.

If the essence of politics is a quest for maintaining or bringing about in the community an order that its proponents consider good, the stage is set for the typical features that politics presents to us day after day. There is likely to be sharp disagreement among different persons and groups of persons about what is good. Some may think, for example, that it is good to make their community more egalitarian by abolishing existing privileges and distinctions. Others may consider it bad to deny the outstanding individuals a special status that elevates them above the crowd; there may be disagreement about what kind of excellence the community should recognize as a basis for granting special status. The social and economic interests of various groups within a community may also have something to do with whether they favor more equality or less (see Chapter 5).

To further their concepts of what the community should be like, people with common ideas and interests get together and form political parties or interest groups. To do so lends more force to their desires in shaping the community. Under normal circumstances, there is already a well-established set of governmental institutions in which the contending groups can get a hearing for their wishes and complaints, and through which issues are resolved according to generally recognized and acceptable procedures. A group can achieve its goals by getting its representatives elected to positions in the governmental machinery or perhaps simply by exercising pressure upon current officeholders.

Once we enter the stage where various groups of differing sizes struggle for dominance in a community, the phenomenon of *power* looms large. Participants (and even observers) may tend to forget the original goal of their political endeavor—the quest for maintaining or for establishing a good social order as they see it. All kinds of groups—local communities, national governments, and alliances of nation-states—constantly feel the lure of the game of power politics, a struggle for dominance or for aggrandizement or for sheer survival. They become absorbed in the study of the means and techniques of this fight for the stakes of power. To survive, it may be necessary to defeat one's rivals and to gain power over the community in order to establish the good order that one favors. Power relationships and the techniques for the preservation and increase of power are an unavoidable part of large-scale politics. Power can be a necessary means to a good end. But the pursuit of power for its own sake—unlike the quest for justice and good order—is a pursuit without end or satisfaction, an aimless kind of perpetual motion, which, in the long run, tends to destroy both the pursuer and those who get in his way. Power does corrupt, most especially when it becomes an end in itself. By contrast, the pursuit of a specific social order favored by a group of people has a definite and satisfactory end. There is no such thing as political "good" in the abstract. And as long as the end is concrete and attainable, it is also possible to devise an appropriate relationship between *ends and means*.

Let us summarize this discussion of the meaning of politics. We began by delimiting the scope of the field. Politics is only one of several social activities of man, though intimately related to his other pursuits. It commands a central phase, though not a monopoly, among his various activities. It affords him the opportunity for exercising some free choice in attaining the basic order of values in society. *Politics is the process through which man orders the society in which he lives according to his political ideas about the ends of man.* One can regard politics as the implementation of high philosophical values or bring it down to earth as does Harold D. Lasswell in his book with the telltale title *Politics: Who Gets What, When, How.* One can find politics in the context of an ideal democracy in which every citizen has an equal say in determining the final choice of a social order, or in the context of an oligarchic society, where a powerful few struggle with each other for supremacy over passive multitudes. It appeared in the static social order of past centuries, when society was likened to the hierarchical order among the heavenly circles, as well as in the never-ending stream of governmental politics by which modern states seek to adjust the society of today to rapidly changing technology. It can be found in the narrow compass of small, self-contained communities like the ancient *polis*, within the large framework of the modern nation-state, or in the greater society of states, international blocs, and continents. The main theme and end is always the same: the allocation of values, of privileges, and priorities. At its best, politics is a noble quest for a good order and justice; at its worst, a selfish grab for power, glory, and riches. The ways and means by which men try to achieve their ideas of the good society vary greatly: they may include the formal institutions of government, with narrowly circumscribed procedures and powers of rule-making, adjudication, and administration; they may include the authority and persuasiveness of elaborate beliefs or ideologies; or they may devolve upon organized groups or the force of armed men. In later chapters of this book, we shall deal with all of these subjects of political science.

What is scientific about political science?

For the politically interested student, it is often very difficult to accept the presence of a neutral, objective science of politics the findings of which may on occasion seem to clash with his own preferences. Politically committed people, in particular, tend to mistake the truths of political science for an all-out challenge to the philosophical beliefs they hold themselves. They are mistaken on two accounts, the nature and extent of political science statements and the question of value judgments to which we address ourselves in greater detail below. As for the nature and extent of scientific statements, for example, a political scientist in his right mind would never state that the Young Trotskyists or the Young Republicans are intrinsically right or wrong, even though he may have his personal preferences. If the political scientist is to remain on the solid grounds, he will have to limit himself to a well-considered description and analysis of the political philosophies or programs involved, leaving it to the political participant to take sides or resort to action. Regarding specific governmental policies or institutions, likewise, a political scientist qua scientist can only state that, given certain circumstances, a specific policy or procedural arrangement will tend to have certain specifiable results. And the political scientist will have to be prepared to demonstrate this very limited statement by detailed reference to cases including those that tend to limit or gainsay his thesis. The political participant, by way of contrast, has an infinitely greater range of statements to make and they will tend to be generically different: "Love those Black Panthers!" "We ought to spare welfare recipients the indignity of a means test," or "Women have just as much right to managerial jobs as do men." These statements of political participants are assertions of preference and hardly require any kind of empirical proof. They are impossible to prove in any case. They are an assertion of the freedom that is inherent in political thought and action.

Why should we be concerned about whether or not political science is a science? Why not just study and learn what there is to learn about politics? There is good reason for concern about the scientific character of the study of politics. In perhaps no other field of scientific study are factual, objective observations by trained minds so likely to get mixed up in the clash of opposing opinions, factions, and interests. Political science is constantly under the threat of being engulfed by politics itself. The political scientist is often accused of taking sides and presenting as the objective result of sophisticated scientific research, or as well-established facts, something which to many people can only be a highly political matter of opinion. It is for this reason—the need to distinguish between verifiable facts and interested opinion—that we must establish the study of politics as a definitive science that is quite capable of bringing forth a body of scientific truths not vitiated by political passion and preference.

Political science is also called the study of politics or of government. These alternative names are often chosen by students of politics who prefer to look on political science as a branch of the humanities—a field of philosophy, a matter of ethics, or an art. In such doubts about the scientific nature of the study of politics there often lies a misunderstanding of the word *science*. Living in an age dominated by the discoveries and practical applications of the natural sciences, we need not be surprised that popular usage tends to draw its scientific criteria from the nature and method of the natural sciences: "If you can't count it, it doesn't count." In reality, however, every science has to draw its methods and criteria from the nature of its subject. Political science or any other social science can no more be expected to conform to the standards of natural science than the methods and criteria of biology need to conform to those of nuclear physics.

More specifically, the denial of the scientific character of the social sciences cites a number of natural science criteria, such as exactness or precision of measurement, the presence of "immutable" causal laws, and the method of laboratory experimentation as inapplicable in the social sciences. But contemporary natural and physical sciences have long abandoned the rigid nineteenth-century notions of immutable laws and unshakable certainties in the realm of dead matter, not to mention the realm of living nature. In many natural science disciplines, scientific truth has become a matter of relativity, probability, and theoretical uncertainties. How much more can we expect, therefore, than approximations and probabilities in a field that deals with human beings, each with a will of his own?

The information necessary for political predictions, furthermore, is often not available in time because the people in possession of crucial pieces of knowledge are usually participants in the game of politics and therefore are unwilling to impart their inside information to an outsider until the decisions have been made. Often, important information does not become accessible until years or even decades later. Yet if we compare the intricate nature of politics with the nature of other subjects, we cannot but marvel at the number of reasonably accurate predictions that political science can make about such things as the outcome of an election, the likely effect of a political measure, or the workability of a constitution under given circumstances.

Similar observations would seem to be in order with regard to experiments and their repetition. To be sure, political science cannot employ laboratories and test tubes, which are not, in any case, the only paraphernalia of natural science. Astronomy, for example, does not use them at all. Every science has a structure of many levels ranging from a bottom step of empirical observation and verification to ever-higher levels of generalization and theory. The instruments of experimentation and empirical research usually have their place only at the lowest level of this logical pyramid of science. The process of developing working hypotheses at the higher levels and testing them by experimentation at the lower levels is what we mean by research. Many of the great scientific innovations of the twentieth century in the physical sciences, for example, were developed by deductive reasoning—from the theoretical level on down to the laboratory test—rather than by inductive reasoning—from the bottom up. The development of a scientific view of an entire subject is a very slow process in which the scientists constantly alternate between induction, that is, generalization from a specific case they examine, and deduction, that is, drawing conclusions about specific cases from the accepted generalizations about the whole subject. It is inherent in the nature of a science that accepted generalizations, or "laws," can be challenged or disproved by new empirical evidence. Consequently, the only thing "immutable" or "unchangeable" about a true science is that it changes its view of the subject in the light of new discoveries over a period of time.

Political science and political science research differ very little from the other sciences in these respects. Here, too, there is a structure on many levels, ranging from empirical observation and testing to the high levels of political philosophy, although the structure may be less integrated than that of many natural sciences due to its age, worldwide ramification, and disputes among different schools of thought. At the empirical level, the observation of political facts and relationships has gone on since time immemorial. To be sure, the gathering and analysis of data were at times unsophisticated and almost always overshadowed by the desire to apply the knowledge gained for practical objectives. In few other aspects of human life has man, from the earliest times, felt such a pressing need to analyze the conditions of his existence and to create an acceptable order out of the natural chaos. Constitutions and governmental policies themselves are in a sense experiments, or bundles of experiments, which test the insight of their authors into the processes of politics much as a new measuring device tests the insights of its designers in fields such as mechanics, electronics, and physics. Depending on the success with which a given political instrument under given conditions achieves the desired result, we may obtain the "experimental proof" of the theories that contributed to its design.

Two further attributes of political science and some other social sciences are sometimes misunderstood as being in conflict with the scientific character of the discipline. One is the method of *understanding*,[1] the other, the role of *value judgments*. Because the political

---

[1] *Understanding* in this context refers to the ability of one human being to put himself into the situation of another to *understand* his motives and to anticipate his reactions. As a technical term it has been used, in particular, by sociologists of the school of Max Weber. See also Theodore Abel, "The Operation Called *Verstehen*," *Amer. Jour. of Soc.*, 54, 1948.

scientist is just as human as the actors on the political stage and his mind resembles theirs both in logic and in irrational urges, he can understand and often predict their actions with an uncanny intuition that would be inconceivable, say, in chemistry. Considering the difficulty of prediction in the social sciences, we should welcome the method of understanding as a useful addition rather than as a flaw. There are also the differences between the realm of matter, where cause and effect rule, and the realm of politics, where intelligent human beings are motivated by goals of action rather than by causes. Consequently, understanding would seem to be the method most capable of revealing such goals and their role in politics.

The question of *value judgments* arises from three circumstances inherent in politics. First, the actors on the political stage have personal preferences and religious or philosophical commitments or goals that guide their actions and have to be accounted for in every analysis of politics. But this fact should not detract from the scientific character of the study of politics. All it means is that values must be studied as well. Second, political scientists themselves have value commitments and prejudices that may at times cloud their judgment, leading them to observe what they would like to see rather than what is really there. This is a regrettable human shortcoming, but it is no argument against the discipline itself. Finally, value judgments enter political science from practical applications. The nature of man as an end in himself, for instance, automatically rules out any kind of negative experiment or exploitative manipulation of human beings. Practical application to the uses of man has introduced values and preferences into other sciences as well. At the same time, there are still wide areas of political science that can be and often are kept free of value judgments. This is the case, for example, with most descriptions of political ideas, situations, and institutions as long as they remain purely descriptive. In the last analysis, the objection to value judgments in political science is really an objection to the nature of politics. Only if human beings were like atoms of matter, devoid of free will and without goals and conscious purpose, could their actions and relationships be discussed without any reference to values.

To sum up, political science may in some ways differ from the physical and natural sciences, which some people insist on regarding as the only true sciences. It does so with respect to the orientation of political man toward subjective ends. It does so also in the method of understanding, an inductive method comparable to the device of introspection, which enables a psychologist to make generalizations about human nature from a knowledge of his own propensities.

Political science conforms fully to a dictionary definition of science as "a branch of study . . . concerned with observed facts systematically classified and more or less colligated . . . under general laws [and including] trustworthy methods for the discovery of new truths within its own domain."[2] Political science commands both factually, empirically observed knowledge and insights of a more theoretical nature. Its method for the discovery of new insights into the realm of politics usually involves both inductive and deductive reasoning in a combination not unlike that which we might find in the natural sciences.

The logic of comparison

Underlying much of the empirical observation and analysis of political scientists is a method of comparison. We attempt to isolate comparable sets of variables and attributes separated by geographic location or the passage of time and then compare them systematically in order to discern similarities and dissimilarities. We may, for example, take gubernatorial elections in the State of California over a period of sixty years and compare them with regard to such variables as the voter turnout, the changing size of the voting population, the kind of campaign employed, or the relation of the candidates to the issues at large. Or we could also use the gubernatorial vote in each county of California in the same year as the *unit of analysis* and compare such variables as population size, urban-rural composition, exposure to campaign efforts, variation from the partisan division in previous elections, and many others. In either case, comparison leads to generalizations about how these variables affect voting behavior in California.

When the investigation is extended to other states as well, the generalizations can describe various determinants of American voting behavior. And if the voting situation, or other sets of variables of political action, could be successfully applied to a reasonably representative sample of countries of the whole world we could even generalize about human political behavior. Admittedly, this is a big "if," and, for the time being, we have to be satisfied with a far more modest scope of generalizations. If we can successfully compare certain sets of variables of political action either among a number of Western nations, or among developing nations, or among the Communist nations, we have already accomplished a great deal.

The logic of comparison operates on many levels of political

[2] Oxford Universal Dictionary, 3rd. ed.

science research, beginning with its role in most of the basic operations of conceptualization and explanation. Human language hardly
permits us to label anything without implicitly comparing it to what
it is not and without relating it to similar phenomena. The sets of
variables of voting behavior or other individual political behavior
referred to above are considered to be at the *microlevel of analysis*
in political science. At a higher level of social complexity, such as
the interaction of organized groups and institutions, we speak of a
middle-range level of analysis and hypothesizing. At this level, needless to say, political causes and effects become so complex as to
make empirical investigation very difficult and generalizations hazard-
ous. The middle range thus is a great challenge to new talent in
political science research.

A still level is the *macrolevel of analysis,* which deals with whole
national political systems or their governments. This level of politics
has always enjoyed a great deal of attention within countries and
in comparative study because of its great importance to people
everywhere. At this level, scientific study is facilitated by the similarity of the functional requisites of independent statehood the
world over. The modern state with its administrative and defense
apparatus and a modicum of representative government is practically
universal today and thus invites comparative study. And there are
many theories which postulate certain basic functions that all macropolitical systems have to provide, such as goal attainment, integration and pattern maintenance, or leadership recruitment, socialization,
interest articulation and aggregation, and the governmental output
functions of the making, application, and adjudication of general
rules.[3] Empirical research at the macrolevel is likely to deal with
materials different from those at the other two levels. The same
can be said of the study of the *intersystemic level* or international
level of political life.

Facts and interpretations

To appreciate political science research, the student should be cau-
tioned particularly about the distinction between research findings
and the broader interpretations which are often attached to them.
Most empirical research in political science, no matter how broadly
intended, allows only rather limited statements to be made with
some claim to objective validity, provided the research has been

---

[3] See, for example, Gabriel A. Almond and James S. Coleman, *The Politics of the
Developing Areas*, Princeton, N.J.: Princeton University Press, 1960, p. 17.

carried out in a sound manner. Researchers and other observers, however, are often tempted to expand upon this narrow base and to place upon it interpretations which by a process of extrapolation, hunches, and preferred beliefs soon go beyond anything that could be said to rest upon the empirical observation.

To be sure, interpretations and speculations should not be discouraged, since it is only with their help that we can attempt to leap across the oceans of ignorance between the small islands of researched territory. The material obstacles to global political science research are too great to expect it to catch up with the swiftly changing scene of politics in the foreseeable future. The realm of research-related speculations also supplies further research with the needed hypotheses and links discrete research operations into a more meaningful whole. Nevertheless, students are well advised to distinguish between what is demonstrable and certain and what is merely likely or probable.

The limits of credibility of the interpretations placed upon research are particularly obvious when interpretations are linked to preferred political action or policies, in other words, to politics itself. Here the poetic license of interpreting what is known with certainty becomes so wedded to what some people would like to believe that it loses all scientific validity. The result often repels other people so violently that they are inclined to reject the well-established political science knowledge along with the obvious bias of the political interpretation. To illustrate, a cigarette commercial proclaimed not long ago, while showing a hundred years of progress of modern women in America, "You've come a long way, baby." This aroused the ire of feminists and many others who felt that the message implied that such progress was quite enough. If we apply our distinction between known facts and political interpretations, however, an analysis of such changes in role and status of American women as may have occurred during the time in question is an entirely separate matter from any political interpretation placed upon it. Such interpretations, moreover, could go in many different directions, depending on the bias or political intent of the interpreter. Given appreciable changes in the role and status of women over a period of time, to begin with, it is a matter of subjective interpretation to say whether these constitute "too little" or "too much" or even any "progress" in the right direction. No method of political science can ever determine this. And even if there is common agreement that the changes constitute "having come a long way," it does not follow with cogent logic that such progress is "enough." Rather, it would be just as logical to conclude that therefore change ought to go on at the same (or a faster or slower) pace, or even that the changes ought to be reversed. The factual finding, in other words, can be interpreted in totally contradictory ways depending on the preferences of the interpreter.

This example of longitudinal comparison can be supplemented with equally dubious interpretations placed upon comparison across national boundaries. It has long been a popular suspicion that comparative study was chiefly employed in order to show that some policy or political relationship was handled better in Great Britain, or in the Soviet Union, than in the United States. More recently the popular argument directed at youthful critics of American society and government has reversed its tune: "If you think this country is not free and democratic enough for you, why don't you go to France, or to China or Cuba and find out what they do with their dissenters." Needless to say, neither one of these lines is a valid application of comparative political science method, which is not meant to be used for such immediate, and transparent, political rationalizations. This is not to say that serious students of comparative politics would not be interested in a detailed comparison of policies and practices regarding the civil rights of dissenters or any other topic, provided the scientific objective is not distorted by ulterior motives.

Finally, a word should be added on the frequent interpretations which refer more or less specifically to historical events. A popular reference point of many a political argument today, for example, is Adolf Hitler's Nazi regime, which is described in some detail in Chapter 14 of this book. It is quite common to hear a fervent plea in favor of legalizing abortion which likens the legal compulsion of women to bear unwanted babies to the worst of oppression under the Third Reich. It is equally common to hear arguments against legalizing abortion liken it to legalized murder and genocide under Hitler. In a similar fashion, student rebels in Europe and America like to accuse their antagonists of "Fascist repression" while the latter liken them to the Nazi students and stormtroopers who took over German universities some forty years ago. In either case the reference amounts to little more than name-calling, and those who use it involuntarily betray their ignorance of the historical situation to which they are referring.

More elaborate historical analogies and interpretations may have great value for illustrating a relationship or for building a hypothesis about contemporary events. But they can likewise never really be said to "prove" or "disprove" anything about the contemporary scene. There are far too many independent variables and relationships for history ever to repeat itself exactly. And, as has often been pointed out, all analogies tend to break down sooner or later.

What is the relation of political science to the other sciences?

Political science is one of several scientific disciplines that concern themselves with aspects of human society and with man's life in society. Among the other scientific disciplines there is, for example, economics, the study of how man manages his resources, produces and distributes wealth, and supplies his wants. The relations between economics and political science have always been very close; in fact, economics at one time was called political economy. Some knowledge of economics, and at times an in-depth understanding of economic conditions and theories, are indispensable to a student of politics if he is to grasp most problems of contemporary politics. He cannot understand the activities of lobbying at the seat of a government without knowing the economic issues at stake; he cannot penetrate the secrets of Soviet politics without some familiarity with Communist theories and the problems of a planned and regimented economy; and he cannot analyze the issues of foreign aid to the developing nations without comprehending the complex economic questions behind them. Conversely, students of economic problems may similarly need to call on the resources of political science.

The study of politics also bears a close relationship to sociology, social psychology, cultural anthropology, and history. Depending on the nature of the particular subject matter at hand, sociology may contribute its knowledge about social stratification, social psychology its grasp of personality, cultural anthropology its insights into the behavior of primitive man, and history its vast knowledge of the past. History and political science, in fact, have much to contribute to each other because of their seemingly parallel interest in the political affairs of man. Whereas history is more interested in recording and understanding the events of the past in their uniqueness, political science strives more for practical lessons that can be drawn from the lawlike recurrence of situations and relationships in history. The student of politics, therefore, first has to study history before he can hope to find any laws in it or draw any practical applications from it. The political scientist must also utilize the resources and skills of disciplines such as psychology, philosophy, theology, geography, and statistics whenever they appear to be of help in the understanding and analysis of the problem at hand.

The frequent need for the student of politics to consult other disciplines results in part from the *basic unity of the life of society*. The various social activities of man are all of one piece because they are engaged in largely by the same people and they take place side by side in the same social environment. Because politics has an ordering function in society, the concern of political scientists is not so much with the recording and analysis of all political happenings in the world as it is with particular problems, crises, maladjustments, and dilemmas.

The problem approach   This problem approach usually requires the unraveling of all the strains and antecedents contributing to a particular crisis. For this purpose, and because the different social activities of man cannot be separated sharply from one another, political scientists may need to call upon these other disciplines for help in analyzing and solving particular problems. To utilize the methods of economics, sociology, or psychology does not imply that the problem has been turned over to these other disciplines, or that it has become an economic, sociological, or psychological problem.

The tool of political understanding   The basic tool of analysis, even while using these other methods, remains political understanding. The extent and significance of each contribution from another discipline to the solution of a problem likewise can be judged only by the standards of political understanding. Statistical methods, for example, are often employed by empirical research in subjects that lend themselves to a quantitative manipulation of data, such as election results and public opinion polls. But it is strictly a question of political science whether or not a research project that uses statistics on political phenomena—in a statistically sound manner—also makes good sense by the standards of political understanding.

The criterion of quantitative relevance   Attention should also be drawn to the quantitative criteria that often decide the relevance of the evidence of other scientific disciplines to political analysis. Generally speaking, the knowledge of psychology or economics does not by itself take on political significance. If psychology should discover, for instance, that John Doe hates his father, this fact in itself is of no interest to political science. Only if a whole nation consists overwhelmingly of men who hate their fathers, or if John Doe becomes Soviet premier or British prime minister, or if such people make up most of the voters who have switched their party affiliation from that of their fathers to the opposite political party, does this fact take on political relevance. Political science usually concerns itself only with events and circumstances that affect many people. The criterion of quantitative relevance is an important part of the criteria of sophisticated judgment in political science.

What are the fields of study in the discipline of political science?

There are several logical ways of dividing the discipline of political science into fields of study. In most political science departments of academic institutions a combination of principles has been employed for designating the major areas of study as well as the individual courses of instruction. Because education for citizenship has always played an important role in the study of politics, a popular way of dividing the fields has been to distinguish between American government and comparative government, the latter usually comprising the study of major foreign governments which the student can compare with his own government, thereby deepening his understanding of the former.[4] International relations or world politics then accounts for what goes on outside the United States and between the nations. A simple geographic division into various area studies has also been used, such as Asian studies, Latin American government, the government of Great Britain and the Commonwealth, and African politics south of the Sahara.

Another convenient method is to follow the levels of governmental organization. There may be courses on metropolitan government, state and local (American) government, American national government, regional organizations—such as NATO or the Organization of American States (OAS)—and international organizations. Another widespread classificatory scheme is one relying mainly on the tradition of distinguishing between the study of political theory and law —constitutional law, administrative law, and international law—and the study of political institutions and processes—domestic, foreign, and international.

Last, but perhaps most interesting, is a collection of more recent fields of interest loosely identified as the political process: political socialization, political parties, policy-making, politics and administration, or just politics. There may be courses on political psychology, political parties, interest groups and public opinion, the legislative or administrative process, and public policy. Many institutions have developed special courses in political behavior: voting behavior, legislative behavior, political sociology, and even administrative and

---

[4] The term "comparative" is used here in a rather narrow sense. Compare the discussion of Aristotle's comparative method (Chapter 2, pp. 38–40, of the present book).

judicial behavior. These courses usually place great emphasis on the utilization of quantitative methods for political science research.

Needless to say, every academic institution will tend to divide the fields and courses according to the past and current interests among its faculty and its students.

CONTEMPORARY TRENDS IN POLITICAL SCIENCE RESEARCH

At the same time that the systematic study of politics is one of the oldest academic disciplines, it has also been transformed drastically time and again by revolutionary upsurges of innovation. Such thinkers as Machiavelli (1469–1527), Rousseau (1712–1778), Marx (1818–1883), and Freud (1856–1939) each emphatically expressed the belief that his insights opened up an entirely new view of social and political reality. Marx and Freud, in particular, were convinced that they had succeeded in peeling off a whole façade of appearances behind which lay a "more real" reality than had hitherto been perceived.

The behavioral approach

The quest of political scientists for more empirical approaches in the first half of the twentieth century, and particularly since World War II, has moved essentially in the same direction. Almost every generation of political researchers in this century found itself dissatisfied with the methods of inquiry handed down by its predecessors, or at least with the way in which its predecessors had communicated their view of political reality. In a succession of attempts at fundamental innovation, different schools have cropped up in turn, emphasizing new methods of studying politics and frequently relying heavily on other social sciences, such as economics, sociology, or psychology.

The most recent wave of methodological innovation in political science, the *behavioral approach*, had been beating on the ramparts of the established methods of political science for the last decade and a half and has now been generally accepted and integrated into the discipline. Whenever new schools of thought clash with older ones, there is bound to be much confusion and mutual recrimination, which may disturb the beginning student of politics. Yet there is hardly a doubt that the conflict and challenge to accept new ideas brought about by the waves of innovation are of great benefit to the development of the discipline. As will be remembered from our earlier discussion of scientific method (pp. 11–14), it is of the essence of a scientific approach that the findings of yesterday and the conclusions drawn from them be open to challenge by new methods and new evidence. Students, therefore, should be encouraged to learn to grasp the new approaches as well as those of the older schools of political understanding.

The most recent trends in political science research, as indicated above, owe a great deal to such earlier schools as the *group approach* of A. F. Bentley and David B. Truman or the *new science of politics* of C. E. Merriam and H. D. Lasswell. Yet they have gone far beyond their predecessors in several significant respects, which rather tend toward the systematization of political science as a discipline. The *behavioral school*[5] in particular developed these points to a state of conceptual perfection that will remain with political science long after the "behavioral mood" of methodological rebellion against the older philosophical, historical, and institutional approaches is forgotten. According to representatives of the behavioral approach, such as Robert A. Dahl, David Easton, and Heinz Eulau, one of the directions of methodological innovation has been the redefining of institutions as systems of related individual behavior or systems of social action. Instead of studying, for example, the United States Supreme Court or Congress, as institutions, members of the behavioral school have turned to the study of the behavior patterns of the Supreme Court justices, and of senators and congressmen.

Observation of what men do　Another aspect of the recent methodological innovations has been their concern with the constraint that the traditional language of political science imposes on the progress of research. Defining politics in such traditional terms as government, power, the state, or authority, Heinz Eulau has argued, makes it difficult to inquire empirically into *what men do* when they act politically. Just as economists approach economic behavior by observing how people produce, buy, sell, exchange, invest, speculate, and consume, so should political scientists study political behavior by studying how man "rules and obeys, persuades and compromises and bargains, coerces and represents, fights and fears."[6]

Use of models, quantitative methods of measurement, computers　A third point of emphasis of the behavioral approach is the stress on method, which has increased the already present trend toward the building of sophisticated *models*, the use of quantitative techniques

[5] The name is not to be confused with the turn-of-the-century psychology of *behaviorism* of J. B. Watson.

[6] Heinz Eulau, *The Behavioral Persuasion in Politics* (New York: Random House, 1963), pp. 4–5.

of statistical measurements and manipulation, and the use of computers in political science research. One of the most common uses of quantitative methods is in opinion polls, but there are many others, such as the correlation of the vital social and economic statistics of a country with its politics. Computers can be used not only to speed up the manipulation of large amounts of quantitative data but also to *simulate* administrative or military processes of decision-making, or even a diplomatic encounter between several powers under known conditions. The general purpose of the great stress on the use of sophisticated research methods is to place political science on a more scientific basis and to allow empirical verification of as many of its statements as possible.

Unity among social sciences   A fourth aspect of the current trend in political science research is the desire to unify the study of political behavior with similarly oriented segments of psychological, sociological, and anthropological research. Such a union could come about through the employment of a common terminology and methodology, such as common models of *decision-making*, the concept of *roles*, and *game theory*. Some sociological methods, such as *structural-functional analysis* and the concept of *social action* of the sociologist Talcott Parsons, have long attracted the interest of political scientists. The extraordinary impact of the study of the politics of the developing countries on the whole discipline has also furthered the cooperation and, at times, the merging of the different social sciences. The comparative study of Western governments at approximately the same level of technology and social organization could still get by with only a legal and institutional approach. But with the great cultural disparities and different stages of development encountered in the study of the new nations, understanding and meaningful comparison require a comprehensive grasp of what cultural anthropology, sociology, economics, and social psychology may be able to tell us about the setting of the politics of a society in transition (see Chapter 12).

Development of empirical theory   Finally, the contemporary trend in political science research has been to devise theoretical systems and models that can account for the observed regularities of political behavior and provide a solid foundation for its further study. Other empirical sciences have long developed such a framework of "empirical theory," without which it is difficult to carry on research and to accumulate research findings in a meaningful way. In political science, however, the presence of centuries of political thought of a high order was considered by many to be an obstacle to theory-building.

Actually, the bulk of classical political philosophy about questions such as the good order of society or the ends of man is not at all incompatible with empirical theory on a middle-range or case level. We need not discard the entire teachings of a great political philosopher because of a few empirically unverified or clearly erroneous statements. Nor is it necessary that we accept his statements just because his general political philosophy may be very impressive. It is possible to separate the different levels of theory according to their function and to give each kind of theory the place it deserves.

A postbehavioral mood? Ever since the late 1960s, there has been talk about a "postbehavioral mood" and a "new political science." The behavioral revolution, indeed, had run its course and most of its methodological and theoretical innovations had become quite accepted in most political science departments. The postbehavioral mood, however, does not constitute a new wave of methodological innovation as much as a time of stock-taking and reappraisal. There has been a noticeable trend back to normative political theory which had been all but forgotten among the behaviorists. And the advocates of a new political science would like the discipline to focus more on matters of acute social concern which they claim, not always justly, have been neglected in favor of knowledge for knowledge's sake by the "old political science."

Whatever may be the long-range impact of these trends, one thing is certain: There is plenty of life in this ancient discipline. Schools of thought contend bitterly over all kinds of issues. Waves of methodological revolution and innovation arise periodically to sweep the discipline. And, occasionally, political passion itself enters the fray or points political science to new directions, generally leaving the discipline none the worse.

CHAPTER 2 CLASSICAL ISSUES OF POLITICAL THOUGHT

From the earliest beginnings of the study of politics, outstanding thinkers have pondered the aims of man in political society. No student of politics today can afford to ignore the broad stream of political philosophy through which these great minds have enriched the Western political tradition over the centuries. We shall therefore trace some of the fundamental concepts of modern political life back to their roots in the political thought of the great Western philosophers. To do full justice to each of some twenty or thirty famous political philosophers, at least a full-year course surveying the history of political philosophy would be necessary. Within this book, we shall have to content ourselves with a selection of seminal ideas that played an important role in shaping the political tradition of the West.

PLATO: GOVERNMENT BY CONSENT OR BY PHILOSOPHER-KINGS?

Athens in the fourth century B.C. was a city glittering with the splendor of great art and culture and teeming with intellectual ferment and interest in political philosophy. Among its citizens (there were also slaves and resident foreigners who were not admitted to citizenship) an egalitarian democracy had developed, which, in some respects, went considerably beyond the standards of political equality found in contemporary Western democracies. A citizen of the Athenian *polis* was entitled to a variety of rights of political participation. He could vote in the monthly town meeting, the *Ecclesia*, and was eligible for jury duty and for various executive offices. In the election of jurors and magistrates, selection by lot and rotation in office played an important role. Terms were short and there were usually provisions against reelection. The Athenians prided themselves on their all-round ability to shine in many different pursuits of life. Because the Greeks valued participation in the life of the *polis* so highly, selection by lot, and other devices, aimed to provide as many citizens as possible an opportunity to hold political office at least once in their lifetime. The skills of statecraft were evidently considered no different from the skills required for other pursuits in which Athenians had shown such happy versatility. Only generals and shipbuilders were directly elected and eligible for reelection, on the theory that the technical nature of these offices made it imperative to gain men of superior skill. This consideration outweighed the demands of fairness toward the many citizens who might have wished to hold such an office for a short time.

Behind the unusual political institutions of Athenian democracy lay the fundamental conviction of the Greeks that citizenship in the *polis* and participation in its affairs ennobled a man and helped him to realize his moral character. The Greek city-states were small by our standards and had the benefit of a social atmosphere of such familylike intimacy and wholeness as we moderns in our vast and impersonal nation-states can hardly imagine. Decisions of public policy could be made upon a thorough discussion among the citizens themselves, who considered their political activities as the most important thing in their lives. In contrast to today, most executive offices required no extensive training and specialization.

Plato was born into an aristocratic family in Athens in 427 B.C. The most important influence molding his character was his friend and teacher Socrates (469–399 B.C.), the great moralist who fell victim to the intrigues of the democratic city-state and, on questionable grounds, was ultimately sentenced to die. The tragic death of his revered teacher, and his own aristocratic origins, led Plato to view with distaste the political egalitarianism and happy versatility of Athenian democracy and to regard the crushing defeat of Athens at the hands of the more disciplined and oligarchic state of Sparta in the

Peloponnesian War as proof of the inferiority of the democractic way of life. He laid down his convictions in a series of famous philosophical dialogues which number among the great literary masterpieces of the world. He also taught his theories in the Academy, a school he founded in Athens. Of greatest interest to the student of politics is his dialogue, *Republic*, although he modified his views somewhat in later writings—*The Statesman* and *The Laws*.

Government by philosopher-king

Plato's *Republic* describes a utopian city-state which is supposed to realize *justice* both in the state and in the lives of its individual citizens. By justice Plato meant a relationship among individuals and groups of the *polis* that allows everyone to engage in the activity for which he is suited best. A just life for the individual is one which fits him into a place in society that develops his special gift to the fullest capacity. Instead of the happy versatility of Athenian democracy, Plato proposed both a differentiation according to aptitudes and a social stratification according to the intrinsic worth of the individual. He divided his utopian society into three classes, according to the inclinations of its inhabitants. Those inclined to material pursuits and pleasures were to compose the lowest class—the merchants, farmers, and artisans. The next higher class, the auxiliaries, was to consist of men and women of spirit, or of physical courage, whose function would be that of defense and of keeping order. Finally, there was to be a ruling class, the guardians, or a single philosopher-king, who had distinguished themselves by superior wisdom and virtue, the qualities required for the extraordinarily difficult tasks of government. An elaborate process of education and selection was to separate and train the young for their roles in these three classes.

What a striking idea this was!—to turn government over to those most outstanding in wisdom and virtue—an idea that is especially pertinent today, when crisis and doubt challenge our most cherished beliefs. Throughout history, men have dreamed of making government and leadership the domain of "natural aristocracy." The Greek word "aristoi" means "the best," and aristocracy would be rule by the best. Plato and Socrates equated reason and virtue: if a man is capable of knowing what is good, he will do it. The philosopher-king is at the same time the most intelligent and the most virtuous man in the country, a ruler of singular ability, and a man so selfless that, according to Plato's *Republic*, he has to be forced to take on the authority of a king rather than spend his time in philosophical contemplation.

The thesis of the philosopher-king epitomizes Plato's position at one end of one of the perennial issues of politics and political philosophy. In the *Republic*, Plato poses the question: "Suppose we do find out what justice is . . . the pattern of an ideal state . . . can this theory ever be fully realized in practice?" And he proceeds to answer as follows:

Unless either philosophers become kings in their countries or those who are now called kings and rulers come to be sufficiently inspired with a genuine desire for wisdom; unless, that is to say, political power and philosophy meet together . . . there can be no rest from troubles . . . nor can this commonwealth which we have imagined ever till then see the light of day and grow to its full stature.[1]

A number of other passages in the *Republic* pursue the same idea, namely that statecraft is an exacting science that calls for the exercise of the highest intellects and not for the gathering of consent by a democratic counting of noses that may belong to both wise and foolish heads. Plato even rejected reliance on the accumulated experience of custom or the laws in favor of the rational faculty of his philosopher-king for discovering political truths.

In *The Statesman*, although beginning to despair of finding true philosopher-kings, he wrote:

Among forms of government that one is preeminently right and is the only real government, in which the rulers are found to be truly possessed of science, not merely seem to possess it, whether they rule by law or without law, whether their subjects are willing or unwilling.[2]

We may be shocked by this disparagement of law and consent, but his position is logically consistent: *If a man truly possessed of wisdom and virtue could be found,* a man who is vastly superior to anyone else in his grasp of what needs to be done in any specific case, what point is there in restraining his judgment with what is, by definition, the inferior judgment of the governed or the vagueness and generality of a law? Ordinary people, in the opinion of Plato and of many rulers and writers about politics since his days, can rarely be expected to penetrate the highly complex issues of politics and arrive at the right decision. In fact, they may often be unaware of what is in their best interest or too inclined to sacrifice their own best long-term benefit for temporary whim or pleasure. Worse yet, democratic organization often invites a multiplicity of leaders each to put forth

[1] Cornford edition, 471c–474b.

[2] H. N. Fowler's translation, 293c.

his own plans and to gather a following. Potentially, every member of a democratic community may wish to be the leader and come up with a different plan for all to follow. In the confusion it is very likely that no leader and no rational plan is followed and the community disintegrates instead into warring factions.

This argument, in one form or another, has reappeared time and again as a challenge to government by the consent of the governed. It is true that this argument has often provided a sophisticated excuse for stark tyranny. On the other hand, it would be simpleminded not to recognize that it has also served legitimate causes and highlighted legitimate doubts about government by consent.

Cases of stark tyranny are too familiar to bear more than a brief enumeration. Throughout history, absolute rulers have claimed to be acting with fatherly concern and circumspection and only in the interest of their subjects even when this assertion was obviously untrue. The terror regime of the Jacobins during the French Revolution was excused by Robespierre as the "despotism of liberty against tyranny," a despotism which had to use terrorism in order to "force men to be free." The Communist establishment of the Soviet Union, and other Communist countries, justifies its rank dictatorship over the masses with its philosopher-kinglike grasp of the alleged truths of Marxism-Leninism.

On the other hand, the paternalism of philosopher-kings can have a legitimate place whenever the basic conditions of government by consent, such as mass education and political maturity, are absent and have to be supplied by the mentally more advanced authority in charge. The mental adequacy of a population to mastering temporary crises of the environment or of new challenges of adaptation or survival is very often in doubt even in well-educated democracies. The concept of an enlightened despotism, which appealed even to such liberal minds as the French philosopher and writer Voltaire (1694–1778) and the British political philosopher Jeremy Bentham (1748–1832), aims in this direction. These men felt that the necessary reforms of their tradition-bound societies could never come about by action of the ignorant populace and hoped instead that kings and rulers might be persuaded to use their power to impose reform. The British idea of an enlightened and responsible ruling class, or an aristocracy constantly replenished with deserving commoners, also is not very far from Plato's concept of the philosopher-king. The development of some of the new nations—from Kemal Ataturk's Turkey to Habib Bourguiba's Tunisia—has led to coercion and dictatorial methods for the purpose, we hope, of furthering the lagging social and economic growth that can someday support a stable democracy. Even colonialism at its best, as only its most determined opponents will deny, contains the possibility of a beneficial paternalism, a trusteeship until the colonial people may be ready for self-government. In each instance, the question of good faith is crucial and can only be determined from case to case.

The question of the philosopher-king is also raised by the transformations that have occurred in politics and government since the days of Athenian democracy. In Athens at the time of Plato, government could still be handled by amateurs; political decisions could be made in discussions among citizens in the streets, in the *Ecclesia*, and in the magistracies. Judicial administration could be taken care of by popular juries, and most other administrative matters by amateurs selected by lot and rotation for a short term of office. It was little more than a hundred years ago, in England and in the United States, that civil administration was still so small and uncomplicated that the civil service was considered a convenient source of sinecures for political appointees. The political functions of ordering society were largely taken care of by self-regulating processes of society. The state did little more than exercise the functions of a night watchman.

Today, a vastly more populous, urbanized, economically interdependent and swiftly changing society has long resorted to turning over more and more of its self-regulation to a growing staff of experts in legislation and administration who direct the processes of change and adjustment. With this trend towards centralized and streamlined government by trained experts has come a restatement of the old Platonic thesis of the philosopher-king: The complexities of the regulation of modern society seem to call for a mastermind capable of planning—for a tightly unified administrative structure, or a brain trust, rather than for a diffuse government attendant upon the untrained minds of the hoi polloi. This has been a particularly persuasive argument in fields such as foreign relations, where the average citizen of a democracy can hardly be expected to know all the facts relevant to the great and fateful decisions that have to be made. It has also sounded convincing during times of severe economic crisis, when the individual citizen came to feel hopelessly at the mercy of vast economic forces and often put his faith into "economic philosopher-kings" inside and outside the government. On such occasions, in fact, the common man often cannot be expected to make an intelligent choice between the dubious economic panaceas of a demagogue and practicable economic alternatives.

In ancient Greece, the decline and eventual overthrow of Athenian democracy appeared to prove Plato right. Perhaps an Athenian philosopher-king could have anticipated and prevented the many ills that befell Athens and brought about the subjugation of all of Greece by foreign powers. Many centuries have passed since the days of Athenian democracy, and again democracy has risen, though this time under rather different circumstances and on a vastly broader scale. Let us examine the argument that government should be by the consent of the governed rather than by the infinite wisdom of a philosopher-king or an enlightened elite.

THE ARGUMENTS FOR GOVERNMENT BY CONSENT

The demand that government should be by consent runs like a red thread through the history of political theory from the Greeks to our day. Among the better known landmarks of this story is the triumph of the English barons over King John in 1215, which resulted in his signing the Magna Charta, a document securing their ancient freedoms and privileges against royal encroachment. Of abiding influence on the development of democratic government in England and America were the writings of the British philosopher John Locke (1632–1704). In his *Second Treatise on Government*, Locke supplied the philosophy underlying the Glorious Revolution of 1688 which forever made the British monarch dependent upon the consent of the representatives of the people in Parliament. Locke took as his point of departure the individual and his natural rights and freedoms, which are prior to society and government. Man enters society by means of a social contract which guarantees his rights and spells out his duties. Government is established as a trust to be operated solely for the protection of individual rights. The people are the supreme authority and their consent is the standard of right policy for the government. As the American Declaration of Independence was to put it nearly a century later:

We hold these truths to be self-evident, that all men are created equal, that they are endowed by their Creator with certain inalienable Rights, that among these, are Life, Liberty, and the pursuit of Happiness. That, to secure these rights, Governments are instituted among Men, deriving their just Powers from the consent of the governed. That, whenever any form of Government becomes destructive of these ends, it is the Right of the People to alter or to abolish it, and to institute new Government, laying its foundations on such Principles, and organizing its Powers in such form as to them shall seem most likely to effect their Safety and Happiness.

Since the time of the foundation of the American Republic, we have been able to gather much firsthand evidence both here and abroad of how government by consent works and where its weaknesses lie. In the old days, disciples of Locke used to point to the selfish or stupid practices of rulers and ruling classes and justify their preference for popular rule by saying: "People are the best judges of their own interest, since nobody will knowingly injure himself," or "Only the wearer can know where the shoe pinches." In the complex world of today, however, it is no longer so easy to know what will injure us and what will help us. In the early thirties, for example, the German people were driven to despair by the Great Depression and voted Adolf Hitler into power. In doing this, they were obviously acting against their own best interest. Rank prejudices against such groups as Jews or Blacks can become the nub of a scapegoating mechanism in times of crisis, if the will of the majority prevails. Other instances of large numbers of people panicking before typical modern crises into suicidal decisions could be cited in order to demonstrate that people often do not know where the shoe pinches. Instead of locating the real source of pain they may even decide to cut off their whole foot in their frenzy to kill the pain.

It also used to be thought that the coming of democracy would automatically eliminate governmental oppression and even wars. It was taken for granted that the majority will of the people would have the public interest at heart and would be peacefully inclined. But government by consent has often meant that a few well-organized interest groups control public policy through lobbying and at the expense of the broad public interest. In highly urbanized and industrialized countries, moreover, government by consent has tended to lead to the unchecked pollution of the environment and to leave a myriad of social tasks undone. The advocates of democracy have also learned that chauvinistic public opinion in a modern democracy can be as greedy and warlike as any absolute ruler with a penchant for territorial aggrandizement. Almost all of the new democratic governments established in Central, Southern, and Eastern Europe after World War I soon turned into oppressive dictatorships.

As a consequence of the emergence of these and other limitations of government by consent, a host of critics of democracy has appeared in the twentieth century. Some of them simply argue in Platonic fashion against majority rule. They contend, for example, that a comparison of the ability of majority and minority to think of the right solution for a given political problem will often show up majority rule as government by a multitude of inferior minds. Many advocates of democracy themselves are in reality advocating a kind of "democratic elitism" in which various oligarchic devices such as representative government make sure that a political elite rather than the demos (people) itself will rule.[3] Other critics of democracy, notably Fascists and Communists, are venomous in their contempt for the procedures of free government that we profess. Instead of democracy, most critics recommend either an autocratic form of government, which omits the consent of the governed altogether because they consider it a nuisance or totally unnecessary, or a totalitarian government, which simulates the consent of the people by propaganda and terror—by the carrot and the whip. Some of the critics wish to discard organized government altogether.

Because of these limitations and criticisms, should we abandon government by consent? Certainly not. Winston Churchill once called democracy "the worst form of government, except for all the others that have ever been tried." Here indeed lies the crux of the matter. It is easy to condemn democratic regimes and their majority rule because of the inadequacies and frequent errors. But what can one expect of rule by a minority? Plato himself in his later years began to despair of finding wise and virtuous philosopher-kings and contented himself, instead, with designing a "second best state" that would be based on good laws. Many political theorists after him have asked the classic question *Quis custodiet ipsos custodes?* (But who is going to watch the guardians?)

We have also to bear in mind that contemporary government has long developed a workable compromise between government by an "enlightened elite" and the principle of consent. This compromise simply consists in the evolution of a staff of experts in the regulation of modern society by legislation, adjudication, and administration. Not only are our legislators, judges, and administrators carefully selected and trained both by formal education and by experience, but they are organized so as to coordinate their individual decisions as if there were only one will behind them. Judges and administrators are organized into hierarchic structures in which the lower levels have to conform to the decisions of higher echelons. The decisions of legislators win effect only by the formal passage of a bill with the majority support of the whole legislative body. Like Plato's philosopher-king, these regulators of modern society can devote their lifetime training and career to thinking about what is best for us. They can also prepare alternative proposals of policy and submit them and their own careers in an election to the people.

To be sure, the element of consent implicit in the choice of a voter in the national elections of a large democratic country may seem

[3] See Chapter 4 for definitions of various kinds of democracy.

small considering the many different issues he will have to approve or condemn in bulk and the many decisions upon which he can exercise little or no influence. A modern republic is a far cry from the direct democratic self-government of the Athenians meeting in their *Ecclesia* or from the New England town meeting of old. But the limited choice of the ballot still holds within itself the power to say "Yes" or "No" to a party, a policy, a set of leaders, in short, the power to "turn the rascals out." As the British political theorist A. D. Lindsay has pointed out in his book *The Modern Democratic State,* this element of consent, however limited, can guide and restrain a democratic government quite effectively. In particular, the people can and do let their government know on crucial decisions what they are prepared to do and at what point they will cease to cooperate with it. In the long run, no democratic government can afford to ignore popular sentiment on an important issue.

ARISTOTLE: THE SCIENTIFIC ANALYSIS OF POLITICS

Although Plato in his quest for the ideal state did important groundwork for the study of politics, it remained for his famous disciple Aristotle (384–322 B.C.) to make the study of politics a systematic scientific discipline. Aristotle's name is connected with the beginnings of almost every important scientific or philosophical discipline of Western intellectual life. In the Renaissance, more than 1,500 years after his death, his towering intellectual stature was still so generally recognized that a great writer on politics, Niccolo Machiavelli (1469–1527), referred to him in his works not by name but only as "the philosopher." The reading public of that age was expected to know who "the philosopher" was.

The ends of man

To Aristotle, politics was the master science. His political insights and the results of his political research are laid down in his *Politics,* which was culled from the lecture notes, so to speak, of students of government in his philosophical school at Athens, the Lyceum. The *Politics* concerned itself both with questions of the ends of man and with the study of actual constitutions and policies and what we can learn from them about the appropriate means to the chosen end. Aristotle considered man a *zoon politikon,* a being meant for life in the *polis.* The ideal state, according to Aristotle, is one of constitutional rule. He defined constitutional rule as government in accordance with three criteria: (1) lawful procedures and well-established customs, (2) government by consent—though not necessarily democracy—and (3) rule in the interest of all rather than in the interest of only the ruling class. Like Plato and other Greek thinkers before him, Aristotle distinguished among three basic kinds of government—monarchy, aristocracy, and democracy—as well as between these and their degenerate forms—tyranny, oligarchy, and mob rule. The criteria for these distinctions are the number of rulers and whether they rule in the common interest or only for themselves. But where government conforms to the precepts of constitutional rule, it was not very important to him whether it was a democracy, an aristocracy, or a monarchy, although he rather preferred monarchy. Aristotle's whole approach to the study of politics was colored by his common sense, his regard for the accumulated wisdom of the ages in law and custom, and his reluctance to engage in speculative flights of fancy about something as precious as the good life of man in the *polis*.

Aristotle's comparative analysis

In addition to these philosophical insights into the ends of politics, Aristotle laid the groundwork for the scientific analysis of politics by his discovery of the comparative method. As a tool of political analysis the comparative method can be compared to the role of experimentation in the natural sciences. The experiment in physics or chemistry, for example, serves to test working hypotheses about the nature of physical or chemical processes under controlled conditions. The factors of a given experiment can be varied in order to permit conclusions about the causal relationship between a given combination of factors and a certain result. One great advantage of the experimental method is that a given experiment can be repeated many times under the same or intentionally varied conditions. The conditions and results of each experiment in the series can then be compared and related to one another; we can draw causal inferences and minimize sources of error.

The comparative method of analysis in political science works in a similar manner: instead of repeating an experiment many times, we try to find as many instances of our "experiment" in real life settings as possible. Then we try to learn by comparison and close observation how the factors in each "experiment" operate, what factors or combinations of factors appear to cause what results, or under what circumstances certain means will achieve certain results. To illustrate:

Suppose we considered the adoption of a parliamentary form of government for the federal government of the United States in order to produce greater cooperation and unity between Congress and the

*executive branch. Such an undertaking has an implicit working hypo-
thesis, namely that parliamentarism under American conditions will
unify these two branches of government without producing any ill
side-effects. To test this hypothesis, we shall have to start out by
giving each of our terms a very concrete and precise definition: What
exactly do we mean by "unifying" in this connection? What are the
"American conditions" relevant to such a change? In what sense can
we speak of two separate branches which we now want to unify?
What ill side-effects would we consider momentous enough to vitiate
even the achievement of this "unified direction"? These secondary
questions already demonstrate the immense complexity of the whole
question. The most important question is still to come: What is parliamentarism? Under what conditions does it flourish? Under what
conditions will it produce the unity we have defined above? What are
the likely effects other than unity that flow from its adoption?*

*To answer the question about the nature of parliamentarism, we
have to collect and analyze the examples of parliamentary systems in
all places and at all times, such as in England in varying versions
since the eighteenth century, in France since the 1870s, in the Weimar
Republic and the Bonn Republic Republic of Germany, and in many
other countries and periods where it was adopted. We would discover immediately that there are considerable differences both in design and mode of operation among parliamentary systems. Some
seem to operate more efficiently than do others. From this diversity
arises the need for a sophisticated scheme of classification that will
order our collection of cases according to the categories most relevant
to our inquiry.*

*Furthermore, we have to examine the settings and conditions under
which these parliamentary systems functioned, and the relation of
parliamentarism under a given set of circumstances to our objective
of effective coordination between Congress and the President. We
may find out, for example, that the party system prevailing in a particular country is crucial to the optimal operation of parliamentary
government. Naturally, then, we have to examine the American party
system in order to learn whether or not this main condition of a
workable parliamentarism is suitable. Needless to add, this part of
our study involves a comprehensive comparative understanding of
what party systems there are and how they function. Only after we
have duly analyzed each case of parliamentary government in its
peculiar setting and ascertained what makes a particular kind of
parliamentarism work well and produce the desired unity of direction,
are we in a position to give a reasonably accurate estimate of whether
or not this kind of parliamentarism would work in the United States,*

and whether it would fulfill the desired goal without undesirable by-products.

During this whole process of "experimenting" by studying the "laboratory reports" of past and ongoing experiments with parliamentarism under varying circumstances, our working hypothesis is likely to have undergone some modification and refinement: We will have become aware of what design of parliamentary government produces the desired result and what others do not. We will have learned what major factors other than the constitutional design affect the mode of operation and the effect of parliamentarism on our objective. Perhaps, the most important conditions for successful parliamentary government lie in the homogeneity of a nation, its constitutional tradition, its national character, the party system, or in the manner in which the change to parliamentarism comes about. We will have learned also to discount interferences with parliamentarism from outside the country or by popular discontent within the political system concerned. To make our working hypothesis meaningful, we have to take for granted that the people of a country want to adopt or continue parliamentary government.

After all this refinement by testing it in "experiment" after "experiment," our working hypothesis will have become a highly sophisticated tool of analysis which will tell us not only whether the United States could achieve unified direction of executive and legislative powers by the adoption of parliamentary government, but it will also reveal whether or not any other given country might adopt it for this purpose and why this system of executive-legislative relations has not worked well in some instances. Last, but by no means least, the tested insights of our whole research operation can be utilized for other inquiries in related subjects.

The comparative method today Today the comparative method is one of the chief tools of political science analysis. Its application need not carry comparison across national boundaries. A good deal of excellent political science research has merely compared institutions or practices of different state governments or local governments within the United States or a particular institution or practice, say, of the 1920s with its counterpart of today. In fact, there is an advantage to limiting comparison to one country or at least to one political region of the world: If we compare settings that are too dissimilar, the significance of the conclusions we can draw may become too vague to be of practical value. Apart from general macropolitical features, little is to be learned from comparing the politics of a nomadic tribe with that of a highly urbanized country. Very often also, the comparative nature of political science analysis is implicit rather than expressed. When we study a single political system, such as our own, and speak about such things as "the separation of powers," "executive prerogative," or why we have a "two-party system," we are often drawing upon comparative study and experience. In fact, it is very difficult to be sophisticated about the study of a single case without the benefit of comparative knowledge, whether or not this knowledge is gained by direct observation or indirectly by training in concepts sharpened by the comparative studies of other political scientists. Political science as a body of well-tested concepts and relationships is, like all sciences, the product of the work of many people over a long period of time. Hence, training in political science automatically transmits to the student the benefits of many insights gained by comparative study.

Aristotle's objective

To return to Aristotle, this major breakthrough toward making the study of politics a science was initiated with his famous collection of 158 Greek city-state constitutions. Unfortunately, all but one of these case histories have been lost, the only survivor being the *Constitution of Athens*, which was rediscovered in 1891. But we can surmise from this case history and from a large part of his *Politics* what his objective was in this first great venture of comparative analysis on a grand scale. He wanted to know the causes that destroy or preserve city-states and make for good or bad government or, in other words, what a statesman should know for his striving after the best and most stable constitution practicable. Aristotle started out by defining a constitution as an arrangement of offices and went beyond the classification into three major forms and their perversions as it was customary at that time. He distinguished between the form of a constitution and the way it was operated; a democracy, for example, might function oligarchically. He also contrasted lawless and law-abiding governments. Finally, he examined the economic and social substructures of his city-state constitutions and drew distinctions according to which social classes were dominant, whether or not the main division was between the rich and the poor, or of an occupational character such as farmers, artisans, and merchants. With this scheme of classification, he arrived at some rather striking conclusions.

Oligarchy and democracy, Aristotle found, were the main types of Greek constitutions in his time. But there were several kinds of each. Different types of democracy could be distinguished—according to whether the masses were encouraged to participate in the conduct of public affairs, or whether they were content with leaving the main decisions in the hands of a few elected officials as long as the latter governed well. The latter version, an oligarchically functioning democracy, appeared to be a fairly stable and satisfactory type of government. Oligarchies likewise can have a small or a broad basis, depending on the number of privileged persons or families holding power. In a democracy, the many poor hold power, whereas in an oligarchy the few rich hold power. Aristotle considered a broadly based oligarchy the better type of oligarchy.

The greatest cause of civil unrest in the Greek states appeared to be the issue of equality. Oligarchies were usually overthrown by the masses sooner or later because equality was denied them. Egalitarian democracies sooner or later turned into oligarchies because there were always some people among the masses who felt that more power should go to those who by merit, birth, or wealth stood out above the crowd. Stability and good government, Aristotle reasoned, might be attained best by regimes that blended the democratic and oligarchial elements as in the two examples mentioned above, an oligarchically operating democracy or a broadly based oligarchy, or perhaps in a constitution by which the few rich and the many poor share power. Better still, if one could find a city-state with a strong middle class, this might well constitute the best condition for good government and stability. For members of the middle class, according to Aristotle, will be more amenable to reason, more willing to submit to or exercise reasonable authority, and more moderate in their policies than the members of either extreme in social rank and wealth.

It is particularly noteworthy that Aristotle's comparative study of the causes of civil unrest in Greece resulted in conclusions that were at variance with his preference for monarchy. He evidently did not allow his preference to prejudice the outcome of his research operation. We should also stress the manner in which he moved from Plato's philosophical and psychological reasoning toward the construction of autonomous variables which he could manipulate in his comparison. This great step from political philosophy to social science, of course, is applicable also to many other issues raised by the political philosophers regarding the role of the individual vis-à-vis the social groups with which he lives or the political community in which he participates. The social science approach to these particular issues has been expanded in the last decade, especially, with the study of *political socialization,* which investigates how a young person grows into the role of the citizen of a given political community.[4] The study of the actual learning and enculturation processes of the young among the socializing agents of a particular society, such as the family, the school and peer groups, and the political system itself is of course on a very different plane from a philosophical discussion of what the individual owes to his political community.

Questions of the political obligation of the individual, or of his social obligation to the groups around him, such as the filial piety advocated by Chinese philosophy, have preoccupied philosophers for more than two thousand years. Does a man really owe it to his country to allow himself to be drafted and maimed or killed in war, any war? Should a man or woman really have to surrender hard-earned income by way of taxation to a government which may not share his or her ideas of what constitutes worthwhile public expenditures? Individualistic societies (that is, societies in which the individual is considered to owe little to the political community) are far more vexed by these dilemmas than collectivistic societies (in which vast political and social obligations are taken for granted) such as China or the Soviet Union, because individualists are reluctant to accept even majority decisions in these painful matters, not to mention the oligarchic decisions of modern, bureaucratized systems. Political philosophers have agonized over these and related matters for centuries and have often tried to respond with elaborate philosophical constructions such as the "organic community," "universal man," "the social contract," or the "invisible hand." Students unfamiliar with the original works of the political philosophers discussed here are well advised to consider carefully the logic of these constructs without attempting to reconcile them with scientific findings or methods. These works are not meant as statements of fact but rather as illustrations of the logic of social life advocated by each philosopher. Radical individualism itself or the collectivistic rationale of Communist or communal societies likewise are philosophical paradigms rather than factual descriptions of how the people in them actually live.

THE INDIVIDUAL AND THE COMMUNITY

When an individual is born into this world, he is not immediately self-sufficient or able to make his own decisions. Even though in his

[4] For a survey of methods and approaches, see Roberta Sigel (ed.), "Political Socialization: Its Role in the Political Process," *Annals of the American Academy of Political and Social Science* (September 1965).

later life he may become a radical individualist and feel beholden to nobody and least of all to his political community, for the first ten or fifteen years of his life he is likely to be utterly dependent on his family. As he grows older and begins to think on his own, moreover, he has already been living for more than a decade as a member of several kinds of groups or communities of varying size: his family, his friends, his school, his neighborhood, his local community, his region, and his country. All of these mold his thinking and way of life. Once he becomes economically self-sufficient and founds his own family, there are other groups of which he becomes a member: occupational or professional associations, trade unions, clubs, political groups, and others. His membership in most of these groups, at least in the smaller and more intimate circles, is likely to engage him not merely in a rational, reflective way, but also on a deeper emotional level where he communicates, imitates, joins group action, and adjusts to group values without giving them much thought. Thus group contacts become the vehicle through which his way of life is transmitted to him from the family group in ever-widening and many times overlapping circles, which finally include the civil society of a modern state.

The organic community

Aristotle was aware of this multiple-group character of a political community and described in some detail how villages are made up of families, and commonwealths of villages. The political community to him is "a creation of nature" and man is "by nature a political animal." Further, "the political community is by nature clearly prior to the family and to the individual, since the whole is of necessity prior to the part." And the great philosopher went on to demonstrate the "natural" character of the state and its "priority" to the individual by asserting that an isolated individual is not self-sufficient, unless he be a beast or a god.

This statement of the position of the individual in the political community is the classical one that has been echoed down through the ages. Among the disciples of the organic concept of the political community were a host of medieval philosophers including such illustrious men as St. Thomas Aquinas (1226–1274) and the British political philosopher John of Salisbury (about 1120–1180), who in his *Statesman's Book* likens the body politic to a human body of which the clergy is the soul, the prince the head, the senate the heart, the judges and provincial governors eyes, ears, and tongue, soldiers and officials the hands, the financial officers the stomach and intestines, and the husbandmen the feet. The implications of such an organic concept are usually fivefold:

1. The organic nature of the body politic usually allows no distinction between state and society. The state is regarded as the political form of society.

2. There is the notion of plantlike growth of the body politic which thereby links the past with the future and precludes arbitrary changes that could upset the "organism."

3. There is a functional division among the component parts of the body politic which can be no more easily exchanged than a man can replace his head with his foot.

4. The interrelation among the parts is God-given and forever fixed, an "organic unity" superior to any man-made kind of harmony.

5. There is no equality among the parts just as the loss of the head of a human body is more consequential than that of a hand.

In the social reality of the Middle Ages, organic notions implied the presence of several unequal classes in society in which birth determined the station of the individual in life. The social order was supposed to be God-given and immutable. The three main classes of society were the clergy, the nobility, and the common citizenry, headed by king and pope. To a medieval mind, they constituted an analogy to the hierarchical order among God and his angels in the heavenly spheres.

The rise of individualism

The concept of the organic community and the position of the individual within it was challenged by the dawn of a new age of individualism in the sixteenth, seventeenth, and eighteenth centuries. It is difficult to determine the causes of this new individualistic attitude toward all spheres of life. But it becomes quite evident in many ways: in religion, with the rise of Protestantism and its new stress on personal, individual religious experience; in economics, with the rise of capitalism, which emphasizes individual endeavor and its rewards; and in politics, with the rise of absolutism on the one hand and of social contract theories on the other. The new individualism meant basically a striving for personal autonomy, independence from the prevailing religious order —the Catholic Church—freedom from the prevailing economic constraints, emancipation from the bonds of the prevailing social and political order. Radical individualism in political philosophy found expression particularly in the idea of a social contract to bind the otherwise completely autonomous individual.

Social contract theories

Theories of *social contract* were not new at the time, nor did they die out with this period. As early as the days of Plato we find philosophers reducing the cohesion of political society to a quasi-contractual obligation among the individuals composing it. Still, at the end of the nineteenth century, the British social philosopher Herbert Spencer (1820–1903) speaks of a social contract in his book *Man Versus the State*. The full flowering of social contract thinking occurred in the age of individualism whose explicit premise was that the individual is prior to the political community and owes it only a limited allegiance. The idea of a social contract was able to reconcile the contradiction between this individualistic premise and the obvious fact that man is born into society and tied to it in many ways. Now political thinkers could speak about a *state of nature*, in which man was definitely a solitary individual, and about man entering civil society by means of the social contract, which spelled out his rights and obligations as a member of society.

A review of the most prominent social contract theories in this connection presents a somewhat confusing picture. There are really three kinds of social contract among which some of the political thinkers make no sharp distinction: (1) There is the social contract which ties isolated individuals into a society (discussed in the preceding paragraph). (2) There is the idea of a contract between people and their rulers, a notion which implies government by the consent of the governed, which was touched upon in our discussion of John Locke (pp. 33–34). (3) There is the Biblical concept of a contract between the people and their God. The first prominent social contract theory of the rising individualistic age, for example, was developed by the French Huguenots, sixteenth-century Calvinists, who were trying to defend their religious freedom against the Catholic monarchy of France. In their pamphlet *Defense of Liberty Against Tyranny*, they used a double contract between the people on the one hand and both God and the king on the other. If the king forced them to break their covenant with God, they argued, he thereby also rendered their social contract with him null and void and freed them from their obligation to obey him. The Huguenots were evidently not concerned with the basic contract that holds society together.

Hobbes's social contract theory A more pertinent example of radical individualism and social contract can be found in *Leviathan*, the work of the British political philosopher Thomas Hobbes (1588–1679). Hobbes takes as his point of departure a grim picture of the *state of nature,* in which man is motivated solely by greed, "vainglorious pursuits," "continual fear, and danger of violent death." It is a state of continuous war of every man against every other man, and human life in it is "solitary, poor, nasty, brutish, and short." To escape this terrible life, men enter society by means of a social contract, which establishes among them an "artificial" (that is, not natural) community. Because Hobbes was an apologist for absolute monarchy, he concludes that the content of this social contract is the surrender of all individual power to the absolute ruler, who is not himself a party to the contract. The only right retained by the individual upon entering society is that of defending himself against the infliction of death, injury, or imprisonment by anyone, including the state. As can be seen, the use of the idea of the basic social contract in political philosophy is not necessarily connected with government by consent as we know it. Radical individualism can be the basis for despotism as well as for democracy.

Locke's social contract theory The social contract theories of this age reached their climax in the thought of John Locke, who described the state of nature in more pleasant colors than did Hobbes. His social contract theory is a combination of the kind of contract that ties individuals together into a civil society with a contractual relationship between the people and their government. It is from the basic social contract, which makes a body politic out of individuals, that Locke derived the basic natural rights of man. Man gives up the state of nature for civil society only for the mutual preservation of life, liberty, property, and the pursuit of happiness, and therefore retains the right to these goods after entering society. In fact, when the people proceed to set up a government on the basis of a trust, its sole purpose is to protect and guarantee those rights to life, liberty, property, and the pursuit of happiness.

It is from the Lockean version of the social contract that the opening phrases of the Declaration of Independence stem:

We hold these truths to be self-evident, that all men are created equal, that they are endowed by their Creator with certain inalienable *rights, that among these, are Life, Liberty, and the pursuit of Happiness.*

This is also the origin of many of the concepts in the American

Bill of Rights, especially those contained in the First and Fifth Amendments regarding the freedoms of religion and of speech and the injunction against depriving a person of life, liberty, or property without due process of law. Lockean thinking likewise makes up the core of the civil rights of most modern constitutions in other Western democracies, beginning with the French Declaration of the Rights of Man, which was proclaimed at the time of the French Revolution and stated among other tenets:

Article II: The end of every political association is the conservation of the natural and imprescriptible rights of man. These rights are liberty, property, security and resistance to oppression.

The underlying idea of this individualistic contribution to the spirit of modern government is that the individual is prior to the community and that, in fact, the political community exists only as a result of the basic social contract which ties individuals together and gives them specifiable rights within the community. In this connection, we must not take the concepts of the social contract and the state of nature too literally or in a historical sense. Hobbes and Locke did not intend to suggest that men actually lived in this state of nature at one time and ended it by entering a social contract. Nor did they mean to imply that the individual, who is born into society, now is given a choice between signing the social contract and returning to the state of nature. The idea of the social contract is merely a means of explaining the priority of the individual to society and the standing of individuals in it. By the same token, Aristotle had no intention of claiming that the *polis* actually antedates the individual and the family when he said that it was prior to them. He just meant that human nature was meant for life in the *polis* and derived meaning only from being a part of the *polis* community.

The return to collectivism

The new age of individualism had hardly begun to flower into actual institutions and guarantees of individual rights, when its tenets were contradicted both in theory and fact by a return to the collectivism of community-oriented life. Although some of the traditions of individualism survive into our time, owing in some cases to their enshrinement in the constitutions or constitutional practices of modern democratic states, the impact of the various new all-pervading and all-demanding communities on the history of the last 150 years has been great. To illustrate this new trend, we shall discuss three outstanding representatives—Rousseau, Burke, and Hegel—of the return to community-orientation as well as its practical manifestations during modern history.

The influence of Rousseau   One of the important influences of the return to collectivism was the writings of Jean Jacques Rousseau (1712–1778), who, in his earlier period, had himself been an individualist. Born in Geneva of French parents, Rousseau grew up without a mother and at sixteen ran away to lead a life of vagabondage and restlessness. His brilliant mind grasped the gradual decay of individualistic attitudes in the spirit of his time and expressed it forcefully and with great emotion. His thought is full of contradictions, though always presented with an air of overwhelming sincerity. As is true of many a modern man, his mind harbored deep inner conflicts, religious and moral guilt feelings, and a fervent longing for a community or place in life to which he could belong, though his unsteady life seemed to belie his writings. Roussea's encounter with the social and literary elegance of the highly individualistic society of eighteenth-century Paris, the glittering cultural and intellectual metropolis of Europe, left him in a state of revulsion against the vanity, the greed, and the selfishness of the individuals who dominated Paris high society and the literary salons. He had more faith in the "common man," as he had come to know him during his years of wandering. Simple in his needs, the common man was free from the corrupting influences of civilization and refinement; instead of the calculating mind of individualistic self-interest, he was possessed of a fundamental sincerity and naïve morality which flowed freely from a compassionate heart, and was as capable of physical courage as he was of lasting personal loyalty and patriotism.

Like Plato and Aristotle, Rousseau believed that a body politic should not exceed a size that allowed the most intimate bonds of friendship and community spirit to hold it together. The ancient Greeks had thought of the ideal size of a body politic as one which would allow all the citizens to gather within earshot of a speaker addressing them at the town meeting. Rousseau agreed with their notion of a tightly knit and all-pervasive community and went to great lengths in his book on education, *Emile,* in talking about what a citizen owes to his community. He even advocated, as did Plato in his *Republic,* a civic religion of patriotism with which the citizens from early youth should be indoctrinated for good citizenship. After developing the role and identification of a good citizen with his small and intimate community, Rousseau applied the same concept to the much larger new community of the modern nation. In this fashion the Platonic idea of citizenship in the *polis* was transferred into a rationalization for the rising tide of nationalism.

In his book *The Social Contract,* Rousseau finally presented his mature thought about the organization and conduct of affairs of his ideal state. The title is somewhat misleading, because his individuals lose all their individual rights to the collectivity upon entering the community. His state enjoys the same organic unity that we have noted with regard to political thought from Plato to the dawn of the individualistic age, except for the inegalitarian implications of the other organic theorists, which he does not share. Rousseau's *polis*, like that of the ancient Greeks, is a source of value and meaningful existence of the highest order. Its common good takes precedence over the interest of any part of it or individual member, and even over the aggregate of individual interests. In fact, the individual member is enjoined to take an active part in the determination of policy aiming at the common good. As every righteous citizen wills the common good, there emerges the *General Will* which is intrinsically moral and the supreme lawgiving power of the people.

The doctrine of the General Will sounds noble in theory, but has been questioned as to its practical applicability. What happens if a part of the people, a minority, should be of a different opinion than the rest regarding what is good for the country? Such disagreements, after all, occur every day in a well-functioning democracy. Rousseau has given a rather disturbing answer to this question. He would prefer to see no "particular associations," no minorities that frustrate the attaining of unanimity. Long debates and dissent are "signs of the decline of the state." Because the General Will derives its moral character from the common good, and the only form of moral freedom for individual members of the community consists in their participation in the formulation of the General Will, there is the implication that dissenting individuals or groups are engaging in something immoral or selfish. Therefore, Rousseau points out, they "have to be forced to be free" or must be coerced to see the light and the truth of the "common good." Perhaps, such a doctrine is practicable within the confines of the town meeting democracy of a tiny village. If applied to a larger community or modern nation, however, it is likely to produce tyranny—a totalitarian dictatorship of the majority or of righteous leaders trampling upon the rights of minorities and individuals.

The influence of Edmund Burke   Another important influence in the return to the collectivism of the community was the British philosopher and statesman Edmund Burke (1729–1797), who is often called the father of conservatism. A brilliant orator and writer, Burke was filled with a deep pessimism about the ability of the individual and his rational faculty to penetrate the mysteries of politics and government. The excesses of the French Revolution of 1789, the most ambitious climax of the radical individualism and faith in natural human rights of the Enlightenment, prompted Burke to spell out fully his conservative views on government in his famous *Reflections on the Revolution in France*. In this work he took issue, in particular, with the boundless human arrogance of the revolutionary leaders who considered themselves so emancipated from religious belief, social conditioning, and historical continuity that they undertook to reconstruct society and constitution with but a few pretentious, abstract theories about the natural rights of something called the "universal man." To Edmund Burke, a constitution was a living thing such as the time-worn conventions of British constitutional life, the historic rights of Englishmen, and the traditions and institutions of a rich national culture hallowed by patriotism and moral sentiment. Political society or the state, he wrote in a famous passage, ought to be considered more

than a partnership agreement in a trade of pepper and coffee, calico or tobacco, or some other such low concern, to be taken up for a little temporary interest, and to be dissolved by the fancy of the parties. It is to be looked on with other reverence; because it is not a partnership in things subservient only to the gross animal existence of a temporary and perishable nature. It is a partnership in all science; a partnership in all art; a partnership in every virtue, and in all perfection. As the ends of such a partnership cannot be obtained in many generations, it becomes a partnership not only between those who are living, but between those who are living, those who are dead, and those who are to be born.[5]

This eloquent tribute to an organic concept of political society places great emphasis on fitting the individual into the stream of national history. As Burke put it elsewhere in his writings:

The individual is foolish; the multitude, for the moment, is foolish, when they act without deliberation; but the species is wise, and, when time is given to it, as a species it always acts right.[6]

By the same token, Burke's political society has no use for democ-

[5] *Reflections on the Revolution in France* (1790).

[6] *Reform of Representation in the House of Commons* (1782).

racy or equality. It is a highly stratified society extending from the privileged nobility down to the last tallow-chandler. Everyone is expected to know his place, and political authority is reserved to the traditional ruling classes, the hereditary aristocracy, and the propertied interests. The temporal establishment, moreover, is suffused with religion and with the loyalty of the citizenry toward the national institutions and traditions. Burke leaves even less doubt than does Rousseau about the turning away, in his times, from the optimism of the Enlightenment about the capacity of the individual to order his political fate by the exercise of his reason.

The influence of Hegel A similarly potent contribution to the return from individualism to an identification with the community was made by the German philosopher G. W. F. Hegel (1770–1831). Hegel shared Burke's horror of the French Revolution, although he had at one time been rather partial to it. He conceived the history of the world and of particular nations as the movement of vast "ideas" and systems of ideas, which is the reason that his type of thinking is called *philosophical idealism*. These ideas evolve and rise to prominence in history, are challenged and fought by opposing ideas, and are finally superseded by a compromise between the old and the new, until this compromise is challenged in turn by the evolution of further new ideas. This method of explaining the events of history is called *dialectic idealism*. Twenty years later a disciple of Hegel, Karl Marx, appropriated the dialectic for his own purpose, turning it, however, "on its head." According to Marx it is not the ideas that manifest themselves in material conditions, but the material conditions that determine the "superstructure of ideas"; hence the term *dialectical materialism*.

Hegel's dialectic idealism amounted to both a rationalization of struggle in history as well as to a moralization of the actions of the struggling individual. History is but a stage upon which the great movement of ideas carries out the dialectical struggle. Individuals and, at times, whole peoples are no more than the instruments through which these ideas manifest themselves and act out their clashes. Hence, there is really nothing better to do for an individual but to try to be at one with the group to which he belongs and with the historical idea that happens to have taken possession of him.

One of the great ideas in history with which Hegel was particularly concerned was the *spirit of a nation* as it gradually evolves over the centuries and makes its mark in the politics of the world. As did Burke, Hegel believed that this national spirit creates the traditions and institutions of the political society in which we live, and good citizenship demands that we honor the sublime reason which this form of the political society, "the state," as both Burke and Hegel call it, has taken. In describing the relation of the individual to his political society, Hegel used such exalted language that he has often been accused of establishing a cult of the state and, in fact, of a German state. Although this point may have been stretched too far, there can be little doubt that he viewed the role of individuals in politics as a most modest one and had no sympathy for the doctrines of natural rights and enlightened individual self-interest. As was true of Rousseau and Burke, Hegel's view of the individual replaces the hard-won individual autonomy of the Enlightenment with an absorption by a larger group: the individual means nothing except as a member of a nation or as the instrument of a great cause.

Collectivism triumphant

In summing up the concrete developments of the days since the late eighteenth century, when the return from individualism to collectivism began, we can draw up a whole list of the different kinds of communities into which the spirit of the times and the advice of prominent philosophers wanted to confine individuals. It is advisable not to overestimate the influence of the political philosophers who rarely contribute more than an articulation of existing sentiments and conditions. First, there was the subordination of the individual to the unrestrained majoritarianism of Rousseau, which idea some recent writers have even suspected as the theoretical foundation of twentieth-century totalitarianism. Second, there was the submersion of individual freedom of decision in the evolving history of a national culture or a great idea, as we find it in Burke and Hegel. Third, we have the appearance of a large-scale nationalism as both a popular movement in many countries and a propensity of thinking of the times which hardly needed any assistance from the writings of a political philosopher. The *nation* as a very demanding collectivistic community, which had to be defended against all enemies—foreign and domestic—or as a nationalistic revolutionary movement for the achievement of an independent nation-state similarly required the individual to sacrifice his rights and self-interest to a larger whole.

Later, in the nineteenth century and also in the twentieth, there were further kinds of community which claimed the subservience of individuals and individual self-interest to the interest of the group to which they belonged. There was, in particular, racism, with a concept of *race* that was supposed to constitute the great collective, whose interests were said to be vastly more important than the happiness of individuals. There was also the "cult of the *state*," which the Italian Fascist dictator Mussolini called "an absolute, a strong organic body," from the service of which the individual citizens derive the importance of their lives. Last, but not least, there was the Marxist idea of *class*, of class consciousness and class struggle, all of which were supposed to be vastly more important than the pursuit of happiness of any single individual.

All of these demanding communities that have tended to supersede the individualistic tradition of Western civilization have been further encouraged by attitudes and reactions to the modern world that are widely current today. Among them is the romantic *cult of group life* which encourages individuals to immerse themselves in a group and its activities. Group life tends to bring about conformity and identification of the individual with the group in a largely nonrational, emotional manner that can circumvent both the moral scruples and the sober judgment of individual reason. Today, it is the fashion to complain about the tendencies of conformism that threaten to choke off the frail flower of individuality. On the other hand, it is also generally realized that radical individualism is a way of life that is immensely difficult in our time—partly because the state of modern industrial society is highly organized; partly because a great many persons lack the individual creativity, the emotional stability and self-confidence, and sometimes even the desire, to avail themselves of individual freedom when they could. Thus counsels of at least a measure of "togetherness" or "belonging" have pointed out quite correctly that a society composed of isolated and lonely individuals is far more likely to fall for a demagogue, a great ideological cause, or a totalitarian dictatorship than would a society in which the individual can fall back upon the emotional support of his group. However, it should be noted that this argument speaks only of a limited kind of engagement in any of the new and old kinds of community of our times and not of the sweeping demands of the communities mentioned above for individual self-effacement and self-sacrifice.

CHAPTER **3** **THE NATION-STATE IN MODERN TIMES**

The modern world has added many additional problems and new solutions to the perennial issues of political philosophy. A word of caution is in order in the discussion of modern issues. It would be naïve to attribute the rise of the modern state and of our democratic age chiefly to conscious efforts on the part of the movements or persons involved. A host of developments and factors combined to bring about the modern state. As the old Kentucky farmer replied to the queries of reporters who asked how he had raised such a huge, prize-winning hog for the country fair: "It jest growed." Let us examine in some detail the major features of some of the problematic developments of our time and the discernible causes for their growth to the present proportions.

STATE AND SOVEREIGNTY

During the last three or four hundred years, no other concept of political theory and practice has been as important as that of the state. Since the days of the Italian Renaissance, the reality of the modern state has forced political philosophers increasingly to take the state into account and to devote their thought to taming this vast new force in human affairs and adapting it to the purposes of man and society.

To understand fully the nature of the modern state, it is necessary that first we consider the circumstances which led to its evolution from its beginnings. Next we shall discuss some of the political philosophers who made an important contribution to the understanding and improvement of the state. Finally, we shall describe some of the accepted theories of the state as it evolved to the present day.

Evolution of the modern state

The modern state began to evolve in areas of Western Europe such as northern Italy as early as the fifteenth century. By the seventeenth century it was a fairly general phenomenon and had taken on an unmistakable form. In the nineteenth century, however, there were still some Western societies which had managed to avoid evolution toward a state form of government, or had, at least, prevented the consolidation of regional developments resembling states. In the twentieth century, statelike forms of government spread throughout the globe, especially since World War II, when even the last "stateless" societies of Africa were reorganized.

Let us consider, for the moment, the kinds of governments there were before the development of the state and in what ways they differed from state governments. The history of government goes back to primitive society, in which politics was shrouded in the mysteries of custom, kinship, and religious authority[1]. From there it was a long way to the rationally organized Greek *polis*, which possessed one important element of the modern state—citizenship—although in a form rather undifferentiated from partnership in the entire social life of the community. There were also the Greek concept of government as a joint enterprise of the community, or "an arrangement of offices," and notions of officeholders as trustees responsible to the community. These political ideas could have blazed a trail toward modern government had the Greek *polis* outlasted the rise of empires around it.

The Roman Republic and the Roman Empire made even greater strides toward the modern state, with its elaborate and rational system of law, its distinction of public and private spheres, and a differentiated concept of citizenship. In fact, the Roman govern-

---

[1] For a contemporary survey see Ronald Cohen and John Middleton, *Comparative Political Systems* (Garden City, N.Y.: The Natural History Press, 1967).

ment came about as close as any organized body politic to resembling the modern state. If it had not been for the basic inability of Rome —a body politic sprung from a typical city-state—to maintain stability and control over a vast multinational empire sprawled around the shores of the Mediterranean and as far north as England, Rome might have become a modern state. As it happened, this vast area could be held together only by alien armies whose generals eventually turned against the republic, made themselves emperors, and at times even turned the Roman Empire into little more than a form of oriental despotism.

Between the fall of Rome and the rise of the modern state lie centuries of political chaos and, ultimately, the rise of the feudal system, a development which reversed the trend toward the crystallization of political concerns. Politics and government once more merged with other social functions, particularly in the typical combination with legal and quasi-property relationships between feudal lords and vassals. Instead of political relations between rulers and citizens or subjects, the feudal lord "owned" land and people and loaned them out, so to speak, to lords of minor rank in exchange for military and other services.[2]

The modern state rose in Europe as a result of a series of incisive political, economic, and religious changes that occured at the decline of the Middle Ages and helped to usher in the Modern Age. Most important among these changes was the rise of European *power politics*, of *absolutism*, and of a new concern of governments for the *internal affairs* of their countries. Several important political philosophers and political leaders of that era also contributed to the elucidation and interpretation of the transformations of European life.

The rise of power politics in Europe

The rise of power politics in Europe was preceded by the decline of the unity and comity which the family of European nations had possessed under the sway of the Catholic Church in the Middle Ages. Religion seemed to lose its hold over the individual ruler as well as its power to prevent or at least conciliate all-out clashes of armed power among the members of this "family of nations." As the ruling dynasty of each individual country achieved greater independence from the European community and its moral guardian,

---

[2] For a good brief survey of the "prehistory" of the modern state, see Robert M. MacIver, *The Modern State* (New York: Columbia University Press, 1955), chaps. I–IV.

the universal church, it generally sought greater national power. With every country fighting either for survival or for territorial aggrandizement, the stage was set for the system of power politics that has occupied a very large part of European history. In this dog-eat-dog world of ambitious dynasties, there was almost constant war, often between great alliances of states that would shift in their composition from one day to the next. For the individual dynasty, the new (or ancient) art of diplomacy had the function of feeling out both friends and enemies in order to anticipate danger as well as to see to it that a country would have powerful allies when under attack. The art of war, likewise, became once more the science of survival that it had been, at times, in the ancient world. The "balance of power" concept was advantageous to the individual state in a bipolar system of alliances, as equal power was pitted against equal power, not allowing either side hope of victory.

Machiavelli's theory of the national interest An Italian writer and diplomat, Niccolo Machiavelli (1469–1527), witnessed and described the rise of the system of power politics among the small Italian states and the powerful foreign invaders of Renaissance Italy. He and his contemporaries were the first to use the word *lo stata*, the state. His famous work, *The Prince*, is a handbook for rulers and would-be rulers on the art of founding and preserving a state amidst the power struggles of his time. The extreme nature of the means he advocated, and his espousal of the doctrine that any means whatever are justified by the supreme end—the attainment and preservation of power—bear witness to the bitterness of the struggle, and its effect on the minds of men. One should also note Machiavelli's deliberate rejection of his predecessors in political philosophy of the preceding four centuries, who never forgot to relate their discussion of politics to religion and individual morality. Such scruples, Machiavelli implied, can be fatal in the battle of states for survival.

Machiavelli's greatest contribution to an understanding of the state as a historical phenomenon lies in the formulation of the doctrine of the "reason of state," or the "national interest," as it would be called today. "Countries are ruled by kings," the Huguenot general and duke, Henri de Rohan (1579–1638) had said, "but kings are ruled by interests." The most important such interest is the survival and independence of a state. A competent ruler is compelled by circumstances to do everything in his power to follow this basic interest.

The effect of power politics on the states The rise of a world of power politics made a deep impression upon each country and its government. Since the supreme interest of the existing states was their survival in a hostile world of constant threat of war, only a standing army could satisfy the pressing need of preparedness for both defense and aggression.

As it happened, many of the European countries involved in this development still had something resembling a constitutional order, including representative institutions in the form of provincial and general estates. These representative assemblies varied widely in their powers. In England they had control over the royal purse and in particular the royal power of taxation. The estates were composed of representatives of the nobility, the clergy, and the commoners, and took a dim view of standing armies and what they might do to suppress the historic liberties of their own people. Since the establishment of standing armies also involved vast new expenditures for which money had to be raised, the estates often clashed with the royal dynasties over issues of what would be called defense policy today.

In England and Sweden, the estates general eventually became modern parliaments. In continental Europe, the representative institutions declined, in the long run, under the impact of a world of power politics which required strong executive control for survival. In some cases, the estates were suppressed with the help of the standing army they had feared with good reason. In this fashion, the new system of power politics also contributed to the rise of absolutism.

The rise of absolutism

The rise of royal power to supremacy and absolute authority overcame the resistance not only of the ancient medieval estates, but also of the other intermediate bodies between the king and his subjects. There was, for example, the universal Catholic Church, which had shared power in the Middle Ages. The development of national churches and the struggle between Protestants and Catholics enhanced secular state power and helped to subdue the resistance of the religious forces on the continent to absolutism. The nobility was another formidable power that had once brought King John to his knees at Runnymede, although it had since fallen on bad days in many parts of Europe. A sustained effort either to uproot noblemen by inducing them to serve the king and enjoy life at his court, or to suppress them by force and economic pressure eventually leveled down aristocratic privileges and at the same time raised commoners to political power and economic accomplishments.

Although the developments in the various countries naturally differed from one another, and in some cases took centuries to come to completion, there was no mistaking the outcome: there arose a fundamental equality before the law which united the citizens, or subjects of the state, on a common political level. With the elimination of the intermediate bodies between a king and his subjects, moreover, the power of the state authority from now on could take direct and equal effect upon all citizens, collectively and individually. In a similar manner, the rising absolutism of France, for example, dealt with such intermediate bodies as historic provinces that had their own provincial estates and with autonomous cities. In a conscious effort to wipe out the old geographic identities, the French even drew new administrative boundaries for their absolutistic state administration and subordinated their local governments to strict administrative control by the central bureaucracy. In this fashion, the French State established its complete, direct and inescapable domination over its entire territory. The centralized nature of territorial control is also a typical feature of the modern state.

Bodin's theory of sovereignty The theory rationalizing the rise of absolutism is generally attributed to the French writer and political philosopher Jean Bodin (1530–1596). Bodin contended that in a well-ordered state there has to be a person, an agency, or a group of officeholders who exercise *sovereignty*, or supreme authority, over all the other persons or agencies of the state. This sovereign— and Bodin was evidently thinking of the King of France—is *legibus solutus*, or above all laws or commands of another except for the laws of God, of nature, and the basic constitutional order. Bodin, it appears, was very much concerned about the disintegration of the French body politic by the religious dissensions of his time between Catholics and Huguenots and may well have meant his theory of sovereignty as an attempt to salvage the political obligation of a French citizen amidst the conflict of loyalties caused by religious civil war. In addition to Bodin's *Six Books Concerning the State*, a number of other writings appeared in the sixteenth and seventeenth centuries which elucidated further aspects of the concept of sovereignty and of the modern state in general. Among them were treatises on the state in international law or the "law of nations" by Spanish Jesuits and Dutch and German Protestants such as Francisco Suarez (1548–1617), Hugo Grotius (1583–1645), Johannes Althusius (1557–1638), and Samuel Pufendorf (1632–1694), who emphasized, in particular, the international aspects of sovereignty: For a country to be sovereign in the international world it has to be independent and in full control of its external relations. Later theories of sovereignty stressed the legal structure of the state and the manner in which legal authority within a state is derived from the locus of sovereignty down through the hierarchy of political institutions. Other theories of sovereignty concerned themselves with the sovereign authority of the state vis-à-vis other social groups within society such as the churches, business establishments, and labor unions.[3]

The concern of governments for internal affairs

The third important strain in the development toward the modern state was the result of a combination of causes and felt needs of the entire period from the declining Middle Ages into the period of absolutism. The stresses of the Modern Age—religious dissensions, economic, and social crises, and the burden of costly wars—led to a new concern on the part of the existing governments for the internal affairs of their countries. And, unlike governments in the Middle Ages, the new governments were not content with accepting the economic order and basic structure of their societies. They deliberately attempted to change and improve the fabric of the society by whatever means appeared to lend themselves to their purposes of unity and consolidation of power.

Unifying the legal systems One of the most significant developments in this direction was the unification of the legal systems of the old feudal monarchies. In England, where legal unification began as early as the twelfth century, it was accomplished by the king's judges, who gradually built up an impressive body of case law, the common law. This law in time became a uniform civil and criminal law in place of what once had been an infinite variety of local versions of customary law under many separate feudal jurisdictions. In later centuries other Western countries followed suit and accomplished legal unification by other means, often by replacing the prevailing system with an entirely new code of law derived from Roman law. The consequences of legal unification always included

[3] It may be appropriate here to point out that the theory of sovereignty is difficult to apply to the United States Constitution. In this document, which appears to continue the older British tradition of the day of the Great Elizabeth, sovereign power was apparently divided not only between states and federal government but also among three coordinate branches, the presidency, Congress, and the Supreme Court. According to Bodin, however, sovereignty is supposed to be indivisible. It does not help to search for sovereignty in the people, because even they are divided into the peoples of the several states and the nation. Nor would Bodin admit that sovereignty can be lodged in a document, the constitution, or in the likewise divided and seldom used constituent power of the amendment process.

the strengthening of the central authorities and often laid an in-dispensable basis of legal uniformity for the benefit of commercial expansion and the growing legal equality among the subjects of the king.

Improving the economy   Another important aspect of this new concern for internal affairs was the increasing interest of govern-ments in the economic well-being of their countries. It was called forth, in part, by a desire to remedy the devastation and impover-ishment caused by an age of terrible religious and other wars, and by the need to improve the economic structure for purposes of taxa-tion—for maintaining standing armies and for conducting wars. In many cases the royal dynasties started glass, chinaware, silk manu-factures, and mining in order to increase domestic production and exports. On some occasions, the new state administrations would undertake ambitious projects of repopulating areas devastated by war or of colonizing new land at home or abroad by encouraging immigration. They also experimented with the introduction of new technical skills, or of new food products, such as the potato in Europe. Governmental activities in the economic realm finally cul-minated in the age of mercantilism, the classic economic intervention-ism of absolute rulers and enlightened despots. Concern for the economic well-being of the country and the policies of mercantilism encouraged outstanding thinkers like Adam Smith (1723–1790) and the French *Physiocrats*[4] to inquire into what really constituted the wealth of nations.

Development of the bureaucracy   Not the least significant mani-festation of the new concern with internal affairs was the deliberate development of an elaborate bureaucracy. Standing armies were a useful device for crushing opposition by force but worse than useless for purposes of day-to-day civil administration. The levying and collection of taxes, especially, required a firm but gentle hand that would not crush the hen that laid the golden eggs. It also required a civil service of high efficiency, training, and integrity. By skillful devices and with the benefit of the experience of centuries of trial and error, the absolute monarchs of Europe developed a career service of the highest quality that became an effective tool of the monarchic will in internal affairs. The monarchs often selected their

[4] An influential group of thinkers founded by François Quesnay. One of Ques-nay's disciples was DuPont de Nemours (1739–1817), founder of the industrial DuPont family in the United States. The Physiocrats were the first to use the term *laissez faire*. They believed in increasing wealth through "granting more freedom of investment, trade, and circulation of goods, though under the plan-ning authority of an 'enlightened despot.'"

civil servants deliberately from among the commoners, who at that time were an underprivileged class. By avoiding the aristocracy with its entrenched distinctions of rank and birth, they could make their selections and promotions increasingly by merit or competitive examination. A high-ranking civil servant, moreover, would owe his career solely to the monarch and would therefore be completely loyal. Special devices, such as rotation in field offices or punishment by transfer to another part of the country, were periodically employed in order to retain the complete control of the monarch over his civil servants.

Once the bureaucracy had fully evolved, the modern state was able to stand on its own feet. The civil administration with its pyramid-like structure, from the administering field office up to the locus of sovereign power, gave the state its characteristic form. Although the presence of monarchy was important to its evolution, the modern bureaucracy of the state easily survived the demise of monarchy. It also survived with hardly a modification the rise of written constitutions, the return of representative government, the coming of democracy, and, in England and Sandinavia, even the advent of socialism.[5]

Summary of the concept of the state

To summarize the generally recognized attributes of the modern state as it has evolved in the West: The traditional definition of the state usually speaks of control over a definite territory and population, and an independent government as its minimal attributes. Two further distinguishing characteristics that apply to most states today may be added: (1) Its unity and distinctness as a form of social organization rest on legal uniformity and unified administrative control,[6] and (2) the link between government and the individual citizen is direct and uninterrupted by intermediary agencies or groups. The state is for all effects and purposes a secular structure that bases its authority on rational relationships rather than on religious or other nonrational authority.

Even this cautious definition may not always accurately describe the changing reality of the modern state. The many stages of its historical growth, intervals of war or anarchy, and most of all, widely varying interpretations of its nature have often served to modify some of the features mentioned above. Self-styled "realists" among

---

[5] For a detailed account, see Carl J. Friedrich, *Constitutional Government and Democracy*, 4th ed. (Boston: Ginn-Blaisdell, 1968), chaps. 1 and 2.

[6] There are some exceptions to this rule, wherever a federal form of government has been adopted. See Chapter 11 of the present book.

both statesmen and political writers conceived of the state as primarily *a power structure*. Where their view prevailed, therefore, the state was often transformed into a primary instrument for the gain and preservation of power. Another school of thought interpreted it as primarily *a legal structure* and engaged in heated controversies over questions of legality and form, or over borderline cases which did not seem to fit the legal definition of a sovereign state.[7] With the rise of the forces of nationalism and mass democracy, many a Western or non-Western political leader and writer would also emphasize the character of the state as *an association of citizens* and its sovereign government as the instrument of the *general will* of the entire people. The latter approach gave the state, which had up to that time been popularly regarded as a hostile tool of arbitrary monarchic rule, a new lease on life. For now it could become the sacrosanct guardian of the *public interest* with hardly an internal modification.

Around the turn of the last century, sociologists developed a great interest in the history and prehistory of the state. Tracing it back to its earliest antecedents, some concluded that the state originated in the conquest of one society by another, with the victor forming a ruling class and protecting its supremacy with the help of the repressive institutions of the state. Origin by *conquest* and a *ruling class* emphasized the power aspects of the state, but should not be confused with the Marxist version of the state as an instrument of class rule whose causes and objectives are strictly economic. Other sociologists placed more emphasis on such aspects of the state as its *monopoly of violence*, by which the state distinguishes itself from all other social groups, or on the underlying social structure of a particular state, or on the values, language, or history that the people of a state have in common.

Political scientists, especially in the United States, have generally been wary of using the concept of the state and have instead concentrated on an analysis of the political institutions, powers, and functions of a particular country. Most recently, political scientists have directed their attention largely to the study of *the policy-making process*, the complicated political process through which a particular people resolves its questions of policy. It would be an exaggeration to say that contemporary political science has discarded the concept of the state. Yet the empirical orientation of current political science research has found the concept to be of limited utility for its pur-

---

[7] Such controversies might arise, for example, over "semi-sovereign states" or the application of the standard definition of a state to federal systems such as that of the United States, where the constituent members of the federal union are also called "states."

poses. American political scientists are also wary of its traditionally authoritarian connotations.

This waning of theoretical interest in the state, however, should not suggest any decline in the real phenomenon for which the word stands. The state has always figured prominently in popular talk in which people designate the state as "they" and as an enemy of "we, the people." This distinction between the state and society differs substantially from the standard textbook definition, which includes the population as a component part of the state. The conception of the state as denoting only the machinery of government—the bureaucracy or the range of governmental functions—is, to be sure, an idea going back to the days when "they" referred to the monarch and his administrators or, perhaps, to a colonial administration. Under those circumstances it was understandable that the public authority would be regarded as an alien, hostile, and dictatorial element, unlike today, when many governments are popularly controlled and representative of the popular will.

Yet even if we prefer to stick to the wider definition of the state, we must concern ourselves with the problems and current controversies raised by the growth of government powers and apparatus to the present level. For the same state, which some consider the vehicle most capable of fulfilling the highest hopes of man, is regarded by others as a threat to the good life, both in its expansion of functions within and in its capacity to threaten the peace of the world outside its borders.

MONISM VERSUS PLURALISM

No discussion of the political traditions of Western society—or, for that matter, of Indian and Chinese society—would be complete without mention of the pluralistic society, a term that needs to be defined in some detail. An examination of the argument for pluralism will also lead us further into the great debate pitting pluralism, or the free society, against monism, which today means either the scope of the activities of the state or the curbing of the influence of special interests.

A free and pluralistic society

Let us assume that a modern society in the Western world could afford to ignore completely the necessities of external security and defense. Let us also assume that this society was made up of such honest and well-intentioned citizens that it would not require any institutions, laws, or police force for the repression of crime or violence. What would such a society be like? How would it operate? Many political thinkers have spun their dreams about such a society —especially the founders of utopian colonies, who often were too optimistic to reckon with the forces of social disorder and international power politics.

In such a society without crime and war, the dominant forces would most likely be the large social groups that are held together each by its major interest in life; the churches and their following; the major branches of the economy (separately, and as organized by trade unions, business associations, and farm groups); the groupings and institutions devoted to education, cultural, and scientific pursuits; and the vast numbers of voluntary associations that dedicate their efforts to public affairs or social life on many levels and along many different lines. Every group within this vast plurality of varied group activities could devote its whole life to the pursuit of its own major interest in the manner suggested by the inner rationale of its particular activity and by its own preference. There would be no outside agency to tell the farmer what to grow, or the steel mills what to charge for their product, or the communal groups how to live, or the teacher what to teach. Everyone engaged in a meaningful activity could savor the inherent meaning of his activity to the fullest degree and could derive the deep satisfactions of doing a job well and of exercising to the fullest his creative ability and good judgment. This is the archetype of a free and pluralistic society as it has been advocated by many pluralistic thinkers, such as the legal historians Frederic W. Maitland in England, Otto von Gierke in Germany, and Léon Duguit in France, the English economist G. D. H. Cole, the English political scientist Harold Laski, and the American sociologist Robert M. MacIver.

To be sure, most of the advocates of pluralism do not deny completely the need for a public authority for such purposes as defense and internal policing. But they see this public authority and its political process as merely another one of the many functional groups of the free society. Hence they withhold from the state all authority to intervene in the spontaneous life of other groups such as business corporations, labor unions, and university communities, except in grave emergencies.

Monism in early societies

Let us contrast this image of pluralism with that of monism. As the word "monism"—from the Greek *mono*, "one"—indicates, the basic concept behind it is that of utmost social unity. Before the rise of the modern state, social unity was often conceived of as the domination of a particular group activity over the rest of a society. Long before politics had even crystallized as a separate social activity, clearly differentiated from others, organized religion or kinship relationships were already cohesive forces of such strength that they alone could completely dominate and integrate a society. Thus originated the early societies in which for thousands of years either political control was exercised by god-kings or priestly castes, and political obligation was confused with religious feelings of dependence, or kinship relations were the social matrix after which all the other relationships were patterned.

The state versus society

In modern times, ever since the political functions were once more differentiated from others and consolidated in the hands of the modern state, the issue between monism and pluralism has taken on a new and more specific form. It was called "the state versus the society," and the battles between the two sides were often carried on under the banners of "the public interest," "good order," or "sovereignty" on the side of the state and of "limited government" or "freedom" on the side of society.

"Society" is the conglomeration and interaction of the many spontaneous and creative group activities. The state is the instrument for ordering and adjusting society in accordance with and by the authority of the will of the sovereign. It is also the largest and most inclusive group of the body politic, counting all citizens as its members. Since most citizens, however, belong to at least one other group, and often a number of other groups, the loyalty of the citizen is likely to be divided. He feels beholden not only to his country, or state, but also to his labor union, his church, his fishing club, or his neighborhood group. These multiple loyalties may coexist without difficulty under normal circumstances. But there comes a time when they may clash, and a citizen may be asked to choose between his government and his church or between his municipality and his business associates.

What typical clashes of this sort are occurring today? A steel factory in a particular locality has for years been polluting the local streams, a local lake, or the air the community breathes, undeterred by the negligible fines levied under prevailing local ordinances. The ecology-minded parts of the community are enraged and pressure their local authorities to get tough with the polluter who in turn is supported by his employees and other local businessmen who are either dependent on his business or fear that similar action might be initiated against their sins toward the environment. In this issue the special interest of the factory community (*pluralism*) is pitted against the common interest of all (*monism*) for a clean environment. Another example is the monistic claim of the larger society to regulate the use of narcotics in self-contained hippie communes or student communities in the United States. Other countries the world over, of course, have comparable disputes pitting the common interest against various pluralistic, special interests. But in collectivistic societies such as the Soviet Union, the issues are at a more basic level, such as whether Soviet Jews will be allowed to worship as they please or whether the Soviet military command will continue to be completely subordinated to the party. It would hardly occur to a Russian citizen to claim exemption from the draft on conscientious objector grounds, nor would a local Chinese community expect its autonomy to be recognized and respected by the higher levels of the party or other authorities. In the United States, by comparison, a growing antipluralistic literature in political science has concentrated on these issues in recent years.[8]

Monists and pluralists One can look at pluralism also as the confounding maze of interests of a social or economic character in a free society. Every one of these innumerable groups of society has a rather clearly identifiable interest that is likely to determine a good deal of its actions. This is true of vast social groups as well as of individual corporations or persons, although larger groups may have internal divergencies of interest and opinion regarding the question of where the group interest lies in a particular situation. A pluralist would contend that society can operate best when every group and every individual are allowed to act according to their own interests. A monist would worry about the chaos resulting from the unrestrained pursuit of individual or group interests by many different agents of the group process. He might be concerned, in particular, about the danger of stronger individuals and groups pushing aside their weaker competitors in an unregulated free-for-all. He might contend that there is such a thing as "the public interest" or "the common good," even if its content is difficult to determine beyond a few general points such as the desirability of order, of general prosperity, or of fair procedures that protect the weak from extinction or exploitation by the strong. Pluralists, by contrast, do not deny

[8] See, for example, the writings of Theodore Lowi, John Kenneth Galbraith, or Peter Bachrach.

the desirability of order in society. However, they believe that many a monist is overly obsessed with creating order, or that too much ordering activity will stifle the creative spontaneity of society. Furthermore, pluralists have an implicit faith in the natural ability of social processes to bring about a reasonable harmony among the various groups and their interests. Adam Smith, the famous eighteenth-century spokesman for economic freedom from state intervention, in fact, assumed that the "invisible hand" of nature would assure harmony among the interests of individuals, groups, and the entire body politic.

Freedom from domination of a group   It should also be noted that much of the pluralistic agitation of the Modern Age stems not so much from a general concern about the expanding sphere of activity of the state as from the efforts of a particular group to free itself from domination by another group that happens to have the authority of the state at its disposal. A typical example of this motivation is supplied by the cry for religious freedom on the part of religious minorities threatened by an established majority religion. The early Christians in the Roman Empire found it necessary to distinguish sharply between what was "God's" and what was "Caesar's," and on occasion they had to pay with martyrdom for their refusal to pay homage to the established religion. The French Huguenots of the sixteenth century, British Protestant sects of the same age, and even some small American sects of today, such as the Jehovah's Witnesses, have had to defend their rights against public authorities acting in the interest of the religious majority. Even disestablishment and the separation of church and state, as the contemporary concern seems to demonstrate, will not set an end to the issues of church-state relations, which are among the most explosive of practical politics.

Laissez faire   Another example of pluralistic motives springing from rather specific interests is the eighteenth-century movement to emancipate the productive economic activities of citizens from state control. A long line of economists and social philosophers from the days of Adam Smith to this day have argued that a flourishing economy depends on the voluntary and self-interested actions of individuals and groups; and that state control and intervention in economic activities prevents the delicate "natural" adjustments of a free economy from taking place. The British philosopher John Stuart Mill gave expression to this fundamental bias against the state when he wrote in his *Principles of Political Economy* (1848):

In all the more advanced communities, the great majority of things are worse done by the intervention of government, than the individ-

*uals most interested in the matter would do them, or cause them to be
done, if left to themselves. . . . Few will dispute the more than suffi-
ciency of these reasons, to throw, in every instance, the burden of
making out a strong case, not on those who resist, but on those who
recommend, government interference. Laissez faire, in short, should
be the general practice: every departure from it, unless required by
some great good, is a certain evil.*

Laissez faire ("let them work it out for themselves") became the
great injunction to the once omnipotent modern state throughout the
nineteenth century as the industrial revolution brought forth a tremendous rise of productive economic activities. The ordering functions of the state were supposed to be limited to those of a night
watchman, who, by discouraging depredation while everyone sleeps,
contributes in an unobtrusive way to the working of the "natural"
economic laws. In the late nineteenth century, in fact, the new giants
of industrial enterprise—the great railroad, mining, manufacturing,
and banking empires—had acquired such vast powers that they could
challenge and at times dominate what was left of the public authority
of the state on all levels. Economic interest and group activities had
won, at least for the time being, a clear superiority over political
considerations of any kind. To be sure, we have since retreated from
this position under the impact of such weighty political events as
worldwide wars—both hot and cold—vast population increases and
the problem of feeding all those hungry mouths, and the menace of
political disturbances caused by the gluts and depressions of an
unregulated economy. But even today, in the 1970s, we tend to agree
with Mill's statement that the burden of proof for the necessity of
government interference in the economy clearly lies with the advocates of such intervention.

Pluralistic freedom for all groups Upon seeing that the proponents
of economic freedom were successful in their attack upon the state,
a host of other groups used this opportunity to claim a similar freedom from state supervision and intervention. Among them were the
churches and religious groups, universities and spokesmen for the
arts and sciences, and voluntary groups and associations everywhere.
In many parts of the Western world, cities and incorporated munici-
palities had long fought for emancipation from the stifling embrace
of the modern state. Now they had a generally accepted premise for
their cause: the limitation of the functions of the state to those of a
night watchman of society. In many cases, pluralistic theorists such
as Maitland, Cole, and von Gierke drew their arguments and illustrations from the example of the Middle Ages, a time characterized by

the inability of the predecessor of the modern state to extend its control over the church, the universities, the guilds, and the free cities. The fundamental bias against the state extended also to the entire Socialist tradition of nineteenth-century thought, which generally tended toward anarchism. Even Karl Marx looked upon the state as merely an instrument for the exploitation of the lower classes and predicted that in the future classless society it would simply "wither away." (See Chapters 5 and 13.)

When we call our own society today "free" and "pluralistic" in contrast to the Communistic societies behind the Iron Curtain, we obviously do not mean to imply superiority or domination by any one group over the state. A business-, labor-, or church-dominated government might signify a new kind of monism. Pluralism only asserts the right to existence and initiative in their own affairs on the part of the many groups that make up society. It does not clash with the maintenance of basic political concerns such as those of defense or of the social and constitutional order by the state. In an advanced pluralistic society, in fact, the problem is often one of safeguarding the "public interest" or "common good" against special interests that are well organized and represented by lobbies.

Monism resurgent

There has been much public concern about the growth of bureaucracy and the intrusion of governmental activity into more and more spheres of formerly private activity. This monistic trend has aroused particularly strong opposition in the United States where, in contrast to most European countries, there is very little of the absolutistic tradition of state omnipotence of the seventeenth and eighteenth centuries. Since much of Big Government, though by no means all, originated in the days of the Great Depression and the New Deal, moreover, many Americans insist on calling this kind of monism, quite inaccurately, "socialism." Monism in the form of Big Government is a phenomenon that occurred in all the countries of the Western world as a result of the wars and economic perplexities of the twentieth century. Although one may be justified in worrying about its impact upon the pluralistic way of life, this new monism is no more likely to retreat or disappear than will the horse and buggy replace our automobiles and airplanes.

Monistic claims, moreover, do not necessarily originate only with governments and bureaucratic establishments. The current wave of antiestablishment criticism in the United States, for example, advocates the determined use of public authority to stop the degradation of the environment, to curb the special interests that frustrate the control of air pollution, and to make the racial equality proclaimed in legislation prevail over the stubborn resistance of certain local interests. There are many foreign and historical parallels for such a monistic thrust from outside the establishment. And it is not unusual to combine monistic claims on some subjects with pluralistic concern about others, such as the freedom of certain groups to determine their own life style.

Examples of extreme monism

Much as one may be troubled by the increase of monism brought about by the broadening of governmental functions, it would be a gross exaggeration to believe that this trend has brought Western countries appreciably closer to the extreme monism practiced by their competitors behind the Iron Curtain. Totalitarianism means that political control is omnipresent and total, extending even into the most remote recesses of human life. A pure Communist economy is completely subject to planning and political control. There is no private ownership of means of production and very little consumer choice.[9] There is, moreover, a vast array of social controls over churches, family life, education and science, public opinion, and even the minds themselves, which, by comparison, makes the annoyance of an American farmer or businessman with governmental regulation, paperwork, and taxes seem petty indeed. Fascist totalitarianism presents the same picture of extreme monism as does Communism, including such strongly unifying devices as an unceasing propaganda campaign and a reign of terror. A third example of extreme monism is that of countries temporarily in the throes of violent revolutionary upheaval and nationalistic passion, such as France and other European nations during the great revolutions from 1789 to 1917, or some of the colonial and excolonial countries of today. While the upheaval lasts, these nations are often convulsed with a passion for unity that brings about violent repression of any stirrings of dissent and even of any counsels of moderation. The extreme monism of nationalistic revolution is not dependent on the state or on its repressive apparatus for the achievement of utmost social unity. Nationalistic revolution can reach the goal of unity by the passion of common action for a common purpose, especially where the passion is inspired and

---

[9] The Soviet economy has allowed minor exceptions to this rule such as small garden plots for members of collective farms. Eastern European economies have increasingly given private incentive and consumer choice a more prominent role than Communist theory had provided. And there have been indications that the Soviet economy is likewise retreating in the same direction.

sustained by violent events, such as a struggle for independence, and by a steady stream of propaganda.

THE NATION-STATE AND INTERNATIONAL ANARCHY

In the preceding section we considered the challenge to the modern state from within, by the tradition of pluralism whose proponents fear that the growing power of the state will in time restrict that personal liberty which is so essential to the good life of individuals and groups. Now let us turn to the challenge from without, which increasingly questions the usefulness of the system of modern states for the welfare and indeed the survival of man in this world. The external aspect of the concept of sovereignty will serve as our point of departure. Next we will examine in contrast to the society within a state of international society among sovereign states. It will be remembered that the impact of wars and the threat on Western society and institutions were major factors in the rise of the modern state. Today, the age of nuclear power, with its potential for total destruction of civilization, automatically raises questions about the institution of the sovereign nation-state and encourages a search for devices for its limitation and replacement.

Sovereignty and power politics

Sovereignty within a state is the supreme authority which is derived from no other authority and requires the consent of no one else. Sovereignty in international relations is complete and undiminished national independence. A sovereign state is equal to any other sovereign state and not subject to any outside authority, not even to that of an international tribunal or a gathering of states in an international organization. The United Nations Charter states that the United Nations "is based on the principle of the sovereign equality of all its Members" and recognizes a sphere of "domestic jurisdiction" which is to be reserved to each member state. External sovereignty, then, permits a people and its government to run their affairs as they please, no matter what they do within their own borders.[10]

With regard to the larger picture of world affairs, the principle of national sovereignty has contributed a great deal to the striking differences between the social relations within a particular nation-state and among the different states. Due to the nature of society and the cohesion of ethnic groups and established ways of life, small,

[10] The only exception to this rule mentioned in the United Nations Charter are enforcement measures of the organization to counter "any threat to the peace, breach of the peace, or act of aggression," as determined by the Security Council.

closed areas have always tended to be better organized with respect to laws, customs, and established government than have larger areas. The forerunners of modern nation-states, the medieval kingdoms, had a greater degree of social order within than had prevailed among the different kingdoms, although these medieval kings were still very far from considering themselves independent of any moral obligation or spiritual overlord beyond their borders. The diversities among the countries and the frictions and misunderstandings among them, however, increased very sharply with the rise of the universal system of national egotisms that is characteristic of sovereignty. The emerging modern nation-states tended to be increasingly well ordered and unified within, but also more and more at odds, if not at war, with one another. Thus arose the system of power politics, constant threat of war, and shifting military alliances, which have persisted with hardly a modification to this day. Inside the modern state, a well-ordered society is oriented toward the pursuit of justice and the blessings of liberty and the good life. Outside, and among the states, anarchy and the law of the jungle reign: the big states gobble up the little ones, and military might makes right.

Let us compare the effect that international anarchy had on the internal affairs of the European nations at the time of the rise of the system of power politics with what it can do to our way of life today. As was mentioned earlier, the development of the state and that of power politics were two factors which mutually reinforced each other. The better a state adapted itself to the struggle for survival among the states, the tougher became the struggle and the greater the need for further adaptation. To fit themselves better for the struggle for survival, the medieval kingdoms in due time exchanged their pluralistic organization for an increasingly monistic one. They transformed the limited office of medieval kingship into that of the absolute ruler of the modern state. They took away the corporate liberties of their free cities, the privileges of their proud nobility, and the rights of representation in courts and estates. They wiped out historical frontiers and ancient rights. The standing armies, which were indispensable for the external struggle for survival in a hostile world, often became the very vehicle of force with which the new royal absolutism centralized and strengthened its government of its subjects. Once power politics had forced absolutism upon Western societies, it took literally centuries for pluralism and representative government to reassert themselves in most European countries.[11]

11 Among the rare exceptions in this development are countries such as England, Sweden, and a few small countries, which for reasons of their own managed to escape the blight of absolutism that lay so heavily on France, Spain, Prussia, Austria, and Russia.

In telling contrast to the rise of powerful states in the West, the traditional soiceties of Asia, the Middle East, and Africa remained in a more pluralistic form of social organization. In such cases as the venerable societies of China and India, pluralistic organization was so extreme and rigid that these countries proved unable, in spite of their size, to mobilize their strength against the far smaller attackers from the West. The degree of monistic organization of the new states of the West facilitated the conquest of less well-organized societies and the creation of colonial empires throughout most of the non-Western world. With transparent rationalizations such as "the white man's burden," the chief instruments of modern monism— armed force and bureaucracy—brought Western domination to these politically "backward" societies. After a few generations of colonial rule native leaders caught on, and the ensuing movements of national independence have since broken up most colonial empires. Some native leaders and their new nations learned the game of monism and power politics so well that their chief preoccupation has become to determine how to dominate weaker neighbors and extend their own dominion.

War in the twentieth century

Today, Western political institutions may appear better developed and so deeply rooted that they could not be overwhelmed overnight by the renewed onslaught of power politics.[12] But the stakes of international politics have also grown much higher, the powers more menacing, the technology of weapons far more destructive. There have always been regional wars and international tensions. Yet, since the beginning of the twentieth century, the rivalries of power politics have become worldwide. There is no longer an oasis, such as the United States in the nineteenth century, to which man could escape from the clash of conflicting interests among the great powers. Two world wars have already been fought, with tens of millions of dead, in order to stop some of the great powers from aspiring to world-wide hegemony. A third war, the Cold War, has been fought since 1947 to contain the expansion of a new superpower, the Communist bloc, which is bent on dominating the whole world. At the same time, the colonial independence movement has led to wars of independence on a global scale, such as the war of 1945–1947 in Indonesia against the Dutch rulers, the war of 1945–1954 in Indo-China, and the war of 1956–1962 in Algeria against their French rulers.

---

[12] There have been prognostications of the coming of totalitarian empires everywhere as the inevitable result of total war, in the writings of Harold D. Lasswell and in Orwell's novel *1984*.

Communist-trained native guerrillas have led nationalist revolts against their own native government or former colonial masters into the pale of the Cold War, as in several countries of Latin America and South East Asia. Dozens of other warlike conflicts between different nations, new or old, or within such countries as Cyprus, the Congo, and Korea, have made our time one in which war seems to be a permanent condition of human existence.

For the United States, the decade of the 1970s opened with the traumatic experience of involvement in a war in which the element of decolonization was inextricably mixed with an unsuccessful attempt to contain the spread of Communism in South East Asia. The magnitude and seeming endlessness of the American military involvement and the domestic upheaval in opposition to it have tended to obscure what expects us at the end of the tunnel: more international anarchy and more wars in which determined aggressors get what they want. And Americans will probably have less leadership abroad because of the erosion of national self-confidence under the trauma of the Vietnam debacle.

War in the twentieth century has come to disregard all the old rules of chivalry, morality, and human decency. The trend began with the *levée en masse* and universal conscription in the days of the French Revolution. With the first great war of the twentieth century, World War I, it had become the "total war" of masses of men and war matériel, not to mention poison gas and hunger blockades. A typical major war is now characterized by the straining of every sinew of national power to the point of exhaustion. All resources are mobilized, the entire economy is strictly regimented, and all manpower (and womanpower) thrown into the balance. In the ultimate contest for national honor or survival there is little regard for human rights and hardly any for human life. Modern warfare does not spare noncombatants—the old and the sick, and women and children. Cities are laid waste. Centuries of culture and civilization can be devastated in a single night. With total war we have returned to the barbarism of the days when hordes of horsemen turned vast cities and stretches of cultivated land into "scorched earth," and slew their inhabitants or carried them away into slavery.

As if the horrors of World War II with its mass slaughter and destruction had not been bad enough, the technology of modern weapons has in the past two decades gone far beyond the V-2 missiles that bombarded London and the atomic bombs dropped on Hiroshima and Nagasaki. The same space technology that can orbit men around the world or take rockets to Mars or the moon may eventually be used to deliver unimaginably powerful 100-megaton bombs to population centers anywhere in the world. The likelihood of nuclear war is further enhanced by the possession of the super-weapon by both sides in the Cold War, and by an increasing number of smaller powers whose governments may actually be more likely to use it in a moment of wrath than the stalemated giants of the Cold War.

The Soviet Union and the United States have long recognized the extreme danger to themselves of starting an exchange of nuclear attacks and have made limited efforts to control the likelihood of an accidental outbreak between each other, not to mention among other nuclear powers. Yet for the past decade and longer, an arms race of nuclear stockpiles and ever-advancing military technology has given both antagonists the power to obliterate each other many times over. A similar arms race between the great powers of 1910—Great Britain, France, Russia, Germany, and Austro-Hungary—was a major cause of World War I.

Even if the nuclear confrontation of the Soviet Union and the United States continues to produce a nuclear standoff in the shadow of which localized conventional or guerrilla wars take place, the impact of power politics on our attitudes, institutions, and way of life is an exorbitant price to pay. It figures not only in the enormous defense expenditures—which could serve a better purpose than the accumulation of stockpiles that will, hopefully, never be used for their original purpose—but also in the growing concentration of economic, industrial, and military power whose monistic tendencies can be viewed as a danger to pluralism and individual liberty. Even worse may be the long-range effect of the nationalistic hatreds aroused on both sides—of a military, or fighting, mentality—which is also at odds with the civilian tradition of peaceful economic, cultural, and religious pursuits that have made Western civilization great.

Attempts to modify the state system

It is against this background of worldwide power politics, unrestrained national hatred and warfare, and the playing with the ultimate weapon, that the efforts to escape the dilemmas of twentieth-century power politics must be viewed. These efforts have moved along different lines but have almost always tended to tamper with the cornerstone of the anarchic system of modern states: national sovereignty.

Collective security   One attempt at cleaving the Gordian knot has been the establishment of the system of *collective security* upon which the League of Nations and the United Nations were built. The underlying theory of collective security is that the member nations have a common interest in maintaining peace and should, therefore, jointly suppress aggressive action by any power or powers against the territory of one of them. The practice of a system of collective security has not always been successful. Among the more successful devices for maintaining peace and deterring aggression have been regional alliances such as the North Atlantic Treaty Organization, and the Organization of American States. The practical weaknesses of a global collective security system have been serious, although perhaps not irremediable. Both the League of Nations and the United Nations have suffered from a structural flaw that is inescapable under the principle of national sovereignty. Coercive action to save the peace required unanimity in the League of Nations. It requires unanimity also among the five permanent members of the UN Security Council. The veto privilege of the great powers in the Security Council and of all states of the old League is based on the premise that a truly sovereign state must not allow itself to be coerced against its will. An enforcement action by an international organization against an aggressor nation, of course, violates the sovereign rights of that nation and can violate also the sovereign rights of other states involved in the coercive undertaking.

Another and no less serious problem raised by collective security is that condemning every design for territorial changes as a present or contemplated act of aggression automatically puts an undeserved air of saintliness on the *status quo*. A desire for territorial change can be legitimate, for example, for the purpose of righting previous wrongs. What is needed, therefore, is a procedure for peaceful change and a tribunal that could rule authoritatively on the merits and legitimacy of a particular claim for peaceful change. Such an authority to provide for peaceful territorial changes, however, would cut very deeply into the sovereign rights of the nations concerned. Let us assume, for example, that an overwhelming majority of the German-speaking inhabitants of the South Tyrol in northern Italy wished to secede from that country and join Austria. No greater interference in Italy's sovereignty can be imagined than if an international organization undertook to judge the merits of this case for secession and, perhaps, facilitated such a territorial change. Yet, short of such a violation of national sovereignty, where could a dissatisfied ethnic minority get a fair hearing? It could only resort to violence, and the other country, Austria, could support it clandestinely or go to war for it. With this last alternative, the vicious circle from national sovereignty to the most stringent form of power politics, international war, is once more complete. Since, in the world of today, small wars are so entangled with worldwide power relationships that they cannot always be confined to a restricted area, such a local minority problem could lead to another world war, another gigantic struggle that would kill tens of millions and destroy whole civilizations.

Disarmament and arms control   Another attempted means for changing the system of power politics is *disarmament*. The underlying theory of disarmament is that no major war and, in particular no aggressive war, can be fought without an ample supply of modern military equipment. Without restraint or limitation on national armaments, there can be no curbing of the mad competition between East and West to pile up ever bigger stockpiles of nuclear destruction and to develop ever more devastating weapons. Disarmament as an alternative to the arms race is an idea that goes back to the nineteenth century and to the naval conferences of the 1920s and 1930s, which sought to establish a ratio among the war fleets of the great powers. Its history also includes the futile attempts to distinguish between "aggressive" and "defensive weapons," or between nuclear and conventional armaments, with the purpose of outlawing "aggressive" and nuclear weapons. Proponents of disarmament generally admit the need for limited national forces capable of maintaining internal order and a measure of defense. "Total and general disarmament," such as the former Soviet Premier Khrushchev proposed, and later spokesmen reiterated, could open the door to a different kind of aggression by Communist guerrilla forces and violent overthrow of governments by the fifth columns that Cuba, Peking, and the Kremlin have sent into many lands. And the Communists are not the only ones menacing the self-determination of small countries in this fashion. Limited systems of arms control, on the other hand, such as measures to curtail the spread of nuclear weapons, and safeguards against war by misunderstanding or against the possibility of major surprise attacks, hold greater practical promise.

Disarmament and arms control may be capable of restraining the arms race between opposing military blocs, but it is no panacea for war. It is quite difficult to come to a disarmament agreement when the stakes are as high as they are today. Even a limited gesture of disarmament such as a ban on nuclear testing between East and West has time and again had to yield the stage to considerations of military and technological advantage. It does not of itself facilitate the peaceful settlement of international disputes. Finally, and perhaps most discouraging, disarmament neither scraps the economic capacity for sudden rearmament nor disarms belligerent minds. Hence, wars can still start and the arms race is only delayed until the outbreak of hostilities.

Again, disarmament impinges upon national sovereignty even where it is voluntarily entered into, for the full use of the national capacity for war and defense is an integral part of that sovereign autonomy that recognizes no limitation or obligation above itself. This becomes readily apparent if one thinks of the controversy over inspection of the extent of Soviet compliance with any plan for nuclear disarmament. It is the sovereign right of a great power to cheat on disarmament provisions for the sake of its ultimate security or even victory, just as the canons of power politics sanction peacetime spying in the national interest. It is for this reason that the West has insisted on foolproof inspections, although such inspections are a most obvious invasion of national sovereignty. The real question arising from the inspection controversy would seem to be: Is it not, in the last analysis, the principle of sovereignty that lies at the root of the dilemma?

International law and adjudication The third remedy against the reign of power politics is logically more consistent and compelling than the stopgap measures of collective security and disarmament. If the relations between nation-states are anarchic and in striking contrast to the well-ordered life inside most modern nations, then the solution to the problem of peace in our time is to make an orderly society out of the international world. Political thinkers and practical politicians have given much thought to this process of civilizing the world among the modern states and, by implication, the external behavior of these states. As the famous Dutch lawyer and statesman Hugo Grotius (1583–1645) wrote in the midst of seventeenth-century power politics:

Among the traits characteristic of man is an impelling desire for society, that is, for the social life—not of any and every sort, but peaceful, and organized according to the measure of his intelligence, with those who are of his own kind . . . this maintenance of social order . . . is the source of law properly so called. To this sphere of law belong the abstaining from that which is another's, the restoration to another of anything of his which we may have, together with any gain which we may have received from it; the obligation to fulfill promises, the making good of a loss incurred through our fault, and the inflicting of penalties upon men according to their deserts.[13]

The first step in the direction of taming the international anarchy was the revival of *international law* by Grotius and his contempo-

13 *Prolegomena,* secs. 6–8.

raries from antecedents going back to the Roman Empire. As Western society has rested securely on a basis of customary law and consensus, they believed, the international society of states ought to be based on rules derived from existing treaties, accepted customs and usages, and general principles derived from natural law—the law above the positive law of particular states.[14]

The idea was good, but the practice at times imperfect, as long as the observance of rules and treaties was a matter of voluntary compliance or enforcement by the aggrieved party taking justice into its own hands. At the turn of the last century, international tribunals of arbitration and a permanent court of international justice were introduced for the purpose of arbitrating or adjudicating all disputes submitted to them. This worked quite satisfactorily in cases in which small nations or small matters were concerned. The big political questions, however, were withheld from the courts and instead decided in the customary manner—by brute force. The resurgence of power politics for worldwide stakes and the brazen imperialistic drive, first of the Axis powers and then of the Communist bloc of nations, moreover, further reduced the uses of international law and the world court. Neither the Soviet Union nor the United States accepted the compulsory jurisdiction of the International Court of Justice after World War II. The superpowers, and even small international lawbreakers, had once more restored the anarchy of naked power politics over the beginnings of an international social order.

International government But the effort at civilizing the savage ways of the international world did not stop with these discouragements. When lawbreakers scoff at the rules and defy the judicial authority of a civilized society, we call for a sheriff, a police force that will strike fear into the heart of the criminal and bring him to bay by force. The idea of an *international police force,* on an expeditionary or permanent basis, had long been discussed before one was actually employed by the United Nations in the Middle East, in Korea, and in the Congo. Were there to be an adequate international police force, the other attempts at restraining the reign of power politics—by means of collective security, disarmament, and international law—would take on a new significance. For now there would be an enforcement agency that could at least in theory restrain an aggressor, inspect compliance with disarmament agreements, or enforce treaties and covenants. Yet the idea of a permanent interna-

---

[14] See also Majid Khadduri and Herbert J. Liebesny, *Law in the Middle East* (Washington, D.C.: Middle East Institute, 1955), vol. 1, pp. 349–372 on Islamic notions of international law.

tional police force, as a last step toward an orderly international society, was evidently premature and resulted in a deep crisis for the United Nations when several large powers refused to pay their share of the enforcement effort in the Congo. There also remain the special privileges of the great powers, who, in the Security Council, can veto any enforcement action against themselves or their interests.

To close the last loophole, consequently, both theory and practice have carried this line of thought to its logical conclusion. International society will come to resemble domestic society only when an international government completes the structure of order and law. From antiquity to this day, political thinkers, writers, and voluntary organizations have thought at great length about such a world government or world state. They developed elaborate designs to ensure the survival of the Western traditions of constitutional government, democracy, and pluralism in a worldwide state.[15] But there has been no serious effort in the direction of establishing such a structure, which would presumably be federal in character so as to guarantee home rule and autonomy to the constituent states. The United Nations is very far from developing into anything like a world government. It is committed to the principle of national sovereignty, which would have to yield to a world government and its new legal norms.

There has been something of a trend toward the establishment of a real international government of a federal character at the regional level, such as among the original members of the European Economic Community (EEC), popularly known as the Common Market. There the participating nations and their governments have been ready to give up some of their ancient sovereign rights to a future common government in exchange for a lasting reign of peace among such age-old antagonists as France, West Germany, Italy, and other European countries. Yet even among the member states of EEC, a single old-fashioned nationalist leader such as President de Gaulle was able to demonstrate how easy it is to ruin the existing goodwill and cooperation by selfish demands for a preponderant position for one of the member states.

---

[15] Western or Muslim universalism are easily matched by the universal outlook of Imperial China. See, for example, Kung-chuan Hsiao, *China's Contribution to World Peace* (Chungking: China Institute of Pacific Relations, 1945), pp. 35–41.

CHAPTER 4 DEMOCRACY AND EQUALITY IN MODERN TIMES

There is, perhaps, no other word in the political science vocabulary which is as frequently used, as crucial, and yet as ambiguous as the word "democracy." As a label for what system various nations possess or to what they aspire, it has been immensely popular, at least since the days of Jean Jacques Rousseau. Even Adolf Hitler at one time claimed to favor a system he liked to call "German democracy"; leaders were to be freely elected but, once elected, would enjoy absolute authority. There have since been many other such unlikely champions of democracy. Before Rousseau, and especially among political philosophers since Plato, democracy was very rare and generally condemned as something closely akin to mob rule or anarchy.

The classic notion of democracy
The reader will recall the description of Athenian democracy (Chapter 2) and its stress on equality and participation. These were the hallmarks of the classical notion of democracy, and we shall en-

counter them again in more recent theories of democracy. However, there were other aspects and assumptions of Athenian democracy which are not always appreciated even though they were crucial to its functioning and survival. First of all, there were the ideals inspiring the Athenian democrats, the concept of the *polis* as a meaningful common concern and of participation as an ennobling, indispensable part of the good life of a free citizen. There was general respect for law and for the established procedures of the system. The law was customary Greek law and the citizens felt a deep pride in it and were anxious to distinguish it from the "arbitrary rule among the barbarians."

While Athenian democracy lasted, moreover, the democrats were a very public-spirited lot who considered their participation worth what must have been a considerable loss of time and effort from their private pursuits. It was this ethical community of values which made it possible for Athenian democracy to flourish. The gradual demise of the civic faith inevitably doomed Athenian democracy even without its conquest by the Macedonians.

The social and economic circumstances of Athenian democracy also deserve mention since they tended rather severely to limit attempts to transfer democracy to other settings. Athens and the surrounding area constituted a rather small state. The exclusion of foreign residents, women, and slaves left a citizen population of perhaps twenty thousand adult males, which was probably still far too many for town meetings of the *ecclesia*. The Athenian democrats, moreover, were relatively prosperous though mostly on a small and equal scale. Nearly two-thirds of them are estimated to have lived on small (five acres or less) farms, small shops, or from laboring skills. The dominant element was certainly not a leisure class supported by slavery, as has sometimes been suggested. It is this social basis of relative equality which made democracy feasible and attractive.

Rousseau drew his democratic design chiefly from the town meeting practices of Swiss rural communes, again a setting resting on the relative social and economic equality of the citizens. There was also, in Rousseau's theories and in Swiss practice, an emphasis on morality and civic faith. To overcome the limitation on the size of viable units of participation, he proposed at one point to federate such self-governing communes into a state large enough to survive in the world of his day. Federation, however, would have involved of necessity a representative mechanism and probably executive organs appointed for longer terms as well, and it would thus have compromised the purity of direct democracy. Rousseau, in fact, took a dim view of representative assemblies such as the British House of Commons because he did not trust elected officials under any circumstances. The British people, he claimed at one time, are sovereign only for a single day, the day of the elections by which they subordinate themselves to the authority of a gathering of selfish men for another legislative term.

Dilemmas of modern democracy

The actual rise of modern democracy, then, followed neither the model of Athenian democracy nor Rousseau's theories of democratic participation except in merely partial aspects of the complex political life of modern nation-states. It is simply not possible today nor has it ever been in the past, for the millions of inhabitants of a nation-state with a large expanse of territory to "govern themselves" in the literal sense of the word. Instead, they have had to be content with the privilege of electing their governors or voting them out of office, and with an indirect, corrective influence on governmental policies.

There is, in particular, a difference in the levels of the modern bureaucratic state at which democratic control can take effect. Classic theory suggests that the real decisions are to be made by the people in assembly and then carried out by a handful of easily supervisable executive officers. Modern conditions instead confront us with a vast and complex governmental machinery guided and supervised by elected officials who periodically have to account for their decisions. As we seek to define modern democracy, then, we should not be ensnared by ringing phrases such as "government by and for the people" which obscure rather than reveal democratic realities. We should look instead for the democratic procedures and controls that should be at work at crucial junctures and key functions of the modern bureaucratic state, such as in the representative process, in the interaction among legislators, between executive and legislature, between administrators and the public, and in the bureaucratic and market mechanisms of the private bureaucracies of a modern society.

The caveat about the big words of democratic self-advertisement, which often mask insufficiently democratic procedures, also applies to such current slogans as "democratization" and "participatory democracy," and to their application to nonpolitical institutions. There is almost always room for making a given political structure more responsive to the influence and control of its constitutents. But the procedures of "participatory democracy" have only very limited application to bureaucratic structures of any sort. Bureaucracies need a free press and professional watchdogs such as legislators or an *ombudsman*, but hardly participatory democracy except perhaps on some matters among the employees of each level. There is also the danger that the clear lines of responsibility may be lost in a maze of crosspressures, thus frustrating the best leverage for making bureaucrats accountable. Holding up a false ideal to the imperfect realities of democratic institutions is worse then a hoax. It negates their legitimacy without being able to put anything in their place.

Nonpolitical applications of democracy

The application of democratic procedures to nonpolitical institutions or settings is in itself a momentous decision. Why should a church, a school, a business corporation, or a family be run in a democratic fashion? It is very foolish to take for granted that, for the greater glory of democracy, they should. If we do decide in a particular nonpolitical area to introduce democracy, such a decision is itself a *politicum* of the greatest importance and will very likely transform profoundly the original relationships in that area. The slogan of "industrial democracy" or of the "democratization" of capitalistic industry is a good example. It epitomizes many of the central concerns of Democratic Socialism (see Chapter 5), especially those of the producers rather than the consumers. When industrial democracy was first proposed, therefore, its intended purpose was indeed the socialistic transformation of private industry by transferring authority from the owners and managers to the workers. Its purpose was obviously not democracy for the sake of democracy.

The democratization of a church or of the family as an institution, or of the schools, likewise have to be carefully pondered, because they are more likely to result in the complete transformation, and possibly dissolution, of the institution than in an enhancement of democracy for its own sake. Of course, churches and parents should be responsive to their charges, but this is not the same as formal democracy. The last few years have seen, in particular, attempts and proposals to democratize higher education in the United States and in many countries of Western Europe. Even apart from the obvious attempts to "reconstitute" classes or whole universities into instruments of revolutionary action, the inspiration of these attempts and proposals has been political, or at least not at all intrinsic to the educational process of transmitting and acquiring knowledge. Using new admissions or testing policies as a lever for the redistribution of privilege in society, for example, is a political goal. This is not to say that the bureaucratic, mass institutional character of contemporary higher education is not in need of potent watchdog and corrective functions to enforce responsibility and to relieve the strain on the masses of students confined for years to the halls of ivy. Nor is it to deny that there should be market-type controls wielded by the student consumers over the quality of the educational products they receive. Again, participatory democracy in the classroom must not be confused with a responsive democratic atmosphere which is very desirable. The voting processes of democracy, however, would hardly improve, and more likely reduce the actual interaction between teachers and students to the level of an educational farce.

THE RISE OF LIBERAL DEMOCRACY

It is important to understand modern democracy in all its faults and glories, in its successes and its limitations, as a historical product which in its details has varied a great deal from period to period and from country to country. Just as in ancient Athens, actual democratic systems are highly dependent on socioeconomic circumstances as well as on the presence of the willingness and ability of the citizens to maintain them. There are enormous differences, therefore, between different periods of the same democracy and even more among democratic countries even if we exclude for the time being such alleged democratic systems as the Communist *people's democracies* or certain developing countries where no devices for the actual control of the policy-makers by the people exist.

Equality of condition

A modicum of equality among the citizens, as in Athens, is a precondition of any democracy. The extreme inequality of class and status in the European Middle Ages, therefore, was a poor soil in which to plant the democratic seed. The same has been true of many a quasi-feudal society of Africa, Asia, or Latin America until rather recently. The rise of the centralized, absolutistic state in Europe tended to prepare the ground for greater equality by leveling down the privileges of aristocracy and church. As de Tocqueville pointed out, equality feeds upon itself, engendering a passionate desire for more equality. But equality alone is not enough and can be present also in a dictatorship or in the graveyard. What democracy requires is a desire for political freedom as well as equality, and it is this remarkable growth of both in conjunction in the Western world which we should examine.

There is indeed no more unprecedented and momentous development in the life of Western man than the steady advance of the masses of people toward a dignified and responsible life for every individual. The beginning of this advance was heralded the day a spokesman for rebellious soldiers in Cromwell's army addressed the following words to his officers:

Really I think that the poorest he that is in England hath a life to live as the greatest he; and therefore truly, Sir, I think it's clear, that every man that is to live under a government ought first by his own consent to put himself under that government.[1]

The road traveled by Western society to the point where the "life of the poorest he" was accorded the dignity due him as a human being, and where his consent became the foundation of government of great powers, was a slow, steep, and perilous one. Looking at the steep and lengthy climb that lies ahead of the developing nations in Africa, Asia, and Latin America today, we may well be inclined to reflect upon both the ardous road which was traveled and the final goal which America and other advanced Western nations have long taken for granted.

To achieve a dignified and responsible life for *every individual*, of first importance is a standard of living high enough to loosen the bonds of dire economic necessity, thus enabling the common man to lead a full, healthy, and satisfying life within the limits of his ability and wisdom. On a mass level, this goal has not yet been approached outside of North America, Australia, Japan, the USSR, and Western Europe. The rest of the Communist countries are still engaged in a determined effort to catch up economically with the West at a high price to human liberty. More than half of the world population today still lives at a level of subsistence not far removed from the bare satisfaction of animal needs. With respect to educational, economic, and technological resources, such countries are many decades removed from a decent living for the masses of their people.

Levels of living condition are difficult to assess when comparing different periods of history. Among countries at a given period of time, a crude comparison can be made on the basis of per capita income per year. In the second half of the 1960s, the figures ranged from about $1500 for the Soviet Union, Israel, Czechoslovakia, and East Germany to around $2000 for most Western European countries, and Australia, Sweden, Iceland, and Canada were approaching $3000. The United States was close to $4000. A number of rather de-

---

[1] A. S. P. Woodhouse, ed., *Puritanism and Liberty*, 2nd ed. (Chicago: University of Chicago Press, 1951), Vol. I, p. 301.

veloped countries, including Japan, Poland, and Venezuela, reached about $900 to $1000 per capita income. Many of the least developed countries achieved $100 or less: Red China, India, Uganda, Tanzania, Guinea, Mali, and Haiti. The figures may not tell the whole story, but it is quite clear that the lower levels also imply an absence of the literacy and mobility which facilitates modern democratic participation.

Between the developing nations and achievement of a decent level of living lies what took two centuries of gradual growth and development in the West, although these nations will not have to invent and develop the machines and can import capital and technical knowledge from the more developed countries. Will the developing nations follow the example of the Soviet Union and Communist China, forcing economic growth by means of a regimented, Spartan life? Is democracy possible under conditions of forced growth? To be sure, Western society also paid a heavy price at various stages of its growth, through senseless wars and the abuses of the early industrial revolution, though rarely as a matter of deliberate public policy. But pluralistic tradition and optimistic faith in the future of man have helped some advanced Western nations to survive the intermediate stages of growth by keeping the door open for errors to be refuted and failures to be overcome. As John Stuart Mill has argued convincingly in his *Essay on Liberty* (1859), there is a necessary and intimate connection between liberty and social progress: where the free creation and exchange of ideas are trampled underfoot, there can be little if any creative change, and material progress becomes a hollow triumph.

The dangers of the transition

A similar caveat applies to the noneconomic aspects of the rise of the common man from traditional obscurity to a future of self-realization of human potentialities. Man lives not by bread alone, although its lack or scarcity can be fatal to his ambitions. Nor is it merely a question of human happiness, for man can be "happy" from intoxicants and pipe dreams. An undeveloped society usually permits only a very small elite to develop its individual potentialities and to lead full and satisfying lives, while the masses are left yearning for education and opportunities for developing their talents, and for recognition of their personal aspirations.

More consequential than the economic development of a society for the growth of a democratic potential is its cultural evolution. As older societies embark on the great transition, conditions of cultural breakdown and disintegration tend to disorient the people and often subject them to mental anguish and despair. To transform their old values into new values hospitable to democracy requires a long and painful process of readjustment. To a people in transition, the advantages of democracy are not as readily apparent as we tend to assume. Their deeply felt yearning for a better life is not economically conceived as much as it is a cultural yearning for new meanings in place of the old socioreligious or politicoreligious ones. For this reason, and not necessarily because of its economic promises, Communism or revolutionary nationalism are often far more tempting to the masses of these nations than is liberal democracy.

It is with this deep yearning for meaning and fulfillment that the greatest dangers of the transition arise. For as long as the real goal is distant and the impatience great, there is no lack of demagogues or of mirages of a paradise nearer at hand. Up until the end of World War I, there was a strong conviction in the Western world that the advance of democracy throughout the world was inevitable, although a little crusading might be necessary "to make the world safe for democracy." Then came the Russian Revolution of 1917, the march on Rome of Mussolini's Fascists in 1922, and a steadily growing number of dictatorships in Central, Eastern, and Southern Europe, until by the time of the Great Depression of the 1930s, democracy was in retreat everywhere. Even in the staunchest Western democracies—England, France, Scandinavia, and the United States—movements and ideologies of the extreme right and left demonstrated their appeal to tens of thousands of men and women disheartened by the economic crisis and taken in by the fantastic promises and propaganda techniques of the demagogues.

The excolonial peoples of the world will be exposed to similar dangers as they face the long ascent ahead. Self-seeking demagogues will attempt to lead them astray—through the lure of Communism, revolutionary nationalism, Fascism, nativist authoritarianism, or other substitute religions which respond to their yearning for a better life—to the short intoxication of rebellion, or to the long hangover of dictatorship. Yet there is a real chance that the lasting promise of the dignified life which democracy holds may gain in appeal and at last triumph as the developing part of the world becomes better fed and better educated.

A DEFINITION OF LIBERAL DEMOCRACY

After three centuries of the march of democracy in the West through such landmarks as the American and French Revolutions, the British electoral reforms, and the progressive era and the civil rights movement in the United States, we live in an age almost universally beholden to at least the word "democracy." Even dictators pay lip service to democracy, and Communist countries call themselves "people's democracies." Yet how can *liberal democracy,* as it is often called, be defined to distinguish it from its imitations? What are the premises or assumptions upon which it is based? What are its weaknesses and who are its critics?

   Abraham Lincoln defined democracy as "government of the people, by the people, for the people." Government *for* the people is reminiscent of Aristotle's distinction between rule in the interest of all and rule in the sole interest of the rulers. But the other two parts are less precise and rather like the literal translation of democracy, rule of or by the *demos,* the people. The nineteenth and twentieth centuries have seen a number of dictatorial regimes with broad, if artificially generated, popular support—from Napoleon I to the "people's democracies." The impracticability of direct democracy in modern nation-states, furthermore, has taught us that the people can govern only indirectly under any circumstances.[2]

The four principles of democracy

These considerations compel us to define democracy very carefully and with a view not only to what it is, but also to what it is not. Four major principles combine to constitute our definition: (1) government by discussion, (2) majority rule, (3) recognition of minority rights, and (4) constitutional government. Let us examine each in some detail.

Government by discussion   First, democracy is government not only by consent, but by individual and rational consent of a representatively large number of citizens. It has also been called government by discussion or by persuasion, for these are the typical ways in which the consent of the governed is gained and reaffirmed. Naturally, the highly technical nature, the volume, and the urgency of governmental decisions make it impractical to consult the people on every detail of every policy. But it remains an indispensable hallmark of democratic leadership that the government does not lose touch with popular sentiment on the major outlines of policy, and that the people are given appropriate opportunities to make effective choices between alternative sets of leaders and policies.

[2] As Robert M. MacIver succinctly put it: "Democracy is not a way of governing, whether by majority or otherwise, but primarily a way of determining who shall govern and, broadly, to what ends." *The Modern State* (New York: Columbia University Press, 1955), p. 198.

A democratic form of government is distinguished by institutions that facilitate the gathering of consent and offer choices. Devices and institutions have been developed in various Western countries that help to accomplish this goal with varying degrees of success. Among the most important are free elections, the secret ballot, devices for the legislative control of the executive branch, and judicial remedies against arbitrary use of governmental power. Informal institutions, such as political parties, voluntary associations, and the media of public opinion, also make vital contributions by providing a meaningful setting in which the individual citizen can make responsible choices.

Among the false versions of democracy which do not meet these specifications is "plebiscitary democracy" or, as it has also been called, Caesarism or Bonapartism. The plebiscites by which the two Napoleons and Hitler secured the acclamation of the masses provided as little meaningful choice as the one-slate elections of the "people's democracies." Neither system is government by discussion or persuasion. Both regimes relied on distortion and coercion for winning consent rather than on discussion and persuasion.

Government by discussion differs from traditional autocracy, in which little effort is made to ask for the consent of the people. In a traditional autocracy the masses are politically dormant, and the government rules by traditional authority and custom. Consent is not necessary because the people do not participate in the making of decisions. The existing leadership is accepted with habitual obedience as long as it rules within the bounds of custom.

Majority rule The second part of our definition is the principle of majority rule. In every body politic, important decisions constantly have to be made at one or more levels. The people must choose among several sets of leaders and thereby among several policies. In a direct democracy, such as in a New England town meeting, the people may also appoint the officers, pass laws, and set up the budget of the community. In a representative democracy there are bodies of representatives—legislatures, committees, and collegial executive or regulative bodies—for example, such as the British Cabinet or the American regulatory commissions. Majority rule means that in all of these decision-making bodies, from the electorate to the last committee, the issues are to be resolved by voting. Majority rule assumes that the units to be counted are equal. Political equality in the electorate—the principle of "one man (one woman) one vote"—constitutes, therefore, one of the oustanding characteristics of democracy. Because most of the older societies were highly stratified into social classes, such as the privileged aristocracy and the lower classes, the principle of majority rule at first appeared to be a revolutionary innovation aimed at breaking down the hereditary class barriers.

Because the electorate never quite embraces the entire population, there arises the question of what kind of suffrage restriction is legitimate and what kind is clearly contrary to the spirit of democracy. The evolution of Western democracy has been in large part the story of the broadening of the suffrage. One by one, over the decades of the nineteenth and twentieth centuries, the voting restrictions of property ownership, race, and sex were abolished. However, some limitations on the suffrage are still considered legitimate, because they exclude from the suffrage individuals who cannot be expected to use their ballot in a rational and responsible manner. Convicted criminals, mental patients, and persons under a legally fixed age fall into this category. The basic assumption is that the suffrage restrictions must rest on objective and reasonable criteria of incompetence in order to be legitimate. There will always be room for disagreement and borderline cases. Often the distinction between legitimate practices and obvious abuses can be determined only by an assessment of the overall factual conditions for democracy in a particular country. For example: If the population of a particular country is composed of 90 percent illiterates, it is plainly undemocratic to base the right to vote on a literacy requirement.

The "people's democracies" of Eastern Europe and Asia enjoy a certain amount of popularity within their own borders, with occasional lapses of which we in the West do not always become aware. However, they cannot be said to meet the criterion of majority rule either in elections, or in their legislative assemblies, or in the origin of these regimes. Their sham elections and manipulated deliberative bodies make a mockery of majority rule. The Communist regimes in every country now under Communist domination arose from the position of a seemingly hopeless minority. Quite aware of the fact that they could nowhere count on a majority, the Communists in practically all of these countries came to power by force and fraud. Even in the Soviet Union, where Communists have been in power for more than forty years, government is still the undisputed monopoly of the Communist party unchallenged by any opposition. The Soviet Union is ruled by a minority of about 3 percent of the total population. This new ruling class has shown no inclination to submit its dominant position to the hazards of majority rule. A similar statement can be made about the traditional autocracies and more recent military or Fascist dictatorships, except that these other nondemocratic forms of government rarely go beyond oral avowals of majority support. Many members of these governments, in fact, profess an unabashed preference for extreme social, political, and economic inequality. It should be mentioned, however, that some of the new one-party states are more difficult to fit into the mold of majority rule because of their communitarian voting patterns. The plebiscites on the acceptance or rejection of the de Gaulle constitution in the former French African colonies, for example, elicited in most cases nearly unanimous decisions in favor or, in the case of Guinea, against. It is not appropriate to expect the conduct associated with majority voting of peoples who prefer a communitarian consensus.

Recognition of minority rights   The third part of our definition of democracy is the protection of minority rights. Although the important decisions on the policy of the whole community should be made according to the will of the majority, there must be limits to what this majority can do to minorities of various description in the body politic. It would be most unreasonable, for example, to permit the majority to punish the minority for its dissent by threats of bodily harm, exile, or expropriation. The Western democracies have, therefore, developed a series of specific exemptions from the organized authority of the majority. An example is the First Amendment of the United States Constitution:

Congress shall make no law respecting an establishment of religion, or prohibiting the free exercise thereof; or abridging the freedom of speech, or of the press; or the right of the people peaceably to assemble, and to petition the government for a redress of grievances.

Congress is the organized representation of the majority will for purposes of government. But Congress is barred from action in these exempt areas, which are considered the special preserve of individuals and groups, inviolable and removed from the authority of the state.

In the early days of Western democracy it was considered sufficient to protect these rights of individuals and groups from action by the state, that is, action by the organized authority of nationwide majorities. Nowadays the concern about what organized majorities may do to defenseless minorities has shifted to the majorities of the population of a member state of the federal union, a local community, a school district, or even just a residential neighborhood. The term *majority* as a numerical concept is dependent upon the number of people included in a particular community, whether it be nationwide, regional, local, or even smaller. Any group of three or more people is capable of forming a majority that discriminates against its minority. Whenever such a group has a public character, such as a district or local government, it can impose its will upon the minority by ordinance or law. The compulsory character of such pronouncements, however, makes them a legitimate subject for the protection of minority rights by judicial or legislative fiat.

Minority issues, unfortunately, are universal among modern nation-states the size of which makes it unlikely that their population would be of the same ethnic stock. The French are not treating their Algerians right, the British are guilty of discrimination toward the colored immigrants from the Commonwealth. The Soviets mistreat their Jews and certain other nationalities, the Czechoslovaks their gypsies, the Nigerians their Ibos, the Sudanese Arabs their black fellow-citizens, the Indonesians their Chinese, and so on. Minority questions periodically erupt in political tensions or, as recently in Northern Ireland, in bloody, uncontrollable clashes.

The ubiquitous nature of these complaints and conflicts, which so often get far beyond anything remediable by legal or procedural means, cannot exonerate the American majority of its obligation to the nation's Blacks, Chicanos, Puerto Ricans, Orientals, and Indians. But it should sharpen our appreciation for the democratic protection of minority rights. Minority grievances take many forms ranging from psychological insults over discrimination in housing, education, and employment to physical persecution and genocide. In our age of verbal overkill, it has become fashionable to equate the lesser complaints with slavery and genocide, a practice that is more likely to shed heat than light on the subject. Legal safeguards of minority rights in democratic countries sometimes fail to be effective against determined majority prejudice or sudden manias of scapegoating. Yet even with their imperfections, these safeguards are worth having because their presence helps to raise the level of awareness of both majority and minority, thus initiating change toward a more favorable climate of opinion. This is the best we can hope for in the permissive climate of democratic politics.

By comparison there is no institutional protection of individual or minority rights in the so-called "people's democracies." The *guaranteed right* to life, liberty, and the pursuit of happiness of individuals and groups has no more place behind the Iron and Bamboo curtains than it had in the Fascist dictatorships of Mussolini and Hitler. In the old, traditional autocracies of yesterday and their contemporary equivalents—countries like Saudi Arabia and the military dictatorships popular in Latin America and Asia—there is also no institutional protection for minorities or the rights of individuals.

Not infrequently, in fact, minorities are pilloried as scapegoats for the grievances of the majority or the failures of the regime.

Constitutional government The fourth major principle of Western democracy is constitutional government, or "government by laws" rather than by men (see Chapter 6 for a detailed discussion of constitutionalism). Democracy is by no means an easy or simple form of government. In addition to a general consensus on the desirability of democracy, it requires an infinitely complex machinery of processes, procedures, and institutions to produce and translate faithfully the majority will into governmental action. Democracy makes enormous demands on the time, goodwill, and integrity of its citizens and public servants. These circumstances bear within them grave dangers to the stability of a democratic republic. Since only mortals—men of flesh and blood—make up democracies, the temptation is often great to cut through the manifold complexities of the machinery in pursuit of legitimate objectives. The rules of the game are suspended initially to permit the quick fulfillment of a popular wish or the effective solution of a tenacious problem. The next time around, the precedent for relaxing the rules has already been set, and this time the object pursued may no longer be so legitimate. Finally, the shortcuts devised by impatient men may be used by their weak or corrupt successors to tear down the elaborate edifice of democratic government.

The only way of lending stability to democratic government that has yet been devised is to set it into a well-rooted framework of laws, into a constitutional tradition that will command a reverence among men that is otherwise reserved to religion. Only where the more significant rules of the democratic game are laid down in law and constitution are they likely to be faithfully observed. Only where there is already an established tradition of law as an integral part of the social order can the latent and self-destructive turbulence of democracy, which political philosophers from Plato to James Madison have feared, be confined to orderly and fairly permanent channels. The same point was made recently by Samuel P. Huntington, who concluded after examining comparative and historical examples that a (democratic) increase in political participation in developing societies was likely to produce political instability unless there was also present a high level of institutionalization. A high level of participation alone, as in a democratic revolution, does not guarantee that democracy is here to stay.[3]

If the successful organization of rule by the consent of the majority

[3] See Samuel P. Huntington, *Political Order in Changing Societies* (New Haven: Yale University Press, 1968).

requires a legal and constitutional structure, this is even more true of the effective protection of minority rights against organized majorities of any size within the body politic. An important aspect of the "sudden passions" of the multitudes in a democracy—about which the *Federalist Papers* expressed concern at the time of the birth of the American Republic—is the violation of the rights of individuals and minorities. Unless these rights are fully spelled out in law and constitution and their protection guaranteed by recourse to judicial or legislative action, the majority will often feel tempted to abuse minorities. In the ordinary course of human affairs, there will always be recurrent economic, social, and political crises. For a short while it may seem very attractive to the multitude to disregard the rights of private property of a few, to suppress unpopular opinions, or to make a particular minority the scapegoat of the frustrations or fears of the whole nation. It is by preventing abuses of this kind that constitutional government makes its greatest contribution to a working democracy.

Again it should be evident from even a cursory look at the "people's democracies," not to mention other kinds of modern dictatorships, that these false forms of democracy possess little constitutional tradition in the Western sense. To be sure, most "people's democracies" have constitutional documents that embody imposing lists of civil rights. But the actual conduct of their regimes and their disregard for the bills of rights in their constitutions have shown the latter to be little more than window dressing. Traditional autocracies, by contrast, may have a constitutional tradition, but they are not likely to be concerned with the rights of individuals and minorities.

Our definition of the formal criteria of democracy, then, is as follows: Democracy is government by discussion, including rational deliberation and open choice, as the word "discussion" implies. Public policy is determined by the principle of majority rule. That is not the same as saying that the numerical majority of the population or even of the eligible voters determines policy. Rather, a majority vote of whatever body is entrusted with making a decision shall prevail, even if a series of such "majority decisions" in the end represents the will of only a minority of the people. Majority rule implies political equality, "one man, one vote," though certain exceptions are widely accepted. The rights of minorities and individuals delimit the sphere of action of majority rule and of governmental activity. They should be generally recognized and effectively safeguarded. Constitutional government, finally, gives regularity and stable procedure to what would, on the face of it, be a rather turbulent, if not chaotic, form of government. Only with the addition of constitutional government can democracy become truly liberal democracy or, as it is often called, constitutional democracy.

ASSUMPTIONS AND PRECONDITIONS OF DEMOCRACY

These four major principles—government by discussion, majority rule, recognition of minority rights, and constitutional government— are the indispensable, minimal criteria of liberal democracy. However, if such a constitutional democracy is to take root and flourish, other unspoken assumptions and favorable conditions are requisite. As will become readily apparent, there is little reason for arrogant pride among democratic nations. Many of these conditions are matters of culture or of economic circumstances which are rather different in the nondemocratic countries of today. Most of the contemporary dictatorships and oligarchies that some Americans look down upon simply lack many prerequisites for democratic self-government at this point in their history. Seen from this perspective, it may indeed be true that dictatorship or oligarchy for them is a stop-gap arrangement on their way toward greater self-government. There is no doubt, judging from their rhetoric, that most of these nations desire to embrace democracy. However, some of their leadership, especially in revolutionary nationalist or Communist countries, define democracy in ways that are dictatorial or even totalitarian. Among the prerequisites of Western democracy are (1) individualism, (2) a cooperative attitude, (3) a capacity for reason and compromise, (4) a stable standard of living, (5) a reasonable amount of social and economic equality, (6) a free pluralistic society, and (7) an empirical attitude. Let us consider these conditions.

Attributes of individuals favorable for democracy

Individualism "Individualism" is a word that has a number of different connotations. As used in this context, it has a dual meaning. It denotes a capacity and willingness to make full use of one's own rights and liberties and a deep regard for the dignity, the rights, and the lives of other men. Minority and individual rights will atrophy if they are not used and defended by the individuals and minorities for whose benefit they have been invented. Majority rule can become rule by a minority when large numbers of citizens fail to exercise their rights of voting and other forms of political participation. Majority rule is out of place in a political system that habitually aims at achieving unanimity. In some of the new nations, notably in Africa, it is customary to argue to consensus rather than to disagree, or to vote in tribal, regional, or national blocs of unanimity rather than as individuals making individual decisions. Where such habits of collective decision-making are culturally conditioned rather than deliberate, and where no procedures exist that allow the voicing of dissent without inviting retribution of sorts, the preconditions for Western, or liberal, democracy are lacking.

There should also be a fundamental regard for the rights of others, which must be ingrained in the social and individual mores of a people, for such regard can hardly be legislated—"The poorest he that is in England hath a life to live as the greatest he." Often the moral training in "living and letting live" is provided by religion. In any case, where the propensity to respect the rights of other people is lacking in individuals, and especially where there is a tendency to gratify one's own ego by humiliating or victimizing others, democracy will have a difficult time establishing itself.

Cooperative attitude   While this kind of individualism—exercising one's own rights and having regard for the rights of others—is very important as a foundation for democracy, it should not be confused with egocentric selfishness. In some cultures, most notably in Latin countries, any attempt at creating a political community tends to conflict with an anarchistic individualism. Raised to distrust persons outside the family, people simply refuse to participate in any common effort. Such selfishness plays havoc with any form of government. In a democracy, however, it breeds anarchy and chaos. Democracy invites anarchy more than do other forms of government because of the extraordinary amount of liberty accorded to every individual.

Yet modern democratic governments are under the same compulsion to maintain a highly organized state having vast functions and an enormous staff as are other forms of government. Hence modern democracy must depend on a constant and voluntary cooperative effort on the part of the multitude of citizens to keep government a going concern through active participation in public affairs. Lacking a widespread willingness on the part of citizens to cooperate in political parties and voluntary organizations, democracy will not work.

Capacity for reason and compromise   More basic even than individualism and a cooperative attitude is the requirement of rationality. Democracy is founded on an optimistic faith in the common man, especially in view of the humble station in life which the

masses of the people occupied before our time: without benefit of
a formal education, illiterate, poor or dependent on the personal whim
of an employer or a landlord, often in agricultural or indentured
servitude, undernourished and heir to numerous diseases and epidemics that modern medicine has now conquered, the common man
before the advent of democracy had hardly a future to look forward
to and had a life span, on the average, only half as long as that of
today. His life was not much different from the Hobbesian description of life in the state of nature: "nasty, brutish and short." His
exterior and, perhaps, at times his conduct made his most typical ex-
ponent in the feudal age, the lowly peasant or *villein*, the evil-minded
"villain" of later drama and epic to this day. These were the people
to whose majority rule democratic thought proposed to entrust the
public interest. These men, it was assumed, possessed enough reason
to know their own interest, enough capacity for improvement to
benefit from education, and enough virtue to do the right thing
once they recognized it. It was a bold dream from which emerged
public education, modern medicine, a high standard of living, and,
last but not least, the training for responsible citizenship by the
exercise of democratic rights. What very few people considered possible in the days of the boorish *villein*, or lowly peasant, today has
come true: the common man has shown a surprising capacity for self-
government when he is given a fair chance and sufficient time to
work out the initial problems of adjusting to the new and unfamiliar responsibility.

Democratic participation on a mass level, however, is not necessarily a result of socioeconomic development alone. As evidence
from a five-nation study of civic attitudes by Gabriel A. Almond
and Sidney Verba has shown, nations with a tradition of strong
lower-class organization in politically oriented unions or political
parties, such as Great Britain, Germany, Italy, and even Mexico,
can boast of substantial lower-class participation in politics. The
United States with its superior economic development, by comparison, has never had much in the way of massive political lower-class
organizations and, consequently, its poorest are a silent, nonpar-
ticipant underclass.[4] There appears to be no substitute for political
mass organizations as a school of democratic participation for those
who need it the most. And there is no reason why developing

[4] See Norman H. Nie, G. Bingham Powell, Jr., and Kenneth Prewitt, "Social
Structure and Political Participation: Developmental Relationships II," *The
American Political Science Review* (September 1969) pp. 808–832. The original
publication of the five-nation study was *The Civic Culture* (Princeton, N.J.:
Princeton University Press, 1963) by Gabriel A. Almond and Sidney Verba.

countries could not make up with massive organization what they lack in socioeconomic development in order to produce democratic attitudes among the masses of their people.

There is another side to this problem when we come to the question of what kind of personality would be desirable for the leadership of a democratic society. New nations such as India often find it very difficult to attract the right kind of people to political careers. Old democracies such as the United States often have the same problem though perhaps on a different level. As recently as 1948, Harold D. Lasswell investigated this subject in America and arrived at a characterization of the "political type" as a person with "an intense and ungratified craving for deference" which he (or she) displaces upon public objects such as "persons and practices connected with the power process." *Power is expected to overcome low estimates of the self.* Lasswell contrasts this political type with the nondestructive, responsive personality of the democratic leader who is thoroughly committed to the values of democratic policy-making.[5]

Conditions favorable for democracy

So far we have dealt mainly with attributes of individuals that create favorable conditions for democracy: individualism, a cooperative attitude, and a capacity for rational self-government. Now let us examine some of the conditions that help to support liberal democracy and, by implication, those which tend to endanger or discourage it.

A stable standard of living It has often been suggested that it takes a certain standard of living to make democracy workable in a particular country. It is true that a starving people may be in no mood to observe the fine points of democratic procedure. On the other hand, it would be difficult to contend that we, for example, are better democrats than our forefathers because we enjoy a higher standard of living. It may be more correct to say that severe economic crises endanger democracy or that excessive economic expectations and impatience for their realization may induce a backward people to prefer dictatorship to democracy. The fall of the democratic Weimar Republic of Germany and the rise of Hitler was caused at least in part by the Great Depression of the 1930s. The so-called revolution of rising expectations among people in the new nations who became aware of the living standard of Western civilization may

[5] See H. D. Lasswell, *Power and Personality* (New York: Norton, 1948).

induce them to view with favor the example of dictatorial Soviet Russia, which in forty years became an industrial power.

A reasonable amount of social and economic equality It has also been suggested by some writers that democracy is linked with social and economic equality: where such equality is present, democracy is said to be a natural choice. Where democracy has been introduced, it is said to bring equality in its train. This is only partially true. It is very difficult to visualize a social and economic equality so complete that not even the differentials of age, sex, and ability would create differences in status. Even the supposedly egalitarian Communists in the Soviet Union have class distinctions between peasants and city workers, not to mention the privileged "technical intelligentsia" and the Communist party itself.

Secondly, equality does not necessarily lead to democracy; it could just as well be the foundation of old-fashioned monarchic absolutism or the plebiscitary democracy of the two Napoleons. To be sure, extremes in economic power or social status can be an obstacle to the workings of democracy. It is also true that some approximation of equality can be conducive to democracy, if the other conditions required are present. But the relationship between democracy and equality in matters other than political is complicated and may vary from case to case.

Thirdly, while democracy has generally arrived long before the present semblance of equality became apparent, the leveling of traditional society was largely the result of economic and social processes rather than of political intervention. If political democracy has done anything to further equality in general, it has been more often in the direction of the equality of opportunity rather than equality itself. Democratic governments have often acted to clear away obstacles in the path of equal opportunities, but they have rarely taken positive steps for the bringing about of equality in general.

A free pluralistic society If any particular form of society has been particularly favorable to the functioning of democracy, it would appear to be a "free," or "open," pluralistic society. An open society allows the existence of a vast number of spontaneous individual and group activities, operating side by side, without much regulation or manipulation by any concentration of power, such as the state. Individuals, business corporations, labor unions, and other associations all look after their own affairs according to their respective needs and life cycles. Where there are clashes of interest or of personality, moreover, they are resolved by bargaining, by the operation of the impersonal forces of the marketplace, or according to majority decision, but not by governmental or powerful private compulsion. Such a free, pluralistic society, it must be admitted, is in some ways wasteful and disorderly. But at the same time it is highly creative and productive, and allows the individual an amount of liberty that no other form of society has ever known. It is for this reason that a free society lends itself well to the purposes of liberal democracy.

An empirical attitude   Speaking of pluralism and the clash of interests brings us to the last precondition of successful democracy: an empirical attitude. A free society is always likely to contain several distinct economic group interests, personal factions or rivaling popular leaders, and ethnic or religious groups. If these groups are to form popular majorities in support of specific government policies, there are likely to be conflicting interests and profound disagreements. There are two approaches to such disagreement on principles. One is that each of the parties to the dispute can view the arguments for its own cause as a vital part of an ideology or a philosophy of life and, like philosopher-kings, insist on calling its own point of view truth and that of the other party error or fallacy. Or the parties in dispute can take an empirical view of the matter: that no one can really know the absolute truth, that the disagreement is merely one of interests or preferences and therefore compromise is in order. The first approach leads to dogmatism and bitter enmity. From the point of view of a philosopher-king, compromise is a dirty business, a watering-down of truth, or an intolerable mixture of incompatible truths. An empirical approach involves a basic reluctance to make up one's mind before all the facts are known. From the resulting mutual regard and consideration there may well flower substantial cooperation rather than stalemate.

THE CRITICS OF DEMOCRACY

This review of democracy would not be complete without a discussion of the numerous criticisms that have been leveled at democracy throughout recorded history. First of all, we must bear in mind that from the days of Athenian democracy until the seventeenth and eighteenth centuries no important political thinker or writer preferred democracy to monarchy and aristocracy. Most of them took Plato's or Aristotle's negative comments about democracy as authoritative, firsthand evaluations, because generally they themselves had no opportunity to see democracy in operation. Their firsthand acquaintance with the lower classes, moreover, tended to dispel any illusions they may have held about the advantages of majority rule. Even among its own proponents, democracy, upon its arrival at the end of the eighteenth century, brought ambiguous reactions. Liberal thinkers, who had long called for more liberty and equality, suddenly saw themselves faced with the routine realities and practical problems raised by this new form of government. Conservative thinkers expressed profound shock at the excesses of popular government in the French Revolution. Yet the coming of democracy was viewed as an inexorable fate approaching the traditional societies of Europe.

Tyranny of the majority

In the 1830s, the French political writer Alexis de Tocqueville visited the United States, which was then at the height of the Jacksonian era of democracy. On his return to France, he wrote his *Democracy in America*, with the air of a man who had looked into the future of his own civilization and was anxious to share his insights with his compatriots. Far from repeating the standard argument of his age against democracy, namely that it was too weak a form of government to withstand the internal and external pressures of the times, he wrote:

The main evil of the present democratic institutions in the United States, in my opinion, arises not from their weaknesses, as is often maintained in Europe, but from their overpowering strength. I am not so much alarmed at the excess of liberty reigning in that country as at the very inadequate safeguards against tyranny.

If an individual or party is wronged [by the majority] in the United States, to whom can he turn for a redress? Not to public opinion, for public opinion constitutes the majority; not to the legislature, for it represents the majority and implicitly obeys its injunctions; not to the executive power, for that is appointed by the majority and remains a passive tool in its hands; the militia consists of the majority in arms; the court jury is the majority invested with the right to hear judicial cases; and in certain states even the judges are elected by the majority.

This new theme of the "tyranny of the majority" became a slogan with nineteenth-century Liberals who were having second thoughts about democracy and equality. One of the more important writers who echoed this fear of the majority and its stifling pressure upon the creative individual was the British political philosopher John Stuart Mill who wrote his *Essay on Liberty* twenty-five years after de Tocqueville's *Democracy in America*. Mill saw in democracy more than just a form of government. He feared the enforced conformity to the tastes and predilections of the unorganized crowd:

Like other tyrannies, the tyranny of the majority was at first, and is still vulgarly, held in dread, chiefly as operating through the acts of the public authorities. But reflecting persons perceived that when society is itself the tyrant—society collectively, over the separate individuals who compose it—its means of tyrannizing are not restricted to the acts which it may do by the hands of its political functionaries. Society can and does execute its own mandates: and if it issues wrong mandates instead of right, or any mandates at all in things with which it ought not to meddle, it practices a social tyranny more formidable than many kinds of political oppression, since, though not usually upheld by such extreme penalties, it leaves fewer means of escape, penetrating much more deeply into the details of life, and enslaving the soul itself. Protection, therefore, against the tyranny of the magistrate is not enough: there needs protection also against the tyranny of the prevailing opinion and feeling; against the tendency of society to impose, by other means than civil penalties, its own ideas and practices as rules of conduct on those who dissent from them; to fetter the development, and, if possible, prevent the formation, of any individuality not in harmony with its ways, and compel all characters to fashion themselves upon the model of its own.

Fear of the mass man   The fears that motivated Alexis de Tocqueville and John Stuart Mill still play a role today. They appear frequently in the form of complaints about the pressure for conformity, by means of which majorities impose their own prejudices and mediocre tastes upon the judgment of individuals. These fears also relate to anti-Black or other prejudices and personal quirks which may be understandable in the individual, but lead to dreadful consequences in the mass. In addition to patterns of discrimination, one consequence may be that the prevailing racist view of Black people permeates their own self-esteem. In the opinion of many Black leaders, conscious effort from a tender age is required to build up Black pride and identity to overcome the effect of prejudicial brainwashing by white people.

These fears also make their appearance in the slogans about the "mass man" and "mass democracy," which can be found in much twentieth-century literature critical of unrestrained democracy, such as Ortega y Gasset's *Revolt of the Masses*. The "mass man," according to this point of view, is a rootless, lonely person, wearing a standard face and conforming to standard notions of behavior until a situation of crisis turns loose his worst instincts under the shelter of the anonymity of a mob. To found democracy upon the rule of the mass man, who is said to be incapable of individual spontaneity, of the responsible use of liberty, and of forming a political community, is to court disaster. Mass democracy is rule by the mob.

In the current wave of criticisms of established Western institutions, liberal democracy has had to take its knocks, too. Some of the attacks have been on the primitive level of shouts of "power to the people" to suggest that existing procedures are not democratic enough. Although a slogan used under widely differing circumstances, such as in referring to the Black or street-people ghettoes near some American universities, is not a sufficiently explicit statement to argue with, "power to the people" raises a set of problems in interpreting democracy which we have not yet considered. It is unclear to what constituency the slogan refers. If it were used by rebellious students of the University of California at Berkeley, for example, it would matter a great deal indeed, whether "the people" in the slogan are the rebels, the whole student body, the people of the ghetto neighborhood, or of the city, the people of the state of California, or of the whole country. Political agitators, of course, find it convenient to be vague about this point, but there is obviously no democratic argument to be made without specifying an appropriate body of people with a legitimate claim in the matter. This question of constituency is equally important in judging jurisdictional disputes in local government or in federal systems from a democratic viewpoint.[6]

Another line of criticism addresses itself to the role of intermediate processes of bargaining and equilibrating among different group forces in democratic policy-making. American democracy, in particular, is said to be based chiefly on this group process rather than on pursuing democratic contents and values in governmental policies.[7] A typical formulation is that of Theodore J. Lowi, who calls the culprit "interest group liberalism" and complains that it "promotes popular decision-making but derogates from the decisions so made

---

[6] A model case of this nature involved the territorial reorganization of two old German states, Baden and Wuerttemberg, into a new South West State in 1952. After a confusing interlude in which zonal boundaries between the French and American zones of occupation divided both states and the Americans had merged North Baden and North Wuerttemberg, a plebiscite was held in the entire territory on the question of union. Over two-thirds of the people in the total area agreed to it and the South West State was formed. Representatives of the old state of Baden, however, brought a suit against the union before the West German Federal Constitutional Court because within old Baden, a majority of the citizens had voted against union. There is no solution to this problem in democratic theory. The court held, however, that the old state of Baden had not survived the collapse of the *Reich* in 1945 and its subsequent division and thus upheld the union.

[7] George D. Beam, *Usual Politics* (New York: Holt, Rinehart & Winston, 1970), attributes this to the Madisonian formulation in *Federalist Papers*, no. 10.

by misapplying the notion to the implementation as well as the formulation of policy."[8] Democratically formulated policies of the government, in other words, are shamefully subverted because organized interests are allowed to interfere heavily with their actual implementation. The informal bargaining corrupts the formal democratic procedure and robs it of its meaning.

Evaluation of arguments against democracy

It may be well to pause here and consider the merits of some of these arguments against democracy. We have already considered Plato's criticism of Athenian democracy (see Chapter 2). It coincides partially with that of de Tocqueville and Mill in that the death of Socrates at the hands of the democratic politicians of Athens is an extreme example of the tyranny and intolerance of the majority. Plato's argument against the happy versatility of the Athenians, however, is tantamount to denying to the masses of humans the opportunity to lead a full, healthy, and satisfying life, which has today become the goal of all the peoples of the world.[9] Plato's elaborate argument for "natural" social inequality, by which the ancients justified slavery on the one hand and aristocratic privilege on the other, is probably the main point in his critique of democracy that appealed to political philosophers until the resurgence of democracy in the eighteenth and nineteenth centuries. The increasing approximation of actual equality today and such unspoken assumptions as rationality, an empirical attitude, and belief in the essential human dignity of every man make it rather apparent that social inequality is anything but "natural."

Modern rootlessness As for the doctrines of the "mass man," it would appear that they are composed of several elements. A large part of the image of the "mass man" is the result of prejudice on the part of the old social and intellectual elites: they no longer find themselves alone and have not yet developed the habit of looking closely enough at their fellow humans of the once lower classes to distinguish in their faces human features very much like their own. Often, writers about the "mass man" and "mass society" will also point to the activities of mobs in action, to extremist movements and to mass psychology. Some of these forms of mass action and mass hysteria appear to be related to the sheer numbers of people who appear as mobs or react irrationally at the same time but indepen-

[8] See his *The End of Liberalism* (New York: Norton, 1969), p. 288.

[9] There is little consolation, in this writer's opinion, in Plato's offer to substitute the happiness of the perfect shoemaker or the perfect carpenter for happy versatility, for these trades are clearly earmarked by him as inferior stations in life.

dently from one another. Although the cruder forms of mob action may disappear with the growth of education and fulfillment of life satisfactions, there will always be a residue of tryannous inclinations of majorities, for which there is no other remedy but training in responsible citizenship and deliberately cultivated habits of tolerance and fairness.

The large numbers of people involved in modern city and industrial life also brings us back to the question of the proper relationship between the individual and the community. Radical social movements often thrive on the loneliness of modern man. They provide a tightly integrated ingroup as a community substitute for him and at the same time focus his aggressive reactions and feelings of insecurity upon a scapegoat, an outgroup. This whole development, however, could perhaps be avoided or minimized if people followed the sage observation of de Tocqueville, who felt that the large number of voluntary associations in America and the willingness of citizens to participate in them was a major stabilizing element in this volatile new society of equals. Voluntary groups can indeed give the lonely individual a feeling of belonging and a sense of community life that may save him from the lure of ingroups of demagogic movements.

Pareto, Mosca, Michels Other critics of democracy have turned their attention to the issue of political equality as such rather than to the nature of the citizens who make up the body politic. Three outstanding European social scientists of the late nineteenth and early twentieth centuries—Vilfredo Pareto (1884–1923), Gaetano Mosca (1885–1941), and Robert Michels (1876–1936)—considered rule by a natural elite an inevitable state of affairs. Pareto and Mosca arrived at their theory of the ruling classes from a study of history. Michels studied contemporary political parties and labor unions and concluded that there exists an "iron law of oligarchy." There are entrenched ruling cliques present in every voluntary association, he concluded, and the rank-and-file members will maintain these cliques in power by sheer apathy and lack of ambition even in extreme cases of fraud or abuse of authority. Many conservatives, the Italian Fascist leader Mussolini, and many of the milder proponents of "racial supremacy" in the American South and in South Africa have believed in such a "rule by natural elites," although the definitions of what constitutes elite status differ widely and are at times diametrically opposed to one another.

The Communist criticism of democracy Communism as an ideology has also found fault with liberal democracy. Its criticism is leveled mainly at the fact that liberal democracy is more interested in individual liberty and political equality than in economic equality. Communists scorn the elaborate devices of constitutionalism, free elections, and the judicial protection of civil rights as a smokescreen of formalities hiding the realities of capitalism—of which they have a concept that is outdated by more than a hundred years. Instead of democracy, they offer a "people's democracy," which is "government for the people" but by the Communist party.

The cult of the irrational   There is a final category of criticisms of democracy that is often implicit rather than directly expressed. It is a cult of the irrational, which finds liberal democracy too rational to be emotionally satisfying. The increasing secularization of modern societies tends to bring on recurrent waves of irrationalism, disgust with civilization, and a yearning for new cults and faiths. Such a wave occurred in the Western world, for example, in the 1920s, when astrology and strange new religions came to flourish alongside quasi-religious, political fanaticisms, and we are in the throes of another such wave now. One strain of this cult of the irrational is to be found in hero worship as it was advocated by the British historian Thomas Carlyle and many other writers and widely practiced by nationalist, Socialist, Fascist, and Communist movements during the last one hundred years. The adoration of the leader or heroic super-man can be reconciled with democracy as little as can similarly sweeping sentiments toward mythical entities, such as the folk spirit or the "Arayan race" worshipped by Hitler's Nazi movement. Dynamic racism goes far beyond a mere assertion of racial inequality and elitism. It uses, instead, pseudoscientific theories of race and history to concoct a fighting creed, or myth, that will inspire a mass movement of malcontents to heroic actions and sacrifices. The fabrication of the "myth" of the Aryan superrace goes back to the pseudoscientific teachings of the French Count Gobineau (1816–1882) and the Englishman Houston Stewart Chamberlain (1855–1927) in the nineteenth century. For Hitler, this myth was a convenient Big Lie on which he could base his Nazi movement and later the Nazi state (see Chapter 14). The Communist movement likewise thrived on a similar myth drawn from the writings of Karl Marx. Among the various Marxist doctrines, those of the class struggle and the inexorable march of history toward the great proletarian revolution proved most useful as a fighting creed (see Chapter 13). A myth is, by definition, not a guide to rational action but a symbol and a vision that can incite to fanatical determination and revolutionary action. There is no place in liberal democracy for myth-makers or myth-manipulators and the barbarian drives which they are capable of bringing out in normally rational human beings. Liberal democracy is the child of the Enlightenment of the eighteenth century, which attempted to bury these rank superstitions and emotional hankerings of modern man and woman once and for all.

Wanted: Better democratic constitutions

As for the current criticisms in Western democracies of "interest-groups liberalism," Madisonian democracy, or pluralistic democracy, their points are well taken for the most part. As forms of government go, liberal democracy is rather permissive toward all kinds of abuses. Self-styled elites and special interests are often able to take crass advantage of it and can entrench themselves in its structure so thoroughly as to turn democracies into self-serving oligarchies. This is particularly true in the United States where the constitution and the usages of government favor the will of special interests and elites over the will of the majority of the people. Parliamentary democracies tend to be less interest-ridden though often more elitist. The specific design of a country's constitution and the details of its institutional practices (see Chapters 6 through 11) have a great deal to do with whether democracy can be made to work as intended. Where abuses crop up and adulterate democracy intolerably, the thing to do may well be a well-considered change in the institutional design or the adoption of a better democratic constitution.

CHAPTER **5** THE CLASH
OF PRINCIPLES:
LIBERALISM,
CONSERVATISM,
AND DEMOCRATIC
SOCIALISM

Politics in the nineteenth and twentieth centuries has been characterized by the appearance of political "isms," or ideologies, with which
vast numbers of people identify themselves in their political attitudes
and actions. We tend to look at contemporary politicians, party programs, and governmental measures as "radical," "liberal," "conservative," "Socialist," "Communist," "Fascist," or "extremist," or in
various other ways. We also use such terms as "right wing," "left-of-
center," or "extreme left"—designations which originated with the
seating order, as seen from the chair of the presiding officer, of the
French National Assembly after the French Revolution. Deputies who
wanted to preserve the old regime sat on the right, whereas those
with a desire to change it drastically sat on the left. Both methods for
identifying political viewpoints are often unsatisfactory, particularly
in the United States, where political labels that were invented in
Europe can easily be misapplied.

The problem of identification is further complicated by frequent
controversies about the true meaning of "liberal" and "conservative,"

and by the manipulation of these labels as political symbols. In this category falls the blatant theft of the label "Socialism" by the Communists and the label "Conservatism" by some contemporary Fascists. There is also the deliberate misuse of such political labels as Communist or Fascist as epithets for a political smear. A major cause of obfuscation is the changing times and the problems that change with them. What was considered an extreme left-wing position at the end of the eighteenth century may well be considered as mildly right-of-center today. What was considered the liberal avant garde in the nineteenth century, Americans may consider conservative today.

Yet when all the confusion is accounted for, there is still ample reason to be concerned with the "isms." Their importance may be on the decline, but they are still a major force in the world today and experience a resurgence every now and then. In fact, Western political civilization cannot be fully understood without a comprehension of the recent ideological forces which gave it shape and affected its values. It may be impossible to determine precisely what a liberal or a conservative is, but we can determine what the meaning of these terms was in a particular country and during the heyday of the movements that bear these names. The controversies about the terms under the changing conditions of today will become more meaningful in historical perspective.

In this presentation the moderate ideologies—Liberalism, Conservatism, and Democratic Socialism—have been separated from the ideological extremes—Communism and Fascism—for several reasons. Discussing ideologies side by side suggests equivalence, analogy, or even choice among them. The extremist ideologies and movements, however, are generally different from their moderate cousins. Inherent in the former is a peculiar dynamism that feeds on individual anguish and social malaise, and a dialectic between the demagogues and the seduced masses which rather defies the rational criteria used in evaluating programs and measures. The dynamics of Fascist or Communist ideology have psychological aspects in the minds of leaders and followers. They also relate to such mechanisms of social pressure as class distinctions or ethnic discrimination. And they owe much of their dynamism to the nature of their advocacy as a highly organized, revolutionary movement. An active member of such an extremist movement, in other words, is not just an advocate of certain philosophical principles but a man or woman deeply committed to the organized effort to keep the movement going and to help it to seize power. Thus, the principles advocated become suffused with an ulterior motive and there is likely to be an ever-widening gap between what the advocate proclaims and what he really intends to do.

Hence it would be very unfair to compare a moderate ism tenet by tenet with its extremist counterpart. Moderate attitudes and philosophies in politics distinguish themselves from their extremist cousins most of all by their insistence on a proper proportion between means and ends. Liberals, conservatives, Democratic Socialists, and other moderates know that using the wrong means can vitiate even the best political ends. Communists, Fascists, and other extremists, by contrast, believe that the end justifies the means and often employ revolting and barbarian methods in pursuit of their goals. The choice may be a choice between democracy and dictatorship, constitutionalism and totalitarianism, humanism and nihilism or the barbarism of quasi-religious persecution and concentration camps. The proper place for the discussion of Communism and Fascism is in the context of revolutionary processes and social disorganization.

There are, of course, many other isms which this book cannot discuss in detail. Almost any noun can be turned into an ism, as in adventurism or interventionism. Some current isms are variations on established themes, as contemporary Trotskyism, for example, is simply a type of revolutionary Socialism or Communism which stresses its independence from the established Communist parties. Sometimes also a well-known ideological label is modified with the addition of the word "radical," as in Radical Liberalism or, in current usage, simply Radicalism. As the origin of the word "radical" indicates, radicals would like to attack the problems of their concern at the root (the Latin word for root is *radix*). Implicit in such Radicalism is often a principled rebellion against Liberalism, or whatever philosophy is being radicalized, on the grounds that liberals have failed to live up to what they have advocated. Frequently, radicals will also undertake a more rigorous reformulation of the original doctrine and they may, in the process, shift the emphasis accordingly. However, Radicalism in actual practice tends to be short-lived, because radicals in the long run either tend to relent in their rebellion or to abandon the original ism for a more extreme political faith. Often it is really the times that change and the rise of a new set of radical rebels that make the old radicals appear to have relented.

Our choice of the five isms discussed in this book was based primarily on their long-range significance in shaping contemporary politics. Once the mainstreams of political doctrine are recognized, the tributaries and offshoots are easily placed in perspective. But there is also another angle which relates Liberalism, Conservatism,

Socialism, and Communism specifically to the evolution of Western societies. These ideologies were originally the ideologies of the major social classes evolving in modern Europe and, more remotely, North America. Liberalism was the outlook of the rising bourgeoisie or middle classes and it became the ruling orthodoxy of America. Conservatism was the ideological reaction to Liberalism of the more traditional parts of European society, the nobility, the churches, and the landowners. The absence of these elements in the United States accounts for the absence of orthodox Conservatism here. Socialism, both democratic and revolutionary (Communism), was the political faith of the working-class movements of Europe which emerged from the industrialization of the major part of the continent. The conditions in the New World relegated Socialism to a minor role here, but it has become eminently successful as a political doctrine, with some modifications, in many new nations of Asia and Africa. Its Communist variant, furthermore, has been given a monopoly position among over a billion people on this planet. However, Liberalism in the form of the principles and institutions of liberal democracy and Conservatism as the natural reaction of traditional elements in societies in rapid transition also are enjoying considerable popularity in the Third World of developing nations.

CLASSICAL LIBERALISM

Liberalism rose in response to an age characterized by the absolutist state, established religion, and a society encrusted with restrictive customs and authoritarian ways. The name "Liberalism," derived from liberty and liberality, is no older than one hundred fifty years. But its antecedents go farther back—to the great intellectual revolution that ushered in the modern age—the age of the Reformation, of science, and of individualism in the broadest sense of the word. The quest for the autonomy of the individual and the appeal to reason that the reformers employed brought the liberal movement from the very first into conflict with the powers that be.

Thus for centuries the contribution of Liberalism was mainly negative, even destructive, in character. Liberalism tended to be preoccupied with the need to remove obstacles in the path of human progress, to break up the bondage of man that society and government had imposed, and to free the enormous potential that was believed to be present in man from the last fetters weighing down his spirit. The attack of Liberalism on established authorities took place over several centuries and in many different fields of human activity.

Liberalism and religion

In religion Liberalism was first directed against the power of Roman Catholicism, when it gave political color to the cry for religious freedom of Calvinists, French Huguenots, and other Protestant groups. It continued to spearhead the struggle as the champion of British nonconformist sects against the established church and its privileges during and after the British civil wars of the seventeenth century. Since that time, Liberalism in religion has fought both for keeping religious worship free of state intervention and for keeping public institutions and government itself free from church influence.

Liberalism and economics

In economics, a field in which Liberalism is associated with such names as Adam Smith (1723–1790) and Richard Cobden (1804–1865), Liberals first attacked mercantilism and other interventionist policies of the absolutist state. Later the rising class of businessmen and industrialists, which headed the attack of the liberal movement upon the old economic order, turned against the remnants of merchant and craft guilds and feudal rights which prevented many potential workers from flocking to the new jobs in early industrial enterprise. Toward the middle of the nineteenth century, British liberals also had to overcome the agricultural protectionism of the old ruling classes in a protracted struggle, which they won with the repeal of the Corn Laws (protective tariff on imports of grain) in 1846.

With the rise of industrial empires and monopolies in the late nineteenth century, the classical liberal movement in Great Britain and elsewhere came to a decisive crossroads in its history. A part of the British movement, for example, left the Liberal party and joined the Conservatives at this point. Others, likewise identifying themselves with the new big business interests, followed the doctrines of "rugged individualism" as they were developed by Herbert Spencer (1820–1903) and the American sociologist William Graham Sumner (1840–1910). A substantial part of the original Liberal movement, however, saw in the rise of monopolies a great danger to free competition. These left-wing Liberals saw little merit in permitting the great "robber barons of industry" to use laissez faire to wipe out their smaller competitors. They also feared the domination of big business over the government and disapproved of the protectionism and tariff and currency policies of big business. During the twentieth century, this part of the Liberal movement also sympathized with

the efforts of labor to organize and, by strikes and collective bargaining, to win security of employment and a higher standard of living in the industrial world. Finally, they took the first decisive steps in the direction of the modern welfare state as early as the beginning of the nineteenth century and again under a Liberal Cabinet before World War I. Prominent Liberals included John Maynard Keynes (1883–1946), who is famous for his theories of "full employment" and "deficit spending," and Sir William Beveridge, whose 1942 report on the "five giants"—"want, ignorance, idleness, squalor, and disease"—presaged many of the measures of the Labour government of 1945–1951.

The two wings of the old Liberal movement are still very much in evidence in the contemporary politics of Western countries. In many European countries, there are Liberal or Radical parties, generally representing the right wing of the original liberal economic ideology. Sometimes there are strong admixtures of left wing, or "Social Liberalism" as in West Germany and England, or whole parties, such as the Italian Republicans (PRI). In the United States, right-wing Liberalism, after the fashion of Senator Barry Goldwater, is an important element in the Republican party, while the left-wing Liberalism of the New Deal and the civil rights legislation of the 1960s is more at home in the Democratic party, even though partisan alignments sometimes refuse to conform to this distinction.

Liberalism and politics

In the field of politics, the drive of Liberalism was at first directed at imposing constitutional restraints, representative government, and individual rights upon the absolutist regimes. In seventeenth-century England, where Parliament had never been completely suppressed by royal attempts at absolutism, the outcome of the struggle was clear parliamentary supremacy over the Crown and, by implication, the rise of popular over royal sovereignty. By contrast, in central Europe in the early nineteenth century, liberals could not hope for more than the imposition of a written constitution and a representative assembly to limit their absolute rulers. Later the issue became the ultimate responsibility of the government toward the people. As this responsibility is primarily enforced through elections, a large part of liberal history in the nineteenth century is the struggle for the broadening of the suffrage. In England, the great suffrage reforms began in 1832 and did not come to their logical completion until the elimination of plural voting in 1947. In the United States, a start was made much earlier, but racial restrictions in the South have not as yet been entirely removed. The struggle for woman suffrage was also an important phase of the liberal effort to make adult suffrage universal.

Liberalism in the social sphere

In the social sphere, finally, Liberalism concerned itself mainly with freeing the individual from restraints imposed upon him by entrenched class distinctions or discrimination on the basis of race, ethnic origin, or sex. There have also been efforts to protect children against excesses of parental authority, and wives against abusive husbands. While the liberal movement did not come around to concerns of the social sphere until a rather late date in its historical development, these matters show, perhaps, the ethical core of Liberalism more clearly than do all the other lines of attack upon the old society. At heart, there is a commitment to the good life of the individual, which can be realized only when all accidental fetters upon his full growth to the measure of his potentialities, his individuality, and his spontaneity have been removed. As the British philosopher Leonard T. Hobhouse put it in his brilliant summary of Liberalism:

> The heart of Liberalism is the understanding that progress is not a matter of mechanical contrivance, but of the liberation of living spiritual energy. Good mechanism is that which provides the channels wherein such energy can flow unimpeded, unobstructed by its own exuberance of output, vivifying the social structure, expanding and ennobling the life of mind.[1]

Attitudes underlying Liberalism

Underlying Liberalism, as in the case of most clearly defined isms, there is a psychological attitude, which we shall attempt to sketch.

Liberalism—A middle-class philosophy To begin with, it must be remembered that Liberalism is a middle-class philosophy. This middle class of business and professional people tends to possess specific character traits, which, in the rigid class structure of Europe, distinguished it notably from the attitudes of the lower classes as well as from the old ruling classes. Members of this middle class were quite individualistic and conscious of their own potential for socially creative activities in business, management, or the professions. The training they received from their families and their own life experience taught them that they had to excel as individuals by using

[1] *Liberalism* (New York: Oxford University Press, 1911), p. 137.

whatever native talents they possessed. They could not, like the old aristocracy, hide behind hereditary rank and distinctions, which tend to discourage initiative and effort. Nor could they disappear into the collective life of the crowd, as did the lower classes. Hence individualism and self-reliance are basic to Liberalism's underlying attitude. It could even be suggested that liberals tend to assume that these traits are universal among human beings.

Belief in the universal man   Liberals generally conceive of man as basically good, though often held back by unfavorable circumstances and restrictive traditions. They believe that there is hidden below the accidental attributes of nationality, social position, or race an essential humanity which makes men everywhere basically alike. Humanism also recognizes essential humanity as the essence of man as a creator able to shape his own fate. This fundamental likeness of men everywhere and under all circumstances implies a fundamental equality among men and logically demands that everyone be tolerant toward people of other religions, races, and nationalities. Humanism encourages understanding even for the criminal, for he is regarded as the product of unfavorable circumstances beyond his control, such as a broken home, a slum neighborhood, bad company, or other forms of neglect or rejection by society in general. It also suggests that the needs of universal man are everywhere alike and, hence, that it is possible to devise a form of government that is most likely to satisfy these universal needs in all countries and among all peoples of the world. By common consensus among Western liberals, this form of government is liberal democracy as we have defined it above (see Chapter 4). And although liberals will not deny that some nations at the present time may not be ready for democracy, they believe it is only a matter of time until all nations are ready; further growth and all-round development will bring every nation of the world to an appreciation of democracy.

The image of progress   Intimately related to the liberal image of human nature is the vision of *Progress*. Liberalism has always viewed the history of particular nations and of the human race in general as an upward movement toward greater perfection. Hence, liberals often take a rather unkind view of the past and what it can teach us. At its worst, some liberal thinkers have contended, the history of the past is a record of crime and folly, at its best a story of errors or of how not to conduct and arrange the relations of society. The liberal attitude is rather contemptuous of the past. "The trouble with history," as Robert M. Hutchins puts it jokingly, "is that it is out of date." Even the present is unsatisfactory. The great hope of liberals lies with the future and they often take it for granted that most important changes in society and government are changes for the better.

Man's faculty of reason   It is inherent in the liberal view of progress that some aspects of typical human behavior seem more desirable to liberals than do others. The most valuable and important faculty of man is his *reason*—his ability to understand and analyze his own situation as well as his physical and social environment. This rational faculty of man is the key to progress and to a better future. If man can understand the conditions under which he lives, he can detach himself from them, and, in the end, subject them to his control. The scientific exploration of the laws of the physical world enabled man to invent machines that make use of this knowledge and make him the master of the universe. The understanding of the world of biology has already doubled the human life-span and promises to solve the problem of food shortage in a perennially undernourished world. The discovery and analysis of the forces which move society, finally, may someday help man to overcome the appalling waste of human and social resources that results from war and social disorganization.

Yet the scientific exercise of individual reason is not the only form of rationality that liberals treasure. Equally important for human dignity is the use of rational choices for purposes of self-government. Man is a free moral agent whose dignity and morality depend on the free exercise of his reason. In fact, the development of individuals, which is inherent in the notion of social progress, consists largely in the growth of their understanding of themselves and of the world around them and, thereby, in their increasing mastery of their own fates. Because undeveloped man is a being enslaved by accidental circumstances of birth and environment, his individual progress can be measured by the emancipation of his rational faculties from the bonds to which the nonrational aspects of his nature have made him heir. Only when he is no longer restrained by hunger, poverty, ignorance, superstition, or disease can he make the free choices of a true moral agent.

By implication, the high regard that liberals have for individual reason is also reflected in their attitude toward irrationality and unguided emotions. Liberals often find it difficult to understand irrational behavior of the sort that manifests itself in pointless belligerence, self-destructive drives, a lust for violence or war, or senseless cruelty. Human emotions going on a rampage when crisis strikes, pulling down what took centuries of effort to erect; entire social classes panicking under the impact of a severe depression and allowing themselves to be driven into the hands of demagogues; primitive superstition, blind faith, or blind personal loyalty; habitual obedience to traditions that have long lost their original function; unquestioning acceptance of traditional inequality or injustice; and, most of all, the morbid infatuation of some nations with a tragic fate, with death, or with a heroic life—all of these belie the most cherished belief of liberals in the rational nature of man. Here, as in many of the points we have already mentioned, we shall find fundamental disagreement between classical Liberalism and Conservatism.

Liberalism, then, is far more than a specific political program designed for a particular situation in a particular country. It is rather like a secular religion that embraces the entire life of the individual, the family, and the state and touches upon law, government, religion, ethics, art, and science. Liberalism is, in a word, the belief in man as a creator and as the master of his own fate.

Hobhouse's principles of Liberalism

At the beginning of this century, the British philosopher of progress, Leonard T. Hobhouse, set forth a classical statement of the principles of Liberalism as understood in its heyday.[2]

1. Civil Liberty. *Both logically and historically the first point of attack is arbitrary government, and the first liberty to be secured is the right to be dealt with in accordance with law. . . .*

2. Fiscal Liberty. *The Stuarts brought things to a head in this country by arbitrary taxation. George III brought things to a head in America by the same infallible method. . . . It means, in a word, responsible government. . . . "No taxation without representation."*

3. Personal Liberty. *At the basis lies liberty of thought—freedom from inquisition into opinions that a man forms in his own mind— the inner citadel where, if anywhere, the individual must rule. But liberty of thought is of very little avail without liberty to exchange thoughts—since thought is mainly a social product; and so with liberty of thought goes liberty of speech and liberty of writing, printing, and peaceable discussion . . . add to these the right of worship in any form which does not inflict injury on others or involve a breach of public order. . . .*

4. Social Liberty. *Liberalism has had to deal with those restraints on the individual which flow from the hierarchic organization of society, and reserve certain offices, certain forms of occupa-*

[2] *Liberalism* (New York: Oxford University Press, 1911).

*tion, and perhaps the right or at least the opportunity of education
generally, to people of a certain rank or class. . . . Once more the
struggle for liberty is also, when pushed through, a struggle for
equality. The "open road for women" is one application, and a very
big one, of the "open road for talent," and to secure them both is of
the essence of Liberalism.*

    *5. Economic Liberty. As time has gone on, men of the keenest
Liberal sympathies have come not merely to accept but eagerly to
advance the extension of public control into the industrial sphere,
and of collective responsibility in the matter of the education and
even the feeding of children, the housing of the industrial population,
the care of the sick and aged, the provision of the means of regular
employment.*

    *If men may make an agreement with one another in their mutual
interest as long as they do not injure a third party (freedom of contract), they may apparently agree to act together for any purpose of
common interest on the same conditions (freedom of association). . . .
The emancipation of trade unions . . . was in the main a liberating
movement, because combination was necessary to place the workman
on something approaching terms of equality with the employer. . . .
On the other hand, the oppressive capacities of a trade union could
never be left out of account, while combinations of capital . . . have
justly been regarded with distrust. . . .*

    *6. Domestic Liberty. The authoritarian state was reflected in the
authoritarian family, in which the husband was within wide limits
absolute lord of the person and property of wife and children. The
movement of liberation consists (1) in rendering the wife a fully
responsible individual, capable of holding property, suing and being
sued; . . . (2) in establishing marriage as far as the law is concerned
on a purely contractual basis, and leaving the sacramental aspect of
marriage to the ordinances of the religion professed by the parties;
(3) in securing the physical, mental, and moral care of the children,
partly by imposing definite responsibilities on the parents and pun-
ishing them for neglect, partly by elaborating a public system of
education and of hygiene. . . .*

    *7. Local, Racial, and National Liberty. A great part of the liber-
ating movement is occupied with the struggle of entire nations
against alien rule. . . . The general tendency of Liberalism is to favor
autonomy, but, faced as it is with problems of subdivision and the
complexity of group within group, it has to rely on the concrete teaching of history and the practical insight of statesmanship to determine
how the lines of autonomy are to be drawn.*

    Somewhat similar questions arise about race . . . [but] . . . until the

*white man has fully learned to rule his own life, the best of all things
that he can do with the dark man is to do nothing with him.*

8. International Liberty. *(1) It is of the essence of Liberalism to
oppose the use of force, the basis of all tyranny. (2) It is one of its
practical necessities to withstand the tyranny of armaments. . . . (3) In
proportion as the world becomes free, the use of force becomes
meaningless.*

9. Political Liberty and Popular Sovereignty. *Underlying all these
questions of right is the question how they are to be secured and
maintained. By enforcing the responsibility of the executive and legislature to the community as a whole . . . is the general answer and it
indicates one of the lines of connection between the general theory
of liberty and the doctrine of universal suffrage and the sovereignty
of the people.*

Needless to say, contemporary liberals may wish to add to this statement of principles, and each of these points leaves much room for
discussion. This is particularly true of what Hobhouse calls "economic liberty," because economic issues always depend vitally on the
circumstances. Liberalism, however, is not so much interested in
maintaining a particular economic system as it is in defending individual liberty and equality against any dangers that may arise from
changing circumstances. This particular observation is very important
also to an understanding of the relation between Liberalism and
Democratic Socialism, and we shall come back to it later, when we
discuss Socialism.

Liberalism on the wane

Any great ideological movement has its weak moments and its crises.
Liberalism in England and in the United States was said to have
reached an impasse in the late nineteenth century, when the rise of
trusts and monopolies called into question its unconditional support
of free enterprise. At that time, as was pointed out earlier, the liberal
movement split into two wings: on the one hand, the tough-minded
Liberalism of Herbert Spencer and William Graham Sumner, who
likened the economic struggle for survival to Darwin's "survival of
the fittest" in the realm of nature; on the other, John Stuart Mill and
the American Progressives, who contended that the true task of
Liberalism was the emancipation of every man from the shackles of
oppression, economic and otherwise. The dispute between these two
schools is still going on today. In the United States adherents of
the Spencer school, such as Barry Goldwater, call themselves
"conservatives."

On the European continent, where Liberalism has always been weaker than in the Anglo-American world, it was challenged, with considerable success, as early as the beginning of the twentieth century by other ideologies, such as Socialism, Fascism, and Communism. A standard argument of its detractors used to be that Liberalism had done its job of bringing about capitalism, national unity or independence, and universal suffrage and was of no further use. Since Liberalism derives much of its political momentum from being a fighting creed, it could, having reached its goals successfully, be given a death sentence, while rival isms are able to dangle further enticing goals before the eyes of the voters. In England, the Liberal party was eclipsed in the 1920s by the Labour party. In the United States, the country which from its very beginning to this day has been the classical country of Liberalism to the almost complete exclusion of any other political philosophy, the 1930s saw such a waning of confidence in the precepts of democracy and Liberalism that John Dewey wrote in 1935:

Democracy has been a fighting faith. When its ideals are reinforced by those of scientific method and experimental intelligence, it cannot be that it is incapable of evoking discipline, ardor and organization. To narrow the issue for the future to a struggle between Fascism and Communism is to invite a catastrophe that may carry civilization down in the struggle. Vital and courageous democratic liberalism is the one force that can surely avoid such a disastrous narrowing of the issue. I for one do not believe that Americans living in the tradition of Jefferson and Lincoln will weaken and give up without a whole-hearted effort to make democracy a living reality.[3]

Resurgence of Liberalism
World War II against Fascism and the Cold War against Communism once more invigorated Liberalism and liberal democracy in Western countries. Within American society, as well as elsewhere in Western countries, numerous problems of oppression, discrimination, and inequality were found to exist, which are likely to keep liberals fighting for their goals for a long time to come. Yet there has also been a renewal of open and covert attacks upon the liberal heritage, partly by Communists and other extremists, partly under the guise of an insincere anti-Communism, and partly under the label of Radical Liberalism, or Radicalism, which has once more proclaimed the "end" or decline of Liberalism.

---

[3] *Liberalism and Social Action* (New York: Putnam, 1935), p. 92.

ORTHODOX CONSERVATISM

If Liberalism rose in reaction to the authoritarian state and society, political Conservatism rose in response to what its proponents considered the excesses of Liberalism and unrestrained individualism. The word "conservatism" was coined from the French *conservateur*, the name given to the French writers and statesmen who advocated a return to prerevolutionary conditions after the fall of Napoleon I. The idea behind the name is apparently the conservation of the *status quo* or of the heritage of the past. The birth of Conservatism is usually dated by Edmund Burke's *Reflections on the Revolution in France* (1790), which excoriated the French revolutionaries for the boundless human arrogance with which they believed they could step out of the stream of historical continuity, and out of their place in society and in God's universe, in order to determine their own fate. Some conservative writers, however, have attempted to trace British Conservatism back to several centuries before Burke[4] and to establish it as a rather timeless attitude toward social and political change that is apt to find proponents whenever great and prolonged changes occur.

However, this should not lead us to confuse Conservatism with a blind reactionary attitude that obstructs social change at any cost rather than accepts or offers constructive ideas as to how society and government ought to be run. To be sure, the conservative ranks have included men like the Frenchman Joseph de Maistre (1753–1821) and his followers, who rejected all compromises short of a complete return to the authoritarian society of old. But generally, Conservatism as a political philosophy is an intelligent and evolutionary approach to social change that is not impervious to the argument for progress; it prefers, however, gradual change to abrupt change, with preservation of the hierarchy of social values which often suffers in the headlong rush into the future. Conservatism also frequently has overtones of romantic nostalgia, a yearning for the "good old times" in which the past is usually seen in a romanticized light.

It should also be noted that in contrast to Liberalism, conservative writings are few and far between. As many a conservative has pointed out, the writing of philosophical speculations about politics is rather at odds with the conservative temperament. Hence a meaningful description of political Conservatism must attempt to place

---

[4] F. J. C. Hearnshaw, for example, has made a reasonable case for carrying it back as far as Henry VIII, or at least to the Cavaliers of the British civil wars of 1641–1660. *Conservatism in England* (London: Macmillan, 1933), chaps. III–X.

more emphasis on the temperamental aspects than on a list of principles or goals. Conservatism, it would appear, not only disagrees with liberal precepts, but questions even the appropriateness of any rational precepts to a subject as infinitely complex as society and government.

The conservative defense of the values of the old society against the liberal onslaught moved along many different lines. Almost every phase of the social and political status quo that was subject to the impact of the changes of the new age found conservative defenders.

Conservatism and religion

In the field of religion, conservatives generally defended orthodoxy, whether or not that meant supporting Catholicism or Protestant fundamentalism against reform, or the established church in England or elsewhere against the proponents of a separation of church and state. Conservatives discovered, in fact, that religious orthodoxy in itself was a value quite apart from questions of faith and truth and hence came to reject religious dissent, sectarianism, and free-thinking out of hand.

Conservatism and economics

In economic concerns, their stand shifted with the changing times, if possible, even more than that of Liberalism. Early in the nineteenth century, their chief concern was with the defense of aristocratic and landed interests, also agriculture, against the onslaught of the industrial revolution, which tended to revolutionize society and devalue most of what was important to the old society. Conservatives were deeply committed to the concept of private property, which to them, and not only for selfish reasons, was the bulwark of stability against rapid change and, not infrequently, also the most durable buttress of the liberty of individuals, families, and entire social classes.

Yet at the same time they felt deeply sympathetic to the new working classes, who were suffering from the abuses of the early industrial revolution. This flirtation of conservatives with the working population was warmly rewarded in 1867 in England, when the Conservative Prime Minister Disraeli embarked on a deliberate policy to woo and enfranchise the lower classes. Subsequently, vast numbers of the new voters voted Conservative and discovered their sentiments for the glories of monarchy and empire. Despite the rise of the Labour party, British Conservatives have retained their appeal to a substantial portion of the workers by their paternalistic attitude toward the lower classes. This attitude, however, in no way prevented Conservatives from active opposition to the power of organized labor in trade unions or Socialist parties.

With the rise of big business and banking empires, an increasing number of representatives of this new big business class parted ways with the Liberal party and joined the Conservatives. The logic of big business and monopoly positions no longer made free competition attractive to them, and their protectionist inclinations found a common ground with those of the old landed gentry and, at times, also those of the working class.

Conservatism and politics

Politically, Conservatism was at first almost exclusively preoccupied with the defense of monarchic and aristocratic privileges against the demands of Parliament and, in particular, the House of Commons. One tends to forget that before the days of Queen Victoria and the enfranchisement of the working classes, the British monarchy in the nineteenth century stood several times on the verge of being abolished and that, before the parliamentary reform of 1911, the House of Lords was a very powerful body. Even today, British conservatives wish to preserve the mystery of God-given authority which underlies institutions such as monarchy and a hereditary ruling class or upper class. They have grave doubts about the underlying assumptions of democracy and prefer responsible leadership by an enlightened ruling stratum of high moral purpose that will rule in the best interest of the country.

The social order

With respect to the general organization of society, Conservatism emphasizes the existence of "natural distinctions," such as differences in intelligence, ability, and character among individuals, social groups, nations, and races. The traditional social classes of a given society, or existing differences in rank, status, and wealth, are often explained by conservatives as being the products of such "natural distinctions." Conservatives also place much emphasis upon the spontaneous groupings of society, such as families, local communities, occupational groupings, and so forth. Because they take a dim view of the pronounced individualism of the liberal tradition, they believe more strongly in the virtues of group life and its inherent rights than do liberals. This strong identification of individuals with the group they belong to has two important implications in the conservative attitude toward politics and society. On the one hand it amounts to a stress on individual loyalty toward the group, the community, or the nation, which may at times lead to a denial of individual rights if they should clash with the interests of the more inclusive group. On the other hand, it has led conservatives to feel protective toward the family and local groups that have felt the disruptive impact of the industrial society most. Conservatives have decried both the uprooting of individuals and the rootlessness of modern society which, in their opinion, tend to lead from the quest for liberty to utter chaos. Once rootless, an individual is subject to more pressures and temptations than his inner restraints can cope with, and his liberty may well become license. Conservatives fear, in particular, the aggregation of rootless individuals into mobs and masses, in which the evil instincts of each individual can win the upper hand in the safe anonymity of the mass and hence lead to violent and destructive mob action. Such rootless individuals fall easy prey to rabble-rousing demagogues.

In summary, Conservatism has been a defensive movement not so much against liberty itself, as against excesses of liberty. As Peter Viereck so admirably expressed it, conservatives feel that

men are not born naturally free or good . . . but naturally prone to anarchy, evil, mutual destruction. What Rousseau calls the chains that hinder man's goodness—society's traditional restrictions on the ego— are in reality the props that make man good. They fit man into a stable, durable framework, without which ethical behavior and responsible use of liberty are impossible.[5]

This framework for the responsible use of liberty is supplied by the collectivity—the nation or the country—over a long period of time, in the form of a constitution, law, custom, and the mores of the community. The "foolish individual," according to Burke, should go along with the "wisdom of the species" by fitting himself into this framework of traditional restraints (see p. 50). Thus conservative philosophy possesses both a psychological and a historical depth that Liberalism cannot match.

Conservatism is also an ethical philosophy, which is often overlooked because of the "pocketbook Conservatism" of some self-styled conservatives and the individual anarchism and social egotism of others who hardly deserve the name conservatives. The conservative tradition has always denounced materialism, or the preoccupation with profit and material gains, as unworthy of the higher values and spiritual goals of life of which human civilization is capable. Instead of the pursuit of happiness, it has championed the traditional

[5] *Conservatism* (Princeton, N.J.: Van Nostrand, 1956), p. 14.

virtues. And in place of mere utility, or of Jeremy Bentham's principle of "the greatest happiness of the greatest number," it has treasured symbolic values such as those of patriotism, glory, beauty, and greatness.

Attitudes underlying Conservatism

Conservative segments of society   As is true of the liberals, a fundamental psychological attitude underlies the conservative temperament. A great variety of people and points of view tend to gather in the conservative camp. To be sure, the conservative attitude may have had its origin among aristocrats, but it also became accepted by other segments of society that suffered as a result of the industrial revolution and the social changes connected with it, such as farmers, handicraft, and small business. With the arrival of universal suffrage, moreover, vast segments of the working classes adopted the conservative point of view, possibly because they had no quarrel with the claims to leadership of the old ruling class or because the symbolism and emotional values of the conservatives appealed to them far more than did the abstract doctrines and complex procedures of the liberals.

The conservative view of man   The images and unspoken assumptions of the conservative temper are diametrically opposed to those of Liberalism. Conservatives think of human beings as basically weak, possessed by evil instincts and desires, perhaps even depraved. In this view there is a grain of religious fundamentalism of several varieties, all of which see man as sinful, or burdened with original sin, and which may tend toward a politically conservative view. It is precisely because of the evil tendencies in man that there is a great need for authoritarian restraints in the form of law, parental or state authority, or other social checks on individual behavior.

Conservatives consider as quite unrealistic the rosy image of human nature that Liberalism draws. They also frown upon the liberal's idea of a universal man, of an essential humanity underlying the accidental attributes of race, of nationality, and of social class that makes man everywhere basically alike. To conservatives, national character, or the character of a race, or the features of a particular class are inherent attributes and hence cannot be shed or exchanged at will. A person's fate depends on these "accidents" of character and no change or improvement is possible. In fact, the only way to improve a person is to improve him morally, or to reinforce his conscience. Here again, conservatives see little point in the liberal panacea of perfecting man by reforming his environment and the institutions of society. These institutions, after all, are a vital part of the traditional framework for the responsible use of liberty. They have grown and developed organically over many generations, embodying the wisdom and experience of the ages. They form a vast and infinitely complex system of delicate social relationships and adjustments. They are so complex, in fact, that it is presumptuous of any individual to believe he understands what makes society and government tick and even more presumptuous of him to expect to be able to reconstruct society according to a speculative ideological blueprint. Hence the shock of Edmund Burke about the French revolutionary leaders, who, after the violent overthrow of monarchy, aristocracy, and organized religion, ventured to recreate society "synthetically," with the help of abstract a priori speculations about the "rights of man." It should be mentioned here that Burke would not have been so shocked had the French acted rather to secure the "historic rights of Frenchmen." Only a decade earlier, in fact, he had sympathized with the American Revolution, caused by such historic rights of Englishmen as "no taxation without representation." But how can anyone claim the rights of that dubious "universal man" without at least being tempted to the most arbitrary choice of particulars?

The rejection of speculative reason   Conservatives are not necessarily anti-intellectual or antirational when they view with distrust the abstract, a priori, or speculative reason, which is Liberalism's key to the future. They think highly of common sense or practical reason. The difference between common sense and speculative reason is apparently that the former merely serves people to adapt themselves to a given setting or, at the most, to adapt the setting in a small way to their purposes, whereas the latter is used for grand schemes of social reconstruction. At the same time that conservatives debunk this sweeping form of a priori reason, they take a kinder view of the emotional life than does Liberalism. There is a wisdom in emotional loyalties, inhibitions, and instincts that often serves a person better than his conscious reasoning would. Furthermore, the impact upon people and politics of such factors as history, national and individual character, and leadership—which to conservatives are the decisive elements of human affairs—is largely nonrational or even irrational.

Hearnshaw's principles of Conservatism

Like Liberalism, Conservatism is far more than a specific political program designed to deal with a particular situation. It is a personal attitude deeply rooted in the subconscious of an individual and of significance not only to his politics but to almost everything he does and thinks. It is a state of mind rather than an ideology. In fact, the spirit of Conservatism is incompatible with the exercise of abstract reason, which a logically complete ideology demands. But this does not imply that it is impossible to discuss Conservatism or to lay down its discernible principles and aspects. The British political writer F. J. C. Hearnshaw has supplied such a list of conservative principles drawn from a penetrating analysis of British Conservatism in the twentieth century as well as in the past.

1. Reverence for the Past. *The conservative . . . feels instinctively that the accumulated wisdom and experience of the countless generations gone is more likely to be right than the passing fashion of the moment. . . . He stands for the universal and permanent things of life; for the ancient traditions of the race; for the fundamental laws of his people; for established customs; for the family; for property; for the church; for the constitution; for the great heritage of Christian civilization in general.*

2. The Organic Conception of Society. *. . . . He has an organic or biological conception of society, as opposed to the inorganic or legal conception prevalent among the philosophical radicals. . . . Hence he is impressed by the need to preserve the integrity of his communal life, which is larger and more enduring than his own brief individual existence; . . . he struggles to maintain the communal identity amid all the changes that time inevitably brings.*

3. Communal Unity. *. . . . Conservatism is utterly opposed to the horrible dogma of the class-war which is one of the most damnable features of Marxism socialism or bolshevism. It denies the existence of any irreconcilable antagonisms in a healthy body politic.*

4. Constitutional Continuity. *. . . . Such a breach in the natural and orderly development of the constitution as occurred in seventeenth century England or eighteenth century France fills the conservative with repulsion and alarm. . . .*

5. Opposition to Revolution. *. . . . The revolutionary, as distinct from the reformer, seeks to destroy existing institutions, not to amend them; to slay and not to cure.*

6. Cautious or Evolutionary Reform. *. . . . Reform is of its very essence. . . . and Burke himself remarked with his usual profound wisdom: "A state without the means of some change is without the means of its conservation. . . ." Conservatism accepts and applies the doctrine of organic evolution.*

7. The Religious Basis of the State. *The conservative . . . recognizes society as existing by the will of God; he regards it as directed and guided by a divine Providence; he considers its end to be akin to*

that of the church itself—namely, righteousness and peace. Hence, as a rule, he holds it to be right and proper that the state should formally and publicly recognize its sacred character by the legal establishment of religion, and by the association of all the most solemn and important acts of government with the august ceremonial of the service of God. "In a Christian commonwealth," said Burke, "the church and the state are one and the same thing, being different parts of the same whole."

8. The Divine Source of Legitimate Authority. *The conservative . . . naturally tends to accept the Ancient Christian view that all legitimate authority is, whether directly or indirectly, divine in its origin. He remembers the cardinal pronouncement of St. Paul: "The powers that be are ordained of God. Whosoever therefore resisteth the power, resisteth the ordinance of God. . . ."*

9. The Priority of Duties to Rights. *. . . The radical concentrates his attention almost wholly on the rights of the individual. . . . As against this one-sided and self-centered assertion of personal rights, the conservative stresses the principle of civic duties. His ideal is public service rather than private gain. He regards the franchise not as a possession which he can claim as his own, but as an obligation which he must exercise in the interests of the body politic. . . .*

10. The Prime Importance of Character. *. . . The conservative . . . is concerned neither for power nor for self, but for character— character both individual and national. He repudiates, in particular, the socialist's gross overemphasis on the influence of environment as a determinant of a man's condition, and stresses that his condition depends very largely upon what he is himself. . . .*

11. Loyalty. *Of all the elements of character which the conservative values and cherishes, loyalty stands pre-eminent. He tends to support men rather than measures; he is devoted to institutions rather than to ideas . . . he is loyal to his family, to his school, to his university, to his party, and to whatever professional group he may be attached. But his larger and supreme loyalties he reserves for his church, his king, and his country, and his empire. . . .*

12. Common Sense, Realism, Practicality. *. . . Conservatism . . . by its balancing common sense, by its instinct for the practical and possible . . . is the party of affairs rather than theories; the party of strong and efficient administration rather than of incessant and ill-digested legislation; the party which adapts policy to circumstances instead of attempting (like the bolsheviks) to fit circumstances into the Procrustean bed of fixed obsessions.*[6]

[6] Excerpted from F. J. C. Hearnshaw, *Conservatism in England* (London, Macmillan, 1933), pp. 22–23. Reprinted by permission of Macmillan & Co. Ltd.

As in the case of Hobhouse's elements of Liberalism, many contemporary conservatives may wish to add to this enumeration or to change the formulation here and there. For Americans, this may apply in particular to the point about the establishment of religion, although popular controversy over such issues as federal aid to parochial schools or prescribed prayers in the public schools demonstrates that the practices of an established church, if not the idea, seem attractive to some Americans.

Another point of considerable interest to Americans in this statement of British Conservatism is the support for a strong and unified state and the anti-individualism of British Conservatism. Here, it should perhaps be called to mind again, that for two reasons there has been little more than a bare trace of orthodox conservative sentiment throughout American history: (1) because of the absence of an aristocracy and (2) because of the strength of the liberal tradition that founded and shaped the American Republic. What American politicians insist on calling "conservative," as we mentioned earlier, is usually the tough-minded Liberalism of Herbert Spencer and of the Social Darwinists.

On the European continent, many conservative parties changed their names in response to the wave of democratization occurring in European politics at the end of World War I. Today, parties such as the French Independents and the dominant part of the German and Italian Christian Democratic parties (called Christian Social or Catholic Conservative in some smaller European countries) and, in their own way, the Italian Monarchists pay homage to orthodox Conservatism. In the Third World, conservative elements are less well organized but almost everywhere strongly represented, especially with movements defending traditional religious practices.

Conflicting views of Liberalism and Conservatism

To contrast once more the clash of principles between Liberalism and Conservatism, one might juxtapose the liberal worship of progress and the conservative preoccupation with order. Order to a conservative means a proper proportion among the different elements of life, or a due respect for the hierarchy of values in the world. Order also implies reverence for historical traditions and customs and an appreciation for the mysteries of leadership and character. Finally, order means also that the life of the individual is fitted into a well-defined framework of restraints in the form of law, customs, and authority.

Whereas liberals are eager for experiment, conservatives are fearful of the unknown and unfamiliar, and suspicious of adventure and unverified theory. Whereas liberals delight in shocking convention and defying custom, conservatives are enamored with the dignity of social rank and authority and with pomp and pageantry. Whereas liberals want to throw open the floodgates to reform and change because they are dissatisfied with the past and even the present, conservatives are largely content with the world as it is and skeptical about change. Their horror of revolutions stems from their belief in continuity, both historical and constitutional, and from their wariness of rash and ill-considered change. The fear of revolution is rooted in their image of the nature of man and society, which Hearnshaw has expressed in inimitable language:

Civilization is a frail flower doubtfully struggling for existence amid a jungle of old luxuriant barbarism; . . . a thin and fragile crust, barely supporting humanity, over molten oceans of volcanic savagery. . . . Man . . . is uneliminated ape as well as undeveloped angel . . . if the development of the angelic element in him demands freedom and opportunity, . . . the eradication of the bestial element calls for the exercise of authority and for the stern enforcement of law.[7]

Anyone who has observed the gruesome spectacles of man's inhumanity to man in the twentieth century would be hard put to scoff at these words as mere rhetoric. Whether the "exercise of authority and the stern enforcement of law" by themselves would be able to eradicate the "bestial element" in man, however, is another question. The theories discussed in our next section have made an attempt to offer a solution to this problem.

DEMOCRATIC SOCIALISM

Whereas Liberalism and Conservatism appear to be fairly precise in definition and, in fact, so complementary as to facilitate comparison, defining Democratic Socialism presents a more difficult task. Far from being a well-defined body of thought, it resembles more a bundle of contributions from many different thinkers and political forces. No Socialist, perhaps, ever held or could logically hold all of these views and conceptions at the same time.

As to a comparison of Socialism with Liberalism and Conservatism, there are a few ideas which Socialism has in common with

---

[7] F. J. C. Hearnshaw, *op. cit.*, pp. 18–19.

both of them. With Conservatism, for example, Socialism shares the collectivist approach, the aversion to individual self-interest, the emphasis on the community as a whole, and in some instances even the preference for a strong state and a closed national economy—all points of common interest that have often made for sympathy and cooperation between conservatives and Socialist causes. With Liberalism, Socialism shares the optimistic view of human nature and the predilection for democracy and equality. Yet it is quite difficult to compare Democratic Socialism as a political philosophy with the other two. Whereas Liberalism and Conservatism are concerned with the whole man and his life in society, Socialists are rather preoccupied with but one issue: how environmental conditions, notably economic conditions, affect the life of man.

Because American popular opinion holds a number of rather misleading notions about Democratic Socialism, we shall start with a statement of what it is not. Although Socialism stresses communal unity, as Conservatism does, it should not be confused with monism, which we discussed in Chapter 3. Similarly, although increased activity by the state and interference in private lives may have resulted from some of the more recent turns of Socialist thought, it is not, as such, an integral part of Socialist philosophy. In fact, most nineteenth-century Socialists distrusted the state, and some wished to abolish it. Governmental centralization similarly is not in itself a Socialist dogma, although the idea of economic planning tends to lead to centralization. Social welfare, too, although it seems implicit in the name Socialism (from the Latin *socius*, "friend" or "companion"), plays a surprisingly small role in Socialist thought. Not only is social welfare much older and more general than the Socialist tradition proper, but it is diametrically opposed to the main goal of Socialism: to create a social and economic order in which "welfare cases" will not occur.

The bulk of Socialist ideas is today quite outdated, having been in part rather fantastic to begin with. The ideas that have survived to this day have shown strength mainly in Western countries other than the United States, where they have had little appeal. Hence, if Socialism is popularly blamed in the United States for every grievance, from high taxes to judicial leniency, the cause of these misconceptions is not owing to Socialism or the Socialists *per se* but rather to the deliberate obscurantism of many a politician (or a special interest group) who prefers to divert public attention from his own activity to that of imaginary entities. In many developing countries, a modified version of Socialist doctrines is very popular.

Democratic Socialism and Communism

A few words are necessary to explain the distinction between Democratic Socialism and Communism, also often glossed over popularly in the United States for lack of concrete experience with movements of both kinds. To begin with, there is an older usage of the word "communism" which antedates the usurpation of the name by the worldwide revolutionary movement started by Lenin and his Bolsheviks. The old communism was generally considered a version of Socialism in which all property is held in common, as was the custom among the early Christians and certain agrarian communes in various countries. The new Communism is an offshoot of Socialism, but vitiated by totalitarian developments, in short, a rather different phenomenon. Furthermore, as we have explained at the outset of this chapter, one of the most important differences in practical politics hinges upon the relationship betwen ends and means. Extreme means such as violence and conspiracy instead of open and rational persuasion automatically vitiate even the most sublimely ethical goals and can change what purported to be a "heaven on earth" into a "hell on earth." The totalitarian nature of a movement like Communism changes the normal criteria of a political philosophy from "Will it work here?" or "Does it make sense?" to whatever the glorious leader decides or what is good for the party, for the Soviet Union, or for Peking.

Furthermore, we have to distinguish not only between Socialist and Communist practices, but also between their theories. This is not an easy distinction to draw, since sometimes both types of theories were advanced by the same thinker, as in the case of Karl Marx (see Chapter 14, pp. 390–392, in which most of his thought is discussed) or were accepted by members of the same organization, as in the case of many of the Socialist movements of the late nineteenth century. The difference between Democratic Socialism and Communism was not settled until the 1920s. It hinges upon several clear criteria. One is the acceptance of liberal democracy as it was defined in Chapter 4—as government by discussion, majority rule, protection of minority rights, and constitutional government. The second is the explicit rejection of the extremist doctrine that the end, in this case the victory of the movement or the utopian society pictured by both philosophies, justifies the employment of any means designed to bring about. Democracy specifically rejects violence and subversion for the attainment of political goals. Finally, there is the positive side of this injunction against extreme means. Democratic Socialism employs gradualistic means for reaching its professed goals. In the practice of twentieth-century politics, two forms of gradualism have been preeminent among the Socialist movements of Western societies. One is the formation of trade unions which better the life of their members by collective bargaining for higher wages, shorter hours, and better working conditions. The other is the ballot box, through which Socialist majorities can elect Socialist governments or get Socialist measures passed. This latter means, of course, is subject to the usual limitations of liberal democracy, such as the consideration of minority rights and of constitutional safeguards, and is dependent upon the winning of majority support.

Evolution of Socialist thought

Now let us trace the Socialist tradition with a historical discussion of its seminal concepts. Socialist thinking and even some practices such as community ownership of certain kinds of property or co-operativism can be found very early in history, in prehistoric times, among the ancients, in the Middle Ages, and with the Diggers of seventeenth-century England, who in protest against economic deprivation started to cultivate some of the common lands in England. But we are mainly interested in the evolution of Socialist thought since the beginning of the industrial revolution. Let us consider, first of all, the vital core of Socialistic thinking, most of which was born in the first half of the nineteenth century.

Demand for social and economic equality If any motive can be looked upon as fundamental to Socialist thought, it would seem to be a veritable passion for equality. Unlike the ambiguous concern of liberals with equality, however, the Socialists were not content with political or even with equal opportunity for every person. They demanded complete social and economic equality on the theory that mere political freedom and equal rights meant very little in a society such as that of the early nineteenth century, in which existing class barriers and differences in wealth and in education drastically reduced the capacity of members of the lower classes to avail themselves of the existing opportunities. One could restate this passion for "real" equality also as a passionate hatred for inequality in any form. To the Socialists, with rare exceptions, inequality was "unnatural" and unjust, and the entire society was in need of complete reconstitution in order to give each person his "natural" due.

Concerns for the social environment Related to this passion for equality was an extreme environmentalism, which went far beyond the mild concern of liberals with reforming the environment in order to emancipate the individual. The influential British social philosopher William Godwin (1756–1836), whose individual anarchism places him rather at the periphery of the Socialist tradition, saw in each individual the inescapable product of his intellectual and moral environment, incapable of sin or crime by himself. Robert Owen (1771–1858), the successful businessman and founder of Socialist colonies, similarly believed that education and the creation of the proper physical and moral environment could produce responsible and enlightened citizens in place of the degenerate wretches among the working classes of the early industrial revolution. He proved his point by transforming the workers' settlement of his own industrial enterprise in New Lanark into a model community much admired in his day. But when he attempted to duplicate his success with self-governing Socialist colonies in various places, including New Harmony in Indiana, his theories met with failure. The idea that people are largely creatures of their environment and that only a total transformation of the social environment would create conditions that are just to every individual, at any rate, remained a part of the Socialist tradition.

Reactions to the industrial revolution   A third, rather general, motive of Socialism was the humanitarian reaction to the economic and social consequences of Liberalism at the time of the early industrial revolution. Socialists took offense at the same abuses as did the conservatives of that period: long hours of work at a mere subsistence wage, unsafe working conditions, industrial diseases, excesses of child and woman labor that were largely caused by low wages, lack of hygiene, of education, and of decent housing for the workers, and also the cutthroat competition among entrepreneurs. However, where the conservatives would have liked to turn back from the industrial age to a more idyllic past, the Socialists clearly recognized in the new technology of factories and machines a means for the future creation of such abundance that there might be more than enough for all. Hence, their humanitarianism did not stop with the desire to put down the glaring abuses of the society of their time, but looked ahead to an age when every member of the lower classes might be enabled to spend his life in dignity and free from the slavery of physical want. They also regarded the previous life of the lower classes under feudalism as not much better than life under the industrial system, with its attendant abuses.

The wastefulness of capitalism   One important aspect of the Socialist reaction to the industrial revolution was its great concern about the enormous waste and inefficiency of the new industrial society, and for that matter also the old semifeudal society. To the French Socialist writer, Count Saint-Simon (1760–1825), inefficiency and waste were for more important than a concern for equality. He was vastly impressed with the possibilities of organization and planning in the new society and proposed to turn over the reins of government to a new elite of bankers, industrialists, engineers, and scientists. Another famous French Socialist writer, Charles Fourier (1772–1837), was troubled by the vision of 300 women, in 300 little houses, cooking 300 dinners in 300 pots on 300 fires for 300 men coming home from work, when three or four women, with one large pot and one large fire, might produce better results.

These criticisms boil down to a general critique of individual and private enterprise, spurred on by the enlightened self-interest of each person as the liberals had envisioned it. In the form voiced by Saint-Simon and most other Socialists, this critique was likely to lead in the end to vast economic regulation and planning of the sort we have encountered in the war economics and in government measures during the great depressions of the twentieth century. Charles Fourier's vision of domestic duplication of effort was an even more basic critique of individualism in living. The pertinence of his critique may not have been new, but in its applications it went far beyond cooperative living and the Socialistic colonies proposed by Fourier. We can find it today in the awesome spectacle of the communes of Communist China in 1958, where dormitories, community kitchens, and community nurseries were designed to free married women for employment in the enormous effort at economic development. We can also find it in the day nurseries and plant cafeterias of Western countries.

Utopian colonies Another aspect of the Socialist reaction to the condition of society was a general predilection for drawing up blueprints of a better society, or even better, for founding colonies upon such blueprints. Every Socialist thinker of that era had a fairly distinct picture of the future form of society, which he either strove to bring about or expected to come about by itself. These visions of the future were determined by the particular complaints of each Socialist school about contemporary society. The future world was envisioned as one of complete social equality, economic efficiency and abundance, altruism instead of egotism, peaceful cooperation instead of all-out competition, and usually the total absence of government.

Often, the future was seen as the establishment of a "natural order" perfectly attuned to human wants and needs. Fourier, for example, drew up an ambitious chart of twelve basic human passions, the "natural laws" of human motivation, and constructed on this basis a world of complete harmony that took into account and utilized every one of these passions as a machine makes use of the physical laws of nature. He contended that the perversion and waste of the society of his day lay in the ignoring of these "natural" passions, which were consequently twisted into selfishness, sin, and crime. Work, too, he thought, could be a most enjoyable activity, if organized to allow for frequent change of occupation so that boredom and drudgery might be banished. At the root of this approach we find the notion that human "nature" and all its "natural" urges are really good rather than sinful, or that a benevolent God meant them to be socially useful. In this fashion, "nature" and "natural laws" are once more set up as superior to the stupidity and injustice of social conventions.

Fourier found many disciples, as did Owen and other Socialist writers, and a number of Socialist colonies were founded and maintained after the principles of Fourierism, Owenism, and also some religious creeds. Founding colonies had a dual advantage. It enabled the like-minded to live in the future utopia they had envisioned. It also served as a tool of gentle persuasion to convince the rest of the public that the Socialists' scheme of thought was workable. Unfortunately, most of the utopian colonies, except for some religious ones, were short-lived. As in today's commune movement in America, the colonists found it difficult to carry on together beyond their initial enthusiasm when they encountered economic difficulties, factionalism, and the disillusionment of aging and generational change.

The Socialist view ·of human nature Another concept central to most Socialist thought is the motion that human nature is cooperative rather than competitive, peaceful rather than aggressive. This "natural" cooperativeness and peacefulness, they argued, made superfluous the political restraints and the incentive of economic necessity that some liberals considered necessary to make people work. The contrast between this image of man and that of conservatives places most Socialist theories in the camp of anarchism. The contrast between the cooperative image of the Socialists and the selfish, competitive one of Herbert Spencer and the Social Darwinists also led to an extensive debate toward the end of the nineteenth century about whether the fundamental law in the realm of plants, animals, and of primitive societies was the "survival of the fittest" or, as the anarchist writer Prince Peter Kropotkin (1842–1921) put it, "mutual aid." To this day, members of Socialist movements often view representatives of the "rugged individualism" of Spencer as psychologically abnormal —aggressive bullies who take pleasure in ruining competitors and suppressing the human dignity of their employees.

Abolition or modification of private property   Another typical element of Socialist thinking during this early period concentrated on the abolition or modification of private property. The distinguishing characteristic of the entire Socialist tradition from its earliest beginnings had been the modification of private property rights in many forms, ranging from cooperativism or common grazing grounds to communal living and ownership of almost everything there is to own. Some of the sentiment about property of nineteenth-century Socialism stemmed from the conviction that land and the goods of the earth are God's or nature's gift to all the people and should be available for everyone's use, without being appropriated by anyone. "Property is theft" was one of the famous paradoxes attributed to Pierre-Joseph Proudhon (1809–1865).

Another important aspect of private property in the Socialist view was that it is one of the mainstays of established society with all its inequalities and therefore a major obstacle to total social reform. Socialists often insist that all substantial wealth is accumulated dishonestly, either by graft and fraud, or by the exploitation of one man by another, or by the "conspiracy of a few greedy individuals against the toiling masses." A third aspect of property that was obnoxious to the Socialists was the idea that property is a boon to individual self-interest. Plato prescribed a community of property, wives, and children for his guardian class precisely to induce the guardians to less selfishness and materialism and more willingness to make sacrifices for the sake of the community. Some Socialists, like Fourier, also extended their aversion to the implements of individual self-interest from private property to the family and to marriage, in the assumption that the abolition of marriage might help to emancipate women. Proudhon on the other hand, despite his slogan, wanted to retain private property and marriage for his small rural communities.

The anarchist strain   As a final point in this summary of the core of the modern Socialist tradition, let us consider the anarchistic strain that runs through most of the Socialist thought of the nineteenth century. The image of cooperative man, as we pointed out above, suggested that governmental restraint was really superfluous. But there was also the conviction that the existing authorities of state and church, and even the legal guarantees of liberty and the representative process, were a part of the conspiracy of the *haves* against the *have nots*. As Karl Marx and Friedrich Engels put it later on, the state was purely an instrument of the rule of the exploiting class over the masses. With the advent of a classless society, there would no longer be a need for the state. It would "wither away" and be replaced by "the administration of things." The anarchistic bias against the state runs like a red thread through most Socialist writings of that period. With some writers, such as Godwin and Proudhon, it became the expression of an underlying individualism. With the Russian revolutionary, Michael Bakunin (1814–1876), it became the destructive raging of a suppressed people against oppression in any form—by social classes, the state, or the church.

This feature also appears in an inchoate form in certain aspects of today's youth culture, the deep suspicion of police and other authorities and the obsession with oppressive "establishments" in school, in adult society, and in the government. This contemporary anarchism complements the other quasi-socialistic features of the counterculture, the stress on good fellowship and communal living, and the aversion to competitive or exploitive drives and the pursuit of material gain.

Later Socialist theories

Against this summary of the core of the nineteenth-century tradition of Socialism, we shall consider the thought and writings of later schools of Socialist thought. Among these are, in particular, the self-styled "scientific Socialism" of Marx and Engels and the stirrings of the awakening working classes.

Marx and Engels Karl Marx (1818–1883) and Friedrich Engels (1820–1895) accepted or took for granted a great many of the precepts of their Socialist predecessors and contemporaries, whom they arrogantly preferred to call the "utopian Socialists." Their own approach, by contrast, they considered to be "scientific Socialism." The implication was that other Socialist thought was of a visionary character addressing itself to the improvement of the whole world, whereas they used the methods of "scientific" analysis to understand the new industrial society, with its rising proletariat, and to project its likely future development. For this purpose they engaged methods of analysis taken from economics, sociology, and history. In economics, Marx is often regarded as the last of the great classical economists. His most distinctive contribution here, for example, was developing further the theory of *labor value* and acquisition as it had passed down from John Locke to David Ricardo, to a point where, in conjunction with Marx's other theories about *economic concentration* and the *impoverishment of the proletariat*, it presaged the *final collapse of capitalism*. Marx and Engels supported this economic argument with an elaborate analysis of the relationship between technology and the ownership of the means of production, and the relations between social classes. All of past history, they concluded from scanty evidence, was the history of *class struggle* between an exploiting and an exploited class. This was the *dialectical* interpretation of history. As far as its scientific hypotheses went, Marxism suffered the fate of most scientific theories. It won little notoriety during most of Marx's lifetime and was soon most successfully challenged and superseded by more sophisticated economic, sociological, and historical theories. Yet, as it turned out, the life span of Marxism was prolonged far beyond its scientific merits by a sheer coincidence of politics. In the 1870s and after, many of the awakening labor movements, most notably in central Europe, made Marxism their fighting creed. During the period between World Wars I and II, its suitability as a fighting creed—rather than its "scientific character"—drew rapt audiences around the entire globe. (See Chapter 14 for a detailed discusion of the nonscientific elements of Marxism.)

Rival schools of Socialism   During the earliest heyday of Marxism in the nineteenth century, many a rival school of Socialism set out to capture or win away from Marxism the newly organized labor movements in Western countries. Marx and Engels had hardly written their *Communist Manifesto* (1847) when Louis Blanc (1811–1882), a French Socialist politician at the time of the 1848 revolution, proceeded on an entirely different course. He saw the salvation of the working class in a strong state that would protect the weaker members of the community against the strong, guarantee jobs, and initiate worker-controlled economic enterprises that would eventually win out over private enterprise. Later, when Marx tried to build up his First Socialist International under his personal control, Bakunin and his followers fought him every step of the way, because they considered him authoritarian and intolerably dogmatic. When the first General German Workers Association was founded in the 1860s, moreover, its leader was not Marx, but a German nobleman, Ferdinand Lassalle (1825–1864), whose views on Socialism resemble those of Louis Blanc in their emphasis on the state and its role in establishing worker-owned enterprises. Lassalle saw the best weapons of the working class in political organization and the ballot box, especially once universal suffrage was achieved. One school of early Socialists in the United States were Lassalleans.

When Marxism had become well established in continental European labor movements, it received a telling blow at the hands of Eduard Bernstein (1850–1932) and his school of "revisionism." Bernstein undertook in the 1890s to revise the Marxist doctrines in the light of the experiences of the labor movement with capitalism. But before we examine this revision more closely and proceed to a discussion of where Socialism as a movement and a philosophy stands today, it may be advisable to discuss briefly the theory and realities of capitalism.

The changing nature of capitalism

In theory, capitalism is the outgrowth of the individualism and rationalism of the modern age. Private entrepreneurs own the means of production and strive—by careful calculation of cost, price, and market for their product—to accumulate further wealth. Since public ownership is limited to a few public services such as roads, sewers, and the mails, economic power is dispersed among many different people rather than concentrated in the hands of the state. The profit motive and competition among capitalists give the incentive for each capitalist to be creative and to engage in socially useful activities to the greater benefit and progress of the whole society. In theory, every citizen of the capitalist society, even the worker, participates in the mutual give-and-take of this system, although he may not be able to contribute anything beyond the work of his body, for which he receives wages. Thus there are many different contributors and many different kinds of contributions in the capitalist system, each of them motivated by individual self-interest.

To assure overall harmony and coordination among the individual participants of the system, the free-market economy provides an automatic regulatory mechanism in the form of the law of supply and demand, which in a thousand ways adjusts the proportion of the supply of services and goods to the demand, and vice versa. By fluctuations in prices and wages, the individual participants in the free market are constantly discouraged from engaging in unwanted activities and encouraged to fill needs of high demand. In a sense, the entire system rests "democratically," so to speak, on the free choice of the sovereign consumer, who is the prime mover of demand. The impersonal mechanism of the marketplace is a powerful authority, nevertheless, which can punish harshly and reward handsomely, according to classic capitalistic theory, as long as the constituent parts of the mechanism function without any restraint whatever. The society of the seventeenth and eighteenth centuries was full of restrictions, which Liberalism sought to remove by its struggle for the different aspects of economic freedom: the freedom of choosing one's job, trade, or occupation; the freedom of entering contracts; and the freedom of property, starting with property in one's person and work.

Capitalism as a system was never attained in pure form even in the nineteenth century, although most of the Socialist thinkers we have mentioned had talked about it as if it had been realized. Political and economic matters are rarely so well ordered that one can summarize them with a simple and logically consistent theory. Neither is it very enlightening, as the Socialists were wont to do, to fight a not yet established system by opposing to its presumed theory a rival theory. Capitalism had not yet penetrated the old precapitalistic society very far, when it was already changing in such a basic fashion as to raise doubts about the analysis by Karl Marx, who was still writing his *Capital*.

Among these fundamental changes in capitalism were the following:

1. The increasing replacement of individual ownership by corporate ownership dispersed over thousands of stockholders.

2. The rising importance of the managers who ran these corporate enterprises with very little restraint by the owner-stockholders.

3. The rise of big businesses whose relative size brought a host of new tendencies that were quite alien to traditional capitalistic enterprise. Bigness proved fatal to smaller competitors and held out temptations of massive economic power unknown to the original small entrepreneur. If one was big, one could try to corner the market, establish a monopoly, fix prices, or bribe politicians.

4. Bigness also implied that each corporation became a tightly organized collective entity with the collectivistic attitude of the "organization man" or the "company family" to match. Instead of being competitive, men in big businesses strove for security and togetherness. This was a far cry from the individualism and self-reliance of traditional capitalism.

5. Bigness meant bureaucratization in business and also in labor, because the vast numbers of workers brought together by large-scale enterprise promptly organized in trade unions. Together with the increasing bureaucracy of government, the upshot of this whole development was a highly organized and bureaucratized society unlike anything the world had ever seen. Such a state of affairs is an inhospitable environment for practical individualism of any kind.

6. The industrial revolution also produced other conditions that tended to reinforce this trend toward collectivism. The allure of jobs in the new industries touched off vast migrations from area to area and, in particular, from the country to the mushrooming big cities. The new metropolises soon experienced a tremendous growth in governmental functions and, as early as the 1860s and 1870s, developed into the small-scale predecessor of today's welfare state. City bosses and reform administrations alike outdid each other in making the big city into a well-functioning collective entity in which government undertook a vast array of services and intervened in the economy whenever it saw fit to do so. Urbanization was further enhanced by the enormous population growth made possible by the consequences of industrialization.

7. Another important result of continued industrial development was the infinite proliferation of the division of labor. Competition encouraged research and inventions and the resulting technology led to ever greater diversity, complexity, and interdependence. Today, for example, a typical consumers' item, such as an automobile, is composed of thousands of parts manufactured by hundreds of different companies. By the same token, each branch of the economy has become so dependent upon the proper functioning of every other branch that, for instance, a strike or a price increase in the steel industry affects practically every person and every business in the United States. This fact of economic interdependence has made economic depressions far more menacing than ever before. It has also been a major cause for governmental intervention and guidance in the economy. And last but not least, interdependence has transformed the national economy into a collective entity upon whose well-being that of every participant depends. The earning power and income of an individual in the American economy today is in most cases strictly dependent upon his role in this collective body.

8. We have saved the rise of economic interventionism and the welfare state until now in order to show the many other developments that tended to converge in this direction. The rise of economic intervention and the welfare state was only in small part caused by Socialist theory and the efforts of Socialist parties or trade unions. It was largely due to such factors as increasing economic complexity and interdependence, urbanization, and the rise of politically powerful industrial empires, which had to be checked, as well as to the impact of great depressions and the war economy of both World Wars. In fact, both the well-administered big city with its public works, services, and planning and the well-organized big corporation with its long-range planning and research and the job security it offered clearly served as the models for the development of national economic planning, public works, and welfare services.

9. Finally, international power politics in the twentieth century has

been aggravated by, and in turn, has accelerated the collectivistic tendencies of mature capitalism. Never before have wars been fought as such all-out contests between national economies, testing their relative resources, productive and inventive capacities, and endurance to the breaking point. The war economies of the nations participating in the two World Wars came the closest that any Western nation has ever come to a completely regimented economy.

These changes in traditional capitalism have affected the character and direction of the Socialist criticisms of the system. In some aspects, they have reduced the Socialist arguments to absurdity. The old cry for a violent revolution, for example, has lost its appeal to rational minds. The workers of today have too much to lose and too little to gain from such an upheaval. Other aspects of the old Socialist critique have been overtaken by the actual developments. The American worker of today has prospered beyond the most fanciful Socialist dreams of the nineteenth century. Some problems of mature capitalism are quite new and baffling to orthodox Socialists. From the point of view of the worker, for example, there is very little difference between working for a giant corporation and for the state in a nationalized enterprise. Both are stiflingly bureaucratic and conformist. Unlike early capitalism, both tend to discourage the worker from indulging in individualism, and both undertake to regulate his life from the cradle to the grave. Hence, contemporary Socialism is faced with a new challenge: How can the individual who is trapped in the bureaucratization and regulation of modern life be once more emancipated and given power and responsibility over his own life? This latter point, as we shall see, has had a profound liberalizing effect upon orthodox Socialism, generally leading modern Socialist theory back to Liberalism, more stress on democracy, and concern for individual freedom.

Bernstein's school of revisionism   Let us now return to where we left off—to the revision of Marxism and earlier Socialist theories by Bernstein (see pp. 141–142) and by other new Socialist schools. As was pointed out above, Marxism had already been well-established among continental Socialist and trade union movements when Bernstein and the adherents of his school of revisionism undertook to review and modify the Marxist doctrines in the light of their experiences with the changing character of capitalism. What seemed to be rank heresy in the 1890s quickly won acceptance among the continental Socialist movements and eventually became the dominant opinion among the democratic Socialists of the world. Only in backward countries with an authoritarian tradition, such as Russia, China, and similarly underdeveloped areas, did another revised version of Marxism, that of Lenin, possess greater appeal to the masses.

Bernstein's revisionism became known "as evolutionary Socialism" in contrast to the revolutionary character of orthodox Marxism. Bernstein dismissed the idea of an imminent proletarian revolution as folly and called the "dictatorship of the proletariat" a "political atavism." Plainly preferring steady improvement to a catastrophic collapse, he rejected one by one the economic theories of Marx as not borne out of the actual developments. It is unrealistic, in his opinion, to speak of only two battling, clearly defined classes, the proletariat and the bourgeoisie, in the face of the great variety of classes that exist. Nor did the concentration of the means of production in just a few hands take place as predicted. He also challenged Marx's theory of surplus value and his economic determinism. Instead of class struggle and class rule, Bernstein preferred democracy, a genuine partnership of all adult citizens in a limited government as their joint enterprise. Liberal democracy was, to his mind, the very substance of Socialism. Such a point of view, it appears, goes even beyond a revision of Marxism and rather leads from Socialism back to John Stuart Mill.

The Fabian Society In England, where Marxism did not arouse much interest until well into the twentieth century, contemporaries of Bernstein founded in 1884 the Fabian Society, which soon rose to prominence with such well-known members as George Bernard Shaw (1856–1950), Sidney Webb (1859–1947), Sydney Olivier (1859–1943), and Graham Wallas (1858–1932). They named themselves after the Roman general Fabius, surnamed Cunctator (the Delayer), who defeated Hannïbal's armies by a strategy of delays and waiting for the right moment, although the Fabians were not an action group but rather a group dedicated to interpretation and propagandizing by lectures and innumerable tracts on such pedestrian matters as "the tenant's sanitary catechism." Fabians were not committed to a very clearly defined course of argument. For a while, they were mainly interested in problems of land ownership such as were raised at about the same time by Henry George (1839–1897) in the United States. Then the Fabians turned more to municipal problems of creating model communities distinguished both by their welfare aspects and their well-organized public services. The Fabians were collectivists, who generally preferred to see individuals as parts of larger social entities. Within their own nation-state, Great Britain, the Fabians envisioned a gradual process of socialization, which would—and, indeed, did—reallocate more and more of the increments of the extraordinary wealth and talents of the few for the benefit of the whole community.

As they argued, neither the rich nor the very talented had a right to the return from their special endowments beyond their ordinary needs. Earlier Socialist theory had already defined the goal as "from each according to his ability, and to each according to his need." This process, however, was limited by a number of specific reservations to which Fabians were strongly committed. The process of "socialization" had to be in accordance with accepted constitutional formulas and democratic procedure. The process also had to be gradual, peaceful, and not immoral in the opinion of the mass of the people. The Fabians, in fact, viewed the process of socialization as rather imperceptible and automatic and would not hear of a definite goal for it as long as the direction was clear. They also favored extended activity by the state if the state was firmly under democratic control.

Guild Socialism   The emphasis on the state and the collectivism of the Fabian Society called forth Guild Socialism, a spirited reaction among spokesmen of the British trade union movement and kindred writers. Guild Socialists felt, as did Marx, that there was an unbridgeable antagonism between the capitalist employers and their workers. Hence they sought salvation in the transfer of whole industries to the control of the trade unions, in which they saw a revival of the medieval guilds. Such a transfer would, in their opinion, not only democratize industry but also offer a pluralistic alternative to the state capitalism of public enterprises. The workers in these industries would no longer be "wage slaves" whose labor was just another commodity to be bought and sold on the marketplace, but partners and shareholders. At the same time, economic enterprise could emphasize such commendable values as a tradition of service and "production for use" rather than "production for profit." To sum up the difference between Fabianism and Guild Socialism one could consider the former as Socialism organized from the point of view of the consumers and the latter as Socialism organized for the workers and producers of goods.

The views of organized labor

With Guild Socialism we have arrived at our first encounter with the proletariat itself, that class of people whose future course Marx and Engels purported to predict. Guild Socialists were not the only part of the organized labor movement that was hostile to the established authorities. One can find similar attitudes also among the Syndicalists of French and Italian trade unionism, who dreamed of the general strike and at time considered acts of labor violence as a purpose in itself. The hostility toward the established capitalist system was also typical of the predecessors of the American Federation of Labor and other trade union movements of that day, who were impeded by personal persecution, nonrecognition, and many a legal device. In the end there emerged "trade unionism pure and simple," interested chiefly in questions such as wages, hours, working conditions, and job security. This trade unionism at its bread-and-butter best was essentially a conservative movement that had no intention of engaging in Socialist flights of fancy, but was content to work out the well-being and general improvement of the working classes within the capitalistic system.

A different impression emerges if we follow the development of Socialist parties in the British Commonwealth and in most countries of Europe as well as in Japan and elsewhere. At the outset, most of these parties were revolutionary and hostile to the existing governments. As the parties grew in size and influence, however, they became more moderate and more willing to play by the existing rules of the game of politics. But they still performed the invaluable service of organizing millions of workers politically and thus forced society to meet many of their demands. By the time the Socialist parties of France, Germany, Great Britain, Italy, and the Scandinavian countries were large enough to be entrusted with governmental responsibility, they had long stopped breathing fire and clamoring for a complete transformation of society. Instead they generally contented themselves with such pragmatic measures as the political and economic situation appeared to require.

A typical case in point is the policy of the Labour government of Great Britain in the years 1945 to 1951. When the Labour party was elected to office, Britain was already a welfare state by the efforts of half a century of Liberal and Conservative administrations. There were also present, as in all Western countries, a number of nationalized enterprises and public services, ranging from the mails to the British Broadcasting Corporation (BBC) and the Central Electricity Board. Earlier in this century, the British Labourites had demanded the complete transformation of society and the total nationalization or socialization—the former meaning transfer to the state, the latter, transfer to municipal or other public corporate bodies, or to cooperatives, as in Scandinavia—of all industry and services. The electoral manifesto of the Labour party in 1945, however, named only a few industries and was content to promise completion of the welfare state in such aspects as taxation and health insurance. Among the sectors of the economy singled out for nationalization were the Bank of

England, civil aviation, telecommunications, the railways, road transport, and inland waterways. Gas and electricity, coal mining, and the iron and steel industry rounded out the list.

In every case, the Labour government gave specific reasons for taking over an industry. In some cases, such as electricity and the Bank of England, Labour was only completing a pattern of governmental involvement of long standing. In others, such as coal mining, the industry was generally acknowledged to be "sick," or in need of such extensive reconstruction and modernization that its owners were unable to raise the capital necessary to restore the industry to health. With regard to other industries, especially public utilities and services and the iron and steel industry, the Labour administration claimed they were bottlenecks. And because these industries were vital to the entire economy, they could not be left to the profit calculations of private enterprise. As it happened, the Conservative party agreed to all of these measures, some of which it had promised to carry out itself if elected, with one notable exception: the iron and steel industry which, unlike the other nationalized enterprises, was only a holding and financing corporation, not an operating one.[8] In a similarly cautious and pragmatic fashion, the Labour government also completed and streamlined the British social security system and transformed the various existing public health insurance measures into its comprehensixe National Health Service. As with the bulk of the nationalized enterprises, the Conservatives have fully accepted these further welfare state measures and have contented themselves with administering this bureaucratic empire while in power.

The same stress on pragmatism rather than on doctrine that we can gather from the actual policies of contemporary Socialist parties in the Western world is evident from their programs. There is a genuine insight to be found in most programmatic pronouncements of recent years that there is no longer any ready-made model of a "Socialist system" that Socialists could attach to their banner. With rare exceptions the programs of the larger Socialist parties no longer advocate further nationalization. The major exceptions are the new nations, in which Socialism is often viewed as useful for economic development. But in the West, there are only a few general ideals, such as the slogan of the French Revolution—"liberty, equality and fraternity"—which is essentially a slogan of liberal democracy, and a willingness to correct and remedy social injustices wherever they may appear. Even the old class system in Europe, which was an

---

[8] As soon as the Tories won power again, they denationalized iron and steel along with road transport, although not without establishing an Iron and Steel Board for the public supervision over this industry.

almost inexhaustible source of Socialist indignation, is conspicuously on the wane. Some observers have spoken of a crisis of Socialism for the last ten years, caused perhaps by the general disappearance of ideological cleavages in Western society or by the fulfillment of traditional Socialist programs and the absence of new ones or merely by the great increase in prosperity throughout the West, Socialism often being regarded as a "hard times philosophy."

No matter from which side one may view it, the reasons for this "crisis" would seem to be hardly alarming. If it is true that the underdog of the early Socialists—the proletariat class—is rapidly becoming an affluent part of the middle class; if it is true that many large Socialist parties and trade unions have made their peace with the rest of society and prefer a spirit of partnership to one of "class struggle"; and if it is true that Western societies are arriving at a new consensus on democracy—individual liberty and minimal standards of living for all—why should anyone mourn the decline of the Socialism of old? On the other hand, there are also new strains of Socialism at hand which are less related to economic needs and class barriers than to life styles and broader perspectives. European student rebels and young professionals are rediscovering a humanistic Socialism beyond the bread-and-butter concerns of the working class, a concern for human alienation and for the sufferings of the Third World.

CHAPTER **6** **THE FOUNDATIONS OF LIBERTY: CONSTITUTIONALISM AND REPRESENTATIVE GOVERNMENT**

As every educated man and woman knows, a constitution is a legal document, a blueprint for constitutional government laying down fundamental institutions, principles, powers, and limits on power for a particular body politic, such as, for example, the United States Constitution of 1787. However, the presence of a written constitution alone is no guarantee of constitutional government. There have been many governments in Western history that were generally acknowledged as examples of constitutional rule, although they possessed no such fundamental law. Great Britain, the fountainhead of much of the modern constitutional tradition, still prefers not to commit its governmental ground rules to a single constitutional document. On the other hand, there have been numerous instances, especially in the twentieth century, where rank tyranny was apparently not at all inconvenienced by the presence of a duly promulgated constitution. It follows, then, that a definition of constitutional government requires far more than a description or classification of the existing national constitutions of various countries. It demands an analysis of the human motivations that produce and sustain a constitutional government, an awareness of the typical devices by which it has been secured, and an understanding of the social conditions that facilitate or frustrate it, as the case may be.

The purposes of constitutional government

There are three great desires of Western political man that have set thinkers and practical statesmen to devising the instrumentalities of constitutional rule.

Desire for stability   First is the desire for constancy, stability, or the internal preservation of the political community—though not necessarily resistance to change or reform—which led men to look at the design of their political institutions as one might look at the construction of a house that is to endure and to serve its purpose well. From this vantage point, makers of a constitution try to build a strong and lasting foundation, perhaps with the aid of religious authority or at least of a quasi-religious regard for the mysteries of secular authority. Stable and yet flexible institutions upheld by carefully selected officers would be the pillars of the edifice. A reasonable regard for human nature and for the implicit consent of the people would determine the floor plan, so to speak, with which the different groups of society and coming generations could live.

Desire for liberty   Second is the desire for liberty, for a reasonable freedom from restraints imposed by the strong upon the weak, or by government upon groups and individuals. This desire gave birth to the idea of limited authority, which has played a seminal role from the beginning of the Western constitutional tradition. More recently, it led to the doctrines of limited government and of government as a necessary evil, spurred on by such concerns as the safeguarding of religious freedom or of individual property rights that were so dear to John Locke and his disciples. One of the politically most significant manifestations of the desire for liberty is its link to the rights of representation. If government is a necessary evil, the liberty of individuals and groups is served best if they play a significant role in the making of governmental policy. Such participation will at least enable them to avert injury to their interests from governmental action.

Desire for justice   Third is the desire for justice—at least in the procedural sense. This is a desire for fair procedures and generally accepted rules, for regularity and predictability in governmental actions, for the general and equal application of the laws to everybody, and for protection against such things as ex post facto laws, self-incrimination, and double jeopardy. It also includes the many other procedural safeguards—briefly named "due process of law"—by which the accused in a criminal trial is given every chance to clear himself until proven guilty before a jury of his peers. It is no accident that the protection afforded the accused in a criminal trial often forms the acid test of constitutional rule, considering that no other form of governmental action can so stringently interfere with the life and liberty of a person as can a criminal court.

It is easy to see why constitutionalism is considered to be such a priceless heritage, if it can satisfy the great human desires for stability, liberty, and justice, which are at the same time among the most basic and the most lofty expectations man has ever placed on government. Yet, constitutional government, as all human contrivances, is not perfect. It has, in particular, one vexatious shortcoming which many social philosophers and social reform movements from Plato to this day have criticized: it cannot offer to each individual or each problem an immediate, ingenious remedy tailor-made to fit the case. It may create a framework within which an individual or a group can work out their own solutions to their problems within certain limits. But it will not supply the solution itself, and its constraints and safeguards of the rights of other people may preclude the attainment of the most obvious solutions. Only Plato's philosopher-king, who is supposed to combine in his person both the ultimate in wisdom and the ultimate in virtue, could be expected to provide the right solutions for each individual and each problem. Despairing of ever finding such a true philosopher-king, generations of Western philosophers and statesmen have instead come up with what to Plato was the "second best form of government": constitutionalism, or the rule of law.

Devices of constitutionalizing government

What have been some of the typical devices by which Western political systems have sought to constitutionalize their governments over the centuries? The chief means were the development of law, the institutionalization of personal rule, procedural safeguards, written constitutions, a system of checks and balances, not necessarily in this order.

Law Law, whether in the form of customary law, judicial precedents, or legal enactments, has been the most important device for the establishment of constitutional government. In fact, the effectiveness of most of the other devices depends on their being embodied in the law and enforced by legal processes.

Institutionalization of personal rule　The institutionalization of personal rule has to do not only with the evolution of permanent governmental institutions from the happenstance of personal authority wielded by historic personages, but also with the limiting of governmental authority. As long as kingship was considered merely a hereditary privilege of the oldest male heir of the royal family or a personal attribute of a particular man on horseback, for instance, it was very difficult to impose any limitations upon the exercise of royal authority. Only when a kingship is regarded as a public office with specific rights and duties can incumbents be held responsible for overstepping their powers or not performing their duties.

Procedural safeguards　Various typical procedural safeguards of constitutional government were mentioned earlier. Fair and generally known procedures of law and government are the very essence of constitutional systems. "Liberty," according to Sir Henry Maine, "is secreted in the interstices of legal procedure." Just as fair procedures in a court trial are meant to give each of the parties in the case a reasonable opportunity to present his side of the case, the procedural emphasis of Western constitutional government affords the persons and parties affected by governmental action a chance to be heard, or equalizes the chances of rival contenders for high office.

Written constitutions　A written constitution is today the most popular, though occasionally abused, device of modern constitutionalism. After a successful revolution, many new nations or new governments have found it easier to adopt a written constitution than to undergo the slow and time-consuming formulation of a constitutional tradition. However, even the best constitutional document will not ensure constitutional government unless the circumstances of its adoption assure it of unconditional authority and adoption occurs in a setting in which a legal tradition and habits of constitutional thinking already prevail. Countries lacking the legalistic style of many Western countries, such as most new nations of Asia and Africa, face a basic dilemma when adopting a constitution. Not only is the new constitution likely to import many alien institutions and concepts without reference to native culture and traditions, but the habit of abiding by legalistic formulas is not so easy to acquire. These new nations might be better off adopting short, declaratory constitutions rather than Western models full of encrusted legalisms which most Asian or African politicians find hard to respect.

Checks and balances　A system of checks and balances, finally, is perhaps the most generally recognized, though by no means an indispensable, feature of constitutional government. The purpose of this system is to weaken power by dividing it among several distinct and autonomous agencies of government, such as the executive, the judicial, and the legislative branches, or the federal and the state governments, which are then expected to check and balance one another. Ancient Sparta featured a double kingship for this purpose. The Roman Republic at one time had popular tribunes who could intercede on behalf of plebeians against actions imposed by the Roman Senate. No constitutional scheme has ever surpassed that of the framers of the American Constitution in the number and kinds of checks and balances superimposed upon one another: federalism, the separation of powers, the different terms of office, the staggered terms of Senators, the manner of election of the President, the senatorial control over foreign relations and executive appointments, the congressional control over the jurisdiction of the United States Supreme Court, and so on. But there is also the government with the most highly developed constitutional tradition, Great Britain, which has practically no such checks and divisions of public authority.

The political constitution   One further word of caution is necessary before we turn to a historical review of constitutional theories and practices. When King John was cornered at Runnymede in 1215 and and forced at the point of a sword, as it were, to sign the Magna Charta, this drastic curtailment of royal power was not effected by means of a legal writ or by a fine turn of phrase in a written constitution. It was brought about by a social force of flesh and blood, the barons, who felt personally injured and threatened by John's usurpation of powers. The most powerful force of the modern constitutional tradition, the *common law*, also made its century-old contribution only because behind it was a group of men—generations upon generations of judges. In the same fashion a kind of political constitution of group forces of society has to be alive and active behind the cold paragraphs and institutional inventions of constitutional documents. Procedural safeguards, whether in court trials or in elections, are best guarded by those who stand to suffer damage from their infringement. Checks and balances come to life only when antagonistic groups and interests attempt to use them in order to check the policy-making authority, which may in turn represent a group or combination of groups. The best checks and balances of modern constitutional government, in fact, have never been written into a constitution and are, perhaps, incapable of legal prescription. They include such things as a well-organized system of political parties of which one (or a combination of parties) runs the government, while the other (or again a combination of parties) plays the role of the "loyal but critical opposition." An equally potent check can be a lively and responsible public opinion, especially as embodied in a free press and a large reading audience.

Because the ruling majority of a modern Western country is often identified with varying groups of economic interest, it has also been suggested that the pluralism of interests and interest groups of modern society is in itself a system of dispersed power and checks and balances: The "outs" can check the "ins" from case to case, or from policy to policy. In this fashion, a wide variety of groups and other social and economic forces supply the *political constitution*, which alone can make the legal contrivances of modern constitutionalism work at their best.

CONSTITUTIONALISM, ANCIENT AND MEDIEVAL

A brief survey of constitutional theories and practices of the Western tradition will demonstrate that not all of the many and and varied contributions to Western constitutionalism were immediately applicable; nor were they always applied to political organization.[1] A large part of the early theories were more in the nature of penetrating insights into the working of political institutions or of idealistic protests against the brutal realities of politics than they were blueprints for constitutional government. In the final analysis, it is the accumulation of theories and practices over some 2,500 years of Western political civilization that has produced the present flowering of constitutionalism at its best.

Constitutionalism in the ancient period

Contribution of the Greeks   Greek lawgivers, statesmen, and philosophers, as far as we know, were the first to experiment self-consciously with different forms of government and to reflect critically upon the ever-changing features of politics and government. Aristotle, who had a deep horror of violent revolution, was one of the first to offer a definition of the rule of law, or constitutional rule. First, it is rule in the interest of all the members of a body politic rather than in the sole interest of the ruler or ruling class. Second, it is rule by means of general laws and according to generally known customs and conventions. Third, the rule of law avoids collision with accepted customs and thus embodies an element of consent rather

---

[1] The role of law and of constitutional notions, of course, was not exclusively limited to the West. See, for example, p. 80, fn. 14.

than being based on force. This definition may be lacking in precision but contains important notions of constitutionalism such as the public interest, the nature of public office, and a constitutional order based on convention.

The mixed constitution   Another important strain of Greek constitutional thinking was admirably summed up by the Greek historian Polybius (204–122 B.C.), who undertook to find out "thanks to what sort of constitution, the Romans subdued the world in less than fifty-three years," namely between the Second Punic War (219 B.C.) and the conquest of Macedon (167 B.C.). Polybius attributed the astounding strength and stability of the Roman Republic to its *mixed constitution*, that is to a mixture of monarchic, aristocratic, and democratic institutions, which he professed to see in the sharing of power by the Roman consuls, the Senate, and the popular assemblies. The Greeks had always believed in a cycle of these three forms of government and their respective, deteriorated versions. According to a generally presumed law of gradual decay, monarchy was expected to turn into tyranny after a few generations; tyranny would be overthrown and replaced by aristocracy, or rule of the best; aristocracy would deteriorate into oligarchy, the rule of the wealthy few; oligarchy would in turn be overthrown and replaced by democratic government; democracy, finally, would turn into mob rule until the eventual emergence of a new king. Polybius apparently believed that the inherent propensity toward deterioration of pure monarchy, aristocracy, or democracy could be halted by mixing these elements. Aristotle's idea of combining oligarchy and democracy (see Chapter 2) for purposes of stability and good government was also an example of a *mixed constitution*, in this case reinforced by the attempt thereby also to balance the influence of the two main social classes in Greek city-states, the many poor and the few rich. Passed on by Polybius, Cicero, and Montesquieu, the theory of the *mixed constitution* came to exercise considerable influence on the Philadelphia Convention of 1787.

The Roman contribution   The contribution of ancient Rome to Western constitutionalism can hardly be exaggerated. To do it justice, however, it is advisable to consider the Roman customs of the republican era and of the principate, at any rate, no developments later than the second century A.D. After this period, the Roman tradition deteriorated and even Roman law fell under the sway of formalism and lifeless abstraction. The earlier Rome excelled, in particular, in its general attitude toward government, in its extraordinary clarity, and in its liberal temper.

The Roman attitude toward institutions and laws can be described as conservative. The Romans prized dignity of bearing (*gravitas*) and steadiness (*constantia*) not only in individuals but also in institutions, whose slow and deliberate growth they preferred to institutional experiments. Institutional change, it was believed, should grow out of the slowly changing consensus among many leading citizens rather than be based on the inventions or innovations of particular individuals. However, the Romans combined this conservative attitude toward law and government with an acute awareness of political realities and, in particular, an *instrumentalist approach* to governmental institutions. Rather than worshipping institutions as purposes in themselves, they judged them by practical standards and were quite prepared to change their design according to the effects desired.

Roman law   Similarly, the typical practitioners of the famous Roman law were wary of legal abstraction and codification. As did the judges of the English common law, they feared that excessive theorizing and defining of the terms of law distracted the attention from the nature of a case, or tended to obscure with empty formulas the living issues of the social relationships on trial before a court. This general self-restraint of Roman jurisprudence and government, however, was not meant to imply a denial or lack of legal or political principles. Rather, and again as in English common law, the unwritten principles of Roman law were much the stronger for not being spelled out in specific wording. And because Roman law during the earlier period was also primarily rooted in judicial decisions and firmly established legal customs, it thereby obtained a flexibility and practcial vitality, which made it the chief force of constitutional government in ancient Rome.

The Roman tradition also distinguished itself by its extraordinary clarity and simplicity. The Roman jurists sharply separated private relationships from public affairs and obligations, and secular law from religious rights and duties. The sphere of rights of the private individual enjoyed a primacy that lent the Roman spirit the appearance (for the times) of an unprecedented individualism. The Romans had not only a love of individual liberty but also a practical legal concept of it that had far-reaching political consequences in such matters as the rights of citizenship, of legal representation and local self-government in the provinces, and of holding and using private property.

Liberty and authority   To balance an excess of individualism, moreover, the Roman way of life featured a strong position for authority and deeply ingrained motives of civic and social cooperation. The place of authority was rooted in the sweeping powers of the *pater-familias* and of the magistrates and other governmental authorities over the individual, balancing thereby individual liberty (*libertas*) with authority (*auctoritas*). Authority in turn was an attribute springing from the deep-seated political consensus of a civic-minded people that affirmed the need for the leading roles of father, magistrate, and Senate and was ever willing to participate in the common tasks of the body politic. Thus a sense of civic duty and clear notions of the nature of authority roles combined to overcome the potential isolation of excessive individualism. The strength of other mores of social cooperation, such as bonds of friendships and kinship, good faith (*fides*), fairness and honesty—both public and private—further cemented together the free individuals of Roman society.

The simplicity of the entire system—its deliberate limitation to a few clearly recognizable themes and the economy of legal and political institutions and relationships—in itself constituted a major factor of stability and balance because it facilitated the task of understanding and safeguarding Roman liberties for the Romans themselves.

The liberal temper of the Roman tradition, finally, manifested itself, both internally and externally, in a manner inviting comparison with that of Rome's neighbors and even of some contemporary states. Toward its own citizens and also toward aliens, the Roman state exhibited from the beginning a humanitarian regard for their personal rights to life and liberty, the inviolability of their homes and property, and the freedom of opinion and of worship as long as these last two freedoms did not involve treasonable actions. Under the influence of Stoic philosophy and its idea of a universal and natural law applying to all men, this humane policy (*humanitas*) became quite similar to what the revolutionaries of the seventeenth and eighteenth centuries called the "universal rights of man." It was also reflected in the procedure at criminal trials about which Governor Festus in the proceedings against St. Paul is said to have stated:

> *It is not the Roman custom to condemn an accused person before he has been confronted with his accusers and afforded an opportunity of defending himself against the accusation.*[2]

Unlike some of Rome's neighbors, and even some states of the twentieth century, Rome refrained from torturing free men for the extortion of confessions and never resorted to the expropriation of private property, not even by means of *eminent domain* or public necessity.

Externally, the liberal temper of Rome colored the sense of mission

[2] *Acta Apostolorum*, XXV, 16.

behind the creation and expansion of the Empire. Unlike the Greeks and Orientals of their time, the Romans did not kill the vanquished peoples, carry them off into slavery, or destroy their settlements. Instead, their famous "Roman leniency" led them to strive to incorporate the defeated nations peacefully into the Empire, allowing them to keep their land and their own laws and rights of self-government under a quasi-federal regime. The great range and duration of the Roman Empire, therefore, was for the nations under it a reign of peace (*Pax Romana*) and stability without equal in the history of man, and it was nostalgically remembered for many centuries after the decline and fall of Rome.

Weaknesses of Roman constitutionalism   This impressive list of the accomplishments of Roman constitutionalism suggests by its sheer bulk that we supply a list of Roman shortcomings. Despite its towering achievements, constitutional government in Rome had gaps and weaknesses that would be considered crucial today. The democratic element of Roman political institutions—the popular assemblies, for example—would today be considered authoritarian and aristocratic in their operation, for no debate or free speech was allowed; they could only vote on what the magistrate submitted to them. The humanitarianism of Rome found little application to women and children, and none at all to slaves until very late in the evolution of the Empire. The legal security of the citizens was also quite inadequate, owing to both the lack of guarantees of the civil rights mentioned above and the difficulty for the citizens to know the laws. The recording of statutes was poor and collections of laws and decrees few and far between; no registers of land ownership were kept, and little effort was made to grant the citizen sufficient notice of his rights and duties under the law. Beyond some basic rules such as the prohibition of ex post facto laws and unwritten rules of judicial procedure, the procedural safeguards essential to modern constitutionalism were as yet inadequately developed. Last, but by no means least important, the constant wars necessary to acquire and maintain the Roman Empire, together with the inadequacy of the old governmental institutions of the city republic of Rome for the administration of a vast empire, had much to do with the decline of the political virtues of the Roman tradition and the eventual fall of the entire edifice. Corrupt provincial administrations and the seizure of power by rivaling generals also could not but undermine the political consensus and the exalted image of authority. The decline of the Senate, the rise of Imperial absolutism, and the momentous social and economic changes resulting from the expansion of Rome—all these finally became landmarks of the decline of Roman constitutional government.

Constitutionalism in the Middle Ages

Constitutional thought and practices in the Middle Ages present a somewhat confusing and self-contradictory picture owing to the survival of the political notions of the late Roman era alongside the more original developments of the time. The medieval concept of kingship, for example, was a curious mixture of late Roman and more typically medieval ideas. The Roman tradition granted absolute authority to the king and considered his will a source of legal authority. The strong belief in customary law and the decentralized character of authority in a feudal society, on the other hand, gave monarchy a character limited by notions of popular consent and respect for the traditional rights and privileges of the subjects. The same law that empowered the king also limited his authority. A good deal of vagueness further reduced the effectiveness of concepts of medieval constitutionalism. The king was often said to derive his legitimate authority simultaneously from election by the princes of the realm, by inheritance from his father, and by divine appointment from God.

The impression of inner contradictions and unresolved questions is reinforced by the contributions of other social forces of the Middle Ages that left an undeniable imprint on the development of constitutional thought and practices, even though they were not primarily political. One such influence was the sustaining faith and self-confidence that built the great cathedrals and inspired the struggle against the infidels. Another was the unifying and moderating power of the Catholic Church, whose moral and philosophical authority sanctioned the social and political order. A more tangible contribution to future constitutional development was the contractual nature of the relation between lord and vassal, their equality before a court of their peers, and the extraordinary decentralization of public authority under feudalism. Finally, there was the rise of free cities and city republics all over Europe, a foreboding of the developments to come. These different strains never coalesced into an integrated political system of the Middle Ages; they supplied, however, the roots of the modern constitutional tradition. The three most significant themes of this development—the law, the doctrine of popular sovereignty, and representative government—merit treatment in more detail.

Omnipresent law The notion of the law, which Oliver Wendell Holmes called "a brooding omnipresence in the sky," was perceived everywhere and in every human and natural relationship. It was recognized by folkways and customs as well as in the elaborate theology of St. Thomas Aquinas, who distinguishes no less than four kinds of law—eternal, divine, natural, and human law—all intimately related to one another. Customary in nature, the medieval law was *not made but found* and antedated any living source of law. Even royal decrees were careful to undertake merely to *declare* this customary law *on the authority of the people and with the advice and consent of their nobles and bishops.* The traveling judges of King Henry II of England, who are credited with the creation of the common law in the twelfth century, also were content with seeking out such principles of the prevailing regional and local customary law as could be applied uniformly throughout the country. Juries similarly had the prime function of bringing to bear upon a particular case the customary sense of right and wrong of their community rather than of creating any new law. Such an all-pervading faith in the customary law, rooted in the people, had a powerful stabilizing and constitutionalizing effect on medieval governments, whose authority was just as much a creature of the law as the privileges of individuals or the corporate liberties of guilds and cities.

Doctrine of popular sovereignty Popular sovereignty was not invented in the Middle Ages, just as the notion of law was not new; however, it took on a new significance it had not possessed before. Roman law, for instance, had clearly held the idea of popular sovereignty, yet somehow sold this birthright of popular government by conceiving of sovereignty as having been ceded irreversibly by the people to the Roman Emperor. The medieval notion of popular sovereignty distinguished itself, in particular, by considering the people of the community to be a fellowship (*Genossenschaft*), or corporate body, that was capable of possessing certain rights, duties, and priviliges. The medieval theologian Nicholas of Cusa (1401–1464), for example, spoke of a divinely inspired popular will of the community to which the ruler must conform: "The voice of the people is the voice of God." The philosopher Marsilio of Padua (1275–1343), in a more practical vein, derived from popular sovereignty essential rights of self-government by which an organized body politic can make its own laws, elect its own rulers, and hold them to account.

Beginnings of representative government Without this notion of sovereignty inherent in an organized body politic, the most original and lasting contribution of medieval constitutionalism—representative government—might not have come to pass. The ancient world had known deliberative assemblies, such as the Roman Senate, but these gatherings did not represent anyone but the persons assembled. It was necessary to conceive of the whole organized community as a body before it could be represented by another person or body authorized to make binding decisions on its behalf. Marsilio proposed such representation not only for political communities but also for the community of the clergy of the medieval church[3] in answer to the demands for the great reform by many voices inside and outside the Catholic Church. Thus arose the conciliar movement of the fourteenth century. In the secular sphere, by similar considerations, representative assemblies arose in many Western countries, especially in Spain, France, and England.

The significance of this new device in the evolution of constitutional government can hardly be exaggerated. To be sure, the functions of these early representative assemblies were different and less crucial than they are today. The early British parliaments, for example, were called infrequently, and they underrepresented, by our standards, the commoners, not to mention the lower classes. Their main function was to consent to new tax levies and to advise the Crown on matters of the king's choosing. But this small beginning cannot obscure the enormous potential of representative institutions for the purpose of gathering consent and facilitating popular participation in government, as a check on executive authority, and also as an important device for the building of national communities.

MODERN CONSTITUTIONAL GOVERNMENT

It remained for the modern period to carry the many promising constitutional ideas and experiments of preceding ages to successful fruition. The foundations had been laid. The goal was clearly in view. But there were still enormous hurdles to overcome—vested interests and class privileges, prejudices and untamed social forces, the menace of economic crises within and of war without. As Edmund Burke put it:

> To make a government requires no great prudence. Settle the seat of power; teach obedience; and the work is done. To give freedom is still more easy. It is not necessary to guide; it only requires to let go the rein. But to form a free government; that is, to temper

---

[3] Marsilio and the philosopher William of Occam (1300?–1349?) even went so far as to call for a representative General Council of clergymen and laity for the reforms of the Church, an idea which clearly heralded the thinking of many Protestant groups during the Reformation.

together those opposite elements of liberty and restraint in one consistent work, requires much thought, deep reflection, a sagacious, powerful, and combining mind.

To make possible this crowning achievement, there had first to come to pass the series of distinctive developments that ushered in the Modern Age of Western civilization: the rise of the modern state, of science and scientific philosophy, of modern economy, and of modern political life. These modern features took several centuries to unfold completely and their evolution did not follow a deliberate or consistent course.

Contributions of the modern state

The rise of the modern state (see Chapter 3), even in its absolutist form, signified a considerable advance over the weak, often disorderly, and poorly organized feudal monarchies with their crazy-quilt patches of legal and property rights crisscrossing over widely varying parcels of land. The modern state brought at least a considerable amount of rational order and simplicity into the prevailing confusion by centralizing governmental authority, introducing legal uniformity throughout the realm, and, at its best, placing the enormous power of the new state at the disposal of enlightened schemes of social and economic development. Although most absolute monarchies stopped short of providing equality before the law and unrestrained individual activity, their spadework of legal unification and effective administration put these goals within easy reach of their successors. Even where violent revolutions overthrew the old regime, as in France, the new regimes owed to absolute monarchies a great deal of their own achievements.

The greatest contribution of the modern state to constitutional government, however, lies in the reaction it caused by its vast accumulation of arbitrary, secular power in irresponsible hands. To be sure, there had been older forms of constitutionalism in the days of weaker government that were content with setting down legal limits and religious restraints upon the rulers of the day. But this older strain pales in comparison to the challenge of bringing the vast accumulation of secular power of the modern Leviathan under control by ever more ingenious devices of enforcing governmental responsibility, of dividing power, or of pitting power against power. First there had to be a strong policy-making authority before the full range of the devices of modern constitutional government could be developed in response.

Modern science

The rise of the scientific attitude also sharpened the sense of politically interested persons for the realities of power and politics. In the same manner that science increasingly strove to explain the natural environment of man solely in terms of cause and effect, political theorists searched for the causes and effects of power and authority. And, in the same way that engineers began to construct clever machines to harness the forces of nature for the benefit of human kind, political leaders conceived of political systems in mechanistic terms and proceeded to set up constitutional schemes according to mechanistic formulas such as the separation of powers or the American federal system. As Alexander Hamilton wrote in *The Federalist*, No. 31:

Of the same nature (as the maxims in geometry) are these other maxims in ethics and politics, that there cannot be an effect without a cause; that the means are to be proportioned to the end; that every power ought to be commensurate with its object.

The most logical course, it appeared, was to check each power with a countervailing power of equal weight or to balance the presumably natural ambition for aggrandizement of the President with that of the Congress, or that of the federal government with that of the states, and vice versa.

Modern political philosophy

Even where modern Western philosophy made no pretensions to scientific method, its contributions to the fabric of thought that underlies modern constitutional government are enormous. Beginning with the humanism of the Renaissance, continuing with the tradition of skepticism and Cartesian doubt, and culminating in the "self-evident natural rights" of the Enlightenment, this philosophical evolution never stopped challenging traditional authority and monarchy by divine right. Finally, the dam of entrenched privileges and venerable prejudices was breached by the British civil wars of the seventeenth century, the Glorious Revolution of 1688, and the American and French Revolutions of the late eighteenth century. In these four great upheavals, the revolutionaries put on their banners those individual rights and constitutional schemes for government by consent that had matured in over two centuries of modern philosophical reflection.

In this account also, we must not forget the role played by the republican tradition of city-states and other republics, ranging all the way from Marsilio's Padua and the intellectual and artistic splendor of Renaissance Florence to the Dutch and Swiss Confederacies. It was through these institutions that the traditions of liberty of the ancient and medieval world were saved from the pernicious feudal and despotic influences around them until the day when modern constitutional government could complete what earlier ages had started. Nor should we forget the example of England, which was the only major European state to sustain the historic rights of Englishmen and their representative assembly. Ever since the seventeenth century, the entire Western world and, more recently, many a non-Western country have drawn on the constitutional experience of the British.

Contributions of modern economy

The rise of modern economy was no less consequential to the development of modern constitutionalism. In centuries of growth, commercial capitalism and, later, industrial capitalism gave rise to a strong and independent middle class, the *classical bourgeoisie*, which became the major social force behind the historic movement toward written constitutions, representative government, and bills of rights in all countries of Western civilization. If this bourgeoisie was also motivated by a selfish concern for its property rights, such motivation hardly detracts from its historic merit as the champion of political freedom against such enslaving forces as feudalism and state absolutism. With the industrial revolution of the late eighteenth and nineteenth centuries, moreover, capitalism fully unfolded its revolutionary character as a force capable of changing the face of the globe, uprooting traditional societies and unlocking the treasures of the earth for human use as no other system in civilized history before it could do.

Rise of modern political society

Last, but not least important in the evolution of modern constitutional government, was the rise of the modern political society. As revolutionary a force as industrial capitalism, which largely caused their awakening, was the rise from centuries of slumber of vast masses of people of the lower classes to political importance. Buoyed up by enormous population increases, these masses rose as revolutionary mobs in the great political upheavals—as great nationalistic movements that could found new states or break up older ones, as the popular armies of the French revolutionary government, as the legions of organized labor, and as the mass parties or the fanatic mass movements of the twentieth century. Owing to this popular mobilization, all modern forms of government feature a considerable degree of popular participation—even totalitarian government does— if only in the form of artificially created enthusiasm and acclamation. Politics in constitutional regimes, moreover, has taken on the characteristic form of constitutional democracy—with rivaling political parties, well-organized pressure groups, and a vocal public opinion.

THE TRADITION OF GOVERNMENTAL RESPONSIBILITY

To understand the development of modern constitutionalism itself, a distinction should be made between the two chief lines along which its theory and practices evolved: the tradition of *governmental responsibility* and the tradition of *checks and limitations on public authority*. Although a detailed account of the specific institutional devices for both purposes is left to Part II of this book, a historical discussion of these two chief aspects of the evolution of modern constitutional government will serve as a means of orientation in the maze of technical detail and historical accident.

The tradition of governmental responsibility to the people is the answer to the practical problem of translating the principle of popular sovereignty into the reality of popular control over governmental authority. Given the predominance of hereditary monarchs and feudal princes on the one hand, and the submerged state of "the people" on the other—masses of illiterate, boorish *villeins*, and a tiny urban bourgeoisie—popular sovereignty at the outset appeared to be a fantastic idea. Yet it eventually became a working reality, within reason, through *the rise of representative processes into the position of the vital center* of modern government in the West. This great triumph of constitutionalization happened during a long painful process of trial and error, of experiments and failures, of penetrating theorizing as well as of pragmatic "muddling through." In the rise of the representative processes to their contemporary central importance, several distinct phases and aspects deserve individual consideration: the rise of parliamentary supremacy, electoral reform and the expansion of the suffrage, the development of the representative group process, and the systematization of the play of political forces to the point where governmental responsibility is so clearly located that the people on election day can pass a meaningful verdict.

Rise of parliamentary supremacy

The rise of the British Parliament blazed a trail for the development of legislative supremacy in most Western countries. It will be taken as an example for the whole development, even though the American experience deviates from it in some important respects. Parliament had a long way to travel from the day when the first Great Council was called to represent the English people in the thirteenth century, to the Restoration period of the seventeenth century, when it became a permanent institution. During this period it wielded some power over the royal purse and occasionally called the monarch to account for matters of general policy but was generally unable to hold kings responsible for their day-to-day actions, short of violent revolution. In a second phase, beginning with the Glorious Revolution of 1688 and the Act of Settlement of 1701, Parliament established the principle of parliamentary sovereignty and hence that the monarchy only ruled at its sufferance. In a third phase, starting in the eighteenth century, practices were developed by which the bulk of executive authority passed from the hands of the hereditary monarch to the hands of a prime minister and his Cabinet who could be overthrown by Parliament at any time without a large-scale revolution. Simultaneously, the development of parliamentary parties allowed Parliament to keep the running dispute between the executive authority and popular opinion contained within the group system inside the halls of Parliament. In this manner, the more subtle, and in the long run far more effective, harness of *political responsibility* replaced the crude control by threat of revolution. Parliaments and legislative assemblies elsewhere largely followed the British example of taming the executive authority of their monarchs. Even in the United States, where the special problems of monarchy ceased along with that institution in 1776, there was long a tradition of legislative supremacy, founded on the legislative monopoly over legislation and finances, a fact which caused Woodrow Wilson to describe American government at the end of the nineteenth century as "Congressional government."

Toward a responsible Parliament

With this victory of Parliament over executive authority won, however, there was still the question of how representative of the people Parliament really was. It was conceivable, after all, that the people had only exchanged one set of irresponsible rulers for another. And so there set in the long process of legislative reorganization and electoral reform that has characterized the last century and a half in most Western countries.

Legislative reapportionment   One aspect of this reorganization was the question of legislative reapportionment, which strove to equalize the basic units of the electorate represented by a seat in Parliament. To this end the electoral reform movement sought to eliminate among the constituencies the "rotten boroughs," which in some cases had sunk into the sea or lost all their population, and to give representation to new industrial towns that had none. Legislative reapportionment is a continuing problem, which at the present time is again very much in the focus of the issues of constitutional democracy in the United States.

Electoral reform   Another aspect of the enforcement of legislative responsibility to the people was the gradual expansion of the suffrage from a narrow property suffrage to all adult males, and, finally, to women and disfranchised minorities. Here, too, the development is still uncompleted in some areas. A third aspect of electoral reform was the choice between different electoral systems such as single-member electoral districts, in which a candidate is elected by a plurality or by a majority on a second ballot, and a system of proportional representation. This choice involves decisions about the nature and purpose of the representative process: Is the chief purpose of elections the mirrorlike representation of popular sentiment or the establishment of a strong moderate government?

Direct democracy   A fourth and last aspect of the strengthening of legislative responsibility to the people unfolded with the development in some Western countries of popular means of direct action, such as legislative referenda, popular initiatives, and recall elections. This phase of the tradition of responsibility developed mainly in countries that practice direct democracy, such as Switzerland, or in which customary channels such as the political parties or the right to petition government for a redress of grievances failed to satisfy the needs of the electorate.[4]

---

[4] In this connection, one could also mention the many reorganization schemes that attempted to make legislatures more responsible, such as the drive for legislative salaries which would enable people from the lower classes to serve in Parliament, shorter terms of office, or attempts to reorganize the internal structure of a legislative assembly in order to eliminate in it the strongholds of organized interests.

The modern political constitution

Even after the full development and perfection of these devices to hold executive power responsible to the elected representatives of the people, and the representatives responsible to those who elect them, the people were still in a very ineffective position vis-à-vis their government. As long as the people were not organized, as long as they faced their government as separate, unrelated individuals, they were unable to oppose specific governmental policies, much less to develop any policy of their own for the government to follow. For this reason, the tradition of *governmental responsibility* required the development of political parties, which organize the like-minded for purposes of making public policy proposals, selecting candidates for public office, and seeking mass support for both. Only after political parties established a link reaching from the formation of popular opinion all the way to the formation of public policy by governmental agencies could popular control of government be said to begin on a day-by-day basis. Because the formation of an intelligent popular opinion also requires a steady flow of reliable information from many independent sources, a free press and other mass media responsible to the public further complete the system of responsible government.

The evolving constitutional system

Owing to the newness of the evolving constitutional system, a great deal of experimenting and constitutional theorizing had to take place. Some experiments are still going on and new constitutional doctrines and theories occasionally evolve. Much of the more recent thought on the subject has gone in the direction of refining and adjusting either the whole system or one of its newer components. A great deal of the literature of American political science during the last fifteen years, for example, has been devoted to determining the proper place of interest groups in a constitutional democracy. Prior to that, a Committee on Political Parties set up by the American Political Science Association issued a report, "Towards a More Responsible Two-Party System," in which the shortcomings of American parties as transmission belts of popular control over governmental policies were listed and suggestions were made for improvement.

There are still many unresolved questions connected with the practical implications of the tradition of governmental responsibility. If the United States Congress is to be made more responsible to the

people, to cite a prominent example, should the individual congressman or senator be chiefly responsible to the voters and organized
interests of his constituency, or should he be under the sway of his
political party, which is meant to be the chief agent of responsibility
toward the entire nation? Owing to sectionalism, localism, and a
heritage of checks and balances, American politics has rarely ventured beyond the first solution, although some American statesmen
and most political scientists would prefer the second arrangement as
more likely to assure governmental responsibility.

This second solution, as it has evolved in Great Britain, is dominated by the two highly centralized and disciplined major parties.
The leadership of the majority party supplies prime minister and
Cabinet and is in full control of the government as long as it enjoys
the support of the rank and file and a popular majority at the polls.
The majority party's controlling position allows it to dominate its
own majority in the House of Commons and to enforce discipline
on every one of its members in Parliament. It also permits the
voters on election day a clear choice between the "ins," who can
be held duly responsible for all that happened under their administration, and the "outs," the opposition party waiting in the wings.
The voter's choice is primarily between the two parties, and their
sets of leaders, not between two popular local candidates of doubtful
effectiveness on the national scene. In this fashion, the British system
can provide for unambiguous governmental responsibility to the
people, whereas the American system allows politicians to dodge
responsibility by hiding behind the multiple checks and balances of
the separation of powers, federalism, Senate-House relationships,
the committee structure, and weak national partisanship.

THE TRADITION OF LIMITED AUTHORITY

Looking back upon the ancient and medieval roots of modern constitutional government, we find that the tradition of governmental
responsibility apparently stems from two concepts: popular sovereignty and representative government. But there is also a second
modern tradition, which is considerably older and goes back to
such venerable ancient and medieval sources as the law and the
mixed constitution. This older tradition was predominant before
the rise of popular government, at a time when the best hope of
taming governmental power appeared to lie in devices dividing power
and subjecting government to the law. In the American system of
government this older tradition is still dominant, although the
tradition of responsibility has asserted itself on significant points,

such as the evolution of the American Presidency into popular and legislative leadership, and the expansion of the suffrage. In Great Britain, in the Commonwealth countries, and on the Continent, however, the older tradition has had to yield the center of the stage to governmental responsibility.

Development of English law and constitutional theory

An understanding in depth of the older tradition of law and other checks on governmental authority requires a brief reexamination of the development of English law and constitutional theory in the twelfth and thirteenth centuries. It was during this time that common law began to evolve as a body of case law, beginning with the decisions of the traveling judges of Henry II. Both this body of law and the royal judiciary subsequently grew into major factors of constitutional development. This was also the time of the origin of Magna Charta, that extraordinary charter of baronial rights and liberties, which soon were expanded to include commoners and even the despised *villein*. Its celebrated thirty-ninth clause,

> *No free man shall be taken, or imprisoned, or disseised [expropriated], or outlawed, or exiled, or in any way destroyed, nor will we go against him, or send against him, except by lawful judgment of his peers or by the laws of the land.*

originally referring only to nobles, was eventually applied to every man. There followed also the self-assertion of the early English parliaments, which for two hundred years insisted that English kings reissue similar charters, some thirty in all. The early parliaments, while they lasted, constituted a strong check on monarchic power, as did representative institutions on the Continent. Very significant for the earlier constitutional tradition were also the writings of the English jurist Henry de Bracton (died 1268), who was perhaps the first writer to systematize the medieval and ancient heritage of law for constitutional purposes. It was he who, among others, presented a doctrine of distinction between a proper sphere of royal powers within which a king was legally supreme and a sphere of recognized rights and privileges of subjects that were solely under the law and therefore removed from arbitrary action by the sovereign. This concept in effect reconciled the Roman idea of absolute sovereignty with the contractual notion of the feudal relationship between lord and vassal, thereby blazing a trail to the granting of rights, liberties, and privileges to noblemen, towns, and corporate bodies. And it ended with bills of rights and solemn gurantees embodied in written constitutions, by means of which a sovereign people granted to its members enumerated rights and liberties.

The unfolding of this half of the modern constitutional tradition had one of its most dramatic moments at the beginning of the English constitutional struggles of the seventeenth century. By this time, the historic liberties of Frenchmen, their representative estates and *parlements* (courts), were already giving way to royal absolutism; the princes of German states had adopted imperial Roman law to suit their desire for absolute power over their subjects; and in England a century of Tudor absolutism had led to the elaborate theory of King James I (1566–1625) that kings rule by divine right rather than by consent or by law. King James's claim to absolute authority, however, was contested by Sir Edward Coke, the chief justice of England, who threw into the balance the whole common law, the independence of the learned judges, and a revived and expensively interpreted Magna Charta, which had been forgotten for several generations. Coke insisted that the common law was a substantially unchangeable constitution setting down both the structure of government and the basic liberties of the subjects. Neither King nor Parliament had any authority to change this fundamental law from which their own rights and duties derived. James dismissed Coke upon this challenge to royal supremacy, although the point was well taken indeed: This historical incident reaffirmed the Western tradition of the *rule of law* in its purest form, as government subject to an overriding law. For the ancients and later modern theorists, this higher law was the law of nature and a part of the cosmic order from which specific *natural rights*, the rights of man, could be deduced. For Coke and the English tradition, it was the historic common law from which "the historic rights of Englishmen" were derived.

The net effect on constitutional government appears to be the same, at least at first glance, whether the historic common law turned out to be stronger and better suited to endure. One important reason for the strength of historic law is that it is judge-made and judge-interpreted; it is tied to the highly trained legal knowledge of an elite, the "artificial reason," as Coke called it, of the learned men of the law to distinguish it from the "natural reason" of King James I, who wanted to render his own justice after prinicples of his own devising. Hence an independent judiciary has become one of the most important features of modern constitutional government. In some countries, such as the United States, judicial independence and the guardianship of the fundamental law of the constitution have led to a mild *judicial supremacy*, a system in which the "high priests"

of the constitution have formally the last word on constitutional
questions.

The evolution of individual rights and liberties

One of the chief strains of modern constitutionalism has been the
evolution of *individual rights and liberties,* a trend highlighted by
the increasing emancipation of the individual throughout the last
centuries. Here the course of development follows several lines:
that of *procedural safeguards,* especially regarding property rights
and the rights of the accused in criminal trials, and the guarantee
of substantive human rights and liberties against governmental interference.

Procedural Safeguards In some common law countries, the procedural safeguards have since been embodied in the all-encompassing
phrase "due process of law," without which no person shall be
deprived of life, liberty, property, or the pursuit of happiness. Among
the important safeguards against the police powers of the state are
the freedom from unreasonable search and seizure, the freedom
from excessive bail and cruel and unusual punishments, the right
to grand jury indictment, the right to a writ of habeas corpus and
to a trial by jury, the right to counsel and a reasonable opportunity
to defend oneself, the right to judicial appeal, and the freedom from
double jeopardy and self-incrimination.

However, this complex system of procedural protection is not accepted in its entirety throughout the Western world. In France, for
example, habeas corpus is not recognized, and class distinctions at
times influence the practices of courts and police. In Western Germany the principle that the accused shall be considered innocent
until proven guilty was formally recognized only very recently in a
reform of criminal law, though it is implicit in Roman law. The
procedure in criminal trials in Roman law countries generally tends
to weight the scales against the accused. In the United States, there
are also frequent controversies about such matters as the admissibility of illegally obtained evidence, jury selection practices, and
the merits of the death penalty. In all countries of the Western
world, even where procedural safeguards are most highly developed,
there are occasional breakdowns in the system in the form of cases
of police brutality, miscarriage of justice, and discriminatory practices
of one sort or another. Procedural devices are only as reliable and
perfect as the persons who administer them: Requiring trial by jury,
for example, cannot prevent juries from rendering wrong verdicts.

Guaranteed rights and freedoms The *substantive rights and liberties* guaranteed to individuals are the hard core of modern constitutionalism:

1. *Freedom of the body.* The primary freedom is what John Locke meant when he wrote in his *Two Treatises of Government,* "Every man has a property in his own person. This nobody has any right to but himself." This freedom of the body that one takes for granted today must be contrasted with such institutions as slavery, serfdom, forced labor, and other kinds of involuntary servitude that were so prevalent in the past and can still be found in some parts of the world. Slavery in the United States was abolished only a hundred years ago. Other typical forms in which this freedom has been incorporated in constitutional campaigns and debates in Western countries have been the free choice of job or occupation, the free choice of spouse, and free movement throughout a country and across its borders, unhindered by iron curtains, armed guards, and walls. Because persons duly convicted of major crimes are usually exempt from this protection against physical restraint, moreover, the security offered by it also depends on the integrity of the whole judicial system. To prevent the abuse of judicial power, there are the procedural safeguards named above and also such protections as the freedom from bills of attainder, ex post facto laws, from trial by special courts, and from other breaches in the formal system of law, which should be general and equal in its application to everyone, with due notice to the persons affected by it, and with known and impartial procdures of adjudication and enforcement.

2. *Freedom of mind and conscience.* The second substantive *freedom* is that *of mind and conscience.* It should be contrasted with the practices of religious intolerance of centuries, the zealotry of moral or patriotic righteousness, or the enormous social pressures toward conformity. In England, the citadel of most civil liberties, the last of the legislative acts discriminating against nonconformist Protestants, Jews, and Catholics were not rescinded until the second half of the nineteenth century. Religious intolerance still exists in many Western countries, especially where there is no separation of church and state. Even in the United States, despite the constitutional guarantee of freedom to worship, there are occasional encroachments on the liberties of small sects and religious minorities as well as frequent debates over the fine line dividing political heresy from conspiracy.

A corollary of the freedom of thought and conscience is the freedom of expressing one's convictions without fear of reprisal, governmental or otherwise. Freedom of speech, of the press, of debate and discussion imply also the freedom to criticize, to question, to challenge, and to say unpopular things, which are important regulatives of political democracy. But this is not to say that there are no limitations on this complex of freedoms. As soon as the freedom of thought turns from the privacy of the mind to the publicity of a thought expressed, there arises also the possibility of injury to others, or to the community at large, which calls for the exercise of restraint—self-restraint or legal restraints and remedies. In times of war or national emergency, moreover, such possible injury to the community is often construed more expansively than in peacetime and linked to such imponderables of national self-preservation as the fighting morale of the troops or the readiness to sacrifice of the people at large. As is true of the previously mentioned liberties, the history of the guarantees of freedom of speech and of the press does not extend very far into the past of most Western countries. Among its landmarks are the failure of the British Parliament in 1695 to renew the Licensing Act, moving pleas for free speech and discussion, such as John Milton's *Areopagitica* (1644) and John Stuart Mill's *Essay on Liberty* (1859), and also contemporary debates such as those on the "management of the news by government agencies," and on the difference between pornography and literature and between seditious propaganda and legitimate protest.

3. *Equal opportunities.* A third substantive freedom is that often referred to as equal access to the advantages and opportunities available in a free society. John Locke, for example, speaks of the right of every man, by "the labor of his body and the work of his hands" to acquire land and other property that are not already owned by someone else. Eeighteenth- and nineteenth-century liberals asserted the freedom to use their property for purposes of capitalistic production, a right to buy and sell as the market, not the government, allows, and a freedom to enter contracts without any restraints whatever. In today's society, people are concerned about their equal access to housing, job, and educational opportunities and about restrictions on this equality of opportunity on grounds of race, sex, or other arbitrary criteria. Although the specific threats to equal opportunity may have changed with the transformation of the economic setting, the basic desire for the pursuit by each individual of his own economic advancement is still the same. Guaranteeing these rights by constitutional law has always been difficult beyond such things as the legal protection of contracts, equal justice under the law, and guarantees of property rights as long as they do not

injure the rights of others or the welfare of the community. Such guarantees may often require special legislation and easier adjudication of wrongs, such as by the Fair Employment Practices Commissions in the United States.

4. *Freedom of political activity.* The fourth substantive freedom evolved by modern constitutionalism is in some ways perhaps the most important because its possession provides the means for the enforcement and expansion of other freedoms. It is the freedom of political activity and includes more specific liberties such as the right to petition the government for a redress of grievances, the right of association for political or economic purposes, and the right to assemble peacefully and to discuss and criticize the authorities. Needless to stress, there are limitations also of these rights based on possible injury to third parties or the public. These liberties, in conjunction with voting rights and representative government, provide the constitutional setting for popular government as we know it.

These four freedoms, together with the procedural safeguards, have been the vital core of modern constitutionalism as it has evolved out of such landmarks in history as the Magna Charta, the common law, the Petition of Right of 1628, the Habeas Corpus Act of 1679, the Bill of Rights of 1689, the numerous bills and declarations of human rights, most notably those of the Virginia Constitution of 1776, the first ten amendments to the United States Constitution, and the French Declaration of the Rights of Man. No respectable national constitution today is without such a guarantee of civil rights and liberties, and no Western government can be regarded as respectable if it does not at least allow a major part of these guarantees to become an enforceable reality. The central importance of guaranteeing civil rights led some European political thinkers and statesmen to refer to constitutional government as *garantisme*. It is the *garantisme*, above all, that distinguishes liberal democracy from the totalitarian regimes and dictatorships of the twentieth century, as well as from the authoritarianism of traditional autocracies before our time.

The act of foundation

There is another element in modern constitutionalism that merits attention—the element of founding a community. The notion of social contract, from the Old Testament to John Locke, implied the assumption of a deliberate act of foundation. The pilgrims wrote into their famous Mayflower Compact:

We whose names are underwritten . . . doe by these presents solemnly and mutually in the presence of God, and one of another, covenant, and combine ourselves togeather into a civill body politick, for our better ordering and preservation . . . and by vertue heareof to enacte, constitute, and frame such just and equall lawes, ordinances, acts, constitutions, and offices, from time to time, as shall be thought most meete and convenient for the general good of the Colonie, unto which we promise all due submission and obedience.

The French revolutionaries of the 1790s were very much attracted to the example of the Roman Republic, which lasted for seven centuries under the spell of a myth of foundation and dated its calendar *qua urbe condita,* "since the foundation of the city of Rome." Hence the revolutionary officials in France adopted such Roman titles and names as "consuls," "dictator," and "senate-consultes," and created a new revolutionary calendar. Many American revolutionaries were looking forward to a similar act of foundation which came, after some delay, with the adoption of the United States Constitution. Before this consolidating act, in the midst of the upheaval, Patrick Henry was in the position to be able to say to the first Continental Congress:

Government is dissolved. . . . Where are your landmarks, your boundaries of Colonies? We are in a state of nature, sir.

After the act of foundation, on the other hand, succeeding generations and administrations, including men who had fought against the adoption of the Constitution, began to look up to this venerable document with a reverence and awe that one can only compare to religious feelings. Thus the inner rationale of the great revolutions had evidently created not only enough emotional energy to overthrow the old order, but also a willingness to sanctify a new authority if it was intrinsically just and moral and laid down in one solemn act of foundation. In a similar fashion, many a new nation of our time has quickly adopted a Western-style written constitution to solemnize the hour of independence with a birth certificate, as it were. By the same token, the federal union of several hitherto separate states has always been deemed to require a written constitution, in the same manner that a solemn marriage ceremony or contract may be necessary for the permanent union of two individuals. In this manner, notions of social contract and the myth of foundation supply much of the inner rationale behind the exalted status of written constitutions. A constitution is a "higher law," at

least higher than ordinary legislation, which is also expressed by such formal characteristics as the difficulty of amendment and the requirement of popular ratification.

The tradition of checks and balances

The last aspect of modern constitutional government, though not the least influential, is the tradition of checks and balances. Its origins, apart from the ancient idea of the mixed constitution, probably lie in the medieval days of the early parliaments. With the evolution of the old institution of kingship into the powerful modern executive branch and of parliaments toward legislative functions, the meaning of the old relationship changed, but the idea was revived by John Locke and the French Baron de Montesquieu (1689–1755) that Parliament should check the power of the king. Locke felt that "the legislative and executive power are in distinct hands . . . in all moderated monarchies and well-framed governments." Montesquieu wrote in the *Spirit of the Laws* that "when the legislative and executive power are united in the same person, or in the same body of magistrates, there can be no liberty."[5] These theories were echoed by the influential *Commentaries on the Law of England* of Sir William Blackstone (1723–1780), which was familiar to the members of the Philadelphia Convention. James Madison, finally, argued in *Federalist Paper No. 47*:

> The accumulation of all powers, legislative, executive, and judiciary, in the same hands . . . may justly be pronounced the very definition of tyranny.

The concept underlying this theory was the mechanistic idea of a balance between several agencies whose incumbents were presumed to be possessed by a natural desire to aggrandize their own power and, in so doing, would "check" one another. Montesquieu was attracted by this idea of checks and balances because of his desire to check and control the vast powers of the absolute French monarch; the farmers of the American Constitution were attracted by it because of their concern about the "passions of the multitude." The entire constitutional edifice of Philadelphia, in its original form, can be interpreted as a long series of checks upon the lawmaking powers of the House of Representatives—presumably the mouthpiece of the popular majorities of the new United States—the Senate, with its staggered terms and mode of election, the Presidential veto,

[5] Montesquieu also stressed the importance of an independent judiciary as an aspect of the separation of powers which is quite generally recognized today.

together with the presumed effect of the electoral college, and the role of the Supreme Court. Federalism, too, was considered a device for dividing and checking power, apart from its other merits—a view also shared by Montesquieu.

The chief objection to checks and balances lies in their conflict with the tradition of governmental responsibility to the people, which demands a single locus of authority that can be easily subjected to popular control. A governmental system that divides power among several branches, two legislative chambers, and two levels of government, if not more, can at best feature as many channels of responsibility as there are independent authorities—a needless complication if not a contradiction in terms. Responsibility, political and even fiscal, is inconceivable without centralization of authority to the point where on election day the voter faces a clear choice between the "ins" and the "outs." The desirable goal of limited government can be achieved also by other means, especially with the help of an appropriately drawn-up constitution.

CURRENT CONSTITUTIONAL PROBLEMS

This survey of the traditions of constitutional government in the West has covered a lot of ground, although it could hardly claim to be exhaustive. Constitutionalism, as we have seen, is above all a tradition of government that is continually developing, animated by a spirit that always seeks for new and better devices to make government responsible and to keep power at the service of human kind, rather than to keep man under the yoke of power. There still remains the task of indicating some of the current points of interest in this constitutional evolution, apart from the spreading and refinement of the existing devices throughout the Western world. Among these current problems are, for example, (1) the extension of constitutional devices to primarily nonpolitical spheres of life, (2) the dilemma of personal freedom in an increasingly bureaucratized and conformist society, (3) the adoption of Western-style constitutions by non-Western nations, and (4) the loss of political consensus in some Western nations.

Constitutionalism in nonpolitical spheres of life

The extension of constitutional devices to nonpolitical spheres of life is not new in principle, as the important role of the conciliar movement and that of Protestant nonconformism have demonstrated in the history of representative government, not to mention the widespread use today of constitutions and rules of order by private clubs and economic associations. The highly organized and bureau-cratized state of advanced industrial society, however, presents new problems of concentrated power wherever one looks—in the economy, in the life of organizations, and in the hierarchies of civil service and giant corporations. In some cases, attempts have been made to control these concentrations of power with the help of devices and schemes mentioned earlier.

In the life of large organizations, such as modern political parties, labor unions, interest groups, and fraternal organizations, their very bigness often presents their members with the same problems of power and responsibility that constitutionalism attempts to solve in the political world. The important representative function of political parties and interest groups in modern constitutional government, in fact, renders all the more crucial the internal structure of these organizations, the integrity of the representative process within them, the responsibility of the leaders to the led, and the safeguard-ing of the rights of minorities and individuals within them. With the growth of big government and big business, similar problems arose for the large number of employees of a single governmental service or big factory. In the private economy, the employee with a grievance now can usually appeal to plant councils, grievance committees, or his trade union for redress against the authorities that govern a large part of his life. In Western Germany, to mention a recent example, an elaborate scheme of "labor codetermination" has been developed from the plant councils, which allows the workers a share in certain management decisions of their companies. In public service there is an even greater need for representative devices and con-stitutional safeguards, bcause the laws of many Western countries prohibit public employees from striking. To mention another perti-nent example, the British civil service features (in addition to unions for the lower ranks) the Whitley Councils, joint negotiation boards composed of higher civil servants and representatives of the civil service unions that can arrive at decisions about most employment matters. All of these institutions and efforts are in the best con-stitutional tradition of the West, although the complex problems of many a nonpolitical setting at times defy the capacity of the con-stitutional approach to make the world of human relationships livable for all.

The dilemma of personal freedom

Another current problem of modern constitutionalism, the dilemma of personal freedom in an advanced industrial society, in part con-siderably exceeds the scope of what constitutional arrangements can do. This is particularly true if one thinks about the fact that personal freedom is meaningful only as long as it is linked with a sense of purpose, a sense of direction derived from individual self-realization, from service to the community, or service to a higher cause. Without such a sense of purpose, personal freedom can be an intolerable burden from which a person seeks to "escape," according to Erich Fromm, the author of *Escape from Freedom*. Modern industrial society is often composed of a sizable number of people without a sense of purpose—people in whom the barren desert of meaninglessness can suddenly explode into whirlwinds of nihilistic destructiveness— or people who take all their direction from the fads and whims of others. Whatever may be the reasons for this growing desert in Western society, there can little doubt that people without a purpose have little understanding or use for liberties and constitutional safeguards and devices. Constitutional government can give a people freedom only insofar as the people want freedom for some great purpose, whether religious, altruistic, or individual self-realization. The pursuit of such a purpose, however, automatically adds a sense of responsibility to the use of freedom. And although purpose and value are beyond the capacity of constitutionalism, responsibility is a concept that is of the essence of the constitutional tradition.

The responsibilities of individuals in Western society have steadily grown over the centuries of rising scientific, technological, and manipulative powers of modern man. Nature, society, and man himself have become almost infinitely subject to change, molding, adjustment, and manipulation. The range of choices of individuals regarding their own lives, their relations with others, the setting in which they are born, mature, and spend their declining years has grown to immense proportions. The role of government as the coordinator and executor of all these decisions of individuals regarding their own lives has become about as central to the interdependent, malleable human world of today as it was, for different reasons, in Athenian democracy.

In this contemporary context, then, personal freedom itself has become profoundly ambiguous. On the one hand, individuals can maximize their freedom best by cooperating with others in joint decisions which, through the representative process, are transformed into governmental policies of far-reaching intervention in their own lives. On the other hand, individuals may shy away from such extensive collective self-regulation and seek their freedom in opposition to its regulatory schemes. Reams of controversial tracts and articles have been written on behalf of both of these schools of freedom, whose directions conflict with each other. In spite of all the acrimonious exchanges of big words and phrases, neither one of these schools can escape the basic dilemma of personal freedom in a society of infinite complexity, interdependence, and malleability. The advocates of collective self-regulation cannot deny that their manner of operation requires a great deal of voluntary conformity to bring about the benefit of specific governmental action. Nor can they deny that the cumulative effect of collective self-regulation narrows the sphere of individual choices and decreases individual differences. Alexis de Tocqueville, John Stuart Mill, Aldous Huxley, and many others have issued pertinent warnings about the brave new world of sameness and tyrannous conformity of humans which might result from collective self-regulation. The advocates of freedom by abstention from government, on the other hand, are proposing an even worse alternative, comparable perhaps to a pilot on a riverboat who leaves the steering wheel because he expects the boat to founder on a rock three hundred miles down the stream anyway. Given the enormous interdependence, the rapid changes, and the constant occurrence of crises in contemporary society, the withdrawal of individuals from collective self-regulation will stop neither river nor boat; it may only set the boat adrift among the eddies, and cause it to founder long before it reaches its place of doom. The highly organized state of an advanced industrial society, moreover makes government only one among several vastly powerful instrumentalities for social regulation—the "private governments" of pressure groups, labor unions, and giant corporations, each intent on pursuing its own exclusive interests. The abdication of "public government" from its task of carrying out the policies decided by a majority of voters would only turn over the regulative powers to minority rule, or in effect, rule by several uncoordinated, competitive, and powerful minorities. In this self-defeating manner, the effort to protect the rights of the dissenting minority against the spread of "collectivism" is, at best, ineffectual and irresponsible, and at worst, undemocratic.

Problems of constitutionalism among the new nations

The third current complex of problems arises from the adoption of Western-style constitutions by many a non-Western new nation. It should be pointed out that such terms as "non-Western" or "undeveloped" raise great problems of definition, quite apart from their connotation of parochial conceit. There are highly developed non-Western countries such as Japan, relatively undeveloped Western countries such as Spain and Portugal, and furthermore, such countries as the Soviet Union, which is half Western and half non-

Western in its geographical location and cultural background. Although the generally adopted terminology may be open to question, there is little doubt about the constitutional difficulties of almost all current undeveloped, developing, and non-Western countries, including boderline cases and, in the recent past, such advanced Western countries as Italy and Germany. Typical examples of the failure of Western-style constitutionalism have been the Latin American countries, which, since the nineteenth century, featured written constitutions, often modeled upon the Constitution of the United States. Until quite recently, many of these states were run by a never-ending series of caudillos and military dictatorships, and seemingly were unable to change their governments in any other way than by violent revolution. The many new nations in Asia and Africa that have won their independence since 1945 similarly adopted written constitutions as soon as their former colonial masters permitted them to do so. However, today, a large number of them are under more or less unabashed military dictatorships, and many are dominated by a single large political party headed by a charismatic leader, such as Sékou Touré of Guinea or Habib Bourguiba of Tunisia.

Why does constitutional government, as we know it, encounter such difficulties in establishing itself in most of these countries? It is not an easy question to answer, considering the number and variety of cases. In any case, naming a few of the most frequent circumstances impeding the development of constitutional government elsewhere will broaden understanding of the conditions conducive to constitutional success in the West.

One of the most pervasive causes for the frequent failure of the adopted constitutions is the existing state of revolutionary social upheaval of the developing societies. In most excolonial countries, the destruction of the traditional way of life began with the coming of colonial rule, speeded up with the first steps of industrialization and urbanization, and was further advanced by involvement in the wars of the colonial powers and the growing appetite for independence. Once independent, these societies become restless for further development and are no more willing to relapse into traditional patterns than advanced industrial nations are willing to go back to preindustrial times. Constant turmoil and the weakening of the old traditions (which played a great role in the growth of Western constitutionalism) in favor of unfamiliar innovations are a poor setting for the gradual growth of constitutional liberty. The adopted constitutions, moreover, are often merely a veneer of cultural Westernization, as is sometimes true of Western-educated native leaders, and an object of hatred by anti-Western segments of society. Individualism, for example, for the sake of which constitutional government has developed impressive lists of guarantees of rights and liberties, is quite alien to most non-Western cuttures. Tribal and family loyalty, not individual self-realization, is the predominant value.

Another relevant factor is often the absence of all-pervading legal tradition such as Western civilization possessed in the Middle Ages, at a time when Western societies were fixed in a traditional mold themselves. The spirit of the law, that "brooding omnipresence in the sky," pervaded private and public relationships in the West long before organized group interests and their political interplay came into being. When traditional Western societies began to form these groups as a result of the economic and political transformations mentioned at the beginning of this chapter, the relationships between these groups and the rules governing the settlement of their conflicting demands were automatically looked on as capable of legal solution. This was the birth of modern constitutional government in the West. Most non-Western societies at present not only lack the stability of legal traditions; they also lack the articulation of groups at a sufficient level of organization and awareness of common interest to have a political life in the contemporary Western sense. Some are just beginning to evolve such groups as an independent middle class or labor unions but are still far from having reached the stable relations among the groups that are a requisite for a "political constitution." The undeveloped group life also fails to check the power of the state. Government is often the most highly organized and hence the most powerful group force present in the new nations, but there are few other groups to impose legal or political limitations upon it or to hold it to account. But even though stable groups may be weak or lacking altogether, temporary mobs of rioters, guerillas, or conspiratorial organizations such as the Communist party can often muster enough strength in a moment of crisis to overpower the government. The governments of non-Communist new nations are strong in relation to the permanent and associational groups of their societies but weak in comparison to the armed forces of revolutionaries within or of other countries.

There is in some of the new nations a substitute for independent groups—well-defined geographical or tribal subdivisions organized into self-governing units. A number of new nations, such as India, have adopted a federal system in order to deal with such geographical units within. Others, such as the former French West African colonies, concluded federal unions among neighboring new nations in order to pool their resources and to increase their political stability. This adoption of federalism is the closest many of these nations have come to an authentic constitutional development. It should be emphasized, however, that federalism is a difficult system to operate for inexperienced hands and that its adoption by the new nations is fraught with special dangers. Many of the larger excolonies won independence in the same accidental geographic confines in which the colony was originally conquered by the white man. These ex-colonies contain within their borders diverse religious and ethnic groups that often strive for separate status as soon as independence is achieved. Where fighting breaks out on a large scale between the central government and various provincial governments, there is little hope for the establishiment of a working federal system. To the extent to which federalism protects tribalism and other feudal arrangements of the traditional or colonial past, furthermore, it can be an obstacle to modern development. In their present state, many of the so-called new nations have not really jelled into national communities; they are little more than a conglomeration of unconnected local communities excited by the agitation for independence from colonial rule.

A further element inconducive to the growth of constitutionalism in the non-Western countries is the prevailing psychological climate. The transition from the traditional society, in which vast masses live an unpolitical life, embedded in customs and usages they need not understand, leaves most people quite unequipped to handle their private problems, much less the ways of politics. So they turn to political action for the satisfaction of such personal needs as a sense of belonging, a need for economic and social security, or a feeling of individual worth, often at the expense of some underdog or outsider. They mistake the excitement of the struggle for independence and the vicarious thrill of following a man on horseback for the essence of politics and are disappointed by the drabness of day-to-day public policy-making and the interplay of group demands.

This immature attitude toward politics applies to almost all the people in a typical excolonial country, though often in different ways. While the masses, for example, may be largely unpolitical, confused and gullible, the small elites—whether military leaders, or old aristocrats, or high priests, or Western-educated intellectuals—tend to be of an intolerant and violent cast of mind that sometimes borders on the totalitarian. In such a climate of opinion, the rule of law and procedural safeguards have little chance to prevail over zealotry and sheer force. Conflicts are settled by riot, assassination, or revolt—if ever they are. Opponents are jailed or murdered rather than permitted, as the "loyal opposition," to criticize those in power. Few are the new nations, such as India, where moderation rules and rights of the opposition are recognized. And long is the road toward a working constitutional system that many of the new nations will have to travel. Some of the old Western nations are still traveling it.

Lack of consensus

The fourth and last current problem of constitutional government is that of the loss or lack of consensus in some Western societies. Marcus Tullius Cicero in ancient Rome defined the essence of political community as a consensus on law. In the nineteenth and twentieth centuries, advocates of constitutional government have rediscovered the importance of consensus from experiencing the effects of losing it. On the face of it, a community of reasonable men ought to be able to solve any problem or disagreement by discussion, vote, or compromise. In practice, however, so many failures and breakdowns have occurred in the recent constitutional history of the West that there is reason to inquire into the nature of political consensus in some detail.

How large a part of the people, it is important to learn, partake of the political consensus in a given country? In a traditional society, there appears to exist a total, all-embracing consensus based on the common culture. In reality, however, the vast masses of the people merely accept their assigned roles in a passive manner, and even the ruling elites rarely consent or participate actively. Once the great upheaval of our age sets in, there are increasing numbers of leaders who actively participate and may establish consensus among themselves, although their communication with the masses of the people is still inadequate. As the great upheaval takes its course, the consensual level is gradually lowered until practically everyone participates in some manner. The final consensus then, if the widening process is not deliberately stopped at one point, is a modicum of agreement among all. This consensus is ideally based on a communications network by which all the participants continuously exchange opinions and make decisions to solve the new problems arising from time to time. Many new nations, of course, have very poor communications and are lacking in literacy.

Next, the extent of the consensus on different subjects requires discussion. No one would suggest that the consensus of a political community should extend to all matters whatsoever. But this immediately raises the question of what matters a political community may safely disagree on without fear of endangering the community.

In the United States, for example, religion has always been considered such a subject, although this has been a sphere in which dissension led to bloody civil strife elsewhere in past centuries. Such basic human rights as the right to life, liberty, and the pursuit of happiness, on the other hand, are not considered by Americans to be open to question, although they were flatly rejected by many Western governments in the centuries before the twentieth. It would appear, then, that the times change and that the disruptive character of an issue is intimately linked to the spirit of the times.

Substantive and procedural consensus Beyond this distinction, one usually differentiates between *substantive* and *procedural consensus.* Consensus on procedures includes, in particular, the rules governing the manner in which decisions are reached and the whole communications network underlying the reaching and maintenance of consensus. The consensus of these *rules of the game* is, therefore, extremely important, sometimes more so than is the consensus on substantive questions. Procedural consensus holds the body politic together and allows reasonable men to reach working compromises on substantive questions. But although some substantive questions may safely be excluded from the substantive consensus, such as religious and cultural matters, and economic interests, there should still remain enough shared values in a body politic to justify the name *community.* The overall consensus must form a dependable framework of common suppositions that one can take for granted in order to allow the normal conflicts of groups and interests to take place within the continuity of the consensual frame.

Now what about the lack or loss of consensus in some Western societies? There have been a series of constitutional breakdowns or crises that can be attributed to the absence of consensus—procedural, substantive, or both. Most of these cases fall into one of three categories: (1) the exclusion of a class of underdogs from the extension of the consensual level to the lower classes, (2) the revolt of the social forces of traditional society against the consequences of industrialization and urbanization, and (3) the decline of civic-mindedness.

Exclusion from the consensual system The exclusion of a group of underdogs from the consensual system by which a constitutional democracy makes its decisions was widespread during the days of the industrial revolution, when courts still banned labor unions as "conspiracies in restraint of trade," and the rising middle classes hesitated to extend the suffrage and other rights and freedoms to the workingman. This exclusion was so deeply resented by the burgeoning labor movement that many of the early trade unions, Socialist parties, and syndicalist movements felt they had to revolutionize society and government by force and to remodel them according to visonary, often utopian, schemes. The Socialist theories discussed in the preceding chapter and even the Marxist tenet of "class struggle" fell on receptive ears, for workingmen tended to associate capitalism, and even democracy, with the callous selfishness and indifference of many individuals.

The gulf between the increasingly powerful labor movements and the rest of society was a severe trial to consensus and constitutional government in all Western nations, the United States and the British dominions having perhaps the mildest cases of this crisis. In other Western countries, revolutions and counterrevolutions broke out, leading in some cases to civil war and dictatorship, in other words, to the complete destruction of constitutional government, as was the case in Spain, in Italy, in Germany, and in Eastern Europe. In Great Britain and Scandinavia, even the deeply ingrained traditions of consensus and constitutional government could not entirely prevent unrest and distrust, at least until Socialist parties had their turn at the helm of the state. In France and Italy, the high Communist vote since 1945 demonstrates that up to a quarter of the electorate still feels excluded and consequently responds with uncompromising hostility against the established order.

The wounds of exclusion are deep and lasting, frequently aggravated by economic misery in the midst of abundance for everybody else, and they rarely heal within a single generation. Beyond the labor problems of old, there is often also exclusion of racial or ethnic minorities from political and economic participation. Frequently, organized labor itself excludes certain groups of people, such as Negroes or migratory farm laborers. These problems can be found in almost every Western country, although they are usually less publicized than they are in the United States. The lack of participation in the common life of society always produces disaffection and bitter hostility toward the consensus of the society on the part of the rejected minority. After all, how can a member of a rejected group take seriously a bill of rights and constitutional liberties that he is not allowed to enjoy?

Revolt against modernity The revolt of the social forces of traditional society against the consequences of industrialization and urbanization can similarly produce extreme disaffection and revolutionary sentiment. In the Weimar Republic of Germany (1919–1933), as well as in Italy, Spain, and Eastern Europe, monarchists, aristocrats, old-style military men, and civil servants, and sometimes the church, the farmers, small businessmen, and craftsmen, were violently opposed to the developing modern society—its big cities and large industries, its labor unions and the advancement of minority rights, and its political mass parties and parliamentary democracy. Similar to the extreme left, the members of these movements not only have rejected the constitutional consensus around them but have done everything to shatter the consensus of their societies by conspiratorial activities and divisive tactics, by sowing distrust against duly constituted authority, and by exploiting existing social, economic, and political grievances. Where they came to power, as in Hitler's Germany, Mussolini's Italy, and a number of other countries, their destructive rage vented itself on political enemies, labor unions, minorities, and in aggressive war upon their neighbors. Needless to add, they replaced constitutional government with dictatorship and, in some cases, totalitarian government. Both types of consensual breakdown, exclusion and antimodernism, demonstrate the dangers to constitutional government of disaffection and rampant emotionalism over real or fancied grievances.

Decline of civic-mindedness The third kind of loss of consensus is less dramatic, but in the long run no less fatal to constitutional government. It is the decline of civic-mindedness in many modern industrial societies. In ancient Athens, democratic politics was almost a full-time job for the citizens eligible to vote in the *Ecclesia* and to serve on juries and in magistracies. Athenian citizens spent much of their day politicking, while women and slaves carried on the mundane tasks. In today's society, however, economic pursuits and private life loom so large that many people fail to keep up with public affairs. The result is a decline of civic-mindedness, which expresses itself both in nonvoting and in lagging efforts by the voters to inform themselves, not to mention the general abstention from more active forms of political participation. Nonvoting in the United States, if somewhat less in other Western democracies, has run as high as 40 percent in Presidential elections and still higher in state and local elections. Representative government becomes unrepresentative and majority rule becomes government by a minority when many voters fail to participate in the political process. Worse still, even those who vote rarely take the trouble and time to inform themselves conscientiously about issues and candidates. The inroads of private life on civic-mindedness are not limited to the United States. When large numbers of citizens no longer care to participate in the exchange of opinion and information that maintains and produces consensus, decisions fall into the hands of determined, well-organized minorities. And as some of the various roles assigned to the participants in the constitutional order, such as the role of voters, of judges, and of policy-makers, are not fulfilled, the entire system begins to crumble.

What can be done to counteract the trend toward a decline of civic-mindedness? In ancient Athens, too, democracy eventually began to suffer from the unwillingness of increasing numbers of citizens to go to the meetings of the *Ecclesia*. The government thereupon ordered public slaves to comb the streets before the meetings, carrying before them ropes freshly painted with vermillion to drive the idlers to the meeting place. Some Western democracies have considered making voting compulsory. These are poor ways of encouraging civic-mindedness. The most promising approach is a strong emphasis on civic education in the schools to build civic responsibility into the character, and recurrent campaigns to encourage civic participation in partisan politics.

PART II WESTERN POLITICAL INSTITUTIONS AND PROCESSES

Part I of this book dealt broadly with the political goals and purposes of the Western tradition over more than two thousand years. To come to grips with the political problems of today, it is necessary to take a closer look at the political institutions and processes that have been developed in the West and are frequently adopted by many of the newer nations. Western political philosophy and constitutional law led to a considerable level of refinement in the design of institutions and legal procedures during the last two centuries and, in some aspects, even earlier. Western constitution-makers and political leaders live in this world of legal institutions and political theory and understand their own actions largely in these terms of reference. Although there are different ways of approaching the study of politics, it is advisable that students of politics master the imposing edifice of the classical theories and institutional designs before they go on to more empirical methods of analysis.

Since the beginning of the twentieth century, the attention of political scientists has increasingly shifted toward recognition of the importance of group processes such as political parties, public opinion, and organized interests both inside and outside the institutional setting we call government. The political scientists, one one might say, proceeded from the study of *government* to the study of *politics*. More recently, and especially as a result of the rise of totalitarian movements and of the growing interest in the politics of the developing nations, political scientists have further broadened their focus in various ways to include the total social system, because it proved increasingly difficult to explain political phenomena without looking at aspects such as the culture and social psychology of a nation, which were once considered to be outside the legitimate scope of inquiry.

The presentation of any subject as involved as the process of government is likely to raise questions of where to start. Most presentations of government simply begin with a description of the forms of the different governmental institutions. Others again prefer to rest their presentation on a discussion of the three governmental functions familiar to the student from his high school courses in American civics—the executive, the legislative, and the judicial functions. A third type of introduction presents the subject by looking in turn at the entire political systems of four or five Western countries, then comparing them. All of these approaches have their strong points, but they also have their weaknesses.

Mere description of the forms of government, for example, may transmit an encyclopedic wealth of detailed knowledge to the student but rarely explains the whys and wherefores of government. Man is a purposive animal. He tends to look at his environment, and in particular at the instruments he has fashioned himself, largely with the questions in mind, What can I do with them? What are they good for? Modern government, in contrast to its more traditional predecessors, is no exception to this rule. Its chief purpose is the *making of policy* for the community it serves. Part II, therefore, is unified by the basic theme of policy-making.

The functional approach with its emphasis on executive, legislative, and judicial functions also has its advantages except that it tends to suggest to the student that the separation of powers, as we know it in the United States, is somehow the natural and only correct arrangement of governmental functions. It will be recalled from the preceding chapter on constitutionalism that the American preoccupation with checks and balances is not widely shared among the other constitutional democracies of the West. The separation of executive and legislative powers, in particular, has long been abandoned by the British and was hardly accepted by many other Western states. Both systems, the American separation of powers and parliamentary government in Britain and elsewhere, can be more readily understood if they are seen in their historical development and in their many variants in different countries. The actual functioning of the systems, moreover, is highly dependent on such things as the party system, the structure of interests, and the role of public opinion in each country. These considerations will determine the orientation of Chapters 7, 8, and 10.

Not all the important political institutions and processes are equally involved in the making of public policy. The chief policy-makers are the key figures of executive, legislature, political party, interest group, and public opinion. The judiciary and the administrative services generally make policy only within the confines of the policies laid down by the former. Yet the design of the judicial and administrative machinery, the quality of their personnel, and the legal fabric underlying the procedure and substance of their actions are also crucial to the performance of their respective functions, both as arms of execution and enforcement of policy and as a corrective of policy where it is needed most— where the power of government most directly affects the lives, liberty, and property of the people. There can hardly be doubt that a lack of integrity and discipline on the part of judges and civil servants (discussed in Chapter 9), will bring any republic to ruin.

The making of public policy also depends in setting and procedure on the geographic condition of the political community for which it is made. Some countries, and especially the smaller ones, are economically, socially, and politically unified enough to entrust the bulk of their policy-making to a central, nationwide representative process that handles all but the purely local concerns of government. Such countries, as for example, France, Great Britain, and Uruguay consequently have a unitary, fairly centralized form of government. Other countries are so large, thinly settled, or divided by geographic, ethnic, or religious barriers that they prefer to split their policy-making into functions that require a national set of institutions, and functions that can be handled autonomously by each incorporated regional community. These countries adopt a federal form of government, which is considered in some detail in Chapter 11, "Federalism and Unitarism." Going a step or two beyond federation are supranational international agencies such as have been established among sovereign nation-states for the purpose of making policy for selected subjects of common concern.

Throughout Part II, no effort will be made to exhaust any particular subject or to cover all the institutions of any specific country. The country-by-country approach of many texts in comparative government has many advantages ranging from "national coverage" to presenting a functioning system within its native habitat. However, this approach can rarely do full justice to each political system within the time and space available, nor will it lend itself to a truly comparative study of specific institutions. It is our purpose to supply a coherent account of the institutional heritage of modern Western government on the basis of topical comparison between different governmental systems. Instead of emphasizing exhaustive detail, we will attempt to transmit mainly the conceptual tools for an understanding of the function of the political institutions. With this equipment, it is hoped the student of politics can approach and analyze with confidence any political system based on the Western tradition.

INTRODUCTION

THE MAKING OF PUBLIC POLICY

Of the three basic functions of politics in human society (see Chapter 1), none is as prominent in the day-to-day concerns of a body politic as the process by which a certain kind of *order* is established or maintained. Within the context of modern government, this ordering process is largely identical with the *making of public policy*. Modern governments and their institutional design are judged by what policies they make, how effectively they make them, and how well their policy-making process lends itself to the larger needs and purposes of modern government.

Public policy-making is the making of decisions by a *public agency*. But this is not all. Policy-making involves a time dimension and a group process within the public agency and between the agency and its public. If policy-making is to be sound, it requires well-established procedures and means of ascertaining the nature of a problem, of thinking up solutions, and of finding out if past measures were successful.

Public policy, finally, requires a well-designed institutional framework which is tied into the representative process and allows for consultation with any party likely to be affected by it. The examples of executives and legislative policy-making in a constitutional democracy will demonstrate this in some detail.

The flow of policy-making

To clarify the concept of policy-making further, it is desirable to arrive at a definition of its chief aspects. Policy in the broadest sense of the word is the deliberate conduct of one entity, a person, a group, or an agency toward another entity, a person, a group, or an agency, over a period of time. A person with a policy may not be very conscious of how and why he is acting as he does. An organized group is more likely to be conscious of the procedures by which it makes policy, especially if internal disagreements frequently occur. A public agency amidst the pressures and crosspressures of organized interests and the representative process of modern democratic government can hardly be unaware that its policy is made up of a long series of individual decisions in which it may often play little more than the role of a broker among the different interests. The unspoken assumption behind any study of policy-making is that even large groups and complex governmental agencies are capable of making policy with the same amount of rational and unambiguous intent as an individual person, or, in other words, that they are capable of thinking and acting with one mind. Such an assumption, naturally, places an enormous burden on the design of institutions, especially if a policy is attributed to an entire governmental system. Yet every day, newspapers will speak of such things as the policy of the United States government toward Laos, or the policy of the Congress toward the steel industry, even when the actual policy followed may resemble a political football that is being punted to and fro between the executive branch and Congress, or between the two houses of Congress, or among the committees and prominent members of either house.

Who makes the policy? A public policy may be ascribed to a specific agency or an officeholder, such as the United States Interstate Commerce Commission or the British prime minister. In practice, it is often very difficult to find out to whom to attribute a particular policy. For example, when British Prime Minister Anthony Eden, in the middle of the Hungarian revolution of 1956, gave the orders for the Suez invasion, it was not readily apparent to outsiders whether this was his decision alone or that of the British Cabinet or of a small group of Tory leaders. The Labour opposition blamed the "die-hard reactionaries" or the entire Conservative party, which at the time held a majority in the House of Commons. To the Egyptians, the responsibility seemed to lie with the entire British people, or with the "colonialist-imperialistic" powers. The Communists attributed the Suez invasion to a conspiracy of "the capitalists" and "imperialist warmongers." People with lively imaginations could, indeed, think up any number of sinister secret societies or conspiracies behind the invasion. This example shows not only the difficulty of allocating responsibility for governmental action but also some of the uncertainty about learning the identity of the origin or the makers of particular policies.

Addressee of a public policy   A particular public policy usually has a definite addressee, a person, group, agency, subject, or foreign state toward whom it is directed. This holds true even if the policy should be one of ignoring a problem or denying recognition to a foreign government. The policy usually derives its generic name from the addressee, such as labor policy, farm surplus policy, or civil rights policy.

An important part of political science research during the last three decades has concerned itself with the content of American public policies in fields of domestic policy. Increasingly, there has also been comparative study of the various economic, social, and cultural policies of different modern governments. The foreign policies of the great powers have always been a subject of interest to historians since the days when the Athenian historian Thucydides (460–400 B.C.) wrote the history of the Peloponnesian War. Governments and governmental agencies have, of course, always concerned themselves with the careful consideration of alternative policies. It should be noted, however, that modern governments have far better resources at their disposal for knowing past policies, considering present alternatives, and estimating future trends and needs of policy-making as compared to their predecessors of a mere 50 or 150 years ago when census data were barely beginning to be collected and policy-making procedures were often crude.

Dynamic nature of the policy-making process   The third aspect of the making of public policy concerns itself with the dynamic nature of the policy-making process. A specific policy is usually composed of a series of decisions over a period of time. Each decision is the result of a process of interaction between individuals, organized groups, and various public agencies, involving consultations, conferences, smaller decisions, communications, and various pressures and maneuvers by interested parties. This process is quite normal in a free society and likely to take place even without the slightest governmental encouragement as long as a reasonable amount of publicity attends governmental actions in the making. The right of petitioning government for grievances, the holding of public hearings, and an inquisitive free press usually give the interested parties sufficient opportunity and early warning of pending governmental action, if it did not, indeed, originate with them.

If the making of public policy to bring effective pressure to bear where and when it matters, and if the resulting policy is to be a public policy—that is, the policy of a government elected by a majority to govern on behalf of all the people, not merely that of these special interests—then the flow of policy-making has to include certain basic phases in order to be fair to all concerned. There is general agreement about what these steps are, although the flow charts suggested vary in some details.

Steps of public policy-making

1. *Taking official notice* Policy-making begins when government takes official notice of a matter, a situation, or a problem. Such a matter might be brought to its attention by one of the policy-makers in executive or legislature, by an administrative agency, by an interest group, by the press, or by the public at large. The matter could involve existing laws or policies, or the regulation of an entirely new field not hitherto touched upon by governmental action.

Taking official notice of a matter may be limited to a statement as vague as, say, "The smoking of marijuana is getting to be a problem." And the commitment to taking some action may go no further initially than saying, "Something ought to be done about it." But even at this step, and more so in the later phases of policy-making, a prime consideration stems from the rules inherent in the constitutional order. What level of government—local, regional, or national—should concern itself with the problem? What particular agency has jurisdiction over it? What basic limitations, such as can be found in the bills of rights of all Western democracies, will inhibit governmental action with respect to the problem at hand?

2. *Fact-finding and consultation* The second step in the flow of policy-making involves both fact-finding and consultation with the interested parties. It is difficult in practice to separate these two, for two reasons: (1) The opinions and attitudes of interested parties in a democracy are among the most important kinds of information required for the making of public policy. Although government may have the power to enforce almost any policy it decides upon, there is very little point in ignoring or offending the sentiments of the

community affected by the new policy. For reasons of economy in government, if for no other reason, it is far better to rely on the voluntary cooperation of a public satisfied with a new policy, or at least a public satisfied that it has been heard, than to rely on enforcement alone. (2) The expert knowledge needed for intelligent governmental action is most likely to be found among the interested parties who are anxious to offer their assistance. To return to the example of marijuana-smoking, who would be more qualified to venture an opinion on its legislative regulation than school authorities, the police, probation and prison officials, youth organizations, and parents? Naturally, the quality of sources of information is crucial to policy-making, and there can hardly be enough effort made to secure independent expertise and to balance antagonistic sources of information against one another.

This second step may involve the holding of public hearings, consultation with organized interests and other agencies, efforts by legislative investigating committees, executive investigators or commissions of inquiry, and invitations to independent experts or specialists to contribute their knowledge. This is also the province of legislative reference services and of the staff of legislative committees.

3. Formulation of alternative policies   The third step is the formulation of alternative policies by the public agencies and often also by the interested parties. At this point, we may say that the *input* of information is tentatively infused with a will, or rather with various desires to control or refashion the subject under consideration. Even if a policy proposal intends only to make a rule of practices that are already customary, there is still that element of a governmental will that can be enforced. At this stage also, there is a tendency for camps pro and con to crystallize, for issues to be stated, and for lines to be drawn for the coming debate. Often the formulation of policies is done by administrators who are not only familiar with the subject but also are aware of the limited choice of practical measures to achieve the various objectives proposed.

4. Public deliberation   The fourth step involves the process of public deliberation on the alternative policies proposed. This phase largely takes place within the governmental institutions and according to the procedures laid down in the constitution and the customs and usages that have grown up around it. The interests and persons promoting a measure and those opposing it battle each other every step of the way. In a political system such as that of the United States with its many checks and balances in government, hostile interests can use every single check, from powerful legislative committees to the Presidential veto and judicial review to oppose an action. In a more streamlined system, on the other hand, such as that of Great Britain, the majority will is so well organized that it possesses what amounts to a practical monopoly on the policy-making process. Nevertheless, the British system allows the major opposing interests their day in court, on the floor of the House of Commons, and in the press without permitting them to obstruct the governmental business. Due to the complexities of deliberation under most Western constitutions, the entire process takes place on many levels and in a number of settings, such as in several committees and on the floors of both legislative houses, in the executive branch, in party and interest group conferences outside government, in the readers' letters and on the editorial pages of newspapers and magazines, at public meetings and, possibly, even among the issues of election campaigns going on at the same time.

5. *Authoritative decision* The fifth step of the flow of policy-making involves making an authoritative decision. A typical example is the final passage of a law by both houses of a legislature and its signing by the chief executive. This is the point at which the choice between the alternative proposals has been made and one policy has been designated as "the public policy." Since a law is a kind of command backed by the power to enforce it, this then may appear to be the final product, the *output* of the policy-making machinery. As will be seen, it is not the end of the flow of policy-making.

Many legislative acts are accompanied or supplemented by administrative rule-making on a high level which may supply a very substantial part of the content of the policy. If the supplementary rules involve broad policy decisions that are likely to be made at the top of the administrative hierarchy, as distinct from decisions of a routine character at the lower levels, then they should be regarded as part and parcel of the deliberative process, along with the making of laws. Similarly, there are executive functions, such as the conduct of foreign relations, that may involve no lawmaking at all or very little of it. Yet they go through the same phases of policy-making as the legislative process, except that the deliberative stake is likely to take place among executive agencies, officials, parties, and interest groups, or even representatives of several powers. The step of making an authoritative decision marks the launching of, say, a new United States policy toward Cuba or a generally understood change of such a policy.

6. *Implementation of the policy* After the authoritative decision come two further steps in the flow whose significance may generally pale before the importance of making a decision. Yet it would

be a gross simplification to ignore them. First, there is the implementation of the policy decided on, a phase requiring both adequate means or organs and a willingness to abide by the decision made at the higher policy-making level. The implementation of a policy may well fall short of success because the policy-makers neglected to supply enough funds or an adequate array of rewards and punishments for enforcement. It may fail also because the administrators, police officers, judges, or military men entrusted with the implementation take a dim view of the policy and have ways of getting around it, either by nonenforcement or by deliberate reinterpretation. In this manner, to cite an example, American courts once nullified the clear intent of early antitrust legislation and reinterpreted the Fourteenth Amendment to permit racial segregation. It is not inconceivable, on the other hand, that the implementation of a policy may on occasion be more effective if those responsible for its implementation substitute their own proven techniques for the ones laid down by the framers of the policy, as long as the intent of the policy is maintained.

7. *Feedback* The final phase in the flow of policy-making is the feedback. When a boy in a game of tag chases another, he does not persist in his original course, but constantly adjusts his course according to the evasive maneuvers of the other boy. This constant adjustment to the changing course of his target is the result of the feedback. A public policy designed to effect certain results may similarly find its goal elusive or discover unforeseen obstacles. Hence, there should be a feedback process by which the policy-makers will be apprised of the shortcomings of their original policy, its failures, loopholes, or unintended by-products. This feedback function is frequently supplied by the implementors, who report their experiences with the administration or execution of a policy, or their questions arising from the adjudication of cases under the new policy. Interested parties, also, may petition or otherwise approach the policy-makers for a reconsideration of the decisions made.

In a sense, then, feedback is very likely to reopen the flow of policy-making from the beginning by getting the government (1) to take notice of the defects of the existing policy; (2) to have new consultations and to accept the new information along with the earlier results of fact-finding; (3) to formulate new alternative policies amending or repealing the existing policy; (4) to go once more through the stages of the deliberative process; (5) to decide on a new policy; (6) to implement this new policy; and (7) to find out how well it works.

It should be clear from this description that policy-making is a continuing process which, from beginning to end, operates in a purposive, rational manner. Therefore, it is always open to the same kind of criticisms that may apply to other kinds of purposive, human endeavor as they may occur in individual life or in the business world. This applies with particular force to political policy-making, because modern politics and government are in some ways still far behind the rational control that has long been brought into the business world and into individual life. A businessman or private individual who substitutes dreams for the reality he has to deal with is readily recognized and often victimized. People in politics, by contrast, are rarely aware of the astonishing extent to which they project their fears and dreams into their view of the political reality. Often both the leaders and the led are prisoners of the same pathetic myths and delusions.

Criteria for judging policy-making

Looking at politics from a strictly rational point of view, then, one can judge governments by the manner in which they have or have not provided for a well-thought-out flow of policy-making. They expose themselves to criticism if in their design they fail to emphasize the central role of policy-making or, to put it differently, the instrumental character of government for the common policy-making of a body politic. They also open themselves to criticism if they fail to provide adequately for all of the phases of the flow of policy-making. They may fall down, in fact, on every one of the seven steps:

1. They may fail to recognize pressing problems or, worse, burden government with tasks better left with private initiative.
2. They may court disaster by ignoring the interested parties or fail to provide for a sufficient "input" of information for their policy-making machinery.
3. They may neglect to recognize alternative courses of policy or fail to tap their full resources for the formulation of well-considered policies.
4. They may shortchange either the majority or the opposing interests during the process of deliberation.
5. They may tend to reach an authoritative decision too hastily or not at all.
6. They may suffer from the poor implementation of good policy or be unaware of the possibility of a subtle subversion of policy at the hands of the implementors.

7. They may have poor feedback or be blind to the fact that only the practice, not good will alone, can measure a policy's worth.

These standards and criteria will be encountered again and again throughout Part II of this book. Other requirements of quality might be made along lines similar to those by which one judges other purposive pursuits of man. Among these requirements might be, for example, a clarity of purpose and procedure, an economy of means, efficiency of operation, effectiveness of policies and, last, but by no means least, the moral excellence of the policy goals. Although the policy-making machinery, like all mechanisms, may be looked at largely in terms of what means are best designed to produce given ends, this does not absolve the student of politics from pondering the worth of the ends. An infamous policy, such as the killing of Jews by the Nazis, or the Jim Crow policies in the South, will become, if anything, more infamous by being clearly conceived and efficiently carried out. A petty or selfish goal, if magnified by the policy-making apparatus of a great nation, will hardly gain greatness thereby. The policy machinery of modern government, like all instruments marshaling vast powers in frail human hands, will never do more, nor less, than to show up the moral quality of the minds that wield it. Policy-making is a moral challenge as great as any that the twentieth century has presented.

CHAPTER 7 LAWMAKING AND LEGISLATURES

The chief instrument for the making of public policy during the last century and a half has been legislative enactments by duly elected legislatures. Laws, large and small, entire civil or criminal law codes, laws to make uniform the court procedures or local government institutions of a new nation-state, laws to give a pension to an invalid war hero, laws to build rivers and harbors with the national tax revenues—a steady flow of laws of every description provides the lifeline of modern governmental activity. This was not always so; in fact, the British Parliament before the nineteenth century was preoccupied with functions other than lawmaking.

It is essential to distinguish between laws and *the law* as the existing fabric of customary law, the vast body of judicial precedents and past enactments. In the present discussion, we shall not be concerned with this legal fabric, which exists at the time the policy-makers formulate a new policy. Instead, the exclusive interest will be focused on how new laws, as instruments of policy, come to pass, and how this legislative process has been organized in various Western systems of government. The policy-making role of political parties, interest groups, and executive-legislative relations will be examined in detail in later chapters.

THE FORM AND ORGANIZATION OF LEGISLATURES

At the center of the "arrangement of offices," as Aristotle used to call it, all Western systems of government feature today a parliament which plays the chief role in the process of making policy by legislation. Although the legislatures of the different countries vary in organization and operation, according to national traditions and in their nonlegislative functions, there are fundamental likenesses among the parliaments of the United States, Great Britain, France, West Germany, and others, which we shall discuss in some detail.

Bicameralism or unicameralism?

The first question of the institutional design that needs to be raised relates to the choice between unicameralism and bicameralism. The constitutional tradition of responsibility clearly suggests that there should be but one legislative assembly in which the popularly elected representatives of the people carry out the will of their constituents to whom, at the next election, they will have to answer for their deeds and omissions. However, only two Western countries— Denmark since 1954 and New Zealand since 1950—and some state legislatures in federal systems, such as Nebraska in the United States, Queensland in Australia, and most of the *Laender* (states) diets of the West German Republic are unicameral. There are a number of approximations of unicameralism; such as the Norwegian *Storting*, which is elected as one body, although it divides subsequently into two bodies for purposes of legislation: the *Odelsting* and the smaller *Lagting*, a kind of permanent senior committee of the whole parliament. The British House of Commons has won such preponderance over the House of Lords, especially since 1911, that the British system similarly comes close to being unicameral in practice.

To the constitutional tradition of checks and balances, of course, bicameralism appears very desirable. Not only can an additional legislative assembly, an upper house,[1] provide a review of the legislative activity, or a check on the "popular passions" and on "the spirit of faction" in the lower house, but it can also bring to bear on

---

[1] Using the terms "first chamber" for the popularly elected and "second chamber" for the upper house can give rise to misunderstanding in comparative study because such countries as Sweden and the Netherlands, for example, assign these names to the two houses of their parliaments in the reverse manner.

the legislative process elements of social organization other than in-
dividualism and mass parties. While, for example, the United States
House of Representatives, the Canadian House of Commons, the
West German *Bundestag*, and the Swiss *Nationalrat* all represent
the individual citizens of their respective countries, the United States
Senate, the Canadian Senate, the West German *Bundesrat*, and the
Swiss Council of States were meant to represent the territorial units
of these federations—the states, provinces, *Laender*, or cantons.
Until recently the upper houses of most American state legislatures
similarly represented counties as if they were the states of a federal
system. But whereas American state senators are directly elected,
a more common procedure among Western upper houses is indirect
election. The upper chamber of the Swedish *Riksdag*, and those of
the Dutch and Belgian parliaments, for example, are elected by the
county and city councils for staggered terms. The Senate (or Council
of the Republic) of the Third (1871–1940), Fourth (1946–1958), and
Fifth (1958–   ) Republics of France have similarly been elected
indirectly by electoral bodies based on local government units. In all
of these cases, the intent of the constitutional design appears to be to
juxtapose an elite of local or provincial notables to the influential
men and organizations that control national politics in the capital
of the country.

There are two further approaches to the composition of an upper
chamber which put a different slant on the basic problem. One is
that of the British House of Lords, which at first glance appears to
be a gathering of men selected according to aristocratic principles
belonging to another age. On closer examination, however, more
than half the peers, not to mention the high judicial and church
officials in it, turn out to be of twentieth-century vintage. They often
represent, in other words, men of high individual merit—former
prime ministers, ambassadors, governors-general, writers, or scientists. The members of the Canadian Senate, appointed for lifetime,
also are supposed to represent an elite. The Royal Italian Senate
before Mussolini's time similarly constituted, in the form of lifetime
appointees of the king, an attempt to balance with "quality" the
reign of sheer numbers of votes in the Chamber of Deputies.

Another view of "quality," in the sense of the elements of composition, but similarly juxtaposed to the representation of individuals, has tried to represent the great vocational and functional groups
of society in so-called economic or social councils. A good example
of such an upper house can be found in Ireland. It is composed of
eleven appointees of the prime minister, six elected by the universities, and equal numbers from five panels representing culture

and education, agriculture and fisheries, labor, industry and commerce, and public services. The Weimar Republic of Germany (1919–1933) and the Fourth and Fifth Republics of France have used economic councils as third chambers which, unlike the Irish Senate, were limited to an advisory capacity in the legislative process.

Once bicameralism is adopted, an issue of great importance is whether the two houses are to be equal in their legislative powers. It would be a cardinal violation of the principles of democracy if the popularly elected lower house were in a weaker position. The opposite, a predominant lower house, would be in keeping with democratic precepts. If there is to be a check on the majorities of the lower house, or if other, nonquantitative elements of social organization are to balance the reign of numbers, it is soley a matter of the discretion of the framers of Western constitutions how strong this check shall be. The British House of Lords is given a delaying period of only one month in the case of a budget bill and twelve months in the case of ordinary legislation, after which the bill becomes law in the form in which the House of Commons passed it. The German *Bundesrat*, despite the emphasis on federalism in the West German Basic Law, has on many subjects of legislation merely a suspensive veto, which can be overridden by large majorities in the lower house. The Dutch upper house, to mention a third method of weakening the check on the popularly elected chamber, is not allowed to amend bills but only to accept or reject them.

The United States Congress, with its equality between the Senate and the House of Representatives, and the Australian parliament are rather conspicuous exceptions to what appears to be the rule. If anything, the United States Senate would seem to be in practice the stronger house. Then there is the example of the Italian, the Swiss, and the Swedish systems, in which the two houses in varying manner share even the control of the executive. More often, however, the parliamentary type of executive-legislative relation makes for the strengthening of one chamber, the lower house, at the expense of the other.

This trend toward focusing responsibility more clearly need not detract from the usefulness of even a weak chamber of review. In fact, being less involved with the partisan alignment for or against the government often allows an upper house to develop its peculiar nature better to the benefit of the entire system of government. The British House of Lords, for example, is a rather weak and anachronistic upper house, although its effectiveness as a chamber of review is generally acknowledged. Reformers anxious to replace it or abolish it outright, however, have come to realize that either alternative would upset the delicate balance of governmental relationships in Great Britain. Abolition would make the House of Commons too strong and any replacement for the House of Lords would be likely to be stronger than the present institution and, therefore, more of a check on the House of Commons than the reformers consider desirable.

Internal organization

The second question of the design of legislatures concerns their internal organization into groups capable of deliberating and of concerting action, such as standing committees or partisan groups. Since a great many different subjects come before a parliament, a division into several smaller, more specialized "little legislatures" seems quite logical. However, there is much more to it.

The United States Congress The standing committees of the two houses of the United States Congress on such subjects as foreign relations, agriculture, the armed services, and so on, are the main legislative agents of these houses and can make or break almost any piece of legislation. Each house tends to accept what its committees lay before it. Committee chairmen are among the most powerful men in Congress. Each house of Congress, therefore, presents a picture of considerable decentralization and fragmentation of legislative power which, under the constitutional tradition of responsibility, is meant to be exercised in a unified manner. In the House of Representatives, the Rules Committee provides a focus of centralized control that can hold back or advance bills, open them up to crippling amendments, or protect them against changes. Before 1911, the Speaker of the House also participated in this controlling function by chairing the Rules Committee and appointing all the members of the standing committees. The seniority system of selecting the members and the chairmen of all committees, on the other hand, detracts from the representative character of such legislative leadership.

Congressional parties are another kind of grouping capable of producing concerted action. The members of both houses are generally elected under the label of a political party. In each house the majority party receives all the committee chairmanships and proportionate representation on all the committees. In the House, the majority also elects the Speaker. Both parties of each house have floor leaders, whips, and steering committees. Yet the prevalence of smaller factions, the paucity of means by which the party leaders can persuade their followers, and the prominence of other groupings and power centers in both houses decisively weaken partisan control. In summary, the internal organization of both houses of the United States Congress frustrates the coordination of legislative policy by an unusual degree of decentralization and fragmentation of power that in practice have led to a certain amount of Presidential legislative leadership despite the doctrine of separation of powers.

The British House of Commons   The organization of the British House of Commons provides an extreme contrast to that of the United States Congress. Following the establishment of parliamentary sovereignty in the seventeenth century, the British House of Commons for a while had fairly strong standing committees on topics such as privileges and elections, religion, grievances, the courts, and trade. With the rise of cabinet leadership from among the membership of Parliament, the Cabinet became the center of power and the topical committees declined, except for a few of more technical function. Today, the House of Commons has only nontopical committees called by the letters of the alphabet, A, B, C, and so forth. The Speaker of the House of Commons, a neutral figure in the partisan sense, routinely assigns bills to them for their consideration and appoints their chairmen who, similarly, are supposed to be neutral guardians of parliamentary practice. Because these standing committees are not topical, they never become the gatherings of interested politicians and experts, which congressional committees invariably are.

Strong partisan control in the House of Commons further contributes to the centralization of legislative authority in the leadership of the well-disciplined majority party in the Cabinet, and in the shadow cabinet of the equally well-disciplined opposition. The centralization of partisan control rests not only on tradition and on the relative smallness and social unity of the British Isles, but even more on the control of the party leadership over the nominations on the party ticket, which, unlike American practice, are not encumbered with primary elections and residence rules. The British habit of voting for the party rather than for the candidate and the powerful, extraparliamentary party hierarchies round out the picture of unified "party government" in Britain. Against this background, the average backbencher in the House of Commons has little choice but to follow faithfully the party line. He can, of course, communicate his dissent to the leadership via the party whips and make his vote felt in the caucus meetings. But, once a decision has been made, he is under severe penalties not to bolt the party on a formal vote.

The French Parliament The internal organization of other Western legislatures can be classified as falling somewhere between the American and British extremes. The French Chamber of Deputies of the Third Republic, and the National Assembly of the Fourth Republic rather resembled the American model in having powerful topical committees and weak partisan control. The latter was due in part to the French multiparty system, in part to the unstable organization of most parties, with the exception of Communists and Socialists. Thus in France the parliamentary executive, the center of power in Great Britain, has always had to be based on a frail coalition of several parties and could hardly assert itself against the other power centers. The constitution of the Fifth Republic curtailed the general powers of the National Assembly substantially, weakened its committees, and separated the greatly strengthened Cabinet from it. These changes have centralized control over the legislative process, but also centered it outside of the National Assembly. The presence of a strong Gaullist faction in the National Assembly facilitates the legislative activities of the Cabinet. The peculiar character of de Gaulle's and now Pompidou's leadership and the two-headed nature of the executive do not permit a comparison between this arrangement and British party government.

Both houses of the French parliament under the Third, Fourth, and Fifth Republics had a *bureau* consisting of a president and a number of vice presidents and other officers. This institution is typical of continental European legislatures. The presiding officers represent the duly constituted and officially registered partisan groups and have the function of scheduling and expediting the business before the house. Needless to say, their importance as a center of legislative authority depends largely on the number and importance of the partisan groups in an assembly. The more groups the less authority.

The West German Bundestag The organization of the West German *Bundestag* approaches the British rather than the French or American model. There is a strong tradition of party unity and discipline that relies on active participation and frequent caucus meetings. From this, one might expect the British type of perfect fusion of executive and legislative branches by party government. However, the majority parties in the *Bundestag* have on occasion exhibited considerable independence and even opposition to their own Cabinet, especially when the deputies felt that they were not consulted on a question of policy. The equivalent of the French assembly *bureau* is here called the Council of Elders. There are also topical committees in which experts and elected representatives of organized interests tend to entrench themselves as in the corresponding ministries. But the party ties are so strong in the committee meetings that the committees are still far from becoming the centers of legislative power that they are in the United States.

The Italian Chamber of Deputies The Italian Chamber of Deputies resembles in many respects the organization of the French parliament before 1940. Party cohesion, outside the Communist party, is weak and vacillating. Committees are powerful and are frequently even given authority, *in sede deliberante* (with authority to decide), to legislate. The President of the Chamber is in a fairly strong position. The individual legislators enjoy a degree of independence found, perhaps, only in the United States Congress. In no other legislature of a large Western country can the members introduce so many private member bills, and nowhere else are they allowed to vote in secret ballots, which allow legislators to bolt their party with impunity on important votes.

Physical settings of legislatures

A third way of looking at the form and organization of Western legislatures is to reflect on the arrangement in the legislative chamber of the facilities for seating the different political parties, the government—if it is allowed to enter the legislature at all—the opposition, the presiding officer, formal speakers, and representatives of committees reporting on matters under their consideration. The physical setting of a legislature can tell us much about the enacting of the legislative drama.

The British House of Commons The British House of Commons, with over 600 members one of the largest lower houses of the world,[2] has seating for only 346 of its members, sometimes forcing the rest to stand or to seek seats in the galleries (see Figure 7.1). In 1943, when the Chamber of the Commons was destroyed by bombs and had to be rebuilt, the government insisted on retaining its original size, because, as Prime Minister Churchill put it:

If the House is big enough to contain all its Members, nine-tenths of its Debates will be conducted in the depressing atmosphere of an almost empty or half-empty Chamber . . . the conversational style

---

[2] Some of the more prominent lower houses, such as the United States House of Representatives, the French National Assembly, and the West German *Bundestag*, have between 400 and 500 members; another group composed of the Swedish, Belgian, and Canadian lower house, between 200 and 300 members; and many others have fewer than 200 deputies.

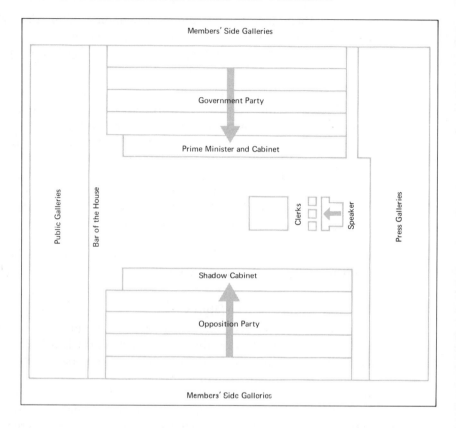

Figure 7.1   Seating arrangement in the House of Commons.

in which so much of our business is done . . . requires a fairly small space, and there should be on great occasions a sense of crowd and urgency . . . a sense that great matters are being decided.

The seats available, moreover, are arranged in the form of five benches, running along both long sides of a rectangular chamber, upon which the members of the majority party and those of the opposition sit, facing each other across the aisle. At one end of the aisle is the throne of the neutral, robed Speaker and a long table at which three clerks sit in gown and wig, all looking down the aisle. The government party sits on the benches to the right of the Speaker. The Cabinet sits on the innermost bench on that side, with the "backbenchers" physically and mentally behind them. On the other side, separated only by the long table and the aisle, is the leader of the opposition and his shadow cabinet, similarly backed by the rank and file of the opposition backbenchers. This setting provides the pattern basic to debate in the House of Commons—the direct confrontation of the two sets of national leaders and their parties. Any member speaking in the House, save the Speaker, is automatically constrained to take his position frankly for or against the government. There is no transition or shading possible between being for or against, as in chambers with a semicircular arrangement. Neither can a member of the House harangue his audience from a raised platform or a rostrum. He has to speak from his seat, when recognized by the Speaker, and generally faces the benches of the other major party, unless he belongs to a third party or if overcrowding and coming late placed him somewhere other than where the seating arrangement intended him to be.

One should, perhaps, pause here and consider also the aspects of the British system that tend to modify such an extreme, black-and-white confrontation between government and opposition. Above all, there is the concept of the *loyal opposition*, whose leader receives a salary from Her Majesty's government for his role of opposing within the framework of agreement and consensus. The idea of a loyal opposition encourages constructive, well-considered criticism and at the same time discourages supporters of the government from accusing critics of disloyalty. Then there are also the many ways in which the two major parties cooperate in the House of Commons, especially through the "usual channels," that is, through contacts between the whips of both parties. Such cooperation is particularly notable with respect to the making of the agenda. Majority and opposition whips regularly confer on what to discuss on the floor of the House, when to discuss it, and how much of the precious time of the House of Commons to allot to the debate of each item. Furthermore, there is the elaborate ceremonial of the House, the polite forms of address, and the deeply ingrained customs for the conduct of debate. All of these taken together have given the House of Commons a sense of solidarity not unlike that of a closely knit club and have tamed many a rebellious new member of Parliament.

Finally, there is the Speaker, guardian of fair play and dramatic director of the great confrontation, who, in comparison to American practice, has a wide array of powers over the debate through his rulings on procedure, his authority to select amendments to a bill for debate and to forestall closure. Despite the superior voting power of the government, he is supposed to refrain from favoring either the opposition or the majority party. His guardianship of fair play and his defense of the privileges of the House against the growing

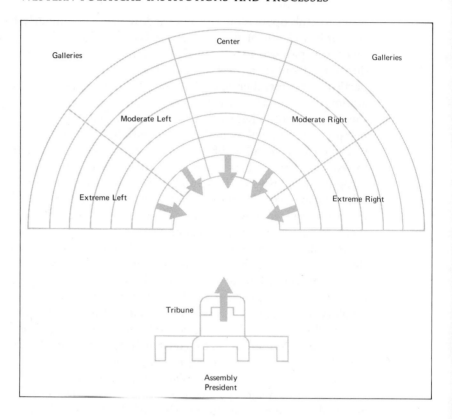

Figure 7.2   Seating arrangement in the French National Assembly.

might of the Cabinet, however, have made him increasingly a guarantor of the right of the opposition to be heard on every item of which it chooses to make an issue. The minority position of the opposition receives further aid and comfort from the powerful British press, which critically observes the conduct of the government during the give-and-take of the debates with the opposition and gives many a clue to the final judges of the governmental record—the voters.

The French National Assembly   The physical setting of the other much-imitated legislature of the Western world, the French National Assembly, presents a marked contrast to the British model (see Figure 7.2). Its shape is that of a semicircular amphitheater, with rising tiers of benches. The foremost benches are reserved to the cabinet ministers and representatives of committees presenting bills for debate. All face the elevated desk of the Assembly President, which is in the center of the semicircle and flanked by the desks of secretaries. In front of the President's desk is the raised tribune, the rostrum from which deputies launch sparkling feats of oratory addressed to the entire chamber. There is no confrontation between government party or coalition and opposition. Instead, the many French parties are seated in a spectrum of many gradations, from the right to the left. The words "right wing," "center," and "left wing," in fact, date from the first National Assembly of 1789 at the time of the French Revolution, when the nobility of the old regime took the seats of honor to the right of the President's chair, while the middle-class advocates of drastic reform sat to the left. Today, these words signify a spectrum of modern attitudes and ideologies so widespread that only the middle portion shares the fundamental loyalty to constitutional order and consensus on the rules of the game which one finds in Britain's responsible majority and loyal opposition. Both extremes in France, a disloyal opposition of Communists and Fascists, are striving mainly to obstruct the government and to make a mockery of parliamentary democracy. Whenever a deputy orates from the tribune in an impassioned manner, the reaction ripples through the chamber according to the ideological shadings rather than as indication of support or opposition to the government. Also, unlike the psychological Rubicon that a British M.P. has to cross when he walks across the aisle to join the other party, a French deputy can wander in and out of the many shadings of partisan opinion with great ease. The ministers, finally, sitting alone on their benches and frequently next to the *rapporteur* of a hostile committee, have none of the "backing" of their own party behind them. On the contrary, they often find themselves the last outpost of the distrusted executive branch, surrounded by the aroused wrath of the entire chamber, which peppers them with *interpellations*[3] and general debates raising the *question of confidence*. It is small wonder that so often, under the Third and Fourth Republics, the ministers quit all too willingly, never quite in their heart of hearts having left the Assembly, to join the dreaded Leviathan, the executive.

Legislatures of other countries   Although seating arrangements are relevant to the life of a legislature, their significance should not be overestimated. Both in Canada and in the Netherlands, for example,

---

[3] An interpellation is a formal question put to a government minister, who has to answer it before the Assembly. His answer is followed by a general debate, ending with a vote. A negative vote at this point is generally construed as a vote of no confidence.

a shape of the lower house similar to the British House of Commons is used. But in Canada each member of the House of Commons has his own seat, whereas in the Netherlands, the different parties sit, according to their political shades of opinion, from left to right. In both houses of the United States Congress, tradition has it that Democrats sit to the right and Republicans to the left of the presiding officer, although their chambers are semicircular. The West German *Bundestag*, whose parties sit from left to the right in an oblong chamber with curved rows of desks, has been toying with the idea of elongating its wings into the form of a horseshoe so that the two major parties, government and opposition, will sit face-to-face.

THE LEGISLATIVE PROCESS

The legislative process is only a part, albeit a very important part, of the entire process of policy-making. Its peculiar place in the making of public policy is demonstrated best by relating legislative activity to steps 1 through 5 of policy-making discussed earlier.

Taking official notice: origin and initiation of laws

The first step by which the policy-makers take notice of a problem in most cases is only informally related to legislation. A large part of the introduction of new subjects of policy-making occurs in connection with the election of the lawmakers. At the time of elections, issues are raised by the contending political parties, by organized interests, in the public opinion media, and by the public at large, which often lead to specific promises and programs to which the lawmakers commit themselves when elected. Other new subjects of legislative interest are brought to the attention of the legislators after the election, by lobbyists for organized interests, and through the channels of public opinion and party organizations outside the legislature.

The third, and possibly the most important, source of new subjects of legislative interest is the executive branch of government, which, in both parliamentary and presidential systems, is vitally involved in the elections and the issues springing therefrom. It is noteworthy also that in Great Britain, in the member countries of the British Commonwealth of Nations, and in most European legislatures, the vast majority of bills that are proposed come from the executive branch. Seven out of every eight bills before the British House of Commons, for example, are government bills.

Three out of every four bills passed by the West German *Bundestag* are cabinet bills. In the United States, the majority of bills are now formulated by the executive branch of the government. Unlike the practice in countries having a Cabinet system of government, no member of the executive branch may directly introduce a bill into Congress. All bills must be introduced through a Senator, a Representative, or a standing committee, generally by the committee chairman. This difference in the mode of operation is due in large part to the separation of powers in the United States Constitution which, by barring the President from exercising more than indirect legislative leadership, encourages a separate set of party leaders in the House and the Senate. However, there is also the example of the French Third and Fourth Republics and the Italian Republic in which, despite parliamentary government, a considerable part of the work of the lower house consisted of bills initiated by individual members and the parties of the parliament.

Some Western constitutions also give the right to initiate legislative action to advisory bodies such as the economic councils or, by means of the initiative, to the people at large. The latter device was developed to some perfection in Switzerland and on the West Coast of the United States, although it can also be found in many other constitutions, such as that of Italy. In the state of California an "indirect initiative petition" signed by a number of registered voters exceeding 5 percent of the last gubernatorial vote will introduce a measure in the legislature. If the legislature fails to act within 40 days, the measure must be placed directly on the ballot, and it will become constitutional law if approved by a majority of the voters. The initiative in Switzerland dates back to the 1830s and crystallized in 1891 as follows: A petition signed by 50,000 citizens eligible to vote can introduce a specific matter or a draft amendment to the constitution to the legislature, which within three years must submit a draft corresponding to the intent of the petitioners, to a vote of the people at large and in cantons. At the cantonal level the initiative is also used for ordinary legislation.

Fact-finding and consultation

Fact-finding and consultation are in large part distributed throughout the stages of the legislative process and frequently take place in an informal manner or during elections. However, there are formal procedures and institutions to insure the effectiveness of both the consultations with interested groups and the gathering of information. The standing committees of the two houses of the United

States Congress, and of the West German *Bundestag* and the French and Italian lower house, for example, provide the concentration of experts and interest-group-oriented legislators at key points in the legislative process; this goes a long way toward facilitating fact-finding and consultation. Informal contacts between legislators and lobbyists have become one of the most pervasive aspects of representative government everywhere. The organized interests often seek to create a public climate favorable to their cause by advertising and other forms of publicity of which the legislator and his constituents sooner or later become aware.

The political parties often provide privileged access to the legislative process to representatives of organized interests who, by campaign contributions, by consistent support, or by personal friendship, have gained an inside track. British political parties, for example, have topical committees which, in consultation with certain interest groups, operate not much differently from legislative committees. Most political parties employ such committees for the drafting of specific planks in campaign platforms. The Christian Democrats of West Germany have a permanent committee structure in which the representatives of interest groups and the party functionaries together determine the course of future farm policy, labor policy, economic policy, and so on. In the same country, the parties will also, on occasion, nominate an interest group official on their party ticket to the *Bundestag*, where he can then join the appropriate committee and take part in the deliberation of policies of interest to his group.

The topical ministries of the executive branch similarly contribute to the information and consultation about measures that fall into their particular field of specialization. Both when a bill originates in the executive branch and when it requires guidance by the Cabinet for its passage, as in Great Britain, the expert knowledge at the command of the topical ministries, as well as their contact with the appropriate interest groups, come to bear on the content of the bill.

In some Western countries there are "regular channels" through which legislative proposals travel as a matter of course. An instructive example is provided by West German practice. Here, Cabinet bills, say, on labor-management relations, routinely follow the triangles of cooperation among the Labor and Economics Ministries, the labor and economic policy committees of the *Bundestag*, and the trade unions and employers' associations. This triangle of topical ministry, topical committee, and interest group is fairly well established in modern pluralistic societies. In West Germany, however, the presence of federalism and the participation of the state governments in the administration and, through the *Bundesrat* (upper house), in the making of federal laws, add a further complication: the labor-management bill also has to be sent to the labor and economics ministers of each *Land* (state), who have their own triangles with the appropriate *Landtag* committees and *Land*-wide interest groups. After a decision by the *Land* Cabinet the bill goes back to Bonn for a vote in the labor and economics committees of the *Bundesrat*, each of which is composed of the topical *Land* ministers or their representatives, and finally for a vote by the entire upper house.

To help with fact-finding and consultations, most Western legislatures use investigating committees for the purpose of gathering information relevant to legislative activity. Some investigating committees concentrate chiefly on the conduct of the executive branch; others concentrate more on activities in society that may be of legislative interest. American investigating committees have inquired, for example, into lobbying and its regulation. The British House of Commons, by contrast, undertakes none of the investigating such as American congressional and state legislative committees carry on. The House of Commons has two standing committees, Public Accounts and Estimates, that are concerned with the financial conduct of the executive and have the power to send for persons and papers. There are also inquiries by the Royal Commissions, appointed by the Crown, which are comparable to some of the Presidential commissions in the United States, such as the Hoover Commissions or the Commission on Civil Disorders. Legislative committees and executive agencies in the United States also hold frequent hearings to which interested groups and executive officials may be invited to supply opinions and information relevant to the policy under consideration. French standing committees can even summon government ministers before them. Finally, individual legislators, legislative committees, and political parties often have a research staff and the services of a legislative reference service or its equivalent at their disposal to help with the gathering of information. Such legislative services and staff are particularly well developed in the United States. If all else fails in any Western country, the individual legislator can always gather his own facts by keeping in touch with his constituency and by burning the midnight oil.

Formulation of alternative policies

The formulation of alternative policies is difficult to isolate as a specific step in the policy-making process because in one form or another it goes on from the beginning to the end of the process. Since policy formulation is a creative act to which human society everywhere attaches great prestige, considerable rewards await political leaders, administrators, and judges, as well as political parties and interest groups, that formulate policies of high quality. Good policy proposals can be the very essence of leadership and political success in a democracy.

Fact-finding and consultation do not necessarily precede the formulation of policy. The initial formulation of policy normally is done in the minds of administrators, legislators, or other public figures after a considerable amount of experience with the problem in question. Quite frequently the seminal concept of the new policy may be derived a priori from the logic of other extant policies, from a partisan philosophy, or from something called "the best American tradition" or "the best French manner," as the case may be. In either instance, there is likely to be a need for the further gathering of information and for extensive consultation with interested groups regarding the acceptability of the policy. If a policy is formulated by an interest group, moreover, there is often a process of policy-making at work which in microcosm resembles that of government itself. When, for example, the Federation of British Industry, or the American National Association of Manufacturers, or their French or West German equivalents try to formulate, say, a policy on foreign trade, they also must take into account a great variety of diverging economic group interests within their own organization and frequently must consult with other organizations such as the respective national chambers of commerce, farm interests, and organized labor, not to mention governmental agencies and key personnel. The officers of an interest group that wishes to secure adoption of the policy often have to spend much time and effort first on selling their own membership on the policy and then on rallying broad support for it from other interested groups. In a typical Western pluralistic society, every organized interest is a little pluralistic group system in itself, each operating much as does the whole pluralistic system of organized groups, among which government is only one of many agencies, though one with special powers to make its decisions stand. In this world of group balances and compromises, the formulator of policies, however brilliant, is likely to fail in attaining adoption of his policy if he is not able to persuade most of the groups concerned to give him support.

Legislative deliberation

Deliberation is the part of the legislative process for which formal constitutional law, standing orders, and other codes of parliamentary procedure have provided in great detail. There are two ways of looking at the process of legislative deliberation. One can either consider it as the careful staging of the grand drama of conflicting interests, groups, and personalities on the floor of the legislature and its organs, or one can follow the process of deliberation by means of a flow chart of the steps through which a specific measure has to pass in order to become a law. The first approach has been touched upon in the previous discussion. Let us now turn to the second manner of analysis: tracing the course of a bill or resolution through a legislature. For the purposes of this discussion, it should be assumed that at the outset of the process, there is at least one complete draft of the bill which may, of course, be changed substantially before the final decision to pass it is made.

Legislative procedure in the United States Legislative procedure in the United States Congress (see Figure 7.3) distinguishes between financial bills, which may originate only in the House, public bills, and special or private bills. All that is necessary for the introduction of a bill or resolution in the House is that it bear the name of a representative, who either hands the bill to the clerk of the House or places it in a box, called the hopper. In the Senate, a senator must first gain recognition of the presiding officer to announce the introduction of the bill. Once introduced the bill is given a number and is referred to one or more of the standing committees. No bill passes Congress without three readings. The first reading is by title only. It is not a "reading" in the strict sense of the word, for all that is required is the printing of the title in the *Congressional Record.*

The standing committee can, after going through its own process of deliberation, with debates, hearings, establishing a subcommittee, and so on, take various types of action on the bill. The committee can amend it, strike out parts, offer an alternative version, or report it unchanged. The majority of bills are "pigeonholed," that is, they are not reported out. To dislodge an unreported bill from a standing committee requires a "discharge petition" supported by an *absolute majority* of the members of the House (for example, 218 in the House of Representatives). When a bill is reported out by a House committee, it is placed on one of three calendars: tax or appropriation measures on the "Union calendar," other public bills on the "House calendar," and private or special bills on the "Private calendar." These calendars are a device for sorting out the vast number of bills and resolutions coming before the House, and in particular for giving the financial bills the important position they deserve.

The place of a bill on one of the various calendars does not automatically bring it to the floor of the House for debate. Most public bills require a special rule or order from the Rules Committee, which can also pigeonhole it indefinitely, as well as determine

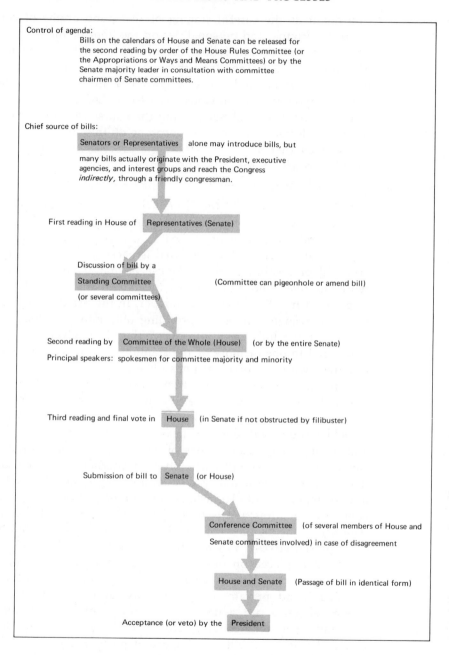

Control of agenda:
Bills on the calendars of House and Senate can be released for
the second reading by order of the House Rules Committee (or
the Appropriations or Ways and Means Committees) or by the
Senate majority leader in consultation with committee
chairmen of Senate committees.

Chief source of bills:
Senators or Representatives alone may introduce bills, but
many bills actually originate with the President, executive
agencies, and interest groups and reach the Congress
indirectly, through a friendly congressman.

First reading in House of Representatives (Senate)

Discussion of bill by a
Standing Committee (Committee can pigeonhole or amend bill)
(or several committees)

Second reading by Committee of the Whole (House) (or by the entire Senate)
Principal speakers: spokesmen for committee majority and minority

Third reading and final vote in House (in Senate if not obstructed by filibuster)

Submission of bill to Senate (or House)

Conference Committee (of several members of House and
Senate committees involved) in case of disagreement

House and Senate (Passage of bill in identical form)

Acceptance (or veto) by the President

Figure 7.3   Lawmaking in the United States Congress.

whether or not the bill is to be open to amendments during the debate. When a bill receives the green light and reaches the floor for its second reading, the House often transforms itself into the Committee of the Whole in order to relax the rules and quorum requirements of its formal sessions. The Speaker steps down and a chairman serves as presiding officer. The House then requires only a quorum of 100 and allows every member who desires to speak five minutes to make his point or to offer amendments. During the debate it is customary to give precedence to the spokesmen for the different points of view in the committee reporting the bill before other members of the House are recognized. The opposition to a measure naturally attempts various dilatory maneuvers, such as demanding time-consuming roll calls, but the role of the Speaker as the instrument of the will of the majority party generally enables the will of a majority to prevail. "Closure" can be obtained by a simple majority vote on the "previous question," which is: "Shall the bill be engrossed [reprinted as amended] and read a third time [for final passage]?"

In the American Senate, whose smaller size and greater continuity make unnecessary many of the arrangements that the House has for expediting business, the Committee of the Whole is no longer used except for treaties. The bill, however, goes through the same procedure of the three readings and the committee stage. Debate is unlimited, except for such general rules as forbidding a Senator to speak more than twice a day on the same subject and "unanimous consent" procedures under which the end of debate is set beforehand. Hence there have been filibusters and also a number of abortive attempts to impose better controls than are provided by the rarely used closure provisions in existence.

Since the versions of a bill passed by House and Senate must be identical, there is often need for a conference committee, a group made up of two members of each house, whose function it is to work out a compromise on the bill and arrive at an identical version agreeable to both. This committee usually includes the chairmen and the ranking majority and minority members of the standing committees in charge of the bill in both houses. The agreed-upon final version is usually accepted or rejected by both houses without further attempts at amendment. Nevertheless, the conference procedure does allow for a kind of renewal of the preceding legislative battles, again giving the leadership of the standing committees involved a particular advantage.

Finally, there is the Presidential veto or the "pocket veto," which is another point at which hostile interests can strike down a bill.

Since the President is the only federal officer who represents all Americans, his veto power, together with his message power and other tools of legislative leadership, are among the few instruments of pure majority will in the American system. Nevertheless, forcing the reintroduction of a bill or the rallying of a two-thirds vote of each house to override a veto also renews the preceding legislative battles in both houses, allowing both sides to reenact their skirmishes with the benefit of broader experience.

Legislative procedure in Great Britain How does the legislative process in Great Britain (see Figure 7.4) compare with that in the United States Congress and, incidentally, very similar proceedings in the American state legislatures? The venerable "Mother of Parliaments," as might be expected, in many procedural matters has actually been the originator of our formulas and customs. The expressions "first reading," "second reading," and "third reading" go back to the practice of the British Parliament before printing was invented. But there are also some significant differences.

The most glaring difference is found in the fact that Parliament today has little to do with the actual formulation of laws. To be sure, Congressmen and Senators also, but rarely, think up and write the laws they introduce, but there can be little doubt about the firm control which congressional committees exercise over the form and content of the measures before the Congress. The British Parliament, by comparison, has been said to be engaged merely in consenting to laws thought up by parties and organized interests, drawn up by civil servants, and guided through the House of Commons by the government. One should bear in mind, however, that the Cabinet and the majority party in the House owe their decisive role to their leadership in the House of Commons and not to an outside source of authority. Parliament may have organized its lawmaking function in a peculiar fashion, but it is still sovereign in Great Britain, if only through its leadership, the Cabinet.

There is the same distinction between financial and other public bills, though both of these major categories, with rare exceptions, now come from the Cabinet. Private members' bills and motions have to take their chance by lot on the rare opportunities provided for them. Finally, there are the "private bills," comparable perhaps to our special bills or to the customary petitions for a redress of grievances addressed to Parliament since the earliest days. For these private bills, there are special quasi-judicial proceedings before the Committee on Unopposed Bills, or the Committee on Private Bills, the latter holding hearings to allow the opposition to be heard.

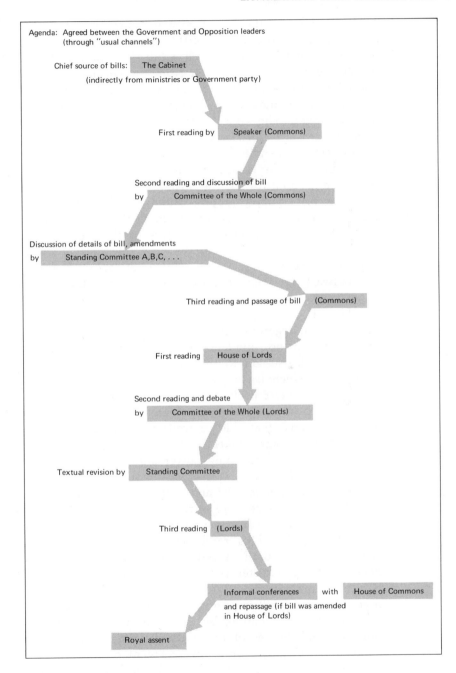

Agenda: Agreed between the Government and Opposition leaders
(through "usual channels")

Chief source of bills: The Cabinet
(indirectly from ministries or Government party)

First reading by Speaker (Commons)

Second reading and discussion of bill
by Committee of the Whole (Commons)

Discussion of details of bill, amendments
by Standing Committee A,B,C, . . .

Third reading and passage of bill (Commons)

First reading House of Lords

Second reading and debate
by Committee of the Whole (Lords)

Textual revision by Standing Committee

Third reading (Lords)

Informal conferences with House of Commons
and repassage (if bill was amended
in House of Lords)

Royal assent

Figure 7.4   Lawmaking in Great Britain (public bills).

Money bills in the British system must originate in the House of Commons, and since the 1911 reform the House of Lords can no longer amend or reject such a bill. But the Standing Orders of the House of Commons bar it from the consideration of any proposal for the expenditure of funds not recommended by the Crown. In practice, this means that budgets are made by the chancellor of the exchequer, who collects departmental estimates and, with the help of Treasury officials, proposes the revenue measures to match the projected expenditures of the next fiscal year. When the budget is submitted to the House of Commons by the Cabinet, the House sits as a Committee of the Whole, either of Ways and Means (revenue) or of Supply (appropriations), to consider it. The size and character of this body, as contrasted to the expertise and efficiency of the far smaller finance committees of the French and American legislatures, tells much about the preponderance of the British executive in the making of the budget, an activity once considered the bulwark of popular government against the executive. This impression is further confirmed by the reluctance of the Cabinet to lift the veil of secrecy from the details of the budget in advance. Its custom of regarding any reduction of items in the budget as an implied vote of no confidence, finally, reduces the role of the House in financial legislation to that of a rubber stamp. Only the loyal opposition, which lacks the votes to do any harm, has much opportunity to assert itself during the debate on the budget and to utilize it for attacks on government policy. On the other hand, it should be noted that this centralization of financial power in the hands of the Cabinet makes for economy in government, in contrast to the diffusion of spending power among, say, the committees of the American Congress.

Nonfinancial public bills and motions in the House of Commons also, in most instances, are introduced by the Cabinet, which tends to preempt most of the time available for debate, even though the number of public bills rarely exceeds about seventy-five a year. According to standard procedure, a public bill or motion is introduced when a minister (who is always a member of Parliament) hands a dummy of the bill to the clerk, who reads its title. Upon the first reading the bill is printed and distributed. The second reading involves the presentation, by the sponsoring minister, of the chief purposes and devices of the bill and gives the opposition to it an opportunity to move for a postponement or to propose alternative solutions to the problems with which the bill deals. The minister is allowed a final rejoinder to the arguments of the opposition. The second reading ends with a vote upon which the tenure of office of the Cabinet depends, if the bill is a Cabinet bill. A negative vote leads to its resignation and, possibly, the dissolution of the House. An affirmative vote indicates the support of a majority in the House for the basic purposes of the bill, whereupon it is sent to the Committee of the Whole or to one of the standing committees for consideration in detail. Unlike American committees, the British committee in question is not at liberty to change the basic purposes of a bill or to pigeonhole it. It must report the bill as soon as possible, depending on the agenda agreed on by the whips of both parties. The report stage allows the entire House to consider and vote on the details of the bill.

It is especially at this point that it becomes necessary for the House of Commons to limit debate and to regulate the number of amendments and motions proposed. The Speaker has the power to silence members who stray from the subject and, by his use of the "kangaroo,"[4] to select amendments for debate. There is also the "guillotine," a timetable for the discussion of the various stages of a bill, which sets a specific time for a vote on each stage, thus cutting off the debate. Closure can be moved at any time, both on the whole bill or any part of it, but must be accepted by the Speaker, who will want to be sure the opposition has had its day in court. These powers and the urgency of the governing majority to get its business done give the Speaker an awesome task of maintaining a fair balance between majority and opposition, and between the front and backbenchers on both sides of the aisle. If it were not for his scrupulous impartiality, the proceedings might easily become a mere show of democratic encounter and compromise for the benefit of the galleries.

The third reading precedes the final adoption of a bill and, at this time, only verbal changes to polish up the bill are in order. The bill or resolution must then be accepted or rejected as it stands. Upon passage in the House of Commons, the bill goes to the House of Lords, unless it has already been passed there, and to the monarch for approval. Since the reform of 1911, and even more so since the Parliament Act of 1949, the House of Lords has lost its equality in legislative power with the House of Commons, which can now override the Lords by passing the bill in question twice (1911–1949: three times) in consecutive sessions, during no less than one year (1911–1949: two years). This still gives the upper house a full veto during the last year in office of a government. The House of Lords

---

[4] The phrase refers to the practice of "leaping over" some amendments in order to select the more basic changes first for debate.

also should not defeat a measure for which the government has received a specific mandate at the preceding election.

Procedure in the House of Lords features the three readings and a standing committee for the revision of public bills. The House of Lords makes much use of the Committee of the Whole and enjoys a reputation for well-considered revision owing to the absence of urgency and of pressure from constituency groups as well as to its ample number of well-qualified former prime ministers, high judges, and other experts in the fine art of lawmaking. The granting of the royal assent to legislation also takes place in the Lords' Chamber to which the Gentleman Usher of the Black Rod summons the Commons. The royal assent is given in Norman French, the usual formula being "La reine (le roi) le veult." Since 1854 the assent has been read, not by the monarch himself, but by three commissioners. There has not been an executive veto ("La reine (le roi) s'avisera") since 1707.

Legislative procedure in France Deliberation in the French parliaments of the Third and Fourth Republics was different in many ways from the British approach (see Figure 7.5, showing lawmaking procedure in the Fifth Republic). The French distinguish chiefly between *projets de loi* (government bills) and *propositions de loi* (private member bills), although the strong *commissions* (committees) of the lower house always took control of either kind as if it were their own. Bills are introduced by being given to the Assembly President, who reads their title, has them printed, and assigns them to the appropriate *commission*. It should be noted that in France, as in the United States, but unlike the procedure in Great Britain, the crucial second reading occurs only after the committee stage. The various topical *commissions* of foreign affairs, of the interior, or of the powerful finance committee, may revise bills in any way they wish and sometimes come up with draft bills of their own. Each committee appoints from among its members a *rapporteur* for studying and preparing a report on each particular bill, a role in which ambitious young deputies invest much effort and take great pride.

The debate on the floor is opened by a speech of the *rapporteur* (or *rapporteurs* if several committees were involved) setting forth the major objectives of the bill for purposes of general discussion. The minister, or other author, of the bill gets a chance to speak only after the *rapporteur*. The recognized party groups of the chamber may designate spokesmen who receive a privileged place on the agenda for the presentation of the views of each party. Individual

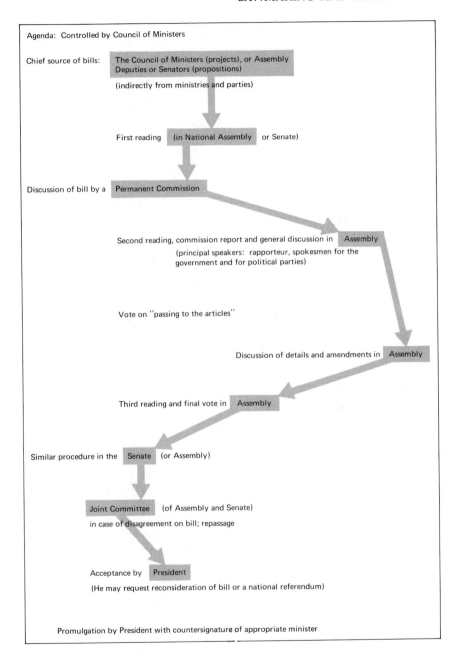

Agenda: Controlled by Council of Ministers

Chief source of bills: The Council of Ministers (projects), or Assembly Deputies or Senators (propositions)

(indirectly from ministries and parties)

First reading (in National Assembly or Senate)

Discussion of bill by a Permanent Commission

Second reading, commission report and general discussion in Assembly

(principal speakers: rapporteur, spokesmen for the government and for political parties)

Vote on "passing to the articles"

Discussion of details and amendments in Assembly

Third reading and final vote in Assembly

Similar procedure in the Senate (or Assembly)

Joint Committee (of Assembly and Senate)

in case of disagreement on bill; repassage

Acceptance by President

(He may request reconsideration of bill or a national referendum)

Promulgation by President with countersignature of appropriate minister

Figure 7.5   Lawmaking in the Fifth Republic of France.

members take their turn in the order in which they have signed in on the President's list of speakers. The general discussion is closed by a vote on the question of "passing to the articles," that is, to a discussion of details, or, if the Assembly disagrees with the committee report, on returning the bill to the committee. Despite its occasional unruliness and the weak regulatory powers of the Assembly President, the French lower house is comparatively efficient in getting its business done. Closure can be voted by a majority vote as soon as spokesmen for and against a bill have been heard. There is also a special procedure of "urgent discussion," which can be invoked by a minister, a standing *commission*, and, formerly, by private members. Under this rule, committees must report within three days, and the debate must follow immediately and continuously until the final vote is taken.

In the Third and Fourth Republics of France, a bill had to go from the lower house to the indirectly elected upper house—the Senate (Third Republic) or the Council of the Republic (Fourth Republic). The Senate had legislative equality with the Chamber of Deputies and acted much the same as did the latter. The Council of the Republic, on the other hand, could initiate laws only in the lower house, and was allowed two months for the examination of bills passed by the National Assembly. Under "urgent discussion" the Council could take twice the time taken by the lower house. In the case of financial measures, it could not initiate any new expenditures or reduce revenues but was allowed the same amount of time to consider the Budget that was used by the Assembly. Before 1954, the Council of the Republic could, by a negative vote of an absolute majority of its members, force the Assembly to override its veto of a bill with a like majority, an undertaking rarely possible in view of the shaky majorities of governments under the Fourth Republic. In 1954, however, this veto power was taken away and replaced with the Third Republic practice of the *navette*, the shuttling back and forth between the houses, for as long as one hundred days, of bills on which there was no agreement.

When the de Gaulle (Fifth) Republic took over from the Fourth Republic in 1958, one of the most prominent features of the new French Constitution was the manner in which the wings of the powerful National Assembly were clipped. Its control over the Cabinet was whittled down decisively (see Chapter 8), its range of legislative activity curtailed, and the other great national institutions—the Presidency, the Senate, and the Constitutional Council—were strengthened at its expense. These changes are also reflected in the processes of legislative delibration; the Cabinet now exercises real control over its own bills. Government bills have priority in either house and can, at the discretion of the Cabinet, be sent either to a standing committee or to a special committee created by the Cabinet, evidently for the purpose of circumventing entrenched committee power. This special committee must bring the bill to the floor within three months. The power of the Assembly to discuss and amend a bill or any part thereof is further hamstrung by the right of the government to object to the discussion of any amendment that has not been considered by the committee. Even more incisive is the right of the government to request that the Assembly or Senate accept or reject with a single vote the entire bill or any part thereof in the form determined by the government. This rule can limit the legislative power of the French Parliament to a mere veto such as the American President has.

There are also special safeguards to assure executive control over the passage of financial legislation. The finance minister introduces the budget, whereupon it is sent to the Finance Commission. The report to the floor has to be in very general terms and there may be no amendments increasing or decreasing expenditure. If the budget for a fiscal year should be delayed beyond its beginning, the government may also request authority to reissue, by decree, a budget identical with that approved for the preceding year.

Legislative procedure in West Germany Lawmaking in the West German *Bundestag* (see Figure 7.6) resembles in many key features the deliberations of the French lower house before 1958. As under the Fourth Republic, for example, the agenda of the *Bundestag* is made up by the *Bundestag* President sitting together with other party leaders of all recognized groups in the Council of Elders.[5] The three readings also follow the French model. The committees are small, but there are many more of them than in France, due perhaps to the German tendency toward specialization and compartmentalization, which also marks the highly technical character of the proceedings in committee. Committee deliberations are generally carried on in closed session, although organized interests are allowed ample contact with committee members. In the plenary debates on a bill, the *rapporteur* and chairman of the reporting committee enjoy some prominence, but not as much as was once the case in France.

---

[5] In the Fourth Republic, the committee chairmen were a part of the council that determined the agenda. In the Fifth Republic, the agenda is determined by the Cabinet.

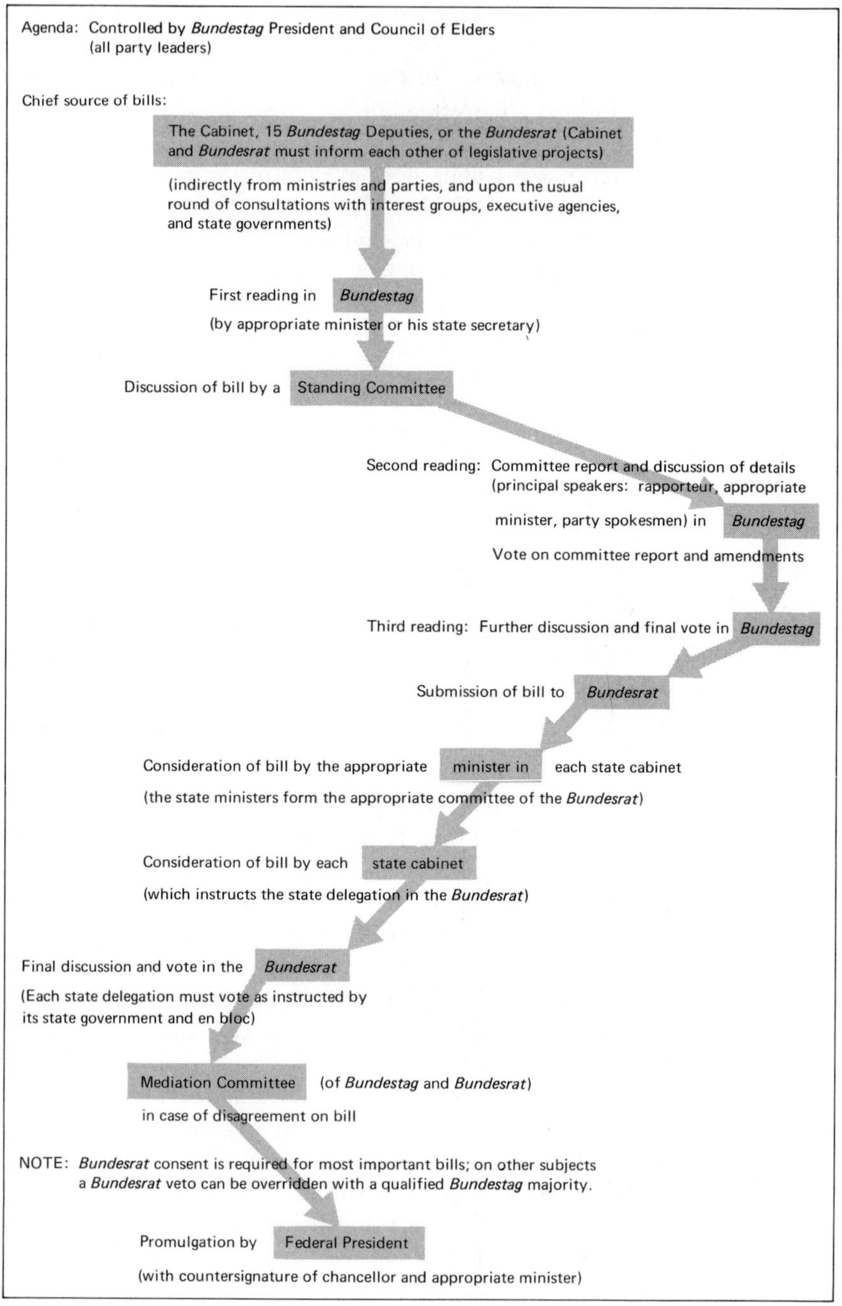

Agenda: Controlled by *Bundestag* President and Council of Elders
(all party leaders)

Chief source of bills:

The Cabinet, 15 *Bundestag* Deputies, or the *Bundesrat* (Cabinet
and *Bundesrat* must inform each other of legislative projects)

(indirectly from ministries and parties, and upon the usual
round of consultations with interest groups, executive agencies,
and state governments)

First reading in   *Bundestag*

(by appropriate minister or his state secretary)

Discussion of bill by a   Standing Committee

Second reading: Committee report and discussion of details
(principal speakers: rapporteur, appropriate

minister, party spokesmen) in   *Bundestag*

Vote on committee report and amendments

Third reading: Further discussion and final vote in   *Bundestag*

Submission of bill to   *Bundesrat*

Consideration of bill by the appropriate   minister in   each state cabinet

(the state ministers form the appropriate committee of the *Bundesrat*)

Consideration of bill by each   state cabinet

(which instructs the state delegation in the *Bundesrat*)

Final discussion and vote in the   *Bundesrat*

(Each state delegation must vote as instructed by
its state government and en bloc)

Mediation Committee   (of *Bundestag* and *Bundesrat*)

in case of disagreement on bill

NOTE: *Bundesrat* consent is required for most important bills; on other subjects
a *Bundesrat* veto can be overridden with a qualified *Bundestag* majority.

Promulgation by   Federal President

(with countersignature of chancellor and appropriate minister)

Figure 7.6   Lawmaking in the Bonn Republic.

Speakers have to enter their names on the President's list. Ministers, *rapporteurs*, and the members of the upper house, the *Bundesrat* (who are usually ministers or high civil servants in the state governments), may speak at any time they desire. The *Bundestag* President presides over the proceedings and can silence, and even exclude for the day, speakers who stray from the subject or become disorderly. In sharp contrast to the tone of technical, expert objectivity of the committee meetings, the speeches from the rostrum to the fully assembled *Bundestag* tend to aim at the galleries and, sometimes, at the microphones of radio stations that have broadcast some of the more important debates.

In financial legislation, the *Bundestag* accords its Cabinet almost as much authority as does the British House of Commons. Only the government may introduce or increase proposals for expenditures or taxes. On the other hand, there is a strong Finance Committee, which can pare down estimates and appropriations, a body far more effective owing to its smallness and concentrated expertise than the British Committee of the Whole.

The West German upper house, the *Bundesrat*, is unlike any other legislative chamber in the West in that it meets in continuous session. Its members are not elected but appointed. They are the delegates (and often Cabinet members) of the state governments and have to vote strictly according to instructions from their governments in a manner not unlike that of an international conference or organization. Consequently, there are state delegations but no political parties in the *Bundesrat*. There are topical committees corresponding to the topical ministries of the *Laender* (states) and the federal government that coordinate the legislative activities of the executive branches on both levels. Each state government has a representative on every committee. Legislative proceedings before the infrequent plenary meetings of the *Bundesrat* consist chiefly of voting on bills that have already been circulated among the appropriate ministries of both levels and thoroughly discussed in committee. Each *Land*, in rough approximation of the size of its population, has 3 to 5 votes that must be cast en bloc. The character of the proceedings only rarely develops into a debate but permits the *Bundesrat* to dispose of ten to twenty bills in a single afternoon. The role of the *Bundesrat* in federal lawmaking is not equal to the role of the *Bundestag* with respect to all legislation, except certain, often more important, kinds of laws. In case of disagreement between the houses, a mediation committee is created, consisting of a representative from each state delegation and a like number of *Bundestag* members, to produce a compromise acceptable to both houses.

Authoritative decision

Authoritative decision in the legislative process is the last formal step in policy-making that needs to be considered here. Decisions are made at many levels, both with regard to parts of a bill and to the whole bill. Some decisions are made even before a fully drafted version is introduced in the legislature. Some occur in the form of votes in committee and on the floor, both on articles or amendments and on the whole bill. The final decision, for which the procedure is usually laid down in the constitution, is the point at which a bill becomes law after having been duly passed by one or two houses of the legislature and signed by the chief executive. Some of these aspects have already been touched upon, especially the stages before submission of a bill to the legislature. The rest require some explanation.

Voting procedures in the United States   In the American Congress there are several ways of voting. The most common method is by a voice vote (viva voce), or the shouting of "yea" or "nay" by the members to indicate their position. If there is doubt, a standing vote may be taken so that the "yeas" and "nays" can be counted. In the House, if one-fifth of a quorum requests it, there is a vote by tellers. Two tellers are appointed, who place themselves in front of the presiding officer's desk and count the "yeas" and the "nays" as each member steps up to the desk and indicates his position. Finally, there is the roll-call vote: the clerk calls off the names and permanently records the votes cast by each member of the House. Due to the pressures of constituency and organized interests, Congressmen and Senators are understandably reluctant to be put on permanent record, except on the most uncontroversial subjects. Roll-call votes are time consuming, which makes them a favorite for groups opposing a measure.

Voting procedures in other Western legislatures   Voting procedures in other Western legislatures differ little from those in Congress. On the European Continent, voting by show of hands is popular both in committee and in the fully assembled house. In the British House of Commons and its Commonwealth equivalents there are also the divisional lobbies into which the M.P.s (members of Parliament) file through "yes" and "no" doors to facilitate counting. This method of voting is also used on the Continent,[6] except that there are three doors—"yes," "no," and "abstention"—because Continental

---

[6] In German usage it is called *Hammelsprung*, which refers to the leaping of sheep over a low barrier to facilitate counting.

practice allows formal abstention; in Anglo-American procedure, the unwilling legislator does not answer the roll call, or he can choose to be absent at the time the vote is taken.

How a bill becomes a law   A bill does not become a law until it has been duly signed and proclaimed by the chief executive, an action which is supposed to follow upon passage through the legislature. In some Western systems of government, the executive has an opportunity at this point to prevent the bill from becoming law by withholding his signature. It will be recalled that the royal assent in Great Britain has become a mere formality during the past two and a half centuries. In the United States, however, the Presidential veto has become an important instrument of legislative leadership. An outright veto involves returning a bill, together with the Presidential objections, to the house in which it originated, whereupon Congress can either attempt to satisfy the objections or to muster a two-thirds vote in each chamber to override the veto. An unsigned bill in the President's hands will become law without his signature after ten days, provided Congress is still in session. As there is usually a very considerable volume of legislation passing through the Presidential office at the end of a session, this provision gives the President a "pocket veto" that cannot be overridden and requires no explanation.

A Presidential veto or pocket veto only empowers the chief executive to accept or reject a bill in its entirety. Presidents have often had to swallow their dissatisfaction with a "rider" tacked onto a bill of which they approve in order to sign the bill into law. The governor of California, by contrast, and the governors of three-fourths of the other states of the Union have, in addition to these veto powers, an "item veto" which enables them to strike out or reduce (but not to increase) any item of appropriations or expenditures in the budget. A few American state constitutions even allow such an item veto to be exercised toward all legislation. Needless to add, the item veto considerably increases the extent of executive participation in lawmaking.

The French President of the Fourth Republic, also, had the function of promulgating the laws within ten days of their passage by Parliament. He could within this period return a bill for reconsideration to the two houses of the legislature. It should be noted, however, that the incumbents of this office evidently regarded their veto powers solely as a means for remedying technical defects in legislation rather than as a tool for Presidential policy. The Constitution of the Fifth Republic of France continued the Presidential power of returning a bill for reconsideration, lengthening the period for executive scrutiny from ten to fifteen days. The Federal President of the West German Republic has not just the right but the duty to refuse his signature to a bill containing aspects of questionable constitutionality. The President of the Republic of Italy, by contrast, has a real veto power, again by returning bills for reconsideration with suggestions for change. Though sparingly used, none of the Presidential vetoes have so far been overridden by the Italian Parliament.

A final note about executive vetoes. Although long in disuse in Great Britain itself, the veto is still very much in use in the British colonies, where governors use it along with considerable decree-making powers on behalf of the Crown. Even in the self-governing dominions of the Commonwealth until the early twentieth century, governors-general appointed by the Crown exercised the power of "reservation," that is, reserving bills of dominion legislatures for the signification of the sovereign's pleasure. On some subjects of legislation, such reservation was obligatory. Before 1900, furthermore, the monarch and his Cabinet in London could "disallow" (annul) dominion laws duly passed by a dominion legislature and assented to by the governor or governor-general of the dominion. This, too, is a power now in disuse.

This concludes our survey of policy-making by means of laws. It should be emphasized again, as at the outset, that lawmaking occupies a central position among the different aspects of the making of public policy. This is the result of two important characteristics of government in the West. First, there is the strong legalistic undercurrent of government and politics, an element quite alien to some of the new nations. The legalistic approach points up the importance of the mechanism for changing the legal rules of the game, or lawmaking. Second, there is a general presumption in favor of largely subordinating other governmental functions, such as administration and adjudication, to the laws made by the legislative process. Although there is some talk of judicial supremacy both in the United States and in West Germany, the bulk of judicial activity in most countries still consists of applying to specific cases the laws made by the legislatures of both countries. While there may also be the specter of executive predominance in America and in France, or of a self-contained administrative state in France and West Germany, the legislative power is still a most potent directive and, at times, corrective force that exercises control over the making of executive and administrative policy.

CHAPTER **8** **EXECUTIVE POLICY-MAKING**

In a discussion of the making of public policy, the temptation is great to limit the discussion to the process of lawmaking by representative assemblies. Yet legislation by representative assemblies as a central feature of government is a modern development dating back not much farther than a century and a half. Before that time, public policy was made almost exclusively by the executive branch. The few parliaments in existence before the French Revolution were not legislatures, but rather courts of law and watchdogs over the raising of public revenues. Thus executive branches had their own policy-making function, which continued even during the rise of legislation by parliaments. In countries with separation of powers, such as the United States, executive policy-making and legislative policy-making remain theoretically separate functions only tenuously tied together by the fact that Congress makes laws—often proposed by the executive—and the executive must carry them out. In countries such as Great Britain and France, the introduction of parliamentary government[1] was meant to make the executive policy-makers re-

1 Parliamentary government is discussed in detail on pp. 257–267.

sponsible to the elected legislative policy-makers. Both executive and legislative policy-making in Great Britain, consequently, are now controlled by one cohesive group of party leaders, the Cabinet. In France, by contrast, the introduction of parliamentary government succeeded only in part, leaving substantial executive policy-making functions still separate.

The significance of executive policy-making today is greater than ever, owing to the enormous increase in governmental functions and consequent bureaucracy. Much has already been said about the role of the executive branches in the drafting, the initiation, and the guidance of legislation. The regular contacts of organized interests with the executive have also been mentioned. There remain four topics for discussion: (1) the bearing the organization of the executive has on policy-making; (2) the areas in which executive branches can make policy with little or no interference from their legislatures; (3) the practice of executive rule-making; and last, but not least important, (4) the varieties of executive-legislative relations in various Western governmental systems.

EXECUTIVE BRANCHES: FORM AND ORGANIZATION

The executive institutions of most Western countries bear a striking resemblance to one another, which, as is the case with the similarities among Western legislatures, is due both to a common heritage and to mutual observation and imitation. The common heritage of all governments in the West, including that of the United States, is one of a monarchic executive being replaced in actual fact, or at least in effective control, by a democratic executive. Aspects of the monarchic executive that were considered, tried, and proven were often retained. In this sense, there are close parallels, for example, between the constitutional position of King George III, the sovereign by divine grace, and the American Presidency, whose authority was derived, at least indirectly, from the new sovereign, the people.[2] The relations of the President with the Senate, especially with regard to foreign relations, were similarly modeled on the king's relation to the House of Lords, down to the formula of "advise and consent." There are similar parallels between the development of the dual executive in Great Britain—king and prime minister—and the Presidency and premiership of the Fourth Republic.

[2] A closer parallel, perhaps, can be found in the Presidency of the Weimar Constitution of Germany (1919), which was modeled after the position of the kaiser before his abdication, again substituting popular election for divine right.

There are also manifestations of national psychology which have made for diversity in the concept of the executive in different Western countries. One can relate, for example, the American image of the solitary, powerful figure of the American chief executive making his lonely decisions to the American image of a man alone pitted against the elements, which has been a popular theme in much American literature. The British cabinet government has often been connected with the British custom of "government by committee," or of always entrusting great decisions to a small group and never to an individual. Then there is the peculiarly French attitude of ambiguity toward authority, which has led French government since 1789 to waver constantly between the two extremes of a quasi-dictatorial executive, such as the two Napoleons and de Gaulle, and of government by assembly. There are also the Germans, who from Bismarck to Hitler, and perhaps to Adenauer as well, appear to have set entirely too much trust in executive leadership. Finally, there is the example of the Swiss Federal Council, whose unique form owes much to the deeply ingrained popular distaste among the Swiss for the showoff, or the man who "wants" to be chief. The Federal Council was modeled after cantonal executive councils and is composed of seven members of the *Nationalrat* (federal diet) elected for a four-year term by this body. The federal councilors are normally reelected as long as they wish to serve and act as one body. The Federal Assembly (both houses) annually selects a new President and a Vice President of the Confederation from among the councilors, thus taking care not to overindulge anyone's love of self. The Swiss share this wariness of ambition or personal preeminence with a number of other Western nations, from the ancient Greeks to the British.

The dual executive

The development of the dual executive is especially pertinent to a discussion of executive policy-making because underlying the theory of the dual executive is the attempt to divide the normal functions of the executive branch into specifically policy-making functions and more symbolic, or ceremonial, functions. Thus the day-to-day policy of the government, the "governing," is done by the British prime minister, the French premier, or the German chancellor, whereas Queen Elizabeth II of England, the Fourth Republic President, and the Federal President of the West German Republic only "reign" as symbols of continuity, of national honor, and of unity.

The Fourth Republic offers a typical example of the division of functions between the two executive figures. The President presided over the French Union, chaired cabinet meetings and the Constitutional Committee, granted pardons, appointed civil servants and ambassadors, signed laws and treaties and, most important, designated the new premier and appointed his Cabinet ministers. One of the incumbents, Vincent Auriol, considered his office the "moral magistracy" of the nation. In spite of this inside role—with a presiding seat on the Council of National Defense and with access to all the diplomatic and other classified documents—the President's political powers were curtailed by the provision that his official acts had to be countersigned by a Cabinet minister. The Cabinet, on the other hand, had the authority over and was responsible for the general policy of the government to the National Assembly, which could and did topple many a premier during the duration of a Presidential seven-year term of office.

The powers and position of the West German Federal President vis-à-vis the chancellor are almost identical with those of the Fourth Republic, with the possible exception, in practice, of appointing premier and Cabinet. Here the French President frequently exercised a real choice among various possible coalitions, whereas his West German equivalent has, so far, stood in the shadow of a strong chancellor. In Great Britain, the division of authority is likewise very similar, although the venerable traditions and the magic of the monarchy have created a curious game of pretense and symbolism in place of the cold language of republican constitutional law. Essentially, the monarch has "the right to be informed, to encourage, to warn," and his (or her) long experience in government and great popularity can make the king or queen an important force behind the scenes. But the few political prerogatives still retained by the Crown have, in reality, long been wielded by the Cabinet, which even writes the royal messages to Parliament and decides all official appointments and acts ostensibly discharged by the monarch.

Functional division of labor

A second important structural aspect of executive institutions is their specialization along functional lines. The American Constitution, for example, makes no mention of a Cabinet. Yet within the first year of the new government of the Union, 1789, Departments of State, Treasury, and War were established. By 1966, there were eleven departments, State, Treasury, Defense, Interior, Agriculture, Justice, Post Office, Commerce, Labor, HEW (Health, Education and Welfare), and HUD (Housing and Urban Development). Each department has within it a number of bureaus, not to mention the many independent administrations and agencies. To cite an example, the Department of Commerce has ten bureaus, dealing with the census, civil aviation, geodetics, inland navigation, maritime affairs, production, patents, public roads, weights and measurements, and the weather.

The British ministry is composed of some seventy agencies, of which about seventeen or eighteen make up a typical Cabinet today. Within this Cabinet, moreover, there is an Inner Cabinet of about half that size. Among the regular Cabinet members are usually the prime minister, the chancellor of the exchequer (treasury), the home secretary (interior), the foreign secretary, the secretaries for commonwealth relations, colonies, and Scotland, the president of the Board of Trade (commerce), and the ministers of defense, labor, and agriculture and fisheries. The French Council of Ministers has been composed of some twenty ministers since 1946. Key ministries were always foreign affairs, defense, finance, justice, and interior, which on occasion have constituted, together with the premier and whatever other ministers they cared to invite, a kind of inner circle for the making of general policy. The West German Cabinet similarly consists of some sixteen to eighteen ministries, among which finance, foreign affairs, interior, justice, defense, economics, labor, and agriculture are the more prominent.

It should be clear from this comparison that executive policy-making requires the same functional division of labor that has produced topical committees—with the notable exception of Great Britain—in legislatures. It is in these individual ministries or agencies that most policy proposals—legislative or other—originate or are worked out in detail. It is here also that ministers or the Cabinet as a body will find the expert knowledge required to transform their plans and wishes into reality. In governmental systems in which most bills come from the executive branch, the individual ministry can also do the actual legislative drafting, owing to the legal training and administrative experience of its career personnel. It will also be remembered how a particular interest group, with the appropriate legislative committee and executive agency, can form a triangle of consultation and cooperation for the purpose of developing a new policy within its particular field of interest. Frequently, when a new ministry or department is established, such as the ministries of agriculture, labor, or economics in most Western countries, this is done in response to the urging of interested groups. The same can be said about the establishment of many a topical committee of a Western legislature and of topical committees in political parties, such as the platform of policy-planning committees of American parties or the agriculture, labor, or economics committees of German or British parties.

Executive coordination

The significance of the functional division of labor in executive policy-making should not obscure the need for coordination and the development of a general policy. Such coordination generally occurs in three ways: (1) political coordination by the executive leader, (2) coordination of departmental policies by cabinet committees or councils, and (3) coordination of the executive by centralization of budgetary powers.

Coordination by the chief executive As chief executives, the United States President, the German chancellor, the British premier, and the French premier must present an image of coherent policies to the public and to the opposition. In the United States, the chief executive runs for office on the basis of such a policy image. In Great Britain and West Germany, the image of the prime minister or chancellor dominates the partisan contest in the elections even though these officials are not directly elected to their posts. The French President of the Fifth Republic has similarly become the chief focus of general policy toward the French public and electorate. Coordination is also facilitated by cabinet secretariats or, in the United States, by the executive office of the President.

The specific manner in which the chief executive coordinates the policies of the different departments or ministers depends also on his relationship to them. President Lincoln could say, when his entire War Cabinet opposed a proposal of his: "The ayes have it." The British prime minister, on the other hand, is only a *primus inter pares*, who must consult with and defer to the majority decisions of his Cabinet even though his preeminence has long been generally accepted. The relationship between President de Gaulle and the individual ministers was rather anomalous in that he left some departments completely to themselves, whereas others, especially defense, foreign affairs, the French Community, and Algeria, were exposed to such frequent interference as to bring about a near eclipse of the premier and appropriate ministers. The President himself, it must be remembered, is not responsible to the French Parliament. The premier of the Fourth Republic was perhaps in a weak position due to several factors, the coalition character of his Cabinet, the impatience of the National Assembly with the executive, and his equality with the other members of the Cabinet. Individual ministers often served under several premiers in succession, thus clearly showing their greater staying power. The constitutional position of the West German chancellor places him in a position somewhere between that of the British and the American chief executive. His Cabinet ministers are subordinated to his policy-making authority. With a strong personality and a legislative majority, Adenauer could dominate and, on occasion, ignore or overrule his Cabinet. Lacking both, his successors have been no more dominant than the British prime minister.

The relative independence of a ministry or executive agency can be gauged not only with respect to the amount of control by the chief executive, but also to the cohesion of the Cabinet or executive branch as a body. In the case of the United States, individual secretaries ofen disagree publicly with each other and on occasion with the President, without violating any accepted customs of executive solidarity. There are, moreover, a considerable number of independent agencies such as the Federal Reserve System or the United States Civil Service Commission, not to mention the powerful regulatory commissions, whose autonomy has been carefully established. On the state level, this lack of executive unity is even more pronounced. A typical example is the state of California where, in addition to the governor and lieutenant governor, the attorney general, state controller, secretary of state, state treasurer, superintendent of public instruction, and the members of the State Board of Equalization, all are directly elected by the people. Under this system, only the gubernatorial control over budget and personnel and what legislative leadership a governor can muster can produce any coordination of policy among these separately elected heads of departments. A look across the Atlantic Ocean shows an extreme contrast in Great Britain, where the Cabinet operates in a spirit of extraordinary unity and solidarity, as well as secrecy. Since responsibility is collective and decisions rest on a firmly implanted consensus that the members of the government are all in the same boat, nobody is allowed to voice his dissent from the majority decision in public. France and Germany are less cohesive than Great Britain, the French Cabinet owing to its coalition character, and the German Cabinet, if not for the same reason, owing to its habits of specialization and of valuing autonomous expertise more than political compromise.

Coordination by Cabinet committees or councils The more or less permanent Cabinet committees or councils comprise a second device for the coordination of departmental policies. In the United States, where the tendency is to set up a new executive agency for every new job, there is, for example, the National Security Council to make general foreign and defense policy. It is composed of the President, the vice president, the secretaries of state and defense, and the heads of the Central Intelligence Agency and the Office of Emergency Planning. They are often joined by the head of the United States Information Agency, the chairman of the Joint Chiefs of Staff, the secretary of the Treasury, and the director of the Bureau of the Budget, as well as by members of the President's staff. An Operations Coordinating Board and the staff of the council help to implement the policy decisions and supervise and report on the implementation by the various departments involved.

The British have favored using Cabinet committees more than has any other system of government. Since 1945, for example, at least five standing Cabinet committees have coordinated government policy for specific purposes, including the Legislation Committee (which reviews all bills issuing from individual ministries and, with the help of the whips and leaders of both houses, proposes the timing and strategy of submitting the legislative program of the government to Parliament), the Defense Committee (which resembles our National Security Council), and the Lord President's Committee (which until 1951 coordinated home affairs). There are also many interdepartmental ad hoc committees that are established only for the purpose of developing a single project or legislative enactment, such as the introduction of the national health service, and are dissolved after they have accomplished their goal.

The French have their Committee of National Defense, a Council on Economic Policy, and *ad hoc* interministerial conferences. In the Bonn Republic the most important ministerial conferences are those among the topical ministers of the federal and state levels, or only among the states, which are fairly permanent and serve to develop agreed policies in each field. Among the best known is the Permanent Conference of *Land* Ministers of Culture and Education, which undertakes to coordinate the *Land* policies of education in the absence of a federal ministry. At the federal level alone, there are frequent interdepartmental meetings below the ministerial level. There are also several ministries, such as that of economic cooperation, justice (for checking the form and constitutionality of bills), and *Bundesrat* affairs whose liaison functions help to coordinate the activity of various ministries.

Coordination by executive budget-making The third and perhaps most significant device for the coordination of the executive departments is the centralization of budgetary powers.

1. *The United States.* In the United States Congress, budgetary proposals used to be introduced by as many as nine different House

committees and altered by fifteen Senate committees with no reference to Treasury estimates of revenues, until the Budget and Accounting Act of 1921 created the Bureau of the Budget. Today, this bureau is a part of the Executive Office of the President, who bears the primary responsibility for coordinating departmental requests and squaring expenditures with revenues. Departmental budget officers on all levels prepare detailed requests that must conform to the overall program of the President and anticipate the likely reactions of Congress. The Bureau of the Budget collects and, as directed by the President, molds the departmental requests into a total spending budget based on Treasury estimates of revenues. The final product of the labors of the bureau is submitted in a Presidential message to the Congress, where the legislative machinery takes over, beginning with the House Appropriations and Ways and Means Committees. Congress has to authorize the expenditures and thus can still increase or decrease items as its own preferences of pressure from constituencies, interest groups, and executive agencies may suggest. Nevertheless, the centralization of budget-making powers gives a considerable measure of control to the chief executive, who can thereby spell out the priorities of a coordinated executive program in dollars and cents. Similar executive budgets are in use in most American state governments.

2. *Great Britain.* In Britain, the departmental estimates go to the financial divisions of the Treasury, which has assistant or undersecretaries specializing in the needs and ways of each spending department and continually confers with departmental representatives until each budget component is whipped into the shape the Cabinet desires. The Treasury also controls taxation and the home civil service. Its proverbial skinflint attitude weighs heavily upon the spenders, forcing them to justify their requests in detail. The fact that the vital money aspects of all government operations go through the hands of the chancellor of the exchequer makes him the second most powerful figure in the Cabinet next to the prime minister. Since the House of Commons is given very little authority over the budget and the House of Lords is given none, cabinet approval for the budget drawn up by the Treasury gives it almost a final character.

3. *France.* The French budget also begins with the collections of departmental requests by the Ministry of Finance which, however, has less authority than the British Treasury or the American Bureau of the Budget to pare down departmental demands. Only the Cabinet, as a body, has this authority, and the coalition nature of French governments is unlikely to allow rigorous budgetary control anywhere. There is, moreover, the powerful Finance *Commission* of the

National Assembly, the "queen of *commissions*," which under the Fourth Republic took firm control of the "executive budget" and turned it into a "legislative budget" at the price of toppling many a Cabinet over budget issues. Under the Fifth Republic the "queen of *commissions*" has been hamstrung with various limitations but has succeeded, on several occasions, in kicking over the traces.

4. *West Germany.* The German budgetary system fulfills the purpose of executive coordination through the powerful Ministry of Finance in a manner similar to that of the British Treasury, without the legislative eclipse customary in Great Britain. There is the same control of the Minister of Finance over departmental requests and also a cabinet veto over any increases in spending that the *Bundestag* may be inclined to vote. On the other hand, the *Bundestag* and, in particular, its Budget Committee as well as the Finance Committee of the *Bundesrat* are given ample opportunity to examine, discuss, and slash items in the budget if they so desire.

EXECUTIVE POLICY-MAKING

This, then, is the setting within which executive policy is made. To begin with, the executive drafts many of the legislative programs that legislatures enact. The executives generally is also given powers and the responsibility of guiding these programs through the legislature. Here are the controls for the execution and administration of these laws, which often require the development of more specific administrative policies within the broad principles laid down by the law. Over and beyond the execution of the laws lie still further areas of executive policy-making, including some which on the surface may seem purely technical or "purely administrative." To cite an example, the American public was not aware of the fact that the United States armed forces were segregated before a 1948 Executive Order of President Truman. Using personnel policy in army and civil service, or antidiscrimination clauses in federal contracts and federally insured loans, also has only recently been employed as a device to assure to all Americans the constitutional rights hitherto denied them. Given the size of the modern executive apparatus and its vast involvement in the activities of society—legally, economically, and otherwise—anything the great Leviathan does or fails to do immediately influences, hurts, persuades, or pressures millions of people, often without any clear intent on the part of the executive leaders. Obviously, it is preferable that such extraordinary powers be used with skill and for deliberate purposes, for which the executive leadership could be held responsible through the democratic process, rather than that they should do damage by mere default or neglect.

Finally, there are the extensive fields of executive activity in which there is very little or no reliance on legislative authorization in the normal course of affairs. Among them are such important fields as foreign affairs and defense, in which some of the most crucial decisions for the survival of a country are made exclusively by executive officials, who may even be in civil service tenure positions from which they can be fired only for cause. Less well known are the extensive promotional and regulatory activities that modern executive branches carry on in economy and society, and in Europe even in culture and in the fine arts. Finally, there are the vast responsibilities of management of modern governments in the West today. They range from the management of the resources of the nation of tomorrow, the purity of its air and water, the wildlife and health of its forests, and its energy sources to the management of such public enterprises as the post office, European railroads, or the vast nationalized or public industries and utilities of Great Britain, France, Italy, West Germany, Switzerland, and Scandinavia.

Executive rule-making

In a civilization as accustomed to legal devices as in the West, it need not come as a surprise that much of executive policy is customarily laid down in legal enactments that for all effects and purposes look like and have the same effect as the laws legislatures make. There are essentially three kinds of such legal directives that can be found in most Western systems of government: (1) general powers of issuing lawlike decrees or ordinances, sometimes contingent upon a state of emergency or legislative authorization; (2) powers of filling in the details of duly passed legislation, either generally recognized or specifically authorized in the laws in question; and (3) administrative rules relating to the management of the administration. These three categories are not always easy to keep apart. Therefore, rather than discuss the practices of executive rule-making according to categories, we shall discuss the practices country by country—in the United States, Great Britain, France, and West Germany. Most of the Western governmental systems closely resemble one or the other of these four systems in executive policy-making practices.

In the United States The power of the American President to issue orders and directives is regarded as inherent in his duty to "take care that the laws be faithfully executed," in his pledge to "preserve, protect and defend the constitution," and in the ordinance-making powers necessary to direct the multifarious activities of the executive branch. The practical use made of these powers is particularly prevalent in those activities that go beyond the mere execution of laws, and have been mentioned above, such as military affairs and the personnel policy of the administration. In the conduct of foreign relations, the practice of concluding "executive agreements" rather than treaties, which would require Senate approval, has long been accepted as an outgrowth of the inherent power of issuing directives in the international field in which the initiative clearly rests in the hands of the President. In wartime or grave emergency, the power to issue executive decrees becomes practically a general legislative power. President Lincoln, upon inauguration, proceeded to raise and spend money and to build up the armed forces of the Union for four months before he even called Congress into session. Later wartime Presidents remained not far behind his example in their use of the war power for enactments normally left to the Congress.

Filling in the details in duly passed legislation is a practice that developed naturally with the rising complexity of the regulatory tasks Congress undertook to tackle by means of laws. In the eighteenth and early nineteenth century, lawmakers could state their intent in simple, broad principles that required little additional clarification. The regulation of the complex aspects of a modern economy and society has raised a multitude of technical difficulties and a need to leave the administrator considerable discretion in applying a law to widely varying circumstances. Hence, Congress has long resorted to tacit or express delegations of the power to fill in details by executive order to the President, or to particular departments or agencies. The Trade Agreement Act of 1934, for example, empowers the President, at his discretion, to lower tariff rates with respect to some countries by as much as 50 percent. The executive orders of the President are published in the Federal Register.

Administrative rule-making is vital to the functioning of any administrative organization. Much administrative rule-making pertains to the internal practices of administrative agencies and may have to do with almost any subject from sick leave provisions to accounting practices. But there is also much administrative rule-making that affects the public. The regulatory boards and commissions issue rules, and altogether there are more than a hundred federal agencies that have the power to make rules and regulations. Congress has attempted to safeguard the public through the Administrative Procedures Act of 1946, which directs the regulatory agencies to publicize their organization and procedures and to give interested parties a fair hearing, right to counsel, and advance notice of proposed rules.

In Great Britain   In Great Britain, the use of executive decrees, properly so-called, has waned, along with the real power of the monarchy and with the functions of the Privy Council, a large unwieldy body that once was the monarch's chief instrument of government.[3] Even proclamations or "orders in council" issued by Queen Elizabeth II are usually made only upon the advice of the Cabinet ministers who are responsible for them to the House of Commons. Typical subjects for an order in council are the granting of town charters or, under the Emergency Powers Act of 1920, the proclamation of a state of emergency for one week, after which period Parliament must confirm the executive emergency powers or allow them to lapse.

The filling in of details in legislation as well as broader rule-making powers are usually provided by delegation of power from Parliament to the Cabinet, the Privy Council, individual departments and agencies, public corporations such as those that run the nationalized industries, and private companies. As a result of this delegation of legislative power, so-called statutory instruments have been issued by departments and agencies at a rate of ten to fifteen times the number of laws passed by Parliament. Interested parties are carefully consulted before statutory instruments are drawn up, and the majority of them must go before Parliament for validation, or possible amendment. The House of Commons has established a Select Committee on Statutory Instruments, which scrutinizes these ordinances and, in case of doubt, brings them to the attention of the House. The making of administrative rules falls in the same category, except that these rules rarely have to undergo scrutiny by Parliament. This lapse of popular control led to severe criticisms, most notably by the Lord Chief Justice Hewart, who, in his book *The New Despotism* (1929), warned against the creation of a bureaucratic power complex with the unrestrained right to make its own administrative rules and decisions in its dealing with the public. Since that time, recourse by injured parties to the courts has again been instituted.

In France   The French have always had a tradition of using executive decrees to a much greater extent than Anglo-American practice

[3] The Privy Council is composed of some 300 persons, including all present and past Cabinet members, Commonwealth prime ministers, and high judicial and church officials. Its functions today are largely ceremonial, with the exception of certain committees of the council, such as its Judicial Committee.

would consider compatible with popular government. In spite of the dominance of the Chamber of Deputies under the Third Republic and of the National Assembly under the Fourth Republic, the number of *decrèt-lois* issued by the executive was quite considerable. Under the Fourth Republic, in particular, the French Parliament twice voted "full powers," first to Premier Paul Reynaud in 1948 and then again to Mendes-France in 1955, to issue decrees covering vast fields of economic regulation, but limited in their duration and effect on the budget. Parliament had to ratify the decrees. In 1958, after the leaders of the collapsing Fourth Republic had called on General de Gaulle to take over power, the Assembly made another grant of full powers to deal with the emergency and to draw up a new constitution. The emergency powers were to be in effect for six months and covered everything except interference with fundamental rights and liberties. The Constitution of the Fifth Republic, by specifically limiting the jurisdiction of Parliement to a list of enumerated subjects of legislation, legalized the stream of *decrèt-lois* of the executive. The *Conseil d'Etat*, a unique administrative tribunal, advises the Cabinet with regard to the form and legality of executive decrees and must be consulted whenever the Assembly grants the government "special powers" to issue decrees for the period of one year. Such powers, under Article 38 of the Constitution, were granted in 1960, after de Gaulle had suppressed the revolt of the French settlers in Algeria. Under Article 16, which has been used only once so far, the President himself can proclaim an emergency and take all steps he deems necessary, upon consultation with the Constitutional Council. His power would undoubtedly include the issuing of executive decrees, but the article specifies also that Parliament shall be in session and cannot be dissolved during the duration of the state of emergency.

As for the filling in of details of legislation, the Parliament has long been in the habit of regulating certain matters by *loi-cadre*, or framework law, delegating an unusually large part of its legislative authority to administrative discretion. The reason for this extraordinary amount of confidence in administrative wisdom and integrity lies in the long tradition of the French administrative state and in the high caliber of civil service personnel who are recruited from the best schools and are specially trained. Administrative discretion also includes the broad departmental powers to issue rules and regulations that are considered an exercise of the police power of the state. The ubiquitous *Conseil d'Etat* again checks the more important rules and regulations for conflict with the laws or with the constitutional liberties of the citizen. Complaints by injured parties are not addressed to the courts, as in Britain and the United States, but to administrative courts and to the *Conseil d'Etat*, which also operates in the capacity of a high tribunal of administrative law. There is in French minds an implicit belief in the integrity and fairness of administrative law, of which the members of the *conseil* are the high priests.

In Germany In Germany, too, executive decree-making power and administrative discretion play a very prominent role. The executive was strong before 1945 because autocratic monarchy was abandoned only as recently as 1918. Administrative discretion still is all-pervasive because, similar to France, the tradition of the administrative state, especially in Prussia, goes back much farther than that of any other modern governmental institution. After the fall of the monarchy in 1918, the Constitution of the democratic Republic of Weimar established a strong, popularly elected President, not unlike the Constitution of the Fifth Republic as presently amended. To this President, the Constitution entrusted largely undefined emergency powers in its Article 48 as an "emergency brake" in case the more responsible politicians were to lose control over the as yet untried democratic institutions of the young republic. As it developed, the crises of the Weimar Republic occurred with such frequency that a veritable flood of Presidential emergency decrees was issued under Article 48 throughout its fourteen years of existence.

During the last years before Hitler came to power, these decrees finally became the only legislative output of the federal government, as the *Reichstag* (Federal Diet) was stalemated by a combined majority of uncooperative Nazi and Communist deputies. Among these emergency decrees were some suspending the civil rights and fundamental freedoms of the citizens, others alternately forbidding and allowing the Nazi storm troopers and other paramilitary groups to parade in the streets, and some replacing the legal (and staunchly democratic) government of the state of Prussia with federal (and pro-Nazi) authority. After Hitler was appointed chancellor, moreover, the *Reichstag* passed the Enabling Act, granting him full powers to suspend parts of the Constitution and to rule by executive decree. After these experiences with executive power, the framers of the present West German Basic Law of 1949 understandably shied away from granting any such decree-making powers to their federal President, who was weakened in other ways also. The Basic Law of the Bonn Republic provides for a "legislative emergency," that is, a state in which the *Bundestag* may be unwilling or unable to pass urgent government legislation, but it is carefully hedged about in several ways: the Cabinet, the federal President, and the *Bundesrat* must agree on the emergency legislation passed in this manner over the heads of the elected representatives of the people in the *Bundestag,* and there is a time limit of six months.

The Cabinet and each ministry also have sweeping powers to issue orders for the purpose of carrying out the laws and of running the administrative apparatus, both of the federation and of the state governments. German practice distinguishes between orders of law (*Rechtsverordnungen*) and administrative rules (*Verwaltungsverordnungen*). The orders of law are generally based on a specific legislative authorization of the Cabinet or a minister to regulate or to fill in the details of a law. They have the force of law. The administrative rules pertain more to the organization and procedures of administrative agencies and their personnel. In the majority of cases, and especially when the administration of federal laws by the state governments is involved, the *Bundesrat* has to give its approval to both—orders of law and administrative rules. The public can have recourse to administrative or to constitutional courts as the case may demand.

EXECUTIVE-LEGISLATIVE RELATIONS

The most conspicuous diversity in the institutional design of legislative and executive policy-making is found in the patterns of executive-legslative relations. The American preference for the separation of powers on the one hand, and the evolution of parliamentary government in many countries of Western Europe on the other, point up a fundamental disagreement about how public policy-making should be organized. The American version of executive-legislative relations is due, in part, to historical accident and circumstance, in part to a mechanistic theory of government. Most significantly also, it reflects the capacity of a single executive figure to hold together a very large and heterogeneous country. An understanding of the different solutions to the problems of executive-legislative coordination in the various Western democracies is vital to an analytical knowledge of Western political institutions.

The single executive—Presidentialism

The historical models for the fashioning of the American Presidency at the Philadelphia Convention of 1787 were the British monarchy in its traditional form and the governorship in many colonies of the British Empire in the eighteenth century, with both of which the

American colonists had had ample experience. It would be an exaggeration and oversimplification to describe the relations between the king and Parliament or between the colonial governor and his legislature as a system of separation of coordinate powers in the sense of the United States Constitution, though separate they were. The king, although exercising traditional royal powers and prerogatives that gave him a preponderant position, was, in fact, in a rather anomalous position because the Act of Settlement of 1701 had once and for all allocated sovereignty to Parliament. His personally appointed representatives in the colonies—the governors—similarly occupied a very strong position vis-à-vis the elected representatives of the colonists, although in subsequent years the trend elsewhere in the British Empire was toward the decline of the governor-general and the rise of a parliamentary executive. The desire of the other British colonists for a parliamentary executive thus served to whittle away the quasi-monarchic authority of the former chief executive and to transfer most of his authority to parliamentary leaders. The American colonists won complete independence from the British Crown at a time when the monarchic executive was still strong, and they consequently modeled their executive upon this example of executive strength except for the matter of election.

At the same time, the mechanistic theories of government of the late eighteenth century, together with a strong preference for as little government as possible, led the framers of the American Constitution to see the separation and juxtaposition of the chief functions of government as an ideal arrangement. The distinction between legislative, executive, and judicial functions goes back to antiquity, but it was for the French political thinker Baron de Montesquieu (1689–1755) to write in his *Spirit of the Laws* (1748):

> *When the legislative and executive powers are united in the same person, or in the same body of magistrates, there can be no liberty . . . lest the same monarch or senate enact tyrannical laws to execute them tyrannically.*

The separation between the executive and legislative branches written into the United States Constitution was, however, never to be so complete as to prohibit cooperation on fundamental governmental tasks. The President still participated in legislation through his message and veto power. The Congress had budgetary control over the executive and could issue legislative commands to it and establish or abolish executive agencies. The Senate, in particular, participated in executive appointments and the making of foreign policy. Neither was the desired antagonism between the two branches intended to be so prevalent as to produce a complete deadlock. During the first three or four decades of the young republic, in fact, the social and later the party ties uniting President and congressional leaders were close enough to keep the separation of power system operating smoothly. As a matter of fact, for a while, the nomination of candidates for President was in the hands of the congressional parties.

But the expansion of the country, the broadening of the suffrage, and the incisive social and economic changes brought about by war and depression soon began to transform the Presidency into a chief focus of national unity for the most disparate and heterogeneous groups at the same time that Congress became more and more fragmented by functional and sectional demands. Nominated as a presidential candidate by a party convention, the typical American President of the last one hundred years has been an outsider to the ranks of national party leaders in the Congress. The senators in the White House of the last decade constitute a new trend which may well lead back to more executive-legislative unity. Before 1960, the President was generally a former governor of a large state, or a popular general of a past war. Nor are the cabinet officers of the President's choice usually selected from among the senior politicians of his party in Congress. The leaders of his congressional party have to accept him as their leader upon whose success the fortunes of the party depend. He may have a following throughout the country and in both houses of Congress, a presidential party, to which he owes his selection on the floor of the nominating convention. But his Presidential party is not identical with the congressional party of the same label. Friction and rivalry develop and soon deadlock threatens even the most popular President, following a brief honeymoon of executive-legislative harmony. Despite his awesome concentration of powers and his mandate for four years from a majority of the voters, the single executive is very much alone with his responsibility to the electorate and to the Constitution, which he swears to uphold in his oath of office.

Although the single executive of the American system appears to have served the United States well, there have been few attempts at imitation among the older constitutional democracies, and none of any permanence. The French adopted the concept of a single executive in 1848 only to find their first President, Louis Napoleon, using the office to become Emperor Napoleon III. Most Latin American nations adopted a Presidential regime after their emancipation from colonial rule, but generally with doubtful results. More often than not, their Presidents became caudillos, and their legislatures little more than rubber stamps of the will of the strongman. At the very least, the Presidents have tended to legislate, leaving their congresses little more than a veto power and no powers at all over the liberally used decree and emergency powers of the single executive. The more recent trend toward closer adherence to the standards of constitutional democracy in Latin America often took the form of abandoning the single executive in favor of a plural executive of the Cabinet or council type. In a sense the position of the charismatic leaders of many a new nation of Asia or Africa today would seem to have much in common with the image of the single executive—more than with that of a prime minister of a Cabinet system, the title some of them hold. Such a comparison would have to rest its case chiefly on the plebiscitary nature of the authority of leaders such as Kenyatta, Nehru, Sukarno, or Bourguiba—on the popular stewardship of their role rather than on their juxtaposition to a congress, or, analogously, to their single, dominant party, which they generally have in far better control than does the President of the United States over Congress.

British Cabinet government

It is one of the supreme ironies of constitutional history in the West that the same British tradition that is largely credited with having originated the separation of powers also gave birth to parliamentary government, in fact, that it began to do so long before the United States Constitution was written. The causes of the development of the "fusion of powers" in the Cabinet can be found both in the rise of parliamentary supremacy and in historical circumstances. The supremacy of Parliament derived from the civil wars of the seventeenth century and the Glorious Revolution of 1688, which put an end to the concept of monarchy by divine right, as well as from the theories of parliamentary sovereignty of the nineteenth century, which refused to tolerate even the appearance of a sharing of sovereign power between monarch and Parliament, despite such formulas as "the King in Parliament," which preface all laws. The concatenation of historical accidents began with the weakness of British monarchs in the eighteenth century, who found it increasingly necessary to select their advisory cabinet from among the leaders of Parliament who could marshal broad support in both houses for the purposes of the Crown. The first two Hanoverians, George I (1714–1727) and George II (1727–1760), felt so handicapped by their ignorance of the language and of the complexities of British politics that they left the conduct of the executive power largely to such skillful cabinet leaders as Sir Robert Walpole (1676–1745), who became not only the first prime minister but also the first head of a Cabinet to be overthrown by Parliament. Still, the executive-legislative relations of British government were not clearly recognized to constitute an entirely new and most desirable pattern until the middle of the nineteenth century, when Walter Bagehot pointed out in *The English Constitution* (1867) that the real power in Great Britain rode not in the royal coach but in a taxicab on the way to number 10 Downing Street. This metaphor signified the transfer of executive, policy-making power from the Crown to the parliamentary executive, the head of what is today the "executive committee" of the House of Commons, the prime minister of the Cabinet.

This was the origin of *parliamentary government*, or *parliamentarism*, the generic name reflecting the derivation of the highest governmental authority from parliamentary supremacy. In its British version, parliamentary government has meant an extraordinary degree of power concentrated in the Cabinet, which sits simultaneously at the apex of the national administrative machinery, in full control of the House of Commons, and at the head of the major party of the land that received a popular mandate at the last general elections. The centralized and well-disciplined nature of British political parties makes this a system of "responsible party government" because the electorate can make a choice between two competing programs and sets of leaders and thereby enforce governmental responsibility in the long run. The emergence of a Cabinet of sixteen to nineteen members within a ministry of some seventy, of an "Inner Cabinet" of eight or nine within the Cabinet, and of the prime minister as the prominent head of what is otherwise a collegial body, further points to the degree of centralization in policy-making. The prominence of the prime minister as government leader, party leader, and steward of the people has become so great that the parliamentary elections, though formally elections to the seats of the House of Commons, are fought largely as a personal duel between the incumbent and the opposition leader, and between their "teams," the incumbent Cabinet and the shadow Cabinet of the opposition party.

The contrast to the American system of separation of powers lies not only in the concentration of powers in one small group rather than in three coordinate branches,[4] but also in the nature of the selection process that brings men to the highest executive offices. In Great Britain, the prime minister and his Cabinet all must have acquired a seat in the House of Commons or the House of Lords before they can become members of the Cabinet. Thus they are

---

[4] The British judiciary is independent but has no power to rule acts of Parliament unconstitutional.

never complete outsiders but can generally look back upon many years of a successful parliamentary career in which they have acquired both plenty of experience and the cooperation of their fellow legislators. The prime minister, in particular, must win a seat in the House of Commons, according to recent custom, which fact has induced many a hopeful contender to divest himself of his aristocratic title and become Sir Alec Douglas-Home (Lord Home) or Quintin Hogg (Lord Hailsham). With respect to the United States, the closest analogy to the British practice would be to select as Presidential candidates the floor leaders of both majority and minority in the House of Representatives and to recruit their Cabinets from among other legislative leaders of either party in the House and the Senate.

Even then it would still take the sharpness of party lines and the cohesion of British parliamentary parties to provide an analogous setting. And the prime minister and Cabinet so selected would have to retain their leading positions in the Congress. It will be recalled what dominant role the legislative organization and procedure in the House of Commons accords to the Cabinet. The Cabinet makes most of the laws and the budget, guides them through the House, has the commissioners of the monarch give the royal assent, and implements the execution of the laws.

The House of Commons, on the other hand, and especially the opposition party, has the duty and ample opportunity to subject the Cabinet to public debate on all matters of policy and administration. More specifically, the parliamentary question hour puts the prime minister and his Cabinet ministers four times a week through a purgatory of written and oral questions on matters, large and small, which inevitably uncover mistakes or abuses and inject them into the editorial columns of the press and, potentially, into the campaign arguments of the opposition at the next general elections. Unlike American Cabinet officers who can claim executive prerogative, the British Cabinet members thus have to be present in person and to account for their policies and the actions or omissions of their departments whenever a member of Parliament demands it of them.

This account would not be complete without mention of the important role of solidarity in British Cabinet government throughout the rise and fall of Cabinets. The Cabinet is a collective body sharing the responsibility as one man. It is not possible for a Cabinet member to carry his dissent from a Cabinet meeting in speeches to the outside as American Cabinet members have been known to do. Neither can the House of Commons vote only one Cabinet minister out of office. Cabinet solidarity requires that the Cabinet sink or swim together, though it can also require one member to be the scapegoat for some common disaster and quietly resign. It is also rather unlikely that a segment of the party in power would break ranks and vote with the opposition to bring down the government however much they may be in disagreement. Since the opposition party is in the minority, then, the government is more likely to fall because of repudiation by public opinion or by covert dissension within the party than by a formal vote of no confidence or of censure. Of course, it may also be forced to call elections because by-elections have whittled down its narrow majority or because the five-year term of the House of Commons nears its end. In any case it is the privilege of the prime minister to choose the time to "go to the people" in such a manner as to favor his reelection. The dissolution of the House by the Crown (only at the request of the Cabinet) is the decisive step in the quest of the prime minister for a new popular mandate. Often the mere threat of dissolution can help to keep the majority party in line behind him. If the prime minister's party loses its majority in the elections, the implication is a mandate for the opposition, even if the opposition did not receive a majority owing to the presence of a third party. The monarch must honor the popular will as customarily interpreted.

French Assembly government

In France, the other great Western European democracy, parliamentary government began in the 1870s, after nearly a century of experiments with various forms of government. There were several basic differences between Great Britain and France that tended to create a rather different setting for French parliamentarism. To begin with, French political parties lacked the discipline and cohesion of their British counterpart. They were often little more than unstable legislative factions with little or no grass-roots organization. There were no two major parties, such as have characterized British politics for more than a century, and at first there was little consensus on the form and procedures of government among the monarchistic and republican groups of various coloration. Furthermore, there was the tradition of the strong state, whose civil service and executive prerogatives dated back to before the great revolution of 1789. Faced with such an unyielding monolith, French legislators and parliamentary parties rarely came to feel that they controlled the government and were responsible for its actions. Instead they seem to have conceived of their role more as that of popular tribunes, representatives of the people versus the state.

Throughout the nearly seventy years of the Third Republic, the Chamber of Deputies grew in influence at the expense of the Senate and of the President of the Republic. One of its first Presidents, Marshal MacMahon, was responsible for much of the decline of the Presidency and the rise of assembly supremacy through his high-handed actions, including an unfortunate precedent that discredited the use of the power of dissolution to discipline the Chamber of Deputies for eight decades. Without this counterweight against the parliamentary weapon of overthrowing the government, however, a forever unruly assembly toppled one coalition Cabinet after the other with awesome regularity. A French social scientist, Auguste Soulier,[5] counted the causes for the fall of more than 100 Cabinets of the Third Republic. Most frequently, Cabinets were toppled by shifts in party strength after an election. Of 28 Cabinets receiving an expression of no confidence, 17 found themselves in the minority at the end of a debate following an *interpellation*,[6] 1 Cabinet was not allowed the establishment of normal relations with the Chamber, 4 resigned after their legislative proposals had been changed substantially, and 6 left office in spite of express endorsement by the Chamber. Another 15 Cabinets quit because the Chamber thwarted their plans by denying them the financial means, and other Cabinets resigned after clashes with the powerful committees of both houses, with organized pressure blocs in the Chamber, or with the President himself. Thus surrounded by hostile agents, the typical French Cabinet tended to see ministerial responsibility involved in every conceivable detail of its short life. Its average tenure of seven to eight months became even shorter toward the latter years of the Third Republic—too short for a minister to establish firm control over the seasoned high civil servants running his ministry, even though some ministers outlived several Cabinets. And the premiers seemed to be almost relieved to lay down their high executive office and to return to their seats in the Chamber, where many other former premiers awaited them.

The onslaught of the Axis powers in 1940 brought the Third Republic to an untimely end and produced the authoritarian Vichy Regime. In 1946, again, a Constituent Assembly, dominated by the Communists, the Socialists, and the *Mouvement Republicain Populaire* (MRP), drew up a new constitution for a Fourth Republic. However, it took a second Constituent Assembly and a second con-

---

[5] *L'instabilité ministerielle sous la troisième République* (Paris, 1939).
[6] An interpellation is a formal question directed at the premier or a minister, who has to reply orally before the Assembly. The reply is followed by a general debate, ending with a vote that may imply a lack of confidence.

stitutional draft to secure the consent of a majority of the voters. The first draft would have established a unicameral legislature with extensive control over the executive. The second draft added a weak upper house, now called Council of the Republic, and other modifications of this extreme design for assembly government. Care was taken to provide for the power of dissolution under circumscribed conditions.[7] The three parties in control during the first years also seemed to be far more cohesive and better organized than those of the Third Republic. An anti-Fascist consensus, which emerged from the wartime Resistance, helped the three parties to operate the new parliamentary system for a while. But soon the Socialists and the MRP lost their electoral strength, and the Communists returned to their irreconcilable opposition of earlier days. The parliamentary system returned to its prewar features of ministerial instability. Governments now fell after an average of five months in office. Unpopular measures and grave decisions, such as those demanded by the Algerian question, were postponed from Cabinet to Cabinet until, in 1958, the Fourth Republic collapsed before the threat of military revolt and civil war.

The procedure of the Fourth Republic for setting up a new Cabinet was the same as that followed before 1940, though it generally took longer. The President of the Republic chose a likely combination of middle-of-the-road parties and designated a prime minister who would then try to strike a bargain with the four or five groups needed to form a legislative majority. The ministers were, for the most part, members of the Assembly to which the Cabinet owed responsibility.[8] The life of the Cabinet inevitably depended on the uncertain agreement of the coalition partners on a few issues and was threatened as soon as unforeseen, divisive questions came up. Cabinets frequently asked for a vote of confidence in connection with important projects and sometimes with minor matters. The Assembly could also take the initiative and prepare a vote of censure that would bring down the Cabinet if supported by a majority.

It will also be remembered that *commissions* of the National Assembly had taken firm control of all pieces of legislation, including Cabinet bills, and even of the budget. Under these circumstances, it was easy for Cabinets to feel thwarted in their plans and to resign in disgust. The *commissions* also took on the job of supervising the

---

[7] The power of dissolution remained in disuse except for one time in 1956 when Premier Edgar Faure invoked it, only to find himself universally condemned.

[8] In the Third Republic, many had been senators and in de Gaulle's Fifth Republic, many have been experts from outside Parliament.

executive and frequently yielded to the temptation to initiate governmental action themselves. At the same time, the use of written and oral questions was not as pronounced in French parliamentarism as in Great Britain. Instead, the French deputies either called ministers before one of the *commissions* to answer questions or used the dreaded interpellation to bring the Cabinet to heel. An interpellation is a question directed at the Premier or a particular minister who has to reply in full. The government's reply is followed by a debate ending with a vote to proceed to the "order of the day." An adverse vote or one requiring the government to take remedial action was quite likely to lead to its resignation.

Thus parliamentary government under the Third and Fourth Republics of France produced a rather different system from that of Great Britain. The names "cabinet government" and "assembly government" are in themselves indicative of the chief differences, whatever the reasons. They also hint at the difficulties of transplanting governmental institutions from one Western country to another, not to mention transplantation to a new nation.

Stabilizing the parliamentary executive in France During the dozen years of the Fourth Republic there was no lack of critics of ministerial instability, both inside and outside the National Assembly. Several attempts were made to strengthen and stabilize the executive, among other devices, by an electoral reform that reduced for a while the large number of Communist deputies in the Assembly. One of the most outspoken critics of the Fourth Republic was General de Gaulle. In 1958, when the parliamentary system broke down in the face of threatening civil war, de Gaulle and his friends were given full powers not only to deal with the crisis but also to rewrite the constitution as they felt should have been done from the beginning. The result of their constructive criticisms and of further developments brought about by de Gaulle is the present constitution of the Fifth Republic whose executive-legislative relations are a mixture of presidentialism and parliamentarism.

It will be remembered how the constitution of the Fifth Republic weakened the powerful *commissions* of the National Assembly and transferred budgetary authority and the control over the legislative agenda to the Cabinet so that a certain similarity to the procedures in England seemed to result. But at the same time, the framers of the new constitution took further steps to make up for the lack of a strong two-party system in France, such as the one that makes Cabinet government possible in Great Britain. Instead of resting the strengthened Cabinet on a coalition of the "old parties" or even on the large Gaullist Union for the New Republic (UNR), they decided to separate it in various ways from the Assembly. Ministers now have to resign their Assembly seats upon appointment and cannot return to them after their Cabinet steps down. Many ministers, as mentioned above, are experts called in from the outside. The Cabinet is still responsible to the National Assembly, but the ways in which the Assembly can control, supervise, and censure the Cabinet have been curtailed so substantially as to make the parliamentary character of the relationship doubtful. There is far less opportunity for the Assembly to upset a Cabinet by frustrating its legislative and budgetary plans, and the Cabinet can be overthrown only by a formal motion of censure, which requires an absolute majority of the deputies as well as a waiting period of forty-eight hours, and which can be used only once in a session. The Premier can stake the fortunes of his government on any bill, which then becomes law unless the Assembly can mount a successful motion of censure within twenty-four hours. The question period, finally, was increased at the same time that the practice of *interpellations* ending with a vote was discouraged. Although it is still possible for an angry Assembly to bring down governments, the present system is hardly one of parliamentary supremacy. In fact, there may be a kernel of truth in the jocular assertion that it is now the government that legislates and the Assembly that has an "executive veto."

Most unorthodox for a parliamentary system, however, was the establishment of a strong Presidency in place of what is ordinarily a figurehead, with largely symbolic and ceremonial functions. The Presidents of the Third and Fourth Republics were elected by Parliament, which fact clearly indicated the source of their authority. The 1958 constitution set up an electoral college of some 80,000 electors composed of more than three-fourths of municipal councilors and mayors. In 1962, however, President de Gaulle changed the election modus to direct popular election, which will give French Presidents a powerful popular mandate, not unlike that derived by Napoleon I and Napoleon III from plebiscites. This method of electing the President, de Gaulle hoped, would remold the French party system into two strong groups, as indeed it seems to have done in the United States. However, de Gaulle's reelection in 1965 and the Presidential elections since that time have given little evidence of such bipolarization in French politics.

Even before this plebiscitary turn, the new Presidency had enough power to constitute the chief focus of authority in the 1958 constitution. The constitution conferred upon the President the guardianship over the functioning of the governmental organs, together with sweeping emergency powers under Article 16. In conjunction with his traditional headship over the entire administration, the armed forces, and the French community, and added to these, his personal prestige as the embodiment of French greatness during the bitter days of defeat in World War II, this grant of powers gave de Gaulle invincible strength in French politics. His successors are unlikely to match this personal preeminence behind the office. Vis-à-vis the once-proud National Assembly, the constitution added a power of dissolution that is solely in the hands of the President and, while sending the deputies home for reelection or defeat, affects neither the Cabinet nor the President, who has a seven-year term. The Cabinet no longer falls with every election. It is selected and appointed by the President and requires no "investiture" by the Assembly, although it can be repudiated by it. The French President has always presided over Cabinet meetings. Since 1958, however, his weighty presence gives him a policy-making role of major importance tending toward the eclipse of the premier and other key ministers. Under President de Gaulle, at least, no premier or foreign minister could be anything but his spokesman and helpmate. Whether President Pompidou and his successors will be able to maintain his system or will prefer to modify its authoritarian features in the direction of more parliamentarism only the future can tell. Pompidou's conduct of the Presidency has already shown a tendency to rely more heavily on the Gaullist party than de Gaulle ever did.

Stabilizing other parliamentary systems

France has not been the only country to experiment with modifications of parliamentary government. Another significant example of such experimentation is provided by the German Republics of Weimar and Bonn, although they seem to have followed a course opposite to that of the French.

Executive-legislative relations under the Weimar Republic of 1919 were patterned, in large part, after the preceding imperial regime which in its last days had allowed its ministers to become responsible to the *Reichstag*, under the impact of impending military defeat. Thus the chancellor and his Cabinet were now to be drawn from a majority coalition of the many parties in the lower house, whereas the *Reich* President would be directly elected by the new sovereign, the people. Having been denied control over the executive for such a long time, the *Reichstag* now introduced French-style questions and *interpellations* with a vengeance. With a multiparty system incapable of rallying majority parties or even stable coalitions,

Cabinets fell as frequently as in the Third and Fourth Republics of France. Rising economic crises and political turmoil in the early 1930s finally made the establishment of Cabinets with a parliamentary majority impossible as the number of seats of Communists and National Socialists, combined, reached a majority of the *Reichstag,* not counting the other parties hostile to the republican constitution. During the last two years before the appointment of Hitler, the Cabinet of the Weimer Republic was forced into complete reliance on the emergency powers of the *Reich* President.

The strong Presidency was thought of by many as the "emergency brake" on the, as yet, unfamiliar processes of party government and parliamentary democracy. This tentative attitude toward parliamentary government marked, also, other aspects of the "improvised democracy" of Weimar. Cabinet ministers, for example, were often selected from among nonpartisan, outside figures or experts rather than from the party leaders in the mistaken belief of thereby escaping the violent factionalism that rent the political community. The second *Reich* President, von Hindenburg, was also an unpolitical figure, who represented the military glory of the past but was quite unable to deal with the political crises before him. The tentative attitude toward parliamentary democracy in the end induced many Germans to toy with the idea of replacing it with a more authoritarian regime, and made even the "constitutional dictatorship" of the emergency powers of the *Reich* President seem like a normal form of government. Thus, parliamentary government in the Weimar Republic met an untimely end, among other reasons, because of the diffidence of the party politicians who were all too ready to leave authority to the strong President.

The Bonn Republic represents in many ways a strong reaction to the weaknesses of the Weimar Republic. Its executive-legislative relations, in particular, show a determination to establish a system of Cabinet government somewhat like that of Great Britain. The framers of the Basic Law of 1949 completely eliminated the strong, popularly elected President of the Weimar model and created instead, with their Federal President, a figurehead weaker than the President of the Fourth Republic of France. At the same time they decided to stabilize the parliamentary executive, the Chancellor, with a novel device: the *constructive no-confidence* vote. The *Bundestag* can overthrow a chancellor only by electing a successor. The theory behind this clause is that an irresponsible opposition, such as the combination of Communists and National Socialists in the early thirties, would thus be unable to topple governments.

In the decade and a half that the West German Basic Law has

been in effect, something very close to a two-party system has supplanted the earlier multipartism, so that there are now a government party or coalition and a unified opposition party lending stability to the parliamentary system. Nevertheless, the *constructive no-confidence* vote still weights the scales noticeably on the executive side with side effects that are not always desirable.

This analysis of the separation of powers system compared with the system of parliamentary government may not have answered conclusively the question of which of the two is better. The answer to this question hinges on the philosophical encounter of theories of constitutional checks and balances with those emphasizing governmental responsibility to the people. A conclusive answer also involves a detailed analysis of the political parties, sectional or other divisions, and legal procedures of a country. What has worked well in Great Britain and the United States may not do so elsewhere. However, some basic relationships should have become clear from this survey. A homogeneous, unified society, with a two-party system of centralized, well-disciplined parties (unlike that of the United States) seems to be well served by parliamentarism. Countries with many parties and great sectional and other diversities, on the other hand, are better off entrusting their executive authority to a strong President. Attempts to combine the two systems seen to create a confusion of authority and to undermine the position of the prime minister.

Policy-making, a challenge to democratic citizenship

One final note on policy-making is in order. As will be recalled, policy-making is by no means confined to official policy-makers, whether legislative or executive. A multitude of more or less organized groups and more or less stable personal relationships, from parties and organized interests to personal friendships and golf course partners, play an important role. Even the staff of legislative committees or the office staff of an executive agency may influence crucial decisions. A receptionist's friendly smile or early morning curtness to a visitor of her legislator or administrator boss may have unforeseen consequences.

In a democratic society, the policy-making process is supposed to involve everyone, from an informed citizenry to interested groups contending over specific issues, from an alert and critical press to lively political grass-roots discussion. In an age of vastly multiplied government functions and enormous governmental power in society, the process of policy-making presents one of the greatest challenges to democratic citizenship. It can be the solemn manner by which free men realize their loftiest dreams of human dignity and individual freedom, or it can be a burdensome tyranny, a meddlesome and yet inefficient machinery through which countless special and local interests prey on the conscience, the dignity, and the pocketbook of the defenseless citizen and taxpayer.

What makes the difference is the enduring concern of citizens and political leaders with the following three questions: (1) Are the policy-making institutions and processes organized as effectively as possible for carrying through the steps of policy-making described above? (2) Are they organized in such a fashion that the electorate can at any time pinpoint responsibility for action or failure to act, and enforce its will in the long run? (3) Is everything being done to encourage the participation of an informed and politically interested citizenry in the process of policy-making? Depending, of course, on an ever-present and ever-new concern with the answers to these questions under changing circumstances, there is ample reason to hope that even big government can be a faithful servant to man's best interests.

CHAPTER **9** JUDGES AND
CIVIL SERVANTS

In comparison to the glamor of policy-making, the roles of judges and administrators, whose responsibility it is to oversee the execution of the policies, may seem subsidiary and dull. On closer examination, however, it can be seen that the functions of courts and public administration go far beyond implementing the policies made by the policy-makers. There is enough leeway within the policies laid down by legislators and executive leaders to allow development of judicial and administrative policies. And there are other salient features of adjudication and administration that lend to these functions an importance far greater than the day-to-day making of public policy.

It is not easy to describe why and in what sense the judicial and administrative functions are more basic to government than something as central as the policy-making process. One reason is to be found, perhaps, in the difference between the words "the law" and "laws." The law is the entire legal order, including statutes and ordinances—those passed yesterday and others passed centuries ago. It includes also the rules of custom, the values of the community, and in particular, its sense of justice. Different legal or judicial systems may vary in their stress on the *positive law*, that is, statutes and acknowledged customs, as compared to abstract notions of justice. But the primary function of a judge in deciding an individual case is *the maintenance of the whole legal order*—to see to it that transgressions are punished, disputes are settled, and justice is done. Judges maintain the whole legal order, whereas the policy-makers only amend it in small ways.

Administration is perhaps too diverse in its tasks to be condensed into a simple definition. Generally speaking, the basic function of the administration is to direct and manage the affairs of government —its personnel, its finances, and its concrete assets. To use a figure of speech, while the policy-makers spend their time thinking up new enterprises and better ways to serve the customers, the administrators mind the store, manage the whole business, and supervise the employees in the discharge of their duties and functions.

LAW AND LEGAL SYSTEMS

Broadly speaking, some kind of law and rudimentary devices for its enforcement have always been present. Living in a human community requires adherence to certain basic rules of conduct. The rules may be evolved by the customs of everyday living and be absorbed by each individual as he grows into his role in society. Law codes may attempt to state what the customary rules are or try to promulgate new ones. Since man is an intelligent being, the rules must be knowable or made known to him, though the extent of popular knowledge of the law will always be limited to what a person needs to know for the purposes of his own life. Because in case of disputes and controversies each party tends to take a rather subjective, if not self-righteous, point of view, no matter how clear and well-understood the rules, an impartial, knowledgeable arbiter or judge is needed to make an authoritative decision.

There are many kinds of law, distinguishable, for instance, by their degree of sophistication. Primitive societies have primitive legal systems. Less developed, agrarian societies require much less in the way of a legal apparatus than highly diversified, urban-industrial or commercial civilizations. One may compare, for example, the 4000-year-old law code of Hammurabi, King of Babylon, or the Twelve Tables of the origins of Roman law with the highly technical nature of typical satutes of today. With the rising complexity of the law, the demands on the professional competence of lawyers also rise, and their selection and training has to be commensurate with their functions.

Kinds of law

Among the categories of different kinds of laws in modern legal systems, the following are of general significance. The distinction between *private law* and *public law* is as old as the Roman law tradition and is still an important division between large substantive areas of modern law. *Private law* concerns the relationships between private individuals and persons, including, for example, conflicting claims to the same property, contractual obligations between individuals or corporations, and obligations arising from marriage or divorce. *Public law* defines and regulates rights and duties of which the state is either the subject (the holder of a right) or the object (of a duty). Public law would include, for example, the right of the state to collect fees, customs duties, or taxes from individuals, or condemnation proceedings to acquire private land for public use. Another example of public law is the individual claim for social welfare under existing legislation that establishes the obligation of the public authorities to disburse certain amounts in case of certain kinds of disability, unemployment, or accident. The distinction between private and public law is particularly important in Roman law countries such as France, where a different supreme court is provided for private cases, the *Cour de Cassation*. Cases of public law are handled by the *Conseil d'Etat*.

Another significant distinction in modern legal systems is that made between *civil law* and *criminal law*, for which some judicial systems provide different courts. A civil law case is normally a dispute between two or more private persons or organizations for decision by a court, say, for breach of contract, defamation of character, or a suit for divorce. Civil law suits can also be brought by a governmental agency against a private party, such as against a contractor. The French *droit civil*, for example, embraces the law of persons, including the protection of the interests of minors, family law, property law, contracts and torts, community property, and estates. Cases under criminal law are invariably brought by the state, with a public prosecutor or district attorney leveling an accusation at the defendant "in the name of the people of the state of so-and-so." Criminal law defines crimes against the public order, such as homicide, rape, or perjury, and provides the appropriate punishment. The verdict is one of guilty or not guilty, and a jury is often employed as befits the one governmental function that can most deeply affect the lives of citizens by taking away their property, liberty, or even their lives.

There are also other categories of law whose spheres have been given to separate courts in some countries. *Commercial law* is the body of usages and statutes that have been developed in centuries of business transactions, fairs, and commerce, often transcending the boundaries of legal systems and even nation-states. *International law*, public and private, similarly, grew from custom, usage, and general notions of law and treaties among states. Unlike most kinds of law, international law lacks the iron hand of enforcement, except through retribution or its threat, or by an international organization, although there is an International Court of Justice and there have long been arbitral tribunals called for special cases. *Constitutional law* of the constitution, including implementing legislation, such as organic laws setting up governmental institutions or defining the relations between them. By its very nature, it is of a higher order than ordinary law, and when in conflict, overrides the validity of the latter. Constitutional law in the form of cases and court rulings is more likely to be highly developed in the few countries practicing judicial review, such as the United States. This is not to say that there is no elaborate constitutional law to be found in a country like France. On the contrary, French constitutional law is spelled out in the legal treatises and textbooks of French law faculties, and occasional rulings of the *Conseil d'Etat* are part of it. In Great Britain, where no court can invalidate parliamentary legislation, the courts can still interpret the laws and their constitutional context in quo warranto proceedings which do produce some case law on the constitution.

Constitutional law is a part of public law and not always clearly separated from *administrative law*. Administrative law consists of the rules and regulations governing the relations and procedures of administrative agencies. It is generally promulgated by higher administrative agencies for the lower levels, and its passage often involves some legislative participation or review. To the extent that administrative law defines the form and organization of governmental agencies, it may coincide with parts of constitutional law. *Labor law* is the outgrowth of less than a century of collective contracts and legislation governing the relations between employers and employees. The complexity of modern tax legislation and the thicket of social security laws in some countries have also led to the growth of *fiscal law* and *social insurance law*, with appropriate tribunals to consider complaints and challenges to state action.

Legal systems—Roman law and common law

The two most widely used legal systems in the Western world are derived from Roman law and from English common law. The differences between the two are fundamental and manifest themselves in many ways. Historical in their roots, even constituting a matter of different temperaments, the different legal systems have often been described and compared by legal experts belonging to one system in terms most unfavorable to the other. Some of the distinguishing labels have borne overtones of bias, despite their explanatory intent, such as when common law writers contrasted the "inquisitorial" procedure of Roman law courts with the "accusatorial" procedure of their own. Sometimes manifestly false principles are attributed to Roman law systems, such as "that the accused is considered guilty until proven innocent." Sometimes also, the comparison has gone no deeper than to aver rather erroneously that Roman law was purely statutory and common law strictly judge-made law. A look at the historical backgrounds of both Roman law and common law may help to clarify some aspects of each.

Roman law We have already encountered Roman law in the discussion of constitutionalism in ancient Rome (see Chapter 6). During the first six centuries, from the origin of the Twelve Tables in about the middle of the fifth century B.C. Roman law was a system very much like the idealized image of common law two thousand years later. Based on judicial decisions and well-established, but unwritten, legal customs, it owed its vitality and flexibility as much to its closeness to the facts of each case as to its reluctance to theorize and to commit its legal notions to verbal formulas. The Roman *ius civile*, after which present-day Roman law is sometimes misleadingly called "civil law," was perhaps the proudest monument to the genius of the Roman Republic.

It was not until Rome had become an absolutist empire and its civilization had passed through centuries of decline that Roman law was codified in the famous Justinian Code in A.D. 533. As further centuries of anarchy and chaos filled the void left by the fall of the Roman Empire, Roman law survived in the form of the canon law of the Catholic Church until its rediscovery at French and Italian universities in the twelfth century. By this time, far more primitive tribal and feudal systems of law had established themselves in some of the new feudal monarchies of Europe. The rediscovered Roman law, annotated by learned jurists, seemed very advantageous to the educated and mercantile classes in the newly rising cities and also to many a feudal monarch who would have preferred the absolute authority of the Roman Emperor to dependence on the vagaries in loyalty of his feudal lords. In the centuries that followed, therefore, Roman law was revived and taken over in varying degrees. It became an influential source of legal method and concepts even where it was not introduced. Areas that once were an integral part of the Roman Empire, such as southern France and Italy, naturally went farthest in this direction, while many Slavic and Germanic states tended to mix local customary law in various ways with the Roman tradition. Its influence reached as far as Scotland and the Scandinavian countries. England, too, was several times on the verge of adopting Roman law, and there is no denying the influence of Roman law thinking on the development of the common law and equity tradition.

The present Roman law countries offer a considerable variety of legal customs and practices because of these differences in historical background. At the same time, they are more alike today than they were two hundred years ago. For in 1804 Napoleon I promulgated the French *code civil,* soon followed by further law codes. The French *code civil* became the model for the legal systems of Portugal, Spain, and the Latin American republics, as well as for Quebec and Louisiana; for Switzerland, Germany, Austria, Belgium, the Netherlands, Italy; for Turkey and Japan, who chose it in their quest for modernization; and also for the colonies and dependencies of the foregoing countries.

Common law and equity The English common law originated at about the same time as the medieval rediscovery of Roman law. It was the result of the efforts of English kings such as Henry II (1133–1189) to centralize judicial authority by means of traveling judges who rode from local court to local court, hearing cases and fashioning a "common law" from regionally diverse legal customs. With the help of court records, a legal profession of high caliber, and great jurists like Henry de Bracton (died 1268), the common law soon became a complete and stable system built on the *rule of precedent (stare decisis),* which means that all principles used in judicial decisions have to be deduced from earlier cases. Such a rule is not as restrictive as it may appear, because precedents can be construed narrowly or liberally, and the facts of two cases are hardly ever alike. The common law system provided uniformity and certainty without depriving the courts of a creative role.

Still, there evidently was enough rigidity and dearth of remedies in the common law to give rise to a second strand in the development of English law: cases in *equity,* by definition a source of judicial remedies dictated by natural law and reason. Where common law would grant damages only afterwards, to cite an example, equity could force a defendant to live up to his contractual obligations or to abstain from conduct that would be injurious to the plaintiff. Writs of equity originally were granted by the king's chancellor rather than by the courts but in time gave rise to a large body of judge-made case law governed by the rule of precedent.

While equity merely complements or mitigates the common law, the needs of changing society for exceptions to the rules led to increasing legislative activity on the part of "the Crown in Parliament." The resulting statutes soon began to govern most of English criminal law and other areas of the law as well. In the United States, likewise, statutes have long occupied vast areas of the law, superseding a large part of what was once exclusively governed by common law and equity. While it is still true that the statutes tend to cover chiefly the exceptions, and the rules and principles are still left to case law, moreover, there has been some codification in several fields of law, including attempts to state or reiterate principles of common law and equity. Common law jurists still insist that theirs is a *judge-made, bench-made, case law,* but they are evidently speaking of a mode of treating and looking at legal problems, a "mode of judicial and juristic thinking" (Roscoe Pound), and a way of teaching the law rather than a pure case law without statutory, "legislative" definitions.

Common law systems spread from England and Wales to Ireland, to the American colonies, and finally to English-speaking Canada, New Zealand, and Australia. Common law also exerted considerable influence on the legal systems of India, the Scandinavian countries, and Israel.

Comparison of Roman law and common law It is evident from the foregoing description of the historical beckgrounds of Roman law and common law systems that they have much in common. The real differences can hardly be stated in terms of the slightly varying mixtures of statutes, judicial interpretation, and case law rather than legal theories. Common law countries have numerous statutes and even some codification; they also have their great jurists and legal commentaries. Roman law countries cannot enforce statutes without some judicial interpretation, and there is a rule of precedent binding lower courts to the decisions of higher courts and creating considerable bodies of case law wherever the law codes have gaps or where recent statutes and older codes form a patchwork rather than the harmonious, comprehensive edifice of a *code civil*. The real difference lies far more in the approach of judges, lawyers, and laymen to the law than in the elements and sources used.

A glimpse of the different attitude of a Roman law judge can be gotten especially from decisions in cases where the statutory law is silent, obscure, or insufficient. In such a case, a common law judge would boldly proceed to state a new rule, perhaps with reference to an obscure and distant precedent, refuse to accept the case for one reason or another, or decide the case on narrow technical grounds without venturing an opinion on issues that he feels not confident enough to judge. A Roman law judge, by contrast, is very reluctant to take on the role of creating a new rule. Since the law specifically compels him to decide the case brought before him in the broadest of terms (a refusal would be considered a denial of justice to the parties before him), he will very likely seek to relate his decision to the existing code, either by interpolating the intent of the legislators as expressed on other matters or by analogy from the logic of other parts of the code, from the context, or from the legal textbooks written by university professors. The training of a Roman law judge, his concept of the role he is called upon to play, and his concept of the nature of the law and the judicial process obviously differ a great deal from his common law counterpart.

Although there also are national differences among Roman law systems and among schools of jurisprudence that put varying stress on sociological understanding, legal positivism, or formalism, the fundamental underlying concept of the law is profoundly rationalistic and aesthetic in nature. Roman law jurists see their own law as *ratio scripta* (written reason)—perfectly rational, harmonious, natural, elegant, even beautiful. There is little of the typical common law emphasis on experience, pragmatism, or the profound respect for the stubborn facts of judicial practice, or concern for the social relationships outside the courtroom. Roman law jurists would be shocked at the statement of Justice Oliver Wendell Holmes that "the life of the law has not been logic; it has been experience." They set their trust more in logic and hence look to the lawgivers and the law professors as a guide rather than to judicial experience with actual cases. In this sense, then, common law is indeed judge-made, litigation-born, a "lawyer's law," whereas Roman law is a "professor's law" and the law of the great codes of law that have sought to draw the whole life of civil society, of crime and punishment, or of commercial transactions each into one comprehensive, perfect code of civil, criminal, and commercial law.

Judicial procedure and organization

The profound differences in attitude and concept of law cannot help but fashion decisively the procedure of law courts in the different countries. Again one should bear in mind, however, that there are considerable differences in judicial procedure and organization among the various Roman law countries and, for that matter, among the common law countries, and even among various states of the United States.

Role of the judge The role of the judge in either system varies with the kind of law at issue. In civil law suits the differences are not as great and, for obvious reasons, not as controversial as in criminal law proceedings. It is in the latter that common law observers have criticized Roman law procedures as "inquisitorial." The role of a Roman law judge, in ancient Rome as well as in prerevolutionary France, was historically associated and sometimes combined with that of the examining magistrate or the public prosecutor, which often meant that provincial judges would initiate the proceedings against an alleged lawbreaker *and* try the case in the first instance. From this precedent grew a concept of the role of the judge in criminal trials, even after the functions of public prosecutors and the judges were separated more carefully,[1] that inspired such labels as "inquisitorial."

Before the trial can begin in a French criminal court today, an *investigating judge (juge d'instruction)* carries out a careful preliminary examination *(enquête)* of the case, including an interrogation of the accused and the chief witnesses and an examination of the evidence. If the *enquête* yields insufficient evidence, the case is dropped. At the trial, the judges (generally more than one) actively participate in the courtroom questioning of witnesses and of the defendant. A French criminal trial thus becomes the public repetition of the preceding investigation with the apparent objective not only of the public prosecutor, but of the judges as well, of proving the defendant guilty according to the definition of the law. Behind this "inquisitorial" conduct of the judges lies a deep belief in the objective truth. Investigating judges regularly confront witnesses whose accounts differ in order to force them to come up with "the true story" of what happened. This search for truth places comparatively little emphasis on procedural safeguards or rules regarding the admissibility of evidence in the trial, in large part because it is the

[1] French judges still can transfer to prosecuting functions and back again with an ease that shocks common law observers.

judge rather than an opposing party that conducts the examination.

Common law procedure in criminal trials has its equivalent to the preliminary examination of Roman law procedure in the proceedings of the *grand jury,* a body of laymen who decide by majority vote whether the evidence against a person warrants an indictment, that is, that he be called to trial in court. A negative finding by the grand jury usually means that the case is dropped. An indictment, on the other hand, leads to the courtroom trial, a battle between the opposing lawyers, in what is termed the Anglo-American *adversary method.* While the lawyers struggle either to prove the case of the prosecution or to rebut it, the judge does not participate actively in the questioning of defendants and witnesses, or in the weighing of evidence. He is, rather, the referee of the match, who guards proper observance of the large body of rules of combat, procedural safeguards, and rules of evidence that have been developed over centuries of courtroom practice. In the end, the judge charges the jury to make the fateful choice between *guilty* and *not guilty.* The common law jury deliberates alone, whereas French juries in the Courts of Assize deliberate together with the judges. Behind the great concern of common law criminal procedure for the rights of the accused there lies, in the last analysis, a deep awareness of the likelihood of judicial error and of the inherent limitations of the human quest for truth.

Although there can be little doubt that common law procedure gives the defendant in criminal trials a better chance to clear himself, this is not to say that it is inherently more likely to procure justice. The adversary method can be credited with a great many historical contributions to individual freedom such as the right to confront witnesses, the right to counsel, to bail, the privilege not to have to incriminate oneself, and many other rights. Herbert J. Spiro interestingly attributes to the adversary method the development of the mental habits of British two-party government.[2] The confrontation of government and opposition, the rules of combat between the two, and the procedure by which the issues of public policy are debated and resolved do suggest a parallel between the courtroom and Parliament.

But judicial systems must stand judicial tests, such as the speedy and inexpensive availability of judicial remedies, the easy and equal access to counsel even for indigents, and the freedom of criminal trials from emotional community pressures. The common law system does not always compare favorably on these counts with French

[2] See Herbert J. Spiro, *Government by Constitution* (New York: Random House, 1959).

judicial practice. There is no statistical evidence that would indicate which of the two systems of criminal trial leads more often to wrongful convictions, but there can be little doubt that common law courts and juries more often let a guilty person go unpunished than is likely to happen, say, in France. On the other hand, the Roman law systems can rarely point to anything even resembling the independence of common law judiciaries from their administrations or ministries of justice.

Judicial organization   Judicial organization in modern states varies according ot differences in national historical tradition and other circumstances. All court systems are hierarchically organized, with *trial courts,* or *courts of original jurisdiction* forming the lowest level of the pyramid. Depending on the seriousness of the matter as determined by law, weightier cases may be assigned for trial to a higher court. A trial court renders a complete decision on the facts of a case, as well as on the law pertaining to it. But if the losing party believes that he can demonstrate errors in law or gross prejudice on the part of the trial court, he can appeal to the next higher court. An *appellate court* then reconsiders the points at issue and has the power to overrule the lower court if it so desires. In common law systems, the appellate courts generally accept the findings of a trial court as to the facts. Because there may be several levels of appeal, a case can be appealed all the way to the highest tribunal, provided each higher appellate court accepts it. The highest courts usually limit their jurisdiction to cases raising fundamental issues of legal interpretation. Most courts with appellate jurisdiction in some matters also have original jurisdiction in others. Even the United States Supreme Court has, in addition to its appellate jurisdiction over cases considered by the lower federal courts, original jurisdiction to hear cases involving ambassadors and other foreign agents and cases to which a state government is a party.

1. *Court Systems in Federations.* A federal form of government may complicate the organization and course of appeals of the judiciary. American federalism has two separate court systems, federal and state, each confined chiefly to cases involving the laws of its particular level of government (see Figure 9.1). But this is not the rule. German and Swiss federalism, and with some modification Canada as well, give their *Laender,* cantonal, or provincial courts jurisdiction over both state and federal law (see Figure 9.2, showing the court system of the Federal Republic of Germany). The federal courts serve only to maintain uniformity in legal interpretation on appeal, though they may also have original jurisdiction over such

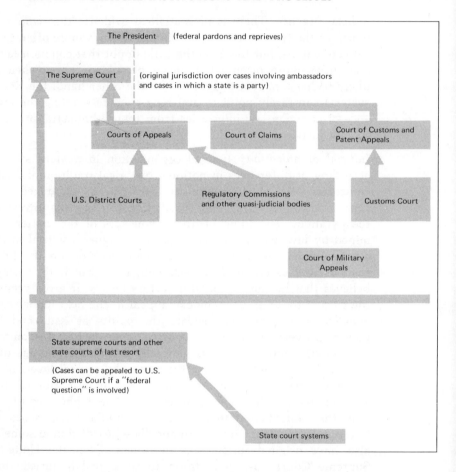

Figure 9.1   The divided court system in the United States.

subjects as disputes among the states or between the federal and state governments. Soviet federalism, by contrast, has a unified, centrally controlled judiciary whose public prosecutors on all levels are responsible to the Procurator General, and the judges are elected by the *soviets* of each level under the guidance of the Communist party.

2. *United States Courts.* There are also considerable differences between court systems characterized by functional divisions and those which provide one court hierarchy for all or almost all cases at law. In practice, the difference is more one of degree than a basic characteristic. Among the United States federal courts, for example,

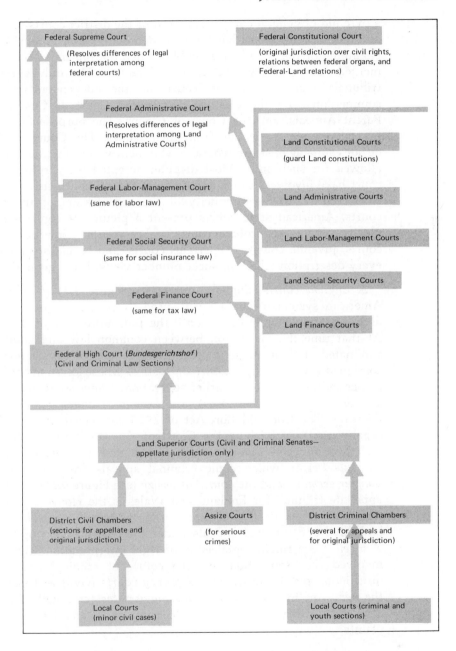

Figure 9.2   Federalism and legal unity: the court system of the
Federal Republic of Germany.

a pyramid of general courts composed of the district courts of appeal, and the Supreme Court has been the dominant pattern from the very beginning of the American Republic, when the Judiciary Act of 1789 merged courts of law and courts of equity. The only specialized tribunals, apart from military courts and the independent regulatory commissions, are the Customs Court, the Court of Customs and Patent Appeals, and the Court of Claims. The purpose of the two first mentioned is obvious from their names. The Court of Claims decides suits against the federal government within the narrow limits allowed for such suits. Most disputes accepted for a ruling of this court have involved claims arising from federal contracts.

In contrast to the simplicity of the organization of the federal courts, American state courts present a picture of confusing complexity. There are probate courts, police courts, domestic relations courts, juvenile courts, magistrates courts, and regulatory boards of every description which in sheer number vie with the general courts.

3. *English courts.* English courts (see Figure 9.3) to whom the American system owes so much, used to be a maze of functional divisions and separate courts until the Judicature Acts of the 1870s. At that time the distinction between common law and equity was eliminated, and the various central courts of civil jurisdiction were combined into the *High Court of Justice,* whose divisions still bear names indicative of their earlier separation: *Chancery* (equity cases); *Queen's Bench* (all civil cases); and *Probate, Divorce and Admiralty Division.* The Consolidation Act of 1925 completed the judicial reorganization, establishing the *Court of Appeals* before which come civil law appeals from the *High Court,* and a *Court of Criminal Appeals* before which come criminal appeals from the *courts of quarter sessions* and the *courts of assize* (see Figure 9.3). The highest appellate tribunal for England and Wales is the *House of Lords,* in which the *Legal Peers* and nine *Lords of Appeal in Ordinary* hear both civil and criminal appeals under the chairmanship of the *lord chancellor* if a fundamental issue of legal interpretation seems to be involved. The separation between courts of criminal and of civil jurisdiction reaches down to the *county courts* (civil) and *justices of the peace* or, in cities, *stipendiary magistrates* (criminal). There are also various regulatory tribunals setting rates and handling complaints.

4. *French Courts.* The French courts (see Figure 9.4) have also been divided into a three-step civil law hierarchy composed of *courts of instance* and of *grand instance, superior courts* and *courts of appeal,* and a criminal law hierarchy ranging from the criminal

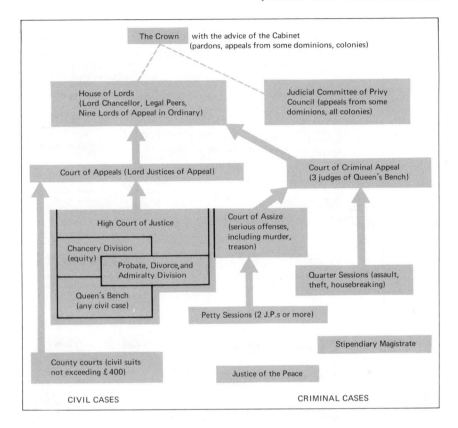

The Crown — with the advice of the Cabinet (pardons, appeals from some dominions, colonies)

House of Lords (Lord Chancellor, Legal Peers, Nine Lords of Appeal in Ordinary)

Judicial Committee of Privy Council (appeals from some dominions, all colonies)

Court of Appeals (Lord Justices of Appeal)

Court of Criminal Appeal (3 judges of Queen's Bench)

High Court of Justice

Court of Assize (serious offenses, including murder, treason)

Chancery Division (equity)

Probate, Divorce, and Admiralty Division

Quarter Sessions (assault, theft, housebreaking)

Queen's Bench (any civil case)

Petty Sessions (2 J.P.s or more)

Stipendiary Magistrate

County courts (civil suits not exceeding £400)

Justice of the Peace

CIVIL CASES

CRIMINAL CASES

Figure 9.3   The court system of England and Wales.

sections of the *courts of instance* and the *courts of correction* to the *assize courts*. The *Court of Cassation*, at the apex of the system of ordinary courts, furnishes authoritative interpretations of the law in its civil, criminal, or petitions sections and can order a case retried by another court of the same level as the one from which the case was appealed. There are also separate *commercial tribunals, councils on labor disputes, children's, farm lease*, and *social security courts*. Serious cases before these specialized courts may be appealed to the civil law appeal courts. West Germany has a similar proliferation of specialized social insurance, labor-management, finance, and administrative courts in addition to the hierarchy of ordinary courts.

The most important rival to the predominance of the ordinary courts in France is the hierarchy of administrative courts. They exercise considerable control over the administrative Leviathan be-

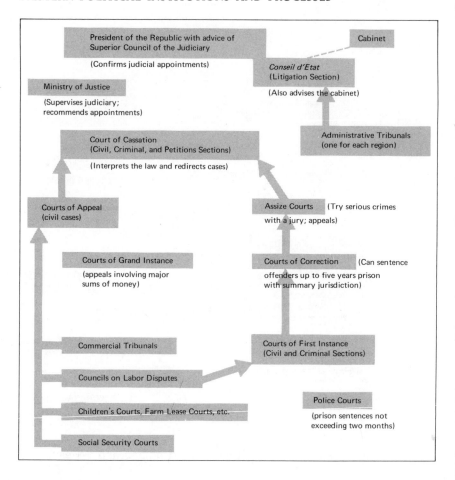

Figure 9.4   The court system of France.

cause, unlike the United States, France's court system is not allowed the practice of judicial review. The Anglo-American practice of not permitting the state to be sued, without its consent, for the actions of its public servants in the course of discharging their duties, is not followed by France, Germany, and other Roman law countries. They have established administrative tribunals to hear complaints and lawsuits of the public involving administrative actions. The defendant in these cases is the state itself, not the state official in charge of the action, as is generally assumed in common law suits of this nature in England or the United States. Malfeasance in office, if present, is tried separately by disciplinary courts that can punish or dismiss a public employee if they find him guilty. In France, each of twenty-four regions has its *administrative tribunal* for this purpose. And the litigation section of the *Conseil d'Etat* can decide appeals from the administrative tribunals. The French (and the West German) administrative courts enjoy the same guarantees of judicial independence as do the ordinary courts at civil and criminal law.

Selection and training of the legal profession

The role of the judiciary within the state and the quality of the justice meted out ultimately depend on the quality and training of the judges and lawyers, who are the main factors of the judicial process. When one speaks of courts as a check upon legislative or executive power, for example, one assumes that the judges and other judicial personnel are so carefully selected and well trained that they can be safely entrusted with the power to overrule legislative or executive decisions. This is all the more important in that it is generally easier to remove or fail to reelect a legislator or executive figure than a judge. With the exception of state court judges in many American states, in fact, judges do not have to stand for popular election or reelection at all. Election for a fixed term by a legislature is more frequent throughout the Western world.[3] Because it is suspected of tying the judiciary to the political alignments in the legislature, this mode of appointment, also, may be of questionable merit. In various countries the most frequent method of appointment or reappointment is by the executive branch according to established standards and procedures and in many cases "during good behavior," that is, for life. From this it follows that there must be well-established methods of training, selection, and outside supervision to assure the integrity and impartiality, not to mention the knowledge and intelligence expected of such a powerful office.

In England In the Anglo-American tradition, judges are recruited chiefly from among the practicing lawyers, and the bond between bench and bar continues in many respects after judges have been appointed. In England, a distinction is drawn between *barristers* and *solicitors*, and judges are selected solely from among the former. The *barristers* comprise a small but highly qualified elite of court lawyers, who are authorized to plead cases in the higher courts. They belong to the historic four *Inns of Court*—centuries-old, voluntary organizations that are half law school and half professional association. The

---

[3] It is used in the Soviet Union, for example, for all but the lowest courts. In Switzerland, the federal legislature elects the federal tribunal for a six-year term. In the United States, this method is used only in three of the states.

Inns of Court train and examine the future barristers and enforce the professional standards of the bar during their entire career. The scholarly, tradition-enshrined background of the bar has ensured a level of judicial ability and integrity that has few rivals in the world. All higher judges are appointed by the Crown in consultation with the prime minister and the lord chancellor; the latter also selects the lesser judges. By the time they become judges, they generally have years of successful practice and experience behind them. The *solicitors* are office lawyers who accept and prepare cases but cannot plead them except in the lowest courts.

In the United States In the United States and the older dominions, no distinction is made between barristers and solicitors. Judges are recruited from the bar, which also polices the profession and supervises the examinations for admission to the bar. Bar associations in the United States are a powerful influence in maintaining and improving the quality of judicial practice and organization. The upperclass composition typical of the British judiciary is far less pronounced in the United States and the Commonwealth. As in England and Wales, the *justices of the peace* and other minor court justices often need not possess any formal legal training. Judges of higher courts generally have had broad practical experience in the practice of law, and often in politics, before they win office. Their background of experience tends to give the man independence of mind, in spite of the partisan ties to which they may owe their office. In particular, common law judges everywhere have developed a remarkable sense of independence from the executive authority, almost a bias against it, even when they have been appointed by it.

In France Being a judge in a Roman law country such as France generally implies membership in a judicial career service patterned after, and often associated with, the general civil service system. The average French judge, upon leaving law school, immediately enters judicial service at the lower levels by passing an appropriate state examination. Far from being an experienced, independent-minded attorney, the typical Roman law judge still reflects the uniformity of approach and sense of proper form of presentation of his humanistic secondary education, as well as the theoretical bent of mind of his law school professors. He starts out in a provincial town and, always sharing the bench with two other judges (except on the lowest level), is quickly absorbed by the esprit de corps of the judiciary, its traditional approach to law, and the formal constraint on the three judges on the bench to hand down a unanimous, *per curiam* decision, without dissenting opinions. The French judicial career is a haven of lifetime security, with frequent promotions for the deserving. It cannot but attract persons seeking tranquillity rather than the competition of the marketplace, and those rather inclined to support the powers that be. At the same time, the highest French courts can boast judges of outstanding ability and a sense of professional perfection that is a source of stability for the entire judicial service. The professionalism and civil service mentality of the French judiciary also shield it from political pressures, which at times lie heavily upon higher common law courts. The expectation of frequent promotion by his superiors, on the other hand, may make a French judge more obsequious than one would expect of an Anglo-American judge, whose judicial career is rarely based on such hopes.

A deep gulf of attitude and temperament separates the French judge from the *avocat* or *avoué*, the French equivalents of barrister and solicitor. The *avocat* ranks in social prestige with the magistrate and the law professor. But unlike the police magistrate (*magistrature assise*) and other judges, the *avocat* is a man of the "free professions," who seeks his fortune in the marketplace. He is responsible for his conduct primarily to his bar association (*ordre des avocats*). In contrast to British barristers, the *avocat* specializes chiefly in the oral development of his case, the *plaidoyer*, which can be compared to a common law trial lawyer's summation of the arguments to the jury. French trial practice gives the *avocat* no opportunity to cross-examine witnesses or to employ the procedural maneuvers for which common law practice is famous. The *avoué* is an office lawyer with certain official functions, who usually acts as the agent of the litigants. French law, as does United States law, permits a person to plead his own case and to offer legal advice and services without any formal training.

The close link between judiciary and administration is also evident in the relations between the judges and the judicial administration (*ministère public*), from the procurators of the lowest to the highest level. The French *procureur* is the equivalent of the American district attorney and attorney general and follows the same course of formal training as the French judge. There is also a certain amount of interchange of personnel between judiciary and procuracy. The personnel of the five-member administrative courts is recruited from among able, experienced civil servants who have had years of firsthand experience with administrative practices without necessarily acquiring a bias on the side of the administration. The more than eighty members of the litigation section of the *Conseil d'Etat*,[4] which

---

[4] The other four sections are smaller and exercise functions such as the drafting of cabinet bills, rendering advisory opinions, and reviewing administrative rules. Their members are recruited in the same fashion as those of the litigation section.

hears appeals from the administrative courts, are selected from two sources: (1) the graduates of the prestigious *École Nationale d'Administration*, which trains the cream of the French top civil service in a highly competitive three-year course from which less than one hundred fifty graduate each year; and (2) transfers from the top echelon civil servants of the ministries, the regional prefectures, or special appointments from outside or from the ranks. The *conseillers* are a body of extraordinary qualifications and prestige.

In West Germany   The West German judiciary and legal profession greatly resemble their French equivalents, with minor exceptions. The similarities were even greater before 1933. The most significant exception to the rule is the personnel of the Federal Constitutional Court, whose members are elected by Parliament and mostly from outside the career judiciary. Both the lifetime career judges selected from other federal courts and the politicians, lawyers, and professors serving eight-year terms on the court must have formal legal training. The diversity of backgrounds, the selection by the political parties and *Land* delegations in Parliament, and the functions of judicial review and guardianship over the constitutional life of West Germany have combined to create a group of high judges unlike any to be found in a Roman law country. Their independent-mindedness reminds observers of the judges of the United States Supreme Court, which may have served as a model in the eyes of the framers of the West German Basic Law and the subsequent implementating legislation which established the Federal Constitutional Court.

PUBLIC ADMINISTRATION

It is fashionable nowadays to deride the "bureaucrats" or the administrative state in general, although not necessarily with malice. This dislike of administration, which is especially widespread in the United States, is based on a fundamental misconception of its origin and nature. Administration, public or private, is merely a derivative of a certain degree of social organization. Just as private persons, in their own concerns of household or business management, develop skills of administration as soon as their concerns become complex and voluminous enough to require well-organized cooperation and awareness of the goals that are to be achieved, so do groups develop an administrative staff and established procedures as soon as their size and functions can no longer be handled in an amateur fashion. *Public* administration is the organization and management of men and materials to achieve the purposes of government.

The origin and nature of public administration

Historically, the full development of any permanent form of administration, public or private, required first of all the evolution of a written language, facilities for record-keeping, and the knowledge of measurements of weight, space, time, and currency, as well as of the rudiments of mathematics. One can conjecture that the building of temples and canals in the most ancient civilizations, and especially the erection of the Egyptian pyramids, were not possible without some semblance of public administration. The conduct of war on land or at sea and the establishment and maintenance of great empires must likewise have required, in addition to brute force and violence, the knowledge of logistics and rational management. During the heyday of ancient Greece, public administration and finance were already well developed. In democratic Athens, magistrates were elected by lot from the citizenry to take charge of the various administrative functions. At the end of their short terms, auditors examined their handling of public funds. The Romans were forced by their own imperial expansion to develop a semblance of large-scale public administration. After the fall of the Roman Empire, the Byzantine, Arab, and Turkish empires further developed public administration and finance to a fine point of perfection, whereas Western Europe sank into the anarchy of feudal, localized, and undifferentiated exercise of governmental power. Only the Catholic Church maintained a much-admired and feared administrative structure of international proportions.

Rational public administration and finance were finally revived in the Renaissance, as the growth of cities and commerce created a need for it and allowed Western Europeans to learn from the Arabs and Byzantines. The rise of the absolute monarchies of France, Spain, Austria, and Prussia, to mention the more prominent, would have been impossible without the adaptation of administrative skill and knowledge of great trading cities—from Venice to Augsburg and London—to the purposes of reorganizing and developing the new monarchies. The absolute rulers and other monarchs aspiring to a similar position systematically centralized governmental power and struggled relentlessly to demolish the autonomy, representation, and even the geographical foundations, of the power of their nobility. They sought to develop the wealth and power of their monarchies by a systematic husbanding and development of their resources and the acquisition of colonies. Most significantly, however, they established a bureaucracy, a civil service based on merit and achievement, often recruited deliberately from among commoners and the lowest ranks of noblemen. A career civil servant thus owed everything he was to the king and felt no loyalty toward the old aristocratic society. A well-staffed and well-organized civil service was a revolutionary weapon and the best instrument for carrying out the will of the sovereign. Next to the standing army, it was the very embodiment of his power.

Much as the establishment and internal consolidation of the new territorial states had enhanced public administration and finance, the following stages of Western political development led to a natural decline. As middle-class revolutions in England and France brought absolute monarchy under control, and commerce and industry began to flower in the eighteenth and nineteenth centuries as never before, liberal ideology came to view public administration as authoritarian and meddlesome. The *laissez-faire* ideal had room only for representative assemblies and, at most, judicial enforcement of the laws, but not bureaucracy. With the waning of the interest in administration, recruitment practices declined and the public service in countries such as England and the new American republic became a sinecure for persons tired of competition in the marketplace or for incompetent relatives and sons of influential families. In the days of the *spoils system* in the United States, administrative offices were used as reward for partisan loyalty and for help during election campaigns. It was evidently assumed that administrative activity required neither a great deal of formal training nor professional standards of conduct.

After long neglect, the interest in rational public administration was once more revived in the latter half of the nineteenth century. Heralded and advanced by a new concern in the world of business and industry for efficient management rather than just efficient machinery, by the application of scientific method to human relationships and society rather than only to nature, the new concern with organization and management soon spread from the private realm to public business. Civil service reforms in England and the United States strove to tackle the most obvious abuses of the decades of neglect. A Civil Service Commission was established in England in 1855, and by 1870, entrance into the Home Civil Service had been restricted to persons who passed *open examinations*. The principles of a career service also spread to the Commonwealth nations. In the United States, the Civil Service Act of 1883 brought the first 10 percent of federal employees under a *merit system;* presently almost the entire federal service and increasing portions of the state and local employees are recruited and promoted according to merit.

On the European continent, the heritage of absolutism had preserved bureaucracy, although there was also a need for streamlining and democratizing practices which were reminiscent of an authoritarian past. In nineteenth-century France, for example, each of the executive departments set down its own standards and rules of appointment, discipline, and promotion. Despite sporadic attempts to pass uniform civil service legislation, it was not until 1946 that an Office of Public Service (*Fonction Publique*) was created in Paris to fulfill functions similar to those of the U.S. Civil Service Commission. The establishment of a federal civil service of Germany in the nineteenth century had first to await the creation of the Empire of 1871. The dominant influence of Prussia, with its deeply ingrained bureaucratic-authoritarian tradition, on the new state served to carry over the patterns of the absolutist bureaucracy to the modern German civil service. This is not to say that the resulting practices were not a model of efficiency and integrity, but they were, however, authoritarian in their relationship to the public.

Administrative management

Modern public administration has attracted the attention of scholars from many disciplines, from whom have come some of the best descriptive accounts of it. One such definition that sets forth clearly the salient organizational characteristics is by Max Weber, a German sociologist writing in the first decades of this century. He describes the criteria of a fully developed bureaucratic organization as follows:

1. Fixed and official jurisdictions of each agency which are regulated by specific rules or laws;

2. Hierarchic organization on several levels in super- and subordination;

3. Extensive, careful and usually secret record-keeping;

4. Professional or at least thorough training for staff members;

5. Separation of domicile from office and full-time devotion to functions of office;

6. Operation according to rather stable and exhaustive rules.

More recent treatises on public administration have also stressed such desiderata as *economy* and *efficiency*. Others have emphasized the importance of developing *democratic techniques* in administrative procedure, especially in dealing with the public. Administration in a setting of democratic government obviously cannot deal with the citizens affected by its actions in the manner of the authoritarian bureaucracies of Prussia or France during the age of absolutism. Even where vital public tasks enjoy the political support of a majority, the administrators cannot ride roughshod over the resistance of a local minority. More specifically, channels must be supplied to process the complaints of citizens and, in serious cases, there must be judicial tribunals that can provide swift redress of grievances, injunctions against threatening damage, or damages for injuries already suffered from administrative action. This is the place for the administrative courts of France and Germany or for equivalent procedures or tribunals in the Anglo-American democracies.

A related demand made upon modern public administration is that it should be *responsive* to the needs and pressures of the society in which it operates. The American sociologist Philip Selznick, for example, showed in his study of the Tennessee Valley Authority that an administrative oranization in a new environment can survive and fulfill its essential functions only by "cooptation," that is, by the reception of new and outside elements into its leadership or policy-making structure. An administrative organization has to win acceptance and support from the local leadership groups of the community in which it is to carry out its task. This is as true of local government functions as of the field offices of the national government. It even applies to the work of U.S. Information Service centers and Peace Corps members in foreign lands. In the case of TVA, responsiveness to the Farm Bureau Federation, the county agents, the extension service of land grant colleges, and the more prosperous farmers also meant that TVA became a part of an alliance of social forces opposed by certain other social forces, such as the low-income farmers and government agencies favorable to them. It also meant that the carrying out of the primary task of TVA, to provide public power, had to be purchased at the expense of some minor goals that were not acceptable to its coopted allies.[5]

Being responsive is not the same as being *responsible*. Administration in a modern democracy must be responsible in many ways. It must be accountable to the courts in case of specific complaints or lawsuits. It must be accountable to public opinion in general and in the particular community where it operates. Still more important is administrative responsibility within the administrative establishment and accountability toward the elected representatives of the people in Parliament. Responsibility within the administrative organization is implicit in the hierarchic order of offices and the subordination of lower to higher officials, or lower to higher agencies, all the way to the top of the executive branch. The lower officials have to carry out the commands and instructions of their superiors

[5] *TVA and the Grass Roots* (Berkeley: University of California Press, 1949).

and are broadly responsible to them for the manner in which they execute their assigned tasks. This responsibility is generally reinforced by a system of rewards and punishments. Rewards take the form of promotion, salary increase, and assignment to more desirable tasks. Punishments range from delayed promotion and assignment to less desirable jobs or locations, to disciplinary proceedings that can result in dismissal, and even to the instituting of criminal proceedings against serious cases of misuse of public office.

In a career civil service, where the individual administrator expects to spend a lifetime at his career, the rewards and punishments can be quite subtle without losing their effectiveness. In fact, drastic measures or a constant threat of dismissal would be more likely to create a poor working climate and feelings of job insecurity that can be just as injurious to productivity in the public service as they are in industry. It is far wiser to engage a person's pride and ambition in his optimal performance than to worry about how to deter him from wrongdoing.

Most qualified civil service positions also link an employee to one of the many professional associations or at least to general civil servants' associations. This pride in one's profession and in doing a job well is supported and encouraged. A government-employed agricultural enonomist, psychiatrist, or carpenter desires the respect not only of his superiors, who may not know how to judge his performance in his specialty, anyway, but he wants to be well thought of by his colleagues outside the government. He would like to be regarded as a competent agricultural economist, psychiatrist, or carpenter. His own striving for perfection and recognition, in other words, encourages him also to do the best he can in his government career. Professional associations similarly help to set high standards of professional conduct and create an esprit de corps among civil servants that is indispensable to the smooth functioning of any large organization and conducive to the best cooperative efforts.

Administrative *responsibility toward the legislature* is generally enforced through the channels of executive-legislative relations. The legislature or individual legislators are not supposed to investigate or demand an accounting of individual administrators or agencies, bypassing the chief executive or the responsible minister, except in formal investigations. They are to hold the President or, in parliamentary systems, the Cabinet as a body, responsible for what goes on in any administrative department. This is the purpose of the question hour in the House of Commons or the *interpellation* in the Fourth Republic of France. In practice, it is not so easy to deter legislators from using their personal influence and administrators from cooperating all too willingly. In the United States, more than elsewhere, legislative meddling in administration, the threat of public investigation of an agency, or threats to its budget have produced a great deal of lobbying and direct appeals to Congress by some administrative agencies, often over the head of the President. Legislative meddling has on occasion also fostered an atmosphere of insecurity among administrators, who are reluctant to put forth their best efforts for fear of legislative reprisal instigated by opposing groups in the administration who draw their friends in Congress into their squabbles.

Finally, administration in a democratic society is also expected to be shaped by the attempt to *realize democratic values*. This realization determines its form, procedure, and general bearing. It also influences its personnel practices, including recruitment. In imperial Germany and in prewar Japan, for example, the civil servants, as a social group, were not broadly representative of the entire populations of these countries. They came from the privileged classes and their sympathizers. Such exclusiveness is, by definition, as undemocratic as the imported colonial service of an imperial power in a colony of different ethnic stock, regardless of the integrity and competence of the alien administration. The realization of democratic values also refers to the content of what administrators do and the philosophy that inspires them. Nowadays most administrative branches possess, in addition to the *line agencies,* which carry out government operations, *staff agencies,* whose function it is to provide planning and advisory services for the policy-makers of executive and legislative branches. It is desirable for the realization of democratic values that both line and staff administrators feel a commitment to the values of democracy and that they use their best talents to advance democracy rather than to obstruct or subvert it.

Civil service systems

As is true of the judicial function, administration stands or falls with the quality of the personnel who occupy crucial positions from the top to the bottom. A well-established civil service constitutes an elaborate system with differentiated recruiting and advancement on several levels and for specialized tasks. The typical civil service has at least three levels—administrative leadership, middle management, and the rank and file. The top executives usually include political appointees, such as ministers, department secretaries, and undersecretaries, who are not part of the civil service proper. This is not to say that these appointees lack the experience and discipline of a long public career. The rank and file may include the vast pool of secretarial and other manpower that is outside the career service. The total number of civilian government employees, including local and regional levels of government, reaches into the millions in the larger nation-states of today. In the United States, for example, federal civilian employment amounts to almost 2½ million persons of every description. West Germany, with a total working force of 25 million gainfuly employed persons, has ¹⁄₁₀ of that number on the payrolls of federal, *Land,* and local governments. For France the number in the public employ is 2.8 million.

The civil service in Great Britain The civil service in Great Britain is composed of three major classes: a small administrative class of no more than 2,500, an executive class of about 70,000, and a clerical class of 126,000.[6] It does not include the large staff of the public corporations, which are made up of the industries nationalized after 1945 as well as a number of older public bodies, such as the BOAC or the Central Electricity Board.

1. *The administrative class.* The administrative class is recruited in part from members of the executive class who have passed special examinations. Its bulk is recruited directly from the cream of university graduates in their twenties. Graduates with first- or second-class honors need only pass an interview; other graduates, a written examination as well. All examinations are geared to test general knowledge in the arts and sciences and well-rounded ability rather than technical qualifications.[7] The administrative class in a very real sense runs each department and, by means of continual interdepartmental contacts and conferences, the entire administration. As top civil servants in each department, they are both advisers and troubleshooters for their minister, whose difficulties with his Cabinet, with Parliament, and with the public they must seek to head off or at least to straighten out once the difficulties have arisen. The administrative class is entrusted with the preparation of plans or legislative drafts for the use of the policy-makers.

2. *The executive class.* The executive class is concerned with the management of most day-to-day government operations, supplying the office directors and supervisors for the most diverse functions.

---

[6] British Information Service, *The Central Government of Britain,* July 1963. These figures do not include the specialist ancillary clerical and messengerial classes, which total another quarter million.

[7] The written examinations give the applicant an opportunity to show his knowledge of obscure technical subjects as well as his general knowledge.

Whereas the members of the administrative class have *staff functions,* the executive class chiefly directs the *line functions.* It is drawn from eighteen- or nineteen-year-old graduates of academic secondary schools, who have to pass an examination and an interview, again along lines suggested by the educational curriculum rather than by technical qualifications. Nevertheless, members of the executive class often acquire a great deal of expertise in a technical or semiprofessional field such as taxation or accounting.

3. *The clerical class.* The clerical class consists of clerical and subclerical workers who are recruited with some secondary education at the age of 16 or 17. The most numerous part of the service classes, its members usually work under supervision and according to the instructions of members of the executive class, keeping records and preparing accounts. They can also become members of the latter, if they can demonstrate adequate qualities by passing an appropriate examination.

In addition to the three service classes and the ancillary clerical pool, the British government has also engaged the services of specialized professional, scientific, and technical personnel. Here the certified formal training and practical experience of an applicant as criteria of employment have been augmented by an interview to gauge the subtler requirements of a public career.

The United States civil service The American federal service has no equivalent of the British administrative class, the highest positions being generally filled by successive administrations with their own political appointees. This procedure is motivated less by considerations of party patronage than by the belief that the "reform character" of the program of each new incumbent in the White House requires a new set of dedicated top-level administrators. Holdovers are rare, though they do occur. The federal career service has a *General Schedule* of eighteen classifications, which range from clerical jobs to professional and scientific positions at the top. Subclerical positions are covered by a separate *Crafts, Protective and Custodial Schedule* with another ten grades.

Recruitment to the federal service is by competitive examinations. At the higher levels, a process of evaluating the academic background and professional experience takes the place of the examinations. A college graduate is usually classified at grade GS–5, or lower middle-management, but can be promoted in time to the top. By and large, it can be said that the lower positions of the American federal service have been comparatively attractive and have competed well with private industry. The higher levels, however, have rarely held their own as compared to the professions and executive positions outside government. Because of the inadequate compensation and the lack of tradition and prestige, able men and women are often discouraged from making government service their lifetime career.

The French civil service The French civil service before World War II was characterized by the differing practices and uneven quality of personnel of the different executive departments. The Foreign Service, the *Conseil d'Etat*, and the Ministry of Finance and the Ministry of Interior have always attracted exceptionally able men, whereas other ministries had to adjust their examination and promotion standards to the meager crop of applicants. Promotions were generally within each department. The reforms of 1945 created two uniform classes of civil servants—the *administrateur civil*, modeled after the British administrative class, and the *secrétaire d'administration*, which corresponds broadly to the British executive class. The civil administrators have the function of preparing legislative drafts and ministerial directives as well as of coordinating the many moving parts of the administrative machinery. They are recruited from among the graduates of the *Ecole Nationale d'Administration*, which handpicks its students from large numbers of applicants under 30, who either have a diploma from a college-level institute of political science or are officials in the service. Entrance is by a single examination that tests general knowledge and intelligence. The course of studies mixes academic instruction and practical experience in administration, social services, and private industry. The *Ecole Nationale d'Administration* also offers refresher and advanced courses for officials of experience. Next to the secretaries of administration, the French service has two more classifications—the administrative clerks and the typists and subclerical workers.

The civil service in West Germany The civil service in West Germany has inherited many of the virtues, but also some of the vices, of the tradition of efficiency, austerity, and the authoritarianism that once made Prussia a byword for bureaucracy. The civil service is divided into four classes of which the higher service (*hoeherer Beamtendienst*) is somewhat more numerous that the British administrative class. Members of the higher service supply planning and advisory services, provide administrative coordination, and, on the highest level, may represent ministers in Parliament or in their contacts with the press. The higher service is recruited almost exclusively from law school graduates, who upon graduation, as is required for the judicial career, have to serve an additional three and one-half years of in-service training, ending with a second state examination in law. The near-monopoly of legal training, and in Roman law at that, must be contrasted with the breadth of background preferred by the British civil service and with the French efforts in the civil service reforms of 1945 to give future civil servants a broad political and social science training. Historically, the German preference for legal training is connected to the nineteenth-century notion of the *Rechtsstaat*, the "administrative state under law," rather than under an arbitrary monarch—a notion more plausible to German liberals at the time than any thought of democracy. In practice, this excess of legalism has tended to make the German civil service unnecessarily rigid and unresponsive to social needs and pressures.

The other classifications of the German civil service are the elevated service (*Gehobener Dienst*), comparable perhaps to the executive class in Great Britain, and the middle and simple services, which include minor executive and custodial or messenger services, respectively. There is also a vast army of white-collar service. The elevated service requires applicants to have the equivalent of a German secondary education and a period of in-service training. For the middle service six years of secondary school and an apprenticeship of one year are expected. The simple service demands that applicants have completed eight years of elementary school and that they have learned a trade. The numerical proportions are clearest when the civil service of both federation and *Laender* are considered, since their service regulations are uniform and the *Land* administrations constitute, by far, the bulk of the administrative state in West Germany. For every two members of the higher service, there are seven of the elevated, five of the middle, and one of the simple service, and about ten white-collar employees without civil service tenure. This breakdown does not include the personnel of the federal mails and the railroads, which makes up about half of the public employees of federation and *Laender*.

The German civil service made a bargain with "the state" almost from the very beginnings of German state bureaucracies. The civil servant would devote his best efforts to executing his job faithfully if his monarch promised to protect him and to take care of him and his family in sickness and old age. Complete protection in the discharge of his duties, sickness and disability benefits, and pension rights, with generous annuities for the widow or the orphans of a civil servant, were the eventual goal. This bargain, not always kept faithfully by the state in the age of monarchy, became the cornerstone of the "well-acquired rights" of civil servants in the republican period. Obligated to the old order by reason of its composition, the

German civil service clung to its privileges rather than becoming a British-style service class responsive to the wishes of the emerging democratic society. To this day, and despite the efforts of the Allied occupation at reforming the German civil service after 1945, the administrators are too defensive to adapt themselves and their training to the changing society around them. Despite their efficiency and relative freedom from corruption, they remain exclusive, aloof, and unresponsive.

This survey has shown some of the administrative services in operation and compared their varying interpretation of the concept of a lifetime career service under a merit system. In European countries, the remainders of class barriers which have fashioned their highly stratified educational systems, also show up in the classifications of their civil service systems as compared to the general schedule of the American federal government. Yet such countries as Great Britain and France have moved with all deliberate speed to democratize in spirit and training their once aristocratic top civil servants. Through scholarships, Great Britain and France have encouraged persons from all social backgrounds to compete on an equal footing for admission to their highest administrative classes and have made it easier to transfer by examination to the next higher class. At the same time, American administrators and social scientists have long been moving in the direction of ever greater professionalization of the federal and some state civil services. More recently, they have given serious consideration to proposals for the creation of a senior civil service analogous to the British and French models.[8] Learning governmental practice and institutional design from one another whenever a need seemed to arise, after all, has always been one of the signs of the vitality and willingness for self-renewal that continue to make the Western community of nations great.

[8] These proposals are discussed in two publications of the Brookings Institution, Washington, D.C.: P. T. David and Ross Pollock, *Executives in Government* (1958); and M. H. Bernstein, *The Job of the Federal Executive* (1958).

CHAPTER **10** POLITICAL PARTIES,
INTEREST GROUPS,
AND PUBLIC OPINION

The institutions of government and the policy-making process of
a given political community do not exist in a vacuum. They are part
of the fabric of pluralistic society. They reflect its social mores,
customs, and explicit beliefs or ideologies. In fact, such governmental officials as judges and civil servants, and legislators as well,
are also important groups of society and of the political process,
along with the numerous other groups that make up social life.
Government and politics are part of what has been called the *group
process*, the life and interaction of the many different kinds of groups
of society—social classes, occupational groupings, geographical communities, any manner of associations, interest groups, and political
parties.

Some general remarks about political and social groups are necessary at the outset. These groups vary widely in distinctness, size,
and character. They also differ in their bearing on government.
Although no noticeable stratification or sizable grouping of society
is without political significance, such groups as political parties, government officials, and interest groups obviously bear a more direct

relation to the governmental process. This relationship can be defined in terms of the functions regularly performed by a given group for the entire sysem. It will be remembered what functions characterize the activities of the policy-makers and what functions are fulfilled by judges and civil servants. The functions of parties and interest groups will be defined below. It should be borne in mind that the highly organized mass parties and mass interest groups of the most advanced Western nations are a rather recent phenomenon. Among these groups are traditional groups, social movements of a nationalist or protest character, and temporary electoral organizations that are set up for the purpose of nominating and electing a slate of candidates and virtually disintegrate at the end of the election campaign. Furthermore, political parties and interest groups are often not sharply distinguishable, either because the existing organizations are not functionally specific or because they are still adaptable to either function: electioneering or the furtherance of their group interest. In the process of political development, both in the now developed and the still developing nations, the appearance of highly organized parties and interest groups indicates the beginning of political modernity. There are some partyless states and temporary lapses in party organization, to be sure, and there are also degrees of organization to set off the more developed from the less developed. The presence of party competition, too, is an indicator of political modernity. One-party systems, generally speaking, are only at the very beginning of modern political development and are considerably less developed than systems with two or more parties. Once a society has reached a certain amount of pluralistic differentiation, it is no longer well served by a monopolistic party system. The Soviet Union has long reached this stage, although the Communist party there seems most unlikely to want to follow the example of liberal reformers in Czechoslovakia and other Eastern European satellites.

The line often drawn by students of government between formal institutions and informal group processes is misleadnig. It is not the neoclassical architecture of the public building and the constitutional clause providing for it that make up an institution. A political institution is defined by its function and the relative regularity of the behavior of the group of persons associated with it: judges, congressmen, administrators, or party members. While it is to be hoped that the patterns of regularity of group behavior in legislative, executive, and judicial agencies will have a good deal to do with the constitutional law, statutes, and rules pertaining to them, the legal structure can never hope to be more than a small part of the patterns of group behavior. The regularized activities of political parties and interest groups are institutions even without the benefit of a legal structure (which, in any case, is often present). Neither is the distinction between public affairs and private relationships,[1] which long kept the consideration of parties and interest groups out of the pale of political science, very helpful when private motives and interests are as intertwined with public functions as in the making and execution of public policy.

PARTY SYSTEMS AND POLITICS

All modern political systems, in the West as well as elsewhere, can be said to have a party system of some sort. Until about two decades ago, before the study of the politics of developing areas encouraged a reappraisal of the study of Western politics, the classification of party systems was deceptively clear and simple. There were three kinds, distinguished chiefly by the number of parties in each. One-party systems were assumed to be dictatorial, two-party systems ideal for stable and responsible government, and multiparty systems somewhat anarchic, but still workable in a liberal democracy. The emphasis on the number of parties was hardly misplaced, considering the importance of stable majorities for the functioning of parliamentary government and for passing legislation that two-party systems promised, and the absence of any political check on the powerholder in one-party states. In the meantime, however, the classification of party systems has become far more complex as the list of the distinguishing criteria has expanded to the point where a "party system" has become literally a mirror for the entire political system of a country at a particular time.

Classifying party systems

Kinds of parties One of the first criteria for the classification of party systems, obvious as it may seem, lies in the kind of parties of which it is composed. A one-party system dominated by a Communist or Fascist totalitarian party obsessed with a violent, ideological drive to conquer the world is not the same as the single party, or nationalistic movement, of a developing nation such as Mexico. The latter may not exactly conform to American notions of liberal democracy, but is often noncoercive and based on considerable efforts to secure consent by patient persuasion and promises

---

[1] Political science in the nineteenth century (and in some countries to this day) ignored political parties as personal factions and friendships, and lobbying as personal corruption.

of social and economic progress for the masses.[2] A two-party system in which one party is totalitarian is very unlikely to operate in the manner familiar in Anglo-American countries. It will either perpetuate the moderate party in power regardless of any misgovernment or corruption on its part, or convert the government into a totalitarian dictatorship if the totalitarian party gets into power. There is also a world of difference between the British two-party system of centralized, disciplined parties, with binding programs, and the two confederations of widely varying state parties of the United States, where the national election platforms resemble each other and mean little. And what about third parties, which sometimes complicate a two-party system by preventing a majority for either major party? Or what if one of the two parties has an overwhelming majority of the vote, while the other is condemned to a perpetual minority status because it is identified with a particular social group, such as a religious or ethnic minority? An adequate definition of a workable two-party system will have to specify more precise requirements than that there should be but two parties.

Multiparty systems require even more critical attention, beginning with the number and relative size of their parties, if the term is to be understandable to a student of politics. At what point, for example might third parties or excessive decentralization into regional components be said to transform a two-party system into multipartism? There is also an important difference between a system of three or four stable parties of comparable size, as in some of the smaller countries of Western Europe, a multiparty system composed of numerous small groups, and a system such as that of India, where the Congress party has a considerable majority alongside a number of small groups. And what about multiparty systems made up of unstable, constantly changing groups that might not even possess any party organization outside the legislature? What about the multiparty façades established by the Soviet Union in East European countries to veil the Communist dictatorships?

A particularly crucial aspect of the composition of multiparty systems is the extent to which the cleavages of the parties correspond to existing cleavages among social classes, well-defined regional, ethnic or religious groups, ideological camps, and distinct economic group interests. The pluralistic society of a modern country is made up of overlapping groups and of individuals who belong to many different groups at once. If the significant groups are mutually ex-

---

[2] See, for example, James S. Coleman and Carl G. Rosberg, Jr., eds., *Political Parties and National Integration in Tropical Africa* (Berkeley: University of California Press, 1966), pp. 1–12.

clusive and antagonistic, then their individual members lose all ties to other groups and to the larger political community. The body politic is split into irreconcilable factions—religious, ethnic, regional, or class-conscious—and will break asunder in civil war or secession. A society composed of distinct religions, or nationalities, or warring sectional or class camps simply cannot entrust the conduct of its politics to parties identified with these groups without inviting disaster.

Homogeneity or heterogeneity of society   This brings the discussion to the second criterion for classifying party systems, the homogeneity or heterogeneity of a given body politic, or the extent to which existing social divisions are a source of political antagonism. Multiparty systems often reflect a way station of a given society along the road to modernization. When industrialization creates powerful new groups and interests, such as industrial entrepreneurs and workers, for example, the emergence of the new group interests need not lead to the establishment of new political parties unless the newly emerging groups encounter attempts at suppression by the social or governmental powers that be. A headlong rush toward national unification or discriminatory treatment of a religious or ethnic minority may also be the most frequent reason for the regional or other minority group to form a political party for its defense. The German multiparty system of the years between 1870 and the 1950s, with its proliferation of class, religious, ideological, and regional groups, is a good example of such party origins.

Once a social base and a party organization have become thoroughly identified with each other, another rigid element has been added to the multiparty system, which will remain long after the causes of its origin have passed into history. Often the parties or the effect of the conflict between them will actually create the nonpolitical organization of their social base, such as labor unions, farmer organizations, and business organizations, which assure the corresponding parties of their clientele. Thus the parties unwittingly help with the *interest articulation* of their society in the throes of development, at the same time dividing it further.

Aggregation of interests   A third criterion for the classification of party systems of all kinds is how and to what extent they labor to bridge the antagonisms between the different groups of society and to rally a political consensus among as many groups as possible. This *aggregation of interests*[3] is most likely more developed in two-

---

[3] For further discussion of the terms *interest articulation* and *interest aggregation*, see Gabriel A. Almond and James S. Coleman, eds., *The Politics of the Developing Areas* (Princeton, N.J.: Princeton University Press, 1961).

party systems or single-party states than in multiparty systems, because in the former two there is more of an incentive and fewer obstacles to winning broad majority support. American political parties often represent aggregational effort in the most explicit form when each endeavors to draw every conceivable social, ethnic, religious, and occupational group into its election campaigns or, at least, not to antagonize any such group if it can be avoided. But again, there is ample room for exceptions. The British two-party system throughout much of the nineteenth century was recruited from the same social stratum and for a while neither party made much of an effort to appeal to the newly arising group interests. It is not unusual for the two parties of a two-party system to enter a tacit agreement to ignore or even suppress a racial or religious minority, even though doing so runs counter to democratic values and beliefs.

One-party systems lack the competition to force the single party to appeal to all groups for support. A Communist party in power, in particular, tends to be an exclusive elite dedicated to the technique of increasing its own solidarity by victimizing certain internal enemies. Only before it gets into power, or when it is still struggling for a monopoly of power, will it cater to the interests of other groups in order to win their support. A Fascist party in power similarly "uses" popular hostility to designated internal or external enemies to increase its own power. This concern overrides all propensities for an aggregation of interests. In developing nations such hostility against seeming remainders of colonialism or alien minorities, such as the Chinese in some Southeast Asian countries or Arabs and Indians in East Africa, may have a similar effect. Even where this is not the case, new nations often may not yet have articulated many interests to aggregate, and the single dominant party recruits itself chiefly from a narrow layer of educated or trained persons.

Multiparty systems, although not ostensibly given as much to interest aggregation as are the two-party systems, cannot quite do without it either. A farmers' party, for example, has to unite a number of very distinct interests, say, of large, medium, and small farmers, wheat and cotton growers, sugar beet farmers, cattle ranchers, grain growers, and perhaps even farm workers, to mention a few of the subdivisions within agriculture. The French party systems of the Third and Fourth Republics used quasi-ideological labels of rather obscure content, such as Radicalism, Left Republicanism, and Radical Socialism, to rally a variety of local and economic interests behind a group of politicians. German multipartism under the Weimar Republic also featured highly organized efforts on the part of the Conservatives (DNVP), Nazis, Liberals, the Catholic

Center Party, and the Socialists, each trying to build an empire by aggregating interests. In fact, the Weimar system might easily have turned into a two-party system had there not been so many such empire-building parties in competition with one another.

Responsible party government A fourth criterion for distinguishing party systems hinges upon the functions performed in relation to governing the country. The theory of responsible party government, for example, presumes not only the existence of two major parties, or two highly cohesive blocs of parties, between which the voters choose with the effect of giving a mandate to one party program and set of leaders, but it also conceives of such a two-party or two-bloc system as a policy-making or problem-solving mechanism which raises, debates, and decides issues of public policy, the final verdict being reserved to the electorate. Finally, it presumes both a governmental system that allows the majority party or bloc of parties full control and the willingness of the parties to take on governmental responsibility in turn.

The assumption that there will be some alternation in governmental authority between competing sets of leaders is rarely a reality, even in two-party systems, not to mention single-party systems or multipartism, where governmental control tends to remain in the hands of the same centrist parties, Cabinet after Cabinet. In two-party systems, persistent third parties, or the rigid identification of each of the parties with a given social base, may prevent a *floating vote* between the two major parties and instead of alternation, create long periods of one-party dominance. Or the two parties may be so decentralized, as in the United States, by federalism and by the separation of powers that their respective national strength becomes an arbitrary sum total of many separate state, congressional, and Presidential contests, which similarly may make for long periods of one-party dominance.

The presumption that the governmental system will allow the majority party to take full control of the government is evidently not necessarily true in the American separation of powers system, which can separate the congressional majority party from the majority mandate (if he has one) of the President. The strong Presidencies of the Weimar Republic and of the Fifth Republic of France seem to have the same effect, and so does the tradition of a strong bureaucratic state as in the Third and Fourth Republics of France. Thus the political parties are denied the harness of responsibility and, implicitly, also a powerful incentive to try to win a popular majority by broad appeals and interest aggregation. They may content themselves with the status of permanent minority parties, who merely represent their constituents vis-à-vis a government they can never hope to control.

The matrix of issues These four criteria for the classification of party systems are not the only ones in use. French political scientists, for example, have suggested a schema of divisions on major issues of policy to explain their particular multiparty system. Taking as issues (1) a pro-Western versus a nationalist versus a pro-Soviet orientation, (2) clericalism versus anticlericalism, and (3) laissez-faire economics versus an orientation toward state economic planning, they obtained almost as many distinct party positions as there are possible combinations:

Communists	pro-Soviet, anti-clerical, planning-oriented
Socialists	pro-Western, anti-clerical, planning-oriented
Democratic Center	pro-Western, clerical, planning-oriented
Radicals	pro-Western, anti-clerical, laissez-faire
Independents and Peasants	pro-Western, clerical, laissez-faire
Gaullists	nationalist, clerical, planning-oriented
Fascists	nationalist, anti-clerical, planning-oriented

If all these three divisions coincided, dividing Frenchmen into only two camps, it was contended, France might have a two-party system.

The impact of institutions Other classifications of party systems suggest the use of different forms of party organization as distinguishing criteria. These forms will be discussed below. Much thought has been expended on ascertaining the extent to which given institutional peculiarities of a country—Presidentialism, federalism, and the electoral system—might influence the form of the party system. The findings have been inconclusive. Although there is general agreement that federalism tends to inhibit party cohesion on a national scale, for example, the presence of sectional differences also may be said to encourage an attitude of compromise and cooperation, thereby enabling political parties to bridge the gaps between the states. American Presidential elections are often credited with preserving the two-party system or at least with insuring cohesion among the national parties; parliamentary government in such federal countries as West Germany and Canada similarly has made a great contribution toward unifying parties or blocs of parties for the creation of majority coalitions at the national level.

The effect of electoral systems The impact of such electoral systems as the American single-member district plurality system—that is, plurality of the vote electing one representative in each district—

which the British and many Commonwealth countries also use, the single-member district majority system with a second ballot (if no candidate receives a majority on the first ballot), and the various types and admixtures of proportional representation have been matters of considerable controversy. Proportional representation, in particular, has been charged with contributing to the proliferation of parties, while single-member district plurality systems are said to "polarize" electoral opinion in each district between no more than two candidates or parties.[4] Polarization in each electoral district is no guarantee of a nation-wide two-party system, because different pairs of opponents in different areas still add up to multipartism in the national legislature.

Although few would deny that proportional representation is more permissive toward new parties and splinter groups than the plurality system (in which even the votes for the second candidate are "lost"), it also happened to be adopted at a time of considerable party proliferation for economic and other reasons. There is also the example of the smaller democracies of Europe, notably of Belgium, where party proliferation was insignificant despite proportional representation. The most obvious criticism of an overemphasis on the electoral system would appear to be that electoral systems can be changed if they seem to produce undesirable results. The French, for instance, developed an electoral system in the mid-fifties that helped them to reduce the Communist representation drastically. West Germany uses a minimum hurdle of 5 percent of the popular vote as a device to deny representation to splinter groups. However, it is difficult to abolish a permissive system like proportional representation, once many new and small parties have acquired a vested interest in it, for even though the small parties themselves may lack the power to dictate the form of the electoral system, they can often forestall change by bargaining or trading their legislative votes on other matters for the support of large parties in retaining the electoral system.

Class and ideology An ideology-class scheme along historical lines of development has long been popular in the Western world. At the beginning of modern party development in the middle of the nineteenth century, the confrontation was between the Liberalism of the rising bourgeoisie and the conservatism of aristocracy and other

---

[4] Single-minded districts with a majority required, and with a runoff ballot, are assumed to lack the polarizing effect, because the parties can wait until the second ballot to conclude the electoral alliances. This system is currently used in France and was quite popular in continental Europe before World War I.

traditional forces. With industrial-urban maturity the working classes began to seek representation through a Socialist party, and a re-alignment split the liberal forces into a left and a right wing. These three or four parties may have been further augmented in countries in which a religious issue, farm discontent, or sectional dissent created additional parties. After World War I, moreover, the bitter-ness of the war and its aftermath added extremist movements of the right and left, Fascists and Communists, at the same time that the class divisions and the inner logic of speaking of "left" and "right" began to disintegrate.

The development of political parties

A sense of alarm has always been felt at the first appearance of political parties in countries ruled by traditional elites. Aristocrats, a land-owning oligarchy, families of long-established wealth, and sometimes also the clergy, automatically held positions of political influence in traditional societies before the onset of the large-scale social mobilization connected with industrialization and urbanization. Where there were candidates to nominate and elect, the traditional elites generally handpicked men to their liking, and their judgment was respected by persons of lower status, who looked up to them. With the onset of social mobilization, however, sufficient numbers of the latter became dissatisfied with their status and resented the ob-vious bias of this handpicking process. If these malcontents concerted their efforts and (1) nominated their own candidate and secured as many votes as they could for him, or (2) formed little discussion groups to dream and talk about the shape of the future, or (3) joined in a clandestine intrigue to exercise pressure where it mattered in the process of selection by the old elite, or (4) formed a con-spiracy for revolutionary action, they originated *a political party*, that ubiquitous institution of modern politics. To the traditional elites and their conservatively inclined followers, such a development was an "insidious conspiracy" against their authority, a threat of anarchy and revolution even if the party was not a revolutionary action group. They even feared that this organization of "nobodies" was about to outmaneuver by sheer numbers their "sterling qualities" of "moral leadership." And with respect to their fears, they were right, although they could hardly turn back the clock. In time they soon discovered that there was no better way to counter the "in-sidious conspiracy" of the party than to organize their own following into a conservative party that could promote their point of view, get their candidates elected, and reward the loyalty of their own supporters.

Parliamentary group The protean character of political parties should be obvious from the foregoing. Parties are a highly spontaneous form of group activity and will adapt admirably well to widely varying tasks and functions, ranging from electioneering to instigating a popular revolution. One of their most frequent points of origin has been representative assemblies, where the requirement of majority support to enact legislation creates the need for an organization that can deliver the vote or give substantial support to a point of view. In eighteenth-century England, the Crown established for this purpose a parliamentary secretary to the Treasury and lord commissioners of the Treasury, who won majority support with gifts, honors, and patronage. These officials are known today as the whips of the majority party in the House of Commons. Patronage, honors, and spoils of office are devices for holding parties together which are in use around the whole world. In Great Britain today, the chief device for insuring discipline among the parliamentary parties is the control that party leadership has over nominations. A legislator who breaks party discipline on an important issue faces the threat of not being renominated for election.

On the continent, some partylike organizations antedated the opportunities for representation in a parliament. Parliamentary parties appeared as soon as representative, or constituent, assemblies were formed. Generally they gathered in ideological camps, taking their earliest names from their meeting places. The Jacobins of the French Revolution, ironically enough, were named after the religious order of the convent in which they happened to take up quarters while serving in the Constituent Assembly. In the Frankfort Constituent Assembly of 1848, in the German revolution, the new parliamentary parties likewise took the names of the hotels where they were meeting, such as the Donnersberg for the far left, the Cafe Milani for a right-wing group. Only much later were the ideological labels adopted by European continental parties, such as Liberals, Conservatives, Radicals, or Progressives.

Registration committee The parties or factions originally confined their operations to Parliament and its equivalents on the European continent, with no partisan coordination of the local nomination and election processes that were often still in the hands of the traditional elites. Electoral reforms, such as the British reform bill of 1832, and the subsequent widening of the suffrage finally created a need for a grass-roots organization of nominating and electioneering committees or caucuses that could mobilize and deliver the vote for as many of the candidates of the party as possible. In the British case, the obvious first step after the reform of 1832 was the establishment of registration societies to get the newly enfranchised voters to place their names on the voting register.

Extraparliamentary organization There followed the establishment of more formal party organizations outside of Parliament under such party leaders as Sir Robert Peel (1788–1850) and Benjamin Disraeli (1804–1881). Finally, there emerged Major Joseph Chamberlain's Birmingham Caucus in the 1870s, the first big city machine in Europe to match services to the community with ward-by-ward organization in an unbeatable combination. A generation later a political sociologist, M. Ostrogorski,[5] could chronicle the rise of the extraparliamentary mass party as a powerful, well-disciplined organization with the evident ambition of controlling the policies of its parliamentary party. Although this latter danger failed to materialize, British parties were not alone in attaining an intensive degree of extraparliamentary organization. On the European continent, parties, intimately intertwined with economic interest groups and other associations, became the object of a devastating critical analysis by another sociologist, Robert Michels,[6] a decade after Ostrogorski. Michels claimed that continental trade unions and Socialist parties, far from being the epitome of democracy, were all suffering from an "iron law of oligarchy" inherent in all mass organization and applicable to Conservative and Liberal mass parties as well.

In the United States, the congressional parties had reached out and begun to build effective extraparliamentary organizations at the beginning of the Jeffersonian era, especially in New York City, where ward-by-ward organization had been introduced half a century prior to the Birmingham Caucus. The great thrust of post-Civil War industrial and urban growth, together with substantial waves of immigration, produced city bosses and machine politics, which, even more than in Birmingham, England, owed their effectiveness to the additional functions of labor union, employment office, and social welfare agency, which parties had to play in this setting. The evils of political machines and boss rule may have been vastly exaggerated by their contemporary critics. But they evidently aroused enough antagonism in the American public to lend success to the Progressive assault upon party organization, which, in the first decade and a half of this century, dealt a mortal blow to intensive party organization with the introduction of congressional and state primary elections in place of the nominating conventions controlled by the parties.

[5] *Democracy and the Organization of Political Parties*, 2 vols. (New York: Macmillan, 1902).

[6] *Political Parties* (New York: Hearst's International Library, 1915). More recent scholarship has cast some doubt on Michels' findings about organizations.

American parties have still not overcome this handicap of half a century's standing,[7] whereas European parties have continued to evolve their partisan ways.

Styles of partisanship A comparison of political parties in the Western world cannot ignore the differences in style and organization which distinguish party politics and party organization in different countries. There are, for example, vast differences among parties on a scale ranging from intensely ideological, doctrinaire parties, such as the Communist parties or European Socialists before the middle of the twentieth century, to such pragmatically oriented parties of many different points of view as the Democrats or Republicans in the United States. There is also a significant contrast between the locally controlled, candidate-oriented party politics in the United States and the eclipse of local roots as well as of the individual candidate in British politics. There is no residence requirement for candidacy in Great Britain which would prevent the party leadership from running deserving nonresident candidates in safe districts. And the British voter has apparently been so well conditioned to partisanship that the individual candidate, whatever his merits, is not believed to be able to add or subtract more than 1 or 2 percent to the total his party would win anyway.[8]

Then there is also the notion of formal membership, which lends most European parties the character of a formal association, whereas American parties do not accord "card-carrying" membership even to their leaders. Political parties in the United States serve more as election-time magnets and landmarks of political orientation for the general public aside from partisan registration in states with a closed primary. European political parties have sometimes been compared to a fellowship of faith or a church. "Outside the party," to rephrase the medieval saying, "there is so salvation." In strongly ideological parties, there is a great desire for frequent meetings of rededication, even for individual assignments of "missionary work." Communist and Socialist parties made even the payment of monthly dues an act of rededication, preferring such frequent demonstrations of faith to the more convenient annual payment.[9]

For the individual citizen of a democracy, party activity affords a

[7] This is also the thesis of James MacGregor Burns, *The Deadlock of Democracy, Four-Party Politics in American* (Englewood Cliffs, N.J.: Prentice-Hall, 1963).

[8] See R. T. McKenzie, *British Political Parties*, rev. ed. (New York: Praeger, 1963), p. 5.

[9] The economic condition of most of the working-class members of the Communist and Socialist parties was also a good reason for preferring monthly rates.

heightened sense of participation. The magnitude of membership may be illustrated by the example of Great Britain, where about 9 million, or more than one-fourth of the eligible voters, are members of one of the three more important parties. In contemporary France, by contrast, there has been far less active civic participation, as indicated by the party membership figures, in part because of the French tradition of *incivisme,* or indifference toward public affairs, and in part owing to the same disgust with "the old parties" that helped General de Gaulle into power and granted him all the plebiscitary requests he demanded. In the Bonn Republic, there has been a similar reluctance to enter into active citizenship, for different reasons. Under the Weimar Republic, German citizens joined the various political parties in numbers not unlike those in Great Britain. But the Weimar debacle and involvement with the National Socialist regime have spread a distaste for politics that has kept party membership down to a small fraction of what it used to be. Hopefully, the negative image of politics among the general public is beginning to decline in West Germany, as indeed it appears to be doing in the United States as well.

Patterns of party organizations

So far we have encountered three basic elements in the evolution of political parties—the parliamentary group, the local electoral or registration committee, and the entire extraparliamentary party organization. The contrast between highly centralized and disciplined parties and parties locally decentralized or, in federal countries, on a state-by-state basis, has also been mentioned. But within these confines and beyond, there are still significant differences in organization and attitude.

Caucus party   The most common type of structure is that based on the local caucus or electoral committees. The caucus party has been a favorite device of middle-class political organization. One caucus is usually enough for a whole electoral district, for which it nominates or renominates a candidate and does everything from fundraising to canvassing to get him elected. This signifies, among other things, a certain atrophy of the party between elections, and the attraction of a volunteer army of precinct workers or volunteers at election time. The caucus itself remains a relatively small group recruited from among the local notables of the party supporters. The two major parties in the United States are of the caucus type, as are the French Radicals and Radical Socialists, and other Liberal or Conservative parties on the European continent.

Sometimes the caucus may be merely the representative council of other associations within the constituency, such as local or ward partisan bodies smaller than, or not coinciding with, the electoral district. More frequently, such a caucus consists of the representatives of ideologically kindred groups, whose primary purpose is not political—such as labor unions, agricultural, professional, and women's associations, and religious lay groups. A General Management Committee of the British Labour party in a particular electoral district, for example, typically consists of delegates of such affiliated organizations as the trade unions, cooperative societies or branches of the Cooperative party, branches of Socialist societies, professional, and other associations affiliated nationally with the Labour party as well as representatives of the ward committees of the constituency. The Labour party, it should be explained, is a party made up, in large part, of indirect membership through affiliated organizations such as the trade unions—who make up the bulk—and, in small part, of individual members. The Catholic parties of continental Europe also seem to prefer the representative caucus in which each of their numerous lay organizations—Catholic trade unions, women and youth organizations, professional and businessmen's associations —can be represented for purposes of nominating and electing suitable candidates. American parties, too, have long tended to bring into membership in the caucus liaison men or women from existing nonpolitical associations and minority groups as well as representatives of affiliated partisan groups such as Republican women's federations or partisan leagues or clubs.

The local caucuses or electoral committees are a part of a larger organization made up, in large part, by election and delegation from the local committees. At the same time, the local committees generally retain their home-grown autonomy, allowing regional or national bodies only a very limited control over local political policies and conduct. This means that the caucuses also fail to establish a strong extraparliamentary party organization which could exert pressure on their parliamentary representatives. Hence the latter can generally proceed as they wish in the distant national legislature. This is particularly true of such caucus parties as the Radical and Liberal parties of Europe and the Democratic and Republican parties in America, where even the discipline of the parliamentary parties is weak. Parties with an indirect, representative caucus, on the other hand, tend to have a stronger organizational framework. The reason for this difference may well lie in the need to spell out in statutory form and to maintain carefully the union of the different constituent elements at all levels of the party organization.

Branch party While caucus parties appear to be more concerned with supplying a cadre organization for political action or a political framework for nonpolitical organizations, there are other forms of party organization that reach out to the masses. One such type is the local branch party, typical of continental Socialist parties. The branch is a fairly large group of individual "card-carrying" members, about fifty to one hundred strong, the faithful of a city ward or small town. Unlike the caucus, the branch features intensive political life between elections. There are frequent meetings, lectures, lively discussions, social activities, educational undertakings, and organized sports, though there has been a decline in activities in the last decade. One is tempted to view life in the branch as that of a little utopian community that envelops many more facets of life in addition to the specifically political ones associated with caucus functions. The individual branch member is, to use the term coined by the late Sigmund Neumann, "democratically integrated" into the body politic.

While the origin of the branch goes back to the need of Socialist parties to educate and train workers for political action, branch-type party organization proved so useful that certain Conservative and Christian Democratic or Christian Social parties also adopted it. For the Conservatives, whether Protestant or Catholic, this choice was dictated by the need to consolidate their following among the lower classes against the appeals of the Socialists. While the Conservatives thus achieved a mass party character, the branch, as such, rarely attained the intensive group life once typical of Socialist branches. In some cases, in fact, it atrophied into a representative caucus as described above. In North America, Socialist movements such as the Canadian New Democratic Party (formerly CCF) and some Democratic and Republican club movements in certain states operate in a manner somewhat comparable to the European branch.

Since the typical branch party has a considerable number of members and frequent, well-attended meetings, it lends itself much better to the operation of organizational democracy than do smaller groups, where personal relationships or infrequent get-togethers tend to subvert the democratic formalities of group life. Branch parties can afford to have open competition for offices, regular discussions reviewing the policies of the leadership, and frequent votes of the mass membership to ascertain the support behind the national leadership of the branch party. If still there are oligarchic tendencies in spite of the maintenance of formal democracy, as Robert Michels and the syndicalists have charged, the reason lies in some of the basic difficulties of mass movements. Mass parties require a bureaucratic apparatus of salaried, full-time functionaries, who, not unlike the civil service of a modern state, need to be checked by elected representatives in party councils or assemblies. Actually this problem is also faced by caucus parties, which have increasingly found it necessary to hire employees for some of their functions. There is no reason to assume that branch party employees are less reliable than those of caucus parties. Also the political leadership of a branch party would not, for any reason of inner logic, have to be more demagogic, except for the historical accident of the last fifty or seventy-five years, during which the caucus parties were generally middle and upper class, whereas the lower classes preferred branch parties. During this period, however, the lower classes—peasants migrating to the cities, workers on their way to a better life—have often exhibited a "working-class authoritarianism"[10] that has invited demagogic appeals or men on horseback.

Branch parties are usually more unified than caucus parties. The branches and constituency organizations are firmly integrated into the well-articulated larger party organization, and lack the intense localism and parochial outlook of the typical caucus. This is not to say that they will not jealously guard their autonomy and statutory rights. But they delight in a sense of solidarity with the whole movement, which comes from intensely shared convictions. Branch parties generally set up a powerful extraparliamentary party which may, on occasion, attempt to dictate the policy of the parliamentary party. The extraparliamentary party at its congress or convention elects the leader and his lieutenants, who may become, if it is a parliamentary regime, the next prime minister and Cabinet, or opposition leader and shadow Cabinet, and thereby also the leaders of the parliamentary party. Tension between parliamentary and extraparliamentary parties, at least with typical branch parties, is not infrequent. It is often a result of the clash of two well-separated worlds— the world of legislative compromise and tactical necessity, and the world of the utopian community of the branch, where political discussion is often more rooted in theory and ideology than in pragmatic considerations.

Cell party Next to caucus and branch parties, there are two forms of party organization that have been adopted only by totalitarian movements of the extreme right and left. One is the *cell party*, the other the *militia type*.[11] The cell was invented by the Communists

[10] See the chapter of the same name in Seymour M. Lipset, *Political Man* (Garden City, N.Y.: Doubleday, 1960), chap. 4.

[11] Except for this last one, the names of the party types have been in general use. See especially Maurice Duverger, *Les partis politiques* (Paris: Armand Colin, 1951; English edition, London: Methuen, 1954), chap. 1.

and has been copied by some Fascist movements. The militia type developed with certain Fascist movements under the influence of militant veterans organizations and their war experiences in World War I and was promptly adopted by the Communists in the 1920s. The militia type also relates to the guerrilla armies of today.

Historically, the cell was probably developed after the model of the clandestine underground organizations under the police state of prerevolutionary Russia. Among the secret societies spreading revolutionary propaganda at factories and schools, and sometimes engaging in terrorist actions, these clandestine clubs were most effective and hardest to detect if they formed small secret cells with very little contact with each other so that the discovery of one small group would not necessarily lead to the discovery and destruction of the whole movement. The Russian Social Democrats, from whom the present Communist party of the Soviet Union is derived, had cells in factories and secret intellectual clubs of a comparable character in the larger cities. When the Bolsheviks came to power after the 1917 revolution, the cells were retained in the party structure and, after the establishment of the Communist International, made mandatory for all Communist parties throughout the world. The cell structure has unique advantages for purposes of infiltrating other organizations such as trade unions, pacifist groups, or moderate parties, and controlling them from within. This, among other aspects, is the chief reason why Fascist and crypto-Fascist movements in Western countries frequently adopt it, too, for the purpose of infiltrating moderate conservative parties—veterans groups, farm groups, and the like.

The typical Communist party cell comprises no more than ten to at the most twenty members. Instead of being based on a geographical area, as is the caucus in the electoral district, many cells are based on the place of work in the factory, workshop, office, or wherever people are brought together by their occupation. Yet there are also area cells side by side with the factory cells, either to unite isolated workers or to bring together people in callings that lack the accumulation of persons typical of industrial life. These area cells are in no way made to correspond to electoral districts—elections being less important to the typical cell party than propaganda, agitation, and the recruitment of new members. Some branch parties in countries that did not allow their members to vote were also little concerned about electoral districts. In the case of cell parties in Western countries, there is a deliberate choice against the processes of democracy and in favor of preparing for revolutionary action. Factory cells have an advantage over area cells—such as street, block, and village cells—in that they tightly unite a small community that is in constant contact for the full length of each and every working day. Cell meetings are full of intense discussion in which ideological fanaticism and activist militancy are fused into a fighting creed that subordinates all other considerations to the determination to do everything for the final victory of the cause.

The typical cell party, especially in Communist movements, features a strongly unified structure based on the exclusive use of *vertical links*. In caucus and branch parties there are, generally, several formal and informal (horizontal) channels of contact among local units. In the Communist cell structure, however, the individual cell has no contact with other cells, but only with the higher echelons of the party.[12] This ingenious system was probably also an outcome of the underground past and still lends itself well to clandestine activity. Not surprisingly, this structure of vertical links serves to prevent any spread, in the party, of schisms or of opposition to the party leadership. Though discussion may be free and untrammeled in each cell, the leadership need not fear that dissent from one cell can "contaminate" the others or that an opposition be formed through grass-roots cooperation. To tip the scales even further, the delegates of each cell to the next higher level and on up to the top are chosen by the party leadership. Far from representing the opinion of the cell toward the hierarchy, each delegate is responsible to the higher echelons to which he must report any unrest in his bailiwick. Such extraordinary centralization of power cannot but breed an entrenched oligarchy feeding upon its own autocratic power, supported by the sway of ideology over the minds of the members and by the strong feeling of solidarity that demands that dissidents accept what they believe to be the verdict of the majority after due discussion at the lower levels. The central leadership also retains special disciplinary powers and devices to purge uncooperative members at any level. This strange combination of free discussion at the grass roots with effective dictatorship within the party is called, by Communists, *democratic centralism*.

Party militia A militia, an important part of a political party, is generally a sign of a society deeply shaken by militarizing experiences such as a major war or civil war, or the expectation of a violent domestic uprising. This was the origin of the Fascist movements of Germany and Italy after World War I, when the experiences of the

---

[12] In France, the next higher level, the *sections*, likewise has no horizontal links, and neither does the third level, the *federations*, until the entire structure ends in the National Congress of the Communist Party. Duverger, *op. cit.*

first major struggle of men and matériel combined with the appearance of well-organized workers' movements demanding a share of power. The obvious strength and striking power on the left called forth vigilante organizations and private armies in both countries, and they eventually proved more than a match for the street fighters of the extreme left. After the first impact of right-wing militancy, to be sure, the German Communists also formed a militia named Red Front. Later on, practically every party of the Weimar Republic was associated with some form of paramilitary organization of doubtful effectiveness. But not even the Communist militia was ever allowed more than a protective role within the party, and the German and Italian Fascist parties always had party cells and even branches right alongside the storm troopers and Blackshirts. A short time after Hitler came to power, moreover, he resolutely cut down the leadership of the militia organization of his party in a savage purge in order to prevent it from becoming a rival center of power to his own control of the party.

A party militia is a private army only in the sense that its members receive quasi-military training, are organized in armylike squads, companies, battalions, and so on, and like to wear uniforms, march in step, carry flags, and flaunt badges. The members are not maintained by the organization but are expected to drill frequently and to be prepared for physical combat with weapons. Even though the ability of a militia to capture control of the streets and to carry out terrorist raids can be a great asset in a situation where the authorities are in sympathy with what they may view as "sincere patriots," as in Italy and Germany in the 1920s, the uses of a party militia are very limited. One can also look at the uses of a militia from the point of view of what it does for its potential members. Sometimes the militarizing effect of a recent war and the thrust of youth revolt together create waves of politically mobilized youth with an enormous urge to march, to demonstrate, and to strike out at their real or imagined foes. A militia need not be in strictly military uniform and ranks in order to give militants a sense of struggle and purpose. The militia may serve as an outlet for the explosive tensions of a situation of impending civil war and may channel expectations of violence into postures of active defense or attack upon the "enemy." It may also provide romantic roles of heroism and knighthood in shining armor to disturbed persons in need of such an escape from the world of reality. But in the last analysis, such private armies are no match for the military power any legitimate government of today can summon. Nor did the two most prominent Fascist dictators, Hitler and Mussolini, owe their ascent to power, to any great extent, to their militias. Even as a device of mobilizing people in the service of political mass movement, membership in a cell is probably more effective in the long run than the militia can ever hope to be.

These four types, then, have been the prevalent forms of party organization in Western countries, often found with different parties side by side and sometimes in combination within the same party. Their adoption by particular parties is determined by the historical setting and environment of social class and by the preferences of the members or adherents for certain patterns of politics and styles of political involvement. Parties in which the caucus is predominant, as we have seen, are well adapted to the prevailing pattern of democratic politics, say, in the United States where life centers around the elections in particular districts. The typical party adherent is content to get involved only at election time, when he attends meetings and may even volunteer his services. Branch parties, constituency associations, and club movements are less tied to the electoral function and devote themselves more to such functions as educating their members and the public in the particulars of the party philosophy. The typical member of a branch party regards its community life, with all the ancillary activities and organizations, as a large part of his own life—political and otherwise. Cell and militia parties, finally, are fighting orders quite divorced from and often contemptuous of the electoral activity normally associated with Western-style democracy. They are best adapted to other forms of political struggle such as agitation, infiltration, and street fighting. The typical member of a cell or militia is completely dedicated to the violent goals of his movement, which overshadow all other aspects of his personal life. This total dedication is a hallmark of totalitarian parties, and has often been compared to religious fanaticism, especially since such movements promise a kind of substitute salvation and often rise as conventional religion declines.

INTEREST GROUPS IN THE POLITICAL SYSTEM

Defining interests and groups

Next to agencies of the *group process* such as political parties or government officials, whose political activity is more obvious, there is a multitude of other groups relevant to the policy-making process. Sociologists offer definitions of many different categories of groups, not all of which are likely to play a role in politics. The problems of defining the nature of groups in politics have been complicated also by the notion of *interest,* a time-honored concept in Western political theory, but somewhat lacking in empirical precision.

Classical economic theory ascribes self-interest as the chief motive to individuals. Theories of international politics generally assume that nation-states have a "national interest." Socialist philosophers such as Karl Marx have reduced all social and political life to the clashing "interests of classes" such as the *bourgeoisie* and the *proletariat.* Many legal theories presume the existence of a "public interest." Political scientists such as Arthur F. Bentley and David B. Truman have placed the understanding of government and politics into a context of clashing group interests, many of which are said to remain latent until stirred up by the actions of other groups or government. The groups themselves originate in response to a threat to their latent interests. Another political scientist, Alfred DeGrazia, points out that all politics is the "politics of interest groups," a politics of disinterest being most unlikely.[13] Yet it appears to be almost impossible to state exactly what we mean by the word *interest.* Where economic relationships are involved, one might still be able to state in dollars and cents how a given individual would profit or suffer damages from a given course of governmental or other action.

But the "interest of a group," as it comes to bear on the political system, is an exceedingly elusive phenomenon. So many subjective and variable factors enter into it that contemporary students of interest groups often prefer to speak about the actual *demands* voiced by a group rather than about its interest. Even the identity and cohesion of a group can be a matter of controversy, as in the case of Marx's hypothetical proletariat, which presents enormous difficulties of definition for purposes of statistics or empirical sociology. Fully organized groups with charters, officers, and "card-carrying membership" are no more likely to have a clear awareness of their "interests" or threats to them than will an informal group defined by a neighborhood or place of work. What matters are perceived by the group or its leadership as involving the "group interest" depends entirely on a complex welter of attitudes, fears, hopes and, very likely, plenty of misconceptions of all sorts.[14] Nevertheless, all kinds

13 In the *Annals of the American Academy of Political and Social Science,* vol. 319 (September 1958), p. 113.

14 The tautological character of some attempts at conceptualizing about groups and interests is, perhaps, clearest when groups or classes are defined by their "sharing of interests."

of groups constantly develop specific notions of where their interests lie and act upon them in the political sphere.

Historically, there have always been groups of various descriptions—family, religious, occupational, ethnic, geographical. However, the passing of traditional society and culture—in a word, modernization—in many countries gave rise to powerful new groups, such as labor unions, business associations, and farm groups. It also changed the goals of existing groups, generally directing them more toward politics, and developed new styles of organized group life not unlike the growth of modern political mass parties.

Highly developed, bureaucratically organized interest associations with, in some cases, nationwide coverage and even mass membership, are not a necessity for a politics of interest groups. Lobbying with governmental agencies was just as lively before the advent of the new groups, in times when individual businesses, industries, and local groups were in the forefront. Before the new associational groups appeared, powerful influence was also wielded by such institutional groups as churches, such anomic groups as street mobs in riots, or the pressure of unorganized ethnic or other social groups aroused by grievances. In many cases, the new groups have given political leverage to the interests of scattered "little men," such as farmers, workers, small businessmen, or to minorities previously ignored by government, and have also given permanence and stability to the relations between groups, such as bargaining or propaganda. Policy-makers in parliaments and administrative agencies consult with the appropriate interest groups as a matter of routine, just as conflicts between management and labor are no longer isolated clashes of uncertain course but follow well-ordered procedures of settlement.

Differences between parties and interest groups

It is generally assumed that there are unmistakable differences between political parties and interest groups that make it easy to distinguish between the two. Among these differences is the willingness of parties to take over the full responsibility for government, to make public policy in all fields of governmental activity, to aggregate interests in the desire to gather broad support, and to recruit and promote candidates for public office. Interest groups, in contradistinction to political parties, are content with promoting their own particular interest and show little desire to pick candidates or to run the whole government. In many cases, interest groups are limited to a geographical area and have a membership restricted to a particular social group or economic group, such as soybean farmers or steel workers, whereas a party strives for nationwide support from all citizens. This view of the differences between parties and interest groups is fairly adequate as it applies to the United States, though with some exceptions. Third parties such as the Prohibitionists, for example, resemble interest groups. There is also the case of American labor in the nineteenth century, when the early labor leaders were divided on the question of whether or not to form a political party or a trade union movement. This is a common experience in the evolution of societies. In the earlier stages of development, the evolving organizations of labor, agriculture, and business often remain undecided for a long time about developing a functionally specific character as an interest group or as a political party. Insofar as interest groups are concerned, there are numerous instances in American politics where they do take an active hand in the selection and promotion of candidates on all levels, especially in local government. There are also frequent cases of groups such as the League of Women Voters, the AFL–CIO, the National Council of Churches, and many others taking a strong stand on issues of public policy far beyond what could be called the narrow focus of their interests.

Outside the United States, the dividing line between political parties and interest groups is harder to draw, even if the parties are highly organized and disciplined and the country is an advanced industrial nation. The British Labour party, for instance, is, to a large extent, composed of trade unions whose members have acquired "indirect membership" in the party. Most Catholic parties on the European continent are inextricably linked up with Catholic trade unions and various Catholic lay organizations. Political parties in the Bonn Republic have developed the custom of nominating officials of certain business and farm groups among their candidates for the *Bundestag*. In two-party systems, the organized interests are often accommodated inside the major parties, whereas multiparty systems, such as the French, often include one or several parties that are really interest groups pursuing their interests by promoting their own candidates and endeavoring to place them into the policy-making institutions.

Kinds of interest groups

This brings us to the relation of interest groups to the process of policy-making. Although the most obvious activity of interest groups in this respect may be lobbying with administrative agencies and legislators, there are a number of important distinctions and circumstances that need to be considered for a better understanding of the role of groups in the democratic process. The basic differences in kind among groups play a role in determining how they can hope to influence government.

First, there are *associations of economic interest,* such as the American NAM (National Association of Manufacturers), the French *Patronat,* the Federation of British Industry, and the German *Bund der deutschen Industrie,* and of course many more specialized groups, organized to wield national influence by means of hired lobbyists and propaganda designed to create favorable public opinion.

Then there are associations of *public service organizations* of varied tasks, including, in particular, European chambers of commerce and, in some countries, semiofficial chambers of handicraft, or agriculture, whose political interest orientation is not always easy to ascertain. The chief function of these groups lies in the local services they perform and evidently not primarily in lobbying, though there may often be a certain amount of propagandizing done almost inadvertently. On the European continent, the chamber organizations also join other business, handicraft, or farm groups to form mighty interest combines, or "summit associations," who then claim to be the "voice of French business" or of "German handicraft" toward government.

A third kind of interest groups is primarily devoted to common professional or occupational interests, such as the American Medical Association, the German Association of Journalists, and the French and German Associations of Civil Servants, which is not to say that they will not lobby or propagandize when their income or professional status seems to be at stake. Associations of civil servants have the added advantage of being inside the governmental apparatus, although this very circumstance may make them suspect in the eyes of the legislature. In countries where civil servants play a great role in party politics, as in Germany and Japan, moreover, there are ample informal ways for the civil servants to wield effective influence.

A fourth type of interest group, not always clearly separable from the third or, indeed, the first we mentioned, are associations formed for the primary purpose of allowing their individual members to bargain collectively with those on whom conditions of their livelihood depend. This type includes labor unions of the industrial (rather than craft union) type, and employers' associations, which are sometimes identical with federations of industry, and sometimes separate. It also includes certain farmers' leagues and associations oriented toward collective action or cooperative solutions to their economic problems. Although this category embraces some of the most powerful mass membership organizations in an advanced industrial society, lobbying with government and direct influence on elections is secondary to their primary purpose. Because early labor and farmers' movements often vacillated between the roles of a political party and an economic association, and because mass organization and intensive group life can encourage an interest in more than one purpose, their relationship to government and politics has tended to change considerably over the years.

A fifth category of interest group is of an *institutional character* and includes government agencies, courts and judges, the personnel of such large establishments as public enterprises, the armed forces or branches thereof, regional and municipal governments, and the clergy of the churches. Whereas the previously mentioned civil service associations may concern themselves with salary scales and standards of promotion, these institutional groups—for example, the employees of the German federal railways, the local government of the French city of Lyons or that of Miami, Florida, the British navy or the Argentinian air force—all may on occasion wish to influence legislatures, lobby with administrative organs, or try to persuade the public through the mass media to support them in their demands. Municipal associations wield great influence in Germany and Scandinavia. The Catholic clergy of France, as elsewhere, have been repeatedly involved in political battles over such issues as religious influence on public education or the status of civil marriage.

In addition to the kinds of interest groups mentioned above, there are many other types, such as veterans organizations, fraternal associations, and such short-lived but forceful phenomena as street mobs or organized demonstrators—all of which may come to exert influence on government. One thing, however, is certain: Interest groups may sometimes take over functions normally reserved to political parties, but in their role toward government they clearly take a different approach. Only parties attempt *to govern*, to take on complete governmental responsibility; interest groups never do. On the other hand, there are some parties that prefer a purely representative role vis-à-vis a government they cannot control. And there are irresponsible parties who prefer to ride out economic or social crises in the opposition while the government parties get blamed for calamities beyond their control. In any event, most interest groups are clearly too limited in their goals and organization to be mistaken for bona fide political parties.

THE ROLE OF PUBLIC OPINION

The changing concept of public opinion

Few expressions in the literature of politics have undergone as extensive changes of meaning as the expression *public opinion*. From the time of the rise of popular government, political thinkers such as Jeremy Bentham, Alexis de Tocqueville, John Stuart Mill, and James Bryce have insisted that in the last resort it is public opinion that makes democracy work. Over and beyond such devices of restraint on government as checks and balances and elections, they reasoned, there has to be an enlightened public opinion to check the government and keep it on its toes. This public opinion, it was assumed, was composed of an independent press and an informed citizenry that took an active part in government by speaking its mind on the issues and policies at hand. From this vital role of public opinion followed further emphasis on the freedom of the press, of speech, and of assembly as functional prerequisites of democracy in addition to their value to personal liberty. Political scientists, therefore, in comparing different political systems never fail to notice the role of the press, the pattern of civic participation, and the presence of government censorship or other restraints, such as the withholding of information or "management of the news."

Since the days of the nineteenth century, political theorists mentioned vast improvements in communications media—radio, film, television, and other efficient devices of communication have sprung up. These new developments do not change the importance of the role of a free and vital public opinion, but they do complicate the task of maintaining it and even more of studying it. It was discovered from the great wars, dictatorships, and social upheavals of the twentieth century that public opinion could be and, indeed, was manipulated on a grand scale by governments and private parties. Governments and the sensationalist "yellow press" whipped nations into a frenzy of hatred toward other nations in the hope of preparing for war. Mass movements and interest groups spread large amounts of propaganda, often of a nature to incite the feelings of men. Press lords and radio orators used the vast new powers of persuasion available to them for purposes other than public information and enlightenment. Most alarming of all, perhaps, was the development of a monopoly on all information in totalitarian movements and dictatorships, which enslaved people by replacing the objective information that would have made them free, responsible individuals with never-ending torrents of ideological propaganda. These developments also turned the interest of political scientists toward studying the nature of propaganda and the dependence of the public on accurate and factual news, for a citizen can participate responsibly in national affairs only to the extent that he can learn what goes on hundreds and thousands of miles away.

Rise of public opinion polls

Since the 1940s, the understanding of the complex processes of public opinion has been broadened and intensified through empirical research utilizing public opinion polls. Learning by trial and error, these empirical studies have progressed from crude beginnings to quite a degree of sophistication. At present they are being used in many Western and non-Western nations, so that it is beginning to be possible to compare the attitudes and political preferences among nations.

One of the first problems that had to be solved was the development of reliable *sampling techniques* that would allow the pollsters to select and interview a small representative sample of respondents and thereby ascertain with reasonable accuracy the opinions of a much larger number of persons. A carefully balanced *quota random sample*—that is, one selected at random while controlling the proportion of registered party voters, members of the various religious faiths, of the main occupational, age, sex, and income level groups to mirror the known proportions of these groups in the entire American population—will produce an accurate picture of the opinions of the whole nation through no more than a few thousand respondents. The smaller the number, the lower the cost of the study.

Another crucial problem that had to be solved was the perfection of *interviewing techniques*. Questionnaires had to be designed that would elicit meaningful and comparable answers from respondents of widely varying background and varying comprehension of the subject at hand. Opinion studies trying to predict the outcome of an election, for example, had to assign the same weight to the opinion of a well-informed respondent as to one who was unfamiliar with some of the candidates and issues but evidently inclined to vote. The interviewers also had to be trained to handle the complex human relations of the interview situation with a minimum of bias or distortion. Finally, methods of the *statistical manipulation* of public opinion data had to be developed to handle more and more sophisticated studies of the subtle processes of opinion formation and change, such as the relationships between opinion leaders and followers, and so forth. At present, the methods of statistical manipulation of opinion data have become so complex and sophisticated as to require the use of computers and a good deal of mathematical training on the part of political scientists who design public opinion studies.

There are many fields of study to which the current methods of public opinion research are applied. The most generally known are polling studies with the object of predicting the outcome of an election. This type of study often uses repeated measurements to yield the changing opinions about parties, candidates, or issues, sometimes with a panel of the same persons asked repeatedly. There is so much demand for election predictions in the various Western democracies that private polling institutes in Great Britain, West Germany, France, Italy, the United States, and many other countries have been formed.

Political scientists are less interested in prediction than in autopsies of elections for what the latter reveal about the way individuals make up their minds, how they view candidates and issues, and how they identify with political parties. Elaborate studies have tried to correlate partisan voting, for example, with age, sex, income, or educational level of the voters, or with occupations or membership in important associations, such as trade unions and the like. Changes in the composition of the adherents of a given party over a period of time can tell much about the changing character of the party, or about the working of the entire political process at the grass roots. Some studies have focused on the exposure of voters to campaign appeals and materials, to newspapers and mass media of known bias, or to the influence of relatives, friends, or co-workers of known bias. Others, again, have attempted to fathom the reasons that keep eligible voters from voting. Nonvoting is a particularly vexatious problem in the United States, where restrictive election laws and a lack of political involvement have kept the turnout even in the Presidential elections as low as two-thirds or less of the eligible voters. But even though other Western democracies may have a turnout of 75 percent to 90 percent in national elections, there are similar problems of nonparticipation at the regional level, and especially in local elections.

One reason why election studies have always lent themselves particularly well to public opinion polls and statistical manipulation of data is to be found in the equality of all individual opinions in the act of voting. A similar equality of opinions prevails also among the members of a legislative body insofar as voting is concerned. For that reason, some political scientists have used polling techniques and other supporting data, such as social background data and recorded votes, for sophisticated studies of legislative behavior. In this manner, they examined, for example, the cohesion of various blocs or factions in national legislatures, or the increasing integration of supranational parties in European regional assemblies, such as that of the Common Market.

Other public opinion studies have dealt with the informal power structure of local communities; respondents are asked what persons they consider to be influential in local politics. Another line of inquiry is the study of political socialization—the processes and agents that get young people or new citizens involved in citizenship roles, partisanship, and other forms of political participation. Each country has what the two authors of a recent comparative study called a "civic culture," a welter of attitudes and ideals regarding the expectations of citizens toward government, their roles as citizens, passive or active participation, and such institutions and organizations of politics as parties, elections, or political leadership.[15] There is no better way to find out more about the civic culture of a country than by interviewing its citizens in a systematic, sophisticated fashion and piecing the results together to sketch a national political profile. Finally, public opinion studies can also focus on political elites of various descriptions, or on the membership of political parties or similar organizations crucial to the process of policy-making in modern governments.

[15] Gabriel A. Almond and Sidney Verba, The Civic Culture (Princeton, N. J.: Princeton University Press, 1963).

CHAPTER **11** FEDERALISM AND UNITARISM

More than half of the inhabited territory of the world today lives under a federal form of government of one sort or another. Among the federal systems are the Western European countries of Switzerland, Germany, and Austria; the United States, Canada, Mexico, Brazil, Argentina, and Venezuela in the Americas; Australia; India, Pakistan, and Malaysia in Asia; and any number of real or planned federations in Africa and the Middle East. Even Yugoslavia and the Soviet Union lay claim to the federal label. Yet though the institution may thrive and more federal systems be added to the number every decade, the definition of federalism continues to be a matter of controversy.

Federations of sorts have an ancient and honorable tradition going back to the permanent leagues of Greek city-states in antiquity and to the Dutch Confederacy of the seventeenth century. They reemerged with great vitality in the United States Constitution of 1787, but in a far more centralized form, characterized by the *Federalist Papers* as a mixture of "federal and national government." This new form of federalism has found many imitators and admirers.

In the meantime, however, the industrialization and urbanization of the more advanced federal countries, and the enormous pressures of the age of world political involvement and worldwide wars have begun to transform federal systems. Some state and local functions, such as social welfare and economic regulation, have had to be transferred increasingly to the federal government. The enormous burdens of defense and foreign policy have become more centralized and top-heavy; some observers have begun to complain that the federal character of the systems is being obliterated. Other scholars feel that the adjustment of the older schemes of federal organization to the necessities of industrialism and the nuclear age involved nothing more than changes in the concept of federalism.

The federal concept has indeed undergone profound changes, although there never was, perhaps, a logically satisfactory definition of federalism at any time during the earlier phases of federal development. The older school of federal theory owed much to the concepts of state and sovereignty as we have encountered them in the thought of Jean Bodin (see Chapter 3). Federalism was defined as the midpoint of a scale running from unitary government to confederation. Unitary government is characterized by the location of sovereignty with the central government. The sovereign Parliament in London, for example, has unlimited power to govern, which it need not share with any local or regional level of government. Confederations, on the other hand, such as the one preceding the United States Constitution, were defined as permanent *unions of sovereign states.* And since the states retained their sovereignty, the central government or Confederate Congress was to have no power over revenues or over the individual citizen and could make important decisions only with the unanimous consent of all the sovereign member states.

This approach gave a satisfactory explanation of unitarism and of confederation but only served to complicate the difficulties of defining the in-between—the mixture of "national," or unitary, and "federal," or confederate—elements. For sovereignty, according to Bodin, is *indivisible* and *exclusive of any rival sovereignty.* It made no more sense to allocate sovereignty to both central and regional governments than to either level, thereby unitarizing or confederalizing federal government. The most sensible explanation suggested that sovereignty was possessed jointly, by the whole federal state, and exercised in different fields by both the central and the regional governments, each directly over the individual citizens. But then again, this explanation tended to fragment "indivisible sovereignty" or at least to suggest that the accepted definitions of state and sovereignty did not fit the complex realities of federalism.

It is small wonder, then, that contemporary writers have tended to express themselves more carefully and without reference to the words "state" and "sovereignty." The late British constitutional theorist A. V. Dicey spoke of federal government as a form of government preferred by those who "seek union rather than unity." The American political scientist Carl J. Friedrich prefers to call it "a union of group selves." Another American political scientist, William H. Riker, speaks of a federal "bargain between prospective national leaders and officials of constituent governments for the purpose of aggregating territory, the better to lay taxes and raise armies."[1]

FEDERALISM AND SOCIETY

The adoption of federal government in preference to unitarism by a particular country is rarely a matter of free choice. When the framers of the United States Constitution set out to establish a "more perfect union" from the loosely confederated states, their plan would have been rejected had they tried to carry centralization to its ultimate conclusion. Neither could the governments of Canada, Australia, Switzerland, the German Empire, India, or Nigeria have been established in unitary form, though a confederate form or separate existence of the constitutent states was imaginable.

The reason for this limitation on the degree of centralization attainable appears to lie in the composite nature of the society enclosed by a *federal community*. Many federations are created from states that have previously led separate lives for hundreds of years. Each of these constitutent states is inhabited by a people with a sense of identity and a feeling of community that continues to exist after the union is achieved. These communities of the several states are the "group selves" of which Carl J. Friedrich speaks, and their identity is preserved to some extent even though their union adds to it a new, national sense of identity and a national feeling of community. In many federal countries, the "group selves" may even be distinct nationalities of different language and customs, as in India, Switzerland, Canada, Nigeria, and the Union of South Africa. Soviet and Yugoslav federalism also can be traced to the many nationalities that make up these countries. Often the sense of regional identity stems from a colonial past, when several colonies or settlements distant from one another were held together by ties to an equally distant, common motherland. The Western European nations involved in economic and, hopefully, eventual political integration

---

[1] *Federalism* (Boston: Little, Brown, 1964), p. 11.

offer a subject for penetrating insights into the persistence of the patterns of identity of the constituent elements of what may some days become a federal union.

On the other hand, a large federal community may start with the "federal bargain" to unite in the face of an external threat, or parhaps for the sake of economic expansion and development. An external enemy or the former colonial masters can do wonders in creating a common interest in joint defensive strength that will overcome the jealous anxiety of the constitutent states for their sovereign independence. The time of seeking a "more perfect union" is also often a time of industrial and commercial growth, a time of searching for a common market uninhibited by tariff barriers between the states, and a time of canal and railroad building that unifies the larger community and further facilitates commerce. And from these activities there may emerge a national consciousness, which, for example, in the decades prior to 1776 led Virginians and New Yorkers to think of themselves increasingly as Americans above all, or that inspired Prussian and Bavarian liberals in the mid-nineteenth century to feel that they were Germans first.

A mature federal system in an advanced industrial society, finally, is a highly complex body politic. Basically, it consists of two or more layers of communities superimposed upon one another, the national community and the regions, living side by side and in various ways intertwined. But there are numerous complications caused in large part by the changes mentioned at the outset. Wars and international involvement tend to intensify national loyalty at the expense of regional identification. Depressions and a highly developed economy likewise increase the dependence of the individual citizen on nationwide big business, big labor, and big government.

Along with the mobilization of resources of large-scale modern industry on a national basis, there are also the migrations from rural to urban areas, and between cities, typical of the industrial age. Migration tends to weaken regional loyalties. The national capital of a federation, say, Berlin in the Bismarckian Empire, would grow into a vast metropolis of millions of new inhabitants. They would find employment with the national government or with the central offices of big business, all the interest groups of the new age, with banking and credit institutions, with transport or other services to the national economy, or with manufacturers of information and popular culture such as the great publishers of books and periodicals and the entertainment industry. Yet the economic and cultural spell cast by such a capital city over a federal country would be dim as compared to that radiating from Paris over France, or from London over

Great Britain. For a thoroughly unitary country such as France not only has, by centuries of tradition, concentrated administration, services, culture, and even fashion in Paris, but also lacks other metropolitan centers of comparable size, such as can be found in the advanced federal countries. The West German part of truncated Germany alone, for example, contains nine metropolitan areas of more than half a million inhabitants each. The United States has about twice that number, including half a dozen that constitute urban complexes of millions of inhabitants. The largest of them, the New York area, for reasons inherent in American history, has come closest to being the capital city in the sense in which Berlin was once the capital of Germany.

Although the growth of a major regional urban center may testify to the capacity of a region for self-contained, advanced economic and social development, these new spatial patterns frequently pay no respect to existing regional boundaries of a federal country. Many a great metropolis grew up next to a state line, spilling over into a neighboring state and, perhaps, appropriating a large portion of it as its economic hinterland. Legions of commuters might work in the city, using services and facilities in the one state, yet live and pay taxes in the other. Some states might not have any notable urban center, and their economies may be under the sway of outside centers. Whole depressed regions or groups of states, in fact, might be in bondage, economically speaking, to a more developed part of the country.

These transformations could hardly help challenging the very basis of federal government and its geographical patterns, the constituent communities of the larger union. In times of economic crisis, as during the Great Depression of the 1930s, plans for territorial reorganization and federal reform were seriously considered by many people in the more advanced countries. Putting the American federal system on the basis of the existing economic regions might have created reasonably balanced and economically self-sufficient constituent units in place of the often purely accidental states of a past age. With strong constituent units of the federal system, the original division of functions between the union and the states could have been maintained and the threat of bankruptcy of some state governments avoided. Instead of territorial reorganization, Americans chose the easy way out of the crisis: governmental centralization in Washington.

An instructive example is provided by the German federal system, which from its very beginnings in the nineteenth century suffered from an imbalance in its geographical structure. From 1871, when the

Bismarckian Empire was established upon confederate antecedents, two-thirds of the territory and population were taken up by the state of Prussia, which had effected the union by superior military force and was economically far more developed than the other dozen and a half states. The smallest of the latter, moreover, were too small to allow even for the full development of local government services, not to mention their being partners with the federal government. With the rise of big government at all levels in the twentieth century, the imbalance in German federalism grew ever more severe. Vital new governmental functions could not be carried out by the smaller states. Instead, these functions had to be administered directly by the *Reich* (federal) government, to the dismay of the larger states that were quite capable of carrying them out. Repeated attempts to break up Prussia into a number of smaller states and to consolidate the smallest units with each other or with neighboring states failed. And so the federal system of the Weimar Republic collapsed in the Great Depression as state governments went bankrupt and the emergency powers of the *Reich* President superseded all traditional divisions of governmental functions.

The West German successor to the federal republic of Weimar is founded on a far more balanced territorial organization, although the individual *Laender* still vary in size, from the city-state of Bremen, with 700,000 inhabitants, to the state of North Rhine Westphalia, with 16 million. But the smaller states are now large and affluent enough for a fruitful partnership with the federal government. Although there is still some interest in territorial reorganization, and the West German constitution provides ways of bringing it about, there is very little likelihood of any reorganization ever taking place. Quite apart from the considerable resistance that attends any territorial change, it should be stressed that the imminence of reorganization in a federal system is a most disruptive influence. It is often better for the territorial status to be settled and stable, even if considerable imbalance and border problems exist, than to have the very foundations of federal government in continuous flux.

DIFFERENT PATTERNS OF FEDERAL INSTITUTIONS

With so large a number of federations of widely varying circumstances and origin in existence around the world, considerable differences in the institutional patterns are to be expected. However, apart from names and minor idiosyncrasies, there is a great deal of similarity underlying the basic design in all federal countries. Apart from the older and looser forms of union, three major variants can be distinguished: (1) the much-imitated Anglo-American pattern, which prevails throughout most of the British Commonwealth, in the United States, and, with modifications in practice, in Latin America; (2) the German type, which resembles federal organization in Switzerland and Austria; and (3) Soviet federalism, which served as a model for Yugoslav federalism. The chief differences between these types lie in the basic concept of the nature of the partnership between the different levels of government. Analogous differences can also be found in the prevalent types of relationships between national and local governments, except, of course, for the inherent autonomy and inviolability of the constituent members of a federation in contrast to the dependence of local government on national legislation.

Relationships between the levels of government

The Anglo-American pattern The distinguishing characteristic of the Anglo-American pattern of federalism is the attempt at complete *separation* of the federal government from the governments of the states or provinces (Canada) in order to make the two levels of government *coordinate* rather than dependent upon one another.[2] (See Figure 11.1, showing the United States pattern.) Though there are differences in the design of American, Canadian, and Australian federalism, these federations have in common the idea that each level of government should be fairly complete in its legislative, administrative, taxing, and judicial powers, and its governmental organs independent of those of the other level of government. To be sure, there have been exceptions. Until the twentieth century, for example, the members of the United States Senate were selected by the state legislatures and governments, a pattern implying dependence even though the senators were under no further control of the state organs once selected for their six-year term. There are also deviations from the idea of independence of governments: in Canada, for example, the dominion executive appoints the lieutenant governors of the provinces and retains certain veto powers over provincial legislation. In practice, however, the tendency has been toward as much independence of the two levels of government—each in its own sphere—as possible.

The German and Swiss pattern The German type of federalism, by contrast, makes no such attempt to separate the levels of govern-

[2] Kenneth C. Wheare in his *Federal Government*, 4th ed. (New York: Oxford University Press. 1963), pp. 2–3, considers this the criterion of all truly federal government.

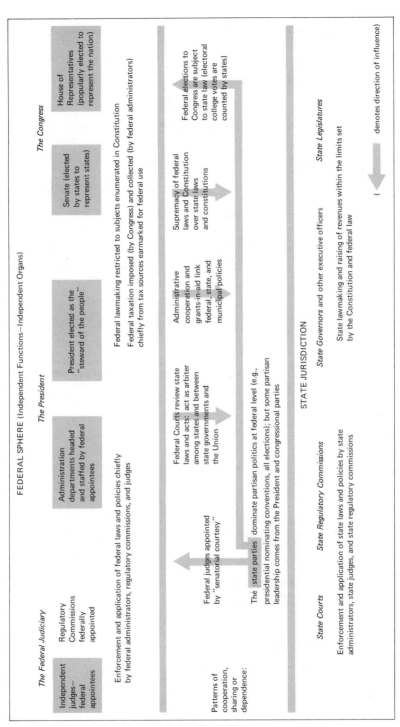

Figure 11.1   The mutual-independence pattern of federalism:
the United States.

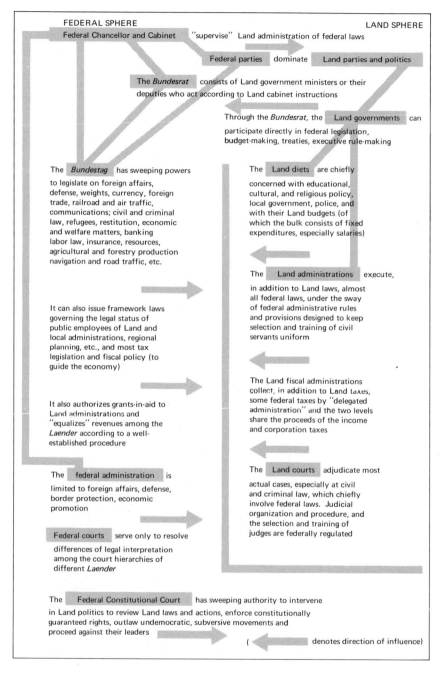

Figure 11.2   The federal-council pattern of federalism:
the Bonn Republic.

ment (see Figure 11.2). On the contrary, the German constitutions of 1871, 1919, and 1949 all established a pattern of intimate interrelation and mutual dependence between the two levels of government. A large part of the explanation for the difference in design of the several types of federalism can be found in the circumstances of origin. The framers of the American Constitution wanted to overcome the inherent weaknesses of the central authorities of the American confederation by creating a strong and independent federal government complete in its governmental powers and enumerated subjects of jurisdiction. Bismarck, the founder of the German Empire, on the other hand, was guided by the desire to give constitutional form to the new Prussian-dominated German nation-state, which his Prussian armies had just unified. Far from wanting to establish a federal government independent of the state government of Prussia, he preferred a design that made the King of Prussia the German Kaiser, and a member of the Prussian Cabinet the chancellor of the *Reich* (federal) government. A second reason for the unusual design lay in the monarchic nature of that federation, most of whose member states were monarchies with underdeveloped institutions of popular government. These state monarchies were willing to delegate the task of making unifying legislation for the new nation-state to a popularly elected federal assembly, the *Reichstag*, but preferred to retain administrative powers and actual control through their emissaries in the *Bundesrat* (federal council). This council resembled the old Confederate Congress of the German Confederation (1815–1867) and became simultaneously the upper house of the federal legislature and the nominal executive council of the federation, both under Prussian domination. Whatever the circumstances of origin, the German type of federal organization appears to have served its purpose well enough to be readopted in 1949 by the Bonn Republic, after Prussia had long ceased to exist and Germany had been truncated.

Four characteristics distinguish the German type of federalism from the Anglo-American pattern as follows: (1) The division of legislative powers between the federal government and the *Laender* (states) places the bulk of legislative authority with the federation, leaving the regulation of only a few subjects, such as education and local government, to the *Laender* diets. (2) At the same time, the bulk of the administrative and judicial powers remains at the *Laender* level, which implies that most federal laws are administered and adjudicated by state authorities. The federal administration is chiefly responsible for foreign affairs, defense, and perhaps raising its own revenues, though even this function can be delegated to the state administrators. The other federal ministries are concerned only with the drafting of federal laws, not with their administration. (3) It is the nature of such a federal system that the federal government has at its disposal certain additional powers that serve to streamline and unify the operation of the entire system. The Constitution of the Bonn Republic, for example, provided for federal courts for the chief purpose of keeping uniform the interpretation of the federal laws by the state courts. The federal government has certain rights of supervising and investigating the administration of federal laws by the *Laender* and can bring complaints before the *Bundesrat* whenever it is not satisfied with the execution of these laws. The federal government has sweeping powers to regulate the selection and training of all civil servants and judges, and to prescribe uniform administrative and judicial procedures and organization throughout all the *Laender*. Finally, Bonn federalism features an elaborate procedure for equalizing the financial resources of the different *Laender* governments similar to the financial equalization procedures in some American states.

All of these special federal powers, it should be noted, are more typical of the national governments of unitary states. But it would be premature to conclude that these features tend to centralize governmental power too much to call this system federal, for there is (4) the *Bundesrat*. This distinctive institution allows the *Laender* governments a degree of direct participation in all aspects of national politics, which no American state or Canadian province can boast. Unlike American Senators, *Bundesrat* members are neither elected nor do they serve a fixed term. They are members or officials of the *Laender* Cabinets. In the *Bundesrat* they cast from three to five votes on legislative bills or administrative rules, depending on the size of their *Land*. These votes have to be cast en bloc and according to the instructions of the *Laender* Cabinets, which have several weeks in which to examine the bill before the house. And although the *Bundesrat* has only a suspensive veto on many subjects of legislation, its consent is required for all matters involving the distribution of power in the federal system and affecting the administration of federal laws by the *Laender*. If some of the foregoing features of the German type of federalism give the impression that the *Laender* governments depend on the federal government, the position of the *Bundesrat* within the federal government easily balances this pattern of dependence with one of federal dependence on the *Laender* governments.

Swiss federalism resembles the German pattern in the distribution of legislative and administrative powers between the cantons and the central government, but the Swiss Council of States resembles more nearly the United States Senate than it does the German *Bundesrat*. Its members are chosen in equal numbers from each canton and serve fixed terms. Most cantons provide for direct election of their councilors for four years, and the councilors are not instructed by their cantonal executives.

The Soviet pattern   The pattern of Soviet federalism is also indigenous and is to be noted chiefly for the ways in which it deviates from some of the basic notions of federalism in the West (see Figure 11.3). The enumeration of these points of difference, therefore, may serve to point up important elements in Western federalism, which are so basic that we tend to take them for granted. One such element is the voluntary, pluralistic character of Western political group life, which is particularly pronounced in federal countries. The exclusive monopoly on power of the monolithic Communist party of the Soviet Union deprives the constituent members of the Soviet federation of the will and capacity to use any autonomous powers that the Soviet constitution may grant them. Another element of most Western federal systems is the deliberate establishment of powerful checks on the central government, both by means of dividing powers between the two levels and of allowing the representatives of a regional minority an effective veto against the actions of a national majority. Such a concept of federal government is alien to the Soviet Union. Neither can we expect from the Soviets the counterpart of the scrupulous adherence of Western governments to their written constitutions. In 1944, for example, a constitutional amendment purported to give the union republics the power to engage in diplomatic relations with other countries and to maintain separate armies. But the union republics have exercised these powers no more than they have ever exercised the right of secession, which is also guaranteed in the Soviet constitution.

The key to Soviet federalism lies in its accommodation of the more than a hundred nationalities that make up the Soviet nation. Before the 1917 revolution Lenin recognized their right to political self-determination, with the result that he could not prevent Finland, Poland, and the Baltic countries from seceding after the revolution. Today the Soviet federal system presents a hierarchic order of national units, of which the highest are the fifteen union republics, followed by twenty autonomous republics and various smaller national units, all subordinated to the Union Republics, yet represented in the Council of Nationalities, the upper chamber of the all-union Supreme Soviet. Thus Soviet federalism is a union of nationalities on several levels, with the rights of cultural self-expression granted to each nationality, but not the rights of political autonomy.

At the same time, the monopoly of the Communist party, the exigencies of rigid central economic planning (scarcely modified by economic decentralization), and collectivization give the Soviet Union a framework more unified than that of most unitary states. In fact, the representative assemblies (soviets) on about five levels, from the local to the national level, do not really possess spheres of competence of their own, but rather tend to carry out the same policies over varying areas of geographical jurisdiction. And the parallel structure of the Communist party takes care that the solidarity and common interest of the "international proletariat" in the many national units of the Soviet federation are not subordinated to the "bourgeois nationalisms" that multinational union would seem to indulge. Unfortunately, the egalitarianism of the Communist ideology has not entirely saved some or all of the other nationalities from occasional discrimination and even persecution at the hands of the Great Russians, the largest of the nationalities by far, and traditionally the oppressor of the others, from the days of the tsar to Stalin.

Federalism and policy-making

Soviet federalism, then, in substance is at the other end of the scale of the three major types of federal institutions. Such a scale can be defined by the degree of true *decentralization* of policy-making powers. The Anglo-American type of federal institutions allows the individual states or provinces to be policy-making centers in their own right on a great variety of subjects, albeit within the framework of federal law and federal constitution. The German type involves the *Laender* governments intimately in national policy-making, but leaves them comparatively little policy-making authority each within its own sphere. Apart from administrative policy and management, only local government, regional planning, cultural affairs, and educational policy remain at their descretion, and even in these subjects the *Laender* policies are under some pressure to conform to uniform practices and standards. The Soviet type, finally, goes one step further and allows its constitutent members practically no policy-making *decentralization*. It aims at *deconcentration*, at devolving the task of carrying out the policies made by the central government upon regional authorities. The supervision by the central policy-makers over the regional execution of their policies, moreover, is carried out with greater efficiency by the Communist party of the Soviet Union than is the awkward process of *federal supervision* of the *Land* administration of federal laws in the Bonn Republic, owing to the deliberate checks of German federalism.[3]

Common features of federal systems

Autonomy of constituent members Aside from the more obvious differences between various types of federal systems, there are many features common to all true federal systems. All of them, for example, are built on the notion that the constituent members, unlike local government units, have certain inalienable rights and immunities such as territorial integrity, which is beyond the purview of the central government. In the older theories of federalism, these inherent rights were associated with such terms as "sovereignty" and the "nature of a state." Sovereign or not, a constituent member of a true federation need fear no unilateral change in its territorial status or borders. Only in the Soviet Union could it happen that several autonomous republics such as those of Kalmyks, Volga Germans, and Crimeans were dissolved in World War II because Stalin feared uprisings there in sympathy with the invading German armies. On the other hand, all federations envision the possibility that grave emergencies or insurrection in a particular state, *Land,* or province of the union might make it necessary for the central government to intervene with armed might and temporarily take over all public authority in the constituent member in question. For the duration of such a state of emergency, then, the inherent rights of the constituent member are suspended and its territory is under the control of the central government as if it were part of a unitary state.

Equality of constituent members It is also customary in most federations to give formal expression to the principle of equality among the constituent members regardless of their size. In some federations, such

---

[3] The three types of federal government, as mentioned above, offer a rough parallel to the three foremost modern types of relationship between local and national governments. Again, there is an Anglo-American type characterized by local government operating autonomously within narrow confines laid down by national or state legislation. Then there is the European continental version, typified by the French system, which gives duly elected local governments more leeway in determining local affairs, but also subjects them to continuous supervision and frequent interference by the officials of the central government, unhindered by any local government equivalent of states' rights. In France, though not everywhere on the continent, local government officials also play a more or less formally recognized role in national policy-making and in the indirect election of organs of the national government. The Soviet type again presents an example of *deconcentration* rather than the creation of local centers of policy-making authority *(decentralization),* as elective councils (soviets) on many levels direct the local implementation of national policies under the watchful eye of the Communist party. See especially Harold F. Alderfer, *Local Government in Developing Countries* (New York: McGraw-Hill, 1964).

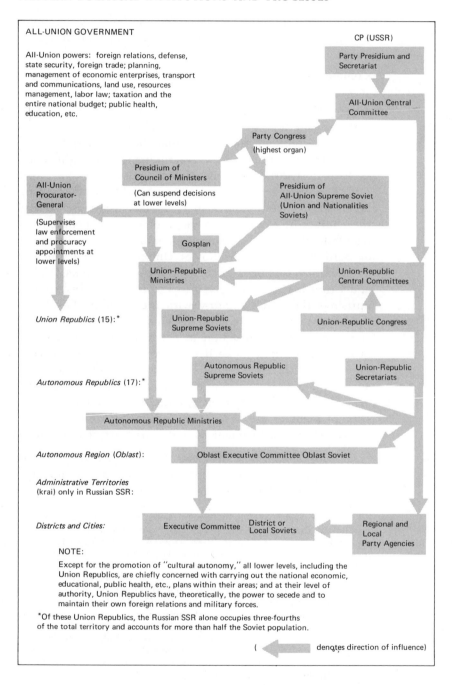

Figure 11.3   The Soviet pattern of federalism: decentralization and the monolithic party.

as the United States and Australia, this is accomplished by giving each state equal representation in the upper house, the Senate. In the Soviet federation, each union republic receives twenty-five seats in the Soviet of Nationalities, despite extreme variations in size, each autonomous republic eleven, and so on, down to the smaller units. In the West German *Bundesrat, Land* delegations vary only between three and five seats, while *Land* populations vary between 700,000 and 16 million. Even in the German Empire of 1871, the Prussian *Bundesrat* delegation was limited to seventeen seats, or one-third of the total, although the Prussian share of the population was two-thirds, and the tiniest dwarf state was also granted a seat. Despite such modifications, the principle of the equality of the constituent members grants a veto to the representatives of a region or group of constituent members whose inhabitants may constitute but a small minority of the total population. To prevent an amendment to the United States Constitution, for example, the opposition need only control the state legislatures of the thirteen smallest states of the union. The United States Senators from the seventeen smallest states suffice to veto an executive appointment or a treaty. In West Germany, where the *Land* governments pass on constitutional amendments through their instructed delegates to the *Bundesrat*, the five smallest *Laender* with a population of less than one-fifth of the total can veto any amendment.

Constitutional interpretation and arbitration Not the least important feature of a well-functioning federal system is the task of authoritative constitutional interpretation and arbitration among the constituent members, as well as between the members and the central government. Federal constitutions may embody careful divisions of powers between the two levels; provide that "full faith and credit" be given to the official acts of one state in all the other states; protect the free flow of interstate commerce against any kind of regional barriers; and undertake to protect the civil and constitutional rights of the citizens of the nation against prejudicial action by any member government. Yet all of these provisions require authoritative interpretation and enforcement, a need which is likely to increase with the age and transformations of a federal system. To be sure, the progression of social, economic, and political changes in a federal system often decides federal disputes, in the long run, by a verdict of the voters, whose consent is indispensable for formal constitutional change as well as for policies that imply such changes. But in the short run, and for federal disputes that are not amenable to an electoral verdict, an arbitral agency is needed that can render an immediate decision.

In the United States, the federal judiciary and, in particular, the United States Supreme Court, have been the principle arbiters of disputes among the states and between the union and a state. As chief interpreters of the United States Constitution, the judicial branch has also enforced the interstate commerce clause, decided questions of jurisdiction between the federal government and the states, and considered cases and controversies involving violations of the rights and freedoms guaranteed to all United States citizens. In Canada and Australia, the ultimate authority in interpreting the constitution long rested with the Judicial Committee of the Privy Council in London. In 1949 the Canadian Parliament designated the Supreme Court of Canada as the final court of appeal in all law suits, including federal disputes and questions of jurisdiction. The High Court of Australia has similar powers, although it can still elect to refer a dispute to the Judicial Committee. In Switzerland, the Federal Tribunal exercises the same function, along with the task of maintaining the uniformity of judicial interpretation of federal law by the cantonal courts, which adjudicate most questions of cantonal and federal law. In German federalism, the first instance for many kinds of disputes among the states and between the federal government and the states has been the *Bundesrat,* the gathering of the representatives of the state governments, which would pass on controversies such as questions of jurisdiction or the alleged failure of a state to perform its obligations. Before 1933, disputes of a legal character could be submitted to a court of state. Since the early 1950s, the Federal Constitutional Court has been the last resort in all disputes involving constitutional interpretation, questions of jurisdiction, and the arbitral function in the federal system in general. Unlike the high courts in federal countries other than the United States, the West German tribunal has sweeping powers of judicial review. It can set aside as unconstitutional not only *Laender* laws and ordinances, as the other high courts can invalidate cantonal or state actions, but also the acts of the federal legislature of West Germany. Like the federal judiciary of the United States, moreover, the Federal Constitutional Court can accept complaints of violations by any local, *Land,* or federal agency against the basic rights and freedoms guaranteed to all German citizens in the Basic Law (constitution) of the Federal Republic.

FEDERALISM AND POLITICS

While it has long been customary to view federalism primarily in static terms—as a set of unchanging relationships or as a system of checks and balances—such a view fails to do justice to the lively forces that create it and maintain it. It will be remembered how intimately federal systems at birth and throughout their lifetime are wedded to the geographical patterns—economic, ethnic, and other— of the social forces whose lives pulsate and seek expression within each region and on the national level. The "union of group selves" can become more unified or less so as these social forces tend toward geographical integration or disintegration.

In the context of modern governmental institutions, in particular, the social forces seek expression and self-government through the process of policy-making. The making of public policy in a federal system focuses on the representative organs and processes of nation and states, provinces, *Laender*, or cantons. Each state capital and the national capital, a set of federal institutions presumes, must have the capacity for an autonomous political life to match the elaborate apparatus of state and national legislatures and executive branches.

National politics and each state politics are presumed to have their own political party systems, which are the prime carriers of this autonomous political life. The nationwide organization and cohesion of each major party of a federal system give a good indication of how much political autonomy is possible within each constituent member and also indicate whether or not the political life of the federation has reached and is maintaining a degree of union commensurate with the unity indicated by its governmental institutions. Examples taken from several well-known federal systems illustrate this point.

The federal structure of political parties

The most glaring example of a federal system whose party system is completely incompatible with federalism is the Soviet Union. With the Communist party in the dominant position as sole, unchallengeable policy-maker on all levels, its monolithic, authoritarian character precludes autonomous politics, for example, in the Ukrainian Union Republic or in any other unit in the Soviet federal system. Thus the Soviet Union is fundamentally unitary, not federal, in character.

On the other hand, there may be federations so new that party organization has not yet reached the degree of national unity which the institutions appear to indicate. To be sure, some federal unions are the result of movements for national unification that are well organized throughout the separate states or colonies before the union is brought about. Other federal unions have been brought about by an informal group of leaders rather than by a political party or movement, or by devolution from former colonial authorities, or by superior force of a hegemonic power such as that of Prussia, which founded the German Empire of 1871. In these latter cases, parties often took decades to develop unified national organizations. During these formative years in Germany, for example, the state parties of the National Liberal party, the nationwide movement in favor of the new union under Prussian leadership, bore widely differing names—a telling indication that their national consolidation was far from complete. Other parties in the states that had been lukewarm about, or opposed to, national unification on these terms took even longer to consolidate their national organizations. Regional differences in the kind and number of parties and the political attitudes and circumstances from state to state exact tribute from even the most unified national party. The Social Democrats, for example, found it impossible to maintain ideological purity and rigidity in the face of the differences of opinion among their affiliates in the various regions of Imperial Germany.

The impact of federalism on political parties

Among the party systems of well-established federations, that of the United States supplies a striking example of how federalism can decentralize political parties when its impact is added to a climate already unfavorable to party politics. Parties in the United States, it will be remembered, suffer from a good deal of prejudice dating from the Progressive era, from the effect of the separation of powers, and from an undercurrent of anarchism frequently associated with a businessman's outlook on life. A hundred years of distrust of government regulation of commerce and industry have hindered the development of any strong, popular policy-making apparatus, such as modern political parties tend to become. The sectional differences of a large and diversified country, the presence of strong, popularly responsive state governments—in short, federalism—have contributed a decisive share to preventing the growth and consolidation of strong national parties in America.[4] Political scientists prefer to describe the major parties of the United States as two confederates of fifty state parties each, thereby indicating that the parties are more decentralized than are the governmental institutions. The national

---

[4] See, for example, James MacGregor Burns, *The Deadlock of Democracy* (Englewood Cliffs, N.J.: Prentice-Hall, 1963), pp. 20–23, 80–86. Also Elmer Schattschneider, *Party Government* (New York: Holt, Rinehart & Winston, 1942) and Arthur N. Holcombe, *Our More Perfect Union* (Cambridge, Mass.: Harvard University Press, 1950).

parties outside of Congress, indeed, have almost no permanent organization and appear to be held together merely by the party names and the quadrennial efforts to get a Presidential candidate elected. Every four years, the Presidential nominating conventions have to perform remarkable feats of compromise to rally the required majority of state party delegates behind one candidate. The party platforms drawn up for the Presidential campaigns likewise are marvels of blandness designed to appeal to such diverse regional elements as Southern and Northern Republicans or Democrats. Regional diversity and the autonomy of each state's politics tend to reduce any ideological difference between the two national parties to Tweedledum and Tweedledee. The two Presidential campaign organizations that temporarily unify the national parties also disband the day after the election, leaving behind nothing more tangible than their campaign debts and, perhaps, a new incumbent in the White House, who symbolically presents a personal image in place of a well-rooted national organization.

Party systems in older federations often mix various elements, especially if they are multiparty systems. In Switzerland, for example, such parties as the Catholic Conservatives, Radicals, Liberals, and the Farmers' party approach the "confederate" character of American parties in their dedication to cantonal politics, although they possess more of a national, extraparliamentary organization and exhibit more partisan cohesion in the National Council, the lower house of the Swiss federal Parliament. The Swiss Socialists, by contrast, show more national consolidation and a more unified structure, with less room for regional caprice, though they would not deny their affiliates a good deal of cantonal autonomy. The Swiss Communist party, finally, is as centralized and monolithic as are Communist parties anywhere. Similar gradations can be found in the party structures of the Weimar Republic and in India. Canada, on the other hand, has a complex system, superimposing the national parties, Liberals and Conservatives, on a motley collection of provincial parties, of which some are affiliated with the national parties and others are not.

Just how autonomous the state and cantonal politics of a given federal system really is cannot be inferred, with certainty, from the structure of the parties, owing to their flexibility and the varying role of individual party leaders. Because the regional organization of national parties and their state or provincial parties generally coincide, at least in part, in the same persons and groups, the degree of autonomy can be ascertained only by empirical observation of cases of dispute, jurisdictional squabbles, the process of nominating candidates for federal office, and the handling of party finances over a period of time.

Partisan impulses of federalism

Another important aspect of the impact of federalism on party politics and vice versa is the intermingling of the relationships between central and regional governments with the interaction between the different parties of the party systems of both levels and with the conflicting group demands characteristic of modern political life. In a well-functioning federal system, especially where two-party systems are operating on both levels, the patterns of opposition between the "ins" and the "outs" or between conflicting interest groups often tend to transcend the levels of government. The party in opposition at the federal level will fortify itself in the state governments it controls. Interest groups not favored with good access to governmental decision-makers at the state level will turn to the federal government for aid and political support, and vice versa. Thus the circumstances of political conflict on both levels become interwoven with federal-state relationships. Individuals and groups advocating states' rights, more often than not, are merely defending interests entrenched at the state level, while others advocate greater centralization chiefly because they are in a strong position at the federal level.

The states' rights posture of Southern Democrats and of many Republicans today, for example, is motivated by the desire to protect certain interests or to maintain political or social control at home. On the other hand, the supporters of federal action—for example, in such fields as urban development, pollution control, or aid to education—frequently represent interests whose demands, for various reasons, have been ignored or rejected by state legislatures. This mechanism is equally at work in other federations. In the Bonn Republic, to cite an example, one of the two major parties, the Christian Democratic Union (CDU), started out as a states' rights-minded party, whereas the opposing party, the Social Democrats (SPD), traditionally gave priority to the needs of the nation over the demands of regional autonomy. After nearly two decades in power in Bonn, however, the CDU had become an advocate of central government power, and the SPD had turned into a staunch defender of regional autonomy and initiative, especially regarding the *Laender* governments under its control until the SPD attained power in Bonn in 1969. In Canada, regional protest movements such as the New Democratic party or Social Credit generally exhibit a fierce pride in provincial autonomy inasmuch as their basic motives generally include efforts to undo within their particular region what they consider to be the deleterious influence of the Eastern financial or commercial interests dominant at the federal level.

There is some question as to whether this identification of oppositional patterns and federal-state relations has the effect of uniting or disuniting a federal union. In the short run, partisan alignments and the conflicting demands of organized interests may well sharpen disputes between the central government and the constituent members, and thereby lessen the federal union. In the short run, partisan alignments and the conflicting demands of organized interests may well sharpen disputes between the central government and the constituent members, and thereby lessen the federal consensus that is supposed to hold the entire system together. But there can be little doubt that the partisan and interest group squabbles sooner or later contribute decisively to the consolidation and strengthening of the union. The history of many new federations has shown, for example, how the completion of the national organization of the movement supporting the union sooner or later similarly forces the antiunionists to organize. It has also shown how the latter eventually come around to accepting the union they once fought, especially if they in turn come to control the federal government. The development of the European economic union by means of the Schuman Plan (ECSC) and Common Market (EEC) also demonstrated the consolidating effect of competition among parties and interest groups. One by one, the parties and groups that earlier opposed European economic union have made their peace with it and have begun to participate in the central policy-making process. Since competition and partisan conflict involve well-defined roles in the whole political system, the opposing groups evidently take their first step toward acceptance of the new federation the moment they take up the challenge of opposing the unionists on issues other than union itself.

FEDERALISM AND THE INTERNATIONAL ORDER

The origin of the word "federalism" goes back to the Latin *feodus* (*-eris*), which means a treaty or agreement among allies. It should not be forgotten, indeed, that historically the alternative to federation was not a unitary state in the modern, democratic sense, but separate, small, independent states. Such separate existence inevitably meant greater exposure to attack or conquest by powerful neighbors, or also the likelihood of destructive, fratricidal war among the separate states.

From their earliest antecedents, leagues and federations have been inspired by fear of a common enemy as much as by an awareness of common bonds. The Greek leagues of city-states were forged under the imminent threat of invasion by such powers as the Persians. And it was war among the city-states, particularly between the two largest, Athens and Sparta, that proved the undoing of Greek freedom and independence. The writers of the *Federalist Papers* similarly conjured the threat of British reconquest and of war among the thirteen states in order to persuade Americans to accept the "more perfect union" of the United States Constitution. The Canadian federation owed much to the fear of American expansion into the Western territories of Canada. The German Imperial Federation of 1871 was born on the battlefields of a war between what had been up to that time the two largest member states of the Confederation of 1815, Prussia and Austria. That war established the Prussian position in Germany, and a second war, against France, consolidated the imperial federation as a new power bloc in European politics, capable of defending itself against outside attack.

At the outset of the present attempts at building a United States of Europe, the motives of union were essentially the same. The peoples of France, Germany, Italy, Belgium, the Netherlands, and Luxembourg were alarmed by the defenselessness of what had been, until then, the hub of world politics against the new superpowers emerging from the war. They feared in particular the Soviet Union, which before their very eyes took over the governments of one Eastern European country after another by treachery and force. They also came to reflect on the futility of centuries of war and power politics among themselves. They could not help but contrast the devastating results of perpetual wars with the rewards of commerce and joint economic development that federation would bring. Viewed in these terms, the alternative between federation and separate existence became a choice between security, peace, and prosperity or external insecurity, internecine strife, and lagging economic development. African leaders who promote the establishment of federal unions or of a Pan-African federation, and the proponents of Pan-Arab federation see the alternatives in the same light. However, even the common awareness of an outside threat is often insufficient to produce federal union over the self-centered particularism of newly independent states. Advocates of worldwide federalism are similarly attracted by the promise of peace among the nation-states and by undisturbed social and economic development. But their appeal, however persuasive and rational, lacks the compulsion of an external threat, at least until such time as the proverbial invasion from Mars occurs.

PART **III** **OUR REVOLUTIONARY AGE**

ON REVOLUTION

Revolution is a word which comes easy to the lips of people today. From revolutionary new can openers and headache pills to the flights of imagination of restless college youth the world over, the word often bears little relationship to the major political upheavals which under the same name have been shaping the world we live in and are still going on today. Whole states and societies have been born in contemporary revolutions and are still sustained by a revolutionary faith while others underwent a thorough reorientation in fear of or in defense against the revolutionary menace. Revolution and counterrevolution characterize large stretches of recent history all over the world.

There is no greater challenge to the student or practitioner of politics than to contemplate the problems of revolution and drastic social change. The political philosopher may plumb the depths of human wisdom, explore the traditions of his society, and come up with what seem to him and his contemporaries the ultimate answers to all questions of political value and obligation. The constitution-makers and other designers of political institutions can devise the most effective checks and balances and design the optimal relationships of responsibility between the governed and their government. But when vast changes rapidly transform the entire social order, or when a major revolution has a nation in its grip, all their philosophical and institutional edifices begin to totter. Values and beliefs change dramatically. The social structure which implicitly underlies most of the traditional philosophies and forms of government undergo a drastic reshuffling. Even the relations between the sexes, or between parents and children, or the patterns of family life, when they change in significant ways, can bring about important readjustments in the processes of modern politics.

We are living in a revolutionary age. In some respects, in fact, revolutionary change can be said to have been going on in the Western world for the past three centuries or more. Violent, large-scale revolutions began to occur as early as the English civil war of the 1640s, which ended with the military dictatorship of Oliver Cromwell and ushered in the age of the Glorious Revolution of 1688, the beginning of the liberation of British government. The American Revolution of the 1770s and the French Revolution of 1789 carried the seeds of discontent and the heady wind of a new freedom far beyond the thirteen colonies and the borders of revolutionary France. By the second half of the nineteenth century, the revolutionary fever had raged through the capitals of most European countries and brought independence, if not liberty, to most of the countries of the American continent.

Industrialism and the great wars of the twentieth century finally spread the great upheaval to the non-Western world. World War I, which brought in its wake the fall of empires and crowned houses in Central and Eastern Europe and in the Middle East, and the Russian Revolution of 1917 were powerful destroyers of tradition and mobilizers of dormant populations. World War II and the Cold War touched off or intensified the great upheaval among the hundreds of millioms of Asian and African peoples, who had up to then patiently endured Western colonialism and their lot in their traditional societies, and started them on the long and difficult journey to modernization.

The age of revolution is far from over. There are still colonies and trusteeships awaiting independence. The newly independent countries are generally internally unstable and externally vulnerable to attack. Major shifts and political realignments occur with disturbing frequency. A revolution that has brought national independence may not have broken down the social barriers within, or created the conditions necessary for rapid social or economic development. There may be movements for another revolution, conspiracies of ambitious men, rebellion fomented from the outside. Even in the older, well-established Western societies, social, economic, and political changes continue at a rapid rate.

There is a natural affinity between revolution and youth for many reasons. To begin with, the period of youth in a person's life is itself one of dramatic change from dependence to autonomy, of a sudden readiness for mobility and expansive development, of departure for great journeys into uncharted regions and unknown experiences. If real revolutions and drastic social change involve an ability to learn something quite novel or to adjust with ease to totally new circumstances, moreover, these are facilities one can hardly expect of people at a later stage in their life cycles. This is even more true of the members of revolutionary movements who may have to dedicate their lives and limbs to their cause through political violence and civil or international wars. As the composition of Communist revolutionary guerrillas, Fascist storm-troopers, and nationalist revolutionary columns shows very clearly, the bulk of the revolutionary militants is young, male, and unencumbered by wife or child. It takes the vigor of youth, and perhaps a little recklessness and love of adventure, to embark on a revolutionary enterprise, or even on the social migration from rural antecedents to the city, or from an old society toward modernity.

Any such intensive and continuing process of change, one would think, would have a definite point of departure, a distinct goal, and a series of steps or stages marking its progress. Discussing the type of society from which come these people making the great journey is the best point of departure. It is the *traditional society* with its traditional forms of social life, economic production, and government, with some variations of course. The stages of development are clouded in controversy and their interpretation varies according to the political allegiance or vested interests of the observer. Communists of various shadings, the nationalistic elites of the developing countries, and the business circles of their former colonial masters give widely varying answers to the question of how and by what steps the great transformation comes about. Their responses differ not only because of their personal involvement, but also because they envisage different goals. Communists see the vast process of modernization as the road toward their visions of a Communist utopia and view the Soviet Union or China, and the advanced Western countries as well, as stages on the way to utopia. Western observers and, in particular, economists like to think of the great journey in stages of economic growth, of social modernization, or of democratization with a goal resembling invariably their own societies. Native leaders dream of their own utopias, which are colored strongly by their cultural traditions and personal backgrounds. What will really come about and by what steps is another question. There is, however, an assumption common to all three—Communists, Western observers, and native leaders— that the process of modernization East or West, developed or developing, is substantially the same process with minor variations and, of course, different starting dates everywhere.

Social scientists, therefore, turn to the study of the transition from traditional societies happening before our eyes, in quest of a deeper understanding of how Western societies developed to their present state. Just as Western observers may read into the process of modernization in excolonial societies what they know and value about their own evolution, one can try to learn to look at one's own history through eyes trained in the empirical examination of modernization in the living laboratories of Asia, Africa, or Latin America. There are, after all, considerable and crucial gaps in the historical understanding of the Western past due to the absence of written records documenting large parts of the social and economic history of the lower classes during the early phases of such transformations as the industrial revolution or urbanization. We cannot, of course, interview the unsung generations of a century ago or more in the West, but we can conduct opinion polls of the views, attitudes, and human problems of the new migrants, say, to Caracas, Calcutta, Lagos, or Stanleyville. Are they not likely to respond in ways similar to the new urbanites of Manchester, England, in the eighteenth century or Berlin, Germany, in the nineteenth century? Might not their political style and preoccupations tell us more about the why and wherefore of English and German politics in a similar setting than reams of musty records and yellowed official documents?

Placing the study of Communism and Fascism in the context of the process of modernization calls for some explanatory comment here. The intimate connection between Communism and social development hardly needs emphasis. Karl Marx was the author of one of the first comprehensive theories of modernization. Even though the Communist movement has long turned away from his doctrines in many significant ways, it is still suspended, as it were, between his idealistic, utopian vision and its own violent and dictatorial practices. What is more, the Communists have turned their chief attention to the developing countries. Beginning with Russia and China, they have committed their best efforts to the exploitation of the anticolonial, nationalistic ambitions of non-Western populations and actively promoted their seizure of power in most of them. Thus Communism, by its own efforts, has become the chief trap for people on the difficult road to modernization.

The connection between Fascism and modernization is far less clear than that between Communism and modernization, in large part because rather heterogeneous movements under widely differing circumstances have been lumped together under the name Fascism. It was long customary to view Communism as the vanguard of modernization and Fascist movements as violent attempts on the part of elements of traditional society to stop modernization by force. Upon closer examination, this interpretation turns out to be, by and large, erroneous. The Communists have generally been the vanguard only for themselves and their own coming to power, thereby inevitably arresting modernization in the end in the straitjacket of dictatorship. Fascist movements, on the other hand, fit the reactionary label only in a few cases, such as in Spain and in Portugal and in some parts of Eastern Europe, where at the time of their rise industrialization and urbanization were still very weak. In countries such as Germany, Italy, France, England, Belgium, and Scandinavia, Fascist movements offered many modernizing and even futuristic appeals, right along with shamelessly exploited traditional feelings and resentments. Seen with the benefit of hindsight, even rank racism and preparation for aggressive war and empire over slave populations, as in Nazi Germany or in South Africa, can be a powerful, if deplorable, solvent for overcoming the barriers and rigidities of a maladjusted society in the throes of modernization. Like all totalitarian dictatorships, however, Fascism tends to encase society in a new straitjacket from which no society seems to be able to free itself without outside help.

CHAPTER **12** MODERNIZATION AND POLITICAL CHANGE

It is nearly impossible to discuss the processes of modernization and political change in a manner entirely free from cultural bias. Each culture tends to see the nature of the values and respective merits or demerits of its traditional society in its own way. It also perceives the dilemmas and alternatives of the great transition in culture-bound ways which may present far greater obstacles than the very considerable economic and technological hurdles an awakening society has to overcome. And as for the goal of modernity, again but perhaps less so, cultural blinders frequently blur or reinterpret what is likely to result. Nevertheless, both native leaders and Western social scientists frequently describe the future of the developing countries in terms of a "spreading world culture" (Lucian Pye), of statehood, nationalism, and democracy in the Western sense. Sometimes, native leaders also include Democratic Socialism in their vision of the future. To be sure, the current realities in most developing polities are still far from a realization of these goals. But the seeming identity of goals encourages us to point out the relationships between modern societies and their politics and to contrast them to traditional societies and politics. There is so much of Western contemporary society and its politics that people growing up in it take for granted that to a student of government, traditional ways and politics may appear at first as quaint and exotic rather than as a way of life similar to that of his ancestors.

MODERN SOCIETY AND DEMOCRACY

The social structure

The first important aspect requiring emphasis is the social structure of a country. Western democracy presumes a great deal of actual social equality among the different layers of society as well as between men and women, and young and old. This is not to say that social stratification is entirely lacking, that there are no social elites, or even that there are no pockets of inequality affecting ethnic minorities, women, or young people. With the passing of traditional society, a modicum of social equality must come about prior to the introduction of the revolutionary doctrine of "one man, one vote." Bringing political democracy to a highly stratified society would precipitate immediate civil war, as the old upper classes would defend their status by force.

The role of the individual

The role of the individual within the groups of society, and especially within his family, is a particularly crucial aspect of advanced modern society. Democracy presumes a highly mobile individual who participates actively and *as an individual* in social, economic, and political life, making his own decisions and taking firm control of his own life. Western societies were by no means always composed of individuals willing and capable of playing this role. In fact, there are still large segments of Western democracies where individuals are still far from being capable of mastering their own fate; most persons, in fact, fail in this respect in some area or at some time in their lives. The individual in traditional societies generally lives largely as a more or less integral part of a group—his village community, tribe, or family clan. Thus most of his decisions are made within the collectivity. Needless to stress, the autonomy of the individual in modern society is also dependent on a vast array of educational opportunities not available in previous ages nor to the underdeveloped, and on the presence of free mass media to communicate the information vital to intelligent political, economic, and social participation.

The reception and utilization of information again requires facilities (such as literacy), habits, and attitudes that were never universal in the West and are still weak in the underdeveloped lands today.

The link between cultural values and democracy

The intimate link between Western cultural values, including the great *religions* of the Western world, and the ideals of liberal democracy should not be overlooked. Western individualism has strong cultural and religious roots reaching back into antiquity. Capitalistic civilization likewise rests on cultural and religious convictions and attitudes at least as much as the law of supply and demand. A different religion or another cultural heritage would profoundly influence the political system a people would prefer. There is also the question of cultural change—the waning of old religious rites in some countries and the effect of acculturation on a given society. The foremost example of acculturation—the Westernization of non-Western civilizations—is a highly complex process whose effect on modernization social scientists have never been able to agree about. Westernization has led to the adoption of Western governmental institutions by most developing nations, but there is considerable doubt as to whether they are operating as they would in a Western setting.

Transportation and communications

Another important aspect of advanced Western society and government that is easily overlooked is its high degree of integrated transportation and communications. Modern government takes for granted the facilities for ranging all over a huge territory and delivering men and supplies anywhere in the nation within a day or two. It relies on the communications network and the fact that it can transmit explanations of what it is doing and why to practically all of its citizens by press, radio, and television. To understand the significance of these facilities one need only go back to the horse-and-buggy days of the early Amemican Republic, or to observe the wearisome efforts by which the government of Iran may try to carry out a program of vaccination among nomadic tribes, or the government of India to bring birth control information to remote villages. The fatal weakness of the central governments of many a Latin American or African country in dealing with rebellion or subversion owes much to the inadequacy of transport and communication facilities.

The urban setting

Few circumstances have such a profound effect on the theory and practice of modern Western government as the urban setting in which the majority of Americans, Englishmen, Frenchmen, Germans, and other advanced societies live. In spite of the widespread lore about the virtues of rural life, Western ways today are predominantly city ways, and democratic practice has to serve city-dwellers as much as anyone. This is not to say that democracy is not possible among a farming people. There have been democracies of agrarian freeholders in history from the days of Greek antiquity. For most traditional societies, however, farming as a way of life formed one of the chief links in the chain around their necks. It often brought the farmers under the tyranny of powerful noblemen and warlords. Even at its best, farming was a kind of enslavement to the soil and the weather. At its worst, it was serfdom of the most stultifying sort, such as could be found in many European countries at the dawn of the modern age. Politically, it rarely made for popular self-government, but more likely for some sort of petty local tyranny by a feudal lord or oligarchy of village elders. Democracy, it would seem, thrives better where masses of well-informed people can unite for action than in the isolation and ignorance of rural life. No aspect of the great transformation is more incisive in the lives of the people of a modernizing society than their migration to the city.

Advanced industrialism

Then there is the connection between advanced industrialism, or sustained *economic growth*, and democracy. Where the industrial revolution occurs freely, that is, without state ownership and regimentation as under Communism, it brings in its wake enormous social changes, which in time transform the politics and government as well. Economists have defined modernization as the state in which each successive generation, if not each decade, experiences drastic changes in technology and, perhaps, in the whole way of life, as distinct from traditional society, where change and economic growth are so slow as to be rather unnoticeable. Being an advanced society, in other words, means being subject to constant, drastic change and transformation as a basic fact of life. The economic growth experienced at the same time supplies the incentives and the working capital for the ever-widening impact of these changes.

Once a high plateau has been reached in industrial development, which is mass consumption, the attainment of private affluence has a powerful, emancipating, and personally satisfying effect on those in the industrial population who, until then, led lives of poverty. With mass consumption, the machine age finally makes good the promise it held out for so long to everyone. Greater individual autonomy becomes possible for all, not just for a small top layer of society.

Pluralistic politics

Democracy, with its frequent elections and enforcement of the responsibility of the rulers toward the ruled, is better adapted to such a situation of continual change than is any other form of government. It allows political change to follow in the wake of social change without bloodshed or even disturbance, once the process of constitutional democracy are well established. And, while allowing the majority to make the big decisions, democracy protects and encourages the complex, pluralistic forces of a rapidly changing society, each to follow its own rationale. The principle of political competition inherent in democracy spurs on all manner of development, not unlike competition in the economic marketplace. It contributes, in particular, to the articulation of group interests in the form of associations and interest groups. Furthermore, it makes for a competitive system of political parties which compete by catering to and aggregating these groups' interests. Among the political parties, the competition also goes on internally, as new groups vie with old over issues of policy and leadership. It is difficult to think of any political system other than democracy in which this pluralistic politics could freely develop and function.

National unity

Finally, the major advanced countries of the West have had the advantage of maturing for centuries into *nationhood*. National unity and the relative homogeneity underlying it have created circumstances more favorable to stability and a political consensus than most "new nations" can exhibit. A sense of national identity lends unity and continuity to most Western societies and helps them to overcome the internal tensions and frictions of the immense journey. Many of the so-called new nations, by way of contrast, are the accidental products of arbitrary colonial boundaries. These nations lack a common language, or culture, or a sense of identity, and frequently face threats of secession within a seizure of parts of territory from without. India, for example, with some seven hundred languages and dialects, still depends largely on the tongue of the former colonial masters for a common second language. Worse still, the entities making up many African or Asian new nations are still of a tribal nature, with archaic forms of headship and a collectivistic sense of identity that demonstrates that a people can become a true nation only after modernization has weakened or broken up older collectivities. There is also the danger that the social and political tensions of modernization in a society fragmented into hostile ethnic groups may become associated with these group tensions. Modernizing Indonesia, for example, is quite difficult enough without the Javanese and non-Javanese suspecting each other at every turn of the arduous road.

TRADITIONAL SOCIETY AND AUTOCRACY

The nature of traditional society

What is this traditional state of society like, from which our own societies once sprang and which can still be found barely stirred by modernization in many parts of the world? Is it the blissful paradise of carefree children happily playing in a world of enchanting rituals under a tropical sun as travelers have often imagined it to be? Or is it a grim, hopeless existence in ignorance and squalor as the statistics of illiteracy, living standards, and poor health seem to indicate? Are these traditional societies not happier as they are now and more so, perhaps, than the more advanced societies, with their harried, regimented affluence which has taken so large a toll in degenerative diseases and mental breakdowns? Less than 5 percent of the people of developing nations, for example, reach a high school level of education at the present time despite the aspirations of their own governments and development agencies which see in massive education the key to modernity. The Catholic reformer and Latin American expert, Ivan Illich, on the other hand, strongly objects to the "American ideology of schooling" which, in his opinion, teaches neither useful skills nor humanly important attitudes but only the importance of "schooling" as a new device for establishing social hierarchies in Latin America. A very similar argument applies to foreign aid for economic development, not to mention military aid to enable native governments to defend themselves against subversion. These are also "American ideologies" which should be pursued only after careful investigation of their likely consequences. It is extremely naïve and rather propagandistic to simplify the extraordinary complexity of foreign aid programs to a question such as:

Should the "rich nations" strain their resources to the utmost in order to relieve the misery and suffering of the "poor nations"? These questions and alternative interpretations reflect not only Western preoccupations and sentimentality, including romantic disaffection from the modern way of life, but also reveal basic misunderstandings about the nature of traditional society.

Types of traditional society To begin with, there are considerable differences between various types of traditional societies. There are still some societies which in anthropological classification belong to an earlier stage than agricultural settlements, namely primitive societies of nomadic hunters and collectors of fruit and edible plants, or nomadic tribes of herdsmen, such as the Bedouins. These peoples are also awakening to the appeals of modernity and show little inclination to go through an agricultural phase before congregating in cities and developing commerce and industry. While most traditional societies were or are agrarian, moreover, there are considerable differences among agrarian societies, depending on such things as the form of land tenure (private or communal), the size and operation of each agricultural unit, the size and character of the village community and its relative isolation from other villages, urban centers, and commercial links. Politically, some agrarian societies were highly decentralized structures of local or regional communities held together by distant feudal obligations, as in medieval Europe, or only by kinship. Where cities and an urban civilization arose, mighty empires such as those of the Near East, Rome, and China developed in time, reached a pinnacle of power and cultural sophistication, and then sank into oblivion—all with little effect on the agrarian society, which generally included at least three-fourths of the population. The cultural achievements in art, drama, and philosophy of ancient Greece, China, and medieval Europe form a strong contrast to those of the more primitive tribal societies then as now. Yet in the technology of economic production and of everyday living *for the masses of the people*, the ancient Greeks or Chinese were a great deal closer to the Fiji Islanders or the Eskimos than to the people of an advanced industrial society.

The static nature of traditional society Traditional society is relatively static, which is not to say that it does not change at all or that there may not occur occasionally a sudden burst of technological progress in a limited sector of social activity. But visible change from generation to generation is so small as to encourage the belief that given forms of social, economic, or political relations are God-given and natural. A thick crust of custom builds up over many generations and provides a restrictive setting into which a person is born and which he will probably not transcend in his lifetime. Sons know that they will never grow beyond the station of their fathers. Women and inferior classes know their place in society and nourish no hopes of emancipation. An air of fatalism pervades the whole culture, often sublimated in religions that place no value on material achievements and promise rewards only in a life after death. The status and privileges of noblemen and other powers that be are accepted without challenge as right and legitimate. Due to the primitive techniques of economic production. there is little opportunity for a person to improve the family fortunes significantly within his lifetime, which further limits the likelihood of the rise of new elites in place of the hereditary nobility.

The village community   The typical human community of traditional society is the village, often coinciding with tribe, clan, or family. Based on the inner rationale of agricultural production, patterns of land tenure, and family structure, the village is a closely knit community in which everyone knows everyone else. These face-to-face relations need not imply love and harmony. Nor is the typical traditional village hospitable to strangers. Contrary to the stereotypes of the friendly *community* (*Gemeinschaft*) as compared to the impersonal relationships of big city or commercial *society* (*Gesellschaft*), the traditional village can be a dog-eat-dog world in which the possessions and honor of individuals and families are jeolously guarded against encroachments or slights.[1] Yet there is generally a web of mutual obligations and cooperation, without which village life would be hard to bear. No more effective sanction of the village community against offending individuals or families can be imagined, in fact, than the withdrawal of all cooperation and mutual aid or, in other words, a boycott or ostracism. Villages in medieval Europe were generally under the control of a feudal lord or monastery, enabling these overlords, with their taxes or services rendered, to live a more agreeable life. Ancient empires similarly used to exact the means for their higher civilization through taxes or services from peasants and subject peoples.

The closest identification of the traditional villager is with the extended family. The clan is not only the most important entity in his life, but it fits him during his lifetime into its heirarchy of age and sex. Women must defer to men, children to parents, younger

---

[1] On this point, see especially Everett E. Hagen, *On the Theory on Social Change* (Homewood, Ill.: Dorsey Press, 1962), pp. 65 ff. Also Edward and Laura Banfield, *The Moral Basis of a Backward Society* (New York: Free Press, 1958).

persons to their elders, and the whole family to its patriarch, who often participates in the government of the village as a member of a council of elders. The close identification with the family lends to the life of the individual a superindividual dimension and a continuity transcending his life-span. But it also prolongs the effect of shame and slight brought upon the family by an outsider or by a black sheep in its midst for an indefinite time. The individual consequently matters but little; honor and family are all-important.[2]

Social class in traditional society   Although three-fourths or more of most traditional societies are made up of peasants, there are other important elements. Other groups on the same level as the peasants are artisans, craftsmen-shopkeepers, and the domestic servants of the elite groups. What anthropologists call the elite groups is in itself highly stratified. At the bottom of these groups there may be such groups as teachers, intellectuals, and professional persons, for example, doctors and lawyers. Persons at the top of their profession occupy a somewhat higher status. The religious and the bureaucratic or military establishments sometimes provide lifetime careers open to all, one of the few channels of social advancement in traditional societies. Although clergy and bureaucracy occupy elite positions at various levels, their highest positions are often reserved to members of the uppermost social elite, the nobility. The nobility, again stratified in several layers, generally derives its status from the large-scale ownership of land over a long period of time. Such a landowning oligarchy is still in control in most countries of Latin America and the Near East today. In medieval Europe, feudal lords derived their fiefs by inheriting name and title or by achievement and loyalty in war or warlike emergencies.

This link between land ownership, the highest value in an agrarian society, and war, the most visible source of drastic change in family fortunes, also created a pattern for the development of society during the transition from traditional society. Military leadership tended to remain the preserve of the nobility of some European countries long after the decline of the power and status of the old top elite had set in. Noblemen and their sympathizers, in fact, made the "warrior" way of life the symbol of the values of traditional society as opposed to the modern-commercial way of a "nation of shopkeeprs," as Napoleon Bonaparte called the British. Middle-class regimes have retaliated by devising civil-military relations in such a way that there would always be civilian (middle-class) control over the real and fancied aristocrats in the military establishment.

[2] See also Robert Redfield, *Peasant Society and Culture* (Chicago: University of Chicago Press, 1956).

Traditional autocracy

Government in traditional societies is generally *autocratic,* which means that it derives its power from itself, or more precisely, from its own traditional authority. The aristocracy rules without any need to derive its consent from anyone else. Where there is a "first family" among the nobility, there may be monarchy, although the monarch generally continues to depend on the loyalty and cooperation of the highest lords of the realm. In medieval Germany these lords even elected the emperor from among their midst.

Traditional monarchy may also be rooted in religious conceptions of monotheism or in philosophical convictions about the intrinsic merits of unity, hierarchy, and single headship. Traditional authority and custom may also sanction the secular power of the church, whose bishops in medieval Europe occupied positions equal to those of the great lords and at times even received a whole region in fief. While authority was underived from below, moreover, there were mutual obligations between lords and vassals, from the king down to the last peasant, which were assumed to bind the lord as much as his vassal. All traditional autocracies were governed by some notion of the duties of a good ruler toward the ruled, often with religious overtones. How well these duties were observed in practice and who would interpret them in any particular case was always a doubtful question to which, in the long run, only constitutional government and representation could give a satisfactory answer.

THE TRANSITIONAL PROCESS

The transitional society

It would be quite misleading to speak of a transitional society in as precise a sense as one can, for example, describe typical features of the various traditional societies. A society enters the transitional phase from the moment its traditional cast is stirred by major, continuing transformations. The development of urban civilization, large-scale commerce or industry, or the rise of empires in traditional society were evidently beginnings of the transition. Only in retrospect, after the burst of a civilization has relapsed into stagnation, can it be said that the transitional process has failed to carry through to a condition of permanent technological change.

It is not impossible that our present modern state of affairs could lapse into stagnation and traditionalism if faced with unsurmountable crises. Even the most advanced industrial-urban societies of our time, moreover, can have pockets of a type of traditional society in which all innovation has stopped for several generations. Such pockets can occur in cities where slum conditions may nurture a constricting subculture of urban poverty that renews itself from generation to generation rather than leads the children toward a better life.

Another reason why the transitional state is difficult to describe is that the transition does not involve all members of a society at once or in a like manner. When the transitional process typically begins, it is limited to particular places and groups of persons, spreading over a long period of time in ever-widening circles to larger areas and more people. There are also considerable differences in the sequence with which different sectors are drawn into the vortex of modernization. A grand classificatory scheme may be developed some day that supplies analytical categories for the various types and stages of modernization. At present, there is not enough information available about the development of societies, though further observation of the developing nations of today may close many gaps. In many respects our own advanced societies are still in the process of transition to we know not what. Until the state of rapid change has entered such regular and mutually reinforcing channels as to become reasonably predictable, the transition will continue.

The breakup of traditional society

Although it may be difficult to supply a schedule of transition, it is possible to discover the chief mobilizing agents that initiate it or keep it in motion. The traditional societies of Western Europe, and many others as well, often broke up and embarked on the great transition because of internal problems they could not master within their traditional framework. A disequilibrium between the social classes caused by famine, epidemics, and other shifts in the basic economic condition of agriculture and crafts might cause acute discontent. Misrule by bad or inept autocrats could trigger revolution. The need for greater national wealth to finance a stronger army or a larger navy or merchant marine in competition with other powers might shift status from the land-owning nobility to the commercial middle class, or to traders and financiers who occupied a low status in the traditional scheme of things. Religious dissension or ethnic friction within a society often gave the disaffected minority a strong incentive to become the *modernizing elite* in order to secure and enhance their position vis-à-vis a hostile majority. The advancement of capitalism by the British nonconformists—the French Huguenots, and the Dutch and Swiss Calvinists—are cases in point. The inner turmoil of civil war or religious struggle often sharpened the intellectual and creative powers of a society to the point where a permanent breakthrough might occur from traditional forms of knowledge based on authority to empirical, scientific knowledge based on experiment and verfication. The scientific outlook is indispensable to the advent of modernity.

The most prominent cause of the breakup of traditional societies is their encounter with more advanced civilizations. The encounter can come through war, conquest, or colonization, but it can also come in subtler ways: by trading contacts, by the communication of technical skills and ideas, and by education abroad. All of these ways can produce feelings of deep anguish and humiliation. Defeated countries have been known to withdraw into their traditional shell, as did Russia in the eighteenth century. It is also true that conquered populations have on occasion assimilated their conquerors and that some colonial peoples have continued their traditional ways seemingly untouched by the presence of their new masters, as happened, for example, in Africa and for a long time in parts of Latin America. Nevertheless, the unsettling impact of conquest—for example, the impact of Napoleonic conquest on most countries of continental Europe or of Western colonialism on the entire developing world of today—cannot be denied.

An instructive example of the reaction to the challenge of foreign conquerors is supplied by China during the last hundred years. The Middle Kingdom was widely admired as one of the most enlightened countries of the world as late as the middle of the eighteenth century, when the onset of the industrial revolution in Western Europe began to wipe out in a few decades the advantage of two thousand years of highly developed civilization and of the Confucian universal state. The leading industrial power, Great Britain, overcame Chinese resistance in the nineteenth century in two humiliating wars. The Anglo-French occupation of Peking and the burning down of the Summer Palace in 1860 jolted the Chinese into a realization of their new situation. Their first response was the Self-Strengthening Movement of the early 1860s of the mandarins who proposed to follow the slogan "learn the superior barbarian technique in order to repel the barbarians" (Wei-Yuan) but limited their imitation of their conquerors to military supplies and technique. It took the defeat of 1894–1895 at the hands of the more modernized Japanese to drive Chinese scholars and officials on to political and institutional reforms after the Western model which they had originally rejected out of hand. And even after the revolution of 1911, the Chinese Nationalists and the Communists still fought for many decades over the best path toward modernization.

Depending on the seeds of modernization already present in a conquered country, and especially on the readiness of potential modernizing elites to take up the cues and to compete with the conquerors, conquest or colonialism appears to be the surest way of breaking up a traditional society, although it may take time. Conquest or colonialism deprives the traditional elite of its status and replaces it with foreign or colonial administrators, who live a relatively modern way of life, even if they take on some of the habits of the old ruling class. Conquest or colonization may introduce modern methods of transportation and communications, of commerce and production, and of management and business administration. The introduction of advanced law, adjudication, and centralized public administration and finance may soon recommend itself to the conquered people. The drawing of members of the native population into the business and administrative operations of the conquerors—and most of all, the introduction of modern self-government of sorts—complete the learning process.

Reactions of societies in transition

Westernization as a typical example of acculturation has its own dynamics in the encounter with less advanced cultures, which varies greatly from one culture to the next. In some cultures, the willingness to adopt Western ways is conspicuous. In others, there is an all-pervasive stubborn resistance to the alien intruders and their evil ways, rooted partly in culture and religion, partly in pride. A third category reacts by splitting into camps of militant Westernizers and resentful nativists, or, like Russia, remains split between the two ways of life to the depth of its soul. There are also significant aspects in the clash between the otherworldly or fatalistic features of traditional religion and what non-Western peoples interpret as the boundless hunger for power and material gain of Westerners. Spurred by feelings of being exploited and powerless, societies in transition often react with an ardent desire to be rich and powerful, equal to or stronger than the colonial masters. This can be a spur to Messianic movements or conspiracy with such foreign powers as the Soviet Union or Communist China today.

The communication of more advanced ideas and techniques to a traditional society rarely leaves much of an impression, except as it may enable modernizing elites to function more effectively. It would be very naïve, for example, to expect democratic ideas to be accepted readily because of their intrinsic merit, because their merit is indissolubly linked to the function they can fulfill in a society. Neither will the techniques of public and business administration or of industrial production find an enthusiastic reception before a great many prerequisites for their appreciation have been met. On the other hand, much of the work of specialized international agencies such the Food and Agricultural Organization and the World Health Organization has an immediate impact. Population pressures caused by the drastic reduction of infant mortality and diseases and unbalanced by adequate measures for birth control and increased food production are dynamite to the traditional society. Traditional agriculture is quite unable to feed the many new mouths, hence the resulting surplus population must move to cities and industrial centers, if there are any, in quest of work and bread.

Migration from country to city, from city to city, from region to region, from job to job, or from one country to another is perhaps the most meaningful symbol of the great transition from traditional society to a new life. War and revolution, oppression and persecution, famine and economic crises have often mobilized vast masses of people and sent them on the road. Uprooted from their traditional ways, they have had to use all their ingenuity to make a new life for themselves with new methods in their new environment. The industrial revolution in the West could never have succeeded without the "industrial reserve army" of uprooted country boys and job seekers. Technological change is far more difficult when skilled workmen are not accustomed to having to change jobs and learn new methods at frequent intervals.

The migration of millions from the Old World to the New meant that the United States or Canada never really had to start with a traditional society, save the Indians. The millions of Spanish, southern Italian, Greek, and Turkish migrant workers in the countries of the European Common Market have a deeply unsettling effect on the traditional remnants of their own socieits when they return. The new city dwellers who live in the slums of big cities, in the *favelas* of Rio, in the *barrios* on the outskirts of Caracas and Mexico City, or in Calcutta, or in the "underprivileged neighborhoods" of Chicago, New York, Los Angeles, London, and Frankfurt, also are a living manifestation of the great transition, They have left their rural homes in body and in spirit and, looking back, see their former life as a miserable existence to which they would not care to return. Yet they have not quite arrived in the city either, where employment problems and slum living give their social life too unstable a basis for full participation in the economic, cultural, and political life of the city. Perhaps their children will make the transition complete and fully arrive in the urban-industrial way of life. Or, perhaps, the lives of the children, too, will be stunted by illegitimacy, inadequate family life, slums, and ignorance.

The mixture of traditional and modern elements

Transitional society is likely to be a strange mixture of traditional and modern elements. There may be patriarchic family life existing side by side with modern industry, or the two may merge to form a patriarchic family enterprise as has come about in many Mediterranean countries. There the *patron* runs family and business with a kind, paternal regard for the well-being of his employees, at least as long as they refrain from joining trade unions or left-wing parties. Modern, scientifically staffed and equipped hospitals may be found side by side with the herb medicines and quack doctors of a thousand years of tradition, as in Communist China. Socialistic doctrines and sophisticated economic planning may coexist with the veil and subordination of women, as in some Moslem countries. Highly refined social science and public administration may be joined with strutting militarism, as in Germany before World War I. Or archaic racial prejudice and the world's most sophisticated space laboratories and rocket launching equipment may coexist, as in parts of the United States.

Since modernization is a long-range affair, extending over many generations and perhaps over centuries, its progress need not be continuous. There may be long lulls, periods of stagnation, and even relapses into an earlier stage of development. The original causes of the breakup of traditional society may disappear, and other causes may propel development along for a while, in turn to be superseded by a third, fourth, and fifth set of causes, and so on. Rectifying the disequilibrium of a traditional society with modern reform generally causes a new disequilibrium, which may call for still further adjustment. Or the reform may mobilize an opposition that eventually may be advancing modernization, too. The zeal of successful modernizing elites is notoriously short-lived. Whether the modernizing elite is a disaffected fact of the nobility, a revolutionary peasant movement, or the disgruntled intellectuals or Western-educated professional people of a colonial society, success and fulfillment of their goals soon tend to blunt their modernization drive and turn them into defenders of the status quo. The famous bourgeoisie of Western Europe, for example, no sooner had broken down the barriers imposed by traditional society on its personal and economic freedom than it began to deny corresponding freedoms to the next class yearning for emancipation—the workers. Working-class parties and trade unions, in fact, had to go through a long struggle before they were permitted a chance to make their own contribution to the modernization of their countries.

Steps of modernization in the West

Modernization in the West has taken centuries up to the present, as compared to the short period of time many a new nation would prefer to spend to achieve modernization. During these centuries, moreover, the slower pace of modernizing the various Western societies forged a social unity that was only partly there to begin with. Modern democratic nations were created in which every individual, man or woman, from a certain age on participated as an autonomous entity in the political, economic, and social life of the entire national community. This devolopment came about in distinct steps: (1) the establishment of the territorial state by a coalition of national elites clustered about the monarchy; (2) economic growth and unification of transport and communication by the bourgeoisie; (3) urbanization and industrialization; and (4) democratization, or the political socialization of the masses by means of representative institutions, political parties, and interest groups. Although literary nationalism and the evolution of national political leaders may often have antedated all but the first of these steps (and in some cases were necessary to attain national unity), real mass participation did not come until all steps were completed.

Frequently there were major obstacles to be overcome, including the restance of traditional elites, or modernizers turned reactionaries, or cultural prejudices against important facets of modernization—such as the medieval horror of usury, or the traditional upper-class view of gainful activity as demeaning. Modernization did not always proceed without violence and bloodshed. There are many kinds of revolution—palace revolts or coups d'état having little bearing on modernization. Unsung revolutions, such as the introduction of centralized monarchy by a coalition of the monarch with middle-class or military elements at the expense of the great lords, have had an enormous impact. The great historical revolutions of Western Europe and Russia have not in themselves been landmarks of modernization, although their ostensible purpose has been to overthrow governments controlled by a reactionary elite in favor of modernizing successors. As historians from Alexis de Tocqueville to Crane Brinton have noted, these revolutions go through a cycle that ends with the

restoration of the old regime with minor modifications unless, as in
the Russian revolution of 1917, well-organized extremists seize power
before the inner rationale of the revolution has led it to return to
its point of departure. Brinton in his comparative study of four great
revolutions notes particularly that all four revolutions seemed to
originate in the discontents of peoples who were economically and
politically on the upgrade, not starving or intolerably opppressed. He
also notes the "disaffection of the intellectuals" and the fatal weakness of the old regimes. Revolutions of this sort, then, happen
almost accidentally. In spite of their fury and violence against the
men and institutions of the old regime, they seem to leave their chief
modernizing impact on the attitudes of the people. Changing the
attitudes of a society that is traditionally custom bound, ascriptive,
hierarchical, and low in economic productivity is, of course, a major
victory for modernization. But such changes could also be brought
about by engaging in a popular war or by such gradual means as
industrialization and urbanization. A colonial revolution or deliberate
movement for national independence or unity, by comparison, is a
more significant major step toward modernization than the great
historical or "social" revolutions of the past.

THE INDIVIDUAL EMERGES

The most significant aspect of the great transition from traditional
society to modernity, and a good measure of the progress of modernization, is the changing role of the individual in the mass. Whereas
the members of the old elite groups change only in minor ways, it
is the common man who has the farthest to travel—first, emerging
from beneath the humus of history, on whose surface heroes and
empires flower, then moving on to the discovery of his own worth
and importance.

What does it feel like to be an ordinary villager in a traditional
society? Daniel Lerner, in a research project on Middle Eastern
countries—since replicated in Latin America, Asia, and Africa—
interviewed Turkish villagers and Jordanian Bedouins and obtained
what appears to be an example typical of traditional society the
world over. Professor Lerner speaks of the "constrictive self" of
the peasant or nomad who would never imagine himself to be or
do anything other than what he is and does and who views the
physical and social world around him as absolutely given—unchanging and unchangeable. Lerner also notes the limited vocabulary,
the exceedingly vague notions of measurements of time, space, and
money, and the reluctance of traditional man to form opinions on

any subject. The "traditional peasant," in contrast to the "transitional person," lacks empathy, mobility, curiosity, and a desire to manipulate things or people. He does not resent his grim poverty. He actually views change as evil and consistently defers to traditional authority in the family and the village. He is illiterate and largely unaware of the world outside his parochial concerns, so much so in fact, he would rather die than have to live outside his village.[3]

Other village studies have related typical ways of child rearing to the pervasive authoritarianism of the traditional personality. Early indulgence and later harsh control are said to inculcate passivity. The Oedipal crisis of young males in the rigid age and sex hierarchy of the traditional family is believed to produce what, in Latin countries, is known as *machismo*, a cult of honor and masculinity on the prowl, an uncongenial cast of mind for cooperation among males, and the basis for a "courage culture," as Lerner calls it, in contrast to "ingenuity cultures," which are more typical of modernity.

What must it be like to be an ordinary woman in a traditional village setting? All the constraints of male existence lie upon her, without the ego satisfactions of *machismo*. In fact, women in traditional society are utterly subject to fathers, husbands, and brothers in addition to all the other burdens they have to shoulder.

What does it take to break the spell of traditional village society, to start the constrictive self upon the road of transition? Would not a major crisis, a lost harvest, an epidemic, a natural catastrophe, or war be more likely to crush rather than to emancipate these men and women living against great odds at the minimal subsistence level? It will probably require a gradual process over several generations, a process that slowly breaks the deadly isolation of the village with trading or traveling contacts, a widening of the limited peasant horizon of everyday experience, perhaps also military conscription and encounters with a distant government or its tax collectors. Because young people are more mobile and capable of changing their attitudes in spite of cultural conditioning, moreover, every new generation means a new chance for change.

One of the greatest obstacles to the social mobility of peasants has been the power of the landowning elite, or nobility, upon whose land peasants work for a pittance all their lives. Most traditional societies have known peasant rebellions, such as those that broke out periodically in tsarist Russia and ended in violence and futility. The oppressed creatures raged against their chains but

[3] Daniel Lerner, *The Passing of Traditional Society* (New York: Free Press, 1964).

never had the leadership or organzation to maintain their temporary advantage. This is one of the barriers of modernization that only political means can overcome. Either an enlightened state breaks up rural feudalism with land reform or the peasants join with other segments of society who do possess the capacity of leadership and organization necessary to break up the large estates. Even after that, as the revolutionary government of Mexico learned earlier in this century, the peasants are still far from able to make the best use of the land they are given. Another vast political, or government, effort is required to teach the peasant how to utilize his land, improve his livestock and crops, raise credit, and market his produce. Despite agricultural extension services and the development of cooperative and community services, the road to something resembling economic freedom on the farm is long and arduous. Even in the industrial societies of the West, only some segments of agriculture have reached a commercially viable status, whereas large parts are still dependent on government manipulation and support.

A shorter road to individual autonomy, economic and otherwise, probably leads from the farm to the city or to industrial centers. Before the young peasant or village craftsman takes this important step, he must have lost much of the traditional fear of change and the unknown. Very likely, he may have learned at firsthand or through friends what life is like in the city. And he no longer would rather die than have to live somewhere else. He must also have an adventurous spirit and perhaps be something of a rebel to want to break with the way of life of his father and grandfathers. Like all true rebels he knows in his heart that somehow he is different from his father and all the peasant ancestors before him. He comes to believe that it is in his power to change his life—a revolutionary idea of the first order in a traditional setting. And he has enough empathy to imagine himself living elsewhere and doing what he may have seen others do far from the village. Thus the individual is born and sets out on the long road of transition.

Long before the peasants of traditional society begin to feel the winds of change, the various elite groups are aware of the great transformation. The great landowners, noblemen, or chiefs have always considered their position a reflection of their natural superiority over the crowd. As they feel the respect and deference due them being withdrawn, they think the whole world is declining and the best moral and aesthetic values are no longer being appreciated. They rail against what they consider to be grasping materialism and against the pervasive rationalism applied to social relations (equality), economics (capitalism), and government (democracy). Some tend to withdraw from this distasteful world, others to lash out furiously at the newly rising social classes.[4] Where the elite is still in political control, however, as in nineteenth-century Prussia and Japan, they may turn to industrialization as a means to greater military power without permitting social and political modernization. The eventual failure of the Prussian *Junkers* in Germany and the fate of Japan both demonstrate that militarism and imperialism can serve only temporarily to postpone social and political modernization.

Traders and financiers, who in traditional society are often disliked outsiders, such as religious minorities—the Jews and Protestants in Europe, the Chinese in Southeast Asia, and the Indians in East Africa—can in time become a basis for a powerful middle class, such as the classical bourgeoisie of Western countries. Thoroughly individualistic and achievement-oriented, they are a modern elite whose commercial, financial, and, later, industrial enterprises have a radical modernizing effect on the whole society but especially on the peasants, to whom they give an opportunity to pursue a new life away from the village. In France and Great Britain and wherever the bourgeoisie was strong enough to mediate between the old elite and the newly rising classes, a framework of constitutional democracy and bills of rights could channel the seething social tensions into political contests rather than into revolution and repression. Unfortunately, most developing countries have lacked such a strong bourgeoise and its moderating role. In some countries, especially in Latin America and the Near East, the military has played a roughly analogous role. Frequently the best-educated and most modern part of a society in transition, the military assumed a paternalistic role, which sometimes even required intervention or supposedly tutelary dictatorship when, in its opinion, civilian government failed to perform its job.

There is also a heterogeneous group in many developing societies today composed of educated, but dependent, persons such as public or colonial employees, schoolteachers, professional persons, and intellectuals. The nationalistic movements largely recruit their membership from this group, which is articulate and sensitive enough to mirror fully the yearnings and dilemmas of the great transition. Fully conscious of the traditional world they have left behind, they often feel a love-hate relationship toward the old customs and traditions. The contact with Western ways has awakened in them mixed feelings of resentment, humiliation, and passionate desire to

[4] See also John H. Kautsky, *Political Change in Underdeveloped Countries: Nationalism and Communism* (New York: Wiley, 1962), pp. 98 ff.

rush their own half-traditional society along the road to modernity. Their frustrated impatience and emotional turmoil frequently make this group receptive to Communist methods of speeding development by dictatorial means. They often combine the traditional authoritarianism and "courage culture" with a quasi-religious yearning for an ideology that explains everything and resolves all ambiguity. They also tend toward a cult of leadership and of hero worship that seems to spring from a deep inner need to personify in the form of a leader the great journey into the future.

And what about the young peasant or village craftsman who has gone to the city to seek a new life there? Where the white-collar groups and intellectuals have theorized and talked about the dilemmas of the *transitional man*, he has lived them, suffered them, and has had to prove his innermost nature against their challenge. Having left the security of the village with great expectations and dreams of riches and adventure, he enters a world where jobs are scarce and poorly rewarded, employers, landlords, and merchants predatory, hygiene and housing very poor, inequalities shocking, and disease and social disorganization always present. The sheer size of cities, their throngs of new migrants like himself,[5] and their diversity of regional tongues and customs are, in themselves, overwhelming. In the mass, moreover, the worst remainders of the traditional past, such as *machismo*, superstition, and authoritarianism, seem to be magnified by the absence of the social control of the village over the behavior of individuals. Not only does the young migrant find crime, injustice, and physical violence rampant, but he may find his own conduct deteriorating, causing him the most acute guilt feelings. He has become an individual who, for better or for worse, determines his own life, indeed. But what a life he leads now! It is so easy in the *anomic* life of urban poverty to sink into a sense of purposefulness, or worse, into crime, alcoholism, and moral degeneration. And yet, what a triumph when our young transitional succeeds! Successful transition to a modern way of life has a naturally reinforcing effect that helps a person to pull himself together, just as failure will surely lure the transitional skeletons out of his mental closet and drive him to the brink of despair and mental disintegration. Causes for personal failure beyond his control surround the migrant at every turn of the road of transition. And from his traditional village past and his ignorance of impersonal social causes such as unemployment, poor housing, or general *anomie*, he is most likely to take failure as a verdict on the worth of his person. The "song of the road," as a

[5] Mexico City, the cities of India, and some of the larger cities of Africa have been growing at a rate of 50 percent or more every decade since World War II.

piece of popular fiction in India called its account of the migration of a family, therefore, is a song of human pathos, a song of great hope and of tribulations that try men's souls.[6]

DEMOCRATIC DEVELOPMENT OR TOTALITARIANISM?

The politics of a modernizing society are perhaps the most vulnerable part and yet are undoubtedly the linchpin of modernization, more so than is economic development, which inevitably stops or regresses whenever the political process breaks down. Members of advanced industrial societies show their modern bias when they assume economic productivity to be as central to a developing society in the early stages as it is in their own world. Once a society seizes upon economic growth as its salvation, it is already well along the road to modernity. The citizens of countries that give foreign aid are far too inclined to think that aid will produce economic growth or even democracy where these features are lacking. Foreign aid is no more likely to have this effect than a large allowance will turn a teenager into a successful businessman or into a person of all-round maturity. First the appropriate attitudes and skills have to mature, and only then will money produce growth and rational behavior. Foreign aid can only speed up growth that is already in progress. Or it can, like the Marshall Plan, supply the investment capital for an existing capacity of skills and achievement-oriented attitudes. And the appropriate attitudes are acquired best by exposure to ongoing economic growth activities or, at the very beginning, some of the causes of modernization already mentioned. Economic growth, then, is simply an integral part of modernization in general and evolves along with it, unless a revolutionary party or regime insists on imposing it by political force and regimentation the Communist or nationalistic way. Unforced economic growth is dependent on the progress of general modernization over a considerable period of time.

Problem areas of political modernization

The chief problem areas of political modernization are the following, not necessarily in this order: (1) problems of unity and consensus; (2) problems of government stability and effectiveness; (3) political communication between leadership and the masses; (4) articulation

[6] See especially the writings of Oscar Lewis about Latin America, S. R. Srinivas on India, and Oscar Handlin on Eastern Europe. Also William McCord, *The Springtime of Freedom* (New York: Oxford University Press, 1965), chaps. I and II.

of interests and organization of political parties; and (5) psychological aspects of political development. These problems will be discussed with regard to the potential for democratic development and for totalitarian dictatorship.

Before we consider each of these problems, a few comments about the historical development of the more advanced societies of the world are in order. As Eugene Staley has pointed out,[7] there is an important difference between countries that developed industrialism by themselves, such as England and Holland, and latecomers such as Germany, Japan, and Russia, where traditional elites or an equally authoritarian Communist dictatorship could introduce or expand industrial development in societies lacking the individualistic freedom and development that had been its prerequisites in England or Holland. The developing societies that today stand at what Walt W. Rostow[8] called the economic take-off stage are also taking over industrialism from without, either at the initiative of colonial masters or of an impatient, modernizing elite in their new governments. The first crucial stages of industrialization in many of the advanced societies, moreover, took place under conditions not of democracy but of oligarchic rule, whether of semifeudal or bourgeois entrepreneurs or the state planners of the Soviet Union. The lower classes who had to suffer most might not have consented to development at this price had they been asked. Even in American social and economic history, where the rule of the oligarchy was by far the mildest owing to democracy and the open frontier, tales of friction and of the woes of industrial workers and farmers abound. Democracy in Europe long remained a mere creed of the bourgeoisie and was not extended to the lower classes until industrialism had reached full maturity. There is a great danger, then, of expecting the politics of developing societies to conform to standards which not even Great Britain observed until she was well along the way on her journey to modernization.

Problems of unity and consensus   The problems of unity and consensus faced by developing societies are partly geographical and partly social. The problems of nation-building and economic development are greatly complicated where there are geographical barriers as in the separateness of East and West Pakistan, or the islands of Indonesia, or unpopulated vastnesses such as have faced

[7] *The Future of Underdeveloped Countries* (New York: Harper & Row, 1961).

[8] *The Stages of Economic Growth* (Cambridge, Mass.: Cambridge University Press, 1960) and by the same author, *Politics and the Stages of Growth* (London: Cambridge University Press, 1971).

Russia, China, and Brazil, and even the United States a century ago. The exhilaration attending the completion of a transcontinental railroad, or of a canal or a highway, opening up an isolated region, bears eloquent witness to the importance of overcoming physical barriers.

Physical barriers are small compared to the barriers between different ethnic elements and social classes. In India the different language communities have caused language riots and demands for autonomy, if not secession. The Austro-Hungarian empire was torn asunder by rising ethnic friction and the agitation of ethnic leaders, each mobilizing his little "nationality" until Eastern Europe was Balkanized, a ready prey for the territorial ambitions of Hitler, Mussolini, and Stalin. Often the social mobilization of one ethnic community is achieved by hatred of or open warfare on another ethnic community, a technique which can become the core idea of totalitarian Fascism when carried to its ultimate conclusion. The social classes of Western Europe from the French Revolution until World War II often constituted warring camps, and the idea of class struggle became the central idea of totalitarian Communism.

One may conjecture that in the course of modernization each ethnic group and each distinct social class of a given society goes through its own, separate process of social mobilization. The differential in modernization between, say, the bourgeoisie and the emerging industrial proletariat may also allow the superior group opportunities of exploitation as well as the ego gratification of evident superiority. The problems posed and the frictions generated are particularly great where large racial minorities, such as white settlers in Africa or the Chinese in Southeast Asia, have played a key economic role, or where a particular ethnic or religious group has been the modernizing elite. The same principles also hold for the relations between neighboring countries. What would Fidel Castro do without the United States, and the Arab leaders without Israel? A differential in modernization between two countries may also invite aggression, colonization, and exploitation by the more advanced of the two. Hatred of and warfare against another nation helps to unite and mobolize one's own nation.

Establishing a basic consensus on such things as the form of government, the rules of the political process, common concepts of justice, or day-by-day policies at home and abroad is an almost impossible task under these circumstances. Some ethnic groups will invariably suspect other groups of wielding too much influence, especially the more advanced ones. Minorities and lower classes will claim that the supposedly neutral government and the assertedly fair rules of political competition are just a smokescreen for an exclusive ruling class. Bitter disputes will ensue over the alleged bias of public policies, especially in the social and economic field. And even if a basic consensus is reached, it is easily lost in the modernizing frictions and rapid change of alignments between the different groups. Is it any wonder that there is a great temptation to turn the violence of factional strife into hatred for a scapegoat, or into war on a neighboring country, which will at least serve to unify the society riven by modernization?

Government stability and effectiveness The problems of government stability and effectiveness are in part related to the presence of a constitutional consensus and agreement on the rules of the game. Constitutional government requires a framework of consensus within which differences between the various interests and proposed policies can be resolved. There must be, in particular, provision made for opposition without penalty. There must also be procedures to facilitate orderly succession between governments. All of these points raise questions with regard to many developing countries today. When we look back on the political development of the advanced societies, the record seems to show, if anything, too much stability. To be sure, there have been periods of turbulence in some countries, which may have led to major crises. But what would really be best for the process of modernization is a moderate, but steady, turnover in government. Periods of stability extended over a decade or more generally signify the entrenchment of a neo-traditional or transitional clique in power that may require a violent revolution to dislodge after years of misrule and graft. This applies particularly to many Latin American countries during the last one hundred years.

Stability and effectiveness of government also define the need for a full-fledged central administration to carry on the business of government with integrity and dispatch. The new nations of today have an especially enormous administrative burden to shoulder, ranging from public health and road building projects to community development and education for millions of illiterates. Their own trained manpower reserves are extremely limited, despite the labor surplus, and have to compete with the needs of economic development, defense, the professions, and other demands. There are also the problems resulting from the premodern attitudes of the available staff—administrative problems of status, nepotism, corruption, and a lack of achievement orientation. The new nations with the most viable administration today may thank the efforts of their past colonial rulers. Yet ultimately a well-developed native administration must grow beyond the colonial precedent. Most of all, it must become politically responsible and responsive to the people. This is the current counterpart of the need for decentralization of the administration of the absolutist monarchies of Western Europe several decades ago.

Communism between leadership and the masses The problems of political communication particularly bedevil the leadership of the new nations today. When a former colony wins independence, the whole array of social forces is generally united by the single sentiment of anticolonialism. The most prominent nationalistic leaders take power. There has been no particular need up to that time to find out what the masses think and what the needs of particular groups among them may be. The desire for independence may not even go very deep among the people. Soon after the honeymoon of national independence, as practical problems confront the new government, it becomes apparent that there are few established channels, such as organs of public opinion or interest groups, that can transmit demands and grievances. There is also a considerable gulf, socially and intellectually, between the modernizing, urban elite from which the leaders spring and the illiterate peasant masses and recent migrants to the city. These two groups are hardly able to communicate with each other and often lack appreciation of the crucial importance of communication. The leaders by their very upbringing and style are not the kind to keep their ears to the ground. They often conceive of their leadership role in quasi-traditional, authoritarian terms as a one-way road. A long-standing pattern of rebellion against colonial authority (often they have spent years in exile or in prison) has made them introverted and has produced a tendency away from realism and toward an ideological cast of mind. Even though they love their people to the point of martyrdom, they know them from subjective introspection only, for they are subject to the social barriers to communication between the groups as much as is any other transitional person. Caught in the cage of their own illusions about the popular consensus or their ideological preconceptions, they may find themselves feted as nationalistic founding fathers today and overthrown tomorrow by the unforeseen outbreak of a peasant revolt, a military barracks uprising, or an urban mob riot. The senseless violence of a riot or assassination by malcontents or mentally unbalanced persons may set an end to their grandeur and glory overnight. Needless to add, the illusions and ideologically tinted perception of the nationalistic leaders also make them easy prey for Communist subversion and take-over.

Problems of lagging interest articulation   A particular problem both
for the stability of the politics of development and for the voicing
of specific demands is the lagging *interest articulation*[9] of most developing societies. One of the reasons for unexpected peasant revolts lies in the absence or weakness of permanent peasant associations to formulate and present demands or complaints to the leaders.
Nor may there be business groups or labor unions of any size to
represent their respective interests until development has advanced
considerably. Even existing institutional groups, such as the Buddhist
clergy in South East Asia, government clerks in India, and the
military in the Near East and Latin America usually disdain formal
organization and take direct action instead on the basis of charismatic leadership.

By the same token, the operation of political parties may resemble
a conspirational net of clandestine groups or a social mass movement and lack many of the attributes typical of a more advanced
stage. To the extent that parties take care of the political socialization
of the citizens of a developing society, such movements may often
induct the individual into membership in a utopian movement instead
of the society in which he lives. There is also a great tendency for
the few organizations that are in existence to exercise far broader
and more ideologically oriented roles than their equivalents in an
advanced industrial society. Labor unions propound ideological doctrines and devote themselves to the election of candidates. Buddhist
monks openly campaign for broad issues of foreign policy. And political party movements may get involved in wage disputes and
strikes—an involvement that the more functionally specific party
organizations of Western democracies have long learned to avoid.

Again there lies a potential for totalitarian development, both
in the indeterminate nature of these groups—whether they are of
the conspirational or of the mass movement type of political party—
and in the prominent role of ideology in the politics of development.
Political parties of developing countries that have a high potential
for democratic development are generally pluralistic leagues and may
even include trade unions, farm groups, and other associations. A
dynamic mass movement that finds itself almost alone in the group
life of a new nation will be tempted to play all of the pluralistic
group roles itself, thus surrounding the individual with its power
over every function of his life. It may even try to take on significant

[9] See also Gabrial A. Almond and James S. Coleman, eds., *The Politics of the
Developing Areas* (Princeton, N.J.: Princeton University Press, 1961) and Gabriel
A. Almond and Bingham Powell, Jr., *Comparative Politics: A Developmental
Approach* (Boston: Little, Brown, 1967).

administrative duties, an alarming development found otherwise only in totalitarian dictatorships.[10]

Psychological aspects of political development The psychological dimensions of political development are, perhaps, the greatest obstacle to the introduction of liberal democracy. Transitional man has no particular predisposition to a democratic way of life, though he may acquire such a predisposition after economic development has run its full course. It is true that village politics in many traditional societies has certain democratic features. The Indian villagers, for example, according to most accounts, are given an opportunity to discuss the decisions made by the council of village elders in a public meeting. Yet the pervasive social stratification, the hierarchy of age and sex in the family, and the collectivism of the village leave their mark on transitional man. Since village ways were a total way of life, he is now prone to accept ideological explanations of the new world around him. Because he has little insight into the necessities and choices of politics, he tends to join politicians and their parties out of a desire for a sense of belonging, rather than to help achieve a clearly conceived policy preference. And because at heart he is still an authoritarian, seeking personal answers to his private problems of the great transition, he worships great personalities, leaders, and *macho* heroes, of whose limitations he does not seem to be aware. Politics to him, moreover, is something psychologically far more satisfying than democratic politics can ever be. It is high drama, the struggle for national independence, the creation of a new utopian society, the machinations of powerful men like the village boss back home, personal loyalty, and group life. All of these features we shall encounter again in the following chapters on totalitarian government.

Democracy, by comparison, must seem drab and uninspiring to the transitional mind. The mechanics of economic growth seem utterly boring and restrictive of individual whim and expression. Real individualism for the average man, at the same time, must seem lonesome and perhaps even a little frightening. And yet the chances of democracy in the developing world may be better than they seem today, provided political development is not intercepted by subversion from without or oligarchic dictatorship from within. Avoiding these mistakes and with the benefit of outside aid, most of the developing nations stand as good a chance as the advanced societies to muddle through by trial and error until liberal democracy can grow firm roots in their soil.

10 See also the M.I.T. study, edited by Max F. Millikan and Donald L. M. Blackmer, *The Emerging Nations* (Boston: Little, Brown, 1961), pp. 68–75.

13 COMMUNIST
TOTALITARIANISM

Viewed against the background of the modernizing process, the modern ideologies of Liberalism, Conservatism, and Democratic Socialism take on a special significance. Each of these ideologies is oriented toward large masses of people who find themselves in the same class position at a particular moment in the progress of modernization. Thus Liberalism springs up as the common view of the world among the new middle-class elites of commerce and industrial enterprise. Conservatism emerges as the common view of aristocrats and other traditional elites who are forced by the liberal challenge to justify their authority and way of life. And Democratic Socialism gains a following as the new working class created by industrialization tries to define its own identity and to fashion the environment to its own liking.

Communism and Fascism also can be fitted into the process of modernization and are intimately related to its stresses and strains. However, there are several striking differences between the role and significance of these totalitarian ideologies and that of Liberalism, Conservatism, and Democratic Socialism. Some of these differences are only a matter of degree. Others amount to differences in basic substance. All of them together make a comparison between, say Conservatism and Fascism or Democratic Socialism and Communism a difficult undertaking. Most of these differences are related to the basic personality makeup of leaders and followers, the prevalence of persuasion or of force, and the fundamental question of human freedom in society. Some of the dissimilarities follow from the stage of modernization of a society, the particular culture involved, or such external facts as war, defeat, isolation, or encirclement.

MODERATES AND TOTALITARIANS

There is a certain reluctance today among social scientists to use the label "totalitarian" on anything or anybody for fear of creating naïve dichotomies of "good" and "bad" politics. Some of this reluctance is based on a genuine concern about the facile anti-Communism popular in the late 1950s and early 1960s rather than on any desire to deny that the particular descriptions of certain "totalitarian" systems are true. This line of argument, in fact, tends to lead us away from objective observation and into the arena of political advocacy for or against particular countries. Another objection to the term "totalitarianism" is, from the political-science point of view, more consequential. The protagonists for this objection are often specialists well-versed in the study of certain Communist or Fascist systems and believe that the stereotype label stands in the way of an appreciation of the considerable differences between the various systems and, for example, between Stalin's and Brezhnev's and Kosygin's Russia. The point is well taken but hardly invalidates the logic of comparing totalitarian regimes and movements of various shadings with definitely nontotalitarian ones. As long as we understand the label to be chiefly a technical term, there is no particular reason to abandon it. The word itself, as it was coined by Mussolini, is quite descriptive, although any other well-understood term for totalitarian politics would say as much.

One of the chief assumptions of the three moderate isms— Liberalism, Conservatism and Democratic Socialism—although varying in emphasis, is that human beings are endowed with reason and deserve to be reasoned with. This is not to say that there have not been lapses in the politics of these moderates where deception or irrational appeals have been used to get results. Yet even the grossest occasional lapses of the moderate politicians in that direction differ fundamentally from the conviction of Communists, Fascists and other extremists that appealing to reason, objectivity in the reporting of facts, and looking at both sides of an issue is a bourgeois, pedantic preoccupation. To Fascists and Communists no stigma attaches to the ruthless manipulation of human feelings, prejudices, and other weaknesses if the employment of such methods will further the power of the movement.

Second, Communists, Fascists and other extremists deeply believe that there can be no such thing as objective truth, that facts can be viewed only through the mirror of the battlelines of the great struggle in which they are engaged. If you are truly one of them, they think, you cannot but view every event, every measure, and every person strictly from the point of view of what they mean to the advancement of the cause. If you are not part of the solution, you must be part of the problem. Wars and riots are viewed as necessary for social change, or in terms of whether the winning side is friendly or hostile to their cause, rather than by the "objective" measure of senseless death and destruction; demonstrably neutral groups and persons are viewed as pro- or anti-Communist, -extremist, or -Fascist; and all the complexities and fine shadings of the political world are reduced to a simple friend-or-foe scheme. This approach is called *dialectical thinking* and goes a long way toward explaining for example, the hold of Communist ideology over the minds of the faithful even in the face of contrary evidence.

Third, totalitarians are distinguished from moderates by a strikingly *Messianic cast of mind.* Taking as their point of departure a preconceived theory of modernization or philosophy of history, they infuse history with strongly religious effects, substituting, however, their own secular aims for the march of the deity through world history. Thus they may long with all their hearts for the salvation of society through a Communist, Fascist, or other utopian revolution, the coming of the Messiah—their great leader—and the beginning of a millennium in the form of a powerful Third Reich, a Communist world, or other utopia. They may look upon their movement as a great crusade against evil and conduct themselves like a fighting religious order, turning their holy wrath upon the "infidels" and also upon heretics in their own ranks and "heretical books."

Finally, totalitarian ideologies, although they are usually predicated on the idea of struggle or conflict in history, never allow for institutionalized conflict in the millenarian society they envisage. Once they take control, they have no use for pluralism, for tolerating dissent or opposition, a system of competing parties, bargaining between labor and management, or such rivals in setting standards and values as independent courts, churches, or independent intellectuals in education or culture. The word "totalitarian," among other things, denotes the completely politicized, monistic character of the society envisaged as well as the totality of political control over all aspects of life. Totalitarians prefer to be masters of the press, the schools, the churches, the economic marketplace, and of all group life. They feel a horror of competition, of ambiguity, of social or spiritual forces beyond their control.

Totalitarian ideologies, then, in contrast to the moderate isms, thrive only under special conditions and require a personality type for their leaders and followers that is rare among Liberals, Conservatives, or Democratic Socialists. The conditions under which totalitarians seem to thrive are conditions of extremely rapid change. It has been discovered, for example, that periods of rapid industrialization and urbanization in various Western European countries have greatly increased the following of extremist philosophies. The sociologist Seymour M. Lipset also demonstrated that the feeling of frustration of workers in pockets of technological backwardness in modern economics such as that of France and Italy encourage a turning to Communism. Fascism, on the other hand, is enhanced by feelings of having suffered an undeserved loss in national prestige, a humiliating defeat or depredation in war, or of wholesale subversion and betrayal everywhere. Conditions of social and economic crisis, accompanied by social disorganization, anomie, and a general loss of a sense of direction seem to benefit both Fascism and Communism.

The personality type most likely to be attracted by a totalitarian ideology has been described by Eric Hoffer as the "true believer," a person with a great longing to believe in a cause and a need to reduce everything to utterly simple dichotomies. He is also likely to be deeply alienated from society, disaffected from its political loyalties, and to feel abused, exploited, or betrayed. An element of paranoia, or a persecution complex, often makes him the victim of an obsessive fear for an all-embracing Communist or Fascist conspiracy, whichever the case may be, which in a free society is said to include almost all governmental and group leadership and to control the press as well. A typical recruit for Fascism or Communism is frequently suffering from severe emotional stress brought on perhaps by the difficulties of growing up (many members of Communist or Fascist parties or militias outside totalitarian countries have been between 18 and 25 years of age), by personal crises of one sort or another, or by being uprooted physically and emotionally from the security of one's old environment. The emotional stress of moving from a quiet, rural environment to the city can be mobilized by a Fascist, revolutionary nationalist, or Communist movement. Communist recruiting also tries to exploit the emotional strain that may result from the encounter of native elites of developing countries, often while studying abroad, with the advanced societies of the West. These stresses and strains are then acted out by engaging in activist causes.

MARX-ENGELS, AN AMBIGUOUS LEGACY

It will be remembered that the teachings of Karl Marx have come in for a great deal of revision and reinterpretation since his death. A substantial part of the movements and parties of Democratic Socialism, in fact, have long paid homage to Marx, though with significant changes on such points as their preference for gradual evolution rather than violent revolution, or for democracy rather than the dictatorship of the proletariat. Actually, the writings of Marx and Engels contain considerable ambiguities on these and other counts and it is no cause for wonder, considering that the formation of different schools of interpretation has continued long after Democratic Socialists and Communists decided to go their separate ways.

Different schools of Communism

Even in the Communist world of today, there are incisive differences that have led occasionally to the suppression of some parts of Marxist writings and to varying emphasis on Marx's different works. The early writings of young Marx, for example, have found great favor with the restless intellectuals of Communist Eastern Europe, who apply his concept of the *alienation of man* under capitalism to the alienation caused by a Communist bureaucracy and police state, aiming their dialectical reasoning even at the holiest of holies, the Communist party oligarchy itself.

In the Soviet Union after Stalin, the Karl Marx most popular was the middle-aged Marx, who wrote the *Critque of Political Economy* and *Capital*—the economist Marx, whose painstaking inventory of economic processes and theories appears to bear more kinship to the problems of an industrial society than either his early philosophy or occasional cries for struggle and violent revolution. In this the Soviet Union has evidently come a long way from the days of the October Revolution of 1917, when Lenin's blueprint for the conquest of power had little reference to production statistics.

Communist China, finally, has little use for Marx the philosopher of alienation or for Marx the industrial economist. Much closer in its state of industrialization to prerevolutionary Russia than to either the countries of Eastern Europe or the Soviet Union today, China prefers Marx the revolutionary, the man who wrote the *Communist Manifesto* and other smaller works, and the sharp interpretations of Marxism by Friedrich Engels, his friend and posthumous editor. Most of all, the Chinese like Lenin's drastic revision of Marxism, which transferred the promise of ruin and rebirth that Marx had held out only to highly industrialized nations to developing countries such as Red China.

Theory and practice

It stands to reason that an enduring concern with worldwide revolution, as is the nature of Communism, cannot be studied merely by examining the system of ideas involved. To be sure, an understanding of the Communist ideology is indispensable to the study of Communism. But the ideology must be seen as part of the total behavior of Communists, their organizations and methods. The ideology of Marxism has undergone enormous changes under the impact of varying social and economic conditions and political needs from the time of birth of Communist parties to their present state of achievement. To these conditions and needs we will now turn our attention.

It was to be expected that a complex social philosophy such as Marxism would change its character as soon as it was brought from the ivory tower of speculation into the realm of political action. Marx himself was of a divided mind in his approach to Socialism— caught between his theory that the process of capitalism would automatically bring about the great revolution and an activist temper that could not refrain from calls for action and attempts to organize an international workers' movement. In the difference between the two there lies the gulf between passivity and political action and the ancient distinction between *revolution by circumstances* and *revolution by plot*. There is little doubt that the basic theory of revolution of Karl Marx is a theory of worsening circumstances, brought on by business cycles and monopolistic concentration and the proletarianization and impoverishment of ever-increasing masses, which finally trigger the revolt against the capitalist system. But the workers' movements that adopted Marxism were led, by their needs for popular agitation and recruitment, to utilize parts of Marx's theories to inspire their followers with the feeling that this revolution could be *plotted*, or at least that its coming could be speeded up.

The need for mobilizing masses of people led Marxist movements to stress the emotionally arousing and prophetic overtones of the original philosophy. The *dialectical interpretation of history* and, in particular, the notion of *class struggle*, was undoubtedly one of the most useful for popular agitation. It could be used for awakening *class-consciousness* in millions of working people who were hardly aware of their common fate. A feeling of common interest and the image of a common enemy, which was necessary for fashioning a combative mass movement, could be created.

The economic doctrine of *surplus value* complemented that of class struggle, since it amounted to a theory of exploitation: If all value is created by labor and if the bourgeois class prospers by taking away part of the value created by the workers in its employ, then low wages are the result of exploitation rather than of low productivity. *Dialectical materialism* rather than the prevailing stress on non-material values further sharpened the confrontation of class interests and lent it an inexorable character undiminished by common bonds of religion or national culture which were, after all, only "super-structures" of the pattern of class rule and exploitation. Finally, Marx's hostility toward the state and its police power, to which he attributed the maintenance of the domination of the working class by the bourgeoisie, imbued the Marxist movements with hatred for all constituted authority and made plotting the overthrow of the state necessary. The phrase "the dictatorship of the proletariat," which hardly occurs in Marx's writings outside of the *Communist Manifesto*, was seized upon by revolutionary Marxist movements who wanted to conceive of themselves as the "vanguard of the proletariat" and to prepare for the coming days of dictatorship both in spirit and organization.

The rise of Bolshevism

Today's Communist party, as distinct from earlier Marxist movements that eventually found their salvation in Democratic Socialism, matured and came into its own in Russia as a result of World War I and of the take-over of the Russian Revolution by the Bolsheviks. As the Russian Communists, through the Communist International (Comintern), dominated and formed new Communist parties in many countries,[1] revolutionary Marxists everywhere took their ways of acting and thinking from the Russian model, both in an effort to meet the conditions for their admission to the Comintern and in

---

[1] In the early 1920s, newly formed groups that wished to be accepted into the Comintern had to subscribe to the famous 21 Points which assured their conformity and loyalty to the Russian-dominated Comintern.

emulation of the strongest Communist party, one already in control of one of the largest countries in the world. These peculiar ways of thinking and acting that were characteristic of the Russian Communists at the time can be understood best by considering their historical background under the tsars.

There are strains in the culture of prerevolutionary Russia that tended toward totalitarian rule. Among them is the religious tradition, with its notion of *Messianic orthodoxy*, the concept that there is only one truth and faith that leads to salvation and that it must be embodied in an institution and spread with dogmatic fervor throughout the world, never allowing dissent or opposition. The *Byzantine idea* of entrusting this crusading mission to the tsar, to make him at once pope and Caesar and his residence the "third Rome"[2] is another aspect of the religious tradition. The Russian tradition of *centralized, absolutist autocracy*—from the Mongol-Tartar empires to Muscovy and finally to bureaucratic absolutism—is another significant pattern. A fourth strain in the Russian culture appears to have been an obsession with unanimity and with group life which pervaded Russian literature and social philosophy long before the rise of Communism. Finally, there has always been the element of Russian *inferiority complex*, which inspired Russian leaders from Peter the Great (1689–1725) to Stalin to prodigious efforts to catch up with their seemingly more advanced neighbors to the south and west. This gnawing feeling of being backward and no match for invading Mongols, Swedes, Turks, Frenchmen, or Japanese had been a powerful spur, long before Stalin's drive to make up, in ten years, for a "backwardness" of "fifty or a hundred years" behind the West. This Russian inferiority complex explains the Soviet fear of "capitalist encirclement" and the extraordinary exultation over the great Soviet triumphs, from rocketry to culture.

The role of the intelligentsia   Even more important than the general cultural setting of prerevolutionary Russia was the climate of the anti-tsarist underground for the formation of the thought and action of the Russian Bolsheviks. Throughout the nineteenth century, Russia had a revolutionary intelligentsia recruited from many classes and concentrated chiefly in the larger cities and at the universities. From the Decembrist Uprising of 1825 to the great revolution of 1917, the intelligentsia planned and plotted for basic reforms and for the abolition of autocracy, serfdom, feudalism, and oppression. Their chief inspirations were the free institutions and great revolu-

2 The second Rome was Constantinople (Byzantium), the capital of the Eastern Roman Empire until its conquest by Mohammedanism in 1453.

tions of the West, even though many intellectuals among them were Slavophiles, that is, convinced of the innate worth of Russian traditions. Whether Westernizers or Slavophiles, they engaged in a long series of abortive underground movements over the years, ranging from starry-eyed discussion circles to bomb-throwing terrorist groups who assassinated tsars, government ministers, and other high dignitaries.

One of the greatest handicaps of the intelligentsia was their inability to obtain the support of the peasant masses that made up the vast majority of Russians. The peasants had their own revolts during that century—violent, destructive, spontaneous, and short-lived. But the peasants deeply distrusted the urban intelligentsia, both before and after the emancipation of the serfs (1861), and even turned in the agitators of the intelligentsia to the government when a Populist (Narodniki) movement sent dedicated members to the villages to win their confidence. The second great handicap was the secret police, the tsarist *Okhrana,* whose agents hounded the conspirators relentlessly, infiltrating their groups and provoking their friends into antigovernment statements and actions.

Deprived of mass support, the revolutionary intelligentsia developed an elitist cast of mind. Force and cunning on the part of a handful would have to replace persuasion and mass revolt. Conspiratorial, undercover activity was the only way to overcome the tsarist police state, its jails, and Siberian exile. In this setting the cell structure still used by underground Communist parties today was an excellent device to minimize losses by detection. If each cell was small and not connected horizontally to other cells, if the identity of each officer of the movement was hidden from the rank and file, even threats and torture of a captured member would be unable to deliver the whole membership into the clutches of the *Okhrana.* That this unhealthy atmosphere of cloak-and-dagger action, double agents, and secretiveness also invited authoritarian, half-mystical leadership and the cynical manipulation of idealistic fellow members seemed a small price to pay toward the great end of all-out revolution. The frustration of even the mildest attempts at reform spawned a vast destructive urge, an irreconcilable, anarchistic hostility against all authority—political, religious, and social —and finally a limitless nihilism toward all values and obligations, including those fundamental to human society. There is perhaps no better witness to the burning determination engendered in the Russian underground than the *Catechism of the Revolutionary (1869),* written by the young anarchist Nechaev. It reads in part:

The revolutionary has no personal interests, no affairs, feelings,
attachments, property, not even a name of his own. . . . He despises
and hates the present-day code of morals. . . . Whatever aids the
triumph of the revolution is ethical; what hinders it is criminal. . . .
All tender, softening feelings of kinship, friendship, love, gratitude
and even honor must be snuffed out in him by the single, cold passion
of the revolution.

There is reason to believe that the totalitarian character of the
Communist movement resulted from the historical background of
the Bolsheviks and later settings and circumstances to a greater
extent than from the ambiguous legacy of Marx and Engles.

MARXISM-LENINISM-STALINISM

The first Russian Marxist group was born into this underground
setting in the 1880s but with an orientation diametrically opposed
to the agrarian socialism and anarchism of other Russian underground organizations. Instead of looking to the peasants for mass
support, it attached its hopes to the swelling ranks of industrial
workers in the Donetz Basin, St. Petersburg (Leningrad), Moscow,
and Baku. By the turn of the century Russian Marxist had formed
a Social Democratic party after the German model. But they soon
began to build a network of clandestine cells among this new proletariat, after the model of the Russian background, for the tsarist
police persecution continued, and the leadership of the elusive organization had to carry on much of its work in exile. At its second
congress in Brussels in 1903, the party split over questions of organization and policy into a narrow majority (Bolsheviks) headed by
Lenin and a minority faction (Mensheviks).

The theory of Leninism

From this time on, Lenin (1870–1924), the son of a school official
and minor aristocrat and brother of an underground terrorist executed when Lenin was 17 years old, began to dominate the reshaping of Marxism into a sharp weapon of conspiracy and revolution.
His principal contributions to Communism were those described
below.

Professional revolutionaries In his essay *What Is To Be Done?*
(1902) he proposed that the party become a tightly knit organization
composed chiefly of professional revolutionaries trained in carrying

on their work and in eluding the secret police. He argued in a fashion quite characteristic of the activists of the old background that such an "organizational weapon," as an American sociologist has called it, would be useful precisely because it could manipulate the development and course of broader revolutionary masses among the workers better than would a broadly based democratic party. His Menshevik opponents continued to prefer democratic organization and nonviolence, but under the circumstances of police persecution, Lenin eventually succeeded in creating his monolithic organization, heading it with a central committee for authoritative policy-making and forbidding the formation of dissenting factions.

When the Bolsheviks came to power in 1917, these dictatorial principles became the law not only among Russian Bolsheviks, but for the whole country. Since the Communist party claimed to represent the entire proletariat of Russia, Marx's flamboyant phrase "dictatorship of the proletariat" (he never thought of a party of professional revolutionaries) became the rationalization for the dictatorship of the Communist party.

Revolution by plot   To understand fully the significance of Lenin's professional revolutionaries, we must recall Marx's theory that the coming of the revolution was primarily a "revolution by circumstances." The circumstances were the economic conditions which would automatically and inexorably bring on the political revolution (*economic determinism*). Lenin, on the other hand, had made of it a "revolution by plot." To be sure, both Marx and Lenin had studied the course of the great social revolutions of the West with fascination; Marx had even participated in the German revolution of 1848. But despite the beginnings of industrialization, Russia, in the early twentieth century, was not ready for even a bourgeois revolution against autocracy and feudalism. Instead, the old regime was shaken to its foundations in 1905 and 1917 chiefly by military defeat, peasant unrest, and extraordinary misgovernment by the tsar and his advisers. Lenin and his professional revolutionaries had little to do with the outbreak of either revolution, but succeeded after the February Revolution of 1917 in seizing power by a skillful manipulation of the discontents of the people and of the weakness of the liberal provisional government. The Bolsheviks came to power by force and fraud receiving only 168 seats out of a total of 808 in the newly elected Constituent Assembly.[3] Thus Lenin won by *a political plot*

[3] Having used the promise of new elections as a tactical device to dissolve Parliament, the Bolsheviks promptly dissolved the Constituent Assembly a month after its election.

rather than by the *economic circumstances* envisaged by Marx to bring on revolution in the most advanced industrial countries—of which Russia was not one. Politics, which Marx had considered merely as a reflection, or superstructure, of the economic development, had won out over economic determinism. The Marxist theory had been stood on its head: The political tail was wagging the economic dog.

Theory of imperialism The third major change introduced into Marxism by Lenin was his theory of imperialism. Borrowed in large part from the writings of a British Liberal and a German Social Democrat,[4] his theory ingeniously picked up the old Russian theme of relative backwardness, coupled with the vision of the sudden conquest of a utopian future far beyond even that of the most advanced Western nations. In his book *Imperialism, the Highest Stage of Capitalism,* Lenin argued that moribund capitalism reaches its most overextended stage when the profit motive drives it to invest its capital in developing areas abroad for a better return. The safety of the investment requires the mother country to make the developing area a colony. The scramble for colonial empires by the advanced capitalist countries, causes, among other things, "imperialistic wars" over markets and colonies. At the same time, the foreign markets artificially prolong the life of overproducing capitalist economies and win over some workers by means of higher wages to the foolish quest for empire. The class struggle thereby becomes international—a struggle between advanced bourgeois nations and a colonial proletariat of developing nations exploited by "international capitalism"—until finally, and with the help of imperialist wars, the weakest link in the chain of worldwide capitalism would snap. The external proletariat of the colonies would experience the revolution first, not (as Marx had written) the internal proletariat of the advanced industrial societies. World War I, Lenin and many revolutionary Marxists believed, was an imperialist war between advanced capitalist nations that would end with worldwide revolution, beginning with some of the colonies. And Russia was a "colony" of France because French capital had financed much of her industrialization. Thus Lenin explained why the great proletarian revolution could happen first in backward Russia, on which Karl Marx had heaped much scorn and derision. And thereby he could also make plausible the coming to pass of the millenarian dream of generations of nineteenth-century Russian reformers and revolutionaries—that somehow

---

[4] See J. A. Hobson, *Imperialism* (London: Allen & Unwin, 1938; first published 1906); also Rudolf Hilferding, *Finanzkapital* (Berlin: Duncker, 1915).

Russia would rise to solve the question of labor and industrialism before the advanced Western countries would.

Lenin's theory of imperialism led to the formation of the Comintern to coordinate the worldwide revolution that never came. It also had a long-range impact, felt chiefly since World War II, as Communist agitation and subversion moved more and more into the developing areas of Asia, Africa, and Latin America, trying to stir up revolution or to infiltrate nationalist movements.

Strategy and tactics The fourth contribution of Lenin was in the field of strategy and tactics. He not only originated a whole new vocabulary of quasi-military terms for policy-making—from battle fronts to advanced and strategic retreat to left- or right-wing deviations, and similar maneuvers—but he also showed himself to be a master propagandist and a consummate tactician, who knew when to advance and when to retreat. No other Soviet leader managed so skillfully to engage the cooperation of peasants, businessmen, and nationality groups with concessions he subsequently withdrew to maneuver his regime through successive economic systems and political poses without ever losing sight of the ultimate goal. No one else, it seemed, could have brought off the delicate task of demanding "all power to the *soviets*" (revolutionary councils of soldiers and workers), when the provisional government held power, and then of taking over and finally subordinating the *soviets* to the party. Lenin's tactical genius and the vocabulary he coined are still integral parts of the Communist array of weapons the world over.

Yet it was also due to this consummate skill that the night of totalitarian dictatorship descended upon Russia when she had hardly tasted democratic freedom. After dissolving the Constituent Assembly and subordinating the *soviets* to the party, Lenin proceeded to suppress all rival parties and the free press, charging in typically dialectical fashion that they were "hostile to the revolution" and generated confusion by "perversion of the facts." The trade unions were made arms of the government and were assigned the task of ensuring increased production. The insurrection of oppositional elements of various description and the abortive Allied intervention brought on the Civil War and a regime of terror that was as savage as any repression in Russian history. A secret police, the Cheka, followed in the footsteps of the tsarist *Okhrana*, with the admitted aim of organized terror. The reins of the party increasingly tightened against deviationist opinions as the smaller circle of the Politburo rose to ascendancy over the Central Committee. A great purge expelled more than a fourth of the party membership in 1921–1922, including many "deviationists" and critics of the authoritarian developments in the party.

There can be little doubt that Lenin established totalitarian dictatorship in his few years of power before his fatal illness (1922–1924). His death momentarily initiated a struggle for power between Joseph Stalin and Leon Trotsky under the guise of the collective leadership of the leading Bolshevik revolutionaries. Eventually Stalin, the general party secretary, succeeded in outmaneuvering Trotsky and driving him into exile. The other old Bolshevik intellectuals were skillfully outwitted and were eventually purged by Stalin, the taciturn general party secretary they despised. For the next twenty-seven years, Soviet Communism was completely in the hands of Stalin (1879–1953), the one-time theology student and son of a Georgian shoemaker, who also impressed his personal stamp upon the Communist movement.

Marxism-Leninism-Stalinism

As compared to the brilliant Lenin and the outstanding theoretical minds among the old Bolsheviks, Stalin was not a theorist, but rather a man of action and manipulation. He quickly built up a powerful machine within the party from his vantage point as general party secretary, while his rivals spent their energy theorizing and orating brilliantly. He is credited with several books on Leninism and on the nationality question, which he thoroughly understood as a member of one of the national minorities of Russia. He also became involved in a bitter debate with Leon Trotsky over the choice between a policy of "permanent, worldwide revolution"and the establishment of Socialism in one country." Stalin favored the latter, although he had argued the former position as recently as a year before the great debate. But his real contribution appears to have been in the realm of concrete policies rather than of philosophical speculation.

Forced economic growth The most significant policy decision of Stalin was the crash program of economic modernization by means of a series of ambitious Five-Year Plans beginning in 1928. First in the program was the expansion of heavy industry to provide a generous basis for the future advanced economy. Second, agriculture was to be collectivized by the pooling of individual farms into large cooperatives (*kolkhoz*) or state farms (*sovkhoz*). Both of these parts of the modernization drive resulted in an enormous cost in human suffering. Between 8 and 15 million resisting farmers (*kulaks*) are said to have died or starved in the collectivization drive, which was never completed. Ruthless regimentation of labor by such means as the labor pass, the incentive system of unequal pay, piecework,[5] work quotas, state-run trade unions, "socialist competition" between individuals and workers' brigades, not to mention the slave labor of millions in concentration camps, was the price of industrialization. The third part of the modernization program consisted of a drive for the recruitment and training of tens of millions of persons for the highly qualified manpower needs of a fully developed industrial economy. Education on all levels and scientific and technical training helped to create the trained manpower for the industrial giant that Russia is today.

Terror total organizational control, propaganda Economic regimentation limited human freedom, but political control became worse as totalitarian dictatorship strived toward the pinnacle of perfection. Secret police surveillance and a net of paid neighborhood informers spread an atmosphere of terror while keeping the slave labor camps filled with a never-ending stream of prisoners to make up for the high death rate under tough working conditions in severe climes. *Total organizational control* drew all citizens into party- or state-run organizations—from the Communist youth and women's groups to professional and workplace groups—and allowed no group an autonomous existence. Propaganda controlled the schools and all information media, and Soviet citizens were isolated against the world outside. An exaggerated cult of leadership was maintained to flatter the eternally morose and suspicious Stalin. His dogmatic infallibility became the chief doctrine of the party, whose members had to follow religiously the zigzag course of the "party line" at pain of expulsion and deportation to Siberia. The great purges of the 1930s decimated party, army, and other groups of specialists. Political justice discovered the ultimate rationale of the totalitarian mania, *"objective criteria of guilt,"* whereby a man could be sent to Siberia because of the class origin or occupation of his father, his own ethnic origin, or because he had been abroad at some time in his life. For reasons understandable only from a reading of fictional accounts such as Arthur Koestler's book *Darkness at Noon* or George Orwell's *1984*, many of the old Bolsheviks on trial in the great purges abjectly confessed treasonable actions they could not possibly have committed. After World War II, Stalin returned to his purging activities in different form until death stilled his paranoid mind.

Premier Nikita Khrushchev gave the world a startling glimpse

[5] Karl Marx, who considered piecework the ultimate indignity of capitalist exploitation, must have turned in his grave.

of Stalin and his brutal regime in his secret speech on the "cult of personality" before the Twentieth Party Congress (1956),[6] which should survive the subtle attempts at re-Stalinization since Khrushchev's political demise. Books like *One Day in the Life of Ivan Denisovich* have described the terrible feeling of isolation by fear and mutual distrust of people in such a society. Boris Pasternak, in *Dr. Zhivago*, lets one of his principals tell how glad he was when World War II broke out and he was drafted and sent to the front. For there at least he knew from which direction the bullets were flying—a condition preferable to that of living from day to day in nameless fear of the midnight knock on the door.

The new orthodoxy A further incisive contribution of the Stalin era to the image of Communism was the introduction of what could broadly be called a *new orthodoxy*. A few examples may illustrate this complementary aspect of the crash program of modernization. Under Stalin, for instance, a new sex morality replaced the exceedingly liberal approach of the old Bolsheviks. Laws governing divorce and abortion were changed from extraordinary permissiveness to strictness. The institution of "socialist marriage" was furthered by party and trade union in a manner caricatured all too well in George Orwell's satire *1984*. The new nation of proletarians was counseled to avoid "bourgeois decadence" in art, music, literature, and personal conduct. Instead, a school of "social realism" was encouraged in the arts, which meant representational paintings of brawny workers and tractor-driving girls, and novels about the love affair of a *kolkhoz manager* with his farm or the thrills of overfulfilling the production quota. In place of freewheeling empirical approach to science, a new "socialist science" introduced favorite practitioners and pet theories selected by the dictator himself in fields such as genetics and linguistics.

Another aspect of the new orthodoxy was a partial return to national traditions and pursuits dating back to the tsars. The slogan "socialism in one country" presaged a new direction which, during the siege of the Axis powers, became a full revival of the patriotic image of Mother Russia. Historical figures such as Ivan the Terrible were rehabilitated and venerated after years of contempt, the old tsarist policy of Russianizing the non-Russian nationalities was renewed, and even anti-Semitism once again became a significant undercurrent of official policies. By the same token, Russia took up

[6] For the full text, see Bertram D. Wolfe, *Khrushchev and Stalin's Ghost* (New York: Praeger, 1957).

the reconquest of such former Russian territories as Finland, East Poland, and the Baltic states, as well as seizure of small countries to the west, south, and east—in pursuance of the old imperial quest for territorial expansion, a sphere of interest, and warm seaports. The subversion of Poland, Czechoslovakia, Hungary, Yugoslavia, Rumania, Albania, Bulgaria, and Greece, as well as the taking over of East Asian territories and Northern Iran, were the goals, most of which were realized during the Stalin era.

Since the Communists insist on Lenin's definition of imperialism, they cannot concede that their post-World War II conquests and aggressions, or for that matter their long-range strategy of further worldwide revolution, are in any fashion comparable to the imperialistic drive of the tsars for territorial aggrandizement. Under Stalin as well as under Khrushchev and his successors, they have continued to woo the developing nations with foreign aid and military assistance, to foment rebellion against native and colonial governments, and to train and equip natives as professional revolutionaries. At the same time, however, the Communists have insisted that uprisings instigated or supported by them, with the hope of taking over, are "wars of national liberation" no different from a bona fide struggle for colonial independence such as that of the United States to win independence from the British Empire. The implication of the phrase "war of national liberation" is that these are *revolutions by circumstances*, which is supposed to induce the West to keep hands off, rather than *revolutions by plot*, even though Communist-trained plotters may be right in the thick of them.

RED CHINA AND POLYCENTRISM

Despite its aggressive talk of world revolution and its support by a gaggle of tiny Communist movements in other countries, Soviet Communism was hardly a threat to the world in the 1920s. The era of the Great Depression in the West and the subsequent assault of Nazi Germany and its allies on the peace of the world at first obscured the effect of the enormous changes that had been wrought in a single generation under Stalin. In spite of the setback suffered in World War II, the Soviet Union at the time of Stalin's death (1953) had emerged as one of the two military superpowers of the world and as an industrial giant almost as advanced as its Western rivals. The Depression and the war years had also helped to strengthen Communist movements abroad considerably, especially in countries under the Nazi occupation after the Nazi-Soviet Pact broke down in 1941, such as France, Eastern Europe, and even Italy.

Communism in Eastern Europe

With the collapse of Nazi power in Eastern Europe, a unique opportunity presented itself for a Communist take-over under the protection of Soviet military power. The Soviet Union, prior to the Nazi collapse, had been able to annex Latvia, Estonia, and Lithuania as well as East Poland and parts of Finland with the help of the Nazi-Soviet Pact of 1939–1941. After 1945, with the Red Army victorious, the Soviets were in a position to dictate the terms of the reestablishment of native governments in the other Eastern European countries. They insisted on "friendly" coalition governments, including both Communists and democratic parties, such as were common throughout postwar Europe and quite acceptable to such democratic statesmen as Masaryk of Czechoslovakia, Tildy of Hungary, and Petkov of Bulgaria. The coalition governments bore names such as National Liberation Front (Yugoslavia, Albania), Fatherland Front (Bulgaria), and Government of National Unity (Poland). But the Communists also insisted on placing their men in key Cabinet positions, such as the Ministry of the Interior—which controls the police—and the Ministries of Defense, Justice, Communications, and Education, in what in retrospect appears to have been a deliberate preparation for their seizure of power. By 1947 the Communists' coups had overwhelmed Albania, Yugoslavia, Bulgaria, Rumania, Hungary, and Poland and were stopped in Greece only by armed might and American assistance. The Communist take-over of Czechoslovakia in 1948 by coup d'état finally opened Western eyes. Typically, Communist coups would begin with the arrest of rival political leaders and the seizure of radio and railroad stations, followed by the use of police and army, and the threat of Red Army intervention, to prevent popular uprisings. East Germany was under Russian occupation from the end of World War II, and, in contravention of Four Power agreements, was transformed into a Communist satellite.

People's democracies   Once in power, the Communists proceeded to introduce their system. They promoted land reform by breaking up the large feudal estates and, in some cases, introduced agricultural collectivization. They started Five-Year Plans of industrialization.[7] Most important, they established the so-called *people's democracies* in the satellites, which feature constitutions without benefit of enforcement, multiparty façades to hide Communist dictatorship, elections without a choice, and representative assemblies composed of

---

[7] In Poland it is a Six-Year Plan.

delegates handpicked by the governments. As in the Soviet Union, all organizations are Communist-controlled, and business, labor, agriculture, and youth are forced into compulsory organizations of government or party, which can control and regiment the society.

The Communist empire But the term *people's democracy* in the subtlety of Communist ideology has also denoted inequality in relation to Soviet Communism, a mere "transitional phase" requiring "guidance" from the "Socialist motherland." Hence nationalism was ruthlessly suppressed among these once so autonomy-conscious Eastern European nationalities, and Communist policy has sought carefully to isolate them economically and culturally from the West to which they had formerly been bound by many ties. The appeals of panslavism and allegations of "capitalist encirclement" and conspiracies of capitalist and foreign agents were included in the propaganda line designed to attract the Eastern Europeans to Russia. Brutal coercion also beat down any resistance to Communism as such, most notably the resistance by the churches. Russian advisers and administrators in considerable numbers, moreover, were placed in the state administrations, on the economic planning staff, and in the Communist parties of each satellite.[8] The Communist Information Bureau (Cominform), the successor to Comintern, subordinated the satellite Communist parties to Russian leadership, while the Council of Mutual Economic Assistance (Comecon), the Communist equivalent of the European Common Market, made sure that the Soviet Union profited from the relationship between itself and its satellites. The stationing of Soviet troops in the the satellites completed what was, even by the judgment of Marxism-Leninism, Stalin's colonial empire.

The beginning of "Goulash Communism" Lenin had predicted the doom of the capitalist colonial empires by pointing to colonies as "the weakest link in the chain of capitalism." Stalin's empire may have lacked a Lenin to theorize about what "the weakest link in the chain of Communist imperialism" might be, but there appeared to be a number of internal contradictions at work. At a very early stage of the Communist take-over in Eastern Europe, Stalin proved unable to prevent Marshall Tito of Yugoslavia from following his own concept of a nationally autonomous Communism or from accepting Western aid. Stalin's death and his subsequent debunking by his successors shook his Communist empire to its very founda-

---

[8] In tiny Albania alone, some five thousand Russians at one time constituted a privileged class no different from colonial adminstrators in the former colonial empires.

tions. Communist parties outside the Iron Curtain faced mass resignations and angrily turned against what they once considered the source of all wisdom. In the satellites, young Communist intellectuals overthrew many of Stalin's personal puppets and began to challenge the wisdom of aping every policy of the Moscow party. In the Soviet Union itself, the oppressive nature of Stalin's reign had evidently nurtured vast resentments, from the military brass down to the last concentration camp inmate, which erupted all at once with his demise. Muzzled writers began to speak out, economic and legal reforms were demanded and obtained, and a series of amnesties freed nonpolitical prisoners. Most significant, the long-denied demand for consumer goods was heeded, demonstrating that Soviet society in the 1950s had indeed come a long way from the state of pre-revolutionary Russia. The demand for a more adequate food supply also uncovered the long-standing inadequacy of Soviet agriculture and led to many attempts at improving and expanding agricultural production rather than concentrating on heavy industry. This was the beginning of "goulash Communism," which soon began to spread to the Eastern European satellites as well. As the Polish uprisings of 1970 show, however, the goulash is still neither cheap nor plentiful.

Peaceful coexistence The successors of Stalin almost immediately proclaimed a foreign policy détente toward both the Western powers and Tito and his emulators elsewhere within the Communist camp. To the West they admitted the possibility of *peaceful coexistence* between Communism and capitalism. This did not imply the abandoning of the long-range goal of world revolution, which is fundamental to the Communist faith, nor even an abjuring of violence, revolution, and war to attain this goal in the end. As Nikita Khrushchev pointed out, and his successors have repeated, peaceful coexistence may even include worldwide disarmament but not the disarming of the Communist fifth columns and revolutionaries plotting the overthrow of governments "in the name of the people" in the developing countries. It did mean, however, that the Soviet Union was no longer a have-not nation ready to risk everything in warlike gambles for revolutionary gain. Soviet leaders now preferred competition in the economic field and in the conquest of outer space. Khrushchev's boast about the Soviet hopes of overtaking the United States economically in another decade accentuated his evident belief that such a triumph would be considered the equivalent, in Communist ideology, of military victory. The declining growth rate of the Soviet economy and the failure to overcome the inadequacies of Soviet agriculture have hardly changed the determination of Soviet leaders to succeed without a suicidal all-out military clash with the West.

The birth of polycentrism   The new attitude of Stalin's heirs toward Titoism culminated in the admission that there could be "more than one road to socialism." This was a major turning point in the history of a movement that had once prided itself on being a monolithic movement based on the monopoly of the Moscow leadership in the one and only way to salvation. And even though the Poznan riots in Poland and the Hungarian Revolution in the wake of the de-Stalinization campaign of 1956 showed the dangers of such a course, and ended with brutal military repression, there was no stopping the development now. *Polycentrism* was born. Every Communist party, whether in Italy, Yugoslavia, or Poland, could use its own judgment as to what policies were best adapted to its particular national habitat. To maintain Communist solidarity, Communist orthodoxy and conformity had to be sacrificed. If Communist Poland preferred to keep hands off the Catholic Church and the individual way of farming, if Tito wanted to experiment with more capitalistic incentives, or if unorthodox Communist mayors in Italian towns wished to promote the economic interests of small businessmen, they had the right to do so.

Nevertheless, polycentrism has had its ups and downs. The most notable relapse into Stalinist patterns was the invasion of Czechoslovakia in 1968 by Warsaw Pact forces led by the Soviet Union. While the exact sequence of cause and effect is still only a matter of surmise, the antecedents of the 1968 crisis are fairly clear. There had been years of attempts at economic liberalization in defiance of Marxist and Communist orthodoxy in several of the satellite countries and, timidly, even in the Soviet Union. In spring of 1968, moreover, the Dubcek government of Czechoslovakia lowered the political controls on free expression as well at a time when the West German government was engaged in an all-out diplomatic offensive to establish friendly ties to various Eastern European countries. The suspicious Soviets evidently considered the reforms of Prague alarming and responded with force. The counterreforms and purges carried out by the new Soviet puppet regime in Czechoslovakia appear to demonstrate that it was indeed the political liberation that the Soviets disliked the most. In the meantime, the Czechoslovak experience has also served as a rude reminder to other satellite countries such as Roumania that there are definite limits to Soviet toleration of autonomous policies.

Chinese Communism

The greatest challenge to the monolithic nature of Communism to date has come from Red China. The coming to power of Communism in the venerable four thousand-year-old culture, the mighty "middle kingdom," which had fallen under shameful Western domination for most of the last hundred years, could have been the greatest triumph of Soviet Communism, an enormous bridgehead in the developing world of nonwhite peoples. Instead it became a festering sore in the side of the Soviet colossus, and possibly a presage of a Communist future not under Russian Communist domination. All of a sudden Moscow had begun to find itself classed vituperatively with the "reactionary imperialists" of the West and considered, at best, a rearguard, not the "vanguard," of the proletarian revolution.

The Chinese background Chinese Communism is in many ways reminiscent of Russia's terrible years, except that everything seems to be carried to such extremes as to make even Stalin appear a moderate. There are few parallels in the history of the two nations. China was shaped by a succession of dynasties and alternated between extremes of anarchy—or the regional rule of war lords—and a highly centralized, bureaucratic government. The tension between these two elements is sometimes considered a possible precedent for the enormous present effort to transform Chinese society. At the height of the venerable culture nurtured by Confucianism, China was distinguished by a brilliant and inventive ruling class that sought to build a utopian great commonwealth of the world ruled by rational ethics. Some observers see in this a precedent for the rule of the Communist party today, which also inculcates party members and private citizens with a deep faith in the rationality and righteousness of the Communist way of life. Another major motive impelling the Chinese today is hatred of the "foreign devils" who preyed on the carcass of the Chinese Empire and sold opium to the people for nearly a century before Chiang Kai-shek established his rule in the 1920s. The "foreign devils" included the Russians, who took away Chinese territory and helped to put down the xenophobic Boxer Rebellion of 1900. Another important historical motive is the pride of a great culture and glorious empire held down by Western "barbarians." Korea, Tibet, and parts of India and South East Asia at one time had been part of the Chinese Empire. Hence the Chinese view them, as the Russians have viewed East Poland and Finland, as really belonging to them.

Rise of the Chinese communists There were Chinese Communists before the Russian Revolution, including Mao Tse-tung himself. With the help of the Comintern they organized the party in 1921 and then joined Chiang's Kuomintang in the hope of seizing power from within his Nationalist movement. When this failed, they withdrew from the urban strongholds of the Nationalists and concentrated instead on remote rural areas and on *agrarian reform* rather than on industrialization.

Having defeated Chiang militarily on the mainland in 1949, the Chinese Communists quickly took over the reins with a United Front government that included other parties, various occupational groups, and national minorities. They proceeded to act according to Mao's pamphlet *On the People's Democratic Dictatorship,* which suggests how the cooperation of some social classes, including the "national bourgeoisie," is to be used for the step-by-step liquidation of the old elites. The next step was to restore the economy and insure the food supply by an "agrarian reform" which included the public execution of 2 million landlords and other persons obnoxious to the regime. After further bloodbaths of "counterrevolutionaries" and "corrupt bureaucrats," the Communists instituted their first Five-Year Plan in 1953. Under this plan, the entire economic structure was re-vamped, almost all private enterprise was nationalized, and the vast pool of Chinese manpower was fully regimented into the great effort to telescope Russia's terrible years into a shorter period. By 1956, moreover, most Chinese farmers had been brought into cooperative farms.

Up to this time, the Chinese Communists had relied on skimpy Soviet aid and technical assistance and succeeded in getting along with both Stalin and Khrushchev. The de-Stalinization campaign of 1956 was viewed with some caution in Peking, although Mao himself was willing to introduce some measures of liberalization. He even invited what he called constructive criticism of his government with his famous "Let a hundred flowers bloom" speech. To the dismay of the party leadership, there ensued student demonstrations and vociferous denunciations of the Communist dictatorship. The party then lashed out angrily against the "rightists" and cowed its critics with thinly veiled threats.

Communes The launching of Sputnik by the Russians and its impression on the rest of the world in 1957 seems to have encouraged the Chinese Communists to become far more aggressive and optimistic about the prospects of world revolution. They persuaded the Soviet Union to help China in the development of nuclear weapons. They began quietly to abandon the peaceful coexistence policy, which they had accepted earlier. At the same time, they began to speak of the "Great Leap Forward" in industry and agriculture. One of the prominent features of this new industrialization drive was the processing of scrap iron in hundreds of thousands of do-it-yourself,

hand-operated backyard steel furnaces. Though their practical significance was somewhat doubtful, this exercise in regimented mass
enthusiasm was impressive. Even more momentous, however, was
the transfer of 550 million Chinese peasants to balanced agricultural-
industrial communes of about 5000 to 6000 families each. This was
the utmost in antlike regimentation for labor, militia training, and
constant indoctrination. Men, women, and even older children were
put in harness to do heavy labor in place of scarce machinery, mostly
in 10- to 12-hour days, and with almost no holidays or leisure time.
Their dormitories were segregated by sex, even including married
couples, and the old people were put in charge of nurseries and
mess halls. The replacement of family life by stepped-up engagement
in socially useful activity and indoctrination was touted as the
advent of "pure Communism" in contrast to the Russian version,
which has always been regarded as merely "socialism, a transitional
phase on the way to Communism" by the Soviets themselves.

As a revolutionary device to transform society, the communes
complemented the long-standing drive to change the traditional relationships of Chinese society with respect to family ties, ancestor
worship, and relation of the sexes. Up to that time mass indoctrination with respect to an attitude of "struggle"—a dialectic pose—
against the old traditions, ancient customs, the old elites, and "Anglo-
American imperialism" had carried the chief burden of mobilizing
the masses for utopia. Personal mobilization beyond the party itself
had been limited to the raising of "volunteers" and neighborhood
brigades for campaigns against rats, mice, flies, and uncleanliness.
But now the mass mobilization was complete, and the old Chinese
individualism was turned into an antlike collectivism both in labor
and in hatred for the foreign powers. Chinese reverence for education
was transferred to work and productive achievement, and Chinese
pragmatism into a utopian, self-sacrificing attitude. Except for occasional unrest and disaffection, the engagement of individuals in
this grand effort of national, Communist self-liberation was deep
and genuine. The average commune dweller really believed that by
his personal engagement and sacrifice, the nation would come a
step closer to salvation, economic and political.

The Sino-Soviet dispute The Russian Communists responded with
deep annoyance to the Chinese claims of a "purer Communism" and
with alarm to the idea of translating the scientific achievements of
Sputnik into political or military aggression. The Chinese reacted
to Soviet reluctance with acid criticisms of "revisionism," or lack of
revolutionary determination, using Tito as a whipping boy for
Khrushchev. In a curious application of the dialectical approach to

statistics, the Chinese Communists also began to set fantastic goals for production and to publish vastly exaggerated preliminary production results in an apparent effort to use the power of positive thinking for the purposes of the Great Leap Forward. Abroad, Russian and Chinese efforts at subverting new nations began to clash openly. There had been squabbles over the Sino-Soviet borders for several years when fighting broke out in earnest at the Ussuri River in the late 1960s. There were repeated skirmishes and casualties and a wave of war hysteria in Moscow and Peking. Although the violence subsided after a while and China has followed a cautious course in foreign policy in spite of her verbal aggressiveness, the conflict is still smoldering under the surface. The Soviet Union and China, moreover, continually accuse each other of secret or overt collusion with "the American imperialists." Even token gestures of Chinese hospitality toward an American ping-pong team and a lowering of American trade barriers toward Peking raise Soviet anxieties by perceptible degrees.

Even though the Great Leap Forward meanwhile turned out to be a failure, due to a succession of natural catastrophes, there is no doubt that ultimately China will rise to the status of a superpower of, perhaps, a billion or more citizens. As the Chinese like to joke, a war between Russia and China might take the following course: "At the first battle, the Chinese would let the Russians take 100 million Chinese as prisoners of war, which would burden Russian facilities to the breaking point. At the second battle another 100 million Chinese prisoners. By the time of the third battle, the Russians would be ready to surrender." The Chinese have been working on nuclear weapons and even launched a satellite, even though Khrushchev withdrew the last Soviet technicians from Red China as long ago as 1960.

As if the country had unlimited energy to waste, China also had to overcome in the late 1960s the staggering upheaval of the great proletarian cultural revolution. Triggered by an internal power struggle between the aging Mao Tse-Tung and the entrenched party elite, the cultural revolution turned into a prolonged clash between the mobilized masses of Chinese youth, the first generation to grow up under Communism, and not only the party hacks but all the remainders of Chinese bourgeois and intellectual pride. Mao and his young cohorts eventually won the power struggle, but the disorders and disruptions were so great that some observers expected centralized control to lapse once more into the regional fiefs familiar from the days of the warlords. Instead, the People's Liberation Army stepped in, sent the youths back to work or school, and assumed quasi-dictatorial powers with Chairman Mao. Somehow, the country pulled itself together and emerged stronger than ever from its political disorders, just as confidently as it had overcome the disastrous economic aftermath of the Great Leap Forward in the early 1960s.

The communes of Red China were first drastically modified, then dissolved into their components, the production teams. Unpopular features such as mess halls, restrictions on married couples, and outlawing the small private backyard plots of peasants were abandoned. Some 20 million people were shifted back from industry to countryside, and some investment diverted to agriculture. Voluminous grain imports from Australia and Canada helped Red China over the worst effects of overreaching itself and of the bad harvests. Eventually, the Chinese may come back to the self-sufficient communes, which even Khrushchev acknowledged, by implication, as the ultimate goal of Communism when he told the Twenty-First Congress of the Soviet party that "a society cannot leap into Communism from capitalism without passing through the socialist stage of development."

Some people may wonder whether China, or for that matter, Russia, ever went through a capitalistic stage. This is purely a matter of semantics, while Communist polycentrism continues to divide the movement. Red China and the Soviet Union are continually at each other's throats, with cries of "left deviationism," "dogmatism," "revisionism," or of what is the true meaning of Leninism. The Chinese newspaper *Red Star* evidently wanted to clue in its readers on the terminology of the tensions of polycentrism when it once wrote:

All Communists must work hard to raise their ability to distinguish Marxism-Leninism from revisionism, to distinguish the way of opposing dogmatism with Marxism-Leninism from that of opposing Marxism-Leninism with revisionism under the cover of opposing dogmatism, and to distinguish the way of opposing sectarianism with proletarian internationalism from that of opposing proletarian internationalism with great-nation chauvinism and narrow nationalism under the cover of opposing sectarianism.

It is small wonder Communists have always preferred to give their professional revolutionaries a thorough ideological training, considering how difficult it must be to keep the revolutionary signals straight.

Marxism aside, however, there is little reason why such a large and gifted nation should have to follow the path to modernization of any other nation. The days are over when the winds of change were blowing only from the West. The Chinese nation has "stood up" and can well afford to stand on its own feet while the propaganda loudspeakers and wall newspapers, and even China's orbiting satellite, exclaim proudly that "the East Wind is Red. "

THE APPEALS OF COMMUNISM

An interest in the understanding of and the need for eventual containment of Communism is bound sooner or later to raise the question of why Communism seems to appeal to so many people. To be sure, not all of the billion or more people living under Communism today have chosen it voluntarily, and many of them would probably vote against Communist dictatorship if they were ever given the chance. Still, there are and have always been millions who have voluntarily joined Communist parties or collaborated with them in many ways. Why do they do it?

Potential recruits to Communism are motivated by different reasons under widely differing circumstances and at different times. There are several distinct social habitats or states of mind that may move some people toward Communism. Some depend on the position of the Communist movement in the society. Others grow out of the temporary strains of industrialization or cultural modernization. Still others may be largely psychological, in accordance with the self-selecting recruitment process of extremist movements.

Different settings, different appeals

An example of the first category is a country firmly under Communist control for a generation or more. A young Russian Communist, for example, is hardly a misfit in his society today. He is rather an ambitious social climber who aspires to membership and high rank in the Communist party much as a young American might aspire to the senior class presidency of his high school or to the top salesmanship award of his company. The time-consuming probationary period which the Russian party imposes on a young Russian before he may become a full-fledged member is designed to weed out the oddball, the unstable, and the superficial, who may appear in great numbers in Western Communist parties.

A young Communist in an Eastern European satellite country, where Communism is often viewed as an alien importation or Russian imposition, by contrast, may well be an opportunist or at least a member of small political, social, or ethnic minority impelled by long-standing grievances against his society to want to wield power over it. This "minority point of view" has many adherents among citizens of societies in the throes of industrialization, although Communism has never been the only ideology offered to this "proletariat."

The Old Bolsheviks of prerevolutionary Russia (in fact, the underground of any oppressive dictatorship, whether it be Fascist, Communist, a traditional autocracy of the more brutal type, or a repressive colonial rule) were practically born into a situation smoldering with hatred and violence between government and revolutionaries. They may have steeped themselves in flights of utopian fancy, philosophical radicalism, and dreams of well-plotted revolution as a result of their situation, but their main motive, the hatred of and desire to overthrow the government, was there to begin with, affecting even the gentlest and meekest soul among them. The repressive government gave them the motive of its own accord by creating the situation.

What about the appeals of Communism or kindred movements in countries that have a democratic government, with procedures that offer a hearing and a chance to get a representative of almost any point of view elected, such as the United Staes? There is a difference between individuals who for personal reasons (for example, longing for a cause) make themselves the firebrand spokesman for an aggrieved group, of whatever description, and members of that group who become extremists in defense of their own group interest; especially as long as social tension, labor unrest, or ethnic discrimination is present. Once these tensons have been resolved, self-recruitment for Communism or similar revolutionary groups becomes an intensely personal matter. Government repression or police brutality against such groups and others, for example, may draw onlookers into extremism—in other words, through a compulsion to protect the underdog. Direct action for a worthy cause may become a way of life, an addiction in which one can indulge permanently only within such a movement.

Communist and similar extremist movements in the various non-Communist countries are very skillful in recruiting new converts by certain techniques of agitation and mobilization. One technique popular with Communists is the infiltration of non-Communist organizations whose goals can be bent to the purposes of the party. Thus, labor unions can be turned into anticapitalistic Communist *front organizations,* peace groups can be made to advocate only peace settlements that favor the Communist side, and underdog associations can be used as a battering ram against the majority establishment. The front organization technique has the advantage that a handful of skillful infiltrators in the right offices can manipulate vast numbers of well-intentioned, seemingly moderate people who are not really in agreement with the extremist group in question. A second technique of recruitment is the manufacture and exploitation of a cause celèbre such as a martyr or a case of patent injustice to a person. The emotions of large numbers of people are deliberately fanned in the hope of attracting converts and to maintain the dynamism of the movement for those already in it. A good campaign over such a cause creates in many potential recruits the outraged feelings and alienation from "the system" that help them to identify with the extremist party.

The same outraged state of mind is the object of psychological observations about why people join extremist movements such as the Communists. Sometimes it is a state of mind unfolding from earlier involvement in libertarian crusades, such as civil rights movements, pacifistic campaigns, or student rebellions which may leave a person hungry for encores. Sometimes, the great longing for a cause stems from a basic personality cast. Great inner tensions, caused by adolscence or certain personality disorders, may be taken out in political extremism and in rebellion against authority in any form, a pattern familiar to us from the background of the assassin of the late President Kennedy. The typical Communist, Castroite, or Trotskyite in the United States, and his equivalent in similar settings elsewhere, also derives his belligerence and militancy from a feeling of deep alienation from the society around him. Quite naturally he is inclined to seek the causes of his personal unhappiness in the society rather than in himself.

Appeals related to modernization

The second category, appeals related to modernization, is perhaps the most obvious, owing to the emphasis of Marx, Lenin, and Stalin on industrialism and the proletariat. Upon closer examination, however, it has been noted that no Communist movement ever came to power in a highly industrialized country and that, in fact, the workers of advanced industrialism are far more partial to trade unions, Democratic Socialism, and other moderate means of bettering their life within the existing society than they are to the Communist promises of revolution and utopia. Neither is it true, as is so often popularly stated, that poverty or a very low living standard, such as prevails in most of the developing countries, automatically breeds Communism. Nor is Communism simply a result of the economic differential per se, which, for example, separates the landed oligarchy of Latin America from the peons, or the "rich nations" from the "poor nations." One of the most perplexing aspects of contemporary Italian politics, to mention an example, has been the increasing Communist vote simultaneous with an unprecedented rise in living standards and employment.

The explanation appears to lie not so much in the economic facts as in how the facts are regarded by the poor peasants, villagers, or proletarians. The peasants of traditional society have lived in the same grinding poverty for thousands of years without crying for professional revolutionaries or the overthrow of the government. In fact, they simply developed a fatalistic way of looking at things. If now they are beginning to question the necessity of such poverty and are searching for ways of changing it, politically or otherwise, this only means that they have already embarked on the great journey to modernization. As *transitionals,* then, they may indeed show all kinds of weaknesses for Communism, whose chiliastic millenarianism they may find emotionally satisfying or whose militant, authoritarian group life may assuage in them the wounds of being uprooted from their traditional existence. It is not only a matter of poverty or riches.

Ethnic tensions may also enter at this stage. The building of self-governing new nations often puts a minority on the spot. This is true, for example, of the well-to-do Chinese minorities of South East Asian countries, who find themselves threatened by the new native governments dominated by other ethnic elements that were once poor villagers while the Chinese merchants prospered. Now many of the Chinese have joined Communist cells in order to seek the support of Red China against ethnic discrimination and persecution. Along similar lines, the Chinese Communists have taken to blatant racist appeals in their campaign to carry Communist revolution into the developing countries of the world. Marx and Lenin might be very much surprised to see their doctrines wrapped in racism, yet there is no denying the effectiveness of this crusade against white colonialism and against the Russians as well.

So effective has been the Chinese appeal to the potential recruits of Communism in the developing areas, in fact, that the Communist beachheads in Latin America and Africa, Cuba and Congo-Brazzaville lean toward China rather than Russia. Eleven Asian Communist parties, including the large one of Indonesia, are definitely pro-Peking. Another 24 pro-Peking groups exist in other countries, including India, North Vietnam, Lebanon, Guatemala, and Peru, and more are established every year. As of 1966, the Russian Communists still had the support of over 70 of the 105 Communist parties of the world, although the Chinese with 17 million and the Indonesians with 3 million Communist party members alone make up close to half of the combined world total of 44 million party members. The Moscow-oriented parties have faced pro-Peking splits in the party leadership in Brazil, Ecuador, Colombia, Chile, and Mexico, not to mention the neutral position taken by the Rumanian, Polish, Italian, Cuban, British, Swedish, Norwegian, and Austrian Communists.

The greater appeal of the Chinese brand of revolutionary Communism to the developing nations also mirrors the similarity of their stages of development. The Soviet Union can show them only what the end result of a determined drive toward industrial development may look like. This is no doubt impressive, but also cause for some suspicion. The Chinese, on the other hand, are more nearly on the same level. Africans, Asians, and Latin Americans can feel more directly the inspiration of the enormous effort of mobilizing the Chinese masses to boost themselves into the twentieth century—an effort they can see in progress—than they can with respect to the Russian effort of forty-five years ago. And they feel the same bewilderment, and perhaps envy, as did Mao in 1956, at the Russian change in attitude toward a liberalized, consumer-oriented economy, which now even resorts to market research and opinion polls in order to ascertain what the consumer wants. Economic man must crawl before he learns to walk, and it requires a fierce determination for him to try to get up on his hind legs if he is to do it within one generation. While the newer Communists may admire the pirouettes of the Russian economy, both the Chinese Communists and those of other developing areas feel that this is their time for fierceness, for the big push regardless of human cost.

Arrested economic development

As for the appeals of Communism to the workers of half-industrialized countries, again there is no necessary correlation between the attractiveness of Communism and poverty, or of democracy and industrialization. Rather, the appeal of Communism hinges upon the special circumstances and crises of industrialization. The coming of capitalism always has a way of destroying the livelihood of masses of people of precapitalistic society without immediately or necessarily giving them new jobs. Communism appears as the result of very rapid waves of industrialization and movement to urban slums, or of arrested industrialization which has bogged down in economic stagnation after having raised all kinds of expectations. This may also explain the rising Communist vote in Italy, as hundreds of thousands of people migrate from the abjectly poor *mezzogiorno* to the north where the jobs are.

In Italy and France, and in the long run in Spain as well, economic stagnation and arrested technological development create intense feelings of frustration and of being held back. The feelings are aggravated by the belief among workers in the small, patriarchal businesses that they are being exploited and not paid as much as are workers elsewhere, while their employers prosper from their efforts. Even at that, Communism might not be attractive on the basis of economic considerations alone, if it were not for the other circumstances of French and Italian life. One is the rigid social class distinctions between workers and the bourgeoisie of businessmen, entrepreneurs, and the professions, and the amount of secretiveness of the upper classes, which make Marxist stereotypes of class struggle and capitalist conspiracy plausible. Another is the deep current of anticlericalism of Latin society, which in each town or village tends to pit a Communist mayor or teacher Peppone against a priest Don Camillo, as in the anecdotes of Giovanni Guareschi. This gives Communism an undeserved status and an idealistic-philosophical appeal as a kind of antichurch religion of social progress, for lack of better alternatives. The ineffectiveness, if not downright corruption, of government and of democratic process is the final straw that breaks the camel's back.

Psychological appeals

As for the psychological aspects, Communism from the days of Karl Marx has held a strong romantic appeal to individuals who want to identify themselves with the social outcast and the underdog. The life of the late Che Guevara is a good example. The speculative, Messianic character of the philosophy has always especially attracted minds of an artistic or scientific bent. Here was social science fiction of the most futuristic kind in action. The "inexorable march of history" toward Communism offered to individuals a heroic role in the making of history. The fear of capitalist conspiracy and, even more, the thrill of engaging in clandestine cloak-and-dagger counterconspiracy with a small number of comrades also have romantic overtones that relieve the feeling of alienation from society discussed earlier.

Finally, one must remember the self-perpetuating character of an extremist movement. A well-established, large Communist party outside the Iron Curtain feeds on the masses of the disaffected and disillusioned. But it does not depend on the passing discontents of the masses alone. It can manufacture new discontents by playing up incidents and new grievances by agitation and propaganda. It can also create a fairly stable, self-renewing subculture of Communist protest, which enlists and keeps whole families, villages, and regions in the Communist fold in central Italy and certain parts of Finland and France. Once the pattern is established, it requires major changes to dislodge it. As the causes of Communism in such a setting are not purely economic, a rise in the standard of living by itself will not make appreciable inroads into the popular following of the Communists. What is required are basic social changes, and political alternatives other than the sterile confrontation of Communism and reaction.

CHAPTER 14 FASCISM AND NATIONAL SOCIALISM

It is difficult for a student of contemporary politics to imagine the rosy cloud of democratic optimism which inspired Western leaders at the time President Wilson set out on his World War I "crusade to make the world safe for democracy." Nothing could stop the advance of democracy now that the thrones of the German kaiser, the Russian tsar, and the Hapsburg and Ottoman empires were falling, not to mention countless smaller potentates. And the peace-makers of Versailles and of the League of Nations confidently proceeded to grant national self-determination to almost all the East European and Balkan nationalities who had long languished under the Austrian, German, Ottoman, and Russian empires, in the hope that these "new nations of yesterday" would become stalwart constitutional democracies. Instead, country upon country in Europe fell under a dictatorship: Russia, Italy, Portugal, all the new East European and Balkan countries except Czechoslovakia, and finally, Germany, Spain, and Austria. Only Western and Northern Europe remained free, and even there, native Fascist and Communist movements tried to replace democratic government with totalitarian dictatorship. By the mid-thirties an atmosphere of gloom had settled over the bright hopes of democracy in Europe.

The gloomy outlook was all the more justified, as the new dictatorships for the most part turned out to be brutal relapses into traditional autocracy, with strong-armed enforcement against resistance or opposition of any kind. In some of the new dictatorships, moreover, a new kind of totalitarian movement was at work which challenged most of the fundamental traditions and values of the West: Fascism, as it came to be called, after the Italian model.

What is Fascism? How did it originate and come to power? How does it fit into the development of modern nations? The definition of Fascism is exceedingly vague, and there is great uncertainty as to which systems of which countries should be included and which left out. The temptation has always been great to misuse the term in polemical intention for all kinds of obnoxious right-wing groups. In the United States today, in particular, the term is often applied to police or governmental repression of left-wing revolutionaries by observers who forget that all the historical Fascist regimes started out as revolutionary mass movements fighting against an establishment. Any reasonable definition of Fascism has to go beyond what Fascists do after they are in power and include what they were like when they were still demonstrating and fighting in the streets (and themselves complaining about police repression). The definition of Marxists, that Fascism is a militant defense of capitalism, a kind of fighting back of the bourgeoisie against the rising proletariat, is a faulty sociological analysis. The safest course may be to attempt a historical reconstruction of the rise of the two best-known Fascist systems, Mussolini's Italy and Hitler's Germany, before we attempt to fashion a definition, and to look at other countries as well.

THE RISE OF ITALIAN FASCISM

Unfinished nationhood

Even though the differences between Italian Fascism and German National Socialism are substantial both in theory and in practice, their circumstances and motives of origin bear many parallels. The similarity begins with the national settings; both Italy and Germany were latecomers to national unification. Neither country was unified until the late 1860s, and perhaps never as completely as, say, France or Great Britain. Substantial outside areas inhabited by ethnic minorities and even majorities of Italians or Germans, furthermore, were claimed by nationalists in both cases. Both felt held back by their geographical position and the conspiracy of other powers, especially of Great Britain, from attaining the status of world powers. The societies of both were still very much in transition between the tenacious holding on to power by a reactionary aristocracy and emerging bourgeois middle-class control. At the same time, and to the great shock of the bourgeoisie, the working classes in the form of strong Socialist parties and trade unions were already knocking at the doors of power. Both countries also felt a deep pride in their past cultural achievements and a bitterness that despite this cultural distinction, presumably less cultured nations seemed to wield the power in the world.

A sense of betrayal

Beyond this, many Italians felt a sharp sense of having been cheated out of their share of the spoils of victory as participants in World War I—a sense that their sacrifices and deprivations had been in vain. They had joined the Allied side late, relying on promises of territorial gains from the presumable collapse of the Austrian and Ottoman empires, parts of which contained Italian minority areas. At the end of the war, however, the intervention of the United States, which had not been a party to the earlier agreements and would not countenance any territorial aggrandizement without benefit of national self-determination, cost Italy a part of the expected spoils of her war effort. Then too, the war had been a deeply unsettling experience for large masses of Italians, most of all for the war veterans, who upon their return had had great difficulty finding employment and a suitable place in a society racked by economic dislocations and social upheaval.

Benito Mussolini, revolutionary Socialist

Mussolini's early background Benito Mussolini (1883–1945), the son of a blacksmith with a passion for left-wing causes, became a revolutionary Socialist at an early age and the editor of the Socialist newspaper *Avanti* by the time he was 29. He had enjoyed a superior education thanks to the efforts of his mother, a schoolteacher. But his pugnacious character and domineering personality were not content with a leading role among the extreme left wing of the Italian Socialists. Advocating Italy's entry into the war in 1914 led to his expulsion from the party and brought him into the immediate political neighborhood of the nationalist agitators, the king, and the army, which he had always attacked before.[1] He never lost his

---

[1] His advocating war when Italy was still neutral should be contrasted with his militant pacifism two years earlier when he had attacked the moderate Socialist leaders for supporting the Tripolitan campaign.

early and strong dislike for parliamentary democracy, church and religion, nationalism, the monarchy, and the army, though he later found it convenient to get along with each of them for a while. The dream of the "general strike" of the revolutionary Syndicalists and the "dictatorship of the proletariat" of Marx and Lenin were dear to him, as they were hated by the moderate Socialists. He also had been deeply involved in the left-wing insurrection of "Red Week" earlier in 1914, when syndicalists, anarchists, Socialists, and trade unions called for a general strike and temporarily seized power in small towns of central and northern Italy.

Left-wing and right-wing appeals   The end of the war found Mussolini and his new nationalist friends riding the wave of national indignation over the lost spoils of victory. "Fiume or death," was the popular battle cry. At the same time he shared the sentiment of the war-scarred generation of veterans that no one who had not been out on the battle front himself should hold power in Italy. And as a third appeal to the masses, he continued to harangue the rising millions of unemployed—2 million by 1919—and other victims of economic crisis and dislocation in the language of revolutionary Socialism, telling them that the Socialist party had betrayed them and that he alone could really help them. Thus he simultaneously courted favor with the right wing and with the masses of what promised to be a major landslide to the left. His right-wing course brought him ample financial support from business, industry, and the landowners, all of whom feared Socialist and anarchist uprisings. His left-wing appeal appeared in such platform promises as equal suffrage for men and women, the popular referendum and iniative, the abolition of monarchy and of all aristocratic titles, dissolution of business corporations and confiscation of "unproductive income," an eight-hour working day, the sharing of workers in profit and management of enterprises, an end to conscription, and universal disarmament.

Founding the blackshirts   As postwar political turbulence came to a boil, Mussolini went all out in support of the seizure of Fiume by the nationalist poet D'Annunzio, adding at the same time such left-wing bait as the transfer of power to workers councils (*soviets*), a minimum wage, more social security, the socialization of the munitions industry, and the sequestration of church properties. At first his opportunism gained him very little support at the polls; the Socialist party and the new Catholic Populists reaped the benefit of the swing to the left. Not to be outdone, Mussolini threw his support behind the great sitdown strikes of 1920, the "Red seizure of the factories," which collapsed after a few weeks, as Red Week had done six years earlier. While the Socialists regrouped their forces and a new Communist party split off and affiliated with the Comintern, Mussolini once more executed an abrupt about-face and intercepted with skill what had by now become a major Red Scare. As industry and landowners contributed more liberally than ever before, he built his militia of black-shirted squads—in contrast to the red shirts of the left-wing activists—into a nationwide terrorist organization dedicated to "saving the country from Bolshevism."

Fascist terror   The first such "fighting squad," or *fascio di combattimento*, had been founded more than a year earlier in Milan and already called him *Il Duce*, the leader. The name *fasci* was derived from the *fasces* of ancient Rome, bundles of birch rods containing an ax with the blade projecting, a symbol of the police and judicial authority to the Romans and the symbol of "sweeping out with an iron broom" to right-wing radicals of all times. The victims of the Fascist squads at first were the Socialists, anarchists, and trade unions. Next were the other democratic forces and the duly elected government of Italy. Systematic raids were made on party and press headquarters of "the enemy" during which all resistance was brutally put down, property was destroyed, whole cities were temporarily occupied, and an attempt of Socialists and trade unions to stop the Fascist terror by a general strike was viciously suppressed. One of the favorite Fascist tricks was to seize parliamentary deputies and other dignitaries, force them to drink quantities of castor oil, and hold them until they would disgrace themselves in public. The government, the police, and the army looked on with indecision, and possibly with the secret hope that they could use Mussolini to destroy the entire labor movement. Pro-Fascist elements in army and government counseled the king to look with favor upon the Blackshirts, although many conservatives viewed Mussolini's antimonarchist, anticlerical record with alarm and disliked his organized violence and the resulting anarchy.

The march on Rome   In the fall of 1922, Mussolini moved with skill and determination for the final coup. In a public speech at Udine, he placated army, monarchy, and his supporters in business and industry by conceding that violence should not be allowed to get out of hand and by expressing his preferences for free enterprise and his distaste for the masses and the proletarians in his movement. For the king he had a promise to leave the monarchy alone, coupled with thinly veiled threats that the "national revolution" might replace the king with his cousin, the ambitious and pro-Fascist Duke of Aosta, if he did not cooperate. Having made certain that neither police nor the army would resist, Mussolini issued his ultimatum a month later and prepared the Blackshirt March on Rome. Egged on by his subordinates not to accept the last-minute compromise offers of coalition Cabinets, he put the plan into operation. With the active or passive cooperation of provincial prefects and garrison chiefs, the Fascists seized arsenals, police, railway and telegraph stations, and sent some 26,000 men to march in three columns on the capital. King Vittorio Emmanuele, who came close to declaring martial law and calling out the army, relented at the decisive moment. Mussolini, who had once more turned down all last-minute compromises, finally arrived by *wagon-lit* from Milan, with a written invitation to organize a government from the king's hand. The "national revolution" of the former revolutionary Socialist agitator had succeeded.

Establishing the Fascist dictatorship

The strategy of the take-over Having become prime minister, Mussolini proceeded with cautious determination toward his final goal— one-party dictatorship. He began with a broad coalition Cabinet which excluded Socialists and Communists only and assured the Italian Parliament that he would strictly adhere to legality. Then he quietly brought the administration and police under his control and began to drop the non-Fascist members of his Cabinet one by one. Parliament was maneuvered first into granting him emergency powers for a whole year and then into passing the Acerbo Election Law, which granted two-thirds of the seats in the Chamber of Deputies to the party that won a plurality of 25 percent or more in the next election, a figure which the new combined Fascists and Nationalists were sure to get, especially since they controlled the electoral machinery. The Blackshirt squads by this time had been organized into a Militia for National Security sworn to loyalty to the prime minister, not the king. In the elections they engaged in such wholesale violence and intimidation that people felt revolted in spite of a Fascist vote of 65 percent. When the Blackshirts finally murdered the most outspoken of their critics, the Socialist deputy Matteotti, the country was outraged, and the opposition parties walked out of the chamber and vainly sought to impel the king to depose the dictator. But Mussolini eventually got the better of them and early in 1925 began to harrass and arrest his enemies through numerous house searches and seizures, ignoring all safeguards of the freedom of the press, of association, and of assembly. A plan to assassinate him gave him the excuse to suppress the Socialists, and soon all other parties, and to complete his control over all oppositional elements.

Authoritarian control Governmental changes in the direction of total authoritarian control were not long in coming. In 1925 Mussolini made himself *capo di governo,* chief of state, with responsibility to the weak king rather than to Parliament. And for the following eight years, he introduced a similar principle into the relationship between central, regional, and local government, replacing elected provincial and municipal councils with appointed "presidents" and "rectories." This reform established in Italy what the German Nazis later called the "leadership principle" in local and regional government, and centralized Italian government enormously. In the years 1926–1927 he also established a secret police, OVRA, with a vast network of paid informers, and assigned a long catalog of political offenses for summary proceedings to military courts which could mete out the death penalty. Starting in 1929 also, election ballots carried a single slate of candidates handpicked by the Grand Council of Fascism, the supreme party organ. The opposition was in jail, in hiding, or in exile. At about this time, enabling legislation empowered the Fascist Grand Council to determine the composition of the Chamber of Deputies and a year later to be the arbiter of all questions relating to the constitution and to the succession to the throne and even to Mussolini, who was the President of the Grand Council.

The Catholic Church made its peace with the Fascists in the Lateran Accords of 1929, which undid fifty years of anticlerical legislation in exchange for cooperation by the church. Many great writers and artists, also, jumped on Mussolini's bandwagon. Thus *Il Duce* as omnipotent dictator was the head; the grand council, the supreme body, and the Fascist party, now called *civil militia,* was the vast network of "capillaries" and vessels through which the lifeblood of the state flowed "from top to bottom." The *fascisti* were organized along authoritarian lines and their members sworn to "carry out without discussion" the will of their *Duce.* Youth organizations and other auxiliaries and fronts multiplied the numbers of the party elite and helped with the recruitment of reliable new members. Old fighters who had been with the party from the beginning of the "national revolution" and promising new members recruited from among the Young Fascists received the best positions within the party organization.

Fascist education At the same time, the schools were made into agencies of Fascist propaganda that all grammar schoolteachers had to instill in their children from a tender age. Textbooks were rewritten to praise *Il Duce* in extravagant terms and to prepare youth for the "reawakening of the spirit of the Roman empire." University professors were required to sign a loyalty oath and affidavit that they were not members of any "subversive organization." Famous composers and dramatists were bribed and bullied[2] into publicly supporting Fascism. Adding to the carefully cultivated image of creativity, fertility, and youthfulness, Fascist youth organizations for three age groups were established: *Balilla* (ages 8–14), *Avanguardisti* (ages 14–18), and *Giovani Fascisti* (ages 18–21), analogous to the Russian Young Pioneers and Komsomol, or the Nazi *Jungvolk* and Hitler Youth. Thus the world was put on notice that the future belonged to the movement, and simultaneously the movement could be sure of an ample supply of recruits who would literally grow up with Fascism (or Communism) and never know anything else.

THE RISE OF GERMAN NATIONAL SOCIALISM

In the rise of Hitler and National Socialism to power, there were many parallels to the rise of Mussolini, except that the timing of the steps and the magnitude of some of the factors differed from the Italian situation. Where Italians were incensed only about a loss of some of the spoils of war, Germans had lost the war itself, and had suffered great deprivations and losses of men. What is worse, many Germans believed that victory had been snatched from their hands by a "stab in the back" by revolutionary Socialists and mutineers, since their high command had lied to them about the state of the war up to the very end. As in the Italian case, also, there was the confrontation between a large group of conservative annexationists in and out of the government, who had welcomed the war and had been so sure of victory that they had compiled long lists of foreign territory for annexation, and the parties who pressed for an early peace.

The latter—the Social Democrats, Democrats, and the Catholic Center party—had opposed the plans for annexations during World War I. Now they took over the government and wrote the ultra-democratic Weimar Constitution. The harsh terms of the Peace Treaty of Versailles, after the Germans had laid down their arms believing in the conciliatory promises of President Wilson, further fanned the flames between two camps: the former annexationists, who also represented the old ruling classes of Prussia and Germany, and the democratic governing coalition, whose representatives reluctantly signed the peace treaty to forestall Allied occupation. German

---

[2] Arturo Toscanini, an early Fascist who became disenchanted with the movement, was beaten up by Fascist bullies when he refused once to add their youth hymn "Giovinezza" to his program.

nationalism was also aggravated by separatist attempts at secession in some of the states; by a Polish invasion with the intention of seizing further territory than the Treaty of Versailles had already taken from eastern Germany; by the Allied demand for very substantial reparations on the assumption Germany had started the war; and by the French occupation of the Rhineland in 1923 for the purpose of exacting the French share when the inflation of the German currency imperilled the cash value of the reparations.

Effect of the war on young Germans

As in Italy, though on a larger scale, the war experience led to the mobilization and militarization of large numbers of young people, especially veterans who could no longer find their place in bourgeois society. Unable to settle down to a job and to raising a family, they became the "eternal marchers" for almost any cause, from a proletarian utopia to a racist Third Reich. Many of them became hangers-on or part of illegal ("black") units of the German army, the *Reichswehr*, which could offer them little help because the Treaty of Versailles limited it to a strength of 100,000 men. Large numbers of them joined the *Free Corps* which fought the Polish invasion. They were comparable, perhaps, to the legionnaires of D'Annunzio who had stormed Fiume. Many played a prominent role in the massive vigilante organizations that sprang up everywhere in response to the Red Scare—the attempts at a seizure of power by the extreme left in various places—of the immediate postwar period. And in the declining years of the Weimar Republic, these masses of mobilized and militarized young men were ready for the paramilitary organizations of all the parties—the conservative-militaristic *Stahlhelm* (steel helmet), Hitler's storm troopers, the *Reichsbanner* (*Reich* flag), and Iron Front of the republican parties, and the Red Front of the Communists. There was violence, intimidation, and street fighting almost every day, especially between the storm troopers and the Red Front, who resembled each other down to their brown and red shirts and their chiliastic romanticism. After Hitler came to power, many of the militia men of the other parties joined his Brownshirts, in part because the paramilitary existence was the only life they knew.

The Red Scare

The Red Scare in Germany had been strong long before the war. As early as 1878, Bismarck, the founder of the German nation-state, outlawed the Social Democrats, with the support of Conservative and entrepreneurial representatives. By 1912 the Social Democratic party had become the largest party on the *Reichstag* and the trade union movement the largest in the world. Yet the Prussian aristocracy in government and army continued to keep Socialists from positions in government, bureaucracy, and officer corps despite the long-evident moderation of the party. Entrepreneurs and management refused to negotiate with the trade unions in a manner that would have implied social equality.

At the outbreak of World War I, government and army officials had long lists of Socialist and labor leaders who were to be arrested at the slightest hint of resistance to mobilization. Instead, the Social Democrats surprised their implacable enemies by cooperating wholeheartedly with the war effort. Only as the war failed to produce the expected early victory, did increasing numbers of left-wing Socialists and pacifists begin to sense the final collapse of "capitalist imperialism" and the coming of utopia. The German revolution of 1918 occurred after the military collapse and was the result of defeat and outrage at the military leadership rather than of any left-wing plot. Still, the revolution overthrew the monarchy in the *Reich* and in the states, and cleared the way for the replacement of all the authoritarian features of the old regime by the parliamentary democracy of Weimar. What made the Red Scare acute at the end of the war were the councils (*soviets*) of workers and soldiers that temporarily held power in Berlin and in some state governments after the manner of the October Revolution in Russia. The exuberant chiliasm of the left-wing mobs of workers and returning soldiers confirmed the bourgeoisie in its alarm and called forth the establishment of the vigilante organizations mentioned above. But as in Italy, the threat of Bolshevism had passed long before a Fascist movement began to capitalize on it. Nevertheless, the German Communist party, larger than anywhere else at the time, grew with the support of millions of voters, drawing as much as 12 percent of the popular vote in 1924 and 17 percent in 1932. And the pacifistic offshoot of the Social Democrats, the Independent Socialists, demanded the immediate socialization of industry during the first postwar years until they rejoined their parent party in 1922. The combined Socialist vote at its highest point stood at nearly one-half of the electorate, larger even than the Nazi landslides of 1932–1933.

Postwar economic dislocation

The economic dislocations of postwar Germany were also far more severe than those of Italy. Runaway inflation set in, and in 1923, with France's occupation of the Ruhr—the industrial heart of Germany—the currency completely collapsed. Millions of small business-men, and pensioners and others dependent on a fixed income were ruined. At that time, the Weimar Republic was on the verge of a right-wing dictatorship by Conservatives, states' righters, and offi-cers, including Hitler, who staged his abortive beerhall *putsch* in Munich. Once before, in 1920, right-wing elements had seized power in a coup d'état that collapsed when the entire labor movement went on a general strike. After a few quiet, even prosperous years from 1925 to 1928, the worldwide Great Depression struck new panic into German business and agriculture. Unemployment, never very low in the Weimar Republic, mounted into the millions, reaching its highest point in the summer of 1932. As the unemployment graphs inched higher, so did the Nazi and the Communist vote until their combined total amounted to more than half of the electorate, thereby sounding the death knell of parliamentary democracy.

Old society versus new society

As in Italy, the old elites of German society became the allies of Fascism in the mistaken belief they could use Hitler to defeat the democratic forces of the hated Weimar Republic, especially the Social Democrats. The struggle between the old society against the new elites and their democratic form of government was particu-larly acute, since the Prussian Junkers, the landowning and military elite of Imperial Germany, had succeeded in feudalizing the national bourgeoisie and in checking the advance of all political moderniza-tion even while industrialization and urbanization were turning Germany into an advanced industrial country. Thus Germany ex-perienced capitalism and industrialism without the liberalizing im-pact of an independent "classical bourgeoisie" such as had formed the great Western democracies. Instead, the energies for social modernization, for equalizing and reconciling the social classes, were directed into a determined drive to become a world power not unlike Italy's entering the war to obtain major territorial gains. When Germany lost the war, people associated with the old ruling classes found it impossible to admit the failure of their drive for world power. Nor could they accept suddenly being faced with the de-mands of the lesser classes for equality and a share in power. The military and the bureaucracy, who were chiefly the preserve of the old elites, could not reconcile themselves to the Weimar Republic and to the fall of the monarchies, the most visible prop of the old order. To make matters worse, the economic crises of the Republican era also brought to a head the smoldering discontent of German small business, artisans, and farmers, who had long felt the effect of industrialization and never knew whether to blame big business or the labor movement for their plight.

Adolf Hitler and the Nazi party

Up to this Gordian Knot of interdependent dilemmas stepped Adolf Hitler (1889–1945), the son of a minor Austrian government official and not even a German citizen until a short time before his appointment as German chancellor. He had misspent his youth in Vienna flophouses, unable to get started in any career of his choosing, brooding over the multinational tensions of Eastern Europe and engaging in fantastic dreams of racism and empire. When World War I broke out, he enlisted, glad to have found something to do.

Left-wing and right-wing appeals After the war the *Reichswehr* retained Hitler as a political agent who had to maintain contact with assorted right-wing groups. He joined one of these groups as its leader, and there grew from various mergers the Nazi party, short for National Socialist German Workers party (NSDAP). The name illustrates the opportunistic intention to catch both the nationalistic right and the socialistic left, quite similar to Mussolini's strategy. Similarly, for party symbols the Nazi party borrowed the red flag from the Socialists, the swastika from the Free Corps, the Nazi salute from the Italian Fascists, and the "Siegheil" from the romanticized ancient German past. Hitler's appeal to the workers was not met with much response until the crisis years of 1931–1932, but his nationalistic line and extraordinary oratorical talent soon gained him many right-wing friends. They wanted to use him as "the drummer" of German revanchism who had the mass appeal they lacked. Hitler's personal ambition went much further than that. In the beerhall *putsch* of 1923, he sought to utilize his highly placed connections for a coup against the state government of Bavaria, to be followed by a March on Berlin of reactionary forces from several states. The beerhall *putsch* led to his arrest and to a jail sentence for high treason. While in jail, he wrote *Mein Kampf*, which was to become the bible of his movement.

When released, after a short period of time, Hitler reorganized his movement into a nationwide organization of hundreds of thousands of members and brown-shirted storm troopers in a bid for broad electoral support. Popular agitation was refined far beyond the "unalterable 25 points" of the original party program. The Nazis continued to stress such program points as their diatribes against the Treaty of Versailles, the call for land and colonies for the "people without space," Pan-Germanism, and a centralized and authoritarian

Reich. On the other hand, the nationalization of trusts, the confiscation of war profits and other income not earned by work, profit sharing in industry, freeing debtors from interest payments, and so on, were meant for the little man and his economic woes. Nazi propaganda went beyond the simple left-right dichotomy implied here and addressed each particular economic and social group with specific promises designed to meet its grievances and hopes regardless of the ensuing contradictions. This careful attention to each group paid off handsomely when the mounting economic crisis in the early thirties produced despair and extreme disorientation everywhere. Most of Germany's other parties were closely tied to the representation of particular group demands to the exclusion of all others.

The scapegoat To understand the electoral appeal of the Hitler movement several aspects which helped it to outdo rival parties at the movement of crisis need to be considered. Such an aspect was the skillful use of anti-Semitism as a tool of manipulation. Hitler had explained in *Mein Kampf* that every successful mass movement needed a "Big Lie" to mobilize the masses. The concept of the class struggle he regarded as the Big Lie of the Marxist movement, for which he had great secret admiration. A Big Lie by definition had to be so enormous as to be incapable of demonstration or refutation. It could only be accepted or rejected on faith. Anti-Semitism had become quite pervasive in Germany, as whole socioeconomic groups in obvious decline were grasping for an excuse for their individual or collective failures. Hitler had a malignant genius for exploiting these delusions: offering the Jews as a scapegoat to those who needed one and playing shamelessly on the paranoid tendencies of people in despair by imputing the "stab in the back" and Versailles, the "menace" of Wall Street finance, Allied "encirclement," Communism and Socialism, all to a worldwide Jewish conspiracy. Anti-Semitism was always present in Nazi propaganda, sometimes hidden behind a genteel façade, sometimes violent, according to what a particular audience could be expected to tolerate. Although Hitler himself was undoubtedly suffering from race phobia, his opportunism was demonstrated by his cleverly restrained use at this point of the underlying implications of a "race struggle" and of a utopian *Reich* of Aryan supermen. Despite his deep contempt for German nationalism as "a bourgeois illusion," he preferred to speak of a "German race" and "German national liberation."

Manipulation of pseudoconservative discontents and phobias Another important element of his appeal was his skillful utilization of the discontents and phobias of German traditionalists. He had an uncanny talent for verbalizing the German farmers' distrust of modern industry, the small towns' distaste for the life of metropolitan centers, the military and bureaucratic contempt for parliamentary democracy, and, since this was the 1920s, not least important, the fears of many an insecure male about women's emancipation and equality. Restless German intellectuals of conservative leanings, aristocrats, and elitist leaders of industry and banking all fell for his skillful use of words. Another aspect of his success with the masses was his ability to create a personal image, a cult of leadership and infallibility which grew from a combination of a natural talent for histrionics and a high degree of megalomania. Mussolini possessed the same ability to a high degree and cultivated his personal cult with slogans such as "The Duce is always right." To the German masses who were for the first time developing habits of mass participation, Hitler and his cohorts were easy to identify with because of their humble origin as compared to the aristocratic leaders of the Empire and the dignified, bourgeois old men who governed the Weimar Republic. Hitler and his movement had an egalitarian and youthful appeal to the masses, who regarded him as one of their own.

Refinement of agitation and propaganda   Finally, the refinement of agitation and propaganda should be mentioned, a field in which the Communists, the Italian Fascists, and the Nazis in Germany showed an extraordinary inventiveness. At a time when mass advertising was still in its beginnings and motivation research an occult art of depth psychologists and novel writers, the extremist sloganeers and propagandists showed a remarkable proficiency in their propaganda techniques. And their appeal as yet was unresisted for lack of public immunity to advertising, such as the public in Western countries has since developed. Propaganda planning and coordination was also an important aspect of Nazi success. Hitler's image of the utmost self-confidence and "iron determination" in the midst of the confusion and helplessness of the government facing the crazily reeling economy had a magic attraction for the despairing masses. The Nazi appeal in the last phase of the Weimar Republic was profoundly irrational, psychologically aimed at the tendency of people in despair to surrender themselves into the hands of a father substitute who will take care of everything and deliver salvation without any effort required of the voter.

The Nazi landslide   The Nazi landslide began in 1930, when the Nazi representation in the Reichstag rose from 12 to 107 seats. It reached its highest crest in July 1932, when 230 of about 600 seats were captured. Then it began to decline slowly, and Hitler might never have achieved power legally had not the republican government been in such a state of disintegration; vital governmental decisions were made by a handful of ambitious conservative politicians and a "kitchen Cabinet" of private advisers to the aging *Reich* President von Hindenburg. After several reshuffles of cabinet leadership—the *Reichstag* had ceased to function as a basis of parliamentary government—Hitler was appointed chancellor by von Hindenburg early in 1933. Hedged in deliberately by a majority of Conservative Cabinet members, he appeared to be safely under the control of more responsible elements. Yet it took him only nineteen months after becoming chancellor to establish his totalitarian dictatorship.

Hitler's policy of formal adherence to legality How did he do it? German historians such as K. D. Bracher, Helmut Krausnick and Wolfgang Sauer have demonstrated the techniques and the steps by which the complete seizure of power was accomplished. The abortive beerhall *putsch* of 1923 taught Hitler that his revolution could be attained only by *formal adherence to legality*, as this would neutralize such formidable opponents as the army, the state bureaucracy, and, perhaps, even the considerable forces of the trade unions and Socialist movement. The appearances of *law and order* could never be allowed to lapse without fear of upsetting the people at large and mobilizing resistance at a critical juncture of the step-by-step advance of the Fascist revolution. Hence the efforts of the Nazi movement were shifted to winning elections rather than organizing another March on Berlin. The replacement of the parliamentary responsibility of Cabinets in the early thirties with Cabinets based solely on the emergency powers of the *Reich* President showed Hitler what to strive for. Once in the driver's seat, he skillfully divided and outmaneuvered the Conservatives in his Cabinet. He quickly moved to gain control of the police power in the large state of Prussia and to secure the cooperation of the army with promises of rearmament.

Establishing totalitarian dictatorship

Passage of the Enabling Act Over the opposition of his Conservative coalition partners he also called new elections which, unlike Mussolini's elections of 1924, failed to bring the Nazis an electoral majority in spite of a stepped-up campaign of terror and harrassment of their opponents. As his luck would have it, a mentally ill

Dutch anarchist set fire to the *Reichstag* before the elections, giving Hitler an excuse to secure an executive decree suspending civil rights and allowing him to remove many political opponents from the arena. With only 44 percent of the popular vote, the Nazis had to continue to rely on Conservative support, which allowed them to hide their own advance behind a façade of a "conservative-national rebirth" heartily welcomed by the army, the bureaucracy, and the bourgeois voters who had switched from the liberal parties. While chief propagandist Joseph Goebbels captured the nationalistic imagination with a solemn rededication of the imperial flag—which was different from that of the Weimar Republic—and a grand spectacle of Prussian tradition at the grave of Frederick II (1712–1786) of Prussia in Potsdam in the presence of the Crown Prince and von Hindenburg, Hitler prepared the infamous Enabling Act. By passing this law two days after the spectacle of Potsdam, the *Reichstag* transferred all its legislative authority to the new chancellor over the sole opposition of the Socialists. The Communists, who in their delusion had closely cooperated with Hitler's schemes to ruin the Weimar Republic, had already been barred from the *Reichstag*.

Purge of the civil service Immediately after the Enabling Act, the new regime set the pattern of moral corruption with a law purging the civil service of Jews and of all other "politically questionable" officials, an open invitation to the lowest motives of ambitious men ready to sell their soul for a little promotion or to turn their petty squabbles into character assassination and dismissal for their competitors. Vast numbers of opportunists of many callings and walks of life soon followed the example of the bureaucracy and jumped on Hitler's bandwagon, removing thereby the last barriers of resistance. Instead of assaulting *law and order* directly, Hitler had simply decided to win the cooperation of the guardians of law and order by corrupting them from within.

Total organizational control The establishment of dictatorial control proceeded rapidly. A few months after the Enabling Act all parties other than the Nazis dissolved themselves or were disbanded. The composition of the *Laender* parliaments was brought into line with that of the *Reichstag* and appointive *Reich* commissioners saw to it that no *land* failed to carry out the will of the Nazi leader. To the extent that the Presidency had ever been much in his way, Hitler simply took it over in addition to the chancellorship when von Hindenburg died in August 1934. The trade unions and white-collar organizations were seized and disbanded and their property confiscated. Thereupon all workers and employees were drafted into the National Socialist Labor Front. The various associations of farmers and manufacturers were likewise "politically coordinated" or voluntarily adopted Nazi leadership, although the direction of the German economy was not assumed by the government until several years later, when the preparations for World War II began on a large scale. At the same time, the Nazi government showed its disrespect for private property by appropriating the property of Jews and political enemies in the same ruthless manner in which civil servants, newspaper editors, and all kinds of professional people had been ousted from their positions to make room for the collaborators of the regime. All private societies and associations were brought under Nazi control; some voluntarily chose Nazi leaders, while others were dissolved outright. Youth organizations were a special target of "political coordination." They were subordinated to Nazi youth authorities and merged with the compulsory Hitler Youth at an early date. Half a year after his appointment, Hitler was in a position to claim: "Now our party has become the state . . . there is no other authority from anywhere in Germany."

Nazi propaganda and education   Yet even total political and organizational control was not enough for the totalitarian ambitions of the Nazi movement. "We want to coordinate the German people with their government . . . we want to work on them until they are completely ours," Goebbels said when his Ministry of Propaganda was established early in 1933. The publicly owned radio stations were transferred from the postal ministry to his, and a Chamber of Culture was established to which all writers, artists, and other creative professions had to belong. The publication of news came under strict surveillance, and editors could function only as long as the censors considered them "politically reliable." The free press of Germany was now a mere mouthpiece of government propaganda, another tool for the limitless manipulation of the captive audience. Education from kindergarten to the university similarly came under complete control of the Nazis, who purged teachers and professors, promoted their own friends to key positions, and reoriented textbooks and the entire curriculum in the spirit of their own pseudoromantic and "heroic" approach. Like the Hitler Youth, the schools were supposed to educate the heroic warriors of tomorrow. In this manner, propaganda and control over press and education complemented political control. Not only would no citizen be allowed to resist or act contrary to the policies of the movement, he was not even allowed to think for himself.

Failure to control the church and the army   There were two major areas, however, in which the Nazi regime never quite succeeded in imposing total control, despite attempts to do so. One was the churches. The Nazis made great efforts to subvert the Protestants in particular, from among whom their main support came, by the establishment of a nominal "German faith" for people of little attachment to their church. The Vatican also felt compelled to conclude a concordat with Hitler, which gave the tyrant his first international recognition and an implied promise of collaboration in exchange for a few paper concessions. But the Nazis could not prevent the growth of a militant Protestant Witnessing Church and dogged Catholic resistance in spite of arrests and the wartime drafting of opposing clergymen into the army. There were thousands of Protestant and Catholic clergymen in Hitler's concentration camps, where they shared mistreatment and death with the political enemies, the Jews,[3] and other categories of prisoners throughout the twelve years of Hitler's reign.

The second failure was in the Nazi regime's attempts to obtain complete control over the German army, which remained almost undisturbed for nearly the first half of the twelve years, living in a world of its own despite—or rather because of—the pro-Nazi views of the defense minister. Beginning with the year 1938, Hitler step by step took over the command of the armed services but again without any penetration in depth. Thus it came to pass that the most active nucleus of the underground resistance, which was otherwise scattered and poorly coordinated in both churches and political opponents in exile and in hiding, established itself in the general staff and officer corps of Hitler's army. It was from among this group that his assassination and overthrow were attempted repeatedly, most notably in July 1944.

FASCIST IDEOLOGY AND REALITY: A COMPARISON

The Italian *fascisti* gave the name to many movements of a similar sort, yet having a considerable variety of aims and policies. Even in the old established democracies, Fascist and quasi-Fascist groups appeared in such countries as Belgium, the Netherlands, and the Scandinavian countries during the period between the wars. They often collaborated closely with the Nazi invaders of World War II. The party militia (SS) formations of the German armies in Russia, in fact, had sizable units composed of Fascists from other European countries. In France, small groups of militants such as the *Camelots*

---

[3] The systematic mass murder of Jewish prisoners took place during World War II, chiefly in the occupied territories of Eastern Europe, where special death camps and mass execution commandos carried out the genocidal policies of Nazi Germany.

du Roi of pre-1914 times and the *Croix de Feu* of the 1930s bore distinctly Fascist features. In Great Britain, the prominent Labour party leader Mosley suddenly left his party and founded a Fascist movement in the early thirties. The current tensions over immigration of colored peoples from other parts of the Commonwealth have again spurred the growth of similar groups in Britain. In the United States, the depression years of the 1930s saw the growth of the Silver Shirts and similar Fascist-type movements, not to mention earlier antecedents. The contemporary scene also harbors a number of groups, including the Ku Klux Klan and the John Birch Society, which bear some Fascist features. In most of the Eastern European countries that gained their independence as a result of World War I, and in Spain and Portugal, Fascist-type movements played a role in the establishment and maintenance of dictatorships. The predominance of aristocrats, military men, and sometimes the church, however, gave most of these movements more of a social class basis and a reactionary character than can be observed with Fascist Italy and Germany. Once the dictatorships were established, typically, they were less deeply rooted in the people, far less repressive, but also thoroughly opposed by any modernization whatsoever.[4]

Salient features of Fascist movements

A comparison of Fascist movements in different countries obviously suffers from their great variety and from the difficulty of arriving at a generally acceptable definition. There has been neither a Fascist International nor any common agreement on issues or ideology. A major difficulty of definition also arises from the fact that the motives and attitudes of Fascist leaders differ greatly from those of the followers. Yet there are telltale features that all Fascist movements seem to share.

The historic inspiration of Communism One such feature is the historic inspiration of Communism on non-Communist, though not very profoundly anti-Communist, persons and groups. Lenin's extraordinary demonstration of how a small elite of dedicated "professional revolutionaries" could seize power in the mighty Russian Empire held an almost irresistible fascination for many an ambitious man who, under widely varying circumstances and for differing goals, decided he could use *the same mechanism for winning power, but* without Communism. This is evident not only from the career

---

[4] There have been Fascist-type movements or regimes also in many countries of Latin America, Asia, and the Middle East. Among the more notable was the Argentine dictatorship of Juan Perón, an admirer of Mussolini.

of such former Socialist leaders as Mussolini and Mosley and the numerous ex-Communists and other former revolutionaries of the left who are prominent in Fascist-type movements, but also from a reading of Hitler's *Mein Kampf,* which clearly shows the link between the historic presence of powerful revolutionary Marxist movements and Hitler's political aims. Far from a desire to defend capitalism or the "German way of life," and equally far from the wish to fight Communism except as a rival to his own power, Hitler seems to have wanted power more than anything else in the world—power to make himself a world historic personage, the *Führer* of a great nation and perhaps of the world, power to win the war the Central Powers lost in 1918, and power to carry his personal phobias to the genocidal end of the "final solution." His blueprint for gaining this power was very simply to imitate the Marxist revolutionaries, especially Lenin, while substituting a different Big Lie for the Marxist doctrine of class struggle.

The content of the Big Lie has always been interchangeable, even with the same Fascist leader. It can be nationalism, the traditionalist revolt, superpatriotism, a quest for empire or "lost" territories, the supremacy of one race or ethnic extraction over another, revanchism for a lost war or civil war, anti-Communism, anti-Catholicism, anti-Semitism, anarchism, pseudoreligious appeals, race phobias of every description, or anything else, depending on the judgment and predilections of the *Duce, Führer,* or *el lider.* It is the deliberate use of a Big Lie for the mobilization of mass support and the adoption of most Communist devices and techniques, often on the pretense of "fighting Communism with its own weapons," which is a hallmark of Fascism.

Exploitation of social tensions and causes   Secondly, and this is an outstanding example of such a Communist technique, Fascist movements seek to exploit social tensions and crises to propel themselves into power. Such tensions may be between races or ethnic groups, and Fascists often exploit these tensions in terms of "white supremacy," or anti-Semitism, or similar group reactions. In multinational areas any ethnic tensions lend themselves to such exploitation. The strains of social and economic transformations may set up certain minorities as made-to-order scapegoats for Fascist manipulation. A powerful fear of strong trade unions or of Socialist revolution, as in most of the more advanced Western countries, can become the Archimedean point for the Fascist overthrow of nonlabor, non-Socialist governments. A pervasive feeling of moral or religious decline in a nation lends itself perfectly to Fascist propaganda, as does economic depression or major setbacks in the foreign policy of a country. Because free societies believe in the pluralistic, untrammeled operation of all social forces, there is always of necessity friction, the result of competition and conflict between groups and individuals. The great democracies of the West have long believed that social friction and competition are beneficial to progress. However, there are many people who are frightened by it, and there can be excesses of such friction that would shock anybody. Here again is a ready-made handle for Fascist agitation: Under the guise of promoting "national unity" or "solidarity," or of removing what in a social crisis may seem to many people frighteningly unorthodox, "un-German," or "un-American" behavior, Fascists make themselves the enforcers of a narrow consensus that culminates in their own grasp of dictatorial power.

Love of violence   A third feature of Fascist movements everywhere has been their consistent love of violence. It could be argued that their model, Communism, also considers violence a natural concomitant of social evolution toward the desired goal. It is true that Communist movements attract a certain type of extremist, militant personality, and that in street fighting, underground activity, and on such violent occasions as the Russian civil war or guerrilla warfare today, there is a needless measure of Communist brutality. Yet it would be difficult to top the extraordinary sadism displayed by the average Fascist goon squad both before and after the Fascists have come to power. The attitude toward violence and brutality as a purpose in itself is a distinguishing characteristic of Fascist movements. Successful Fascist parties have indeed had a constant problem of how and when to restrain their bloodthirsty bullyboys, and when to turn them loose to administer the castor-oil treatment, and to engage in street brutality, armed raids, and election day violence. Both Mussolini and Hitler took a certain pride, as do Fascists elsewhere, in assassinations and grisly deeds committed by their followers. The Nazis also believed that the use of violence and brutality separated the men from the boys in their movement. By brutalizing prisoners and concentration camp inmates, for example, a storm trooper had to demonstrate his dedication and his contempt for the scruples of religion and civilized society. The Fascist attitude toward violence and savagery, as a famous theologian put it, marks Fascism as completely pagan and outside of Western civilization, whereas Communism appears more like a heresy within the Western tradition.

Attitudes toward war and conquest   The Fascist attitude toward wars and the quest for empire is related to this attitude toward in-

ternal violence. Where other political movements and civilized society have shrunk away from manifest belligerence and greed, or
have at least gone to great lengths to conceal their motives from both
themselves and others, Mussolini spoke openly of Italy's *sacro ego-
ismo* and blithely pursued obvious paths of territorial aggrandizement. The Nazis likewise felt contempt for the "bourgeois scruples"
of the other German parties and social groups about war and their
concern for peace and international law. Instead of following the
precepts of civilized society, they indoctrinated the people, through
education and propaganda, with their glorification of war.[5] The rise
of Fascism owed indeed a great deal to the mobilization of vast
masses of people in World War I—the first gigantic war between
groups of national war machines employing millions of men at home
and at the front. The role of veterans organizations, the Free Corps
of Germany, D'Annunzio's legionnaires, and the armed and uni-
formed marching columns of paramilitary organizations of right and
left bear witness to the militarization of society. There is in the
barbarism of modern warfare, as seen from the point of view of the
individual soldier, the same shortcut between the emotion of hatred
and deeds of violence which characterizes Fascist behavior in civilized
society. The only difference, and not a profound one, is that modern
societies have outlawed such shortcut action (except on the screens
of television and motion pictures), while in war between nations it
is still considered eminently proper and patriotic. Fascism is a kind
of invasion of the savagery of international war into the orderly
community life of a society.

Contempt for constitutional democracy   A related aspect of Fascist
movements the world over is their utter contempt for democracy and
constitutional government. The imposition of rules of the game, such
as considerations of decency or fairness on the "internalized warfare"
of the Facists naturally strikes them as ridiculous. They are prepared
to yield only to force. But they are perfectly willing to use the
methods of democratic competition to win power and the privileges
and freedoms of democracy for the purpose of ruining democratic
government and of abolishing its freedoms.

The authoritarian personality   This cynical contempt for democracy
is rooted in the authoritarian cast of mind of Fascist leaders and fol-

[5] The glorification of war and violence is well exemplified by Mussolini's slogans:
"He who has steel will have bread! Nothing in history has ever been won without the shedding of blood! It is better to live for one day like a lion than a
hundred years like sheep! War is to the male what childbearing is to the
female . . . a minute on the battlefield is worth a lifetime of peace." The Nazis
found similar formulas to impart a heroic view of life to young and old.

lowers. The typical Fascist, not unlike the typical Communist, if perhaps in a slightly different way, possesses an "authoritarian personality," which means, among other things, that he has failed to develop to the maturity in mental outlook which characterizes the typical political moderate. In particular, his relationship to his parents, to authority, and to government has failed to reach a mature and stable balance, and this is reflected most dramatically in the cult of leadership. The authoritarian tends instead to vacillate between abject submissiveness and rebellion toward established authority, to combine open submision with repressed rebellion, or to hate his own government in the same unreasoning, unconditional way as he may love his leader or the police. The typical authoritarian personality, according to the research of Theodore W. Adorno and other sociologists and psychologists, is also prone to violent prejudices and phobias. In his authoritarianism and prejudice, the typical Fascist surrenders his will and judgment completely to his leader and allows himself to be used as a tool rather than acts as an individual capable of reason and wisdom. This transformation of individuals into mere instruments, however voluntary, of a brutal will to power is also at odds with the Western tradition, according to which every human being deserves to be treated as a purpose in himself.

The cult of leadership Fascists love the security and escape from responsibility which they feel they gain by committing themselves unconditionally into the hands of a leader or group of leaders. This basic attitude also has its concomitants in their view of human inequality and their distrust of reason. The leader or party elite is evidently possessed of special qualities which the Fascist follower feels he himself does not possess. By the same token, the self-chosen leadership has no compunctions about using its presumable superiority to the last consequence in the manipulation and disposition of its "inferiors." This manipulation involves more than the ruthless exploitation of tensions between different groups of the "inferior masses" for increasing the power of the elite. The effect of power on the mind of the Fascist inevitably includes the temptation to play God—to be master over life and death, over war and peace, and over the historic fate of whole nations. If one can use anti-Semitism or racism to gain power, one can also decree the historic catastrophe of an arbitraily chosen scapegoat. In fact, one can enhance one's reputation for infallibility by first predicting catastrophe or war and then making sure it occurs.

The *voluntarism* of Fascism—the view of the world in which everything happens only according to the *will of the leaders*—

sounds the death knell of the liberal notion of reason. The faculty of reasoning, which was thought to unlock the doors to true individual freedom for every human being by helping him to understand and to master his fate, is unreal, even suspect to Fascists. The Fascist leader owes his authority not to reason but to his *charisma*, a quality beyond rational explanation. And the followers do not win salvation by thinking, but by blind obedience. "Believe! Obey! Fight!" was a slogan as typical of the Italian Fascists as of the Nazis, and it was never considered to be up to the man in the street to question why or what for.

Fascist ideology

So far we have discussed what Fascist movements seem to have in common, despite widely varying circumstances. The points mentioned add up to a bundle of attitudes and techniques, or to character traits, but hardly to anything like an ideology. This raises the question whether Fascism ever possessed an ideology in the narrow sense of the word, which is, after all, an important part of any system of totalitarian government. It is the ideology, a dialectical, black-and-white explanation of the evolution of the social world and a promising vision of the future, that lends a dynamic, self-renewing unity to totalitarian movements and gives them direction beyond the immediate tactical and strategic expediencies of seizing and holding power. In the contradictory appeals of Mussolini—to the right and to the left, for and against nationalism, for and against war and empire, for and against the monarchy, for and against the "Red Seizure of the Factories"—there was no continuity or consistency to lend stability to a fighting creed; these lay only in the life and struggle for power of the movement itself and of the man.

Mussolini's doctrine   Mussolini was very much aware of the need for an ideology and strove to supply a statement of doctrine in an article appearing in the *Enciclopedia Italiana* ten years after he came to power. In it he stressed an anti-individualistic, antiliberal, anti-Socialist idea of an "all-embracing state, outside of which no human or spiritual values can exist" and which "interprets, develops, and potentiates the whole life of a people." This doctrine of an absolute state above all groups and individuals was rather at odds with the Fascist reality of the personal role of the leader, the command of the Grand Council of the Fascist party over the state, and Mussolini's compromises with monarchy, army, and church. More to the point were statements of the Fascist disbelief in the possibility of world peace, international organizations such as the League of Nations, the pursuit of happiness, democracy and equality, economic liberalism and "harmful" civil liberties, as well as his statements of faith in authority, order, direction, in an expansive, imperialistic spirit, national collectivism, and a strong state with totalitarian ambitions. But seen as a whole, Mussolini's doctrine hardly amounted to a fighting creed that could have inspired his movement or the whole country. In 1938, after years of foreign policy adventures and Italian-German cooperation on the side of conservative-Fascist insurrection in Spain, Mussolini suddenly added anti-Semitism to his official program. His motive might have been an effort to conciliate Hitler, whose seizure of Austria he had not been able to prevent, or perhaps admiration for Hitler's Big Lie, which had worked so well for the Nazi dictator. But racism failed to evoke much of a response among the *fascisti* or Italians at large. It only embroiled Mussolini in open controversy with Pope Pius XI, which ended only when the latter passed away in 1939.

Nazi ideology—the German way of life? Most other Fascist movements did as poorly in developing an ideology as did the Italian Fascists. German National Socialism succeeded in developing a fighting creed, though nothing comparable to the strength and flexibility of Communist ideology. There have been many attempts in the Western democracies, especially spurred on by World War II, to fathom the roots of Nazism. Some writers even insisted that National Socialism was the epitome of German traditions going back to Martin Luther, Frederick II of Prussia, or to the philosopher Hegel and the romantic period of German literature. Others saw in it reincarnation of Prussian absolutism and militarism, or of the strutting arrogance of the kaiser, whom the Western democracies had defeated more than two decades before the Nazi menace. These interpretations, written in the passion of war and in the shock over the Nazi atrocities uncovered at the end of the war, were immensely flattering to the coarse bullies of the Nazi movement, who were generally quite unfamiliar with and rather hostile to the cultural traditions of their own country. Hitler himself, with a formal education far more limited than that of many of his half-educated lieutenants, is credited with the exclamation: "When I hear the word 'culture,' I feel like drawing my revolver."

Superpatriotism Worse yet than crediting the neobarbarian revolt of Hitler with philosophies and cultural trends far beyond his ken, such an interpretation agrees with Nazi apologists that the liberal Germany of the 1848 revolution, the Catholic Germany of the Center party, the mass following of the free trade unions and Social Democrats, and the German art and literature of Heinrich Heine, Felix Mendelssohn-Bartholdy, Thomas Mann, and German expressionism were all somehow "un-German" and alien. The cultural traditions of Germany are no more to blame for the rise of Hitler than are the ancient Romans for Mussolini's boasts of resurrecting their glory. This is not to say that the Nazis and their apologists did not strain to the utmost to seem more patriotic and to claim more historical German figures for their very own than anybody else. It is typical of Fascist movements everywhere to conduct themselves in accordance with the Big Lie: the more superpatriotic they pretend to be, the more they intend to subvert the body politic; the more conservative they pretend to be, the more they are engaged in the ruin and corruption of the traditions, conventions, and institutions of their society. It was not atypical of the Nazis to set up an extremely narrow consensus on what was supposed to be "genuinely German"[6] and to initiate a crusade against "un-German" activities so defined by the Nazis as to coincide with their scapegoats and enemies. The smokescreen of the "conservative-national rebirth" at the time the Nazis were consolidating their dictatorship is a typical example of their real attitude toward "genuine Germanism": It was merely another Big Lie to them.

Racism—Hitler's basic ideology The underlying ideology of German National Socialism, apart from the attitudes shared by other Fascist movements, was racism. There is a basic difference between prejudice and phobias toward people of other ethnic stock or religion or social or cultural background, such as may thrive in an insecure or disturbed mind, and the political ideology of racism. Prejudice has its own dynamics, which can range from stupid jokes and discriminatory action to acts of violence and pogroms against the minority singled out as the out-group.[7] Strong emotional prejudice may of course predispose masses of people to accept a racist ideology, and may indeed stand behind the attempt of the originators of racist ideologies to rationalize their wild fears with labored theories. But it does not lead to acceptance of racist ideology any more than does the predicament of industrial workers lead to acceptance of Marxism.

The basic ingredients of a racist ideology, as with Marxism, are a few shreds of ill digested and wrongly applied sociological evidence upon which the prejudiced mind seizes with a hunger born from

[6] The slogans and images of this simon-pure "Germanism" was generally taken from the Conservative parties, and literature, but given a sly modernistic twist.

[7] On the "nature of prejudice," see especially the book of that title by Gordon W. Allport (Garden City, N.Y.: Doubleday, 1954).

deeply seated inner needs. An inferiority complex or a desperate yearning to feel superior to someone may induce people to be fascinated by statistics or popular clichés singling out a particular group as generally inferior in moral conduct, education, or social status, or as otherwise odd. Especially if the group in question is highly "visible," or considered highly visible because of the prevailing patterns of prejudice, a group stereotype quickly hardens into the image of a "race" in which the prejudiced persons project qualities of laziness, immorality, or uncleanliness which they suppress in themselves, or even their secret dreams of wealth and power.

Race—man's most dangerous myth   The scientifically dubious concept of "race" is the key term for the ideology of racism; for Marxism it is economic "class." And just as Marxist would-be revolutionaries had to start out by trying to awaken in the heterogenous mass of different kinds of laborers, dependent craftsmen, and white-collar employees a common "proletarian class-consciousness,"[8] racists such as Adolf Hitler and his lieutenants had to designate a "good race" and a "bad race" and to propagandize these notions. In his early days, Hitler's inspiration used to be race theories which pitted a blond, blue-eyed race against a dark-haired, brown-eyed one —not very satisfactory for dark-haired young Adolf—or Austrians of Germanic stock against a conglomeration of Slavic, Latin, and other "inferior breeds."

On becoming a political agitator in the strife-torn Weimar Republic, he changed his two opposed "races" to the "genuine Germans" versus the Jews, who had long been a favorite scapegoat of German and Austrian conservatives and traditionalists. This was understood by Germans and foreign observers to be a kind of integral German nationalism and identification with the national ambitions defeated in World War I. In actual fact, Hitler had nothing but contempt for German nationalism, which he associated with the national unification movement of the liberal bourgeoisie of the nineteenth century. Once he was in power and became interested in enlisting the support of foreign Fascist movements in his international power politics, he increasingly favored the replacement of the image of the "German race" with an "Aryan race" which allowed him to include non-German Fascists among the elect of his "new order for Europe."

[8] The strange contortions of thought about what to include and what not are particularly obvious whenever Marxists had to divide farm laborers, farm tenants, small, medium, and large farmers into friend or foe, or in developing nations where there may be neither industry nor proletariat but only chieftains, and tribes or villages.

Biological determinism   The Aryans were a hypothetical prehistoric people whose existence was suggested by nineteenth-century linguists when they discovered that many of the principal languages of Europe and Asia were closely related. Following earlier precedents of French aristocrats trying to set themselves off from the common people as a superior "race," the French Count de Gobineau and lesser lights then argued that the Aryans must have been a blond, uniquely gifted "master race" whose conquest of less talented, dark-complexioned peoples started civilization and culture everywhere. Hitler's racist writers thereupon started "scientific" investigations of such questions as whether the art of the great ancient civilizations depicted its gods and heroes with blond hair and "Nordic features." Gobineau went on to suggest that the great cultures had declined because the Aryan conquerors diluted their genetic heritage by intermarriage with the "lesser breeds." Thus, instead of the laws of economics, as with Karl Marx, it is the inexorable laws of biology and in particular of genetics that have worked the triumph and doom of mankind from time immemorial.[9]

Racist policies   In a pattern familiar to contemporary America, the fear of intermarriage with whoever was declared the "bad race" became linked up in popular agitation with all kinds of secret sexual fears and phobias. In the Nuremberg Laws of the Nazis, analogous to the South African *apartheid* legislation and American miscegenation statutes, intermarriage between Germans and Jews was outlawed, existing marriages dissolved, and severe penalties imposed on sexual contacts between the "races."

The Nazis also purged the public service, the press, business, and the professions of Jews and subjected their own officeholders to the requirement of having to document their non-Jewish parentage three generations back. This again involved the Nazis as had occurred in other racist regimes, in the difficulty of defining the elusive concept of "race" in individual cases. The popular stereotypes were of very little help and the eternal laws of genetics only helped to confuse the bogus issues created by racism with inconclusive complications such as the infinite shadings of mixed parentage and the total absence of reliable, empirically measurable, objective standards of the biological identity of either "race." In the end, the totalitarian state relied on such nonbiological criteria as the religious affiliation listed in the civil register, the family name, denunciation by "Aryans," and volun-

---

[9] Some earlier race theories, including one having great influence on young Hitler, gave theological formulations to anti-Semitism as well as to other racial theories of the elect and the eternally damned.

tary individual or collective confession of the "objective guilt" of having been born a Jew, punished in most cases by exile or imprisonment in a concentration camp and possible death.

Genocide As the Nazi war machine spread its power to other European countries with sizable Jewish populations, Hitler had his cohorts establish further concentration camps there and round up Jewish men, women, and children, with great brutality, presumably for segregated resettlement and forced labor. In reality, however, they were being shipped to their death. The systematic genocide of about six million human beings was the ultimate consequence of the ideology of racism.

TOTALITARIAN GOVERNMENTS COMPARED

Whenever totalitarian movements such as National Socialism, Fascism, or Communism have come to power, they have sought to establish a totalitarian dictatorship. The result has varied somewhat according to the degree of their dominance; for example, in Italy power had to be shared to some extent with monarchy and church. It has also varied according to the availability of the technological and bureaucratic apparatus necessary for total control, and according to the degree of wholehearted cooperation extracted from the population by propaganda and fear. Where totalitarian government has reached a state of completion, as in Stalin's Soviet Union, Red China, Hitler's Germany, and somewhat less so in Fascist Italy, it has constituted a distinctive form of government basically different from traditional autocracy, the old empires, modern bureaucratic absolutism, or democratic government. In the following pages, totalitarian government as a self-contained system will be described. This is not to imply that Communist and Nazi totalitarianisms are exactly alike. They differ in their goals, their ideologies, their role in the process of modernization. But they had in common such salient features as (1) a single, half-deified leader of extraordinary authority; (2) a passionately dedicated and peculiarly organized mass party in control of the government bureaucracy as well as of all organizations of society; (3) a propaganda monopoly over all communications media and the educational system; and (4) an elaborate system of terror and fear.

The exalted authority of the leader

Though the idea of dictatorship generally suggests the presence of a single dictator with absolute power, most dictators and despots in history did not actually rule by themselves but always with the active cooperation of other established repositories of power, such as the nobility or landowning oligarchy, the church, or the army. In totalitarian systems it was long assumed to be the party or a top group of party leaders that made or sanctioned the policy decisions. Ample evidence, however, has been adduced to show that Hitler, Stalin, and Mussolini at their peak did in fact hold enormous and autocratic power by themselves, derived from no other body and wielded over their own lieutenants with even greater arbitrariness and harshness than over the people at large. No other chief executives of modern nations have had such awesome and irrevocable authority to make major policy decisions on the spot without having to justify them to anyone, least of all to the façade of representative institutions such as the Nazi *Reichstag* or the Supreme Soviet, which are, at best, sounding boards for the speeches and proposals of the leadership.

The leader and the ideology The exalted authority of the leader is in large part due to his function as the author or chief amender of the party ideology, or, in the Communist case, the only man with the authority to suppress or reinterpret parts of the original doctrine. Since the ideology is the mental prison of the party members (or their vehicle for reaching the yearned-for utopia), being the infallible pope of their substitute religion, the prophet of their chiliastic hopes, is a godlike role within their world.

The power to determine policy within the extraordinarily fast-moving totalitarian apparatus is similarly momentous, especially since policy and propaganda are so closely linked that skillful dictators can make a game of constantly presenting their audience with overwhelming and exhilarating surprises. The cult of leadership with which propaganda and education indoctrinate the masses until even small children constantly sing the praises of the great and glorious leader in extravagant terms puts the party under pressure, too. Soon even the rank and file begin to believe that Stalin made the sun shine and the grass grow, and that Hitler was the greatest general of all times. The constant outpouring of propaganda about the leader and his policies creates a hypnotic atmosphere of inexorable victory and salvation about the man that few people can escape.

Relationship between dictator and party Further light is shed upon the roles of Hitler and Stalin by examining the relationship of both with their respective parties. Both Hitler and Stalin carried out periodic purges and shakeups of their parties and other functionaries with the evident aims of (1) getting rid of potential enemies and laggard lieutenants, (2) striking fear and anxiety in the hearts of their followers and other persons, and (3) preventing the power structure from ever settling down and developing local or functional cliques capable of making their own decisions. The biggest of the purges, Hitler's purge of the original storm troopers (SA) and Stalin's great purges of the 1930s, were quite bloody and claimed thousands of victims executed or tried on trumped-up charges, including plots of murder more likely originating with the dictator himself. These purges in both cases served to make the dictator the sole authority within his own movement by killing off his rivals.

The leader and his lieutenants   The late political scientist Sigmund Neumann also drew attention to the quasi-feudal relationship of the leader and his lieutenants, who were entrusted with enormous tasks of administering crash programs, marshaling resources, or reorganizing the secret police. There are numerous testimonials to the abject fear with which the lieutenants and closest associates regarded the morose disposition of Stalin and the tantrums of Hitler. And yet the lieutenants enjoying the confidence of the great man for a short time would give their all to their task and work with a zeal and ruthlessness in clearing all obstacles in their path as if they had to build utopia in a day. To make their status even more insecure and their work more difficult, Hitler had a disturbing habit of creating overlapping jurisdictions and duplicating assignments so that the various lieutenants constantly had to fight each other over their execution of assigned tasks. A grotesque variation of the constitutional device of checks and balances, this technique continually kept the lieutenants off balance and allowed Hitler to promote or ruin them by small shifts of jurisdiction. As a result, Nazi totalitarianism was an administrator's nightmare of built-in conflicts and frustrations, and the seemingly all-powerful lieutenants were rarely more than puppets on Hitler's strings. Needless to add, this relationship is an agreement with the leadership cult of Fascism, and in practice it is nothing new for Communism. For Nazis and Communists alike, the leader was the highest personification of the Aryan "race" or of the "vanguard of the proletariat," whereas the lieutenants were at best exalted mortals.

The totalitarian mass party
The broader circles personifying the Aryan "race" or the "vanguard of the proletariat" are usually referred to as the totalitarian party, although it would be more appropriate to speak of a quasi-

religious, quasi-military order. Unlike democratic parties, Communist or Fascist parties will not accept all comers, but carefully screen recruits and punish members by expulsion without a public trial. Totalitarian parties also practice authoritarian control from the top down without the open elections, political responsibility, or publicity characteristic of democratic parties. As will be recalled, it was Lenin who designed the structure of the Communist party in order to meet the conditions of underground survival in the tsarist police state. Nevertheless, Communist parties in democratic societies, where they are allowed to operate freely, use the same cell structure, the same "democratic centralism," and the same mode of half-legal, half-illegal operation for their professional revolutionaries.

Fascist parties by definition have copied Lenin's "organizational weapon," along with other Communist methods, and share the intense merging of individual wills into the larger whole united behind the leader. The Nazis unconditional *"Führer,* command us, and we shall follow you" and Mussolini's slogan "Believe! Obey! Fight!" mirror the character of life within these parties. Moreover, Communist and Fascist parties do not change their basic structure on coming to power. Their dynamic stride unbroken, they do not turn from revolutionary fighting columns against the established order into tame, responsible government parties. Instead they remain "the movement" bent on revolutionizing society and the world.

There is a difference in that Communist parties, more than is true of Fascist parties, have insisted that they maintain "internal party democracy," even if they will not submit to free elections on the outside. The triennial party congress in the Soviet Union contains delegates from all organizations of the party and has the power to elect the Central Committee as a kind of party legislature, flanked by the presidium (Politbureau) as party executive and the secretariat as the party administration, a structure repeated on the lower levels of the "federal" organization of the party. The formal structure glosses over the fact that power is utterly centralized, internal "elections" are preceded by nomination from the top, and there are levers of power at the disposal of the leader, such as the secret police, which can undercut any attempt by oppositional elements to derive authority from anyone except the leader himself. Stalin, after the purges, was as much in solitary control of the remainder of his party as Hitler ever was. His successors have been able to manipulate Central Committee and Presidium from the post of general secretary and to oust rivals decisively, though such ousters no longer occur by blood purge, but by appointment as ambassador to

Outer Mongolia or overseer of tractor stations, or by retirement to the status of an "unperson."

The party and the state bureaucracy   The relationship of the totalitarian party to the state bureaucracy furnishes other significant differences between Communism and Fascism. In both systems the party is careful not to merge with the state but to maintain its greater mobility and secrecy of decision-making processes behind the façade of official officeholders. In the Soviet Union, however, and probably in Red China too, the state administration and its ubiquitous functions were created for the most part by the Communist regime, which seems to have set a pattern of direct supervision and initiative on the part of the party. Perhaps the enormous, sluggish bureaucracy of the Soviet state could not be made to perform its tasks if it were not for the bureaucratic leadership exercised by the party, which on all levels organizes "socialist competition," local and regional propaganda and production campaigns, and spurs on or punishes wherever necessary. The party itself gathers its members in periodic sessions of self-criticism and mutual dressing down that extends to all details of personal life and to the performance of party obligations twenty-four hours a day, to the point of complete self-effacement. While party members may share the satisfaction of being part of an enormous, constructive effort and of riding the powerful wave of the future, they are not to enjoy their power in the form of public accolades or even in the leisurely life of a privileged class.

The Nazi and Fascist parties, on the other hand, started in countries with fully developed bureaucracies to which they added but little. They contended themselves with the political coordination of each administration, ousting hostile officials and filling all key positions with their own men or politically reliable fellow travelers. This often meant that an uncouth anti-Semite with a grade-school education would become minister, state secretary, or lord mayor, with a well-trained administrative assistant by his side to translate his ranting commands into the legalistic officialese understood by the career service. Despite the political coordination, the civil service continued, as did the army and a large part of the professions, to regard itself as an island of expertise somehow exempt from political involvement. This putative autonomy frequently led to conflicts and clashes with minor party decisions and officials, a condition which led the political scientist Ernst Fraenkel to call the Nazi system a "dual state," in which the state bureaucrats often carried the day on a particular issue. It is difficult to follow his assumption of duality or of a superior position for the bureaucrats, considering that on issues relating to the goals of the Nazi revolution and on police control functions, no conflict was ever tolerated by the party. Italian Fascism in its early days gave "the state" a more prominent role in line with Mussolini's stress on state absolutism but later left less and less doubt about who was boss. The state authority in the hands of party leaders on many levels and the submissiveness of German and Italian bureaucrats to authoritarian rule rather weakened any bureaucratic opposition to party demands in any case. Nazi and Fascist functionaries, in contrast to the Communists, tended more toward public splendor and glory and would not brook as much control over their private lives by their comrades. They often seized perquisites of wealth confiscated from political enemies and Jewish citizens and indulged in as much conspicuous consumption and high living as any self-chosen elite in history. Unlike working toward a Communist utopia, which evidently requires a relatively Spartan life, the crusade for a racist utopia, or for the resurrection of the glorious Roman Empire, seemed to allow its crusaders a generous advance on the pleasures of neo-Roman living to come.

Membership of the party If the totalitarian party is the elite of totalitarian society, it is of interest to know what proportion of the total population is regarded as worthy of this elite status. As long as the party is still competing with other parties, it is likely to grow as fast as it can find recruits. Once in power, however, one would expect it to tighten its requirements. Then again, whenever a great struggle requires mass mobilization, the party may take in large numbers of volunteers, or draft recruits, only to contract its membership once more after the struggle is over. The Russian Communist party grew rather slowly until the time of the first Five-Year Plan, 1928–1933, when its membership rose steeply to $3\frac{1}{2}$ million. The purges cut deeply into the numbers but were followed by recruitment from among the graduates of Communist youth organizations, until the "great patriotic war" against the Nazi invaders boosted membership figures to a peak of 6 million. Then Soviet leaders began to worry about diluting the revolutionary elite of their party, and there followed scattered purges and a period of very slow growth. The latest word on membership is a figure of 10 million, which would indicate rapid growth once more, though for unaccounted reasons. It is conceivable that a certain measure of liberalization in general may also lead to a loosening of the restrictions on entering the party. A Soviet percentage of from 2 to 5 percent of the population can be compared with 2 to 3 percent for Red China, which amounts to no less than 17 million Communists, according to some observers.

Mussolini's Fascists started with roughly 1 million members, or 2 percent, at about the time his rule became totalitarian and the party closed the gates of admission. But after 1932 government employees were forced to join and it became almost impossible to hold any important position in business or the field of culture without being a member. The annual initiation of hundreds of thousands of *Giovani Fascisti* and the dropping of membership requirements for members of the armed forces during World War II boosted the total to nearly 5 million, or 11 percent, in 1943. Later Mussolini tried to return once more to a small elite of true "believers and fighters." However, there was a much smaller cadre of ½ million Fascist militia men who, together with the "old fighters," youth leaders, and the party's inner circle, constituted the real Fascist elite.

The Nazi party also increased rather indiscriminately from about 1 million when Hitler was appointed chancellor as the first big waves of bandwagon acrobats and opportunists came in. The 1937 law requiring all government officials to join the Nazi party produced the same bloated condition as in Mussolini's party. By then it became clear that the real elite was Heinrich Himmler's storm troop militia (SS), although even that inner core was diluted when it seemed expedient in 1943 to encourage the lagging enthusiasm of the common soldier by transferring whole army units to the armed SS.

Youth, labor, and peasants These figures and percentages do not include the auxiliary organizations of the totalitarian parties. The Fascist and Nazi youth organizations included practically all youngsters and had as many as 8 and 10 million members, respectively, at their highest point. The Young Communist League of the Soviet Union, wtih a membership of 18.5 million in 1956, is not far behind in mass coverage[10] and probably far superior in active dedication on a mass scale, whereas the Nazi and Fascist organizations had left real ideological indoctrination to small core groups. Even more substantial in number, though neither voluntary nor with the easily misused idealism of youth, were the compulsory labor organizations which Nazis, Fascists, and Communists fashioned from the free trade unions into instruments of party control over the vast millions

[10] This figure does not include the Little Octobrists and Young Pioneers, the Communist organizations for youth between the ages of 6 and 14. There is also a Communist Youth International, which, under the name World Federation of Democratic Youth, claims to have over 80 million members.

of workers. The Nazi Labor Front had 25 million members; the Soviet trade unions may well have over 40 million by now. A third very large sector of the population that came under direct totalitarian control were the peasants.[11] Both Communism in Russia and China and their satellites and German and Italian Fascism placed heavy emphasis on promises to the peasants and received generous support in return. With only grandiloquent praises of the peasant way of life made by the Fascists, and a passing phase of land distribution made by the Communists, the peasants were most cruelly deceived. The Communists next collectivized or communized the land, thereby achieving effective control over the peasants. The Nazis regimented agricultural production, in "the battle for food," and bureaucratized agriculture by turning the autonomous chambers of agriculture into state organizations subordinated to the quasi-corporate *Reich* Food Estate. With Mussolini's Fascists, regimentation for "the battle for food" and the attempt at autarchy were less severe, since he did not touch the estates of the landed oligarchy; 87 percent of the rural population continued to live marginal lives in wretched poverty.

Total organizational control Party control over the entire organizational and associational life, from women's auxiliaries to athletic clubs and discussion societies, completes the picture of control over the citizens of a totalitarian society. But there were also economic controls including the labor pass, the complete, centralized economic planning typical of Nazis and Communists, and the quasi-corporatism of German and Italian Fascism. A medieval, even Platonic scheme of representation by vocation, corporatism is an anachronistic governmental scheme in modern industrial society, a system which found favor also with some Catholic Conservative parties. To Mussolini and Hitler, it was a crude equivalent of what the *soviets* had been to Lenin: a welcome pretext for undermining the authority of democratic parties and parliaments. Corporate representation could also be used to dissolve the feelings of antagonism between management and labor. Fascist joint management-labor "syndicates" or the National Socialist Labor Front granted the management the "leader principle," albeit under state control, and flatly outlawed strikes. The *Reich* Food Estate was another such syndicate encompassing everyone engaged in the production, processing, and distribution of food.

[11] In prerevolutionary Russia, the peasants composed about 80 percent of the population; in China, more than 80 percent; in Italy, about 60 percent; in Germany, about 30 percent.

Propaganda monopoly of communications

The third distinguishing feature of totalitarian governments is their propaganda system based on a monopoly of all means of communications. Propaganda and terror are opposite poles between which there exists what the political scientists Carl J. Friedrich and Zbigniew K. Brzezinski have called the "psychic fluidum," the peculiar atmosphere of totalitarian dictatorship. Life is lived by the carrot and the whip —by the enticement of a glorious millennium to come and by the gripping fear of the midnight knock on the door and being hauled away to a secret death or worse. One can well imagine the state of mind of man living in a totalitarian environment.

The dynamic nature of propaganda..George Orwell, in his novel *1984*, has painted a persuasive picture of the continual pounding of totalitarian propaganda emanating from his "Ministry of Truth" on the eyes and ears of people, directing their feelings of love toward Big Brother and their hatred at the traitor Goldstein and at whichever of the two foreign superstates they are supposed to be fighting at the time. Orwell also emphasized the breathless, day-to-day existence from yesterday's propaganda theme to today's, while the past is constantly and systematically rewritten and its record, clippings from newspapers and periodicals, is dropped into the "memory hole," to be incinerated into oblivion. The extraordinary volume, the emotional, hate-filled character, the dynamic, breathless pace of totalitarian propaganda are among the characteristics setting it apart from other forms of advertising or persuasion. Like the workers' brigades of Chinese communes who were inundated with propaganda while working, eating lunch, during daily military drills, and during the periodic indoctrination sessions, man in a totalitarian environment is supposed to be constantly unsettled, mobilized, and militarized until he completely identifies with the "struggle" against the foreign devils and internal enemies, and for ever higher work quotas and production goals in agriculture and in industry. At the same time, continual brainwashing places him completely in the power of the totalitarian movement and crowds the last thought of resistance, the last mental reservation, from his mind.

Control over all mass media Another indispensable aspect of totalitarian propaganda is its monopolistic character. Every totalitarian dictatorship to date starts out by seizing control and imposing conformity of all mass communications media—the press, radio, books, motion pictures, and even of the publicly spoken word of church sermons and lectures—to the official propaganda line. Since totalitarian politicizes everything from economics to family affairs, sports, and culture, no subject or source of influence or persuasion is exempt from the centralized propaganda machinery. In addition to the establishment of total control over all domestic sources of information and opinion, the monopoly of the official propaganda mills is completed by the erection of impenetrable barriers to outside sources of information. The Iron and Bamboo curtains, among other things, signify a general ban on the movement of persons, newsprint, books, and movies across the borders, which both prevents news about the realities of totalitarianism to trickle out and maintains the monopoly over information within. Nazi Germany even imposed the death penalty for listening to foreign radio stations during World War II.

Controlling the perception of reality Since modern man can know most of his information about the world he lives in only indirectly through the mass media, the absolute monopoly of, say, Joseph Goebbels' Ministry of Propaganda and Public Enlightenment really amounts to control over knowable reality itself. If the totalitarian propagandists suppress all mention of "un-German" culture traditions or personalities long enough, they will be forgotten. If the propagandists decide to make Stalin post facto one of the leaders of the October Revolution, and to omit the role of Trotsky, this becomes the only known record of history Russians have. If Mussolini wanted his people to think that it was the Abyssinians who first attacked Italian regiments, that is all Italians knew about it. To create an excuse to invade Poland, Hitler had members of the Gestapo and SD (Security Service), dressed in Polish uniform, stage simulated border raids at various places. To lend authencity to the plans, condemned prisoners, clad in Polish uniforms, were left dead on the ground at the scenes of the "border incidents." Then the press and others were taken to the scenes so that Hitler could "prove" to his people that he had been provoked into the attack on Poland. Prophesy and fulfillment, provocation and reaction, even love and hatred, can be similarly manipulated. Hitler could first instruct his fifth column of Fascist professional revolutionaries to incite ethnic friction in Czechoslovakia and then move in with armed might to "rescue our German brethren from Czech hatred and atrocities," as his domestic propaganda put it. Mussolini and Stalin could cause a spate of atrocity stories about any neighboring country, to precede armed aggression there, in order to insure strong popular backing for any act of "retribution," even invasion. Is it any wonder that the Chinese hate Americans when they are constantly told about American imperialism and brutality? What very few persons there may be who are capable of supplying information contrary to the propaganda line hold their tongues under the threat of terror. They can trust no one, not even their friends and their Komsomol- or Hitler Youth-trained children.

The levels of propaganda   Far from a crude repetition of ideological doctrines, totalitarian propaganda has been a highly sophisticated tool manipulated by professionals for maximal effect and with the tactical flexibility required by the zigzags of the party line. Since a totalitarian society is organized in many concentric circles that differ in their involvement with the movement as well as in their knowledge of and tolerance for its true aims, the stream of propaganda messages has to be carefully matched to what the particular recipients should know and are likely to believe. All denizens of totalitarian society, except for the leader himself, are objects of propaganda, but on different levels. Party leadership, militia units, and the secret police or concentration camp guards are the most "in" and are allowed to know the closest approximation of where the movement is going. The party rank and file is at the next highest step of the degrees of totalitarian knowledge, but it is already under the deceptive influence of the Big Lie. Party auxiliaries, government officials, and functionaries of the quasi-corporate structure form the next lower ranks in the hierarchy of knowledge, where the smokescreen of lies gets even thicker and better attuned to what these respectable people can be expected to fight for. The public at large forms the next step, and finally there comes the foreign press and well-wishers in front organizations around the world.

Communist or Fascist totalitarian propaganda is pitched at different levels. For example, the top layer may understand an appeal to domestic vigilance and aggressiveness abroad to be a pure power play, or an indication of a hard-line policy to come, while the rank and file of Communists may think they are gloriously battling for the worldwide utopia. The Russian public may cooperate, because they believe current sacrifices to be their patriotic duty and to insure a better life for their grandchildren. Foreign observers may be led to regard the same Soviet foreign policies in question as a promotion of "national liberation" for the long-range benefit of world peace and freedom, and the domestic measures as the rise of a democratic and socialist "new civilization." There is no need to keep the message uniform or even consistent. Communist propaganda in the United States after World War II was presented to the general public as "20th century Americanism," while the party leadership was under obligation to serve the interests of the Soviet Union. Half a decade earlier, when the propaganda line changed with the collapse of the Nazi-Soviet Pact, Communist agitation[12] suddenly shifted from ardent pacifism and isolationism—"The Yanks are not coming"—to the call for warlike intervention in Europe: "The Yanks are not coming too late." In the same manner, Hitler managed his complete take-over behind such smokescreens for mass consumption as pseudo-conservatism and the "national rebirth." At a later point, it was vital to his success to proportion his anti-Semitic propaganda very carefully, according to how much harrassment and persecution of Jewish fellow citizens any particular public could be expected to tolerate at a particular time. Patterns of prejudice come in many shadings, and the dictator knows how to escalate his discriminatory actions, from the infamous Nuremberg Laws to systematic, large-scale genocide, without arousing alarm among his people.

The system of terror and fear

Directly complementary to propaganda is the totalitarian system of terror and fear. Totalitarian government is "permanent revolution," a constant struggle for an immensely ambitious future, and involves constant efforts to impose changes on resisting people and conditions. Totalitarian ideologies are wedded to "eternal, scientific laws" of historical evolution, economic or biological, and deal in "objective enemies" who, as in a science fiction novel, will not allow the restless mad scientist peace of mind until he has found a scientifically effective but diabolical way to dispose of them. When the madness that is "scientific ideology" seizes upon the method called totalitarian government, the ultimate, inevitable upshot is concentration camps in which human beings are treated as the refuse of the historical evolution posited by the totalitarian ideology. Marx spoke only of "expropriating the expropriators," that is, the capitalists, and Hitler's predecessors generally advocated, at the most, expropriation and segregation or forced emigration of the objects of their ethnic phobias. Violence was anticipated in either case only for a short revolutionary transition. But totalitarian dictatorships seem to drift inexorably toward stepping up the terror, institutionalizing violence and detention under inhuman conditions, and toward feeding not only the "objective enemies" designated by the ideology but constantly new categories of madly invented "objective enemies" into the man-eating machinery of the terror.

---

[12] Communists distinguish between "propaganda," the designing of arguments and their presentation, and "agitation," the pure demagogy of devising potent slogans and reaching a large audience.

The passion for unanimity and conformity

Totalitarianism as a form of militant mass mobilization is not content with propagandizing a passive audience. The people must respond with enthusiasm to the drives and mass appeals of the party. They must turn out with ardor for the sham elections and plebiscites of the regime, for which they are subjected to the most intense agitation by millions of party activists and youth organization members, who thereby also rekindle their own enthusiasm and crusading spirit. By thoroughly agitating, browbeating, arousing, and terrorizing their captive audience, the totalitarian leadership achieves control over minds and passions, resulting in 90 and more percent acclamation in elections and plebiscites in totalitarian systems. The passion for unanimity becomes a passion for total conformity of the people.

The hypnotic effect of mass enthusiasm Frequent repetition of the exercise makes acclamation and emotional transport a conditioned reflex. The dissenter in this raging sea of shouts of *Sieg-Heil!* or *Duce! Duce! Duce!* finds himself an isolated human being—cut off from all contact with his fellow man. At first he may feel he is the only sane person in a mob of maniacs. But then he too may succumb to the passion for unanimity when the mob, sensing a stranger in their midst, begins to turn on him as an unwelcome outsider. Or, perhaps, he may question his own sanity and succumb to the desire to belong when he is faced by the judgment of the totalitarians that he is a social misfit doomed by history or genetics. Dissenters who manage to flee the totalitarian country, and even jail and concentration camp inmates, develop a defense mechanism curiously patterned by the propaganda and policies of the regime. Unable any longer to judge issues dispassionately, they simply negate whatever the regime asserts and identify themselves with everything it condemns, including "foreign agents" or "creeping Communism" or "creeping capitalism," as the case may be.

Utter conformity in the party The passion for unanimity is most oppressive within the totalitarian party and, most of all, within such elite formations as the Nazi SS or its Fascist or Communist equivalent. Members are rated strictly by their enthusiastic performance and total conformity. Individual quirks or a lack of zeal, not to mention dissent, are reasons for expulsion and punishment. The search for deviants and dissenters, as with the public at large, makes terrorists of everybody and poisons the atmosphere at the most relaxed social gatherings and even in the family. Once a victim is found, whether real or fancied, the compulsion of his pursuers to relieve their tensions by directing their aggressions toward him is so violent that he cannot expect from them the slightest human feeling toward him. Seen from this angle, concentration camps and massive purges are a perfectly logical consequence of the "psychic fluidum" of totalitarianism quite apart from the possible economic benefit of slave labor and the need to punish dissenters. The brutality of the concentration camp guards is also an integral part of the fluidum, as well as a chance for the elite to show its zeal. As the commandant of the Nazi death camp Auschwitz testified, in a world in which your government and party leaders unceasingly preach hatred and violence against a minority, killing them becomes a natural thing to do.

The reign of fear Terror also becomes internalized as a half-conscious motive of fear. A person learns what not to do and say, and when not to ask questions. Just as the obedience to laws is in large part a habit of convenience, a matter of taking the path of least resistance rather than conscious acceptance of their justice and legitimacy, the rules of survival in a totalitarian environment make cowards of men. Most encounters of the average citizen with totalitarian injustice are so petty that he can postpone a showdown or evade the question unless he is directly victimized. And yet by taking the path of least resistance, a man becomes so implicated by his own silence from step to more incisive step that finally he can no longer say "No" when a decision big enough for a showdown arises. Thoroughly disoriented by his half-conscious fear, he finally uses all his ingenuity to invent excuses and rationalizations for his own passivity, rather than using it for revolt.

Secret police and terror The revolutionary tasks at hand, finally, require the presence of direct compulsion to remove the obstreperous and to "protect the people" against the subversive effect and activity of the old (bourgeois or landowning oligarchy) society, the Jews, or the foreign agents of the "worldwide capitalist (or Jewish) conspiracy." In the Soviet Union, the long succession of secret police organizations, Cheka, GPU, NKVD, MVD, and MGB, had to arrest and detain first the "bourgeois enemies," then foreign agents, Trotskyites, the millions of *kulaks* who resisted farm collectivization, persons guilty of nonfulfillment or "sabotage" of production quotas, the officers, bureaucrats, and party members purged in the 1930s and, every now and then, the leaders of the secret police itself, lest they become a menace to the regime. During and following World War II, the intelligentsia of Russian-occupied and satellite territories was seized, put in concentration camps, or liquidated outright without the usual test in a labor camp of whether they were an "incorrigible" part of the "objective enemies" of the Communist regime. The categories of victims are determined according to "objective criteria" by the mad scientist—categories such as Polish officers for the Katyn massacre, Lithuanian collectors of foreign stamps, and Hungarian students of Esperanto. While the Soviet secret police has been curbed somewhat since the fall of Stalin, there is plenty of evidence that it is still active and vigilant.

Italian Fascism not only started with the terrorist raids of the blackshirted militia, but in a way never quite managed to subdue their violence into the unified system characteristic of Soviet terror. Instead, the secret police, OVRA, was a state agency only partly staffed with party members and in competition with the political investigation of the party militia which also ran the special tribunal for trying anti-Fascists. Those who incurred the wrath of party or state were either confined to their locality or to the penal islands, the Italian equivalent of concentration camps. But while sporadic violence was often present and there was the usual totalitarian atmosphere of mutual fear and distrust, setting neighbor against neighbor and inviting volunteer informers and anonymous denunciations, the Italian terror never quite took on the appearance of the mad scientists systematically filing away "objective categories of enemies." German Fascism was more successful in subordinating the lust for violence of the original storm troopers (SA) to the goals of the regime in the blood purge of 1934.[13] Their successor organization, Himmler's SS, eventually gained complete control of the secret state police (Gestapo) and also operated the concentration camps, where anyone could be kept in "protective custody"—ostensibly to protect him from the wrath of the people—whenever and for as long as the SS desired. Death from beatings, malnutrition, random bruitality, "execution while escaping," and physical exhaustion from work was frequent, though mass genocide was generally committed at death camps or by execution commandos in the occupied territories of the East. The inmates of the camps were marked according to "objective categories" including political prisoners,[14] Jews, gypsies, criminals, homosexuals, and asocial elements. "Objective categories" in the Nazi system also played a role in the

---

[13] This was not the main purpose of the purge, which was to eliminate the SA as a rival to the power of the party. The SA was also noted for Socialistic leanings.

[14] This category included prominent members of other parties, opponents of the regime from among the churches and every walk of life, and members of the underground resistance to Hitler.

treatment of captive nationalities and in the *euthanasia* program of killing the "incurably ill."

There was also the usual atmosphere of fear and distrust. As in the other totalitarian countries, a legion of paid and volunteer informers helped the secret police. In the German-occupied territories, in contrast to the quiet and unobtrusive efficiency of NKVD and MVD, Gestapo and SS were notably unable, in spite of their public brutality, to prevent the organization of underground sabotage and guerrilla fighters. The guerrillas tied up whole German armies and otherwise injured the German war effort. In this as in many other things, Communist totalitarianism appears to have been a more mature and better organized totalitarian terror system, though we have to bear in mind that Nazi totalitarianism was fortunately destroyed from the outside after a mere dozen years of functioning, half of which were absorbed in the war effort. And since totalitarian dictatorships at their most brutal and successful have a way of accelerating their stormy course, there is no telling what diabolical "perfections" would have been in store for captive Europe had Nazi Germany won the war.

The United States and the Weimar analogy

Far from merely being a concern of historians, our knowledge of German National Socialism is frequently challenged by historical analogies. In addition to the popular comparisons of police or governmental repression of student militants to stormtrooper action and, conversely, of the militants to the Communists in the 1920s and 1930s, there is now a more sophisticated analogy abroad, comparing the contemporary American scene with the declining years of the Weimar Republic. Some observers, for example, have drawn attention to the abandon with which the new left today continually assaults the old liberals of the civil rights movement of the mid-1960s and of the New Deal. The Chicago demonstrations against the Democratic Presidential convention of 1968 were a good example of how radicals tend to hate moderates far more than they hate the conservatives or even the far right. In the last years of the Weimar Republic, likewise, the German Communists concentrated their hatred on Liberals and Social Democrats, whom they insisted on calling "social Fascists," rather than on the Nazis or the ultraconservatives. Political polarization was at least as acute as it has been in the United States in recent years.

Other observers even liken the American student rebels and their campus revolts to the takeover of Nazi students at several German universities in 1929/1930, three years before Hitler even became chancellor. There are indeed many surface similarities in techniques, in the righteous bullying, in the idealism displayed, and in the conscious rejection of reason in favor or emotion and "right" feeling. Most tellingly, the militant infatuation with political violence as a means to the envisaged ends can be compared to the Fascist fascination with violence. However, the argument significantly omits major differences in goals. The pacifism and antiracism which characterize the goals of American students were certainly lacking in the Nazi militants. The similarities in attitude tend to consist mostly of typical features of modern youth movements.

Apart from a few superficial similarities, then, the Weimar analogy does not hold water and deserves to be emptied of the verbal exaggerations which are so popular today. Just as it may be necessary to remind ourselves that current office-holders, college administrators, or sheriffs are by no stretch of the imagination in the same class of villains as Adolf Hitler, Eichmann, or Stalin, we should also realize that however obnoxious student militants of the 1970s may seem, they are not like the stormtroopers nor the Communists of old. The verbal overkill characterizing the end of the 1960s and the beginning of the 1970s can only obscure the most elementary distinctions of fact if we indiscriminately identify such things as current racism with the genocide of the Jews in the Third Reich, or totalitarian terror and concentration camps with the eagerly sought confrontations of students with the police, or some rather minor indignities and disruptions by militant students with the rampant brutality of Nazi or Fascist goon squads. Political or historical comparison is devoid of all good sense and significance without exercise of sane judgment.

CHAPTER **15** WORLD POLITICS
IN THE AGE
OF REVOLUTION

The extraordinary social upheavals and economic and political revolutions of our age have transformed the nature and scope of international politics as well. What used to be little clusters of competing or peacefully coexisting peoples and powers on different continents has become one worldwide system of politics from which no country can isolate itself. Far-flung economic interests and warlike clashes between nations have long reached from one continent to another and twice in this century have drawn the whole world into global wars. Huge semitraditional empires ruling over many ancient civilizations and traditional peasant societies have been jettisoned into small national communities by the processes of mass mobilization, nationalism, and war. Great colonial empires rose as a result of the internal upheavals and collapsed for the same reason within the span of a few generations. Newly independent nation-states seek admittance to the stage of world politics every year and have to be integrated into the wobbly mechanisms of the international community for the preservation of peace.

The reader of this book has already encountered in earlier chapters some of the problems and dilemmas of international politics in the revolutionary age, most notably in the critical discussion of the concepts of state and sovereignty[1] and of the institutional devices such as international law and organization that seek to modify the international system of sovereign states. The present discussion will concentrate on the social forces that have made the international politics of this age the politics of power, violence, and instability— in particular *nationalism* and *imperialism*. It will end with a consideration of the outlook for international politics in the near and distant future.

THE DRIVING FORCE OF NATIONALISM

What is a nation? Solidarity among people sharing a common language, faith, or history, and loyalty to one's homeland and ruler are as old as the hills. But the words "nationality" and "nationalism," at least in their modern meaning,[2] are more properly associated with the processes of political development and social mobilization discussed in Chapter 12. In the Middle Ages and even in the Renaissance, most Western Europeans still attached far more importance to their ascribed social status than to being Frenchmen, Englishmen, or Germans. The first glimpses of a rising national consciousness can be gotten from a few Renaissance intellectuals such as the poet Dante and the historian Machiavelli.

The birth of liberal nationalism

On a mass level, identification with the nation did not come until the age of the great revolutions. The French Revolution, in particular, gave the word *nation* its modern meaning. The nation was the true source of all authority as opposed to the traditional rights of monarchy, church, and nobility. The *bourgeoisie* claimed to represent the entire nation and seized power on its behalf. Thus revolutionary nationalism became wedded to revolutionary Liberalism, and *liberal nationalism* was born. For the next fifty years and longer, liberal nationalism was the fighting creed of middle-class movements striving for the liberalization of their social order and for national unification or emancipation among such peoples as the Germans, Danes, Poles, and Italians.

[1] See Chapter 3. See also relevant passages in Chapters 5, 11, 12, and 14.

[2] By common consensus, scholars also like to apply the terms to such ancient peoples as the Greeks and Hebrews, although the elements of a modern nation are not all met.

The ambiguities inherent in nationalism

From the beginning, however, liberal nationalism harbored profound ambiguities, if not irreconcilable contradictions. In spite of the nationalistic overtones, the creed of the French and American revolutionaries had been cosmopolitan. As the armies of Napoleon carried the gospel of the French Revolution over the battlefields of Europe, they professed to bring national and individual liberty to all the peoples whose governments they defeated. Yet while the liberal-national creed fell on willing ears, the defeated nations could not help but see in the French armies alien conquerors establishing a self-serving empire. Thus French nationalism engendered a German nationalistic reaction, Italian nationalism, and similar movements everywhere whose antagonism to French imperialism often outweighed their liberal inspiration. To be sure, the liberal nationalism of the American Revolution had also been greatly enhanced by hostility to British imperialism, and the French revolutionaries never received more mass support than when the armies of foreign monarchs invaded France to snuff out the revolutionary challenge to the old order. But the process of social and political modernization in America, Great Britain, the Low Countries, and France was sufficiently advanced at the time to give Liberalism a broad and lasting base unlike conditions in Italy, Germany, on the Iberian peninsula, or among the Slavic peoples.

Where national unity still had to be achieved against the resistance of princes and sovereign states, as in Italy and Germany, the strength of the traditional forces exacted crucial compromises from the liberal-national movements. National unification could be attained only with the cooperation of such forces as the kings and aristocratic establishments of the strongest states—such as Prussia in Germany or Savoy in Italy—who were most unlikely to be won over by appeals to democratic sentiment. And so the weakness of Liberalism and the expediencies of unification combined to permit the survival of strong authoritarian elements and to lend a halo to such brute military force as was necessary to overcome the resistance to unification. None of the prominent figures of the struggles for Italian or German national unification in the 1860s, in fact, could be called a liberal democrat. Many of them were rather conservative diplomats, or strident nationalists, or military heroes.

Liberal nationalism among such peoples as the Poles or the modern Greeks, whose nationhood required liberation from the Russian, Prussian, Hapsburg, or Turkish empires, was similarly far more nationalistic than liberal. They thought of liberty more in terms of liberation from an alien yoke than as a new internal social order. Like many prominent Italian and German nationalists, they put collective liberty above individual liberty, although their quasi-colonial status tended to imbue them with a pervasive antiauthoritarian effect. In this, the "unredeemed" nationalities of nineteenth-century Eastern Europe resembled the nationalism of the new nations of today, except that the aspirations of social, economic, and political modernization of the latter are more concrete and purposeful than were the quasi-religious dreams of national salvation of nineteenth-century *Europa irredenta*. The *modernizing nationalism* of former colonial peoples in Africa, Asia, the Middle East, and Latin America is clearly oriented toward the forms, goals, and procedures of modern civilization, which has universally challenged the survivals of traditionalism. By comparison with a substantial part of the European antecedents, then, the contemporary "new nationalism" is more liberal than that of nineteenth-century Central, Southern, or Eastern Europe.[3] But then, this comparison is with nineteenth-century standards of political authoritarianism rather than with twentieth-century liberal democracy. The leadership of most developing countries today tends to be libertarian mostly with regard to freedom from external domination. This is particularly true of brutal dictatorships such as Haiti under the late Doc Duvalier or Communist North Vietnam or North Korea, where executions are the routine method of dealing with resistance or opposition.

The deepest ambiguity of liberal nationalism lay in the definition of the term *nation* and in the nature of the attitudes to be inculcated toward it. Nations, like individuals, are products of heredity and environment, though the heredity is clearly cultural rather than biological. Where a people had experienced a common fate under a common government for centuries and within clearly defined boundaries, as in France or England, it seemed easy to assume that national communities were one of the "givens" of the human condition, eternal verities only now uncovered. The poets of a nation would rhapsodize about its attributes, glories, and traditions. Historians inquired into past manifestations of its character and often invented whole prehistories that more properly belonged to the realm of myth and folklore. But what about the identity of a nation of people who, like the Germans, had for centuries existed in many different states and even under different flags, including those of neighboring coun-

---

[3] This comparison is often wrongly drawn between the new nations and contemporary European Liberalism or lost in the consideration of the gaps between theory and practice of the new nations. It is not fair to expect the new nations to live up to every fine point of constitutional democracy.

tries? What if some parts of what one nationalist movement claimed to be one great nation wanted to be little nations unto themselves? The larger Pan-Arab nation promoted by the late President Nasser of Egypt included several smaller nations such as Morocco, Tunisia, and Iraq, which have their own, less inclusive, nationalist movements and, in some cases, smaller nationalities within, such as the Kurds of Iraq. Or what if large areas, as in Eastern Europe, are populated by such a mixture of awakening Magyar, Slavic, Teutonic, and other nationalities as to make the drawing of ethnic boundaries impossible or to lead to the Balkanization of whole regions into states so small they cannot survive?

Nationality as a principle of political organization makes some sense when there is present a large, contiguous community united by consciousness of national identity and loyalty. Under such optimal conditions, nationalism can direct the enormous energies released by the massive social mobilization taking place on the way from traditionalism to modernity into constructive channels for building a nation-state and reorganizing society. In particular, nationalism can serve to marshal the forces necessary to achieve independence from alien control or national unity as prerequisites to the development indicated above. Where national identity is doubtful or controversial, however, nationalism can become a destructive force. Young nations, like young individuals, can suffer identity crises so severe that they are led into extremely asocial, aggressive behavior.

Especially when several ethnic communities inhabit the same area, nationalism is bound to awaken appetites for power that increase ethnic friction to the point of discrimination, persecution, even genocide, unless violence can be restrained and a more inclusive political faith takes the place of nationalism. There are many nations that are composed of several ethnic communities, have more than one religious faith and several languages. Switzerland, the Philippines, and India demonstrate that relatively stable national communities with an abiding sense of loyalty can be built on such a basis. But first there must be inculcated a more inclusive nationalism, and feelings of exclusiveness or superiority must be expunged from the public mind.

The rise of integral nationalism

The ominous development of European nationalism in the late nineteenth and early twentieth centuries bears testimony to the ambiguities and dangers inherent in nationalism. As middle-class movements became increasingly conservative in reaction to the rise of Socialist movements, the uglier aspects of nationalism came to the fore both in domestic and foreign policy. Movements and spokesmen for *integral nationalism* arose, beginning with the French *Action Française*. Integral nationalists were obsessed with the integrity or "purity" of the nation, an obsession that implied a desire to purge it of "alien" elements in culture and population. Ugly scandals occurred such as the Dreyfus Affair and other anti-Semitic manifestations and actions. Carried to a biologically motivated extreme, integral nationalism amounts to racism demanding, as it were, the establishment of a "pure French race" or an "Anglo-Saxon race" or a "German race." In this form, its theories and sentiments were picked up after World War I by Fascist movements and writers.

In foreign policy, nationalism became the aggressive assertion of one's national interest or national rights, regardless of the conflicting rights of other nations. The wounded pride of a nation defeated in war, such as the French at Sedan (1870) and the Germans in 1918, became a powerful spur to aggressive action. The sense of competition for colonies or for foreign markets or for a proper place among the great powers stirred up nations and induced them to prodigious efforts and a yen for using force against one another. Worship of one's own nation all too often came to be accompanied by loathing for the "inferior breeds." Nations who had minorities living in the area of neighboring countries demanded large cessions of territory, regardless of what other ethnic stocks might be living there or what other nations might claim the same territory. Latecomers to the race for colonies, such as Germany and Italy, also claimed to be inhibited in their development by a lack of "living-space" which they demanded from neighboring countries or from the established colonial powers. This was the setting of crass national egotisms of both the have and have-not powers among whom the World War I broke out.

Although the principle of national self-determination played an important role in the peace settlement of 1919, at least on the side of the victorious Allies, a few years later the defeated powers as well as some others who felt cheated out of their just national claims once more went on a rampage of aggressive nationalism. Japan plunged into Manchuria (1931) and later into China (1937); Italy seized Fiume (1921) and, under Mussolini, grabbed Ethiopia (1936) and Albania (1939); Hitler's Germany remilitarized the Rhineland (1936) and seized Austria (1938), Czechoslovakia (1938–1939), and West Poland (1939); and the Soviet Union helped itself to East Poland (1939), the Baltic countries, and parts of Finland and Roumania (1940). The League of Nations could not stop the resurgence of power politics until a second great alliance of powers in World War II beat down what had by then become an unabashed drive for empire by the three Axis powers, Italy, Germany, and Japan.

Contemporary nationalism

Having observed the debacle of one hundred fifty years of nationalism in Europe, few observers will look at contemporary nationalism with anything but a jaundiced eye. The postwar leaders of continental Europe have tried to bury the ghost of nationalism underneath the foundation of an economic and political union of European states. The attempts of President de Gaulle of France to shore up the national grandeur of his country in the traditional manner had about them a curious air of anachronism and were promptly abandoned by his successors. The revival of national feeling in Eastern Europe, to be sure, spells liberalization and national emancipation from the Soviet Empire in the original tradition of liberal nationalism, though still without the full ramifications of the liberal faith.

The national independence movements of Asia, Africa, the Middle East, and Latin America similarly are motivated by the desire for liberty. Yet there is abundant evidence that with many of them the nation-building energies of the great transformation tend to get bogged down in ethnic divisions that pit Africans against Africans, Arabs or Indians, or Malays and Javanese against Chinese communities.

As national leaders face the usual drab postindependence problems, and their newly born nations experience the postindependence letdown, also, the temptation is great to turn on neighboring countries. An awakening nation, after all, is one of the largest and most excited in-groups imaginable, and it is not surprising that the intense in-group feeling should feed off hostility against out-groups, or at least against the colonial powers of yesterday. In this unstable situation, causes for conquest or empire-building are easily found. Indonesia claimed distant ethnic kinship and collaboration with the colonialists for its war on Malaysia. President Nasser of Egypt promoted his Pan-Arab union by pouring out vast torrents of radio propaganda and by exporting Egyptian schoolteachers and other trained personnel to the less-developed new nations of Africa. Some African nationalist leaders similarly sought to build up their own power by intervention in the troubles and insurrections of other countries such as the former Belgian Congo. And so it seems that the new nationalism of today is just as likely to develop in the wrong direction as did nationalism in the Western Europe of yesterday.

IMPERIALISM, OLD AND NEW

Nationalism is the modern manifestation of the great transformation on a mass scale; imperialism, on the other hand, can be traced back to the dawn of history. To be sure, some of its conditions and goals today may differ from earlier antecedents. The frequent use of the word "imperialism" as an epithet, and in particular according to Lenin's formula, has tended to obscure its meaning and to suggest that it is chiefly a modern phenomenon. But the establishment of the Egyptian, Assyrian, and Persian empires and, in fact, almost all the historical drives for empire until that of Napoleon I, antedated modern capitalism and most manifestations of modernity. Most of the colonial empires of recent times were acquired by countries undergoing a phase of modernization, which is not to say that the motive for acquisition necessarily reflected modern, rational objectives.

Definition of imperialism

Because there is some controversy regarding the concept of imperialism, a broad definition is in order. The word "imperialism" comes from "empire." An empire properly so-called is a large, multinational (or multiethnic) state wherein there is a mother country, privileged nation, "race," or otherwise distinct group to which the other nations, groups, or areas (colonies) are subordinated. Large state organized in a federal manner, even a world federation, are not empires, and neither are international organizations such as the United Nations. Policies aiming at the establishment of an empire or at its expansion over further subject peoples are imperialistic.

Similarly imperialistic are policies that attempt to defend the imperial relationship by force or threat of force against persistent challenge on the part of one or more of the subject nations, groups, or areas. This is not to say that empires cannot be or have not been benevolent or even beneficial to the peoples under their power. They can at times be and have been benevolent. But there comes a time when the subject groups or nations will demand their self-determination. By definition, the right of self-determination includes that of being the sole judge of whether or not to remain under an imperial power, no matter how benevolent or enlightened. It is natural for the rulers and the ruled to disagree about the legitimate nature or objectives of imperial rule. Legitimate rule implies a large measure of acceptance by the ruled, and there may often be doubt in the development of aspirations toward autonomy as to the point in time when a subject people definitely no longer accepts the legitimacy of the rulers. The use of force or threat of force by the rulers against the population at large is generally a telltale sign that their legitimate authority to rule has been eroded.[4]

Imperialistic policies, while implying the "desire" of a whole mother country and its population to exercise direction over another people, generally are the brainchildren of imperialistic politicians, pressure groups, or popular parties or movements. Imperialistic leaders and movements mostly orient their policies to existing political communities, for example, by promoting the subordination of India to Great Britain in a British Empire or by insisting on a forceful repression of Indian demands for autonomy. But imperialists can also be dedicated to the establishment of an utopian empire of a not-yet-extant master community over yet-unorganized subject populations. Declining empires, such as those of Turkey, Austro-Hungary, or the colonial empires in Africa or Asia, often give birth to such imperialistic movements aiming at the establishment of new —pan-Turkish, pan-German, or white European—empires of a newly postulated master race over slave populations constituted by the barely awakening new nationalities in their domain or even beyond the old imperial borders.

These revolutionary movements are imperialistic in a sense different from the imperialism of the international Communist movement. Whereas the advocates of a master race crudely assert their goal of domination, the Communist movements smuggle in imperialism through the back door. Although they speak of liberating subject peoples from alien, colonial, or class rule, they promote this liberation not by appealing to the reason of the populace but rather to their emotional hatreds and fears, by subversion, infiltration of nationalist movements, terrorism, and violence. Where Communists have come to power by force or deception, as in Eastern Europe after World War II, moreover, they quickly turned their own theory of Communist development into a rationalization of imperialism: The "less advanced" people's republics of the satellite nations, as a matter of course, had to accept the domination, guidance, and economic exploitation of the "more advanced" USSR. A similar relationship existed until very recently also between the Russian Com-

---

[4] This rule of thumb has its pitfalls in the challenge of small extremist minorities to generally accepted imperial authority, as in French Algeria in the 1950s, when nationalist terrorism engendered French counterterror, and the legitimacy of French authority progressively lost credence.

munist party and Communist parties elsewhere. The uses of force in suppressing satellite rebellion and earlier rebellion against opposition within the international movement itself was a clear indication that imperialism by any other name is still imperialism. The history of Russian "federalism" was similarly revealed as imperialistic from the moment nationalistic leaders and movements in the member states were violently stamped out.

The drives behind imperialism

What is the dominant motive of imperialism in its various forms? There have been so many imperialistic phenomena under such complex situations that it would be foolish to seek the explanation in any one isolated factor. The history of how particular empires were acquired, maintained, and defended against challenges from within generally falls into several phases of which only some deserve the name "imperialistic." Even during the drive for acquiring, expanding, or defending, say, the British Empire, there were often competing groups and leaders in sharp disagreement on the issues of imperialistic policy. Often, substantial numbers of Englishmen opposed new acquisitions, called the empire an unnecessary burden, or fought bitterly any attempt to stop the advance of the British colonies toward independence. A search for causes, therefore, should at least place as much emphasis on the individual motivation of imperialists as on the broad social factors.

Desire for power According to Joseph Schumpeter,[5] much of the drive behind imperialism can be reduced to atavistic, aggressive instincts and the desire for power that have motivated imperialists from the days of the ancient empires. Frequently the driving force was a warrior caste that sought to maintain its domestic social status and dominant position by recurring aggressions abroad. Its victories would add new territories and subject peoples to the realm. The tribute exacted and the treasures taken from the vanquished added to its domestic power and prestige, as well as to its ability to embark on future aggressive ventures. The atavistic overtones of aggression and desire for power are as present in modern imperialism as they were in ancient times, albeit hidden under a veneer of respectability and proper procedure. Only in wartime, or when a hostile imperialistic drive has threatened a country's territory, the civilized peoples of modernity may drop their restraint and act as their warrior forebears did. Although deeply shocked when the totalitarian dictators

[5] See his book *Imperialism and Social Classes* (New York: Kelley, 1939). Also available in paperbound edition (New York: World Publishing, 1955).

of the period between the two World Wars brazenly demonstrated their desire for territorial aggrandizement by open aggression upon weaker neighbors, the civilized world was much less squeamish about its own colonial policies.

Desire for prestige An element of the same atavistic instinct is also the sense of prestige and grandeur that often spreads imperialistic feelings among the masses of the population. The imperialistic drives of a Napoleon I, a Mussolini, or a Hitler would have been inconceivable without the pride that masses of common soldiers and the population at large took in their military triumphs. The officer corps of professional armies tend to be deeply offended by the loss of colonies, whether they are given independence peacefully or as a result of a lost colonial war. Substantial elements of the French army and civil service, for example, were motivated to join the extreme right wing by their reaction to the loss of Indochina and Algeria. Their embittered resistance to Indochinese and Algerian self-determination was a good example of imperialism.

Economic motives The economic motives of imperialism have often been the subject of controversy among scholars and statesmen. There can be little doubt that economic motivation plays a very important role in contemporary imperialism. Nobody can deny that it is the expectation of greater profits or of easier access to wealth that drives economic enterprise and individual settlers or businessmen to seek their fortune in less-developed lands. The history of colonial empires of the modern age has also given many example of the process by which the enterprises or settlers then persuade their governments back home to take over the country in which they have acquired possessions or are carrying on business operations. When empires disintegrate, finally, the settlers and investments from the mother country frequently become the chief obstacles to a painless transition to self-determination. In all of these instances, individual economic self-interest is a major factor.

At the same time, however, the importance of other motives and the complexity of the situation tend to gainsay the validity of grand economic theories of imperialism. Although individual economic enterprises in less-developed areas or colonies may be very profitable, for example, few colonies as a whole have been profitable. The great "race for colonies" among the Western powers at the end of the nineteenth century and the beginning of the twentieth century was only in small part motivated by economic considerations. It was instead a competition for the pride and glory of empire and for greater power in relation to rivaling empires. Atavistic instincts far outweighed the role of capitalism as a spur to imperialism. Once individual economic interest or settlement and colonization has led to the establishment of colonial rule, this change in itself creates a welter of noneconomic relationships and considerations, such as the politics of empire at home, in the colony, and among the imperial powers. Individuals or economic enterprises are far more willing to sacrifice their stake in a foreign area and to withdraw than are great powers willing to give up their control once it is established. Here again prestige and power, or a loss of face at home and abroad, are weighed more carefully than are dollars and cents.

Racial or ethnic stratification Where large settlements of people from the mother country occur in a less-advanced area of ethnically different stock or different color of skin, factors of personal relations and attitudes are likely to take on pivotal importance. The large colonies of Europeans in South Africa, Southern Rhodesia, Kenya, and Algeria present patterns quite different from those of other British or French colonies. Prejudice and discrimination, combined with the economic skill and power of the Europeans, tended to establish patterns of rigid racial stratification in these areas, culminating in the South African system of *apartheid*. Although the European settlers generally ended up with the more desirable land and the most productive businesses, the social dynamics behind the developing relationship were not economic in character but rather based on prejudice and power. The aspirations of the native population for equal voting privileges, not to mention self-determination, were consequently received with wild fears of violence and native revolution, and not only fears of economic loss.

These unproven expectations naturally led to thoughts of counter-revolution and attempts at establishing racist dictatorships of white supremacy. In Kenya alone, wiser counsel prevailed after some initial repression. The native demands for *uhuru* (freedom) were granted, and the remaining Europeans live and carry on business in Kenya in harmony with the native population. The good example of Kenya unfortunately failed to assuage the fears of the Europeans in Southern Rhodesia, who seceded from the British Crown in the face of British threats and a boycott by all major powers, including the United States. Their expectations of violence and native take-over are evidently driving them inexorably toward the pattern of the Union of South Africa, where racism and fear have already induced the government to abrogate most of the individual rights and freedoms sacred to the Western constitutional tradition. In Algeria, years of civil war and terror from both sides precipitated a series of severe political crises in metropolitan France, culminating in repeated attempts by the French *colons* in Algeria and their friends in army and civil service to seize power in France. The astute maneuvering of President de Gaulle, who came to power as a result of a major crisis and was presumed by the *colons* to favor their cause, finally ended the Algerian crisis peacefully. The *colons*, however, were mindful of the legacy of violence and preferred to emigrate from Algeria rather than to put the Algerian promises of cooperation to the test.

Ideological imperialism   There is a great difference between the acquisition of colonial empires over a long period of time and the sudden flash floods of imperialism associated with the revolutionary ideologies of our time. The British, Dutch, Belgian, and French empires were acquired over a period of several generations and largely, to use the phrase of the British historian Sir John Robert Seeley, "in a fit of absent-mindedness." Individual greed and pursuit of glory, the differential in the stage of development between colonies and mother country, and reasons of state and imperial power politics provided the changing fabric of motives that built and maintained these empires for a century or more. Napoleon I, by contrast, carried the creed of the French Revolution in a brief decade of imperialism all over continental Europe, not unlike Alexander the Great more than two thousand years earlier, who in the same brief span of time conquered a vast empire for Hellenic civilization, interethnic brotherhood, and his personal sense of divine mission. The powers threatened by Napoleon and the French revolutionary ideology struggled to establish a battle line of *containment* for the flood of ideological imperialism, much as the Western powers have been attempting to contain the spread of Communism to further areas since 1945. Behind the theory of containment there stands the hope that the fever of revolutionary ideology will eventually cool and its fires burn out. Napoleon was defeated by a grand alliance of enemies when his armies were depleted and overextended and the sense of revolutionary mission was lost in nationalistic antagonisms. Hitler's racist empire in Europe was built in a few years and was contained and brought down in an equally short period of time by a similar grand alliance. The Communist empire, too, has lost its monolithic character and shows increasing signs of disorganization, if not disintegration.

The driving force behind ideological imperialism is obviously not a matter of economic motivation or, in most cases, even of a differential in the sages of development. It is, rather, the power of the fanatically held belief in the worldwide mission of the particular ideological movement that inspires soldiers, guerrillas, and partisans to sacrifice their property, personal freedom, and perhaps even their lives, in the service of the conquering ideology. The presence of large numbers of persons who are uprooted and disoriented, perhaps transitionals in a developing society, and hence easy converts to ideological imperialism, is also crucial. The closest analogy to this fanaticism can be found, perhaps, in the Christian crusades of the Middle Ages, or the triumphant march of the Islamic religion over a large part of the known world. Like all fanaticism, ideological imperialism tends to be rather blind with regard to ends and means, and destructive to antagonist and protagonist alike. Yet mankind tends to judge ideological imperialism largely according to the merits of the ideology advanced rather than according to the number of people slain or robbed in its pursuit. There is a utopian, chiliastic streak in most men, no matter how modern and rationalistic, that makes them forget scruples and caution in pursuit of an inspiring dream.

THE OUTLOOK: NEITHER PEACE NOR WAR

It should be clear from the foregoing discussion of the social upheaval of modernization and its impact on international politics that the forecast for the future of world affairs is stormy. In the phrase of the title of a book by the British historian Hugh Seton-Watson, there has been "neither war nor peace" since 1945, though the guns have been silent much of the time. The state of instability in world politics between war and peace is likely to continue for as far ahead as one can see.

Major causes of international instability

Impact of modernization process The most important sources of international instability are the internal processes of mass mobilization and modernization in many new nations, which are likely to go on for many more decades, with many newly born nations still to come. All the problems of development—economic, social, and political, the search for national identity and unity, and the slow construction of constitutional, or better yet, democratic stability—have an immediate impact upon international politics. Their influence on the foreign policy of new nations has often expressed itself in a strong preference for neutralism and isolation from the conflicts of world politics so that a new nation may work out its internal problems without being disturbed. However, there have also been frequent examples of countries in the throes of modernization whose governments deliberately chose to exploit external aggression and hatred of other nations to deal with domestic crises. Picking on a national outgroup helps to unify the ingroup, thereby overcoming the universal problems of achieving and maintaining national unity. Many a dominant upper class also has sought to evade the demands for equality by the masses by advocating a virulent anticolonialism or aggression against a neighbor country.

Wars in an age of mass mobilization are easy to get into: Conflicts are ever present, and all that an aggressively inclined government has to do is not to press for a peaceful settlement of its international disputes. Popular sentiment will invariably side with its own government and convince itself of the just and largely defensive nature of any war. While hostilities are in progress, moreover, the government and its supporters can silence or even persecute their internal opposition as being disloyal at a time of national emergency.

Role of the differential of development   The weakness and instability of some new nations also invite aggression and manipulation by stronger powers who may have something to gain in the process. This is especially true of the inevitable differentials between countries in varying stages of development that underlie most modern colonial empires, including the Communist bloc. It is ironic to see how the nationalism of some Western nations eventually turned into an imperialistic drive for a colonial empire over less developed lands, only to sow the seeds of modernization and nationalism among the colonial peoples as well and to usher in the process leading to their eventual emancipation. If ever there comes a time when all nations have developed to a comparable level and the differentials of development have disappeared, this may well signify the end of international instability.

Rearguard battle of colonialism   The second and third major causes of international instability are two kinds of imperialism: the rearguard battle of colonialism and totalitarian imperialism. There still exist colonial empires that have barely begun to feel the winds of change, such as that of Portugal, and remainders of other colonial empires that have as yet to undertake the difficult ascent to independence. Now, more than ever, attempts at repressing broadly based nationalist movements are a threat to international peace. The new nations of Asia and Africa have long formed a powerful bloc that naturally takes the side of the nationalist movements. The Communist nations are anxious to use the colonial struggle to promote their own goals. The Western powers, including the "first new nation," the United States, are stuck with the label of "colonialists" by association. The South African system of apartheid is similarly a threat to international peace in that it creates a neocolonial empire in which the carefully segregated white European communities rule over communities of other stock. It is hardly surprising that the Afro-Asian bloc sympathizes with the aspirations of the nationalist movement in South Africa.

Threat of totalitarian imperialism The threat of totalitarian imperialism has been no less acute and intermittently a greater menace to peace than has been the rearguard battle of colonialism. "Today we own Germany, tomorrow it will be the whole world" was the closing line of a popular marching song of the Nazi party. Totalitarian government in Italy, Germany, the Soviet Union, and China[6] invariably has implied persistent efforts at militarizing the whole society and teaching all citizens from a tender age to hate and attack certain foreign nations. Fascist Germany maintained subversive fifth columns in many countries, including the United States, toward the day a worldwide Fascist order would be brought about by war and revolution. The Communist International and its successor organizations have similarly organized and maintained subversive parties the world over that were most useful both as fifth columns and where conditions allowed Communist take-overs, as in Eastern Europe in the years 1946–1948.

The totalitarian mentality lends to this form of aggression its typical features. Unlike rearguard colonialism, it is not content with rule over limited possessions but thinks in global, total terms. And in characteristic manner, totalitarians will strain their last material resources and personal sacrifices for the pursuit of the utopian empire.[7] Thinking in terms of the revolutionary dialectic, moreover, they are almost impossible to discourage. What they cannot conquer today they will tackle again tomorrow, and the day after tomorrow and so on, in spite of temporary setbacks, ever straining toward achieving the final triumph. The dialectic of the revoluntary struggle, whether Fascist or Communist, in fact obliterates the traditional separation between foreign and domestic politics. Persecuting hostile classes or "races" within, or battling foreign powers, is all part of the same revolutionary struggle. Civil war and international war, domestic revolution and worldwide revolutionary imperialism are

---

[6] Even such a small totalitarian state as Cuba under Castro has embarked on carrying its own kind of revolution to other Latin American countries.

[7] The self-styled Third Reich of the Nazi movement was such a vision of empire, the word Reich "meaning" empire.

inseparable. Victory abroad, in fact, is more important than domestic success. Victory in the worldwide revolutionary endeavor is the highest goal to which all other concerns and considerations must be sacrificed. It is precisely the single-mindedness of totalitarian imperialism that makes it such a formidable foe for nontotalitarian countries.

Totalitarian imperialism and development The nuclear stalemate between East and West has shifted the external threat of totalitarian imperialism to the developing countries. There the battle for the minds of men goes on in a setting dominated by the transitional personality and the social problems and maladjustments of the great transition. To the relatively authoritarian mind of transitional man, liberal democracy is as visionary and utopian as Communism. The latter, in fact, holds a quasi-religious appeal mixed with secret promises of power that democracy cannot match. By the time a transitional society has developed the kind of balance and maturity required for the appreciation of democracy, the totalitarian cadres may have seized power. The best strategy of countering totalitarian imperialism, consequently, consists in political delaying tactics, or containment, coupled with a concerted effort to speed up social and economic development. This is the rationale behind much of the Western policy of political (and at times military) involvement in devoloping areas and behind foreign aid.

Unfortunately, the task at hand presents enormous difficulties of understanding in the Western democracies on the part of the broad public, which must support the policies of their governments. If the challenge were a matter of aggressive war or an open drive for totalitarian empire as in World War II, their patriotic feelings could be engaged and they would understand what is at stake. But the people are ill equipped to recognize the totalitarian threat in what may look superficially like a bona fide nationalist movement or like the American war of independence. Unable to comprehend the challenge abroad, the people of Western democracies are tempted to lapse into a posture of isolationism or to demand either a quick, all-out victory or Western withdrawal. They also demand of the transitional, non-Communist, native politicians and their people the conduct and procedures of an advanced democratic society or else that the West should abandon them to the greedy hands of totalitarian imperialism. It is false alternatives such as these that are likely to lose the battle of containment.

Totalitarianism in Western countries The popular understanding of the threat of totalitarianism at home in the Western democracies is almost as weak as the understanding with regard to the developing areas. The preceding chapters about the characteristics of totalitarian government in general, and Communist and Fascist movements in particular, should leave but little doubt in the mind of the reader about the differences between totalitarian and democratic approaches. A political party can be Conservative, Liberal, or Democratic Socialist, and adhere to constitutional democracy. But if it adopts Lenin's organizational weapon and models its organization and methods on those of the Communist party, whatever may be its excuse, it is *totalitarian in intent* beyond a reasonable doubt. If an organization goes out of its way to exploit group tensions, irrational fears, and a feeling of social or national decline, or instigates hate campaigns against a scapegoat or between "races," as the public defines them, such action is incompatible with the basic assumptions of democracy —and it is at least incipiently totalitarian. In Western democracy, moreover, any attempt to impose a narrow orthodoxy, a "genuine Germanism" or "Americanism" on a free, pluralistic society—along with the banning of "un-British," un-French," "un-German," or "un-American" elements—is a danger signal. This is even more true if a group is dedicated to violence and intimidation or to the advocacy of wars of aggrandizement and empire, the irrational glorification of a leader, an irresponsible elite, the cult of the group, or authoritarianism. None of these elements fits into the patterns of moderation and of getting along with one another—patterns that are necessary for democratic politics. They are all capable of contributing to the rise of a totalitarian dictatorship, complete with a totalitarian *Führer* and his party, and with the "psychic fluidum" of incessant propaganda and terror.

The differences between democratic political behavior and totalitarian politics are so clear that they can be recognized through all manner of smokescreens and deceptive Big Lies. Totalitarian movements need not be a domestic menace so long as they are forced to compete in a bona fide manner with democrtic parties. Proper identification and popular knowledge of how they operate are generally adequate for the people to judge them.

Totalitarianism and modernization   The appeal of totalitarianism to the developing nations, which in another generation may constitute three-fourths of the powerful nation-states in the world, differs only in degree from its appeal to the more advanced nations. Totalitarian dictatorship in a context of social, cultural, and economic development signifies that the inevitable antagonisms of a developing society are suppressed by force. Communism in this respect is totalitarian rule by a modernizing elite that solves all problems of resistance by terror and propaganda. Fascism of the traditional variety, such as under Salazar in Portugal or Franco in Spain, means that moderniza-tion has been arrested by a totalitarian dictatorship of the traditional elites. Italian and German Fascism had some elements of this too. But in an already fairly advanced society, Fascist totalitarianism and aggressive war can also be, among other things, a powerful solvent of social and cultural obstacles to modernization, such as class dis-tinctions, social inequality, cultural roadblocks, or the deadlock of labor and management, and hence can have some long-range benefits, even though the totalitarian movement may have intended nothing more than to put on a show of Four-Year Plans, colossal stadiums, and the draining of the Pontine Marshes near Rome.

In either case, the price of totalitarian development is an exorbitant one to pay for the gains. One great liability of totalitarian develop-ment is the damage to the political fabric and civic culture, for in the wake of totalitarian mass mobilization, responsible democratic participation is almost as difficult to reestablish as if the populace were still in the slumber of traditional society. It takes a generation to uproot the false values and bad habits taught by totalitarian dic-tatorship. The greatest price to pay, of course, is freedom itself, for totalitarian dictatorships are almost impossible to dislodge, once they are established, except by conquest from outside.

How to combat totalitarian imperialism

How then can the peace of the world be protected against the en-ormous imperialistic drive that moves totalitarian parties to spread their gospel and power by military force and subversion throughout the world? The very nature of the Communist and Fascist menace makes compromise impossible or only a temporary strategic ex-pedient for a totalitarian movement. Like a religious crusade, but with modern weapons, armies of soldiers, and trained native profes-sional revolutionaries, they are as invincible as were the crusades of the Middle Ages and the expansion of Mohammedanism.

Opposing force with counterforce At times, it may seem that the best that free nations can hope to accomplish is to band together and oppose force with counterforce in the hope of at least containing the quasi-religious crusaders of today in the territories they already hold, until the distant day when totalitarian government may be beset by crisis, and captive nations can once more reach for their freedom.

Disarmament and arms control Yet there are many other crucial points at which people in the free world can try to head off what often looks like an inexorable development toward war and totalitarian victory. One is the determined effort at containing the technological escalation of military weaponry by disarmament and international agreement. Timing and tactical delays can be crucial to the course of major conflict. It is not at all utopian to hope to control the level of conflict by prior and continuing agreement. Arms control and disarmament is a field of knowledge in which much more research still needs to be done before its possibilities and limitations are fully uncovered. It is also an area in which an enormous amount of publicity work is required to inform a fatally ignorant public throughout the world that still believes the perennial alternative to be a choice between peace and war. Pacifists, no less than the congenitally belligerent, need to be persuaded that it is not necessary to choose between a peace under intolerable conditions and a brutal war. As long as nations are unwilling to accept *peace at any price* and as long as interests continue to conflict at an international level—that is to say perhaps forever—arms control and disarmament offer viable alternatives to either uncontrolled armed conflict or the peace of abject surrender.

The settlement of international disputes   Another vital area where the assault of totalitarian imperialism can be especially intercepted or contained is the setting—psyhological or institutional—in which international disputes are dealt with. If the history of the League of Nations and its breakdown in the 1930s can teach us anything, it is the importance of the impact of the prevailing climate of opinion upon the governments of countries bent upon revising the status quo. Setting up institutions for the peaceful resolution of international conflicts—such as the United Nations, the International Court of Justice, and other international organizations and tribunals—is not enough. Their legitimacy depends upon their actual acceptance and utilization in all specific cases as a matter of course. As long as the great powers regard the United Nations, or the World Court, as fortresses to be conquered and used in the furthering of their own foreign policy designs, the full potential of these institutions will not be realized. At the same time, there must be considerable readiness to tell the aggressors of tomorrow that they will not get away with any attempt to solve vexatious international problems by force. It was the psychological and institutional weakness of the League that failed to deter brazen aggression in the 1930s.

The political future of the world
Against the backdrop of this panorama of forces and of mechanisms to deal with them, there emerges a glimpse of the political future of

the world. Providing that catastrophies can be delayed and eventually sidetracked, what will the political world look like a half century or seventy-five years from now? By then, hopefully, the age of mass mobilization and nationalism will have run its course. All nations will have as much self-government as they desire. The differentials of development and the clash of cultural traditions may have been modified to the point of disappearance.[8] Spurred on by free trade, tourism and cultural exhange, and the exchange of scientific information, people may understand each other better than they do now. From such understanding and reduction of conflict, one can conjecture, greater mutual respect and toleration will flower. A great upsurge of popular scientific method will be necessary in any case to solve such threatening problems as the population explosion, the inadequacy of the food supply, and the economic development of backward areas.

Thus, a new age will dawn—an age that will be more scientific and rational, and also more tolerant and democratic, than ours or any that preceded it. With due respect to collectivities such as the new nations, it will also be a more individualistic age. Its individuals will receive the recognition due them for their individual merit and achievement, or the punishment due them for their individual guilt; and never again will the collective condemnations that have so often camouflaged the worst deeds of our time be tolerated.

[8] So far, the statistical indicators suggest the opposite, namely that the "rich nations" are getting richer and the poor cannot even keep step with their pace of advancement.

SELECTED BIBLIOGRAPHY

Paperbound editions are indicated by PB; some of the works listed have been published in both hardbound and paperbound editions.

CHAPTER 1 **THE STUDY OF POLITICS**

BARKER, ERNEST. *Reflections on Government.* New York: Oxford University Press, 1942. (PB: Galaxy, Oxford U. Press.)

BLUHM, WILLIAM T. DAVID EASTON, ED. *Theories of the Political System: Classics of Political Thought and Modern Political Analysis.* Englewood Cliffs, N.J.: Prentice-Hall, 1965.

CURTIS, MICHAEL, ED. *Nature of Politics.* (PB: Avon, Hearst Corp., New York.)

DAHL, ROBERT, A. *Modern Political Analysis.* Englewood Cliffs, N.J.: Prentice-Hall, 1963. (PB: Prentice-Hall.)

EASTON, DAVID. *A Systems Analysis of Political Life.* New York: Wiley, 1965.

ECKSTEIN, HARRY, AND DAVID E. APTER, EDS. *Comparative Politics, A Reader.* New York: Free Press, 1963.

EULAU, HEINZ. *The Behavioral Persuasion in Politics.* (PB: Random House, New York, 1963.)

FRIEDRICH, CARL J. *Man and His Government.* New York: McGraw-Hill, 1962.

LERNER, DANIEL, AND HAROLD D. LASSWELL, EDS. *The Policy Sciences: Recent*

Developments in Scope and Method. Stanford, Calif.: Stanford University Press, 1951. (PB: Stanford U. Press.)

LOWENSTEIN, KARL. *Political Power and the Governmental Process.* Chicago: University of Chicago Press, 1957. (PB: U. of Chicago Press.)

MACKINDER, HALFORD J. *Democratic Ideals and Reality.* New York: Holt, Rinehart & Winston, 1942. (PB: Norton, New York, 1962.)

MEEHAN, EUGENE J. *The Theory and Method of Political Analysis.* Homewood, Ill.: Dorsey Press, 1965.

RANNEY, AUSTIN, ED. *Essays on the Behavioral Study of Politics.* Urbana: University of Illinois Press, 1962.

SORAUF, FRANCIS J. *Political Science: An Informal Review.* Columbus, Ohio: Merrill, 1965. (PB: Merrill.)

VAN DYKE, VERNON. *Political Science: A Philosophical Analysis.* Stanford, Calif.: Stanford University Press, 1960. (PB: Stanford U. Press.)

YOUNG, ROLAND, ED. *Approaches to the Study of Politics.* Evanston, Ill.: Northwestern University Press, 1958.

CHAPTER 2 **CLASSICAL ISSUES OF POLITICAL THOUGHT**

ARISTOTLE. *The Politics.* TRANS. ERNEST BARKER. New York: Oxford University Press, 1946. (PB: Galaxy, Oxford U. Press.)

BARKER, ERNEST, ED. *The Social Contract: Essays by Locke, Hume, and Rosseau.* New York: Oxford University Press, 1951. (PB: Galaxy, Oxford U. Press.)

BATE, WALTER J., ED. *Selected Writings of Edmund Burke.* New York: Random House, 1960.

EBENSTEIN, WILLIAM. *Great Political Thinkers.* 3rd ed. New York: Holt, Rinehart & Winston, 1960.

FROMM, ERICH. *Escape from Freedom.* New York: Holt, Rinehart & Winston, 1941. (PB: Avon, Hearst Corp., New York)

HAVELOCK, ERIC A. *The Liberal Temper in Greek Politics.* New Haven, Conn.: Yale University Press, 1957. (PB: Yale U. Press)

LINDSAY, A. D. *The Modern Democratic State.* New York: Oxford University Press, 1947. (PB: Galaxy, Oxford U. Press)

LIPSON, LESLIE. *The Great Issues of Politics.* 2nd ed. Englewood Cliffs, N.J.: Prentice-Hall, 1960.

MACPHERSON, CRAWFORD B. *Political Theory of Possessive Individualism: Hobbes to Locke.* New York: Oxford University Press, 1962. (PB: Oxford U. Press)

PLAMENATZ, JOHN. *Man and Society.* 2 vols. New York: McGraw-Hill, 1963.

PLATO. *The Republic.* TRANS. F. M. CORNFORD. New York: Oxford University Press, 1945. (PB: Oxford U. Press)

SABINE, GEORGE H. *A History of Political Theory.* 3rd ed. New York: Holt, Rinehart & Winston, 1961.

STRAUSS, LEO. *Political Philosophy of Hobbes.* Chicago: University of Chicago Press, 1952. (PB: U. of Chicago Press.)

THORSON, THOMAS LANDON, ED. *Plato: Totalitarian or Democrat?* Englewood Cliffs, N.J.: Prentice-Hall, 1963. (PB: Prentice-Hall.)

VEREKER, CHARLES. *The Development of Political Theory.* London: Hutchinson, 1957. (PB: Harper Colophon, New York.)

CHAPTER 3 **THE NATION-STATE IN MODERN TIMES**

BRIERLY, JAMES L. *The Law of Nations.* 4th ed. New York: Oxford University Press, 1948.

CASSIRER, ERNST. *The Myth of the State.* New Haven, Conn.: Yale University Press, 1946. (PB: Yale U. Press.)

FRIEDRICH, CARL J. *Constitutional Government and Democracy.* Boston: Ginn, 1950.

GIERKE, OTTO. *Political Theories of the Middle Ages.* TRANS., WITH INTRODUCTION BY F. W. MAITLAND. London: Cambridge University Press, 1900. (PB: Beacon Press, Boston.)

GOODSPEED, STEPHEN S. *The Nature and Function of International Organization.* New York: Oxford University Press, 1959.

JOUVENEL, BERTRAND DE. *Sovereignty: An Inquiry into the Political Good.* Chicago: University of Chicago Press, 1957. (PB: U. of Chicago Press.)

KISSINGER, HENRY A. *Nuclear Weapons and Foreign Policy.* (PB: Anchor, Doubleday, Garden City, N.Y., 1958.)

KOHŃ, HANS. *The Idea of Nationalism.* New York: Macmillan, 1944. (PB: Macmillan.)

LASKI, HAROLD J. *The Grammar of Politics.* London: Allen and Unwin, 1925.

LIPSON, LESLIE. *The Great Issues of Politics.* 2nd ed. Englewood Cliffs, N.J.: Prentice-Hall, 1960.

MACHIAVELLI, NICCOLO. *The Prince.* New York: New American Library, 1952. (PB: Mentor, New American Library.)

MACIVER, ROBERT M. *The Modern State.* New York: Oxford University Press, 1926. (PB: Oxford U. Press.)

MACIVER, ROBERT M. *The Web of Government.* New York: Macmillan, 1951.

MARITAIN, JACQUES. *Scholasticism and Politics.* New York: Macmillan, 1940. (PB: Image, Doubleday, Garden City, N.Y.)

MORGENTHAU, HANS J. *Scientific Man vs. Power Politics.* Chicago: University of Chicago Press, 1946. (PB: U. of Chicago Press.)

WALTZ, KENNETH N. *Man, the State and War.* New York: Columbia University Press, 1959. (PB: Columbia U. Press.)

CHAPTER 4 **DEMOCRACY AND EQUALITY IN MODERN TIMES**

BARKER, ERNEST. *Reflections on Government.* New York: Oxford University Press, 1942. (PB: Galaxy, Oxford U. Press.)

DAHL, ROBERT A. *A Preface to Democratic Theory.* Chicago: University of Chicago Press, 1956. (PB: U. of Chicago Press.)

EBENSTEIN, WLLIAM. *Today's Isms: Communism, Fascism, Socialism, Capitalism.* 4th ed. (PB: Prentice-Hall, Englewood Cliffs, N.J.: 1964.)

EHRMANN, HENRY W. ED. *Democracy in a Changing Society.* New York: Praeger, 1964.

FRANKEL, CHARLES. *Democratic Prospect.* New York: Harper & Row, 1962. (PB: Harper Colophon.)

LINDSAY, A. D. *The Modern Democratic State.* New York: Oxford University Press, 1947. (PB: Galaxy, Oxford U. Press.)

LIPSET, SEYMOUR. *Political Man: The Social Bases of Politics.* Garden City, N.Y.: Doubleday, 1959. (PB: Anchor, Doubleday.)

LIPSON, LESLIE. *The Democratic Civilization.* New York: Oxford University Press, 1964.

LIPSON, LESLIE. *The Great Issues of Politics.* 2nd ed. Englewood Cliffs, N.J.: Prentice-Hall, 1960.

MACIVER, ROBERT. *The Web of Government.* New York: Macmillan, 1948. (PB: Free Press, New York.)

MAYO, HENRY B. *An Introduction to Democratic Theory.* New York: Oxford University Press, 1960. (PB: Oxford U. Press.)

MILL, JOHN STUART. *Considerations on Representative Government.* (PB: Gateway Editions, Regnery, Chicago, 1962.)

NIEBUHR, REINHOLD. *The Children of Light and the Children of Darkness.* New York: Scribner, 1960. (PB: Scribner.)

RIEMER, NEAL. *The Revival of Democratic Theory.* New York: Appleton-Century-Crofts, 1962.

SARTORI, GIOVANNI. *Democratic Theory.* Detroit: Wayne State University Press, 1962. (PB: Praeger, New York.)

THORSON, THOMAS L. *The Logic of Democracy.* (PB: Holt, Rinehart & Winston, New York, 1962.)

TOCQUEVILLE, ALEXIS DE. *Democracy in America.* 2 vols. TRANS. PHILLIPS BRADLEY. (PB: Vintage, Random House, New York.)

CHAPTER 5 **THE CLASH OF PRINCIPLES: LIBERALISM, CONSERVATISM, AND DEMOCRATIC SOCIALISM**

General

BURNS, EDWARD MCNALL. *Ideas in Conflict.* New York: Norton, 1960.

EBENSTEIN, WILLIAM. *Today's Isms: Communism, Fascism, Socialism, Capitalism.* 4th ed. (PB: Prentice-Hall, Englewood Cliffs, N.J., 1964.)

GRIMES, ALAN P., AND ROBERT H. HOROWITZ. EDS. *Modern Political Ideologies.* New York: Oxford University Press, 1959.

WATKINS, FREDERICK M. *The Age of Ideology—Political Thought, 1750 to the Present.* Englewood Cliffs, N.J.: Prentice-Hall, 1964.

Liberalism

CASTELL, ALBUREY, ED. *John Stuart Mill—On Liberty.* New York: Appleton-Century-Crofts, 1947.

GIRVETZ, HARRY K. *The Evolution of Liberalism.* (PB: Collier, New York, 1963.)

GREENE, THEODORE MEYER. *Liberalism: Its Theory and Practice.* (PB: University of Texas Press, Austin, 1957.)

HARTZ, LOUIS. *The Liberal Tradition in America: An Interpretation of American Political Thought Since the Revolution.* New York: Harcourt Brace, 1955. (PB: Harvest, Harcourt Brace Jovanovich.)

HOBHOUSE, LEONARD. *Liberalism.* (PB: Galaxy, Oxford University Press, New York, 1964.)

RODMAN, JOHN H. ED. *The Political Theory of T. H. Green.* New York: Appleton-Century-Crofts, 1964.

RUGGIERO, GUIDO DE. *The History of European Liberalism.* (PB: Oxford University Press, London, 1927.)

Conservatism

HAILSHAM, VISCOUNT. *The Conservative Case.* (PB: Harmondsworth, Middlesex, Eng.: Penguin, 1959.)

HEARNSHAW, F. J. C. *Conservatism in England.* London: Macmillan, 1933.

KIRK, RUSSELL. *The Conservative Mind.* (From Burke to Santayana.) Chicago: Regnery, 1954. (PB: Regnery.)

ROSSITER, CLINTON L. *Conservatism in America.* 2d rev. ed. (PB: Vintage, Random House, New York.)

VIERECK, PETER. *Conservatism: From John Adams to Churchill.* (PB: Anvil, Van Nostrand Reinhold, New York, 1956.)

VIERECK, PETER. *Conservatism Revisited.* (PB: Free Press, New York, 1965.)

Democratic Socialism

ABRAMS, MARK, AND RICHARD ROSE. *Must Labour Lose?* Baltimore: Penguin, 1960.

BERNSTEIN, EDUARD. *Evolutionary Socialism.* New York: Schocken, 1961.

CHILDS, MARQUIS. *Sweden: The Middle Way.* New Haven, Conn.: Yale University Press, 1936.

COLE, GEORGE D. H. *Socialism in Evolution.* (PB: Penguin Books, Harmondsworth, Middlesex, Eng., 1938.)

CROSLAND, C. A. R. *The Future of Socialism.* New York: Schocken, 1963. (PB: Schocken.)

EBENSTEIN, WILLIAM. *Today's Isms: Communism, Fascism, Socialism, Capitalism.* 4th ed. (PB: Prentice-Hall, Englewood Cliffs, N.J., 1964.)

GAY, PETER. *The Dilemma of Democratic Socialism: Eduard Bernstein's Challenge to Marx.* New York: Columbia University Press, 1952. (PB: Collier, New York.)

GRAY, ALEXANDER. *The Socialist Tradition: Moses to Lenin.* London: Routledge and Kegan Paul, 1946.)

HAYEK, FRIEDRICH. *The Road to Serfdom.* Chicago: University of Chicago Press, 1944. (PB: U. of Chicago Press.)

HEILBRONER, ROBERT L. *The Great Ascent.* New York: Harper & Row, 1963. (PB: Harper Torchbooks.)

JENKINS, ROY. *The Labour Case.* Harmondsworth, Eng.: Penguin, 1959.

LANDAUER, CARL. *European Socialism.* 2 vols. Berkeley: University of California Press, 1959.

MORGAN, H. WAYNE. *American Socialism 1900–1960.* (PB: Prentice-Hall, Englewood Cliffs, N.J., 1964.)

MYRDAL, GUNNAR. *Beyond the Welfare State.* New Haven, Conn.: Yale University Press, 1960.

ROBSON, WILLIAM A. *Nationalised Industry and Public Ownership.* London: Allen and Unwin, 1960.

SCHUMPETER, JOSEPH A. *Capitalism, Socialism and Democracy.* 3rd ed. New York: Harper & Row, 1950. (PB: Harper Torchbooks.)

SIGMUND, PAUL E., ED. *The Ideologies of the Developing Nations.* New York: Praeger, 1963. (PB: Praeger.)

CHAPTER 6 **THE FOUNDATIONS OF LIBERTY: CONSTITUTIONALISM AND REPRESENTATIVE GOVERNMENT**

AMERY, L. S. *Thoughts on the Constitution.* 2nd ed. London: Oxford University Press, 1953.

ANDREWS, WILLIAM G. *Constitutions and Constitutionalism.* New York: Van Nostrand Reinhold, 1961.

ARISTOTLE. *The Politics.* TRANS. ERNEST BARKER. New York: Oxford University Press, 1946. (PB: Galaxy, Oxford U. Press.)

BAGEHOT, WALTER. *The English Constitution.* London: Oxford University Press, 1936.

BARKER, ERNEST. *Reflections on Government.* London: Oxford University Press, 1942.

BAYLEY, DAVID H. *Liberties in the New States.* Chicago: Rand McNally, 1964.

CASTBERG, FREDE. *Freedom of Speech in the West.* Dobbs Ferry, N.Y.: Oceana, 1960.

CORWIN, EDWARD S. *The "Higher Law" Background of American Constitutional Law.* Ithaca, N.Y.: Cornell University Press, 1955. (PB: Cornell U. P.)

CORWIN, EDWARD S. AND JACK PELTASON. *Understanding the Constitution.* 3rd ed. New York: Holt, Rinehart & Winston, 1964.

FINER, HERMAN. *Theory and Practice of Modern Government.* 4th ed. London: Methuen, 1961.

FRIEDRICH, CARL J. *Constitutional Government and Democracy.* Boston: Ginn, 1950.

GELLHORN, WALTER. *American Rights.* New York: Macmillan, 1960.

KIRCHHEIMER, OTTO. *Political Justice.* Princeton, N.J.: Princeton University Press, 1961.

LIPPMANN, WALTER. *Public Philosophy.* Boston: Little, Brown, 1955. (PB: Mentor, New American Library, New York.)

LOEWENSTEIN, KARL. *Political Power and the Governmental Process.* Chicago: University of Chicago Press, 1957. (PB: U. of Chicago Press.)

MCCLOSKEY, ROBERT G., ED. *Essays in Constitutional Law*. New York: Knopf, 1957.

MCILWAIN, CHARLES HOWARD. *Constitutionalism, Ancient and Modern*. (PB: Cornell University Pres, Ithaca, N.Y., 1958.)

MACRIDIS, ROY C., AND BERNARD E. BROWN. *The De Gaulle Republic: Quest for Unity*. Homewood, Ill.: Dorsey, 1960, 1963.

MERKL, PETER. *The Origin of the West German Republic*. New York: Oxford University Press, 1963. (PB: Oxford U. Press.)

MILL, JOHN STUART. *Considerations on Representative Government*. (PB: Gateway Editions, Regnery, Chicago, 1962.)

NEUMANN, FRANZ. *The Democratic and the Authoritarian State*. New York: Free Press, 1957.

SPIRO, HERBERT T. *Government by Constitution*. (PB: Random House, New York, 1965.)

WATKINS, FREDERICK M. *The Political Tradition of the West*. Cambridge, Mass.: Harvard University Press, 1948.

WHEARE, KENNETH C. *Modern Constitutions*. New York: Oxford University Press, 1951.

WORMUTH, FRANCIS D. *The Origins of Modern Constitutionalism*. New York: Harper & Row, 1949.

WRIGHT, GORDON. *The Reshaping of French Democracy*. London: Reynal & Hitchcock, 1948.

ZURCHER, ARNOLD J., ED. *Constitutions and Constitutional Trends Since World War II*. 2nd ed. New York: New York University Press, 1955.

CHAPTER 7 LAWMAKING AND LEGISLATURES
AND
CHAPTER 8 EXECUTIVE POLICY-MAKING

ADAMS, JOHN CLARKE, AND PAOLO BARILE. *The Government of Republican Italy*. 2nd ed. (PB: Houghton Mifflin, Boston, 1966.)

ANDREWS, WILLIAM G. *European Political Institutions*. New York: Van Nostrand Reinhold, 1962. (PB: Van Nostrand.)

ANDREWS, WILLIAM G., ED. *European Politics I*. New York: Van Nostrand Reinhold, 1966.

BAILEY, SYDNEY H. ED. *Parliamentary Government in the Commonwealth*. New York: Philosophical Library, 1952.

BAILEY, SYDNEY D. *British Parliamentary Democracy*. 2nd ed. (PB: Houghton Mifflin, Boston, 1962.)

BEER, SAMUEL H., AND ADAM B. ULAM. *Patterns of Government*. 2nd ed. New York: Random House, 1962.

BOYER, WILLIAM. *Bureaucracy on Trial*. Indianapolis: Bobbs-Merrill. (PB: Bobbs-Merrill, 1964.)

BROGAN, D. W., AND DOUGLAS V. VERNEY. *Political Patterns in Today's World*. (PB: Harcourt Brace Jovanovich, New York, 1963.)

CARTER, BYRUM E. *The Office of Prime Minister*. Princeton, N.J.: Princeton University Press, 1956.

CARTER, GWENDOLEN M., AND JOHN H. HERZ. *Major Foreign Powers.* 4th ed. New York: Harcourt Brace Jovanovich, 1962.

CARTER, GWENDOLEN M., AND ALAN F. WESTIN, EDS. *Politics in Europe.* (PB: Harcourt Brace Jovanovich, New York, 1965.)

CHRISTOPH, JAMES C., AND OTHERS. *Cases in Comparative Politics.* (PB: Little, Brown, Boston, 1965.)

CODDING, GEORGE ARTHUR, JR. *The Federal Government of Switzerland.* Boston: Houghton Mifflin, 1961.

COLE, R. TAYLOR. *European Political Systems.* 2nd ed. New York: Knopf, 1959.

CORWIN, EDWARD S., AND LOUIS W. KOENIG. *The Presidency Today.* New York: New York University Press, 1956.

CRICK, BERNARD. *Reform of Parliament.* London: Weidenfels & Nicolson, 1964. (PB: Doubleday, Garden City, N.Y.)

DAALDER, HANS. *Cabinet Reform in Britain 1914–1963.* Stanford, Calif.: Stanford University Press, 1963.

DRAGNICH, ALEX N. *Major European Governments.* Rev. ed. Homewood, Ill.: Dorsey, 1966.

EHRMANN, HENRY W., ED. *Democracy in a Changing Society.* (PB: Praeger, New York, 1964.)

FENNO, RICHARD F., JR. *The President's Cabinet.* Cambridge, Mass.: Harvard University Press, 1959.

FRIED, ROBERT C. *Comparative Political Institutions.* (PB: Macmillan, New York, 1966.)

GODFREY, E. DREXEL, JR. *The Government of France.* 2nd ed. New York: Crowell, 1963. (PB: Crowell.)

HAMILTON, HOWARD D., ED. *Political Institutions: Readings in Political Science.* (PB: Houghton Mifflin, Boston, 1962.)

HASTAD, ELIS. *The Parliament of Sweden.* London: Hansard, 1957.

HEIDENHEIMER, ARNOLD J. *The Governments of Germany.* 2nd ed. (PB: Crowell, New York, 1966.)

HERMENS, FERDINAND A. *The Representative Republic.* Notre Dame: University of Notre Dame Press, 1958.

HUGHES, C. J. *The Parliament of Switzerland.* London: Cassell, 1962.

HYMAN, SIDNEY. *The American President.* New York: Harper & Row, 1954.

INTERPARLIAMENTARY UNION. *Parliaments.* CODACCI PISANELLI, ED. London: Cassell, 1962.

JENNINGS, SIR IVOR, *Cabinet Government.* 3rd ed. London: Cambridge University Press, 1959.

KOGAN, NORMAN. *The Government of Italy.* New York: Crowell, 1962. (PB: Crowell.)

LIDDERDALE, D. W. S. *The Parliament of France.* London: Hansard, 1951.

LOEWENSTEIN, KARL. *Political Power and the Governmental Process.* Chicago: University of Chicago Press, 1957.

MACKINTOSH, JOHN P. *The British Cabinet.* London: Stevens, 1961.

MACRIDIS, ROY C., AND BERNARD E. BROWN. *Comparative Politics, Notes and Readings.* 2nd ed. Homewood, Ill.: Dorsey, 1964.

MACRIDIS, ROY C., AND BERNARD E. BROWN. *The De Gaulle Republic: Quest for Unity.* Homewood, Ill.: Dorsey, 1960, 1963.

MACRIDIS, ROY C., AND ROBERT E. WARD. *Modern Political Systems: Asia.* Englewood Cliffs, N.J.: Prentice-Hall, 1964.

MACRIDIS, ROY C., AND ROBERT E. WARD. *Modern Political Systems: Europe* Englewood Cliffs, N.J.: Prentice-Hall, 1963.

MAVRINAC, ALBERT. *Organization and Procedure of the National Assembly of the Fifth French Republic.* London: Hansard, 1960.

MOODIE, GRAEME C. *The Government of Great Britain.* 2nd ed. New York: Crowell, 1964. (PB: Crowell.)

MORRISON, HERBERT. *Government and Parliament.* 3rd ed. (PB: Oxford University Press, New York, 1964.)

MULLER, STEVEN, ED. *Documents on European Government.* (PB: Macmillan, New York, 1963.)

NEUMANN, ROBERT G. *European and Comparative Government.* 3rd ed. New York: McGraw-Hill, 1960.

NEUSTADT, RICHARD E. *Presidential Power: The Politics of Leadership.* New York: Wiley, 1960.

PICKLES, DOROTHY. *The Fifth French Republic.* New York: Praeger, 1960. (PB: Praeger.)

ROSE, RICHARD. *Politics in England, an Interpretation.* (PB: Little, Brown, Boston, 1964.)

SPIRO, HERBERT J. *Government by Constitution.* New York: Random House, 1959.

STORING, JAMES A. *Norwegian Democracy.* (PB: Houghton Mifflin, Boston, 1963.)

THOMSON, DAVID. *Democracy in America Since 1870.* 4th ed. (PB: Oxford University Press, New York, 1964.)

VERNEY, DOUGLAS. *The Analysis of Political Systems.* London: Routledge and Kegan Paul, 1959.

WAHL, NICHOLAS. *The Fifth Republic.* New York: Random House, 1959.

WHEARE, KENNETH C. *Government by Committee.* London: Oxford University Press, 1955.

WHEARE, KENNETH C. *Legislatures.* (PB: Galaxy, Oxford University Press, New York, 1963.)

YOUNG, ROLAND. *The American Congress.* New York: Harper & Row, 1958.

CHAPTER 9 JUDGES AND CIVIL SERVANTS

ABRAHAM, HENRY J. *Courts and Judges.* New York: Oxford University Press, 1959.

ABRAHAM, HENRY J. *Judicial Process: An Introductory Analysis of the Courts of the United States, England and France.* Magnolia, Mass.: Peter Smith (PB: Oxford University Press, New York, 1962.)

BARKER, ERNEST. *The Development of Public Services in Western Europe, 1660–1930.* London: Oxford University Press, 1944.

BERMAN, HAROLD J. *Justice in the U.S.S.R.* Rev. ed. Cambridge, Mass.: Harvard University Press, 1963. (PB: Vintage, Random House, New York.)

CHAPMAN, BRIAN. *The Profession of Government.* London: Allen and Unwin, 1959.

DAVID, RENE, AND HENRY DE VRIES. *The French Legal System.* Dobbs Ferry, N.Y.: Oceana, 1958.

ENSOR, ROBERT C. K. *Courts and Judges in France, Germany and England.* London: Oxford University Press, 1933.

FINER, HERMAN. *Theory and Practice of Modern Government.* New York: Holt, Rinehart & Winston, 1949.

FREEDEMAN, CHARLES E. *The Conseil d'Etat in Modern France.* New York: Columbia University Press, 1961.

FRIEDRICH, CARL J. *Constitutional Government and Democracy.* Boston: Little, Brown, 1941.

HOLMES, OLIVER WENDELL. *Introduction to the Common Law.* Rev. ed. Boston: Little, Brown, 1923.

JACKSON, RICHARD M. *The Machinery of Justice in England.* 3rd ed. London: Macmillan, 1960.

KELSEN, HANS. *The Communist Theory of Law.* New York: Praeger, 1955.

KIRCHHEIMER, OTTO. *Political Justice.* Princeton, N.J.: Princeton University Press, 1961.

LANDIS, JAMES M. *Administrative Process.* New Haven: Yale University Press, 1938. (PB: Yale University Press.)

LA PALOMBARA, JOSEPH. *Bureaucracy in Political Development.* Princeton, N.J.: Princeton University Press, 1963.

MACKENZIE, W. J. M., AND J. W. GROVE. *Central Administration in Britain.* London: Longmans, 1957.

MERTON, ROBERT K., AND OTHERS. *Reader in Bureaucracy.* New York: Free Press, 1952.

MEYER, POUL. *Administrative Organization: A Comparative Study of the Organization of Public Administration.* Copenhagen: Nyt Nordisk Forlag, Arnold Busk, 1957.

MORSTEIN MARX, FRITZ. *The Administrative State.* Chicago: University of Chicago Press, 1957.

PFIFFNER, JOHN M., AND ROBERT V. PRESTHUS. *Public Administration.* New York: Ronald, 1960.

SCHUBERT, GLENDON. *Judicial Policy Making.* Chicago: Scott, Foresman, 1965. (PB: Scott, Foresman.)

SCHWARTZ, BERNARD, ED. *The Code Napoleon and the Common Law World.* New York: New York University Press, 1956.

SCHWARTZ, BERNARD. *French Administrative Law and the Common Law World.* New York: New York University Press, 1954.

SCIGLIANO, ROBERT G., ED. *Courts.* (PB: Little, Brown, Boston, 1962.)

SIFFIN, WILLIAM J., ED. *Toward the Comparative Study of Public Administration*. Bloomington: Indiana University Press, 1959.

SISSON, C. H. *The Spirit of British Administration*. New York: Praeger, 1959.

STRAUS, ERIC. *The Ruling Servants*. New York: Praeger, 1960.

WALDO, DWIGHT. *Study of Public Administration*. (PB: Random House, New York, 1955.)

CHAPTER 10   POLITICAL PARTIES, INTEREST GROUPS, AND PUBLIC OPINION

ALFORD, ROBERT R. *Party and Society*. Chicago: Rand McNally, 1963.

ALMOND, GABRIEL A., AND JAMES S. COLEMAN. *The Politics of the Developing Areas*. Princeton, N.J.: Princeton University Press, 1960.

ALMOND, GABRIEL A., AND SIDNEY VERBA. *The Civic Culture: Political Attitudes and Democracy in Five Nations*. Princeton, N.J.: Princeton University Press, 1963.

BEER, SAMUEL H. *British Politics in the Collectivist Age*. New York: Knopf, 1965.

BLAISDELL, DONALD C., ED. *Annals of the American Academy of Political and Social Science*. Vol. 319 (September 1958).

BONE, HUGH A., AND AUSTIN RANNEY. *Politics and Voters*. New York: McGraw-Hill, 1963.

BRAUNTHAL, GERARD. *The Federation of German Industry and Politics*. Ithaca, N.Y.: Cornell University Press, 1965.

BULMER-THOMAS, IVOR. *The Two-Party System in Great Britain*. London: Phoenix, 1953.

BURNS, JAMES MACGREGOR. *The Deadlock of Democracy*. Englewood Cliffs, N.J.: Prentice-Hall, 1963.

CAMPBELL, ANGUS, AND OTHERS. *The American Voter*. New York: Wiley, 1960.

DAHL, ROBERT A., ED. *Political Oppositions in Western Democracies*. New Haven, Conn.; Yale University Press, 1966.

DUVERGER, MAURICE. *Political Parties*. London: Methuen, 1952. (PB: Science Editions, Wiley, New York.)

ECKSTEIN, HARRY. *Pressure Group Politics*. Stanford, Calif.: Stanford University Press, 1960.

EHRMANN, HENRY W. *French Labor from Popular Front to Liberation*. New York: Oxford University Press, 1947.

EHRMANN, HENRY W., ED. *Interest Groups on Four Continents*. Pittsburgh: Pittsburgh University Press, 1958.

EHRMANN, HENRY W. *Organized Business in France*. Princeton, N.J.: Princeton University Press.

FRIEDRICH, CARL J., AND ZBIGNIEW K. BRZEZINSKI. *Totalitarian Dictatorship and Autocracy*. Rev. ed. New York: Praeger, 1964.

GOODMAN, WILLIAM. *The Two-Party System in the United States*. 3rd ed. New York: Van Nostrand Reinhold, 1964.

HODGKIN, T. *African Political Parties.* (PB: Penguin, Baltimore, Md., 1961.)

KEY, VLADIMIR O. *Politics, Parties and the Pressure Groups.* 5th ed. New York: Crowell, 1964.

KORNHAUSER, WILLIAM. *The Politics of Mass Society.* New York: Free Press, 1959.

LAKEMAN, ENID, AND J. D. LAMBERT. *Voting in Democracies,* 2nd ed. London: Faber, 1959.

LANE, ROBERT E., AND D. O. SEARS. *Public Opinion.* New York: McGraw-Hill, 1964.

LA PALOMBARA, JOSEPH. *Interest Groups in Italian Politics.* Princeton, N.J.: Princeton University Press, 1964.

LAPONCE, J. A. *The Government of the Fifth Republic.* Berkeley: University of California Press, 1961.

LEISERSON, AVERY. *Parties and Politics.* New York: Knopf, 1958.

LIPPMANN, WALTER. *Public Opinion.* New York: Macmillan, 1944. (PB: Free Press, New York.)

LIPSET, SEYMOUR M. *Political Man.* Garden City, N.Y.: Doubleday, 1960.

MCDONALD, NEIL A. *The Study of Political Parties.* Garden City, N.Y.: Doubleday, 1955.

MCKENZIE, R. T. *British Political Parties.* New York: Praeger, 1964. (PB: Praeger.)

MACKENZIE, WILLIAM J. M. *Free Elections.* London: Allen and Unwin, 1958.

MICHELS, ROBERT. *Political Parties.* New York: Hearst's International Library, 1915. (PB: Free Press, New York, 1966.)

MUNGER, FRANK, AND DOUGLAS PRICE. *Readings in Political Parties and Pressure Groups.* (PB: Crowell, New York, 1964.)

NEUMANN, SIGMUND. *Modern Political Parties.* Chicago: University of Chicago Press, 1956.

OVERACKER, LOUISE. *The Australian Party System.* New Haven, Conn.: Yale University Press, 1952.

POTTER, ALLEN. *Organized Groups in British National Politics.* London: Faber, 1961.

ROSE, RICHARD, AND ARNOLD J. HEIDENHEIMER, EDS. *Comparative Political Finance.* Special issue of *The Journal of Politics.* Vol. 25, No. 3 (August 1963.)

RUSTOW, DANKWART. *The Politics of Compromise.* Princeton, N.J.: Princeton University Press, 1955.

SCHATTSCHNEIDER, ELMER E. *Party Government.* New York: Holt, Rinehart & Winston, 1942.

SORAUF, FRANK J. *Political Parties in the American System.* Boston: Little, Brown, 1964.

TRUMAN, DAVID B. *The Governmental Process.* New York: Knopf, 1951.

WEINER, MYRON. *Party Politics in India.* Princeton, N.J.: Princeton University Press, 1957.

Note: See also the bibliographies for Chapters 7 and 8.

CHAPTER 11 FEDERALISM AND UNITARISM

AIYAR, S. P. *Federalism and Constitutional Change.* London: Oxford University Press, 1956.

THE AMERICAN ASSEMBLY. *The Forty-Eight States.* New York: Columbia University Press, 1955.

BIRCH, A. H. *Finance and Social Legislation in Canada, Australia and in the United States.* London: Oxford University Press, 1955.

BOWIE, ROBERT R., AND CARL J. FRIEDRICH. *Studies in Federalism.* Boston: Little, Brown, 1954.

BRECHT, ARNOLD. *Federalism and Regionalism in Germany.* New York: Oxford University Press, 1945.

CODDING, GEORGE A., JR. *Federal Government of Switzerland.* (PB: Houghton Mifflin, Boston, 1961.)

CREPEAU, P. A. *Future of Canadian Federalism.* Toronto: University of Toronto Press, 1965. (PB: U. of Toronto Press.)

FRIEDRICH, CARL J. *Man and His Government.* New York: McGraw-Hill, 1963.

GOLDWIN, ROBERT A., ED. *A Nation of States: Essays on the American Federal System.* Chicago: Rand McNally, 1963.

HICKS, W. K., AND OTHERS. *Federalism and Economic Growth in Underdeveloped Countries.* London: Allen and Unwin, 1961.

HUGHES, CHRISTOPHER. *The Federal Constitution of Switzerland.* London: Oxford University Press, 1954.

INSTITUTE FOR STUDIES IN FEDERALISM. *Essays in Federalism.* Claremont, Calif.: Claremont College, 1963.

LIVINGSTON, WILLIAM. *Federalism and Constitutional Change.* London: Oxford University Press, 1956.

LOWER, A. R. M., AND OTHERS. *Evolving Canadian Federalism.* Durham, N.C.: Duke University Press, 1958.

MCMAHON, ARTHUR W., ED. *Federalism: Mature and Emergent.* New York: Columbia University Press, 1955.

MCWHINNEY, EDWARD. *Comparative Federalism.* Toronto: University of Toronto Press, 1952.

MILLER, J. D. B. *Australian Government and Politics.* London: Duckworth, 1954.

MORLEY, FELIX. *Freedom and Federalism.* Chicago: Regnery, 1959. (PB: Regnery.)

PINNEY, EDWARD L. *Federalism, Bureacracy and Party Politics in Western Germany.* Chapel Hill: University of North Carolina Press, 1963.

RIKER, WILLIAM H. *Federalism.* (PB: Little, Brown, Boston, 1964.)

SCHLESINGER, RUDOLPH. *Federalism in Central and Eastern Europe.* London: Routledge & Kegan Paul, 1945.

WELLS, ROGER H. *The States in West German Federalism.* New York: Bookman Associates, 1961.

WHEARE, KENNETH C. *Federal Government*. 4th ed. (PB: Oxford University Press, New York, 1964.)

Note: See also the bibliographies for Chapters 7 and 8.

CHAPTER 12 **MODERNIZATION AND POLITICAL CHANGE**

ALMOND, GABRIEL A., AND JAMES S. COLEMAN. *The Politics of the Developing Areas*. Princeton, N.J.: Princeton University Press, 1960.

ALMOND, GABRIEL A., AND G. BINGHAM POWELL, JR. *Comparative Politics: A Developmental Approach*. Boston: Little, Brown, 1966. (PB: Little, Brown.)

APTER, DAVID E. *The Politics of Modernization*. Chicago: University of Chicago Press, 1965.

ARENDT, HANNAH. *On Revolution*. New York: Viking, 1963. (PB: Compass, Viking.)

BANFIELD, EDWARD, AND LAURA BANFIELD. *The Moral Basis of a Backward Society*. New York: Free Press, 1965.

CARTER, GWENDOLEN M., ED. *Five African States*. Ithaca, N.Y.: Cornell University Press, 1963.

COLEMAN, JAMES S., ED. *Education and Political Development*. Princeton, N.J.: Princeton University Press, 1965.

COLEMAN, JAMES S., AND CARL J. ROSBERG, EDS. *Political Parties and National Integration in Tropical Africa*. Berkeley: University of California Press, 1965.

EMERSON, RUPERT. *From Empire to Nation*. Cambridge, Mass.: Harvard University Press, 1960.

HAGEN, EVERETT E. *On the Theory of Social Change*. Homewood, Ill.: Dorsey, 1962.

HALPERN, MANFRED. *The Politics of Social Change in the Middle East and North Africa*. Princeton, N.J.: Princeton University Press, 1963.

JANOWITZ, MORRIS. *The Military in the Political Development of the New Nations*. Chicago: University of Chicago Press, 1964.

JOHNSON, JOHN J. *Political Change in Latin America*. Stanford, Calif.: Stanford University Press, 1958. (PB: Stanford U. Press.)

KAUTSKY, J. H. *Political Change in Underdeveloped Countries: Nationalism and Communism*. (PB: Wiley, New York, 1962.)

LERNER, DANIEL. *Passing of Traditional Society*. New York. Free Press, 1958, (PB: Oxford U. Press.)

MCCORD, WILLIAM. *The Springtime of Freedom*. New York: Oxford University Press, 1965. (PB: Oxford U. Press.)

MAIER, JOSEPH, AND RICHARD WEATHERHEAD. *Politics of Change in Latin America*. New York: Praeger, 1964. (PB: Praeger.)

MILLEN, BRUCE H. *The Political Role of Labor in Developing Countries*. Washington, D.C.: Brookings, 1963.

MILLIKAN, MAX F., AND DONALD L. M. BLACKMER, EDS. *The Emerging Nations:*

Their Growth and the U.S. Policy. Boston: Little, Brown, 1961. (PB: Little, Brown.)

ORGANSKI, A. F. K. *Stages of Political Development.* New York: Knopf, 1965. (PB: Knopf.)

PENNOCK, J. ROLAND, ED. *Self-government in Modernizing Nations.* Englewood Cliffs, N.J.: Prentice-Hall, 1964.

PICKETT, LEWIS P., JR., ED. *Problems of the Developing Nations.* New York: Crowell, 1966.

PYE, LUCIAN W. *Aspects of Political Development.* Boston: Little, Brown, 1946.

PYE, LUCIAN W. *Politics, Personality, and Nation Building: Burma's Search for Identity.* New Haven, Conn.: Yale University Press, 1962. (PB: Yale U. Press.)

PYE, LUCIAN W., AND SIDNEY VERBA. *Political Culture and Political Development.* Princeton, N.J.: Princeton University Press, 1965.

ROSTOW, WALT W. *The Stages of Economic Growth.* London: Cambridge University Press, 1960.

SCHWARZ, FREDERICK R. O. *Nigeria. The Tribes, the Nation or the Race.* Cambridge, Mass.: MIT Press, 1965.

SINAI, ROBERT I. *The Challenge of Modernization.* New York: Norton, 1964.

SPIRO, HERBERT J. *Politics in Africa.* Englewood Cliffs, N.J.: Prentice-Hall, 1964.

VON DER MEHDEN, FRED R. *Politics of the Developing Nations.* Englewood Cliffs, N.J.: Prentice-Hall, 1964. (PB: Prentice-Hall.)

WARD, BARBARA. *The Rich Nations and the Poor Nations.* Englewood Cliffs, N.J.: Prentice-Hall, 1964.

WARD, ROBERT E., AND DANKWART A. RUSTOW. *Political Modernization in Japan and Turkey.* Princeton, N.J.: Princeton University Press, 1964.

WEINER, MYRON. *The Politics of Scarcity.* Chicago: University of Chicago Press, 1962.

CHAPTER 13 COMMUNIST TOTALITARIANISM

ALMOND, GABRIEL A. *The Appeals of Communism.* Princeton, N.J.: Princeton University Press, 1954.

ARMSTRONG, JOHN A. *The Politics of Totalitarianism: The Communist Party of the Soviet Union from 1934 to the Present.* New York: Random House, 1961.

ARON, RAYMOND. *The Opium of the Intellectuals.* (PB: Norton, New York, 1962.)

BAUER, RAYMOND A., AND OTHERS. *How the Soviet System Works.* (PB: Vintage, Random House, New York, 1960.)

BOBER, N. M. *Karl Marx's Interpretation of History.* 2nd ed. (PB: Norton, New York, 1965: first published 1927.)

BORKENAU, FRANZ. *World Communism, A History of the Communist International.* New York: Norton, 1939.

BRAHAM, RANDOLPH L., ED. *Soviet Politics and Government: A Reader* (PB: Knopf, New York, 1965.)

BRUMBERG, ABRAHAM, ED. *Russia Under Communism*. New York: Praeger, 1962 (PB: Praeger.)

BRZEZINSKI, ZBIGNIEW K. *Soviet Bloc: Unity and Conflict*. Cambridge, Mass.: Harvard University Press, 1960. (PB: Praeger, New York.)

COHEN, ARTHUR A. *The Communism of Mao Tse-tung*. Chicago: University of Chicago Press, 1964. (PB: U. of Chicago Press.)

CROSSMAN, RICHARD, ED. *The God That Failed*. (PB: Harper Colophon, New York, 1950.)

DALLIN, ALEXANDER, AND ALAN F. WESTIN. *Politics in the Soviet Union: 7 Cases*. (PB: Harcourt Brace Jovanovich, New York, 1966.)

DEUTSCHER, ISAAC. *The Trotsky Trilogy*. 3 vols. New York: Oxford University Press, 1954, 1959, 1963.

DJILAS, MILOVAN. *The New Class*. New York: Praeger, 1957. (PB: Praeger.)

EBENSTEIN, WILLIAM. *Today's Isms: Communism, Fascism, Socialism, Capitalism*. 4th ed. (PB: Prentice-Hall, Englewood Cliffs, N.J., 1964.)

EBENSTEIN, WIILAM. *Totalitarianism: New Perspectives*. (PB: Holt, Rinehart & Winston, New York, 1962.)

EINAUDI, MARIO, AND FRANCOIS GOGUEL. *Communism in Western Europe*. (PB: Cornell University Press, Ithaca, N.Y., 1951.)

GYORGY, ANDREW. *Communism in Perspective*. Boston: Allyn and Bacon, 1965. (PB: Allyn & Bacon.)

GYORGY, ANDREW, ED. *Issues of World Communism*. (PB: Van Nostrand Reinhold, New York, 1966.)

HAZARD, JOHN N. *The Soviet System of Government*. 3rd ed. Chicago: University of Chicago Press, 1964. (PB: U. of Chicago Press.)

HOLT, ROBERT T., AND J. E. TURNER. *Soviet Union: Paradox and Change*. New York: Holt, Rinehart & Winston, 1962. (PB: Holt, Rinehart & Winston.)

HOOK, SIDNEY. *Marx and the Marxists*. New York: Van Nostrand Reinhold, 1955. (PB: Anvil, Van Nostrand.)

JOHNSON, CHALMERS A. *Peasant Nationalism and Communist Power*. Stanford, Calif.: Stanford University Press, 1962.

KOESTLER, ARTHUR. *Darkness at Noon*. New York: Modern Library, 1941. PB: New American Library, New York.)

LEITES, NATHAN. *The Operational Code of the Politbureau*. New York: McGraw-Hill, 1951.

LOWENTHAL, RICHARD. *World Communism: The Disintegration of a Secular Faith*. New York: Oxford University Press, 1964. (PB: Oxford U. Press.)

MAYO, HENRY B. *Introduction to Marxist Theory*. (PB: Oxford University Press, New York, 1960.)

MEAD, MARGARET. *Soviet Attitudes Toward Authority*. New York: Morrow, 1955. (PB: Schocken, New York.)

MEYER, ALFRED G. *Communism*. Rev. ed. (PB: Random House, New York, 1962.)

MONNEROT, JULES. *Sociology of Communism*. London: Allen and Unwin, 1953.

MOORE, BARRINGTON, JR. *Soviet Politics—The Dilemma of Power: The Rise of Ideas in Social Change.* (PB: Harper Torchbooks, New York.)

NORTH, ROBERT C. *Chinese Communism.* (PB: McGraw-Hill, New York, 1966.)

OLIVA, L., JAY. *Russia and the West from Peter to Khruschev.* (PB: Heath, Boston, 1966.)

PETERSON, WILLIAM, ED. *The Realities of World Communism.* (PB: Prentice-Hall, Englewood Cliffs, N.J., 1963.)

RIGBY, T. H., ED. *Stalin.* (PB: Prentice-Hall, Englewood Cliffs, N.J., 1966.)

SCHAPIRO, LEONARD. *The Communist Party of the Soviet Union.* New York: Random House, 1959.

SETON-WATSON, HUGH. *The East European Revolution.* New York: Praeger, 1961.

SKILLING, H. GORDON. *The Governments of Communist East Europe.* (PB: Crowell, New York, 1966.)

STUCKI, LORENZ. *Behind the Great Wall.* (PB: Praeger, New York, 1965.)

TRISKA, JAN F., ED. *Soviet Communism: Programs and Rules.* (PB: Chandler, San Francisco, 1962.)

ULAM, ADAM B. *The New Face of Soviet Totalitarianism.* Cambridge, Mass.: Harvard University Press, 1963. (PB: Praeger, New York, 1965.)

ULAM, ADAM B. *The Unfinished Revolution.* New York: Random House, 1961.

VALI, FERENC A. *Rift and Revolt in Hungary, Nationalism Versus Communism.* Cambridge, Mass.: Harvard University Press, 1961.

WINT, GUY. *Communist China's Crusade.* (PB: Praeger, New York, 1965.)

WOLFE, BERTRAM D. *Khrushchev and Stalin's Ghost.* New York: Praeger, 1956.

WOLFE, BERTRAM D. *Three Who Made a Revolution.* Rev. ed. Boston: Beacon, 1955. (PB: Dell, New York.)

Note: See also the bibliographies for Chapters 7, 8, and 10.

CHAPTER 14 FASCISM AND NATIONAL SOCIALISM

ABEL, THEODORE. *The Nazi Movement.* (PB: New York: Atherton, 1966.)

ADORNO, THEODORE W., AND OTHERS. *The Authoritarian Personality.* New York: Harper & Row, 1950.

ALLPORT, GORDON W. *The Nature of Prejudice.* Reading, Mass.: Addison-Wesley, 1954. (PB: Anchor, Doubleday, Garden City, N.Y., abr. ed., 1958.)

ARENDT, HANNAH. *Eichmann in Jerusalem: A Report on the Banality of Evil.* Rev. ed. (PB: Compass, Viking, New York, 1965.)

ARENDT, HANNAH. *The Origins of Totalitarianism.* 2nd ed. Magnolia, Mass.: Peter Smith, 1958. (PB: Meridian, World Publishing, Cleveland, Ohio.)

BARBU, ZEVEDEI. *Democracy and Dictatorship.* London: Routledge & Kegan Paul, 1956.

BAUMONT, MAURICE, AND OTHERS. *The Third Reich.* New York: Praeger, 1955.

BELL, DANIEL, ED. *The Radical Right.* Garden City, N.Y.: Doubleday, 1963. (PB: Doubleday.)

BETTELHEIM, BRUNO, AND MORRIS JANOWITZ. *Dynamics of Prejudice.* New York: Harper & Row, 1950.

BROSZAT, MARTIN. *National Socialism.* (PB: Clio Press, Santa Barbara, Calif., 1966.)

BUCHHEIM, HANS. *The Third Reich.* (PB: Koesel, Munich, 1958.)

BULLOCK, ALAN C. *Hitler, a Study in Tyranny.* Rev. ed. New York: Harper & Row, 1964. (PB: Harper Torchbooks, Harper & Row.)

DE GRAZIA, SEBASTIAN. *The Political Community: Study of Anomie.* (PB: Chicago, University of Chicago Press, 1948.)

EBENSTEIN, WILLIAM. *Today's Ism's: Communism, Fascism, Socialism, Capitalism.* 4th ed. (PB: Prentice-Hall, Englewood Cliffs, N.J., 1964.)

FERMI, LAURA. *Mussolini.* Chicago: University of Chicago Press, 1961. (PB: U. of Chicago Press.)

FRIEDRICH, CARL J., ED. *Totalitarianism.* Cambridge, Mass.: Harvard University Press, 1954. (PB: Universal Library, Grosset & Dunlap, New York.)

FRIEDRICH, CARL J., AND ZBIGNIEW K. BRZEZINSKI. *Totalitarian Dictatorship and Autocracy.* 2nd ed. Cambridge, Mass.: Harvard University Press, 1965. (PB: Praeger, New York.)

FROMM, ERIC. *Escape from Freedom.* New York: Holt, Rinehart & Winston, 1941. (PB: Avon, New York.)

HALPERIN, WILLIAM S. *Mussolini and Italian Fascism.* (PB: Anvil, Van Nostrand, New York, 1961.)

HEIDEN, KONRAD. *Der Fuehrer, Hitler's Rise to Power.* Boston: Houghton Mifflin, 1944.

HOFFER, ERIC. *The True Believer.* New York: Harper & Row, 1951. (PB: Mentor, New American Library, New York.)

KRACAUER, SIEGFRIED. *From Caligari to Hitler.* (PB: Noonday, Farrar, Straus & Giroux, 1959.)

LIFTON, ROBERT JAY. *Thought Reform and the Psychology of Totalism.* New York: Norton, 1963.

LOWENTHAL, LEO, AND NORBERT GUTTERMAN. *Prophets of Deceit.* New York: Harper & Row, 1949.

MOSSE, GEORGE L. *The Crisis of German Ideology.* New York: Grosset & Dunlap, 1964. (PB: Universal Library, Grosset & Dunlap.)

NEUMANN, SIGMUND. *Permanent Revolution.* New York: Praeger, 1965. (PB: Praeger.)

NOLTE, ERNST. *Three Faces of Fascism.* (PB: Holt, Rinehart & Winston, New York, 1965.)

PAYNE, STANLEY G. *Falange, A History of Spanish Fascism.* Stanford, Calif.: Stanford University Press, 1961.

ROGGER, HANS, AND EUGENE WEBER, EDS. *The European Right.* Berkeley: University of California Press, 1965.

ROTHFELS, HANS. *The German Opposition to Hitler.* London: Wolff, 1961.

SHIRER, WILLIAM L. *The Rise and Fall of the Third Reich.* New York: Praeger, 1955. (PB: Crest, Fawcett, Greenwich, Conn.)

SNELL, JOHN L., ED. *The Nazi Revolution.* (PB: Heath, Boston, 1959.)

STERN, FRITZ. *The Politics of Cultural Despair: A Study in the Rise of the German Ideology.* Berkeley: University of California Press, 1961. (PB: Anchor, Doubleday, Garden City, N.Y.)

VOGT, HANNAH. *The Burden of Guilt: A Short History of Germany, 1914–1945.* TRANS. H. STRAUSS. (PB: Oxford University Press, New York, 1964.)

Note: See also the bibliographies for Chapters 7, 8, and 13.

CHAPTER 15 WORLD POLITICS IN THE AGE OF REVOLUTION

ALEXANDER, ROBERT J. *Communism in Latin America.* New Brunswick, N.J.: Rutgers University Press, 1957.

APTER, DAVID E., ED. *Ideology and Discontent.* New York: Free Press, 1964.

ARON, RAYMOND. *The Great Debate, Theories of Nuclear Strategy.* Garden City, N.Y.: Doubleday, 1965.

BAARGHOORN, FREDERICK C. *Soviet Foreign Propaganda.* Princeton, N.J.: Princeton University Press, 1964.

BINDER, LEONARD. *The Ideological Revolution in the Middle East.* New York: Wiley, 1964.

BLACK, CYRIL E., AND THOMAS P. THORNTON. *Communism and Revolution, the Strategic Uses of Political Violence.* Princeton, N.J.: Princeton University Press, 1964.

BOSSENBROCK, WILLIAM J. *Mid-twentieth Century Nationalism.* Detroit: Wayne State University Press, 1965.

BRIMMEL, J. H. *Communism in Southeast Asia.* New York: Oxford University Press, 1959.

COBBAN, ALFRED. *National Self-determination.* Chicago: University of Chicago Press, 1948.

CRABB, CECIL VAN METER. *American Foreign Policy in the Nuclear Age.* 2nd ed. New York: Harper & Row, 1965.

CRABB, CECIL VAN METER. *The Elephants and the Grass, A Study of Non-Alignment.* New York: Praeger, 1965.

DALLIN, ALEXANDER. *The Soviet Union at the United Nations.* New York: Praeger, 1962.

DEUTSCH, KARL W., AND WILLIAM J. FOLTZ, EDS. *Nation-Building.* New York: Atherton, 1963.

DOOB, LEONARD W. *Patriotism and Nationalism: Their Psychological Foundations.* New Haven, Conn.: Yale University Press, 1964.

ETZIONI, AMITAL. *Winning Without War.* Garden City, N.Y.: Doubleday, 1964. (PB: Anchor, Doubleday.)

GIBSON, JOHN SCHUYLER. *Ideology and World Affairs.* Boston: Houghton Mifflin, 1964.

GOODMAN, ELLIOT R. *The Soviet Design for a World State.* New York: Columbia University Press, 1960.

GRAEBNER, NORMAN A., ED. *The Cold War: Ideological Conflict or Power Struggle?* Boston: Heath, 1963.

HAYES, C. J. H. *Nationalism: A Religion*. New York: Macmillan, 1960.

HILSMAN, ROGER, AND ROBERT C. GOOD. *Foreign Policy in the Sixties: The Issues and the Instruments*. Baltimore: Johns Hopkins Press, 1965.

HOROWITZ, IRVING LOUIS. *Three Worlds of Development, The Theory and Practice of International Stratification*. (PB: Oxford University Press, New York, 1966.)

KAPLAN, MORTON A., ED. *The Revolution in World Politics*. New York: Wiley, 1962.

KEDOURI, ELI. *Nationalism*. New York: Praeger, 1961.

KOHN, HANS. *The Age of Nationalism, The First Era of Global History*. New York: Harper & Row, 1962.

KOHN, HANS. *Nationalism, Its Meaning and History*. New York: Van Nostrand Reinhold, 1955.

KULSKI, W. W. *International Politics in a Revolutionary Age*. Philadelphia: Lippincott, 1964.

LAQUEUR, WALTER Z. *Communism and Nationalism in the Middle East*. New York: Praeger, 1956.

LERCHE, CHARLES O. *The Cold War and After*. Englewood Cliffs, N.J.: Prentice-Hall, 1965.

LESSING, PIETER. *Africa's Red Harvest*. New York: Day, 1962.

LISKA, GEORGE. *Europe Ascendent, The International Politics of Unification*. Baltimore: Johns Hopkins Press, 1964.

MCKAY, VERNON. *Africa in World Politics*. New York: Harper & Row, 1963.

MACKINTOSH, J. N. *Strategy and Tactics of Soviet Foreign Policy*. New York: Oxford University Press, 1962.

MEIGS, CORNELIA L. *The Great Design, Men and Events in the United Nations from 1945 to 1963*. Boston: Little, Brown, 1964.

MEZERICK, AVRAHAM G., ED. *Colonialism and the United Nations*. Vol. 10, No. 83. New York: International Review Service, 1964.

MORGENTHAU, HANS J. *Politics Among Nations*. 3rd ed. New York: Knopf, 1964.

NEEDLER, MARTIN C. *Understanding Foreign Policy*. New York: Holt, Rinehart & Winston, 1966.

NIEBUHR, REINHOLD. *The Structure of Nations and Empire*. New York: Random House, 1960.

PENTONY, DEVERE E., ED. *China, the Emerging Red Giant*. San Francisco: Chandler, 1962.

PENTONY, DEVERE E., ED. *Red World in Tumult: Communist Foreign Policies*. San Francisco: Chandler, 1962.

PERHAM, MARGERY F. *The Colonial Reckoning*. New York: Knopf, 1962.

PINDER, JOHN. *Europe Against De Gaulle*. New York: Praeger, 1963.

RIVKIN, ARNOLD. *The African Presence in World Affairs*. New York: Free Press, 1963.

SCHUMAN, FREDERICK LEWIS. *International Politics, The Western State System and the World Community*. New York: McGraw-Hill, 1958.

SETON-WATSON, HUGH. *Nationalism and Communism*. London: Methuen, 1964.

SETON-WATSON, HUGH. *Neither War Nor Peace.* New York: Praeger, 1960.

SHULMAN, MARSHALL DARROW. *Beyond the Cold War.* New Haven, Conn.: Yale University Press, 1966.

SIGMUND, PAUL E., ED. *The Ideologies of the Developing Nations.* New York: Praeger, 1963.

SILVERT, KALMAN H., ED. *Expectant Peoples, Nationalism and Development.* New York: Random House, 1963.

SNYDER, LOUIS L., ED. *The Imperialism Reader.* New York: Van Nostrand Reinhold, 1962.

STRACHEY, JOHN. *The End of Empire.* New York: Random House, 1960.

THORNTON, ARCHIBALD PATON. *Doctrines of Imperialism.* New York: Wiley, 1965.

TEUTSCH, HANS E. *Facets of Arab Nationalism.* Detroit: Wayne State University Press, 1965.

WHITAKER, ARTHUR PRESTON, AND DAVID C. JORDAN. *Nationalism in Contemporary Latin America.* New York: Free Press, 1966.

WHITAKER, GEORGE U., ED. *Nationalism and International Progress.* San Francisco: Chandler, 1961.

Note: See also the bibliographies for Chapters 3, 12, 13, and 14.

INDEX

INDEX

72 73 74 6 5 4 3 2 1